PURCHASING & SUPPLY CHAIN MANAGEMENT

PURCHASING & SUPPLY CHAIN MANAGEMENT

ROBERT M. MONCZKA
ROBERT B. HANDFIELD
LARRY C. GUINIPERO
JAMES L. PATTERSON
DONALD WATERS

SOUTH-WESTERN
CENGAGE Learning™

Australia • Brazil • Japan • Korea • Mexico • Singapore • Spain • United Kingdom • United States

SOUTH-WESTERN
CENGAGE Learning™

Purchasing and Supply Chain Management

Robert M. Monczka, Robert B. Handfield, Larry C. Giunipero, James L. Patterson and Donald Waters

Publishing Director: Linden Harris

Publisher: Thomas Rennie

Development Editor: Jennifer Seth

Content Project Editor: Lucy Arthy

Manufacturing Manager: Jane Glendening

Senior Production Controller: Paul Herbert

Marketing Manager: Amanda Cheung

Typesetter: Macmillan Publishing Solutions, India

Cover design: Adam Renvoize

Text design: Design Deluxe

For product information and technology assistance, contact **emea.info@cengage.com**.
For permission to use material from this text or product, and for permission queries, email **clsuk.permissions@cengage.com**.

The Author has asserted the right under the Copyright, Designs and Patents Act 1988 to be identified as Author of this Work.

This work is adapted from *Sourcing and Supply Chain Management*, 4th Edition, published by South-Western, a division of Cengage Learning, Inc. © 2009.

British Library Cataloguing-in-Publication Data
A catalogue record for this book is available from the British Library.

ISBN: 978-1-4080-1744-9

Cengage Learning EMEA
Cheriton House, North Way, Andover, Hampshire, SP10 5BE, United Kingdom

Cengage Learning products are represented in Canada by Nelson Education Ltd.

For your lifelong learning solutions, visit **www.cengage.co.uk**

Purchase your next print book, e-book or e-chapter at **www.CengageBrain.com**

Printed by Seng Lee Press, Singapore
1 2 3 4 5 6 7 8 9 10 – 12 11 10

BRIEF CONTENTS

CONTENTS

PREFACE

This is a new European edition of the standard work by Robert M. Monczka and his colleagues, which is now in its fourth American edition. It is based on personal experience, research and discussions with purchasing managers from many industries around the world. This edition brings together a broad range of material to give a comprehensive view of purchasing. It describes the core activities and places these within the context of an integrated supply chain.

The book describes what purchasing managers do, and how they make decisions in this key area of business. The purchasing function has changed dramatically in recent years, and has grown from an administrative task, to an integrated function with a major strategic role. The book shows how managers develop relevant purchasing strategies and operations that contribute to overall business objectives.

The book does not assume any previous knowledge or experience of purchasing, and it gives a comprehensive introduction to the subject. It achieves a variety of objectives, helping readers understand:

- the function of purchasing, the variety of activities that it performs and the areas for which it is responsible

- the various demands placed on purchasing by other business functions

- the impact of purchasing on competitive success, profitability and other measures of organizational performance

- the ethical, contractual and legal issues faced by purchasing staff

- the development of purchasing from its origins in simple buying decisions, into a complex function with an increasingly strategic role

- the influence of purchasing on other major functional activities, including product design, information systems, e-commerce, manufacturing planning and control, inventory management, human resource management, financial planning, forecasting, sales, quality management and many other areas.

This edition builds on the contents of previous US editions and includes extra coverage of topics that have become more important, including cross-functional teams, performance measurement, supplier integration into new product development, electronic procurement, supplier development, total cost of ownership, reverse auctions, enterprise resource planning, third-party logistics, negotiation, contracting and emerging practices. At the same time, less relevant material has been removed.

Previous editions have focussed on procurement practices in the USA, while this book takes a strongly international view. The material and examples are drawn from global organizations. It has also moved away from the manufacturing emphasis, recognizing that most readers will work in the huge service sector. This itself is such a diverse area that we have deliberately not restricted our view, and discuss the role of purchasing in any type of organization.

Audience

Purchasing & Supply Chain Management is broadly aimed at students in any college and university course who need an understanding of purchasing in its most general sense. They may be attending specialized courses with titles like purchasing, procurement, material acquisition, materials management, sourcing management and other similar titles. Alternatively, the book can provide supporting material for more general courses, such as logistics, supply chain management, operations management and e-commerce. It can be used for courses at all levels including undergraduate, postgraduate and professional courses. The text is also suitable for professional readers, including buyers attending training seminars and executive education.

Structure of the book

Each chapter of the book follows a common format with a review of contents, learning objectives, the main material divided into coherent sections, a chapter review, case study, discussion questions, references and additional reading. Within the text are numerous 'Learning from Practice' boxes to give real illustrations of the ideas, worked examples and definitions.

The whole book is divided into 18 chapters that provide a thorough coverage of purchasing. The subject is developed in a coherent way, starting with a review of the context of purchasing, moving on to show how strategies set the general direction of the function, and then considering a series of decisions about how the strategies are achieved. These include the organization of procurement, choice, evaluation and development of suppliers and generally how purchasing is done.

- Chapter 1 introduces the ideas of purchasing and supply chain management and defines the underlying concepts.

- Chapter 2 describes a typical purchasing process, including the objectives and responsibilities of purchasing and how these are achieved.

- Chapter 3 shows how firms design purchasing strategies to give the long-term direction of the function.

- Chapter 4 looks at alternative ways of organizing purchasing.

- Chapter 5 examines the development of purchasing as an integrated function and the way that it interacts with other functions and organizations.

- Chapter 6 discusses the type of policies that senior managers in most firms design to guide the activities of purchasing.

- Chapter 7 sees how suppliers are evaluated and selected.

- Chapter 8 reinforces the idea that with global sourcing, suppliers can be located anywhere in the world.

- Chapter 9 describes how appropriate development leads suppliers to give world-class performance.

- Chapter 10 focusses on strategic cost management and associated analyses.

- Chapter 11 describes how firms can manage and improve the quality of items that they buy.

- Chapter 12 deals with the negotiations that are an inevitable part of purchases.

- Chapter 13 reviews the fundamentals of contracting, describing the contents and structure of a legal agreement.

- Chapter 14 looks at the type of legislation that is likely to affect procurement in most legal systems, and the related ethical concerns.

- Chapter 15 focusses on the stocks of materials that accumulate as materials flow through supply chains.

- Chapter 16 highlights the specific concerns of procuring services, particularly logistics and professional services.

- Chapter 17 examines the role of supply chain information systems and the growing impact of e-commerce.

- Chapter 18 looks at the alternative measures of purchasing performance and the way that these are used.

ABOUT THE AUTHORS

Robert M. Monczka is Distinguished Research Professor of Supply Chain Management in the W. P. Carey School of Business at Arizona State University. He is also Director of Strategic Sourcing and Supply Chain Strategy Research at CAPS Research.

Robert B. Handfield is Bank of America University Distinguished Professor of Supply Chain Management in the College of Management at North Carolina State University. He is also Co-Director of the Supply Chain Resource Cooperative.

Larry C. Giunipero is Professor of Marketing and Supply Chain Management at Florida State University.

James L. Patterson is Associate Professor of Operations and Supply Chain Management for the College of Business and Technology at Western Illinois University and served as founding director of WIU's Quad Cities Executive Studies Centre.

Donald Waters was Professor of Operations Management at the University of Calgary Business School and now runs a company whose main interests are in management research, analysis and education.

WALK-THROUGH TOUR

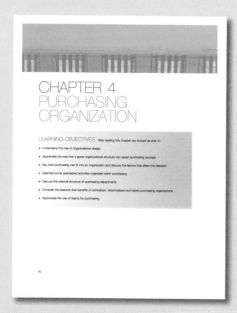

Learning objectives bullet points at the start of each chapter indicate the main ideas that will be covered in the text.

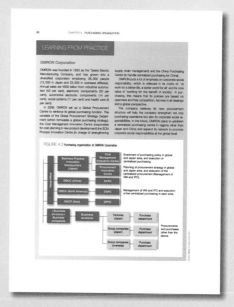

Learning from Practice boxes provide practical examples of key concepts and issues.

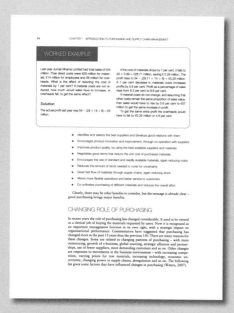

Worked examples detailed solutions to problems are demonstrated clearly and thoroughly.

Key terms are highlighted and explained in full in the margin and in a comprehensive glossary.

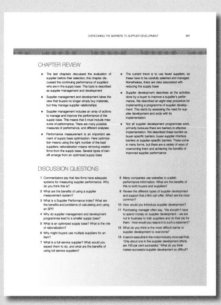

Chapter review each chapter ends with a summary that provides a thorough recap of the key issues, helping to assess understanding and revise key content.

Case studies appear at the end of each chapter to reflect the main concepts of the chapter in a real-world situation.

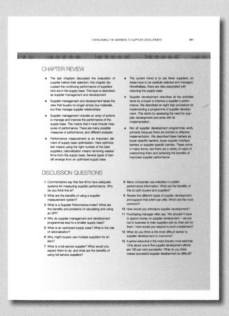

Discussion questions are provided to check understanding of the themes and issues raised in each chapter.

Futher reading and comprehensive references allow you to explore the subject further, and act as a starting point for projects and assignments.

ABOUT THE WEBSITE

Purchasing & Supply Management contains new and revised material, with additional content in the associated website at **www.cengage.co.uk/waters**. This website includes PowerPoint slides, TestBanks, additional cases and other material to help instructors and students use the text more effectively and experience the purchasing process in real time.

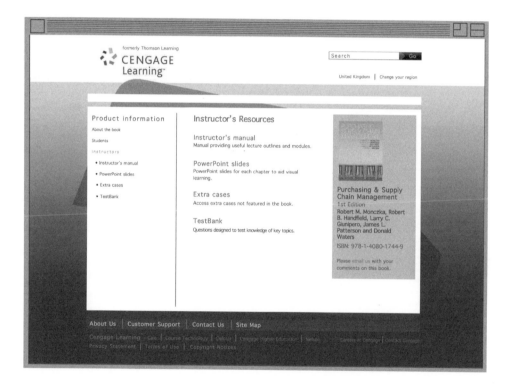

CHAPTER 1
INTRODUCTION TO PURCHASING AND SUPPLY CHAIN MANAGEMENT

LEARNING OBJECTIVES After reading this chapter you should be able to:

- Appreciate the flows of materials through an organization

- Understand the roles of operations, materials and logistics

- Identify the separate activities of supply chain management

- Review the importance of supply chains and their management

- Describe the role of purchasing as a key element of supply chain management

- Discuss the reasons why purchasing is an important function in every organization

- List the benefits of good purchasing

- Review the development of purchasing as a management function

THE CONTEXT OF PURCHASING

This book looks at the way that organizations buy their materials. In principle, we all know what buying means, as we do it every time we go into a shop and hand over money in exchange for something that we want. But imagine that you had to buy 20 Airbus A380s, or new computer chips that had to be designed especially to meet your company's production next year, or transport to move goods regularly from northern China to the Czech Republic – or any large or complicated purchase. Purchasing can be very complicated and expensive. This book gives an introduction to the diverse area of purchasing.

We have to start our look at purchasing by giving some context. For example, we have to discuss the type of things that organizations buy, exactly how they buy them and how they move through supply chains. We start this by reviewing the flow of materials needed by an organization.

Every organization buys materials from suppliers, uses these in operations to make products and passes the results on to customers (as shown in Figure 1.1). Materials come in many different forms that include raw materials, components, equipment, information, utilities, money and other resources – and there are many types of operations that include manufacturing, serving, transporting, selling, training, etc. The main outputs are the organization's products. For example, La Boulangerie Restaurant uses food, chefs, kitchen, waiters and its dining area; its operations include food preparation, cooking and serving; the main outputs are meals, service, customer satisfaction, etc.

It is easiest to imagine these activities in manufacturers like Toyota, Hewlett Packard, Carlsberg and Bayer that make tangible goods, but the same principles apply in organizations that deliver services, such as Lufthansa, MasterCard, Vodafone and Axa. They all have a core set of operations that take different materials and convert them into products (Waters, 2002). There was a traditional distinction between manufacturers and service providers, but you can see that this is rather misleading, as every product is really a complex package that contains both goods and service. For example, Ford manufacture cars, but they also give services through warranties, after-sales service, repairs and finance packages. McDonald's give a combination of goods (burgers, cutlery, packaging, etc.) and services (when they sell food and look after the restaurant). HSBC give a banking service, but they also deliver cash, cheque books, statements, credit cards and a range of other goods.

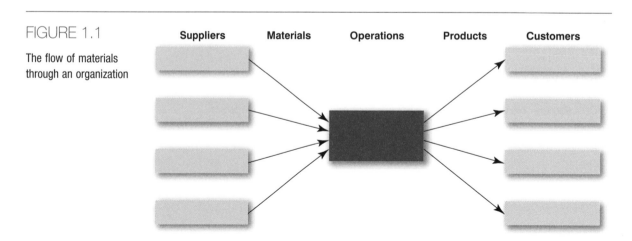

FIGURE 1.1

The flow of materials through an organization

A much better picture has organizations making a spectrum of products. At one end of this spectrum are products that are predominantly goods, such as cars, washing machines, clothes and furniture; at the other end are products that are predominantly services, such as education, banking, transport and internet services. In the middle are products with a more even balance, such as restaurant meals, hospitals, landscape gardeners and some websites.

We now have a basic view of organizations:

1 Acquiring various types of materials.

2 Using these in operations to make products.

3 Delivering finished products to customers.

We can characterize these three as 'buying, making and selling' – in the way that General motors spends $100 billion a year buying materials, uses these to make ten million vehicles, and sells them to customers around the world. In this book we focus on the first of these, discussing the ways that organizations buy – or more generally acquire – all the materials they need. This is an essential activity in every organization. But it is only one step in organizing the flow of materials from suppliers and on to customers.

Flow of materials

Every organization has to acquire materials for its operations, whether it is a manufacturer buying parts from suppliers, a retailer with deliveries of goods from wholesalers, a television news service collecting reports from around the world, a health service organizing supplies of medicines, a restaurant buying food from markets, a market research company collecting information from customers – or any other organization. To be completely general, we describe all these various inputs as materials. Sometimes these are obvious – for instance, when a power station buys coal from a mine, a construction company organizes a delivery of concrete, or a manufacturer buys computer chips. At other times they are less clear, such as a company buying legal advice, insurance or market information. Everything that an organization needs for its operations has to be acquired, and this includes raw materials, components, parts, equipment, spare parts, information, commercial services, expertise, consumables, energy, transport, money, utilities – and anything else you can think of.

Materials
Are all the diverse mix of things that an organization needs to perform its operations.

You can imagine materials flowing into an organization from different suppliers, moving through the operations and then on to customers. These flows need careful management, and the function responsible is logistics (Waters, 2009).

Purchasing as part of logistics

Logistics consists of a series of related activities, each of which contributes to the overall movement of materials. You can imagine these separate activities by considering the movement of materials through an organization, which typically involves the following (Waters, 2009).

Logistics
Is the broad function responsible for all aspects of the movement and storage of materials on their journey into, through and out of an organization.

Purchasing The flow of materials into an organization is usually initiated by a purchase order sent to a supplier. This means that a purchasing department finds suitable suppliers, negotiates terms and conditions, organizes delivery, arranges insurance and payment and does everything needed to get materials into the organization.

Inward transport is responsible for the movement of materials inwards from suppliers to an organization's receiving area. For this managers have to choose the type of transport (road, rail, air, etc.), find the best transport operator, design a route, make sure that all safety and legal requirements are met, get deliveries on time and at reasonable cost and so on.

Receiving accepts materials into the organization, making sure that materials delivered match an order, acknowledging receipt, unloading delivery vehicles, inspecting materials for damage and sorting them.

Warehousing moves materials into storage and makes sure that they are available quickly when needed. Warehousing also takes care of stored materials, giving the right conditions, treatment and packaging to keep them in good condition until needed. This is particularly important for, say, frozen food, drugs, alcohol in bond, chemicals that emit fumes, animals and dangerous goods.

Stock control designs policies for managing inventory. It considers the materials to store, stock levels, investment, customer service levels, order sizes, order timing and so on.

Order processing deals with the orders submitted by customers and ensures that their deliveries are properly organized. This forms a key link between an organization and its customers, and it affects the broad area of customer service.

Order picking finds and removes materials from stores and gets them ready for delivery to customers. Typically materials needed for a customer order are located, identified, checked, removed from racks, consolidated into a single load, wrapped and moved to a departure area for loading onto delivery vehicles. Labels and shipping documents can also be prepared at this point.

Packaging is used to make sure that materials are properly protected for their onward movements and are easy to move.

Material handling moves materials through the operations within an organization. It moves materials from one operation to the next, and also moves materials into and out of storage. The aim of materials handling is to provide efficient movements, with short journeys, using appropriate equipment, with little damage, and using special packaging and handling where needed.

Outward transport takes materials from the departure area and delivers them to customers (with concerns that are similar to inward transport).

Recycling, returns and waste disposal Even when products have been delivered to customers, the work of logistics may not be finished. Sometimes there can be problems with delivered materials – perhaps they were faulty, or too many were delivered, or they were the wrong type – and they have to be collected and brought back. Sometimes associated materials such as pallets, delivery boxes, cable reels and containers (the standard 20 foot long metal boxes that are used to move goods) have to be returned to suppliers for re-use. Some materials are brought back for recycling, such as metals, glass, paper, plastics and oils. And some materials cannot be recycled but are returned for safe disposal, such as dangerous chemicals. Activities that return materials back to an organization are called **reverse logistics**.

Reverse logistics
Occur whenever materials are returned by customers to their original suppliers.

LEARNING FROM PRACTICE

Malaheim Kessinger

Malaheim Kessinger is a food wholesaler, delivering to supermarkets in northern Europe. Although it does not routinely separate logistics costs, the managers of one warehouse did some calculations to judge their scale. They used some estimates, opinions and simplifications, but feel that they have a reasonable starting point for further analyses. The following figures show the costs incurred for each €10,000 of net sales.

a. Cost of sales. €5,800
   – being the cost of purchasing items that are sold-on to customers, including administration of the purchasing office.

b. Transport inwards. €300
   – cost of bringing goods from suppliers and delivering them to the warehouse

c. Other costs of delivery to warehouse. €400
   – a general category that covers all other costs associated with supplier relations

d. Warehousing and handling. €600
   – costs of receiving materials, checking, sorting, moving to the warehouse and storing

e. Stock financing €100
   – cost of financing stock, including debt charges.

f. Sales force. €1,200
   – including salaries and all other costs of the sales office.

g. Special promotions. €300
   – including presentations, visits and samples

h. Delivery to customers. €500
   – costs of taking goods out of the warehouse and delivering to customers

i. Debt financing. €250
   – costs of financing plant and equipment

j. Information processing. €200
   – including all aspects of order processing

k. Returns and recycling. €50
   – cost of recovering pallets and any other materials returned to the warehouse

These figures are open to interpretation, but an initial estimate is that transport (b + c + h) accounts for 12 per cent of sales and warehousing (d + e) a further 7 per cent.

Location Logistics activities are typically spread over many locations – perhaps with stocks of finished goods held at the end of production, in regional logistics centres, in local warehouses, in customers' stores or a range of alternatives. Managers have to find the best location for each activity, with related questions about the size and number of facilities and their relationships. These decisions set the underlying structure of supply chains.

Communication Alongside the physical flow of materials is the associated flow of information about products, customer demand, materials, movements, schedules, stock levels, availability, problems, costs, service levels and so on. The Council of Supply Chain Management Professionals highlights the combination of materials and information flow in their definition:

> Logistics management (is the function) that plans, implements and controls the efficient, effective forward and reverse flow and storage of goods, services and related

information between the point of origin and the point of consumption in order to meet customers' requirements (The Council of Supply Chain Management).

In different circumstances, many other activities can be included in logistics, such as sales forecasting, demand management, production planning, quality management, overseas liaison, third party operations and so on. All of these activities must work together to ensure a smooth and efficient flow of material.

SUPPLY CHAIN MANAGEMENT

We have focussed on the movement of materials through a single organization – but no organization ever works in isolation. Specifically, each acts as a customer when it buys materials from its own suppliers, and then it acts as a supplier when it delivers materials to its own customers. For instance, a wholesaler acts as a customer when buying goods from manufacturers, and then as a supplier when selling the goods to retailers. A component maker buys raw materials from its suppliers, assembles these into components, and passes the results on to other manufacturers.

Then products move through a series of organizations as they travel from original sources of raw materials through to final customers of finished products. Milk moves through a farm, tanker collection, dairy, bottling plant, distributor and supermarket before we buy it. A toothbrush starts its journey at an oil well, and then it passes through pumps, pipelines, refineries, chemical works, plastics companies, manufacturers, importers, wholesalers and retailers before finishing in our bathrooms.

Upstream
The tiers of suppliers in front of an organisation moving materials in.

Downstream
The tiers of customers after an organisation receiving its products.

Each organization describes activities in front of it – moving materials inwards from suppliers – as upstream; those after the organization – moving materials outwards to customers – are called downstream. Upstream activities are divided into tiers of suppliers (shown in Figure 1.2). A supplier that sends materials directly to the operations is a first tier supplier; one that send materials to a first tier supplier is a second tier supplier; one that sends materials to second tier supplier is a third tier supplier, and so on back to the original sources. Customers are also divided into tiers. One that gets a product directly from the operations is a first tier customer; one that gets a product from a first tier customer is a second tier customer; one that get a product from a second tier customer is a third tier customer, and so on to final customers. Then a manufacturer might have a sub-assembly company as a first tier supplier, a component maker as a second tier supplier, a materials company as third tier supplier and so on. It might see wholesalers as first tier customers, retailers as second tier customers and end-users as third tier customers.

FIGURE 1.2 Activities in a simple supply chain

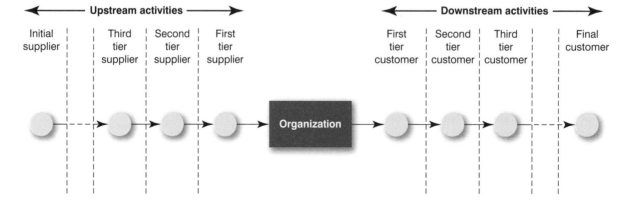

Every product has its own unique supply chain. A supply chain in Cadbury's starts with cocoa beans growing on farms and ends when hungry customers buy bars of chocolate. A supply chain for Diesel jeans starts with someone growing a field of cotton and ends when you buy them in a shop. The supply chain describes the total journey of materials as they move 'from dirt to dirt' (Cooper *et al.*, 1997).

In reality, supply chains come in a huge variety of configurations. Some are very short and simple – such as a cook buying potatoes directly from a farmer, or a manufacturer selling directly to final customers. Others are very long and complicated, with a large number of members. Each member of the chain can buy materials from many different suppliers and sell products to many different customers, so a supply chain converges on a key organization as raw materials move in through the tiers of suppliers, and it diverges as products move out through tiers of customers (illustrated in Figure 1.3). And loops and different types of transaction can make supply chains surprisingly complicated. For instance, when you buy a jacket it has a long journey that starts with a farmer growing cotton – but many chains merge as buttons, polyester, dyes, patterns, packaging and other materials join the main

FIGURE 1.3 Typical supply chain around a manufacturer

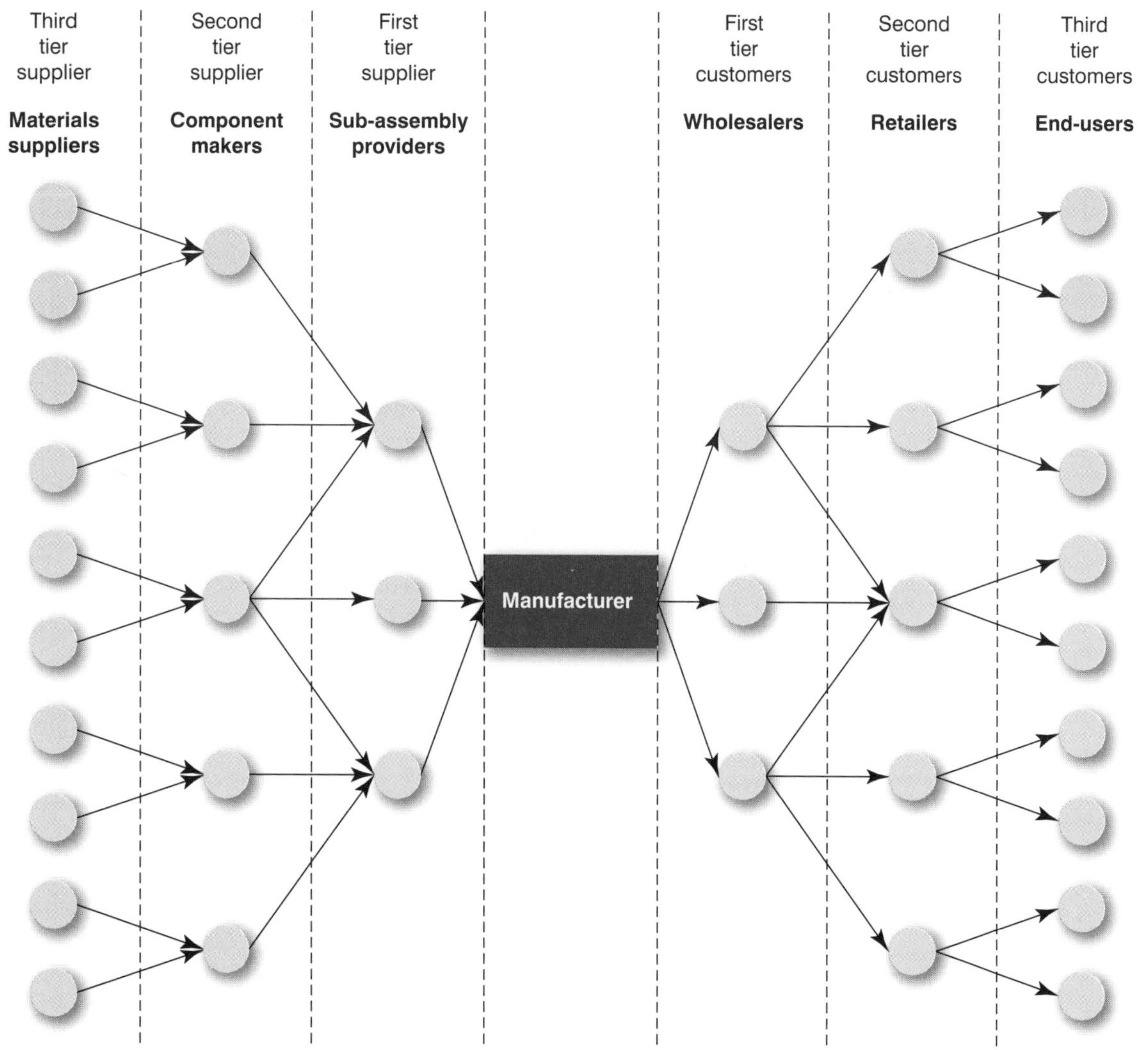

Third tier supplier	Second tier supplier	First tier supplier		First tier customers	Second tier customers	Third tier customers
Materials suppliers	**Component makers**	**Sub-assembly providers**		**Wholesalers**	**Retailers**	**End-users**

Manufacturer

process (each of which can involve its own complex series of manufacturers, merchants, agents, brokers, distributors, transporters, branches, wholesalers, retailers and other intermediaries).

An organization can work with many – often thousands – of different products, each of which has its own supply chain. So the French company Carrefour is Europe's largest retailer and comes at the end of tens of thousands of supply chains; Mittal's steel is used by countless other companies, Microsoft's systems are used for huge amounts of information transfer. The supply chain for a product like a car is very complex, spanning many suppliers, different types of operations, geographical locations, technology, types of customers and so on (with Figure 1.4 suggesting a very simplified view).

FIGURE 1.4

Simplified view of the supply chain for car assembly

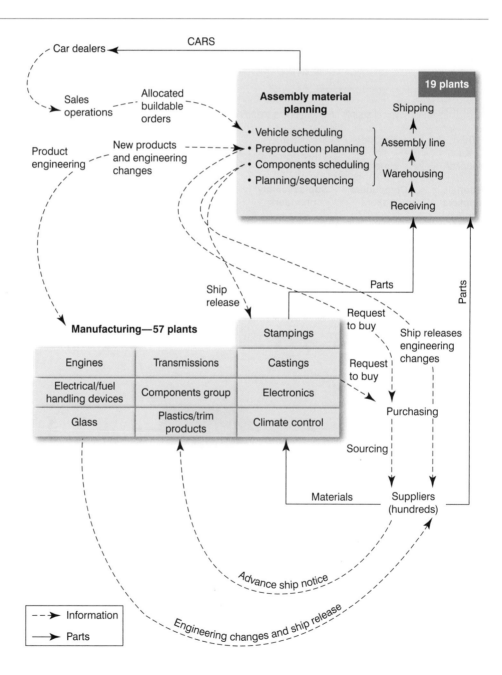

Different terms

Some people argue that the term 'supply chain' does not reflect the real complexity, and they prefer to talk about supply networks or supply webs. This reinforces Peck's (2006) view of a complex 'flow of materials, goods and information (including money), that pass within and between organizations, linked by a range of tangible and intangible facilitators, including relationships, processes, activities and integrated information systems'. People may also describe a supply chain in terms of a process when they emphasize the operations, a logistics channel when they emphasize marketing, a value chain when they look at the value added, and a demand chain when they consider customer satisfaction.

Porter's (1985) view of a value chain is particularly well-known, and is summarized in Figure 1.5. This considers the series of value-adding activities that leads to satisfied customers and draws a distinction between primary activities (inward logistics, operations, outward logistics, marketing, sales and customer service) and support activities (business infrastructure, human resource management, technology development and purchasing). Some people argue that a value chain is a broader concept (as everyone within an organization works in the value chain – but not everyone works in the supply chain). And the basic model can be criticized for limiting the role of operations, separating consumer service, excluding key functions, nor reflecting the real flow of materials, focussing on a single organization rather than a linked network of firms, and so on.

The different terms people use to describe supply chains generally show semantic preferences rather than real differences of principle. We know that materials move through a complex series of organizations and operations between original suppliers and final customers – and in this book we stick to the usual convention of describing this as a supply chain.

We have said that logistics is responsible for the movement of materials, and this definition leads to an alternate title of supply chain management. Generally, 'logistics' and 'supply chain management' refer to the same function and the terms can be used interchangeably. This is the view of the Chartered Institute of Logistics and Transport who define logistics as, 'the time-related positioning of resources, or the strategic management of the total supply chain' (Chartered Institute of Logistics and Transport, 1998–2009).

Supply network, supply web
Alternative names for supply chains.

Process, logistics channel, value chain, demand chain
Give different views of supply chains.

Supply chain
Consists of the series of activities and organizations that materials move through on their journey from initial suppliers through to final customers.

FIGURE 1.5 Porter's value chain

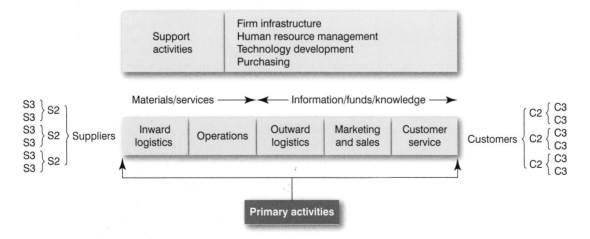

Breakfast cereal supply chains

At first sight, breakfast cereal producers have relatively straightforward supply chains. They buy grains from farmers, process these into their distinctive products and pass the results on to customers. But if you look at the list of ingredients on a typical packet of cereal you see that the producers need more than cereal. For instance, Kellogg's Crunchy Nut lists the ingredients as 'maize, brown sugar, peanuts, sugar, honey, barley malt flavouring, salt, glucose-fructose syrup, niacin, iron, vitamin B6, riboflavin, thiamine, folic acid and vitamin B12 (Kellogg, 2009)'.

Cereal producers also need associated materials, such as board to make the packets, labels, plastic wrapping and so on. And they also have to buy all the services, such as transport, equipment suppliers, finance, market information and so on. Each of these has to move through its own supply chain to reach a Kellogg's plant, where the cereal is manufactured, packed and sent to distributors who move the cereals to retailers and on to end customers.

The result is a surprisingly complex number of transactions and flows of material, information and money, a simplified version of which is shown in Figure 1.6.

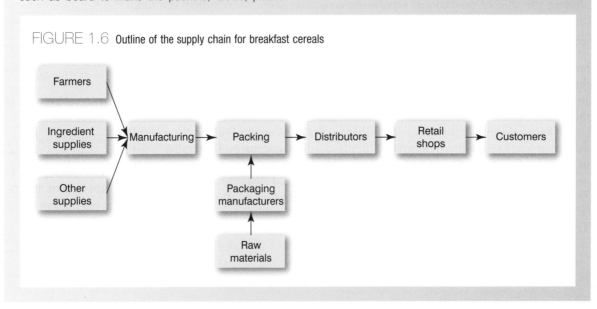

FIGURE 1.6 Outline of the supply chain for breakfast cereals

PURCHASING

Purchasing
Is responsible for acquiring all the materials needed by an organization. It consists of the related activities that organize the flow of goods, services and other materials from suppliers into an organization.

Any movement of materials through a supply chain needs some trigger to actually initiate the flow. This is usually given by a purchase order, which is essentially a message that an organization sends to a supplier, saying, 'We have agreed terms, so send us the following materials.' In response the supplier delivers the materials requested, and is paid an agreed amount.

Purchasing is the function responsible for issuing purchase orders and initiating the flow of materials.

We have to be careful with terms here, as many transactions are not simple purchases, but include rental, leasing, contracting, exchange, gifts, borrowing and so on. It is really more accurate to talk about the acquisition of materials, or more

Source: Based on Carpentier M. (2009) e-Business at the restaurant, Presentation at the Food Purchasing Forum, Nice.

LEARNING FROM PRACTICE

Girot's Fish Restaurant

Marcel Carpentier is the owner and chief chef at Girot's Fish Restaurant in Marseilles. Every morning he goes to the fish market to see what is looking good, and then plans the menus he will feature in the evening. These menus need a range of other ingredients, particularly fresh vegetables. Marcel has a program on his computer that allows him to select recipes and the number of servings needed, and then it lists the ingredients to buy. In the past, Marcel would take this list to his suppliers, select the produce, discuss conditions, pay in cash and take the ingredients back to his restaurant. Now the program connects to his regular suppliers' websites and allows him to submit orders automatically. When the suppliers receive Marcel's orders, they understand his requirements and deliver ingredients late in the afternoon. In the very few instances that there have been problems, this gives Marcel enough time to get replacements. His account with the suppliers is automatically paid at the end of every working week.

commonly procurement. Some people argue that purchasing describes the actual buying, while procurement has a broader meaning which includes different types of acquisition (leasing, rental, contracting, etc.) as well as the associated work of identifying and selecting suppliers, negotiating, agreeing terms, expediting, monitoring supplier performance, analysing orders, material administration, developing purchasing systems and so on. But these differences are largely semantic – and we are interested in the principles rather than drawing artificial boundaries around functions. Here we follow the usual custom of using 'purchasing' and 'procurement' interchangeably as including all the activities needed to acquire materials.

> **Acquisition of materials, procurement, supply management**
> Alternative terms for purchasing.

Purchasing organizes the transfer of materials and arranges the change of ownership and location, but another function – usually transport – actually delivers them. So procurement is largely concerned with processing information – it passes information backwards to describe what customers want, and it passes information forwards to say what suppliers have available. It forms the key link between buyers and sellers, making sure that organizations get 'the right materials, from the right suppliers, in the right quantity, in the right place, at the right time, with the right quality'. To achieve this, purchasing departments need a range of skills that start with assessing the needs of internal customers, move through all the detailed transactions of acquisition, and finish with follow-up after delivery. We discuss these skills in the rest of the book.

Strategic purchasing

The basic activities of purchasing often seem to be shorter-term rather than strategic. This has been the traditional view, but it is misleading as procurement has a major impact on an organization's long-term performance and even its survival. Imagine a village garage that finds it can only buy supplies of petrol from its wholesaler for 5 per cent more than a local supermarket is selling it to customers – put simply the village garage does not have much future in selling petrol. In the same way, planning the way that materials are acquired, ensuring availability of scarce resources, developing relations with suppliers, designing systems for material acquisition, supporting the organization's broader strategies, moving to global sourcing, introducing e-business and a host of other activities all have a strategic impact.

LEARNING FROM PRACTICE

General Electric

General Electric (GE) is one of the world's largest corporations, and is a major supplier of aircraft jet engines. In 2004, a British Airways Boeing B-777 aircraft taking off from Houston's George Bush Intercontinental Airport experienced an in-flight emergency when an engine manufactured by GE caught fire. According to GE and National Transportation Safety Board (NTSB) documents, the cause of the malfunction was a fatigue crack in a high-pressure turbine blade. The failed blade caused a severe vibration in the engine, which ultimately damaged an oil seal, allowing engine oil to enter air lines. Subsequently, the plane's cockpit and passenger cabin were filled with smoke and fumes. The flight crew declared an emergency and made an immediate landing back in Houston.

The problem arose because a casting for the turbine blade had been misidentified with an incorrect part number. Because of this mistake, the turbine blade remained in service far beyond its specified limits, allowing the fatigue crack to appear. And GE's in-plant inspections designed to prevent such an error were found to be inadequate. An internal investigation showed that employees had failed to notice the error when they processed the part and cleared it for installation. The error ultimately cost GE $8 million and made it the subject of an NTSB investigation.

Source: Editorial (2004) GE errors linked to plane fire, Cincinnati Inquirer; Wolfson A. (2004) Madisonville GE plant's mistake linked to jet fire, Courier-Journal.

The recognition that purchasing is not just an administrative task, but has a strategic impact has been at the heart of purchasing development in recent years. Some people have felt that the old term of purchasing is inadequate to describe this new trend, and prefer to use **supply management**, which the Institute for Supply Management defines as, 'The identification, acquisition, access, positioning and management of resources and related capabilities an organization needs or potentially needs in the attainment of its strategic objectives (Flynn et al., 2006).' Unfortunately, this term can be rather confusing, so we will generally avoid it.

WHY PURCHASING IS IMPORTANT

The main argument for the importance of purchasing is clear – every organization needs a supply of materials; purchasing is responsible for organizing this supply; so purchasing is an essential function within every organization. To put it simply, purchasing forms an essential link between organizations and gives the trigger for moving materials through supply chains.

This leads to the second argument for the importance of purchasing, which says that it affects broader organizational performance. If purchasing is done badly, materials do not arrive, or the wrong materials are delivered, in the wrong quantities, at the wrong time, with poor quality, at too high price, low customer service and so on. If it is done well, purchasing can give a significant competitive advantage. A former vice president of AT&T summarized this view by saying that, 'Purchasing is by far the largest single function at AT&T. Nothing we do is more important (Tully, 1994).'

Many features of an organization's products originate with their purchase of materials. For instance, the features of a Dell computer depend on the efficient purchase and delivery of Intel chips, Seagate hard drives, Radeon video cards, Microsoft software, Canon scanners and so on. If purchasing were done differently, Dell's products would also be different. Unfortunately, Coca-Cola noticed this effect in 1998 when some of its production from a Belgian bottling plant was contaminated (Deogun, 1999). Their chief scientist said that the problem was quality lapses at the plant that allowed contaminated carbon dioxide to enter final products. Coca-Cola did not test the gas when it arrived, assuming that the supply was pure; the supplier did not test the gas, as Coca-Cola had not asked for an analysis to verify the quality. A mistake in purchasing had serious effects on final product quality. A similar problem occurred with a consignment of heparin (used to thin the blood and prevent clots after surgery) which has been linked to four deaths and 350 allergic reactions in the USA (Fairclough and Burton, 2008). Baxter International bought the heparin from Scientific Protein, who in turn bought it from small suppliers in China, where there was difficulty in monitoring product quality.

A firm's operations can also depend on the services offered by suppliers. For instance, a supplier that guarantees fast delivery of materials can reduce a product's lead time and increase availability – while an unreliable supplier makes it difficult to deliver products as promised. And when there is co-operation between firms and their suppliers, there can be dramatic improvements to product designs. For instance, when purchasing managers are involved in the design of new products they can suggest standard components rather than specially tailored ones, more readily available materials, materials with shorter lead times and cheaper alternatives that reduce costs. Empirical evidence suggests that companies which involve purchasing managers early in their new product development plans reduce material costs by 20 per cent, improve material quality by 20 per cent, and reduce product development time by 20 per cent. Car makers have noticed this effect, where surveys in the 1980s suggested that better management of supplies gave Japanese car makers an advantage of $300 to $600 a car over their US counterparts (Taylor, 1994) – and surveys some 20 years later found that Japanese companies still pay much more attention to supplier relations and gain a significant cost advantage (Verespel, 2005).

Despite other benefits, the suggestion that better purchasing gives lower costs is still a dominant factor for many managers. Surveys suggest that in a typical manufacturer 50 per cent of the cost of goods sold is spending on material (Industry Week, 2007) – and this often rises high as 70 per cent (Lysons, 2000). Raw materials are becoming relatively more expensive and manufacturers outsource more of their operations, so the amount they spend with suppliers is steadily rising. As a result, a relatively small improvement in purchasing costs can give a substantial benefit. Suppose that a company buys raw materials for €60, spends €40 on operations and then sells the product for €110. It clearly makes a profit of $110 - (60 + 40) = €10$ a unit. Now suppose that procurement negotiates a 5 per cent discount on materials. Materials now cost $60 \times 0.95 = €57$, and with the same selling price the €3 saving goes straight to profit. The profit on each unit now jumps to €13 – with a 5 per cent decrease in materials costs raising profit by 30 per cent. Using the same reasoning, Philips Electronics found that a 2 per cent reduction in their purchasing expenditure increased their return on assets by almost 16 per cent (Philips Electronics, 1999).

Benefits from good purchasing

We know that purchasing is an essential function and have reviewed some benefits from doing it well. Before moving on we can summarize these benefits and say that good purchasing:

- Provides an efficient service to internal customers (who are all the internal users for whom materials are acquired)

- Gives a reliable flow of materials into an organization, ensuring that they are available when needed

WORKED EXAMPLE

Last year Jumail Alhama Limited had total sales of €54 million. Their direct costs were €29 million for materials, €14 million for employees and €6 million for overheads. What is the effect of reducing the cost of materials by 1 per cent? If material costs are not reduced, how much would sales have to increase, or overheads fall, to get the same effect?

Solution

The actual profit last year was $54 - (29 + 14 + 6) = €5$ million.

If the cost of materials drops by 1 per cent, it falls to $29 \times 0.99 = €28.71$ million, saving € 0.29 million. The profit rises to $54 - (28.71 + 14 + 6) = €5.29$ million. A 1 per cent decrease in materials costs increases profits by 5.8 per cent. Profit as a percentage of sales rises from 9.3 per cent to 9.8 per cent.

If material costs do not change, and assuming that other costs remain the same proportion of sales value, then sales would have to rise by 5.8 per cent to €57 million to get the same increase in profit.

To get the same extra profit the overheads would have to fall by €0.29 million or 4.8 per cent.

- Identifies and selects the best suppliers and develops good relations with them
- Encourages product innovation and improvement, through co-operation with suppliers
- Improves product quality, by using the best available suppliers and materials
- Negotiates good terms that reduce the unit cost of purchased materials
- Encourages the use of standard and readily available materials, again reducing costs
- Reduces the amount of stock needed to cover for uncertainty
- Gives fast flow of materials through supply chains, again reducing stock
- Allows more flexible operations and better service to customers
- Co-ordinates purchasing of different materials and reduces the overall effort

Clearly, there may be other benefits to consider, but the message is already clear – good purchasing brings major benefits.

CHANGING ROLE OF PURCHASING

In recent years the role of purchasing has changed considerably. It used to be viewed as a clerical job of buying the materials requested by users. Now it is recognized as an important management function in its own right, with a strategic impact on organizational performance. Commentators have suggested that purchasing has changed more in the past 15 years than the previous 150. There are many reasons for these changes. Some are related to changing patterns of purchasing – with more outsourcing, growth of e-business, global sourcing, strategic alliances and partnerships, use of fewer suppliers, more demanding customers and so on. Other changes are responses to movements in the business environment – with increasing competition, varying prices for raw materials, increasing technology, economic uncertainty, changing power in supply chains, deregulation and so on. The following list gives some factors that have influenced changes in purchasing (Waters, 2007).

LEARNING FROM PRACTICE

John Deere

Source: Based on Smock D. (2001) Deere Takes a Giant Leap, Purchasing, pp 26–35: www.jdsupply.deere.com; www.deere.com; www.johndeere.co.uk

John Deere is a manufacturer of farm and construction equipment with headquarters in Moline, Illinois. The company puts a lot of emphasis on the efficiency of its purchases, as you would expect in a company with sales of $30 billion and material purchases that amount to 70 per cent of production costs. Their Achieving Excellence Programme is 'a significant part of the process in our supply management strategies' with an objective 'to drive continuous improvement and provide mutual benefits to both John Deere and our suppliers'.

But purchasing was not always so efficient, and in the 1980s they had problems with long lead times that could leave customers waiting up to 6 months for equipment. Competition from more nimble companies meant that such delays were no longer acceptable, and the company urgently looked for ways to speed things up.

A new management team soon realized that a key step was to reduce the number of suppliers. The company had moved heavily towards outsourcing non-core operations, and was buying from more than 14,000 suppliers, with more than 80,000 in their database. Each business unit within the company did its own purchasing, with little co-ordination of effort.

Then in 2000 the company spent $7 million on a drive to develop long-term relationships with a small number of core suppliers. And senior managers could soon report that, 'The hard dollar return was $22 million. There's also a big soft-dollar return on things like lower inventory and reduced floor space. But the most important benefit is the building of deep, loyal trust with suppliers.'

John Deere improved its purchasing procedures, with specialists analysing purchases for the whole company and assigning items to one of four categories – unique items, critical items, generics and commodities. Then the best procedure was designed for purchasing each item. For example, local sites could buy items that are only used at their location, while company teams would co-ordinate purchases of items that were used more widely.

An increasing emphasis on costs meant that managers could identify a supplier with higher than expected costs – and then send a team to improve performance. Other improvements looked at education, training and development of e-procurement. The early initiatives developed into an Achieving Excellence Programme, with an emphasis on continuous improvement. The objectives of this programme can be summarized as:

- Developing mutually beneficial and profitable relationships with suppliers that allow the company to achieve its mission
- Using quality improvement and cost management to control total spending
- Providing objective measures that can be used for strategic sourcing decisions
- Presenting accurate and timely information about performance – and recognizing suppliers that give outstanding performance
- Encouraging continuous improvement – sharing resources whenever necessary
- Strengthening communications between John Deere and their suppliers, assisting with technical support, innovation and expertise
- Integrating supplies to all John Deere processes

Changing management attitudes

- **Recognition** that purchasing is an essential function that has a strategic impact and must be managed properly

- **Identification** of the high costs of procurement – with improvements bringing significant benefits

- **Increasing concerns** about risk to extended supply chains and their vulnerability to accidents

- **A movement away from confrontational relationships** and towards increasing co-operation through alliances, partnerships, collaboration and other arrangements

Changes in the nature of markets

- **Fiercer competition** forcing organizations to take every opportunity to improve operations
- **Global operations** meaning that new competitors are continually entering established markets – a trend that is encouraged by free trade areas such as the European Union (EU) and North American Free Trade Area
- **Power** in the supply chain moving downstream to retailers and customers
- **Concentration of ownership** meaning that a few large companies with economies of scale dominate many industries

  Other changes in retail markets, such as 24-hour opening, home deliveries, out-of-town shopping malls, retail parks, telephone and on-line shopping

Changes in the nature of customers

- **Growing emphasis on customer satisfaction** – and recognition that this depends on purchasing
- **More knowledgeable customers** who can use new technology like the web to compare products offered by widely dispersed suppliers
- **More demanding customers** who want higher quality, lower costs, faster delivery and generally better service
- **More diverse customers** who use advanced communications to state clear and precise requirements

Changes in business operations

- **New types of operations** – such as just-in-time, lean operations, time compression, flexible manufacturing, mass customisation, virtual operations, etc.
- **Improved communications** allowing electronic data interchange (EDI), electronic fund transfer (EFT), e-commerce, bar coding, radio frequency identification (RFID), improved contacts with trading partners, electronic point-of-sales-data (EPOS), global positioning, satellite navigation and so on
- **Broader effects of technology** giving improved vehicle design, automated warehouses, driverless vehicles, new materials for packaging, etc.
- **Organizations focussing on their core operations** and outsourcing peripheral activities to third parties

Changing views of society

- **Growth of the service** – and information – economy at the expense of traditional manufacturing
- **Changing attitudes towards transport,** with growing concerns for road congestion, air pollution, climate change, environmental damage, waste disposal, road construction, safety and a host of other green issues
- **Deregulation of transport** to increase customer choice and competition

This may seem like a long list, but it is by no means comprehensive and only begins to describe the pressures for changes to purchasing. Other pressures include economic uncertainty, uncertain market conditions, political changes, deregulation of business, rising costs, shortage of skilled staff, fluctuating exchange rates, industrial disagreements, potential accidents, wars, change of ownership and a whole host of other factors.

Development of purchasing

Purchasing managers have to respond to these pressures, or else more entrepreneurial competitors gain an advantage. The main thrust of the change is that purchasing has moved from an essentially administrative or clerical task to a core management function. Historically, people working in purchasing had an ordered and predictable life; when someone in their firm wanted materials they came to the purchasing department and asked them to send out orders. For larger orders the purchasing department asked a shortlist of suppliers to submit competitive tenders, and then they generally accepted the cheapest bid. This routine approach worked until innovative competitors began to introduce new ideas that were based on worldwide searches for the best suppliers, closer relationships with chosen suppliers, long-term contracts, supplier participation in product development, sharing information with trading partners, integration of activities along supply chains and a host of other ground-breaking ideas. These brought dramatic reductions in cost, improvement of quality, reduced lead times, better reliability and other related improvements.

Senior managers soon recognized that purchasing could be dramatically improved, so they began to demand changes – with efficient procurement not seen as a luxury, but as an essential part of normal operations. These new requirements changed both the type of people working in procurement and the methods that they use.

Of course, our suggestion that purchasing had a stable and unchanging history is a gross simplification, and we should give a brief review of its evolution. This goes back to very early roots, where the need to acquire materials has been around throughout history, and the purchasing transactions were formalized with the introduction of money. However, our interest really starts much later, perhaps with Charles Babbage's reference in 1832 (Babbage, 1832) to the importance of purchasing and his description of a 'materials man … who selects, purchases, receives and delivers all articles required'. By 1887 an early book on purchasing – 'The handling of railway supplies; their purchase and disposition' – was written by the Comptroller of the Chicago and Northwestern Railroad (Fearon, 1968; 1989). He discussed purchasing issues that are still relevant today, such as the importance of buyers having technical knowledge and the need to centralize purchasing in a single department.

By 1905 'The Book on Buying' (Fearon, 1968; 1989) outlined the broad principles of procurement, and organizations gradually gave more attention to the subject over the first half of the 20th century. There was additional impetus during the Second World War when organizations struggled to obtain the scarce resources that they needed. However, this progress was not universal and in 1953 Hill noted that, 'For many firms, purchases were simply an inescapable cost of doing business which no one could do much about … the purchasing function has not yet received in full measure the attention and emphasis it deserves (Hill, 1975).' In 1964 Henderson could still say that executives neglected procurement as they did not consider it important for mainstream problems, and they found it hard to imagine a company being successful through good procurement. He summarized the position by saying that, 'Procurement is regarded as a negative function; it can handicap the company if not done well but can make little positive contribution (Henderson, 1964).' Many organizations certainly improved procurement as a way of reducing costs, but there is no doubt that other functions such as marketing and finance overshadowed purchasing.

The early 1970s brought economic disruption with the price of oil tripling, widespread shortages of products and inflation reached historically high levels. There were shortages of raw materials for manufacturers, national economies moved into recession and there was widespread disruption of industry. These conditions encouraged new interest in procurement as firms struggled to find the materials they needed to keep working – and a distinct function of purchasing emerged. For the first time this had agreed responsibilities and objectives, and it brought efficiencies by focussing on multiple sourcing, competitive bidding, forceful negotiation of conditions, tendering based on price, arm's-length relationships with suppliers and short-term contracts. However, these practices that dominated in the 1970s could not cope with conditions that emerged in the 1990s, and purchasing had to deal with the pressures for change that we listed in the last section. The main response has been towards a strategic, integrated view of the flows of materials, money and information. Purchasing became a part of an integrated logistic function with an aim of contributing to broad organizational objectives. Ammer (Ammer, 1974) felt that purchasing could only be taken seriously when it actively contributed to broad organizational objectives, with purchasing managers playing a part in non-purchasing decisions.

More specifically, relationships with suppliers moved from adversarial to co-operative, recognizing that all members of a supply chain want long-term, mutually-beneficial trading arrangements. This in turn led to supplier development, supplier involvement in product design, full-service suppliers, total cost procurement, strategic alliances, e-procurement, collaborative forecasting and planning, information sharing and a host of other initiatives.

Current position

We can draw three important conclusions from this review of changes to purchasing.

1 Purchasing has continually evolved in response to changing conditions. It has developed new methods and moved into new areas to give an essential service that works within the supply chain of every organization. This innovation is continuing in response to changes in the business environment.

2 The importance of purchasing is growing. It is increasingly seen as a strategic function with a major impact on organizational performance and success.

3 Purchasing is becoming a more integrated part of logistics, and a core function for the operations within an organization.

Future changes

Of course, nobody knows exactly what will happen in the future, but we can assume that some of the current trends in purchasing will continue. There are far too many of these trends to look at in detail, but it is reasonable to expect that:

- The role of purchasing will continue to expand as it responds to changes in the business environment

- Performance will improve continuously, in terms of lower costs, faster response, higher quality products, more customers satisfaction and so on

- The strategic role of procurement will become clearer, as it gives competitive advantages in more organizations

- Purchasing will become more integrated with other functions, as firms focus on the overall process of achieving customer satisfaction

- The organizational structure of the purchasing function will continue to evolve

- Relationships with suppliers will become more important as firms use long-term contracts with a few key sources

LEARNING FROM PRACTICE

Trelawney Garage

Brian Trelawney was the third generation of his family to run the village garage near Truro in Cornwall. Brian earned his income from the traditional mix of motor repairs and maintenance, petrol sales, a forecourt shop and sales of a few second-hand cars. The garage had generated reasonable, but variable, returns for over 80 years.

In 2006 a new supermarket opened in Truro, including a service station. Within the first week, Brian noticed that his petrol sales had fallen to almost nothing, and with less passing trade the sales of his forecourt shop were also hit badly. The basic problem was that the supermarket was selling petrol at a lower price than Brian was paying his wholesaler.

Brian rang the wholesaler to see what was happening, and particularly if the supermarket was running a loss-leader that would soon finish. The wholesaler replied that, 'No, the supermarket is not selling petrol at a loss. They buy in huge quantities and negotiate very good terms from the refinery. They buy straight from the refinery, and avoid wholesalers and other intermediaries. They have efficient operations and work with small profit margins.' Brian was understandably worried and asked the wholesaler about negotiating a new agreement. The reply was not encouraging. 'The supermarket buys petrol from the refinery cheaper than I can. Then I have to cover all my costs. Believe me, I want you to sell as much petrol as possible to increase my own sales, but I just cannot make any more savings, and I don't see how we can compete on price.' Brian could not think of any way of competing, particularly as the supermarket's service station was open 24 hours a day and was easier for customers to get to. Three months later he was very pleased to accept an offer for his whole site from a developer who demolished the garage and built an estate of new houses.

- More non-core activities will be outsourced, putting greater demands on their procurement

- The skills needed by purchasing staff will continue to change – and attracting, developing and retaining people with these skills will become more important for organizational success

- E-commerce will continue to grow, with more efficient communications and information systems

- New methods will be used for measuring the performance of purchasing and its suppliers

We could continue with a long list to show what purchasing will probably look like in the future, but you can already see that it is a rapidly changing function. We describe its progress in the rest of the book.

CHAPTER REVIEW

- All organizations can be viewed in terms of buying materials from suppliers, doing operations to add value, and then distributing products to customers. This suggests three core functions of 'buying, making and selling'

- Materials are all of the things needed by an organization's operations, ranging from tangible raw materials through to intangible information

- Logistics is the function responsible for all movement and storage of materials on its journey from original suppliers through to final customers

- Purchasing forms part of the broader logistics function and is responsible for acquiring all materials. It initiates the flow of materials through supply chains, and includes all the related activities that organize the acquisition of materials from suppliers

- Purchasing is an essential function in every organization. The way that it is done has a direct effect on organizational performance, ranging from product quality to delivery reliability. It is particularly important in financial performance, typically accounting for half of an organization's costs

- Despite its importance, purchasing has not always had its fair share of attention. Interest only really grew towards the end of the 20th century – and it has mushroomed in the past few years. Purchasing has now developed into a key management function that is continuing to grow in importance

DISCUSSION QUESTIONS

1 Is it true that every organization supplies products to meet customer demand?

2 What are the core activities in every organization?

3 What is logistics? Why is its importance as an integrated function increasing?

4 Is there any real difference between a supply chain and a value chain?

5 Porter's model of a value chain describes purchasing as a support activity. What exactly does this mean?

6 Where does purchasing fit into the broader area of logistics or supply chain management?

7 Why has purchasing become increasingly important in recent years?

8 How can good purchasing affect the success of an organization?

9 What skills do you think people working in purchasing need?

10 What other areas in an organization benefit from purchasing involvement?

11 Purchasing continues to develop as a key management function. What challenges do you think it will face in the future?

REFERENCES

Ammer, D. S. (1974) Is your purchasing department a good buy? *Harvard Business Review*, March–April, pp 136–158.

Babbage C. (1832) On the economy of machinery and manufacturers, (2nd edition), London: Charles Knight Publishing.

Chartered Institute of Logistics and Transport, (1998–2009) Members' Directory, London: CILT and website at www.ciltuk. org.uk

Cooper MC., Lambert D.M. and Pagh J.D. (1997) Supply chain management, *International Journal of Logistics Management*, 8 (1): 2.

Deogun N. (1999) Anatomy of a recall: how Coke's controls fizzled out in Europe, *The Wall Street Journal*, June 29, p A1.

Fairclough, G., and Burton, T. M. (2008) In China, gaps found in drug supply chain, *Wall Street Journal*, February 21, pp A1, A14.

Fearon, H. (1968) History of purchasing, Journal of Purchasing, February, pp 44–50.

Fearon H. (1989) History of purchasing, *Journal of Purchasing and Materials Management*, pp 71–81.

Flynn, A., Harding, M. L., Lallatin, C. S., Pohlig, H. M., and Sturzl, S. R. (editors) (2006) Glossary of key supply management terms (4th edition), Institute for Supply Management, Tempe, AZ.

Henderson B.D. (1964) The coming revolution in purchasing, reprinted *in the Journal of Purchasing and Materials Management*, Summer 1975, p 44.

Hill J.A. (1975) The purchasing revolution, *The Journal of Purchasing Management*, Summer, pp 18–19.

Industry Week. (2007) Census of manufacturers, Cleveland, OH: Penton, OH and website at www.industryweek.com

Kellogg. (2009) Ingredients of Crunchy Nut cornflakes, Kellogg Company and website at www.kelloggs.co.uk

Lysons K. (2000) Purchasing and supply chain management (5th edition), Harlow, Essex: FT/Prentice Hall.

Peck H. (2006) Supply chain vulnerability, risk & resilience, in global logistics (5th edition), Waters D. (editor), London: Kogan Page.

Philips Electronics (1999) Purchasing becoming supply chain management, Quality Matters, January, issue 94.

Porter M.E. (1985) Competitive advantage, New York: The Free Press.

Taylor A. (1994) The auto industry meets the new economy, *Fortune*, September 5, pp 52–59.

The Council of Supply Chain Management Professionals (formerly The Council of Logistics Management), promotional material and website at www.cscmp.org

Tully S. (1994) Purchasing's new muscle, *Fortune*, February 21, pp 56–57.

Verespej, M. (2005) Detroit Needs a Different Driver, Purchasing, April.

Waters D. (2002) *Operations management* (2nd edition), London: FT Prentice Hall.

Waters D. (2009) Supply chain management – an introduction to logistics (2nd edition) , Hampshire: Palgrave Macmillan, Basingstoke.

Waters D. (2007) Trends in the supply chain, in Global logistics (5th edition), D. Waters (editor), London: Kogan Page.

FURTHER READING

Many journals and magazines cover aspects of purchasing. Some of these are specific, such as the *Journal of Purchasing and Supply Management, International Journal of Purchasing and Material Management* and the online magazine purchasing. com. Others cover broader logistics, such as International Journal of Logistics Management, Journal of Supply Chain Management and Focus on Logistics and Transport. Other journals, perhaps describing operations management or marketing, have some articles that cover specific aspects of purchasing. It is useful to do a search for related articles – and if you search the web for 'purchasing' you get about a billion matches. Some useful articles to get started are:

Anderson M. G. (1998) Strategic sourcing, *International Journal of Logistics Management*, 9(1): pp 1–13.

Ellram L. M. and Carr A. (1994) Strategic purchasing: a history and review of the literature, *International Journal of Purchasing and Material Management*, 30(2): pp 10–20.

Giunipero L., Handfield R., and El Tantawy R. (2006) Supply management's evolution, *International Journal of Production and Operations Management*, 26(7): pp 822–844.

Gonzalez-Benito J. (2007) A theory of purchasing's contribution to business performance, *Journal of Operations Management*, 25(4): pp 901–917.

Harrington L.H. (1997) Buying better, *Industry Week*, July 21, pp 74–80.

Larson P. D. (2002) What is SCM? And where is it? *Journal of Supply Chain Management*, 38(4): pp 36–44.

Narasimhan R. (2001) An empirical examination of the underlying dimensions of purchasing competence, *Production and Operations Management*, 10(1): pp 1–15.

Rozemeijer F. A., van Weele A. and Weggeman W. (2003) Creating corporate advantage through purchasing, *Journal of Supply Chain Management*, 39(1): pp 4–13.

Sprague L.G. (2007) Evolution of the field of operations management, *Journal of Operations Management*, 25(2): pp 219–238.

There are also a number of books on procurement, and you might like to look at, such as:

Baily P., Farmer D., Jessop D. and Jones D. (2004) Purchasing principles and management, London: Financial Times Prentice Hall.

Burt D. and Dobler D. and Starling S. (2002) World-class supply management (7th edition), New York: McGraw-Hill.

Carter R.J. and Kirby S. (2006) Practical procurement, Liverpool: Liverpool Academic Press.

Emmett S. and Crocker B. (2008) Excellence in procurement: how to optimize cost and add value, Liverpool: Liverpool Academic Press.

Lysons K. and Farrington B. (2005) Purchasing and supply chain management (7th edition), London: Financial Times Prentice Hall.

van Weele A. (2004) Purchasing and supply chain management (4th edition), London: Thomson Learning.

Leenders M., Johnson F., Flynn A. and Fearon H. (2005) Purchasing and supply chain management (13 edition), New York: McGraw-Hill.

CASE STUDY

Purchasing in Warmionsko Powiat

Warmionsko Powiat is a county in the industrial north of Poland. Public services in Poland have traditionally been bureaucratic, with standard procedures and inflexible regulations passed down by higher levels of government. Although conditions have changed since the political reforms of 1989, and particularly since Poland joined the EU in 2004, purchasing in Warmionsko Powiat council still tended to be a clerical, paper-based activity. Then in 2007 they appointed a new Procurement Director who wanted to introduce contemporary, entrepreneurial ideas about purchasing. The Director outlined his aim by saying, 'The main thrusts of our purchasing department should be to use technology to simplify and automate repetitive activities, to improve communications and flows of information, to provide a centralized and trusted service for our customers, to design efficient systems, to add value and lower costs and to develop strategic alliances with leading suppliers.'

In the past, purchasing was typically initiated by an internal customer who would choose a product and supplier, and then ask the purchasing department to send out an order. The process was almost entirely manual, based on hand-completed paper forms and the postal service. Larger purchases needed three competitive bids, but some people thought that this was just a bureaucratic hindrance to introduce unnecessary delays. The new Procurement Director found that purchasing staff were experienced and skilled at administering the existing procedures, but they were swamped with paperwork. They clearly needed more efficient systems – and ironically, they often knew what was needed, but had no time to develop their ideas.

The Director's first step was to prioritize their objectives and establish ways of achieving them. In particular, he found ways of quickly reducing their current workload so that they could divert attention to designing more efficient procedures. After 6 months, they had made significant progress, including an interactive website for internal customers. This eliminated many paper forms manual entry of information, tedious manual transfers of data between different forms and most of the associated errors. The staff also developed a list of approved suppliers who had direct links to their website, eliminating time-consuming searches for suppliers of basic products. A parallel suppliers' website gives complete information on how to do business with the council and entry forms for relevant processes.

The system is increasingly popular with internal customers who are changing from their traditional view of, 'We know what we want, so why do we need central purchasing?' And the purchasing department can now consolidate separate orders, remove inconsistent prices, use their buying power, negotiate better terms, eliminate duplicate spending and improve the management of service contracts. A small illustration of these benefits comes from snack vending machines around the buildings. Previously, eight departments had each installed machines at different times and from different suppliers. The new system resulted in 26 machines being rented from a single supplier, who reduced prices and returns a share of profits to the council.

The council now has three categories of purchase:

1 *Automated buying* – where customers purchase material directly from a designated supplier, such as office supplies.

2 *Competitive bidding* – where the purchasing department has to research and evaluate alternative bids, such as computer systems.

3 *Contracted services* – where the council and suppliers work together to find the best solutions, such as dining services.

These arrangements all need different – but close – relations with suppliers. The Procurement Director is developing these with a set of guidelines to:

● Look for collaboration and teamwork rather than conflict, emphasising that both sides can benefit from the trades

● Establish long-term relationships with the best suppliers

- Actively work together to improve operations in both the council and suppliers

- Create common goals, procedures, communication systems and measures of performance

- Use clear contracts which show who is responsible for even the most basic actions

Questions

- What do you think were the main features and problems with the old purchasing systems?

- How has the new system overcome these?

- What other changes would you expect to see in the future?

CHAPTER 2 PURCHASING ACTIVITIES

LEARNING OBJECTIVES After reading this chapter you should be able to:

- Appreciate the aims of purchasing

- Describe the responsibilities of purchasing

- Describe four enablers of good practice in purchasing

- Discuss the steps in a standard purchasing process

- Understand how organizations can improve the efficiency of their purchasing

- Describe some specific ways of improving purchasing performance

- Appreciate the role of e-purchasing

OBJECTIVES OF PURCHASING

This chapter describes the activities that are normally included in purchasing, and which form the **purchasing process**.

The usual activities included in the purchasing process include identifying user requirements, describing the products they need, searching for suitable suppliers, negotiating terms, ensuring prompt delivery, expediting and so on. The challenge for purchasing is to ensure that these activities are done effectively and efficiently – widely described as achieving **purchasing excellence**.

We have to remember that that purchasing has a strategic role, which is broadly to help the organization achieve its mission. This strategic aspect of purchasing defines a set of long-term objectives, and these are generally variations on the following six objectives.

Purchasing process
Is the set of related activities and procedures that are used to acquire materials for an organization.

Purchasing excellence
Suggests that efficient procurement gives a competitive advantage.

Objective 1: Support organizational goals and objectives

Perhaps the single most important objective for purchasing is to support broader organizational aims. This may seem obvious, but remember that purchasing goals may not always be aligned with organizational ones. For instance, a company might have a policy of moving towards global sourcing, while purchasing would prefer the benefits of using local suppliers; or a firm might form an exclusive partnership with a single supplier, while purchasing would prefer other companies to submit competitive quotations.

This objective implies that purchasing must give overriding support for organizational objectives, which transcend its own aims. Then a company might have an aim of reducing the amount of stock held in its supply chain. Purchasing can work with suppliers to organize smaller, more frequent deliveries that give lower stock levels. This may increase purchasing's administrative costs, but will improve the company's balance sheet and overall operating costs.

Objective 2: Develop integrated purchasing strategies that support organizational strategies

The purchasing function often fails to design strategies that are aligned with the strategies of other functions, or even the broader organizational strategies. There are several reasons for this. Firstly, purchasing has traditionally been seen as a lower level support function, so its staff may still not be invited to join senior corporate meetings. Secondly, senior management has been slow to recognize the benefits that effective purchasing can bring. However, both of these are changing rapidly, and purchasing is being integrated within the strategic planning of most firms. This brings benefits that include a new view of problems, access to a pool of expertise and a source of market intelligence. This market intelligence can be particularly important, and it comes when purchasing:

Monitor supply markets, identifying the main suppliers, new entrants, mergers, global sources, etc.
Monitor emerging trends in markets, watching material price changes, shortages, new products, etc.
Identify critical materials needed to support company strategies, particularly during new-product development.

Develop alternatives for ensuring supplies of key materials, and contingency plans if there are problems with primary supplies.

Supporting the organization's need for a diverse and globally competitive supply base.

Objective 3: Support operational requirements

Purchasing must efficiently perform its traditional role of acquiring materials to satisfy the needs of internal customers. Here, materials include all the raw materials, components, parts, information, services and everything else that an organization buys: internal customers are all the users within the organization who need the materials. So purchasing must ensure an uninterrupted supply of materials by:

1   Buying materials from the right sources.

2   At the right price.

3   With specification that meets user needs.

4   In the right quantity.

5   Delivered at the right time.

6   To the right user.

Purchasing must provide a good service of its internal customers, or else they lose confidence in the function and look for ways of avoiding it. Commonly unhappy users start buying materials themselves to avoid a purchasing department – a practice known as **maverick or backdoor buying.**

Maverick or backdoor buying
Occurs when departments buy materials themselves without consulting the purchasing department.

Objective 4: Using purchasing resources efficiently and effectively

Purchasing managers always have limited resources – including people, facilities, money, time, information and knowledge. They have to use these resources efficiently by:

- Determining appropriate staffing levels

- Developing and keeping within budgets

- Providing professional training and opportunities for employees

- Ensuring high utilization of capacity at facilities

- Designing operations that give high productivity

- Monitoring performance and continually looking for improvements

- Doing anything else needed to increase efficiency and effectiveness

Their aim is always to design better purchasing operations that need fewer resources to deliver the service they need.

Objective 5: Supply base management

An important job of purchasing is to select, develop and maintain a suitable set of suppliers – which is known as the **supply base**. This means that purchasing must keep abreast of current conditions in supply markets to:

- Ensure that current suppliers are competitive

- Improve and develop existing suppliers, particularly those who are falling behind competitors

- Identify new suppliers who can provide good service and join the supply base

- Develop new potential suppliers whose performance is not yet good enough to join the supply base

Supply base
All the suppliers that deliver materials to an organisation.

This objective needs purchasing to work closely with suppliers to improve their existing capabilities and develop new ones. This is particularly important when firms use more outsourcing and pass some responsibility for key operations to suppliers.

LEARNING FROM PRACTICE

Nestlé

Source: Based on Nestlé (2004) Principles of purchasing, Nestlé S.A., Vevey, Switzerland; www.nestle.com

Nestlé was founded in 1866 by Henri Nestlé and is now a leading supplier of food, health and nutritional products. It is one of the world's best known brands, with products including coffee, bottled water, breakfast cereal, baby food, ice cream, chocolate, pet food and many others. Annual sales are more than CHF £100 billion and the 250,000 employees work in almost every country in the world. The company's overriding priority is, 'To bring the best and most relevant products to people, wherever they are, whatever their needs, throughout their lives.'

A huge company like Nestlé spends a lot on purchasing, which it describes as, 'The strategic sourcing of materials, goods and services most appropriate for the purpose for which they are intended at the lowest total cost of ownership.' Within this it describes a series of objectives for purchasing, which we can summarize as:

1 Actively participating as the first link of integrated supply chains.

2 Delivering a sustainable, quantifiable, competitive advantage for Nestlé.

3 Ensuring both high quality supply and satisfaction for all internal clients.

4 Consolidating orders to increasing Nestlé's purchasing power.

5 Fulfilling the company's requirements for materials.

6 Contributing to growth and profitability of the company.

7 Seeking continuous improvement in the performance of suppliers.

8 Developing supplier relationships which emphasize added value.

9 Fostering competition among suppliers.

10 Monitoring the performance, reliability and viability of suppliers.

Objective 6: Develop strong relationships with other functions

Traditionally, firms have not designed organizational structures that encourage interaction between functions. In the extreme, this leads to the silo effect, where each function sees itself as working independently, rather than working together as parts of a larger organization. However, since the 1990s the problems of such fragmented organizations have become clearer, and firms have moved towards more integrated structures, with closer relationships between functions.

Purchasing clearly needs close links with other functions, as this is where their internal customers work. But there are obviously other reasons for having close working relations. For instance, when a manufacturer has problems because of poor components bought from a supplier, then purchasing must work closely with manufacturing to assess the effects of the problem and finds ways of solving it. Similarly, when marketing start a major advertising campaign, purchasing have to work with them to ensure that the advertised price is achievable and that service levels can be met.

RESPONSIBILITIES

All functional groups have responsibility for certain tasks within their organizations, and these are loosely described as their span of control. For purchasing, the span of control includes those tasks for which the purchasing department is ultimately responsible and has final authority to make decisions.

Purchasing's span of control

The span of control for purchasing is established by senior management policies, so there are differences between organizations. However, the four most common tasks included are choosing suppliers, reviewing materials bought, acting as the primary contact with suppliers and deciding how to make a purchase.

1 **Evaluate and select suppliers.** This is one of the most important tasks of purchasing, as it ensures that materials come from the most qualified suppliers. It is important to retain this task and avoid maverick buying, where internal users bypass purchasing and approach suppliers directly, or suppliers contact the users to deal with them directly. Superficially this may seems reasonable, but there are many disadvantages to having isolated groups doing their own purchasing. The only way to ensure that procurement is done properly and the organization is getting the best deals, is to go through an efficient purchasing department.

 Of course, this does not mean that purchasing works in isolation to identify and evaluate potential suppliers, but it should routinely ask for advice from knowledgeable users. And it does not mean that suppliers' sales staff cannot talk to anyone who is not in purchasing. But it does mean that only purchasing staff have the final say, can make commitments to suppliers and sign contracts. In practice, even these rights are not so clear as more organizations use multi-functional sourcing teams with representatives from different functions making a joint decision.

2 **Review materials bought.** Purchasing's span of control also includes the right to review material specifications and say what materials will be bought, although other functions, such as design and engineering often dispute this. Purchasing staff must have the expertise about materials and their markets that gives them the right to

question specifications given by users. For example, purchasing may question whether a lower-cost standard part works as well as an engineer's specially designed one. The right to question material specifications also helps avoid a common problem, where users define specifications that only their preferred supplier can meet. Another benefit is that purchasing may find different users requesting very similar materials, and by making small adjustments they can combine orders and get lower unit costs.

3   **Act as the primary contact with suppliers.** Some organizations have a policy of only allowing contacts between suppliers and purchasing staff. This might make sense from a control standpoint, but other functions may need detailed discussions about their purchases, and these are best handled by direct contact. So this policy is becoming more flexible, allowing efficient and accurate communications between suppliers and internal users, without any intermediaries. Nonetheless, purchasing must still act as the primary contact with suppliers, with controlled access by other functions.

4   **Decide how to make a purchase.** A purchasing department's span off control also includes the right to determine how to make a purchase. For instance, they can decide whether it would be better to award a contract after competitive bidding, through single sourcing, alliances or some other procedure. These initial decisions are followed by others. For instance, if they use competitive bidding, how many suppliers should they approach to submit bids? If they use single sourcing, which suppliers are chosen? Whichever route is chosen, there are inevitably negotiations with suppliers over terms and conditions, and these should be led by purchasing. Again, this does not mean that purchasing should work in isolation, but they have ultimate responsibility for managing the procurement process.

Four enablers of good purchasing

We have outlined the aims of purchasing and its span of control. Organizations clearly want good performance in these areas, but this does not just happen and it needs careful management. In particular, people talk about enablers that allow and encourage good purchasing – and inhibitors which prevent it. We could add many things to list of enablers and inhibitors (a theme that we develop in later chapters) but here we mention four of the most common enablers (shown in Figure 2.1). Human resources, organizational design, information technology (IT) and measurement are all needed to achieve purchasing excellence.

1   **Human resources.** You can often hear managers say that, 'Our most valuable asset is our employees.' This is certainly true for purchasing, with Figure 2.1 suggesting some of the skills needed by purchasing staff. Another view (Giunipero and Handfield, 2004) suggests that the five most important areas of knowledge are:

●   Supplier relationship management

●   Total cost analyses

●   Purchasing strategies

●   Supplier analyses

●   Competitive market analyses

Maintaining staff with the right skills needs a sound human resources strategy that includes training and developing existing staff, and recruiting new people from other functions and organizations who can fill specific skills gaps.

FIGURE 2.1   Four enablers of good purchasing management

I.

Business requirements and guiding principles
Total quality management, Supply chain integration, Total cost management, Globalization, Flexibility and responsiveness, Reduced cycle times

II.
Enabling capabilities support the development of strategies and approaches

Human resources	Organizational design	Information technology	Measurement
Supply chain staff who have the ability to: • view the supply chain holistically • manage critical relationships • understand the business model • make fact-based decision-making • practice advanced cost management • understand electronic business systems.	Organizational designs that feature: • centrally led supply teams • executive responsibility for co-ordinating purchasing activities • co-location of supply personnel with internal customers • cross-functional teams to manage purchasing processes • supply strategy co-ordination and review sessions between business units • executive buyer-supplier council to co-ordinate with suppliers.	Real time and shared IT systems that support: • demand planning • order commitment, scheduling, and production management • distribution and transportation planning • material replenishment • reverse auctions • electronic data interchange.	Include supply chain measures that: • use data from visible sources • quantify what creates value • use goals that change over time • use benchmarking to establish performance targets • link to business goals and objectives • feature efficiency and effectiveness measures • assign ownership and accountability.

III.

Purchasing and supply chain management strategies
Global sourcing, Supplier quality management, Long-term contracting, Early supplier design involvement, Joint improvement activities, Outsourcing, Alliances and partnerships, On-site supplier-managed inventory

2   **Organizational design.** Managers have to design an organization structure for the purchasing function that allows it to achieve its objectives. This includes the division of the function into separate units, the relationships between these, formal systems of communication, allocation of tasks and responsibilities, co-ordination, control, authority and so on. Basic organizational structures are described in familiar organizational charts, but these give an incomplete picture. The reality is that organizational design is much more complex than the charts suggest, and informal arrangements are often as important as the formal structure (Champoux, 2000; Trent, 2003). In practice, the purchasing function is often organized into teams (a theme that we return to in chapter 4).

3   **Information technology.** In recent years there has been a surge in IT developments. This allows, for instance, integrated supply chains with much closer collaboration between members and improved material flow. A major impact on purchasing has allowed e-purchasing, which uses the internet for at least some of the purchasing process (in the way that you can buy books from Amazon.com or auction things on eBay). The software for e-procurement largely focusses on either purchase planning or purchase execution (Kalkota and Robinson, 2000). Planning software seeks to improve

forecast accuracy, optimize production scheduling, reduce working capital, shorten cycle times, cut transportation costs and improve customer service. Execution software replaces the traditional paper transactions of procurement with automated ones (we return to this theme in chapter 17).

E-purchasing has developed from **Elecronic Data Interchange EDI** which allows the electronic transfer of information between buyers and sellers. For example, EDI allows networks to track the position of an item at any point in its journey, or to exchange real-time information about customer orders, or to make cash transfers using **Electronic Fund Transfer EFT**.

4 **Measures of performance.** Measuring performance is a key part of management, as it shows how well things are being done. Then we can get an objective view of how well purchasing is being done at the moment, how this compares with competitors, how it compares with planned performance and performance achieved in the past and how we can improve things in the future. Unfortunately, it seems easy to measure performance – but there can be problems including the use of too many measures, different views about the best measures, constantly changing performance, old data, inconsistent procedures to take measurements and so on (Hofman, 2006). There is certainly no definitive list of procurement measures that can be used in all organizations.

The main benefit of measuring performance is that it gives positive facts to work with, rather that subjective views. A secondary benefit is that it passes objective information to other members of a supply chain. For instance, when a firm monitors a supplier's performance, it can describe its requirements exactly and say how well these are being achieved. The supplier knows the exact measures are being used, and by implication what the customer considers most important, and it can look for ways of improving its performance in these areas. One survey suggests that 70 per cent of firms believe that openly measuring suppliers' performance noticeably improves their performance (Porter, 1999). As well as checking for satisfactory performance, such measures can allow firms to recognize outstanding supplier performance in the way that United Technologies presents its 'Key Supplier Awards' (Avery, 2007).

Electronic data interchange (EDI)
The automatic exchange of information between remote computers.

Electronic fund transfer (EFT)
The automatic transfer of money between accounts.

LEARNING FROM PRACTICE

FedEx Corporation

FedEx Corporation consists of an integrated group of businesses that provide worldwide services for transportation, e-commerce, information, logistics and related services. It is a market leader that employs 300,000 with annual revenues of $40 billion. The name Federal Express has been around since 1971 when the parcel delivery company was founded by Frederick Smith. But the current FedEx Corporation was only formed in 1998 when it started acquiring other companies and diversifying into related transport and information services.

Purchasing within FedEx is organized as a central facility for all related companies. Then instead of each company having its own contract for, say, office supplies, they negotiate a single corporate contract. The basic purchasing process in FedEx has seven steps (shown in Figure 2.2).

Step 1. A user sends a requisition for an item. Then a sourcing specialist or team decides whether it is worth spending time and money on a full supplier evaluation. If the requisition is for, say, €200,000 a year it is probably not worth doing a full supplier evaluation. Then the user can use a simple automated purchase system. However, for larger items (remembering that FedEx operate 675 aircraft and 80,000 vehicles through 2,000 offices and 30 major transport hubs) the team starts to examine existing and potential suppliers,

Step 2. Purchasing consider all the information available and decide their overall approach. Is it best to use

FIGURE 2.2   FedEx purchasing process

Sourcing process	Selected activities
Profile the sourcing group	• Confirm user requirements • Develop category definition • Define basic characteristics • Understand industry and supply markets
Select sourcing strategy	• Assess bargaining position • Evaluate alternative strategies • Select appropriate approaches and techniques
Generate supplier portfolio	• Identify qualified suppliers • Determine supplier value-added capabilities • Develop supplier 'short list'
Select implementation path	• Verify and adjust sourcing strategy • Develop implementation plan
Negotiate and select suppliers	• Plan negotiation strategy • Evaluate supplier proposals • Conduct negotiations with suppliers • Recommend sourcing decision
Operationalize supplier integration	• Plan and implement transition to new suppliers relationships • Link key processes • Conduct joint process improvement activities
Benchmark the supply market	• Monitor market conditions • Assess new technology and best practices impact • Conduct benchmarking activities • Determine appropriateness for re-examining category

the usual approach of a request for proposal? Does the company need to maintain existing relationships? Is it time to renegotiate terms?

Step 3. Conduct an in-depth search of suppliers. Which suppliers can satisfy user requirements, service levels, etc.? The aim here is to develop a shortlist of potential suppliers to receive a request for quotation.

Step 4. Take another look at the purchasing procedure. Has anything appeared that will need changing – perhaps cancelling the "RFQ" and negotiating with a preferred supplier or using a reverse auction?

Step 5. Finalize details of the purchase, select the supplier, negotiate terms and deliver a purchase order.

Step 6. Update systems with the supplier and purchase details, integrate purchasing information, note any conflicts and resolve them.

Step 7. Monitor the supplier performance and benchmark it against other suppliers.

A benefit of having a single corporate procurement system is that FedEx can easily change conditions across the entire company. For example, if a sudden spending freeze prevents the purchase of new computers without senior management approval, this can be introduced with a simple adjustment to the system.

Source: Based on www.fedex.com

THE PURCHASING PROCESS

When someone in an organization wants to acquire materials, there is a fairly conventional method for them to follow, which describes the **purchasing process**. This includes all the activities that a buyer performs to acquire material, from identifying a user's needs through to paying for delivered material.

Purchasing process
The activities used to acquire materials.

The steps in this process vary in different organizations, and they vary with the size of purchase, its importance, time available, quality demands and whether it is a repeat or new purchase. You would not expect purchasing by a national government to be handled in the same way as a small software company – and you would not expect Electricité de France (EDF) to put the same effort into buying routine stationery that it puts into acquiring a new power station. Nonetheless, there is a common thread to all purchasing, and we will describe a general process with six main steps (illustrated in Figure 2.3).

FIGURE 2.3 **The purchasing process**

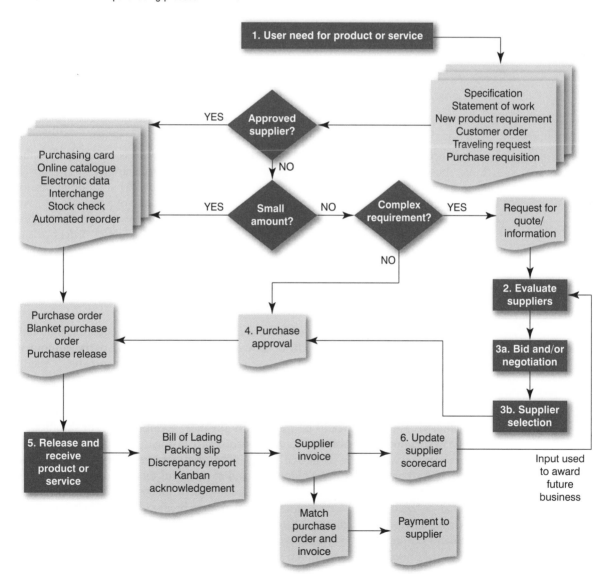

1   Recognize user need for materials.

2   Clarify needs.

3   Identify and select a supplier.

4   Approval, contract and purchase order.

5   Receive materials.

6   Measure and manage supplier performance.

Each of these steps needs documentation, which provides the information flow through the supply chains. Historically this documentation has been a time-consuming, manual process, but it is now largely automated through EDI. Most organizations use EDI to manage the information flows, which means that they generate documents automatically and electronically transmit them to other members of the supply chain. This brings considerable benefits, including:

- A virtual elimination of paperwork and manual handling of documents

- Faster flows of information – and materials – through supply chains

- Better communications both within and between organizations

- Fewer errors

- Lower administrative costs for purchasing and other operations

- Freeing up time in purchasing departments to consider more strategic issues

When some of the EDI is organized through the internet, it is generally described as e-business. However, this – and the various related – terms are used very loosely, and at one extreme e-procurement might mean that all the steps are done through the internet, or at the other extreme one step involves some use of a website. For very small or routine purchases it is not worth going through any complex procedure, and it may be better to bypass purchasing departments with direct orders to suppliers. E-purchasing gives an ideal format for such simple buys.

Recognize user need for materials

The purchasing process begins with the recognition that a user needs some materials. As always, these materials might be raw materials, components, parts, equipment, spare parts, information, commercial services, expertise, consumables, energy, transport, money, utilities or virtually anything else.

Often a purchasing department knows about purchases some time in advance, when it makes planned repeat orders, or has forecasts of future demand for items. Ideally, all purchases would be planned in advance, giving long-term stability and time to sort out any problems. For this reason, purchasing departments should work with internal customers to design longer-term plans of likely requirements. However, not all purchases can be planned ahead of time and sometimes there is a whole set of new requirements (such as materials for new products) or sudden unexpected demands (such as spare parts for equipment that breaks down). Even when purchasing has forecast demands, there are the usual uncertainties caused by varying demand or unexpected conditions.

So user needs may be planned or unplanned, but they always form the starting point for the purchasing process. The next step is to define specifications that show exactly what users want and when it should be delivered.

Clarify needs

Internal customers pass their needs to purchasing in a number of ways that include purchase requisitions, statements of work, forecasts, external customer orders, routine reordering, stock checks, bills of materials and many other forms. The key point is that someone who is authorized by the purchasing department has to submit some kind of requisition document. The person who sends in the document need not be the actual user – which often occurs when only departmental heads have authority to requisition materials needed by staff in their departments. In practice, information about material needs is usually passed to purchasing using one of the following documents.

Purchase requisition or *statement of work*. The most common document used to ask a purchasing department to acquire materials is called a **purchase requisition**. You can imagine this as a printed form, but it is more likely to be a computer-generated order form, or a less formal message passed by email, note in the internal mail, telephone or word-of-mouth. Whatever form the requisition takes, it should contain at least:

Purchase requisition
Document to request purchasing to buy materials.

- A detailed description of the materials needed

- Quantities and date required

- Delivery details

- Estimated unit cost

- Account to be charged for the purchase

- Date of requisition (to monitor the purchase process)

- Authorization to make the purchase

When a service is needed, rather than goods, the requisition form might appear as a **statement of work (SOW)**. Rather than give a description of materials, this lists the work to be done and the type of service provider who can do it.

Statement of work (SOW)
Document describing a service that purchasing should acquire.

For routine, off-the-shelf items, a requisition or SOW may contain all the information that purchasing needs. However, for technically complex or non-standard items, purchasing may need more information about specifications, perhaps including the grade of material, method of manufacture, detailed measurements, tolerances, quality levels, people doing the work and so on. These detailed requirements may refer to industry standards that are widely agreed and well-understood. A variation on this uses 'market grade', where different suppliers offer competing products that meet market requirements. Specifying a specific brand is useful for proprietary materials, or when there is some advantage in using a particular supplier's products. Then a computer manufacturer might specify a DVD drive that conforms to industry standards, a hard disk drive that is market grade and a branded Intel Core 2 Quad processor.

These three descriptors give an effective shortcut for describing user's needs to suppliers, but they cannot be used when there are no agreed standards. Then three methods of supplying the descriptions would use explicit specifications, performance characteristics or details for building a prototype. Explicit specifications give a detailed list of features that an item must have, and might describe the required performance, materials used, manufacturing process, physical dimensions or pretty much anything else. For instance, when NASA purchased the heat shield tiles for space shuttles, it provided specifications for each tile that included the exact dimensions, performance required, materials to be used, manufacturing steps, quality checks and so on. Rather than list the specifications, an alternative is to describe the performance characteristics needed, focussing on the outcomes rather than the precise designs that will deliver it. When Amazon.com use parcel delivery services that guarantee next day delivery, they are only concerned with the results and not the detail of how these are achieved. The assumption is that suppliers are experts in their products and know how to meet customer's needs. The third way of giving details is to provide a prototype, which is better at showing the look and feel of a product than drawings or written descriptions. For instance, a company buying specialized software might design a prototype package, including sample input, output and report screens to give a clearer idea of what it wants.

In practice, purchase requisitions and SOWs are generally used for routine orders that are transmitted through an online requisition system. Figure 2.4 shows the procedure for creating a purchase requisition. Approving it, converting it into a purchase order and ultimately preparing for delivery and payment.

Customer orders. Customer orders can directly trigger a need for more materials. You can imagine this in a wholesaler, where demand from a retailer reduces stock levels and triggers an order for replenishment from a manufacturer. Then purchasing effectively passes the order backwards to a supplier.

Forecasts. Market forecasts can also signal a need for material. For instance, a forecast that suggests a rising demand for a product can signal a need for additional materials.

Reorder level system. Inventory management systems monitor the stocks of all items, as well as operating characteristics such as costs, forecasts of demand, lead times, variability, average stock levels, service level, investment, etc. The system uses this information to calculate a reorder level for each item. When the actual stock declines to this level, the inventory management system sends a message to purchasing that it is time to replenish the item.

Stock checks. Although inventory management systems record the amount of each item currently in stock, there can be differences between the amount recorded and the amount actually available. These differences might be caused by damage, theft, deliveries or withdrawals that were not properly recorded, deterioration, errors in product identification codes and so on. To find such differences between the notional stock records and the actual stock available firms do checks to count the physical stocks. When the physical stock of an item is below the system amount, this may trigger a request for another order from suppliers.

New product development teams. When purchasing is part of a new product development team, it can see product designs at an early stage and identify the type of materials that will be needed. Then it can proactively look for items and their potential suppliers, rather than waiting for a request from operations. This leads to faster product development times with better supplier evaluation and selection. It also gives an opportunity for purchasing to identify difficulties with acquiring certain materials, or suggest changes that would allow standard, cheaper or more readily available items to be substituted.

Identify and select a supplier

After the description of materials has been finalized, there are three alternatives. Either the materials can be made internally by the organization's own operations, or

FIGURE 2.4 Purchase requisition flow

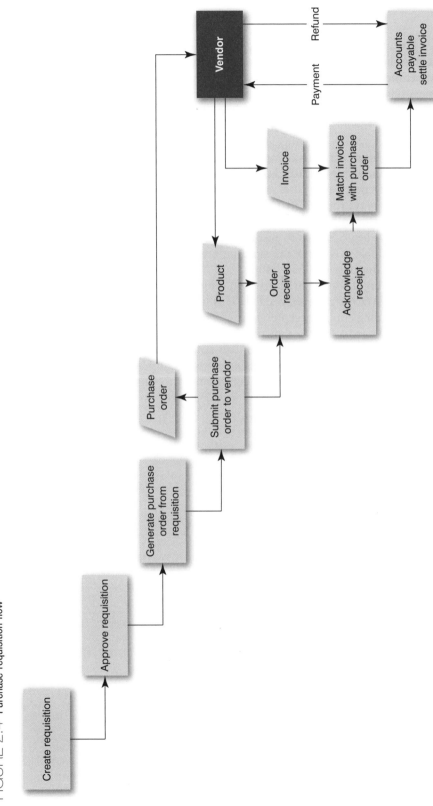

they can be bought from an existing supplier that already has a working relationship with the organization, or no existing supplier may be able to meet the demand and the organization has to find a new one. The first of these may not need purchasing input, but needs more operational scheduling and planning. With the second alternative, purchasing should move smoothly as there is already a qualified supplier with a history of successfully working with the organization. The third alternative is most complicated as the organization has to find a new supplier.

Sometimes an internal user may specify a supplier with whom they have some business relationship, and when the materials are relatively unimportant this may be a reasonable option. For the smallest purchases it may not be worth using the purchasing function, and then users can go straight to suppliers. We have already mentioned this maverick buying, and this is reasonable – and even to be encouraged – when there is little cost or risk. For example, if internal customers quickly need a box of paper, it is probably best for them to go and buy one from a local stationery store. However, maverick buying uses suppliers that have not been checked or approved, and there is always the risk that they are not acceptable traders. When there is any significant cost or importance involved, materials should only be bought from suppliers that have been checked to ensure that they are properly qualified. This checking of potential suppliers is one of the most important tasks of procurement, and mistakes here can be damaging and long-lasting.

The selection of a supplier starts with a long-list of potential suppliers who may be able to deliver the material needed. This list may be generated from a variety of sources, including company representatives, existing or previously known suppliers, information databases, trade directories, competitors' suppliers, trade journals, advertisements and so on. The next job is to consider the long-list and reduce it to a manageable short-list stage. For this buyers will consider the suppliers' expertise, past performance, product designs, commitment to quality, management experience, technical ability, costs, delivery performance, financial security, flexibility, innovation, technology used, management systems and a whole series of other

LEARNING FROM PRACTICE

Purchasing at the design table

When firms design new products, they have to consider the purchase of all materials needed to make them. Many companies now understand the importance of involving purchasing at an early stage of product development. The traditional approach of designing a product, and then hoping that purchasing can get all the materials needed is no longer acceptable.

'We (involve purchasing) before the creative process,' says a Senior Communications Manager at Daimler. 'Basically, before we start developing a vehicle, we want to have everyone involved.'

Maytag, a leading manufacturer of domestic appliances, found it best to involve purchasing during the initial concept phase of new product development. 'We quickly realized that for us (purchasing) helped

drive innovation, so we had to have purchasing representation in research and development,' a procurement director of the company explained.

The Chief Purchasing Officer (CPO) at Freescale Semiconductors stated that, 'Buyers need to have early involvement in the design process.' Then they become closely involved with product design, contribute to product delivery, understand the materials needed and generally combine the skills of purchasing and engineering.

A supply manager at Sciconic sums this up by saying, 'New product design groups need to know what materials are available and how they work. Input from purchasing at an early stage is the best way of getting this.'

Source: Based on Milligan B. (2000) What purchasing brings to the table, *Purchasing*, pp 54–60; Varzamis M. (2006) Procurement and design mesh at Freescale, *Purchasing*.

factors. These factors are weighted in a supplier evaluation process (which we describe in chapter 7) and the overall best performers are put on a short list. Typically a buyer will look for a short-list of between four and six potential suppliers.

Buyers now have to choose the best supplier from the available short-list, and there are two ways of doing this – competitive bidding and negotiation. Competitive bidding means that an organization sends out a **request for quotation or proposal (RFQ)** to all companies on the short-list. This RFQ invites companies to submit a bid for a purchase contract. The RFQ contains the information that suppliers need to develop an accurate quotation, including a description of the item, quantity wanted, date needed, delivery location, quality requirements, whether the buyer will consider substitute offers, date for returning the quote and so on. Those suppliers who feel that they can meet the requirements specified in the RFQ submit a bid to the buyer, giving details of their products, costs, contact person, payment terms, delivery details and all other relevant information. Then the buyer can compare the quotations received and select the best. This seems a simple step, but it is notoriously difficult to compare bids that specify different products, made in different ways, with different quality, costs, lead time, reliability, materials, finances and terms and conditions.

Request for quotation or proposal (RFQ)
Document to collect terms, conditions and other information from potential suppliers.

Competitive bidding is most effective when:

- Orders are large enough to justify the effort involved
- Specifications are clear and give potential suppliers enough information to estimate accurately the work and costs involved
- The marketplace is competitive, with enough qualified sellers wanting the business
- Buyers only ask for bids from a short-list of qualified suppliers that want the contract and who will offer competitive terms
- Enough time is available for suppliers to evaluate and respond to the request for quotation
- The buyer does not already have a preferred supplier

Electronic bidding tools have become more popular as a way of reducing administration, with a popular one described as a **reverse auction** or an **e-auction**. These have a buyer describing its requirements on a dedicated website and qualified potential suppliers going online to submit bids for the business. Each supplier can usually see a summary of competing bids, and to win the contract they have to submit a lower – or somehow better – one. These are somewhat ruthless affairs, but reverse auctions can drive down prices when there is a competitive market.

Reverse or e-auction
Auction run through a buyer's website.

Sometimes there are not enough qualified suppliers to form a short-list – or maybe the specifications are so complex that the buyer and sellers need more detailed negotiations. Then buyers might approach a very small number of companies – often one – and ask for a request for proposal (RFP). In principle an RFP is identical to a request for quotation, but some people say that they describe more complicated purchases and need more issues to be covered in the response. When the buyers get these responses back they can negotiate terms and home-in on a final contract. This approach is used when:

- Any of the criteria listed for competitive bidding are missing (for instance, the item may be technically complex with only vague specifications)
- For some reason, competitive bidding is not an appropriate way of choosing a supplier
- The purchase requires agreement about a wide range of factors, including price, quality, delivery, risk sharing, finance, technology, product support, etc.

- Face-to-face negotiations lead to more understanding and better results

- The buyer wants early supplier involvement

- It is difficult for suppliers to determine the likely risks and costs

- Suppliers need a long time to develop and produce the items

Whichever route is taken – competitive bidding or negotiation – the aim of this stage is to select a single supplier, and hopefully develop a long-term trading relationship with increasing co-operation. If this does not happen, it may be a sign that things are not really working and another supplier might be needed.

Approval, contract and purchase order

This stage is concerned with the administration of the actual order, which is usually based on a **purchase order**.

Purchase order
Is the legally binding document that triggers the delivery of materials. It is the contract between a buyer and seller.

Traditionally the front of a purchase order gives all relevant information about the purchase – specifications, quantity, quality, price, delivery date, method of delivery, delivery address, purchase order number, due date and so on. Then on the back of the order are the standard legal conditions. When you buy something, you may well skip over the standard conditions – the small print on the back of an order – but these are important and purchasing departments always have to look at them in detail.

When purchase orders were printed on paper, firms had a cumbersome process for moving anything up to nine copies around their administration systems. Now purchasing is likely to email a purchase order to the supplier, who returns a receipt to acknowledge that it has arrived and that the terms are agreed. In legal terms, sending the purchase order constitutes the buyer's contractual offer, while the receipt constitutes the seller's contractual acceptance. Although each country has its own unique legal system, this procedure of making an offer and having it accepted is the critical element of most legally binding agreements.

Copies of the purchase order are sent to concerned stakeholders – or as the information is maintained on purchasing's database this really means that the stakeholders are given access to relevant parts of the database. These stakeholders include people who do the following activities:

- *Accounting,* to control cash flows and obligations. Suppliers send an invoice asking for payment, and then accounting match this to an order, check that the delivery has been made, and then arrange payment

- *Users,* who are the internal customers who need the materials, and they authorize a receipt to say that the expected materials have arrived according to agreed terms and that payment can be made from their departmental budget

- *Receiving* to accept deliveries into an organization. They have a schedule of expect deliveries, what they should contain and what to do with them – with formal procedures describing what to do when a delivery does not match a purchase order

- *Quality management,* to check delivered materials and make sure that they reach agreed levels of quality

- *Transport,* who arrange delivery of the materials either using the firm's own vehicles or contract transport

- *Expediting,* who monitor deliveries and take follow-up action for those that are late or likely to experience problems

Some materials are only bought once, and then a purchase order is used for a spot buy. But many items, such as components used for manufacturing, are ordered repeatedly from the same supplier. Rather than send out a series of separate purchase orders, it is better to replace them with a single blanket purchase order. This is an open order, perhaps effective for a year, which covers all purchases of an item during this period. In effect a blanket order says, 'We have agreed terms, now send deliveries when we request them over the next year.' Then ordering an item needs a simple, routine message – a material release – to arrange another delivery. When they have been set up, the administration of blanket orders is much simpler, so they are often the preferred way of ordering.

Blanket orders are often linked to production plans, so they might specify actual orders for the first 3 months, then likely orders for the next 3 months, followed by forecast orders for the next 6 months. This is a common pattern with blanket orders typically covering a year at a time, though they may be used for shorter periods. In practice, organizations are looking for longer-term alliances and partnerships, so the period covered is increasing. But longer-term contracts can bring their own problems, especially when conditions change quickly and unexpectedly, so buyers usually reserve the right to cancel a blanket order using an escape clause.

The key point about all purchase orders is that they are legally binding documents. They define contracts for the purchase of materials described, and also explicitly state the terms and conditions of purchase, the roles and responsibilities of buyers and sellers and how conflicts will be resolved. It follows that purchasing staff must understand the legal aspects of business transactions is part of their core knowledge. Once a contract has been agreed and signed, purchasing staff are responsible for ensuring that all the terms and conditions are met. If the contract terms are breached in any way, purchasing staff are also responsible for resolving the subsequent disputes.

Blanket purchase order
Order covering several deliveries over an extended period.

Material release
Message to arrange another delivery with a blanket order.

Receive materials

When an order has been placed and administered, the next step concerns the actual delivery of materials. For goods, this means that they are transported, arrive at the buyer, are received, unpacked, sorted, inspected, moved into storage and the purchasing system is updated to acknowledge their arrival. For services, receiving means that specified jobs have been completed according to the terms of the purchase order. When this is confirmed, an acknowledgement can be sent.

In principle, the receipt of materials should be routine, and just-in-time (JIT) systems remove all the receiving administration by taking steps to ensure that deliveries always arrive in good order. However, there can be problems and purchasing should monitor deliveries to make sure that things are going as planned, or else expedite an order when it seems likely to be delayed.

Receiving materials into an organization needs three important documents – a packing slip, Bill of Lading and receiving discrepancy report.

Packing slip is provided by the supplier and lists the contents of a shipment. It gives a description of the items in a delivery, along with information about the destination, buyer, purchase order and so on. When a delivery arrives, the receiving department use this document to compare the materials specified in the slip with both the purchase order and the items actually delivered.

Bill of Lading is used by transport operators to record all the information they need for a journey – including a summary of the materials, ownership, transport to be used, routes, terms of trade, delivery dates and so on. For example, a Bill of Lading may say that a carrier is delivering three boxes to a buyer on a certain date, and that these boxes are owned by the buyer – with details of the boxes' contents given in the packing slip. When a delivery is made, the receiving department confirms that the delivery matches the Bill of Lading, and this helps protect the carrier against claims that goods were damaged or lost on the journey. Of course, this does not protect the carrier against later claims of concealed damage that a user only discovers after opening a shipping container. It is often difficult to establish responsibility for concealed damage – as the buyer may blame the supplier or the carrier, the carrier may blame the supplier or say that damage occurred with the buyer after delivery, and the supplier may blame the carrier or the buyer.

Receiving discrepancy report lists any inconsistencies noted by the receiving department which purchasing has to investigate and resolve. Material discrepancies usually note that the wrong amounts were delivered, but they can also find wrong items, damaged goods, poor quality, incorrect labelling or other problems.

Once materials have been delivered the buyer will arrange payment to the supplier, with the accounts payable department typically transferring funds from the buyer's bank account to the supplier's using EFT. At the same time, all relevant records are updated to show that the purchase has been completed. These records accumulate over time and they allow the purchasing department to monitor various aspects of purchasing and delivery, and to identify trends in performance.

Measure and manage supplier performance

The overall purpose of performance measurement is to improve the purchasing process, and particularly supplier performance. Performance measurement over time allows buyers to assess the efficiency of a supplier's operations, see whether this is changing over time, compare performance with other suppliers, ensure that agreed targets are actually met, make comparison with industry norms, identify areas that need improvement and anything else that relies on objective measures.

All supplier activities should be monitored, but a common question asks how often it should be summarized and reported. Is it best to give feedback every week, month, quarter or year? There is little consensus about this, but the most common reporting frequency for routine reports seems to be monthly or quarterly. Needless to say, firms notify suppliers immediately when something goes wrong. Supplier performance measurement is an important part of the purchasing process, which we discuss in more detail in chapter 18.

LEARNING FROM PRACTICE

University of Southern Queensland

The University of Southern Queensland (USQ) was opened as an Institute of Technology in 1967 and became a university in 1992. It has since developed its research and postgraduate programme, expanded its international profile and grown as a multi-campus institution – based on campuses in Toowoomba, Hervey Bay and Springfield. The University now has over 26,000 students, including 7,500 international ones from 120 countries.

The procedure for purchasing at USQ is described in a detailed manual. It is based on four categories of purchases – less than $5000, between $5,000–

10,000, between $10,000–100,000 and more than $100,000. We can illustrate the general approach by the 16 steps needed for purchases of $5,000–10,000, which starts when a Purchasing Officer (PO) receives a request from a user. Various forms are completed, but the system is automated and works through EDI with virtually no paper used.

Step 1 Official purposes. The PO ensures that the planned acquisition is for official university purposes.

Step 2 Planning. The PO makes an initial assessment of the amount of effort needed to acquire the items, making sure that too much time and effort is not put into minor purchases. Some market research may be needed to collect basic information about the planned acquisition, including suppliers and estimated costs.

Step 3 Adequate procurement delegation. Based on their research, a PO checks that they have enough authority to acquire the item. If they have this authority they move on to step 4: if the item is too expensive and the PO does not have enough authority, they refer the job to a more senior PO or to the University Procurement Administrator.

Step 4 Investigate available budget funds. The PO makes sure that the specified budget has enough funds for the acquisition.

Step 5 Investigate university sources. The PO checks whether there are any internal sources for the item, in which case the PO uses the Internal Order System to arrange a delivery. The most common internal suppliers are the Refectory, Building and Facilities, Media Services and Printing. When there is no internal source, the PO initiates external sourcing.

Step 6 Determine the evaluation criteria. The PO determines the most appropriate criteria to evaluate the acquisition, which is usually value for money. However, other criteria may be important, such as urgency, quality or availability.

Step 7 Mandatory standing offer and/or panel supply arrangements. The PO must check whether the acquisition is covered by a mandatory standing offer and/or panel supply arrangements. If it is, then the PO must acquire the item from the specified supplier, and move on to step 11.

Step 8 Non-mandatory standing offer and/or panel supply arrangements. There are also be non-

mandatory – or preferred – standing offer and/or panel supply arrangements, and the PO checks the benefits of using these relative to the benefits from using other suppliers. If the PO decides that the best deal comes from using the non-mandatory arrangements, they move on to step 11.

Step 9 Invitation to suppliers. When a supplier has not been chosen in steps 5, 7 or 8, the PO sends invitations to offer out to enough prospective suppliers to ensure that the university gets value for money.

Step 10 Decision process. The PO compares replies from the invitations to suppliers in step 9, using the evaluation criteria defined in step 6, and decides which supplier offers the best deal.

Step 11 Consideration of legal implications. The PO has to consider various legal implications of an offer, such as contractual agreements, warranties, maintenance agreements, Workplace Health and Safety and licensing requirements. Before any agreements are signed the PO has to clear these with the University Legal Officer.

Step 12 Complete the Requisition Form. When the choice of supplier has been finalized the PO completes a Requisition Form which sends a message to the University Financial Systems that a purchase is to be made.

Step 13 Generate purchase order. Details of the requisition are transmitted to the Financial System which produces an official University Purchase Order and sends it to the chosen supplier.

Step 14 Order expediting. This is needed when the PO believes that it is necessary to confirm – or usually to overcome difficulties and speed-up – delivery of the order.

Step 15 Goods receipt. When the delivery is made, the PO ensures that the Goods Receipt transaction is entered into the Financial System. This informs the Accounts Payable Section that the delivery has been completed and they should pay the supplier.

Step 16 Payment to supplier. Payment to the supplier is made when the Finance Department have both the Goods Receipt transaction and an invoice from the supplier.

Source: Based on USQ (2007) Purchasing manual, USQ, Toowoomba, Queensland.

EFFICIENT PURCHASING

Firms clearly want an efficient purchasing process that minimizes the amount of time and effort spent. One approach to this suggests that purchasing should spend most time on expensive and important items, and put little effort into routine and cheap ones. One study of maintenance, repair and operating purchases reported that the average cost of goods bought was $50, but administration raised the total cost of a transaction to $150 (Antonette *et al.*, 2002). A similar study in the US government reported 1.1 million purchasing transactions with an average administration cost of $300. It makes no sense to have the cost of processing an order higher than the price paid for materials – but you will find that this actually happens in many organizations.

A general approach to improvement

We can start by describing a general approach to improving purchasing efficiency, and then consider some specific steps. This general approach is based on a plan-do-check-act cycle (Waters, 2009), which has a team of people going around to search for things that could be done better, using the cycle:

plan – looking at the existing purchasing process, collecting information, discussing alternatives and suggesting a plan for improvement

do – where the plan is implemented and data is collected on performance

check – which analyses the performance data to see if expected improvements actually appeared

act – if there are real improvements the new procedures are made permanent, but if there are no improvements, lessons are learnt and the new procedures are not adopted

The team is continuously looking for improvements, and at this point they return to the beginning of the cycle, and start looking for other improvements. This cycle is a good starting point, but a more detailed approach has the following steps.

1 Make everyone aware that procurement needs to continually improve, describing the reasons, alternatives and likely effects. Get senior management support for initiatives.

2 Examine current operations, identify the aims, measure performance, check how well the aims are being achieved, identify problems and weaknesses.

3 Use benchmarking and other comparisons to identify potential improvements.

4 Identify specific areas for improvement.

5 Design better purchasing operations using the knowledge, skills and experience of everyone concerned.

6 Discuss the proposals widely and get people committed to the new methods.

7 Design a detailed plan for implementing the improvements, anticipating likely problems rather than waiting for them to happen.

8 Make any necessary changes to purchasing's organization, systems, facilities, etc.; give appropriate training, set realistic goals and show how these can be achieved.

9 At a specific point, implement the changes.

10 Monitor progress and control the results, giving support and encouragement, discussing progress, problems, adjustments, etc.

11   Remain committed to the new methods while they are giving improvements – but accept that they are only temporary and continually look for further improvements.

This seems a rather formal list, but it is based on simple principles – analysing where you want to go and how you can get there. In reality, most improvements make a relatively small adjustment to operations which can be easily absorbed, causes few disruptions and avoids major trouble. A stream of such small adjustments builds a momentum for improvement that can give dramatic results – and make sure that procurement is continually getting better.

Specific types of improvement

Step 5 in the improvement cycle above designed better purchasing operations. Each firm looks for improvements in its own way and depending on its own circumstances – but there are some standard ways that many firms find useful (Trent and Kolchin, 1999).

Electronic data interchange. We have already seen that EDI allows remote computers to exchange information. Industry standards are now almost universal for EDI and it is the most widely used means of improving procurement, both eliminating steps in the purchasing process and making remaining steps easier. It is now a standard part of purchasing, with a survey in 1993 predicting that 65 per cent of all purchasing transactions would soon use EDI systems (by 1997 the actual figure was still only 32 per cent – but continuing to grow).

Online requisitioning systems. These are internal systems that link –through intranets or the internet – various users directly to the purchasing department. When users want purchasing's involvement in acquiring materials they can use standard templates for various types of message. The result is a fast and reliable means of communication that replaces the traditional paper form, internal memo, email or telephone call.

Online ordering systems. This uses the internet to link a purchaser's system to a supplier's, and can transmit routine orders. This is particularly useful with blanket orders, where an automatic material release sent to the supplier's order-entry system can trigger another delivery. Advantages of online ordering systems include:

- Faster order input giving shorter lead times
- Allow automatic orders, especially material releases for blanket orders
- Fewer errors in orders
- Ability to automatically track orders
- Immediate order acknowledgment from the supplier, along with details of delivery
- Batching of orders from multiple users into a single online order

E-Purchasing. This is a broad set of purchasing activities that involve some use of the internet. At a basic level, this might involve procurement managers transmitting orders through their supplier's website. At a more sophisticated level virtually all purchasing procedures are automated and organized through the internet. Surveys (Cummings, 2002; www.BarclaysB2B.com) suggest that by 2002 over 60 per cent of UK companies used e-procurement, and 80 per cent of European managers soon expected to use it regularly. When a major software company introduced e-procurement it estimated the costs shown in Figure 2.5, giving a return on investment (ROI) of 400 per cent a year (Waters, 2009). Such savings alone are a significant reason for moving to e-procurement, but it also brings the advantages of:

- Allowing instant access to suppliers anywhere in the world

- Creating a transparent market where products and terms are readily available

- Automating procurement with standard procedures

- Greatly reducing the time needed for transactions

- Reducing costs, typically by 12–15 per cent

- Convenient access to markets that are always available

- Outsourcing some procurement activities to suppliers or third parties

- Integrating seamlessly with suppliers' information systems

The two main types of e-procurement are described as B2B (where one business buys materials from another business) and B2C (when a final customer buys from a business). Other options include B2G (business to government), C2C (consumer to consumer) and even B2E (business to employee). In 1998 the future of B2B was clearly signalled when both General Motors and WalMart announced that they would only buy from suppliers through e-procurement. By 2002 the value of B2B passed a trillion dollars and continued to rise strongly (MRO Software, 2001).

Ordering through electronic catalogues. You are probably familiar with B2C transactions, where we buy books, music, software or travel from company websites. The dominant format has online catalogues that you use to choose products, and then order forms to make your purchase. Between 1999 and 2002 the number of people using these in the UK rose from 2 million to 6 million (Rushe, 2001). The main benefits of electronic catalogues ar their powerful search capability and low transaction costs. However, forecasts that the majority of shopping would soon be done through the internet were mistaken and by 2007 'e-tailing' probably accounted for 5 per cent of retail sales.

Online auctions. C2C transactions are growing largely through online auctions, where customers bid against each other for products. The best known of these is

---

FIGURE 2.5

Savings by moving to
e-procurement (costs in
€ per transaction)

Process step	Original cost	Cost with e-procurement
1. Create detailed requirement	17.2	9.3
2. Approval process	5.5	2.7
3. Check requirements	20.2	0
4. Order processing	54.4	6.8
5. Receiving	10.3	2.9
6. Internal delivery	35.0	13.0
7. Payment process	23.6	0.6
Total	**166.2**	**35.3**

eBay, with 276 million registered users trading goods worth $60 billion in 2007 (www.ebay.com). Although still smaller in scale, online auctions are becoming more common for B2B. We have already mentioned these in the context of reverse auctions, where a company publishes its requirements and asks suppliers to bid; the supplier that gives the best bid before the end of the specified auction time wins the contract.

E-Marketplaces. As the systems that support e-purchasing become more sophisticated, firms have expanded their scope, starting with buying exchanges. With these, a major company creates its own, private networks for dealing with suppliers, and they only trade with members of this network. Potential suppliers apply for access, which they are only given when they meet certain requirements. General Motors, Ford and DaimlerChrysler initially formed their own trading networks, but merged them when they recognized that they dealt with common suppliers and it was easier to work in a single market (Simson *et al.*, 2000). Buying exchanges evolved into *e-marketplaces,* which are large websites that allow easier interactions between businesses. Essentially potential buyers and sellers enter the e-marketplace, and the system helps them find each other and looks after all the transactions and payments. This makes B2B faster, easier and cheaper. E-marketplaces often specialize in specific industries or types of product.

Longer-term purchase agreements. These are often a result of partnerships or strategic alliances and – while both sides continue to benefit from the arrangements – can last for many years. Such agreements reduce transaction costs by eliminating the search for suppliers, making purchasing routine, reducing the need for periodic reviews, gain benefits from collaboration, encouraging blanket orders and so on.

Allowing users to contact suppliers directly. We have already mentioned that there is little point in having expensive purchasing departments involved in buying low-

Source: Based on Handfield R. (2006) Best practices in the procure to pay cycle, *Practix*, Centre for Advanced Purchasing Management, Tempe, AZ.

LEARNING FROM PRACTICE

Purchasing improvement

In 2006 a limited study of senior purchasing managers asked for recommendations to improve the purchasing process. This does not give a comprehensive view of process improvement, but it identifies some management concerns. Apart from technical features, such as increasing internet use and more flexible system, there were a number of other common themes, including:

- Robust and standardized processes that are simple to use
- The essential need for continual training
- Clear definitions of the roles of different people

- Customer and supplier relationship managers who can help with transactions and liaise between users and suppliers
- Simplified and automated procedures for dealing with transactions
- Standardized systems that can talk to each other without reconfiguration
- Improved forecasting to help plan the purchasing of materials
- Simpler catalogues and easier interfaces to streamline purchasing

value, routine purchases, and it is often more efficient to let users buy items themselves. This is particularly true with e-purchasing that allows users to make fast and easy searches for products – and it shifts responsibility for these routine transactions from purchasing to users. Usually, there is some ceiling, with items of lower value bought directly by users, and items of higher value referred to purchasing.

User procurement cards. When users can contact suppliers directly, transactions can be made easier by a procurement card, which is essentially a company credit card that internal users can use with suppliers. It provides a convenient way of purchasing items that are not included in other purchasing systems, and with users making decisions they can bypass purchasing completely. The transactions are controlled, perhaps to specific suppliers or up to a limited value, and the money comes from departmental budget. Such systems have been found to reduce the average cost of a transaction from over \$80 to under \$30 (Trent and Kolchin, 1999).

CHAPTER REVIEW

- The basic aim of purchasing it to ensure a supply of materials needed by an organization. Within this, there are a series of other objectives, including supporting organizational aims, developing purchasing strategies, supporting operational needs, using purchasing resources efficiently, supply base management and developing strong relationships with suppliers.

- Purchasing's span of control describes the functions for which it is ultimately responsible. Four important ones concern the choice of suppliers, decisions about materials bought, to act as a primary contact with suppliers and to decide how to make a purchase.

- Good purchasing does not just happen, but it needs careful management. This can be viewed in terms of enablers that allow or encourage good purchasing, and inhibitors which prevent it. Four leading enablers are human resources, organizational design, information systems and performance measurement.

- The purchasing process describes all the steps needed to acquire materials. There is no single approach to purchasing, and the best process varies with conditions. However, most purchasing is based on a process with six main steps – to recognize user need for materials, clarify needs, select a supplier, submit a purchase order, receive materials and manage supplier performance.

- Each step in the purchasing process has associated documents which provide the associated flow of information. These documents are largely automated through EDI or e-purchasing systems.

- Organizations continuously strive to improve their procurement. There are many was of doing this, with one approach using a team to systematically search for and implement new procedures. There are also standard ways of improving performance that range from using e-purchasing to moving purchasing staff to work with suppliers.

DISCUSSION QUESTIONS

1 How can a purchasing department affect organizational performance?

2 What exactly is an 'internal customer'? Who are purchasing's internal customers?

3 Why and how might a purchasing department contribute to broader organizational strategies?

4 What tasks are typically considered within purchasing's span of control? Why is it important for purchasing to have authority in these areas?

5 What are the four main enablers of good purchasing? What are the main inhibitors?

6 How do purchasing departments become aware of user requirements?

7 How does procurement's anticipation of material purchases through their involvement in new product development teams differ from their traditional role of reacting to user needs?

8 What are the main documents and templates that would be provided by a suite of e-procurement software?

9 Why is it important to measure and monitor supplier performance?

10 What is the difference between a purchase order and a blanket purchase order? What are the advantages of blanket purchase orders?

11 How do JIT operations reduce the need for certain purchasing documents?

12 How does the purchase of capital equipment differ from the purchase of routine supplies?

13 Should non-purchasing staff be allowed to talk directly to suppliers?

REFERENCES

Antonette G., Sawchuk C. and Giunipero L. (2002) *Purchasing plus* (2nd edition), New York: JGC Enterprises.

Avery S. (2007) UTC General Procurement presents Key Supplier of the Year Awards, *Purchasing*, March 15.

Champoux J. E. (2000) Organizational behavior: essential tenets for a new millennium, Cincinnati, OH: South-Western.

Cummings N. (2002) UK leading the world in e-procurement, *OR Newsletter*, March 9.

Giunipero I. and Handfield R. (2004) Purchasing education and training II, Tempe, AZ: CAPS Research.

Hofman, D. (2006) Getting to world-class supply chain measurement, *Purchasing*, October 1 and website at www.purchasing.com

Kalkota R. and Robinson E. (2000) Business 2.0: roadmap for success, Boston, MA: Addison-Wesley.

MRO Software (2001) Supplying the goods, London: MRO Software.

Porter A. M. (1999) Raising the bar, *Purchasing*, January 14, pp 50–44.

Rushe D. (2001) www.basketcase, *The Sunday Times*, September 2, p 5.

Simson R., Werner F. and White G. (2000) Big three carmakers plan net exchange, *The Wall Street Journal*, February 28th, 2000.

Trent R. J. (2003) Supply management organizational design effectiveness study, Working paper, Bethlehem, PA: Lehigh University.

Trent R. J. and Kolchin M. G. (1999) Reducing the transaction costs of purchasing low-value goods and services, *Tempe, AZ: Centre for Advanced Purchasing Studies*.

Waters D. (2009) *Supply chain management: an introduction to logistics* (2nd edition), Basingstoke, UK: Palgrave Macmillan.

www.BarclaysB2B.com, May 2009.

www.ebay.com, May 2009.

FURTHER READING

Angeles R. (2003) Electronic supply chain partnership: reconsidering relationship attributes in customer-supplier dyads, *Information Resources Management Journal*, 16(3): pp 59–84.

Antonette G., Sawchuk C. and Giunipero L. (2002) E-Purchasing plus (2nd edition), New York: *JGC Enterprises*, Goshen.

Billington C. and Jager F. (2008) Procurement: the missing link in innovation, *Supply Chain Management Review*, January.

Croom S.R. (2000) The impact of web-based procurement on the management of operating resources supply, *Journal of Supply Chain Management*, Winter, pp 4–14.

Croom S. (2001) Restructuring supply chains through information channel innovation, *International Journal of Operations and Production Management*, 21(4): pp 504–515.

Giunipero L. C. (2000) World-class purchasing skills, *Journal of Supply Chain Management*, 36(4): pp 4–10.

Guinipero L.C. (2000) Purchasing plus: changing the way corporations buy, New York: JGC Enterprises.

Handfield R. (2006) Best practices in the procure to pay cycle, Practix, *Centre for Advanced Purchasing Management*, March, Tempe, AZ.

Hirsch C. and Barbalho M. (2003) Toward world-class procurement, *Supply Chain Management Review*, 5(6): p 75.

Martinson B. (2002) The power of the P-card, *Strategic Finance*, 83(8): pp 30–36.

Neef D. (2001) e-Procurement: from strategy to implementation, Upper Saddle River, NJ: Financial Times Prentice Hall.

Palmer R. J., Gupta M. and Davila A. (2003) Transforming the procure-to-pay process, *Management Accounting Quarterly*, 4(4): pp 14–22.

Rudzki R. A. (2008) Supply management transformation: a leader's guide, *Supply Chain Management Review*, March.

Slone R. E., Mentzer J. T. and Dittmann P. J. (2007) Are you the weakest link in your company's supply chain? *Harvard Business Review*, September.

Sabri E., Gupta A., and Beitler M. (2006) Purchase order management best practices, Fort Lauderdale, FL: J. Ross Publishing.

Smock D. A., Rudzki R. A. and Rogers S. C. (2007) Sourcing strategy – the brains behind the game, *Supply Chain Management Review*, May.

Wang Fu Industries

Organizations buy many different items, with the details of the purchasing process often depending on the type of materials. Here 'materials' can include raw materials, components, parts, equipment, spare parts, information, commercial services, expertise, consumables, energy, transport, money, utilities – and anything else you can think of.

Wang Fu Industries uses a traditional classification of materials, and uses slightly different procedures to purchase each category. For instance, raw materials are largely ordered JIT with material releases triggered automatically by the product tracking system; capital goods purchases often involve an extended bidding process.

The classification used by Wang Fu has:

- *Raw materials* such as oil, steel, wood, cotton, potatoes, etc. The feature of a raw material is that the supplier has done little work on them to transform them into finished products

- *Semi-finished products and components* which are items on which some processing has already been done, such as car panels, glazed windows, hard drives, memory chips, wheel bearings, etc. These are variously described as parts, components, sub-assemblies, assemblies, subsystems and systems

- *Finished goods* which are finished items that a firm needs to support its operations (such as telephones, cars, paint, etc.) or to sell on to the next tier of customers.

- *Maintenance, repair and operating (MRO) items* which include anything that does not go directly into an organization's product, but which are still essential for continuing operations. These include spare machine parts, office and computer supplies, cleaning supplies and general consumables

- *Production support items* which include the materials needed to pack and ship final products, such as pallets, boxes, containers, tape, bags, wrapping, inserts, etc.

- *Services* which range from legal services through to gardening. Common services include equipment maintenance, machine repair, data entry, accounting, catering, cleaning, market surveys, consultancy and so on

- *Capital equipment* for assets that are used for some extended period, such as warehouses, material handling equipment, manufacturing equipment, computer systems, etc. These purchases tend to be less frequent, more expensive and sensitive to prevailing economic conditions

- *Transport and third-party services* where a third party (say a transport company) offers a service to link two other parties (the supplier and the buyer). Most firms outsource transport and other parts of logistics to third party providers, which is generally continuing to grow rapidly

Questions

- Can you think of other categories of purchases that Wang Fu have not included in their list?

- What kind of purchasing process is likely to be used for each category of item?

- How do you think the purchasing process will develop in the near future?

CHAPTER 3
PURCHASING
STRATEGY

LEARNING OBJECTIVES   After reading this chapter you should be able to:

- Understand the nature of strategic decisions

- Discuss the strategic importance of purchasing

- Link a purchasing strategy to broader organizational strategies

- Describe a general procedure with five steps for designing a purchasing strategy

- Appreciate the use of specific analyses such as spend, portfolio and SWOT analyses

- List different types of purchasing strategy

- Discuss the way that sourcing strategies evolve over time

STRATEGIC DECISIONS

Some management decisions are very important, with widespread consequences felt over many years; other decisions are less important with consequences felt in a small part of an organization for a few days or even hours. We can use this importance to classify decisions as long-term strategic, medium-term tactical, or short-term operational (Waters, 2006).

Decisions at all three levels are made in every organization. For instance, Carnival made a strategic decision to offer holidays on cruise liners, tactical decisions about the liners' schedules, and operational decisions about the food bought in each port. The University of South Africa made a strategic decision to offer distance learning courses, a tactical decision to offer a particular course next semester, and operational decisions about the time various modules were posted.

A rough guideline suggests that strategic decisions have effects over the next three to 5 years, tactical decisions have effects around a year and operational decisions have effects up to a few weeks – but the scale of these decisions varies widely. For instance, a strategic decision for Electricité de France (EDF) considers the number of power stations it needs over the next thirty years and involves costs of billions of Euros – while a strategic decision for a village store looks a year into the future and involves costs of a few thousand Euros. Whatever the scale, the important point is that organizations need decisions at all three levels.

A traditional – and much simplified – view says that senior managers make the strategic decisions that set their organization's overall direction. They define its purpose and lay the broad principles of how to achieve this. Middle managers analyse these broad concepts and make tactical decisions about the actual work that is done. They form a link between abstract aspirations and positive actions, describing the actual jobs to be done. Junior managers make the operational decisions that ensure work is actually completed according to the plans

There is rarely a clear boundary between the levels of decision, and they often blur into one another. However, we should give a warning here. People gain status by dealing with higher level decisions, so there is a tendency to exaggerate a decision's importance – typically with medium-term decisions labelled as strategic. For instance, one wholesaler relabelled its entire purchasing department as 'Strategic Supply Management' staffed by 'Executive Supply Managers'. Their reasoning was that everyone in purchasing contributed to the long-term success of the organization, and they would feel more confident talking to suppliers at any level. There is no need to artificially promote decisions, as they all play an essential role. Purchasing would not get far if everyone really did plan its strategic direction, but no-one was left to order the materials needed tomorrow.

Purchasing and strategy

Purchasing needs decisions at all three levels – strategic, tactical and operational. Surprisingly, this realization has come relatively recently as purchasing decisions were conventionally limited to operational, or at best tactical questions. Now purchasing is increasingly recognized as having a strategic impact. For instance, if purchasing mistakenly places a long-term contract with an unreliable supplier, it can affect customer service, product quality, costs, sales, profit – and ultimately the firm's survival.

The strategic decisions made by purchasing fit into the broader decisions made within an organization. We can show their exact position on a standard model (shown in Figure 3.1) which has four levels of strategic decision (Waters, 2006; Vancil and Orange, 1975).

Strategic decisions
Are long-term decisions that have major consequences throughout an organization.

Tactical decisions
Are medium-term decisions that have less serious consequences for parts of the organization.

Operational decisions
Are short-term decisions that have relatively minor consequences for specific activities.

FIGURE 3.1

Different levels of strategy

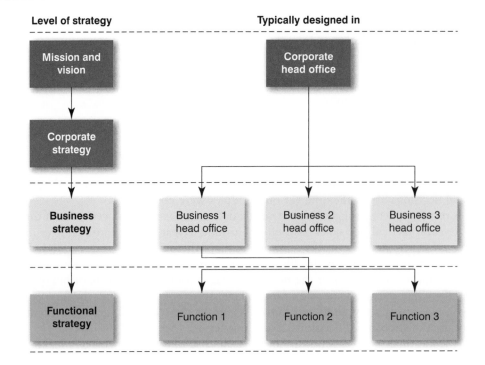

1   *A mission* or *vision,* is a concise, unambiguous statement of an organization's purpose and aims. It shows what the organization is going to do and achieve – and by implication, what it is not going to do.

2   *A corporate strategy,* adds details to the mission and shows how a whole enterprise will achieve its mission.

3   *A business strategy,* shows how each business unit will compete within its industry and contribute to the broader corporate strategy.

4   Each of the major management functions within a business has its own *functional strategy,* to show how it will contribute to the business strategy.

Together, these strategies are all co-ordinated and work together to ensure that the organization achieves its overriding aims.

A purchasing strategy is one of the functional strategies – alongside a marketing strategy, finance strategy, operations strategy and so on. Its aim is to give the long-term direction of purchasing, and show how this will help the organization achieve its broader aims. For instance, when a company has a strategic aim of improving profitability, a purchasing strategy could show how the function will reduce costs; when a firm wants a faster delivery to customers, a procurement strategy shows how the time spent on its part of the supply chain can be reduced.

ALIGNING PURCHASING AND BUSINESS STRATEGIES

Strategies are not just a set of decisions, but they include all of the factors that affect long-term performance – such as culture, infrastructure, resources, expertise and so

LEARNING FROM PRACTICE

FinnAirr

A basic decision for purchasing is what components a manufacturing company should make for itself, and what it should buy from suppliers. This always needs a balance of the benefits of maintaining control over essential supplies, and gaining potential cost and other benefits of purchasing from expert suppliers. There is a clear trend for companies to outsource more of their non-core activities, so that they can focus on core operations. The parallel growth of global sourcing means that suppliers are often located a long way from other operations.

FinnAirr is a manufacturer of industrial 'temperature-controlled environments' – which loosely translates as refrigeration and air conditioning equipment. In the 1990s they began outsourcing operations to local suppliers. These started with the usual legal services, maintenance, information processing, transport, etc. Then by 2000 they were outsourcing more activities,

with components made in China, Brazil and Indonesia, and information processing outsourced to India. In 2003 they made a major decision to close down an old and expensive plant in Sweden, and buy major components from a supplier in China. This collaboration worked very well, giving lower costs while maintaining high quality.

Then in 2008 the company felt the effects of the approaching global financial crisis. Managers realized that it could not continue with its existing operations, so they took the major decision to close down all European production, and buy finished products – with their own brand name attached – through an alliance with the supplier in China. FinnAirr now only has a sales force that continues selling their products, and an administrative staff who organize the flow of finished goods from the factory in China to their customers.

Source: FinnAirr (2009) Publicity material. FinnAirr, Helsinki.

on. Walker *et al.* support this inclusive view in their definition of strategy as 'A fundamental pattern of present and planned objectives, resource deployments and interactions of an organization with markets, competitors and other environmental factors (Walker et al., 2002).' A simplified view of these contents says that an organizational strategy describes:

1 The purpose of the organization.

2 An expansion of this into a series of objectives.

3 Plans to achieve these objectives.

If we consider a complex corporation, senior managers design a corporate strategy that shows how the whole organization can best achieve its mission. They look for answers to questions (Waters, 2006):

What values does the organization have, and how does it interact with stakeholders?

How can it keep growing and improving?

How much diversification or integration should there be?

Which industries and product segments does it work in?

Which business should it maintain, grow or contract?

Which businesses should it start, acquire, close or sell?

What are the relationships between the separate businesses?

What is the best allocation of investment and resources among businesses?

When the complex corporation is made up of a number of business units, each has its own business strategy. Senior managers in each business analyse the corporate strategy from their own perspective, and ask how they can best contribute to its success, asking:

What type of products do we make?

Who are our customers and how can we satisfy them?

Who are our competitors and how can we get a competitive advantage?

What geographical areas are our markets and operations in?

How much vertical integration should we have?

What are our long-term targets for profitability, productivity and other measures of performance?

How innovative are we, and how do we change over time?

A primary concern of senior purchasing managers is to align the purchasing strategy with the broader corporate strategy – and more specifically with the business strategy. For this they have to analyse the business aims and translate them into specific goals for procurement. These goals set the direction of purchasing and they set the context for more detailed tactical and operational plans.

Integrative design

The alignment of strategic purchasing objectives with business ones is clearly important, but it is notoriously difficult to achieve. For example, the business aim of 'reducing costs' may need detailed analysis and planning to become a purchasing goal of 'using e-procurement to reduce administrative costs'. Companies that manage this most successfully achieve strategic alignment using an integrative procedure. This means that the purchasing strategy is designed by – or at least has a significant input from – those people who are responsible for its implementation. And their decisions are made in the context of higher strategies.

> **Strategic alignment**
> Occurs when all the strategies in an organization support each other and work coherently together to achieve the overall mission.

An organization's mission is the starting point for its strategies. Corporate managers analyse this and take into account their competitive strengths, capabilities, competitive pressures, customer requirements, economic conditions, etc. to add details and define the corporate strategy. Business managers analyse this, work together to add details and define the business strategy. Purchasing managers analyse this, work together to add details and define the purchasing strategy. Then lower managers analyse this, work together to add details and make their tactical and operational decisions. In this way the ideas from the mission cascade down through all the levels of the organization to give a coherent set of decisions. The result is integrated decisions that support each other and work towards the common mission.

Figure 3.2 illustrates how strategic alignment might be achieved in a particular company.

Approaches to designing a purchasing strategy

A purchasing strategy has to go beyond broad principles of simply promising 'higher efficiency' or 'lowest cost' and it has to say how these aims will be achieved. Every organization designs its own strategies, so they come in a huge variety. The basic requirement of a purchasing strategy is to ensure that the process of acquiring materials helps achieve the business aims. So a useful starting point for designing a

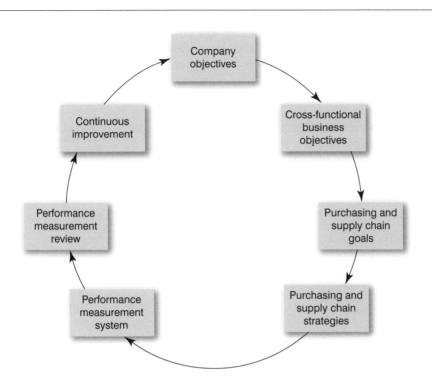

FIGURE 3.2

Integrative strategy
design

purchasing strategy is to analyse the business objectives that show what purchasing has to achieve. These business objectives usually include four features:

Measurement. Quantifiable aims are much more reliable and easier to manage that qualitative ones. It is much easier to work with an aim of 'reducing defects to ten parts per million' where we can measure performance and plot progress, than one of 'being a leader in quality products' which is largely a matter of opinion. Another important point is that absolute measures are often of limited use. For instance, even if you know that the sales of a shop are €1,000 a square metre a year, this tell you very little about its performance. Relative goals are more useful as they compare performance with fixed markers, typically competitors' performance, industry averages, targets or historical values. The sales of our shop are more useful if we know that they are 10 per cent higher than last year, but still 5 per cent lower than the main competitor.

Specificity. Some people suggest that there is a difference between objectives (which tend to be stated in broad, general terms) and goals (which are stated in more specific terms). Then 'we will give the best customer satisfaction' is a very broad objective that is difficult to manage, while 'we will reduce complaints by 3 per cent by the third quarter' is a specific goal.

Time frame. The time within which objectives must be achieved. Some people suggest that this is the major difference between a goal (which has to be achieved within a specified time) and an objective (which does not have a timescale). Then 'becoming the market leader' is an objective, while 'increasing market share by ten per cent this financial year' is a goal.

Focus. Aims may be stated in terms related to the external business environment, or else they may be internally focussed and show how resources will be used. For instance, the statement that 'we will be one of the three largest providers of . . .' has an external, customer focus, while 'we will invest 10 per cent of revenues in new technology' is internally focussed and shows how resources will be used.

Analysing the business objectives from a purchasing perspective is an important step in designing a purchasing strategy. This forms part of a larger procedure which we can describe in the following five steps (illustrated in Figure 3.3) (Waters, 2006).

1   *Analyse the purpose of the business* – which is summarized in its strategy, including a set of objectives, goals, procedures, performance measures, etc. This analysis defines the broad aims to be achieved by purchasing.

2   *Analyse the purchasing function* – including demands on its services, current state of operations, capabilities and particularly its strengths and weaknesses. This gives a detailed picture of the internal features of the procurement function.

3   *Analyse the environment in which the procurement function works* – including details of the broader organization, customers, competitors, economic conditions, likely future changes and particularly the opportunities and threats. This gives a detailed picture of the external environment in which procurement works.

FIGURE 3.3

Steps in designing a purchasing strategy

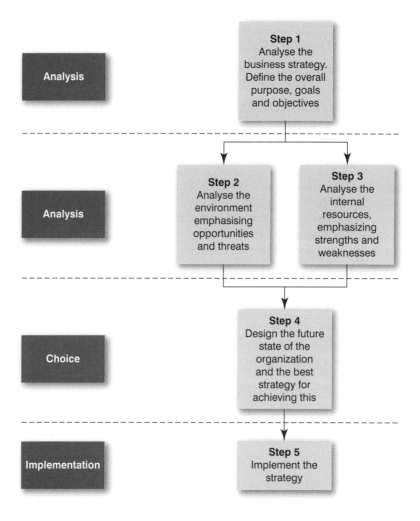

4   *Design the supply strategy* – to identify the best future state of procurement, and design policies for moving from its present state to this desired future one. Several strategies might move the function forward, and managers have to compare the alternatives and choose the best.

5   *Implement the results* – taking related decisions and actions through all levels of the function, monitoring progress, checking results and making adjustments.

This approach is traditionally summarized as 'analysis, choice and implementation' with steps 1 to 3 forming the analysis, step 4 forming the design and step 5 forming the implementation.

We should emphasize that there is no single best purchasing strategy that managers are trying to find. In any situation, there are many options and variations, and managers are trying to design a strategy that they think will be successful, rather than identify a notional 'optimal' one. In the same way, there is no single best way of designing a strategy. There is no straightforward recipe that automatically leads to a good strategy, and managers always have to use subjective argument and judgement. The results depend on their skills and expertise.

However, there are some useful guidelines to help managers design strategies. We will discuss some of these in relation to the five step approach shown in Figure 3.3.

STEP 1 – INITIATE STRATEGY DESIGN

We said that the first step is to analyse the business strategy, but this already makes some assumptions. For instance, it assumes that there is already someone waiting to design the strategy, and they have the necessary authority to implement it. So we should really take a step backwards and consider the preparation needed to initiate the design process.

Most strategic design projects have a 'champion' who provides leadership and takes the initiative to get the work started. For this they:

1   Get the support of key stakeholders, especially senior management; without their commitment there will be little progress.

2   Spend start-up money on resources to check current practices, identify problems, collect data, do research, train people, etc.

3   Build a business case for the strategy design project, assessing the costs, benefits, work to be done, contribution to company objectives, etc.

4   Sustain the initiative as it moves through the early stages.

The project champion who leads this effort is likely to be from purchasing, but sometimes they come from other departments, particularly finance. A survey suggests that 89 per cent of senior executives view supply chains as critical or very important to their company, with finance executives especially concerned (Accenture, 2003). Their control over budgets means that they increasingly add procurement to their responsibilities. Chief financial officers are in a good position to help design procurement strategies, as they wield significant corporate power but are not bound to any of the competing functions in procurement. The president of UPS Consulting says that they can bring 'a certain degree of coherence to what may be a fragmented reporting structure', and because they manage funding allocations they 'probably are in a critical position to be able to manage the trade-offs that should be made' (CFO Research Services, 2003).

At some point the project champion generally hands over to a project manager from purchasing who assembles a team, organizes the work and makes sure that the design is completed. This manager needs the usual project management skills of team building, leadership, decision-making, influencing stakeholders, compromising to reach a consensus and so on. An early requirement of the project manager is to write a project charter which gives a clear statement of the project aims, work to be done, budget, schedule and responsibilities.

At this point the foundations of the project have been laid, and the team responsible for designing the strategy can start their real work. With the model described earlier, this means analysing the business strategy from a purchasing perspective. The business strategy acts as a driver for the purchasing strategy and leads to purchasing goals and operations.

STEP 2 – ANALYSE THE PURCHASING FUNCTION

The purpose of this step is to develop a detailed view of current purchasing operations, and where the function should be heading in the future. A useful starting point for this is a review of current spending, described in a **spend analysis**.

Spend analysis
Examines and categorizes the spending done by purchasing.

Spend analysis

Published accounts show an overall cost of purchases, but this is an aggregate figure which has to be analysed to show the details of what was bought, who bought it, who supplied it, how much it cost and so on. This is often a revealing analysis as managers find that different business units are buying the same product with different terms, that they pay different amounts, that the same product is bought from several suppliers and so on. A spend analysis helps to improve purchasing efficiency by answering questions like:

What did the business buy over the past year? This is the basic analysis which shows the products bought. It also identifies opportunities to standardize products and reduce the number bought, switch from tailored to standard products, consolidate purchases, etc.

How much did the organization spend on purchases? This figure is essential for financial control and calculating the cost of goods sold. We have already seen that purchased materials typically accounts for more than 50 per cent of the cost of goods sold.

Did the business receive the right goods and services that it paid for? This is clearly an important question as continuing operations depend on having the right materials delivered.

Which suppliers received most business? This determines the strategic importance of each supplier – and identifies opportunities to consolidate orders from different parts of the organization, reduce the number of suppliers or exploit market conditions to get better terms.

Were invoices accurate and in agreement with purchase orders, contracts and statements of work? This checks that suppliers meet the financial requirements of their contracts.

Did each part of the organization spend its money on products and services as budgeted? This information helps with planning budgets and controlling spending.

A spend analysis shows the patterns of purchases and is an important planning document for managers in finance, operations, marketing, purchasing and accounting. Despite this, many firms struggle to do a comprehensive and accurate analysis, largely because it is based on a lot of transactional data that has to be properly recorded and analysed. Another problem is that accounting conventions, systems and procedures often vary across an organization, and it becomes difficult to reconcile different types of figures. Such problems are overcome with streamlined e-procurement, and the Aberdeen Group suggest that 'best-in-class' firms are more likely to actively control their spending, and this gives lower costs, fewer errors, fewer suppliers, more e-business and a range of associated benefits (Aberdeen Group, 2005).

Portfolio analysis

A variation on the spend analysis is a **portfolio analysis**, which describes a classification of purchases (shown in Figure 3.4)

The premise of portfolio analysis is that every purchase can be classified into one of four categories – routine commodity, bottleneck, leverage and strategic. This classification suggests the strategic importance of each type of purchase, with materials in the strategic and leverage quadrants generally offering the greatest opportunities for improving performance. Logically, the majority of purchasing's efforts and resources should be spent on these areas.

Routine commodity is characterized by many standard items with low price, and many suppliers competing through price. Typical examples are stationery, office cleaning services, vehicle repair, meals, petrol and so on. Routine commodities are

Portfolio analysis
Classifies different types of purchases.

LEARNING FROM PRACTICE

Promentia Avisoriala

Promentia Avisoriala (PA) offers a range of financial services, mainly to small and medium sized companies. They often perform spend analyses for clients who are extending their e-procurement systems, and they have developed standard procedure with the following steps.

1 Review the materials bought and define the main categories of products and suppliers.

2 Extract data from transaction records and find the amounts spent on each of these product and supplier categories.

3 Put the product categories in order of reducing amounts spent. This is a Pareto or '80/20' analysis, which shows that the 20 largest categories typically account for 80 per cent of total

spending, and these generally give the greatest opportunity for savings.

4 Find the number of suppliers for each category of product and sort these into descending order. Those categories at the top of the list have most suppliers and offer greatest opportunities for rationalization and savings.

5 Find the average amount spent with each supplier. Low average spending generally means that there are too many suppliers.

6 Find the amount spent with each supplier and sort these into ascending order. Rationalization might remove those suppliers with the lowest spending.

7 Consider the pattern of spending and systematically look for improvements.

Source: Promentia Avisoriala (2009) Company promotional material, Milan

FIGURE 3.4

Categories for portfolio
analysis

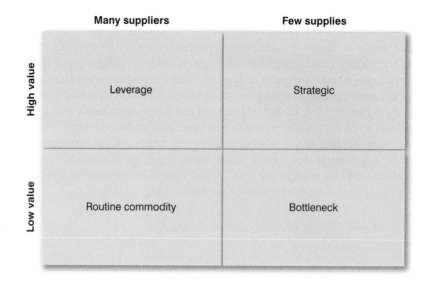

readily available, but because there are so many purchases they can use a disproportionate amount of administration. So the focus of purchasing is to reduce the
effort and overhead costs. They can do this by reducing the number of products
bought in this category by standardization, consolidation of purchases, substitution
of standard products and eliminating tailored items. GlaxoSmithKline standardized
some purchases when it found that its R&D group was using 50 different types of
Bunsen burners and beakers, because individuals had acquired particular preferences while at university. An alternative is to simplify the procurement process
using electronic tools (EDI, automatic ordering systems, on line catalogues, purchasing cards and any form of e-business). Staples reduced ordering costs to its
customers by consolidating purchases of office supplies made by company procurement cards (a type of corporate credit card) from their website catalogue.

Bottleneck occurs when a niche supplier is a sole source of some materials, and
specifications are so strict that no substitutes can be used. Such items need not be
expensive, but high performance or other unique features limit the number of suppliers. The product is usually important to the buyer, so they want to maintain
supplies. Sellers have a dominant position, which they will certainly exploit, and
purchasing can try to avoid this by changing specifications to allow new suppliers,
moving to standard products and continually scanning the market for additional
suppliers. Relations with the current supplier can be improved by using supplier
development, which we discuss in chapter 9.

Leverage is when there is a medium-to-high expenditure, but more suppliers limit
the supply risk. Items here are often industry standards that are purchased
throughout an entire organization. By combining the requirements of different units,
purchasing can negotiate a better deal with a few suppliers, ensuring them significant business over an extended period. Such arrangements give stability to suppliers who can use more efficient operations with lower unit costs and overheads. In
return, suppliers are often expected to maintain a high level of service that might
include management of on-site stocks, just-in-time deliveries, flexibility to respond
to changing conditions, shared cost reductions, etc. A growing trend is to use
e-auctions for such items.

Strategic includes unique, customized and expensive materials that are critical to an organization's success, but are only available from a few critical suppliers (such as speciality chemicals, developing technology, specialized software, aero engines, etc.). Because of the small number of suppliers, it is generally difficult to switch between them, so purchasing looks to develop long-term relationships that support and develop suppliers' capabilities that can give mutual benefits. According to Nelson, 'If you develop the right relationship with your supply base, you can have 10,000 additional brains thinking about ways to improve your product and generate cost savings. And that is very powerful! (Nelson, 2007)'.

STEP 3 – ANALYSING THE SUPPLY ENVIRONMENT

Having described the details of procurement, the next step for strategy designers is to consider the environment in which it works – and this broadly means an understanding of the relevant market places. In the same way that you do research before buying a car (such as reading reviews of vehicles, going to local car showrooms, finding consumer reports, checking advertisements in local newspapers, etc.) purchasing teams do the same type of market research on their suppliers. This is a critical activity to understand suppliers, their capabilities, products, conditions and general capacity to satisfy customer requirements. To make an informed decision about sourcing, buyers need:

- Information on current expenditure by product and supplier, which defines the organization's requirements and comes from the spend analysis

- Market research to assess current conditions in relevant markets, including the key suppliers, their performance, competition, capacity, pricing policies, patterns of customer demand, environmental and legal concerns, technology requirements and any other relevant information

- Changes in the market, including new prices, suppliers likely to enter or leave, new technology, economic changes, changing customer demands, changing strategies, etc.

This information comes from many sources. Primary data is specially collected by the purchasing firm (or maybe a collection agency that they employ), with sources including:

- Related websites which give many different types of data (with differing reliability)

- Trade journals, which give up-to-date pictures of what is happening in different industries

- Company annual reports and publicity

- Government statistics reviewing current conditions and trends

- Investment analyst reports, and other commentators on an industry

- Libraries of newspapers, books and reports

- Interviews with experts and trade consultants

- Conferences, seminars, talks and other presentations

- Suppliers, including all their staff and not just sales people

Primary data is guaranteed to be fit for its purpose and up to date – but it can be expensive to collect and analyse. The alternative is to use secondary data, which has already been collected for other purposes. If you want to find the opinion of suppliers about a certain proposal, you can collect primary data by running a survey of suppliers, or secondary data by finding opinions that have already been published. Secondary data is available from the same sources as primary data, and it has the clear advantages of being cheap and easy to collect. However, it has not been collected for a specific purpose, so it may not provide the specific information needed, and it is often outdated.

Analyses of the business environment

The data collected can be used in a number of formal analyses of the business environments, with one of the best known described as Porter's five forces (shown in Figure 3.5) (Porter, 1985). This classifies the major factors affecting competition, and purchasing managers can then design strategies that work best under these. The five forces are:

1   *Current competition* – including current competitors, size of companies, industry growth, capacity utilization, exit barriers, product variety, cost of changing suppliers, etc.

2   *New entrants who may enter a market* – including global operators expanding into new markets, entry barriers, economies of scale, government deregulation, availability of a skilled workforce, access to critical technologies, patents, customer loyalty, etc.

3   *Substitute products particularly using developing technology* – including the performance of substitute products, relative price, cost to customers of transferring, buyers attitudes, etc.

4   *Power of buyers* – including the number of buyers, volumes bought, cost of changing suppliers, price sensitivity, product differences, availability of substitutes, brand identity, effects of quality, customer profits, etc.

FIGURE 3.5

Porter's model of competitive forces

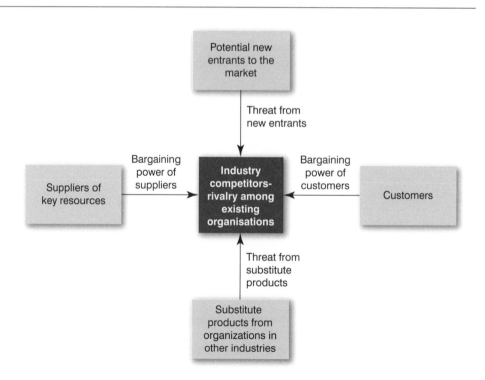

5 *Power of suppliers* – including prices, ability to pass on price increases, availability of key technologies or other resources, threat of forward or backward integration, industry capacity utilization, economies of scale, etc.

Many other possible analyses of the business environment are possible, with a SWOT analysis defining the Strengths, Weaknesses, Opportunities and Threats particularly widely used for strategic design. When we described the internal features of purchasing we said that they often emphasize internal strengths and weaknesses; now an environmental scan can identify opportunities and threats. If we combine these we get a view of:

Strengths – that the organization should build on and develop into competitive capabilities

Weaknesses – that it should try to overcome

Opportunities – that it should take advantage of

Threats – which it should try to avoid.

The aim of this analysis is to review broad external conditions so that purchasing mangers can include a set of appropriate responses in their strategy.

STEP 4 – DESIGN A PURCHASING STRATEGY

The first three steps use various analyses to describe conditions, and now the strategy design team can start the process of designing a strategy that works well within this context. Each organization is somehow unique and will work best with its own strategy that is tailored to its specific conditions. However, there are common patterns to strategies and many have, for example, a strategic aim of reducing operating costs. Some other common aims are described below.

Strategic aims

A purchasing strategy defines many aspects of operations, but it is based on the achievement of aims – and the plans, policies, culture, resources, decisions, actions and other factors that are needed to achieve these aims. So purchasing managers have to take the broader business aims and translate these into more specific purchasing ones. The following examples suggest some ways of starting this process.

Business aim of cost-reduction – leads to typical procurement aims of:

- Reduce unit costs of items bought

- Reduce overheads and administration costs

- Reduce stock levels and associated holding costs

Business aim of introducing new technology to operations – leads to typical procurement aims of:

- Automate more purchases

- Increase use of websites and e-business

- Improve EFT systems

Business aim of introducing new products – leads to typical procurement aims of:

- Enhance joint problem solving with suppliers
- Faster qualification of suppliers for new materials
- Improved market awareness

Business aim of reducing the supply base – leads to typical procurement aims of:

- Reducing the number of suppliers used
- Developing a set of strategic partners
- Greater standardization of components

Business aim of improving product quality – leads to typical procurement aims of:

- Extending total quality management principles to suppliers
- Getting total quality management (TQM) certification
- Eliminating errors and mistakes

Such aims – and the many alternatives – only form one part of the strategy, but they lay the foundations for the other parts. For instance, a strategic aim of lowering unit costs leads to other decisions for encouraging a 'lean' viewpoint, developing a culture of eliminating waste, building long term relationships with suppliers, global sourcing, e-procurement and so on. So setting the aims defines how an organization will work, and what other elements have to be included in the strategy. And when purchasing managers define their aims, they also have to say how these aims will be achieved.

LEARNING FROM PRACTICE

Ford Motor Co.

In 2005 Ford announced plans to overhaul its $90-billion-a-year global purchasing process to offer larger, long-term contracts to a smaller group of suppliers. This move aimed at saving the company billions of dollars a year.

Initial plans to streamline purchasing identified seven major suppliers who delivered $35 billion of purchases for 20 key parts such as seats, tyres and bumpers. A starting point for Ford's plan was to cut the number of suppliers by more than half. Such moves would have a profound effect on the industry, where globally there are estimated to be 5,000 direct suppliers of parts to the motor industry, with combined sales in excess of $500 billion.

This is part of a major rethinking within an industry where many of the key players made huge losses with the economic downturn that began in 2008, and they effectively went bankrupt, filed for bankruptcy protection or had their shares downgraded to junk bonds.

Source: McCracken J. (2005) Ford seeks big savings by overhauling supply system, *Wall Street Journal*, p. A1

STEP 5 – IMPLEMENT THE STRATEGY

The benefits of designing a good strategy only appear when the strategy has been implemented. This implementation means taking all the necessary actions to ensure that designed changes are introduced and operations are performed as planned. This includes establishing tasks to be done and the schedule for doing them, assigning responsibilities for the tasks and ensuring adequate resources are available.

At this stage, the design team may disband, but at least one member of the team usually continues to work with suppliers with a title like *supplier relationship manager*. This person monitors the performance of the new strategy, and makes sure that it works as planned. This monitoring might involve:

- Conducting regular review meetings – at least annually – to check that strategies are still aligned with an organization's business objectives

- Checking that key objectives are being achieved. If they are not being achieved, what is the contingency plan? If the objectives are being achieved, is there an opportunity for further improvements and more demanding objectives?

- Identifying changes, such as new market conditions, that suggest some adjustment is needed to the strategy

- Assessing internal customers' views of the strategy. Are they satisfied with what is happening? If not, can the strategy be adjusted to improve the situation?

LEARNING FROM PRACTICE

Twelve Sourcing Strategies

Research has identified 12 key purchasing and supply strategies that firms should focus on to achieve competitive success in the future. These strategies provide a focussed approach to achieving purchasing excellence:

1 Outsourcing and globalization of supply with greater focus on risk management.

2 Enhanced supply chain integration and collaboration with strategic suppliers.

3 Increased information sharing and transparency, both internally and with suppliers.

4 Purchasing becoming more integrated with other functions, processes and customers.

5 Enhancing the quality, number and execution of purchasing strategies with a focus on value.

6 Ensuring the adequacy of purchasing strategies as a means of obtaining and accelerating innovation from suppliers.

7 Requiring suppliers to take a greater role in cost management by providing value-adding services.

8 Providing common customer-focussed measurements across the supply chain.

9 Developing e-sourcing to include paperless invoicing and knowledge management.

10 Taking a leading role in sustainability and environmental protection.

11 Strategic sourcing with activities located at sites worldwide, and with decentralized global execution.

12 Human resources strategies that focus on identifying, hiring and developing highly talented, flexible, and globally oriented people.

Source: Based on Monczka R. M. and Petersen K. J. (2007) Supply strategy implementation: current state and future opportunities, CAPS Research, Tempe, AZ.

- Collecting external suppliers' views and input, with feedback on their performance and future expectations

- Sharing results with top management and all other stakeholders

TYPES OF PURCHASING STRATEGY

We mentioned earlier that although every organization designs its own unique strategy, they often follow common themes, such as lowering costs or improving service. The following list describes some of the most common themes.

Supply base optimization

Supply base optimization is the process of determining the best number and mix of suppliers. With current trends, this usually means reducing the number of suppliers. The implication is that those suppliers that cannot meet new demands for 'world-class performance' or who fail in some other way are eliminated from the supply base. Unfortunately, when firms look for major reductions to their supply base they may have to drop suppliers that are actually performing quite well, but who are perhaps small or chosen for some other arbitrary reason. This adjustment is continuous, to reflect changing circumstances (we return to this theme in chapter 9).

Total quality management of suppliers

TQM is an approach – and management philosophy – designed to ensure that products have the highest possible levels of quality. Some specific tools of TQM include quality at source, six sigma methods, statistical process control, quality audits – and a broad range of others. A key element of TQM is that a company cannot make perfect quality products itself, unless its suppliers also provide materials of perfect quality. So TQM requires suppliers to develop a philosophy of zero defects and continuous improvement (which we describe in chapter 11).

Supply chain risk management

Supply chain managers are putting an increasing emphasis on risk management (Waters, 2007), perhaps encouraged by a series of disruptive events such as hurricanes, terrorist attacks, fires, diseases, hijackings, accidents and economic downturns. Although not all risks can be predicted, many sources of potential disruption to supply chains can be managed better.

This strategy is particularly relevant as firms increasingly outsource operations to China, India and other low-cost countries. Such global operations offer benefits like lower costs and greater market access, but the hidden risks of extended supply chains are often not fully considered. A survey by BusinessWeek (www.businessweek.com) identified supply chain disruptions as the single biggest threat to companies' revenue streams. Despite this, strategies to mitigate the effects of supply chain disruptions are still at an early stage of development. This is an area of growing concern, with more firms actively looking for strategies that protect the movement of materials through supply chains.

Global sourcing

Global sourcing means that purchasing staff view the whole world as a potential source for goods, services and materials. In practice, few industries have true global sourcing and they generally take a more limited view that includes some international operations. Nonetheless more firms are developing strategies that see the world as a single market and source of materials. This global view brings immediate benefits in cost and quality, but it also gives products greater exposure, allows an exchange of technology, increases the number of potential sources, satisfies counter-trade requirements, establishes a presence in new markets and so on.

Of course, there can be considerable barriers to global sourcing, such as import quotas, exchange rate fluctuations, transport costs, lack of experience with international business practices, cultural differences, complex logistics, etc. chapter 10 considers some more aspects of global sourcing.

Longer-term supplier relationships

There is a trend towards longer-term relationships with suppliers which last over many years. These relationships range from informal arrangements with preferred suppliers, through shared information and product development, and on to formal partnerships and vertical integration. The aim is clearly to identify suppliers with performance that is somehow exceptional, and then take advantage of their superior performance over the long term – essentially finding the best supplier and then using them in preference to others. Within the portfolio analysis described earlier, this approach is most appropriate for materials that are described as strategic.

Early supplier design involvement

This has key suppliers participating at the earliest stages of new-product development. The involvement may be informal, but usually involves participation in cross-functional product development teams. This strategy recognizes that suppliers have considerable expertise, and they can offer more than the basic production of previously specified items. It seeks to maximize the benefits received from using the supplier's design capabilities. This strategy is discussed in detail in chapter 6.

Supplier development

Sometimes an existing supplier cannot meet new demands, or its performance deteriorates for some reason and then the customer's obvious option is to transfer its business to another supplier. But there may be reasons why this is not appropriate – and in the extreme there may simply be no alternative suppliers. An alternative is to work with the supplier and help them improve their performance. For instance, if a supplier cannot meet quality standards, it may be best to work together to design new procedures for improving results. Empirical evidence suggests that buyer-seller teams working together can accelerate supplier improvement more quickly than actions taken independently by the supplier. The basic motivation behind this strategy is that supplier improvement and success leads to longer-term benefits for both buyer and seller.

Total cost of ownership

Total cost of ownership (TCO) considers all the cost considerations of acquiring and owning materials beyond the price, production and transport costs. It includes various other costs associated with a purchased item, such as penalties for late delivery, poor quality, recycling and disposal costs. Identifying the TCO can be difficult, and open to some disagreement. However, strategies based on the findings can give better decisions as they take a broader view of costs, with variances from plans analysed to determine the cause and find a solution.

LEARNING FROM PRACTICE

BTR Engineering

BTR Engineering is an international manufacturing and engineering company that operates in more than 40 countries. Its best known products are parts for the automotive industry where it works in the highly competitive area of original equipment manufacture for major automotive systems. To remain competitive, the company has developed a strategy of involving suppliers early in new product development. Senior managers view supplier integration as a critical strategy for their continuing success.

BTR's main reasons for using a supplier integration strategy include:

- *Ownership* – with early involvement of suppliers ensuring their ownership of their part of the development

- *Design* – as suppliers often have greater expertise in their product, they can customize materials for new products

- *Long-term support* – encouraging suppliers to negotiate long-term arrangements, with incentives to invest and improve their delivered products

- *Focus* – with BTR using more outsourcing and suppliers providing whole sub-assemblies

- *Cost reduction* – to reduce delivered costs, perhaps including holding stocks in suppliers' warehouses to eliminate their own

- The company uses various practices, tools and methods for developing its supplier involvement strategy

- Cross-functional teams for supplier selection and strategy planning

- Effective processes to identify and select potential candidates to enter the supply base

- A best practice manager is put into each new product development team

- Technology sharing with suppliers

- Regular formal meeting for developing and enhancing trust between stakeholders

- Cost information sharing

- Location of buyer staff within BTR, either permanently or over an extended period

Using these methods, BTR has consistently had the active support of suppliers in new product development, and this has helped them achieve significant benefits. For instance, they improved measured quality by 5 per cent and reduced new product development time by 25 per cent over a 12-month period, and reduced total production costs by 20 per cent over a 24-month period.

Source: Based on Monczka R., Handfield R., Ragatz G., Frayer D. and Scannell T. (2000) Supplier integration into new product/process development: best practices ASQ Press, Milwaukee, WI.

E-reverse auctions

An e-auction is an online, real-time auction between a buying organization and a group of prequalified suppliers who compete to win orders. The materials needed must have clearly defined specifications, and then potential suppliers bid against each other on specialized websites until the lowest – or somehow best – bid received during a scheduled period wins the order. This time period is usually only about an hour, but extensions are usually allowed if bidders are still active at the end of the initial time (Beall *et al.*, 2003). E-Auctions are discussed in chapter 17.

EVOLUTION OF SOURCING STRATEGIES

Not surprisingly, purchasing strategies have changed over time. We can describe these changes as an evolution through four phases, with Figure 3.6 summarizing the four phases in terms of supply chain integration. In principle, an organization moves

1. Beginnings	2. Moderate development	3. Limited integration	4. Fully integrated supply chains
• Quality/cost teams • Longer-term contracts • Volume leveraging • Supply-base consolidation • Supplier quality focus	• E-auctions • Ad hoc supplier alliances • Cross-functional sourcing teams • Supply base optimization • International sourcing	• Global sourcing • Strategic supplier alliances • Supplier TQM • Total cost of ownership • Parts/service standardization • Early supplier involvement • Pull systems	• Global supply chains • External customer focus • Shared information and visibility • Cross-enterprize decision-making • Full service suppliers • Early sourcing • E-systems

FIGURE 3.6

Stages in purchasing strategy development

through these four phases as it becomes mature and develops more sophisticated purchasing strategies. So the four phases plot the development of purchasing strategies in general, and within particular organizations.

Phase 1: Beginnings

In the early stages of strategy development, purchasing is seen as a low-level support function. Procurement staff take a short-term view and place orders when requested by internal customers. Relations with suppliers are viewed as short term and adversarial. Purchasing staff react to complaints when deliveries are late, quality is poor or costs are too high, and this response is essentially the only impetus for change. The resources for improvement are limited, usually because the highest-ranking supply managers are still fairly junior and typically report to more senior managers in operations or logistics. The primary role of purchasing managers is to ensure that there is enough supply capacity, with performance measures focussing on efficiency and price reduction. Information systems focus on individual locations or facilities and primarily record transaction data.

In phase 1, purchasing managers tend to focus on supply base optimization, and pay some attention to quality management. These are the basic strategies and in a sense represent the building blocks from which increasingly sophisticated strategies can develop.

Phase 2: Moderate development

This second phase of strategy development occurs when an organization begins to co-ordinate parts of supply management across regional or even worldwide locations. Buyers may be responsible for entire classes of materials, with integrated systems and databases helping co-ordinate activities. The main purpose of this co-ordination is to establish company-wide agreements that consolidate orders and reduce unit costs. These eventually emerge as single sourcing and long-term trading agreements. At this stage, limited cross-functional integration is also occurring.

The strategies most often used in phase 2 are supply base optimization and TQM (like phase 1). Over time these can steadily improve supply management, but the rate of change may not be dramatic. However, these basic strategies are now joined by others that encourage long-term contracts, developing strategic supplier relationships that focus on customer needs. Essentially, phase 2 has buyers establishing closer relationships with critical suppliers, while still continuing to optimize the supply base and quality.

The purchasing department may now be judged by its achievement of competitive objectives, with suppliers seen as an essential resource. This encourages the growth of informal channels that begin to integrate the actions of procurement with operations, marketing, accounting, etc. Some of this may occur through infrequent cross-functional team meetings.

Phase 3: Limited integration

This phase is characterized by purchasing initiatives like concurrent development, lead time reduction, supplier development and early supplier involvement. More specifically, formal moves are made to integrate suppliers early into product and process design, with suppliers becoming actively involved in purchasing decisions. This gives a strong external customer focus, with customer-oriented measurements used to check performance and identify areas for improvement.

Purchasing is now viewed as a key part of the organizational structure, with an important strategic contribution. It is judged on the basis of its strategic contribution, and resources are made available according to these long-term requirements. Extensive functional integration occurs through design and sourcing teams that focus on joint product development, building a competitive advantage and total cost analysis for products. Systems, including global databases, are used by all functional groups and a start is made on total cost modelling.

Phase 4: Fully integrated supply chains

In the final and most advanced phase, purchasing has assumed a strategic orientation, with the senior procurement executive reporting directly to corporate heads. There is a strong external focus, with organizations demanding better performance from their suppliers – and taking aggressive actions to improve supplier capability and accelerate their rates of improvement. Examples of such aggressive actions include development of global supplier capabilities, full service suppliers, and adopting a broad perspective of procurement that encompasses the entire supply chain as an integrated system. These measures involve very close co-operation – and even direct intervention – in suppliers' operations and systems.

Senior managers now emphasize the core activities that add greatest value to the organization, while components of the value chain are outsourced to third parties. Certainly, non-value-adding activities – such as purchase order follow-up and expediting – have been automated so that purchasers can focus on their strategic role.

This fourth phase allows very efficient processes, based on close working, shared information and removal of waste – but the reality is that very few organizations have yet reached this point. There are a variety of reasons for this, including the complexity of higher-level strategies, the large investment needed to implement the strategies, lack of commitment, incomplete supply base optimization, obstructions from suppliers and staff who lack the necessary skills and knowledge. However, those firms that come close to completing this move from having purchasing as a supportive administrative role to an integrated strategic function, gain considerable benefits. These include price reductions, higher quality, improved delivery performance and a supply base that is better than the competition's.

LEARNING FROM PRACTICE

Source: Based on Morgan J. (2003) R. Gene Richter: The man who made supply strategies work. Purchasing

Black and Decker

Black and Decker (B&D) moved on from being a relatively small hand tool maker when it bought the small appliance division of General Electric. Purchasing within the new company had a more significant role, and its mission was 'to out-buy the competition at home and abroad'. This mission was backed-up by a strong buying strategy which the supply director, Gene Richter, built on the cornerstones of:

A supplier for each major commodity. This meant that one supplier delivered the lion's share (usually more than 70 per cent) of the demand for each item. This maintained competition while giving most of the benefits of single sourcing.

Long-term agreements. These ran from 3 to 5 years with renewals each year. Initially about 20 per cent of B&D's purchases were covered by these agreements, but the aim was to extend this each year.

Centralization of key commodities. A centralized purchasing function was established to oversee purchases in key commodities to make global purchasing more efficient. Key commodities were defined by ones with high value, few suppliers, strategic importance, criticality to quality or high technical content.

International buying. B&D buying teams pursued global sources, with enough market and technological intelligence to allow an effective strategy.

These strategies were presented as formal documents. Richter used to say that having a written strategy 'really makes a difference over having a strategy that's just rolling around in your head'. The benefits of written strategies came, for instance, when negotiating with suppliers and purchasing staff could immediately see if a particular stance would help achieve strategic aims.

Changing the strategies had many effects, not all of them foreseen. For instance, purchasing used to be almost completely decentralized, with staff in each plant essentially going their own way. Often this meant that plant purchasing managers were unwittingly competing against each other for limited materials. Another effect was that the supply base was suddenly expanded. Like many other companies, B&D had been reducing their supply base for many years, but they had to reverse this policy when existing suppliers could not meet new, increased demands.

CHAPTER REVIEW

- Decisions are made at different levels within an organization. Strategic decisions are the long-term ones that set the organization's overall direction. They form the context for lower tactical and operational decisions

- There are four different levels of strategic decision – mission, corporate, business and functional strategies. A purchasing strategy is one of the functional strategies

- The overall aim of a purchasing strategy is to set the long-term direction of procurement, and to show how the function will contribute to the business strategy. Strategic alignment means that purchasing works with all other strategies to achieve the organization's overriding aims

- There is never a single best procurement strategy that managers are looking for, nor is there a simple recipe for designing a strategy. These depend on the judgement and skills of managers

- However, there are some guidelines for designing strategies, based on a model with five steps. The first of these initiates the design by assigning responsibilities, analysing the business strategy, setting goals, etc.

- The next steps analyse the internal procurement (including a spend and portfolio analysis) and the external business environment (including SWOT analysis)

- After the analyses the strategy design team move on to actually designing the strategies, where they look for the best policies to achieve the supply aims. It is important to remember that the strategy contains both the aims and the means of achieving them

- Strategies only become effective when they are implemented, so this is the last step of design, followed by continuous monitoring and control

- Each organization designs its own unique purchasing strategy to suit its particular circumstances – but there are some common themes. These include supply base optimization, global sourcing, longer-term supplier relations, TCO and so on

- Purchasing strategies have evolved over time, as the purchasing function has developed. We described four stages in this development that moves from a low-level activity to an integrated function with strategic impact

DISCUSSION QUESTIONS

1 Why has supply management traditionally not been involved in corporate strategic planning?

2 How would you set about designing a purchasing strategy?

3 Describe a set of procurement goals that might be aligned with the business objective of a car assembly plant, 'To be the number one in customer satisfaction.'

4 What are the practical difficulties of conducting a spend analysis?

5 Where might paper clips, machine tools, aero engines, personal computers, fuel, computer chips, printers, polystyrene cups, paper, custom-designed networks fall within the portfolio matrix? Under what circumstances might these items fall into different quadrants of the portfolio analysis matrix, or move from one quadrant to another?

6 Under what conditions might you consider single-sourcing for an item in the 'leverage' category of the portfolio matrix?

7 Discuss some advantages and disadvantages of different types of information you might obtain from websites. Which types of site are likely to be more reliable than personal interviews?

8 What analyses might you do during the initial stages of designing a purchasing strategy?

9 Why must organizations develop suppliers? Is supplier development a long-term trend or just a fad?

10 Supply base optimization must occur before long-term contracts can be signed. What are the implications of this statement?

11 How long do you think it takes a company to design a purchasing strategy?

12 Give some examples of companies that you think fit into different stages of supply strategy development

REFERENCES

Aberdeen Group (2005) Best practices in category management, Boston, MA: Aberdeen Group.

Accenture (2003) A global study of supply chain leadership and its impact on business performance, Fontainbleu, France: INSEAD White Paper.

Beall, S., Carter, C., Carter, P., Germer, T., Hendrick, T., Jap, S., et al. (2003) The role of reverse auctions in strategic sourcing, CAPS Research, p. 7.

CFO Research Services (2003) Paying attention: Chief Financial Officers get involved in managing more supply chains, Traffic World, September 2.

Nelson D. (2007) Interview for North Carolina State University research study on design for order fulfilment.

Porter M. E. (1985) Competitive advantage, New York: The Free Press.

Vancil R.F. and Orange P.F. (1975) Strategic planning in diversified companies, Harvard Business Review, January–February, pp 81–90.

Waters D. (2006) Operations strategy, London: Thomson Learning.

Waters D. (2007) Supply chain risk management, London: Kogan Page.

Walker O.C., Boyd H.W. and Larreche J. (2002) Marketing strategy (4th edition), New York: Irwin McGraw-Hill.

www.businessweek.com

FURTHER READING

Avery S. (2003) Rockwell Collins takes off, *Purchasing* 132(3): pp 25.

Buchanan M. (2008) Profitable buying strategies: how tout procurement costs and buy your way to higher profits, London: Kogan Page.

Craighead C. W., Blackhurst J., Rungtusanatham M. J. and Handfield R. B. (2007) The severity of supply chain disruptions: design characteristics and mitigation capabilities, *Decision Sciences*, 38(1), pp 131–156.

D'Avanzo R., von Lewinski, H., and van Wassenhove, L. N. (2003) The link between supply chain and financial performance, *Supply chain Management Review*, 27(6), pp 40–47.

Handfield R. (2006) Supplier market intelligence, Boca Raton, FL: Auerbach Publications.

Handfield R., Elkins D., Blackhurst J. and Craighead C. (2005) 18 ways to guard against disruption, *Supply chain Management Review*, 9(1), pp 46–53.

Handfield R. and Krause D. (1999) Think globally, source locally, Supply chain Management Review, Winter, pp 36–49.

Handfield R. and McCormack K. (2005) What you need to know about sourcing in china, *Supply chain Management Review*, 9(5), pp 56–62.

Monczka R. and Trent R. J. (1995) Supply management and sourcing strategy: trends and implications, Tempe, AZ: Centre for Advanced Supply Management Studies.

Tyndall G. (1998) Ten strategies to enhance supplier management, *National Productivity Review* 17(3), p 31.

CASE STUDY

El Misr Parcel Delivery Service

El Misr Parcel Delivery Service (EMP) has a head office in Cairo, from where it organizes a parcel delivery service around Egypt and other countries of the Middle East. It's main competitors are the large international operators, such as FedEx, UPS and DHL – and as they guarantee a next day service, EMP has to match this.

Farouk Rakshi is the director of corporate procurement for EMP, and is responsible for all purchasing strategies and long-term issues that affected the company. Recently the purchasing group has been attracting criticism from senior managers for its lack of vision. In particular, the operations department has been more progressive in developing customer-focussed strategies aligned to the corporate strategy, while procurement seems to be stuck with ad hoc procedures based on dated policies. The result has meant that sourcing strategies are inconsistent and sometimes conflicting. For example, while one department was working at developing a partnership with a key supplier, another group was buying similar items on short-term contracts using competitive bidding to get the lowest possible price.

Farouk told a recent departmental meeting that. 'We need to get our act together. Each supply group is doing its own thing, while reinventing the wheel every time we make a purchase. We are not consistent. We are not developing strategies that align with company aims. We are not learning from experiences or talking to other departments. We don't even know who our suppliers really are let alone talk to them.'

Although he sounded convincing, Farouk was troubled by the criticisms of procurement. He knew that different sourcing groups used widely divergent approaches, and these sometimes appeared inconsistent – but they may be responding rationally to the demands put on them by internal users and conditions in the supply market. He was not really sure that they could use standard procedures for all purchases.

Nonetheless, there might be benefits if EMP could develop a strategic process to guide the various purchasing groups. This process would clearly have to be flexible and robust enough for all sourcing groups to use. Perhaps a starting point would be classifying purchase requirements into different categories. Then each purchasing group could adjust the general model to allow for their own categories of purchases. Low-value office supplies would use a different procedure to expensive aircraft parts, but all working within the same supply strategy.

Questions

- What process could EMP use to design improved strategies? How could they develop such a process and what resources would they need?

- How could they segment purchase requirements? How would this segmentation fit in with the strategy developed?

- Identify 10 types of materials that EMP might need and say where they fit into your classification. Now discuss the approach to purchasing that you recommend for each item.

CHAPTER 4
PURCHASING
ORGANIZATION

LEARNING OBJECTIVES After reading this chapter you should be able to:

- Understand the role of organizational design

- Appreciate the way that a good organizational structure can assist purchasing success

- Say how purchasing can fit into an organization and discuss the factors that affect this decision

- Describe some specialized activities organized within purchasing

- Discuss the internal structure of purchasing departments

- Consider the features and benefits of centralized, decentralized and hybrid purchasing organizations

- Appreciate the use of teams for purchasing

ORGANIZATIONAL STRUCTURE

Some of the strategic decisions for purchasing that we reviewed in the last chapter affect the structure of purchasing departments and their relationships with other parts of the firm. The way that procurement is organized can have a significant effect on performance, but when people look for improvements they tend to jump to the obvious methods involving IT, e-business, outsourcing, cost management, strategic relationships and so on. They often miss the fundamental option of making sure that purchasing is organized in the best way to achieve its aims. This requires organizational design.

> **Organizational design**
> Is the process of evaluating options and selecting the structure, formal communications, division of labour, co-ordination, control, authority and responsibility that best achieves the organization's aims.

Organizational design effectively sets the infrastructure, defining the way that an organization is divided into separate units, what each of these units does, who they report to, their interactions with each other, systems they use and so on. You can imagine the formal structure as described by a series of organization charts, but this does not give the whole picture of the way that the organization actually works. There are always informal processes and cultural behaviour that are not shown on the formal charts, but can play a significant role. This means that the design of an organization is much more complicated than drawing a few lines and boxes on an organization chart (Champoux, 1999).

An effective organizational design allows and encourages efficient purchasing. Here we describe the foundations of design by considering the division of an organization into separate units, and the relationships between these units. In particular we look at:

- Purchasing's position within the overall organizational structure

- The internal organization of the purchasing function

- The placement of purchasing authority

- Using teams as part of the organizational structure

- Evolving views of organization

LEARNING FROM PRACTICE

McGurk and Gallaher

McGurk and Gallaher is a small, but long-established independent financial advisor. Their three main offices are in Edinburgh, London and Dublin, each of which works largely independently.

In 2005 the Dublin office appointed a new manager, who immediately set about installing new administrative systems and improving the company's e-business. Surprisingly, at the end of the first quarter they found that purchasing and administrative costs had increased by 7 per cent . The office manager was asked to investigate and she found that the new systems in Dublin were not compatible with the existing systems in Edinburgh and London. This meant that the offices not only worked independently, but they were incapable of close co-operation.

In 2009 the office manager was promoted to take over the administration of the whole company. Now she installed the same systems in all three offices, and connected them to work as a single integrated unit. The efficiencies of this integrated unit reduced administrative costs by 14 per cent in the first 6 months of working. For example, each office had hired its own legal advisors when they were needed, but the new unit signed a long-term contract with a single law firm who offered a better service and lower costs.

The lesson is that when managers give a poorly organized department new technology, they still have a poorly organized department – and the real answer is to improve the way that it is organized.

PURCHASING'S POSITION WITHIN THE ORGANIZATIONAL STRUCTURE

A formal organizational structure serves several purposes. Firstly, it shows explicitly the units into which the organization is divided, and the relationship between each of these units. This sets the scene, showing who reports to whom and the various levels of authority. Each unit in the structure has a specified role, so the second purpose of structures is to show the work that is assigned to each unit and its corresponding responsibilities. A third purpose shows how the broader firm arranges its communications and integrates decisions across functional groups.

We start looking at the organizational structure of purchasing by seeing where it fits into the whole organizational hierarchy. This is an important decision because it defines purchasing's place in the organization, how it is connected to other functions and generally suggests its status and influence. The head of purchasing often has a title such as Purchasing Director or CPO. When this person is a company director, member of the corporate board or is at some other senior level, it inevitably means that purchasing has more influence and power. In these organizations, the highest purchasing manager is at the same level as the heads of other functions, such as finance, operations and marketing. In other organizations you have to do a careful search before finding an individual responsible for purchasing, suggesting that it is the responsibility of a junior manager and has no real influence in the organization.

We have said that the trend is for purchasing to become more important, so it is moving up the organizational hierarchy and becoming more visible. A 16-year-study by Johnson *et al.* (2006) showed that CPOs now have greater responsibilities, report higher in the organization and carry more significant titles than their predecessors.

Factors affecting purchasing's position in the organizational hierarchy

Many factors can affect the status of purchasing, not the least of which is the calibre of people it employs. However, the three main considerations are likely to be past practices, the type of industry and value of materials bought.

History. Perhaps the single most important factor in determining purchasing's position in the organizational hierarchy is its past practices and performance. Historically, purchasing had a low status and was considered largely an administrative chore. It is always easiest to maintain the status quo, so this is still the situation in many firms. Although purchasing is receiving greater attention in more progressive firms and moving up the hierarchy, this needs positive action from senior managers. So you can find more less adventurous firms where purchasing maintains its original position, and more progressive ones where procurement has moved to centre stage and has a very high status – and firms at every position in-between these two extremes.

Type of industry. Some industries are not as dependent on a reliable supply of materials as others – and a firm of management consultants, for example, does not need such sophisticated purchasing as a just-in-time manufacturer. Those industries that are more reliant of purchased supplies will inevitably give purchasing a higher status than industries with few material needs.

Total value of materials bought. In many manufacturing companies 70–80 per cent of their operating costs are attributed to buying materials. This alone should raise the status of purchasing – especially when compared with service companies where materials contribute as little as 10 per cent of operating costs. So the value and size of the procurement effort directly affects its importance and status.

Other factors. Many other factors can play a role in determining the position of purchasing. For instance, the ideas of a company founder exert a strong influence on an organization's formal design, especially when the founder still plays an active role in the business. If the founder of a new high technology company has a marketing orientation, the firm probably gives less attention to procurement; if the founder has an engineering orientation, purchasing will get more attention for its role in product and process development; if the founder has a commitment to environmental protection, purchasing may have a high status because of the need for careful trading with specially chosen suppliers. These arguments can apply to any senior managers and not just founders – and a strong executive with an interest in procurement can raise its profile and put in the effort needed to develop the function.

The type of material purchased also affects procurement's position. We have suggested that routine purchase of everyday commodities is quite different from the one-off purchase of expensive items. So purchasing is likely to have more status when it deals with larger and more complicated items. And when product designs and specifications frequently change, purchasing needs much closer contacts with other functional groups – and is likely to share their higher organizational positions.

One final factor that we should mention is the ability of purchasing to influence the organization's performance. For instance, purchasing in a company might affect competitiveness by its ability to buy materials at such low prices that they gain a competitive advantage – and consequently purchasing assumes a higher position in the organization. Just-in-time manufacturers rely completely on purchasing to deliver a steady supply of materials, and when this supply is interrupted operations immediately stop; so it is not surprising that they put a lot of emphasis on procurement and give it a high status.

To whom does purchasing report?

Bloom and Nardone (1984) reported that 'During the 1950s and early 1960s, a high percentage of the purchasing departments reported in a second-level capacity to the functional managers, most commonly production and operations.' In other words, purchasing was generally seen as a junior part of another function. By the 1980s, the reporting level had risen and studies in the USA suggested that almost 35 per cent of organizations had CPOs appointed as senior executives to lead their own departments (Fearon, 1988). Purchasing was becoming a distinct function with a higher status. This trend continued with further surveys in the USA suggesting that by 1987 44 per cent of CPOs were at senior levels, rising to 61 per cent in 1995 and 70 per cent in 2003 (Johnson and Leenders, 2007). Interestingly, smaller firms seemed to lead this movement. In almost 90 per cent of smaller firms, the most senior purchasing manager reported to either the chief executive or one level below, compared with 65 per cent for medium and large firms (Trent, 2003). Of course, this may not really be surprising as smaller firms have simplified structures that allow easier access to senior managers, and they have fewer levels of management so more functions will always report directly to the chief executive.

Figure 4.1 illustrates three common places to find purchasing in an organizational hierarchy. In part (a), purchasing is an upper-level function with its own vice president who reports directly to the president. In part (b), purchasing is a level

FIGURE 4.1 Purchasing at different organizational levels

(a) Purchasing as an upper-level function

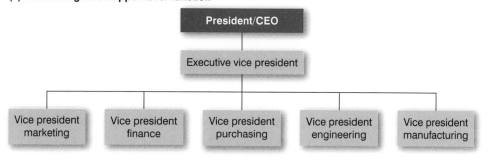

(b) Purchasing as a second-tier function

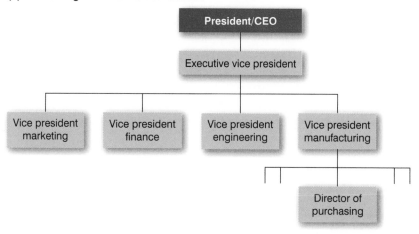

(c) Purchasing as a lower-level function

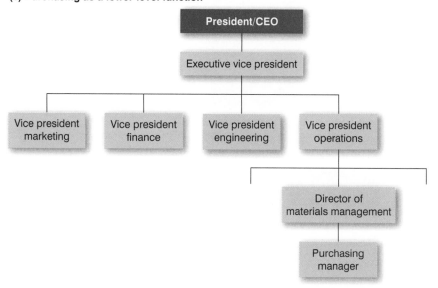

lower, with the CPO not at vice president level. Purchasing is now a part of a larger function and it reports to the vice president of this function. This is probably the most common pattern at present. In part (c), purchasing is at an even lower level with the CPO at least two levels from the president.

LEARNING FROM PRACTICE

OMRON Corporation

OMRON was founded in 1933 as the Tateisi Electric Manufacturing Company, and has grown into a diversified corporation employing 36,000 people (13,000 in Japan and 23,000 in overseas affiliates). Annual sales are ¥800 billion from industrial automation (43 per cent), electronic components (20 per cent), automotive electronic components (14 per cent), social systems (11 per cent) and health care (9 per cent).

In 2006, OMRON set up a Global Procurement Centre to reinforce its global purchasing function. This consists of the Global Procurement Strategy Department (which formulates a global purchasing strategy), the Cost Management Innovation Centre (responsible for cost planning in new product development) the SCM Process Innovation Centre (in charge of strengthening supply chain management) and the China Purchasing Centre (to handle centralized purchasing for China).

OMRON puts a lot of emphasis on corporate social responsibility, which is reflected in its motto of, 'at work for a better life, a better world for all' and its core value of 'working for the benefit of society'. In purchasing, this means that its policies are based on openness and free competition, fairness in all dealings and a global perspective.

The company believes its new procurement structure will help the company strengthen not only purchasing operations but also its corporate social responsibilities. In the future, OMRON plans to establish a centralized purchasing centre in regions other than Japan and China and expand its network to promote corporate social responsibilities at the global level.

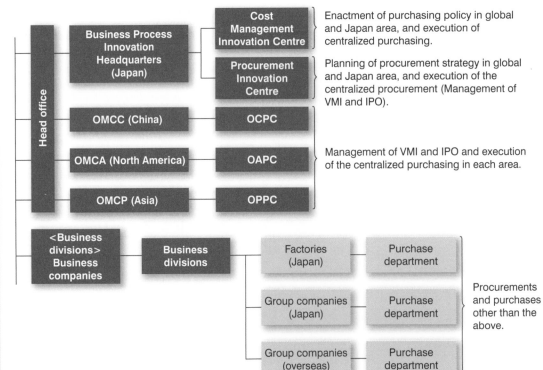

FIGURE 4.2 Purchasing organization at OMRON Corporation

Source: Based on www.omron.com

Of course, you could ask if the reporting level of purchasing is important provided it is done efficiently. One study found that having a higher-level CPO who makes regular presentations to the managing director has a significant effect on the achievement of procurement objectives (Trent, 2003). In general, the higher that purchasing is in the corporate structure, the more likely it is to achieve its goals, and the greater the contribution it makes in supporting broader organizational aims.

ORGANIZING THE PURCHASING FUNCTION

Having set purchasing's position within the business, we now have to consider its internal organization. Each function has its own organizational structure, and Figure 4.3 shows the basic structure of a technology company's sourcing office in China. From this you can see how the function is divided into specialized purchasing units, which fit into the formal reporting structure.

Specialization within purchasing

It is neither efficient nor practical to have all purchasing staff doing every job within the department. Instead, purchasing departments in larger organizations are usually divided into distinct units, each of which specializes in a particular type of activity. Then people develop skills in a particular aspect of purchasing, and the whole process is more efficient. The number of specialities varies with their type of work, but

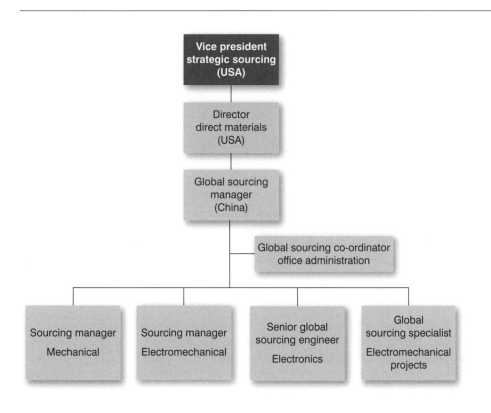

FIGURE 4.3

Organization of the International Purchasing Office in China there are typically four major types: sourcing and negotiating; purchasing research; operational support and order follow-up; and administration and support.

Sourcing and negotiating identifies potential suppliers, negotiates with selected ones and performs the actual buying of materials. In larger organizations this group is sub-divided so that buyers are responsible for a specific range or type of item. For instance, one section might be responsible for buying all capital equipment, or metal parts or waste removal services. Some expensive items always need more effort and involve extensive negotiations, so specialized buyers usually work in teams to negotiate such contracts.

Purchasing research develops long-term materials forecasts, conducts value analyses, assesses supplier capabilities and analyses the cost structure of suppliers. It builds a detailed picture of supply markets, which needs continuing monitoring, research and updating. These tasks might be done by the sourcing group who generally have considerable knowledge of the area, but a specialized research team can produce a more objective and comprehensive view.

Operational support and order follow-up does a range of activities that support the day-to-day operations of the purchasing function. For instance, when orders hit some kind of problem such as delays in delivery, expediters try to sort things out. When follow-up is needed after an order, perhaps because of quality concerns, this group is again involved. And they might do routine jobs such as sending material releases to suppliers arranging another delivery. Some of these routine tasks are being streamlined and automated – especially through e-procurement – so the number of purchasing staff doing these jobs is falling. This is generally a welcome trend, as operational support is an overhead that gives a poor use of buyers' time.

Administration, strategy and support is responsible for developing the policies and procedures for purchasing staff, administering and maintaining the purchasing information system, determining staffing levels, developing department plans, organizing training for buyers and developing systems to evaluate purchasing performance. The group is largely responsible for ensuring that the purchasing department continues to run smoothly.

Purchasing department activities

Purchasing departments are generally divided into units that reflect these four core types of activities. But there are often more units that are responsible for specific activities. Purchasing departments now do much more than the traditional buying of materials, and its role continues to expand, so there may be many types of specialized unit. The following jobs are commonly done by a purchasing department, and they have to be housed within the organizational structure. Clearly, this list shows a general view, and every purchasing department does not do all of these tasks – but some do many others.

Buying. By definition, a primary responsibility of the purchasing function is to buy materials. This is a broad term describing the purchase of raw materials, components, finished goods, services from suppliers or anything else needed. The purchase can be a one-time requirement or the release for materials against an established purchase order. We described the tasks done for purchasing in chapter 2.

Expediting. This is the process of contacting suppliers to determine the status of shipments that are either overdue, or will soon become overdue. Expeditors take the necessary action to avoid any related problems. These actions include doing nothing if the delivery will actually arrive on time, arranging emergency transport, approaching an alternative supplier, warning operations to reschedule jobs and cancelling orders which will clearly not be delivered. Expediting rarely adds value to purchasing, but it is generally accepted as an essential service that adds unavoidable overheads. Many organizations recognize that any expediting indicates that something has gone wrong and either suppliers are not performing as required, or else they are not getting timely data from purchasing. To avoid these problems – and reduce the expediting overhead – organizations have to work more closely with suppliers (which we discuss in chapters 9 and 14).

Inventory management. Purchased goods are usually scheduled to arrive some time before they are actually needed, to add an element of safety. Then they are put into stocks of raw materials in front of operations, with subsequent stocks of work-in-progress and finished goods. Inventory management controls these stocks and makes sure that the right amounts are held and kept in good condition so that they are available when needed. Basic methods of inventory management look for ways of minimizing costs by balancing the costs of holding stock with the service give (Waters, 2003).

Transportation. Purchasing can become involved with transport in two ways. Firstly, it can take an active role in obtaining transport services for the organization, typically to deliver its final products to customers. Then it does the usual purchasing tasks of identification of potential suppliers, evaluation, negotiation, selection and so on. It can also be involved in arranging the movement of purchased items into the organization. This is usually organized by the supplier – or by the purchaser when they have special requirements, knowledge or some other strength in the area.

Managing counter-trade arrangements. Sometimes materials are not purchased for cash, but are part of an agreement to exchange goods. For instance, farmers traditionally take their grain to a miller who is paid with a part of the flour. Such trades often become bartering, and in some companies this becomes a specialized activity. We should give the warning that this is not the same as reciprocal purchasing, where an organization will only buy materials from a supplier that in turn buys some of its finished products. Counter-trade is a convenient means of payment and it still allows choice; reciprocal purchasing allows no choice as it limits business to suppliers who agree to make a return purchase.

Insourcing or outsourcing. There is often a choice between making some component, say, internally or buying it from an external supplier. Purchasing is often responsible for analysing this decision. For certain items, such as standard commodities, this analysis is straightforward – and few companies would go through the formalities of deciding whether to buy diesel for delivery trucks or refine it themselves. However, for other items the insourcing or outsourcing analysis has a strategic important that goes beyond simple cost comparisons. Purchasing's role in make-or-buy analyses is an important one, which we discuss in chapter 10.

Value analysis. This is a tool for improving operations that considers an item's designed purpose in relation to its cost. Value is essentially the ratio of purpose over cost – or value for money. The objective of value analysis is to raise value either by reducing the cost without sacrificing any functionality, raising functionality without increasing cost or raising the functionality by more than the corresponding increase in cost.

Purchasing research and materials forecasting. Purchasing often has responsibility for anticipating changes in material and supply markets. This means that on the demand side they analyse historical demands for items and forecast likely future requirements. These can be used for detailed purchasing plans. On the supply side purchasing has to do research to assess the supply market, cost and price analyses, supplier evaluation and design corresponding procurement policies.

Supply management. In the first chapter we mentioned that supply management is often described as a broad approach to managing the supply base that takes a long-term view and requires purchasing staff to work directly with those suppliers who can guarantee superior performance. Such supply management involves a combination of purchasing, production, quality management, long-term alliances, co-operation between internal functions, achievement of mutual goals and an end to adversarial relationships.

Other responsibilities. Purchasing can also assume a variety of other responsibilities such as receiving, warehousing, managing company travel, production planning, commodity futures trading, global transportation, economic forecasting, sub-contracting and so on.

Separating strategic, tactical and operational purchasing

In chapter 3 we reviewed the differences between strategic, tactical and operational decisions. In reality, there are no clear distinctions between these levels, but we can say that managing day-to-day operations is quite different from managing longer-term strategies. The skills and knowledge needed to negotiate a contract are different to those needed to plot the long-term aims of procurement and its contribution to the business strategy. People often describe strategic tasks as most important, but this is only partly true as decisions are needed at all levels. Strategic decisions are needed to plot the long-term direction, tactical decisions are needed to translate these into medium-term actions, and operational decisions are needed for the day-to-day work of purchasing. If any of these are missing, the function will cease to work.

The standard way of ensuring that every level of job gets enough attention is to assign responsibilities to different levels of staff – creating the traditional organizational hierarchy. Strategic decisions are made by senior managers so they become – almost by definition – more important. However, when people are pressed for time, strategic plans inevitably take second place to more immediate needs – suggesting that they actually become less important.

Figure 4.4 suggests some differences in types of strategic and operational purchasing decisions, and tactical decisions would straddle these two. In a large organization the group responsible for strategic direction is often part of a central sourcing group at corporate headquarters, while the lower levels are devolved to each site or plant (Trent, 2004).

Vertical and horizontal organizations

Having defined the building blocks that form a purchasing department, the next question is how they fit together. The current trend is to move away from a vertical structure, where each function is largely distinct and divided into many layers with work and information moving up and down. Instead, firms are using a more horizontal structure, which has fewer layers, with work and information being managed

- Manage relationships with critical suppliers
- Develop electronic purchasing systems
- Implement company-wide best practices
- Negotiate company-wide supply contracts
- Manage critical commodities

Strategic sourcing activities

- Manage transactions with suppliers
- Use e-systems to obtain standard or indirect items through catalogues
- Source items that are unique to the operating unit
- Generate and forward material releases
- Provide supplier performance feedback

Operational activities

FIGURE 4.4

Strategic and operational purchasing decisions

LEARNING FROM PRACTICE

University of Liverpool

The University of Liverpool was founded 1881 as University College Liverpool and in 1892 its new Victoria Building earned it the title of the original 'red brick university'. After an adjusted name it has grown into one of the UK's leading research-led universities with 21,000 students and 4900 staff.

The main teaching and research work is divided into six faculties and about 50 academic departments. Supporting these are the usual university services of library, finance, computing, accommodation, health, human resources, safety and so on. Among these services is procurement, organized as part of the finance department.

Procurement at Liverpool has the overall aim of supporting the University's mission of 'excellence in education and scholarship and in pure and applied research'. In particular, this means ensuring value for money purchases and the best use of resources. Then procurement's guiding principles say that it will:

- Be committed to effective procurement
- Support the training and skills development of those involved in procurement

- Improve the use of procurement management systems and information systems
- Identify and disseminate information and advice on good procurement practice
- Promote and participate in co-operative procurement arrangements that contribute to delivery of its mission
- Measure the performance and effectiveness of procurement

The finance office at Liverpool is divided into four broad areas:

- Management accounting
- Financial operations
- Purchasing
- Internal audit

The purchasing office is responsible for disseminating and implementing a purchasing policy throughout the University. All purchase orders are routed through this office to give a degree of control. The structure of the purchasing department is shown in Figure 4.5.

Source: University of Liverpool (2009) Prospectus, Liverpool; www.liv.ac.uk

FIGURE 4.5 Organization of purchasing at the University of Liverpool

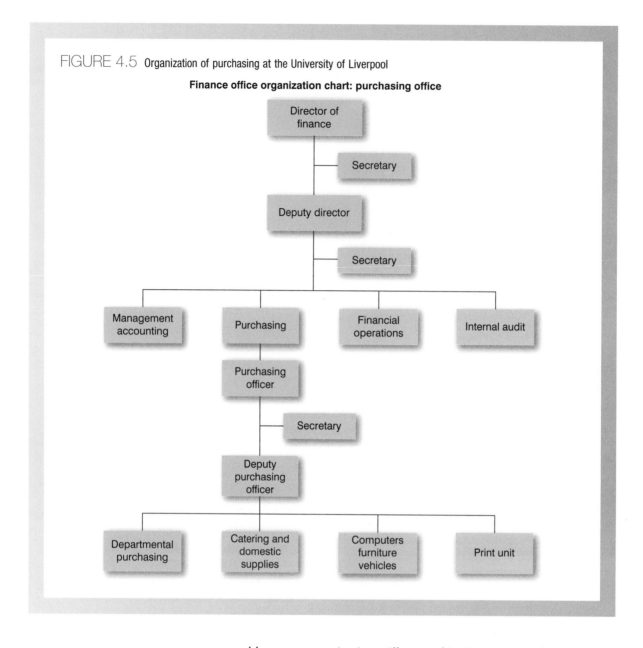

across groups and between organizations (illustrated in Figure 4.6). The main benefit of a horizontal structure is that it eliminates many of the hierarchical, functional and departmental boundaries and eases information and work flows.

Purchasing is following the trend towards more horizontal structures, with the majority of firms using cross-functional teams to manage at least part of the purchasing process. Empirical surveys from the 1990s suggested that almost 80 per cent of firms organized purchasing by items bought, with only 20 per cent using more horizontal teams that focus on final products. Ten years later, the number organizing by products had reduced to 65 per cent, with a corresponding increase in horizontal structures.

In practice, few organizations choose purely vertical or horizontal structures, and most adopt some mixture that captures the best features of each. The results have certain broad features, which include flattened hierarchies for faster decision-making, freer flow of ideas, cross-functional teams to pursue new opportunities and

FIGURE 4.6 Vertical and horizontal organization structures

The vertical organization

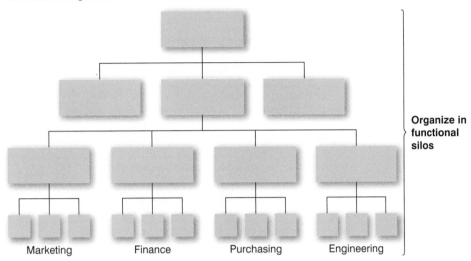

Organize in functional silos

Marketing   Finance   Purchasing   Engineering

The horizontal organization

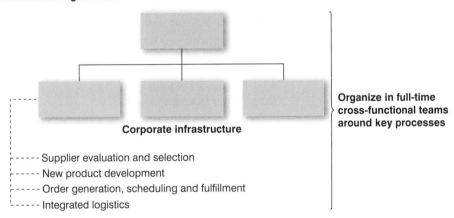

Corporate infrastructure

Organize in full-time cross-functional teams around key processes

- - - - - Supplier evaluation and selection
- - - - - New product development
- - - - - Order generation, scheduling and fulfillment
- - - - - Integrated logistics

sharing of ideas. Probably the most common hybrid structure has centralized strategic design, co-ordination of major spending categories and some support activities, with decentralization of most of the actual procurement. A Head Office provides a core of corporate support, while actual buying is largely devolved. All of the purchasing activities can be co-ordinated with a free flow of information through the internet, intranets, and information sharing systems.

A US survey in 2003 (Trent, 2003) asked procurement executives about specific organizational design features that they expected to use within the following 5 years. The results are summarized in Figure 4.7, which shows the top 12 expected features, and this gives a reasonable picture of current practices and trends. A key finding is that procurement is expected to rely extensively on teams, including commodity teams (for buying particular types of product), teams to manage the procurement process and new product development teams. Another finding is that new product development teams will increasingly include purchasing staff. A third finding was that purchasing staff would be increasingly seconded – or 'co-located' – to work closely with internal customers. Figure 4.8 suggests some of the benefits that this can bring.

FIGURE 4.7

Purchasing
organizational design
features

Specific individuals assigned responsibility for managing supplier relationships	5.06
Physical co-location between procurement and key internal customers	4.78
Centrally co-ordinated commodity teams that develop company-wide supply strategies	4.62
Formal procurement and supply strategy co-ordination and review sessions between functional groups	4.61
New product teams that include procurement representatives	4.61
Lead buyers to manage non-commodity items or services	4.53
Physical co-location between procurement and technical personnel	4.51
Regular strategy/performance review presentations by the chief procurement officer to the president or CEO	4.50
New product teams that include suppliers as members or participants	4.49
A higher-level chief procurement officer who has a procurement and supply-related title	4.46
Formal procurement and supply strategy co-ordination and review sessions between business units	4.42
Cross-functional teams that manage some or all of the procurement and supply process	4.27

Scale: 1 = Do not expect to rely on;
       4 = Expect to rely on somewhat;
       7 = Expect to rely on extensively.

FIGURE 4.8 Benefits of co-locating purchasing staff

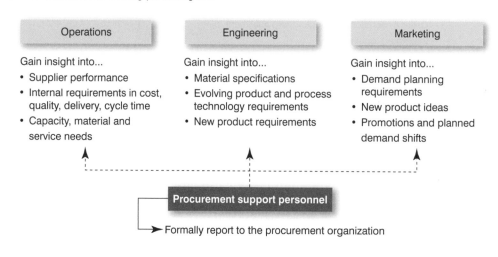

Operations

Gain insight into...
- Supplier performance
- Internal requirements in cost, quality, delivery, cycle time
- Capacity, material and service needs

Engineering

Gain insight into...
- Material specifications
- Evolving product and process technology requirements
- New product requirements

Marketing

Gain insight into...
- Demand planning requirements
- New product ideas
- Promotions and planned demand shifts

Procurement support personnel

Formally report to the procurement organization

PLACEMENT OF PURCHASING AUTHORITY

Placement of purchasing authority refers to the location of its decision-making, and particularly the choice between centralized and decentralized organizations. If a senior purchasing executive at corporate headquarters has authority over the

Source: Aeppel T. (2007) Global scramble for goods gives corporate buyers a lift, Wall Street Journal.

LEARNING FROM PRACTICE

Global Sourcing

Firms are looking further afield in their search for global suppliers. Manitowoc Company, a large maker of cranes, is searching the world for goods – tyres from China, bearings from the USA, chassis parts from Poland and so on. At Manitowoc, purchasing has been given executive level status, with a senior executive who can lead and manage complex outsourcing and global sourcing decisions, who can establish global supplier relationships and who is knowledgeable about various foreign cultures.

The company recognized that it had to establish this purchasing executive post to be in charge of procurement for its 41 facilities in 14 countries across three divisions. Improving procedures with better performance, ensuring dependable supply from worldwide sources, and redesigned organizational structures – all in support of globalization – are the main thrusts for the future.

majority of an organization's purchases, the organization has centralized authority. If authority for the majority of purchases is at divisional, business or site level, then an organization has decentralized purchasing authority.

Organizations all lie on a spectrum, at one end of which are firms with complete centralization of purchasing, and at the other end are firms with complete decentralization. Most firms lie somewhere between the two extremes, and we have already mentioned the most common model that has certain decisions centralized (perhaps strategy design, selection of suppliers, purchasing of major capital equipment, training, co-ordination, communications, etc.) and the bulk of purchasing devolved to local buyers. There are many variations on the type of activities that are either centralized or decentralized.

The best pattern is different for every firm, and it varies over time. In the 1970s centralized purchasing was popular, with a large staff at corporate level having complete control and doing virtually all the procurement activities. Unfortunately, this model often developed into bloated central organization structures, which made decision-making slow and unresponsive. So firms moved towards faster, more agile decentralized purchasing in the 1980s. Better communications and IT encouraged firms to decentralize all the activities that could be dealt with better by local staff, and centralize only the core tasks.

The real challenge is to know which activities to keep centrally and which to devolve. A common solution maintains some of the actual purchasing centrally, and devolves the rest. A hybrid structure combines centralized purchasing for items that are bought for several business units with decentralized purchasing for other items. A survey in 2004 (Giunipero and Handfield, 2004) suggested that some kind of hybrid structure was the most common arrangement among large firms (used by 54 per cent of respondents) but the trend was towards centralization assisted by better communications.

Centralized purchasing
Has all the actual purchasing done centrally, typically in the corporate headquarters.

Decentralized purchasing
Devolves all purchasing decisions to local facilities.

Factors affecting the choice of structure

The degree of purchasing centralization depends on many factors, including the total value, type of organization, nature of materials bought and scope of purchasing responsibility. Other factors that determine the best amount of purchasing centralization include the following.

Overall business strategy. If the organization's strategy is to be responsive to customers in different markets, a more decentralized approach is better. Conversely, if the organization's competitive advantage comes from low costs and efficiency, it is more likely to get economies of scale from a centralized structure.

Similarity of purchases. When fairly similar items are bought across the whole organization, they can be combined into larger orders to get more influence over suppliers, and firms are likely to favour centralized purchasing. Conversely, when purchases are very different across business units, there are benefits from decentralization.

Total purchase value. As the amount spent on purchases increases, they become more significant to the firm and there is greater pressure to centralize, allowing more control by senior managers.

Geographical spread. In the past, greater geographical dispersion of operations inevitably meant more decentralized purchasing, as it was the only way of getting fast decisions. However, technology has reduced this effect, allowing information visibility and faster decisions regardless of locations.

Overall management philosophy. If upper management is committed to decentralization, they will try to decentralize procurement as a matter of principle. Clearly, when a management philosophy believes in greater central control, then more centralized procurement will follow.

Advantages of centralized purchasing

Central purchasing can give many possible advantages, such as its use of standardized procurement procedures. The following list shows the most common benefits.

Consolidation of purchase volumes. Traditionally the main advantage of centralized purchasing has been to consolidate purchases from different parts of the organization into larger orders, and then negotiate more favourable terms. Practically, the central function might do a spend analysis to estimate the total amounts of common items that will be ordered, and then negotiate terms with the best supplier – but then it leaves the actual ordering to decentralized procurement, specifying that they use the chosen supplier. Centralized buying can accumulate services as well as goods, so a company-wide contract for transport, legal services, catering, post delivery, etc. can both reduce costs and give more uniform, consistent performance across locations.

Reduce duplication of purchasing effort. Centrally controlled purchasing reduces the amount of duplicated effort. Imagine a company with 10 locations and a completely decentralized purchasing structure. When each unit want to buy, say, a new computer, each has to follow the whole purchasing process – repeating the process ten times when centralized purchasing would only do it once.

Standardization. This ensures that the same type of products are bought throughout the organization – so that each location does not have incompatible systems, different quality standards or slightly different products. This also applies to internal procedures, so that the whole organization can use consistent ordering process, supplier evaluation, purchasing training manuals, communications protocols and so on.

Co-ordination of purchasing plans and strategy. As purchasing is becoming more strategic in its outlook, it plays a greater role in broader strategic planning. The strategic planners link corporate, business and purchasing strategies into unified plans. This needs a central group that is responsible for developing – and working with – purchasing strategy at the highest corporate level.

Co-ordination of purchasing systems. Procurement's infrastructure includes a number of systems for purchasing, e-business, planning, communications, data warehouses and so on. As these systems all have to work together to achieve broad business efficiency, it is important that they are all integrated. The design, co-ordination and integration of systems needs central leadership.

Developing expertise. Purchasing staff cannot become experts in all areas of purchasing, especially as the function becomes more complex and sophisticated. A central purchasing group becomes large enough to get economies of scale and allow specialized expertise to develop. This expertise, which is available to the whole organization, might be in:

- Purchase negotiations
- Identifying global sources
- Legal issues
- Quality management
- Finance and performance measurement systems
- Supplier relationship management
- Competitive market analysis
- Lean operations methods
- Supplier development
- Total cost analysis
- Team building
- Data analysis and information systems

Managing company-wide change. Every organization works in an environment that is continually changing. They have to respond to these changes, and purchasing can take a leading role in many types of initiative. But major initiatives need senior management support, so they are much more likely to succeed when this support is centrally organized. You can imagine this effect in two companies – the first with centralized procurement, while the second has, say, 80 highly decentralized units. The decentralized company will struggle to initiate any change because each unit has its own ideas and practices, support for corporate initiatives is largely voluntary and corporate work is not a priority. On the other hand, the centralized company has few problems getting the units to support new initiatives, either through direct control or influence.

Advantages of decentralized purchasing

The advantages of decentralized purchasing are based on flexibility and local knowledge to respond quickly to local conditions. Some of the most common benefits of decentralized purchasing include the following.

Speed and responsiveness. The ability to respond quickly to user requirements has always been a major justification for decentralized purchasing. Despite improving communications and logistics that can deliver materials with very short lead times, most purchasing managers agree that decentralized purchasing allows greater responsiveness and flexibility. This is such an imbedded view that many firms automatically resist any centralization, fearing that it will give less flexible responses and these will inevitably be slower.

Understanding local needs. Decentralized purchasing staff have a greater understanding of local needs and the features that make them in some way unique. Purchasing staff become familiar with the products, processes, business practices and requirements of the closer customers. This familiarity often allows buyers to anticipate the needs of departments it supports, while developing solid relationships with local suppliers. With increasingly global operations, this kind of local knowledge is especially important in building a competitive advantage.

Product development support. In firms where new product development occurs at the divisional or business unit level, decentralized purchasing can become involved with the products at an earlier stage. Then they can work with designers to discuss local requirements contact known suppliers and get them involved in the product design, evaluate longer-term material requirements and search for substitute materials.

Ownership. Decentralized purchasing often gives intangible benefits, loosely described as ownership. This means that staff give more support to a local business unit and feel a personal commitment to particular, smaller-scale operations. An extension of this says that business unit managers are responsible for the profitability of their unit, they feel an ownership of the unit, so they should have authority over a core area like purchasing.

A hybrid purchasing structure

We have already mentioned the study in 2003 (Trent, 2003) which considered the organization of procurement in a sample of 172 American manufacturing companies. Some more results are shown in Figure 4.9, which shows the current organization and expected changes over the following 5 years. While most firms use some kind of hybrid structure, there is a shift toward greater centralization, encouraged by improved communications, e-business and other technology that has reduced the effects of distance.

Hybrid organizations look for the benefits of both centralized and decentralized buying, and they can take many forms. These forms are known by different names, but we can summarize the main options as follows.

Lead division buying. This occurs when different operating units within a company buy common items, often because they make the same products (such as a company that makes electrical transformers at several different plants). The company does a spend analysis to identify common items and the plants that buy them. Then it appoints a lead negotiator for all purchases of the item, who is generally the buyer at the unit with the largest expenditure or the greatest expertise in the item.

Regional buying groups. These work best with a geographically dispersed organization, but with some localized concentrations. For example, a company may work throughout Europe, but with concentrations of facilities in Spain and Denmark. Then facilities within a geographical region (such as Iberia and Scandinavia) work together to buy common items. Regional buying groups are normally used for large-volume items common to all facilities – or for locations that do not have their own purchasing staff.

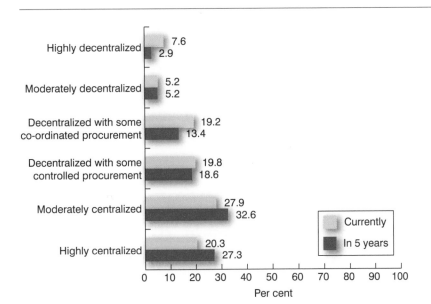

FIGURE 4.9

Centralization of purchasing

Global buying committees. When a key commodity is purchased by many business units, they can form a global buying committee to co-ordinate all of their purchases. For example, a diversified firm with interests in defence and car parts industry might have a steel-buying committee to manage its global purchase of steel. Corporate headquarters generally lead such committees, with every affected business unit having a representative on the committee.

Corporate purchasing councils. When purchasing is largely centralized, with a few purchasing staff devolved to business units, purchasing councils give a way of co-ordinating purchases, as well as sharing expertise. A purchasing council consists of a group of devolved buyers who purchase similar items at their various facilities, with corporate staff overseeing and co-ordinating their activities. The council takes over some purchasing activities from individual companies, so it meets as necessary to share information and divide up associated work.

Corporate steering committees. Steering committees are similar to councils except that they tend to be more advisory and less involved in actual purchases. These committees meet periodically and discuss strategies and tactics for the company's main commodities. Steering committees often invite major suppliers in for discussions, and they provide an opportunity for staff from various operating units to meet and discuss buying plans in decentralized units.

USING TEAMS AS PART OF THE ORGANIZATIONAL STRUCTURE

Organizations have been increasing their use of teams to solve problems for more than 25 years. In purchasing, teams are used to evaluate and select suppliers, develop purchasing strategies, analyse patterns of demand, develop supply plans, develop supplier relationships and a stream of other activities.

But not everyone agrees that teams are inevitably more effective. Teams can certainly give benefits in many different circumstances, but they often have undesirable

LEARNING FROM PRACTICE

Tyco International Ltd

A centralized purchasing organization has a CPO at the top, supported by staff at lower levels of the hierarchy. This traditional model works well for companies with one business, but it can be limiting to diversified corporations with many business units – and it fails to capitalize on the individual strengths that each business unit can bring.

Tyco International is a diversified company incorporated in Bermuda and with operations in more than 60 countries. Its main products are based around safety and security – such as fire protection, anti-theft devices, traffic management and so on – with annual sales of more than $20 billion. It has developed a procurement organization that gives its individual business units the flexibility they need, while centralizing certain core tasks. Co-ordinating purchasing has been a challenge in a large conglomerate that developed through numerous corporate acquisitions. The director of corporate sourcing said that, 'There was a time when Tyco was acquiring four to five companies a week, but it wasn't devoting a lot of resources to integrating those companies.'

In 2003 Tyco had no real corporate procurement organization, and each of the diverse business units did its own sourcing. When new managers started to consider the corporate procurement function, the differences between Tyco's business units began to appear. Some companies had well-integrated and efficient sourcing teams – and others did not. And each company had so many divisions, often working in multiple locations, that even identifying the purchasing stakeholders was not easy.

Running any corporate-wide initiative in such complex circumstances was difficult, and the new managers' first step was to create a working team to make progress. This considered the ideas of visibility, stakeholder mapping and team development. More specifically, it designed a standardized purchasing process with seven steps:

1 Understand internal spending and external markets.
2 Create an approach for going to the market.
3 Consider the supply base and identify all viable suppliers.
4 Decide the most appropriate purchasing tactics.
5 Conduct aggressive negotiations and select suppliers.
6 Implement supplier agreements.
7 Monitor the market and supplier performance.

Once this standard process was in place, Tyco collected information to customize procurement in each business unit, referred to as 'stakeholder mapping'. This had six-steps to:

1 Define the stakeholders and their needs and concerns.
2 Identify the key decision-makers and their methods.
3 Review the measurement and reporting structure.
4 Assess the maturity of the existing team, activities and structure.
5 Address the team's skill and resource gaps.
6 Look for synergistic opportunities.

This information was used to develop customized sourcing teams – but rather than enforce a standard pattern, each team could have its own features. This gave a standard structure for reporting, but with a lot of flexibility to deal with specific conditions. For example, with IT spending, the users – who are experts in the area – co-ordinate and run the purchasing process with minimal support from purchasing staff. The energy sourcing team is more centralized, and achieved $17.5 million in savings over 4 years.

Source: Atkinson W. (2007) Tyco customizes its sourcing organization to fit business needs, Purchasing; www.tyco.com

side-effects. In particular, they can waste the time and energy of members (needing more effort from many people to get results), enforce lower performance standards (by accepting the lowest common levels), create destructive conflict within and between teams, hide or obscure responsibility for decisions, make bad decisions and so on. Not everyone is a natural team player and teams can also exploit, stress and frustrate members – sometimes all at the same time (Hackman, 1987).

If we accept the obvious point that making teams a major part of the organizational structure does not guarantee success, then we have to decide the circumstances in which teams will be successful. Much of the success or failure of teams rests on an organization's ability to ask the right questions about using them. Figure 4.10

FIGURE 4.10 Some questions for planning teams

Identify appropriate team assignments

Do assignments justify the use of teams?

Has the proper team model been identified (for instance, part-time versus full-time membership)?

Does senior and functional management support the use of a team?

Form work team and select qualified members and leader

Have core members and temporary members been identified?

Do members have the proper skills, time and commitment to support the team?

Have team sponsors identified and selected a qualified team leader?

Are users or suppliers part of the team?

Do members understand their formal team roles?

Determine member training needs

Have team member training needs been assessed?

Is appropriate training available?

Identify resource requirements

Are resources provided or available to support the team's work?

Determine team authority levels

Have authority levels for the team been determined?

Have team authority levels been communicated across the organization?

Establish team performance goals

Has the team established performance goals?

Determine how to measure performance and reward participants

Are procedures and systems in place to assess team performance and the contribution of members?

Are there reporting channels to team sponsors?

Is team performance linked to performance reward systems?

Develop team charters

Has a formal charter been developed that details team mission, tasks, objectives, etc.?

Has the charter been communicated throughout the organization?

identifies some types of questions that purchasing managers should ask when they are considering the use of teams.

Teams may be the best way of tackling some purchasing projects, but there are major hurdles that can affect their use. The first comes from the team membership, where many organizations routinely form teams with part-time members. These members work within the organization's existing functional structure, and then have additional duties arising from team membership. The resulting matrix organization makes it difficult to get commitment from members who face conflicting demands on their time. The team demands work from its members – but their boss says that they have to do their normal work within the function. The alternative has teams staffed by full-time members – perhaps on secondment from their normal jobs – but these are more expensive and difficult to administer.

A second hurdle is a failure in many organizations to recognize and reward the effort that team members put into their assignments. Traditional reward systems are based on functional work, and this actively discourages people from moving away from their core duties to join a team. When team members are given inadequate recognition for their efforts, they will direct their energy toward areas that are more readily rewarded. Many companies have not grasped this basic principle, that participation in team work creates conflict when members are take away from the main activities that are recognized and rewarded.

A third hurdle relates to business culture. Many people simply do not work as well in teams as they do as individuals. This may have a cultural basis, where some cultures place group needs above individual needs, and others reinforce the drive of individualism (Hofstede, 1984). But the result is that some people are most productive co-operating and working as a team, and others feel that it stifles individual creativity – and can even be uncomfortable and threatening.

We have mentioned three significant barriers to effective teamwork, but this is clearly not an exhaustive list. The reality is that a host of barriers may affect a specific team at a given time in any organization. Purchasing leaders must understand how to use this demanding – but often difficult – structure to work effectively.

CHAPTER REVIEW

- A properly designed organizational structure is essential for the purchasing function. This structure describes the units that make up an organization, the activities done by each and the relationships between them

- The organization of purchasing affects the function's overall efficiency and performance. A good organizational structure will allow and encourage purchasing success

- A basic question asks where the best position of purchasing lies within an organization. There are several options available for this. The one chosen depends on several factors, including past

purchasing operations, type of industry, value of materials bought and so on

- A subsequent question asks how the purchasing function itself is organized. This concerns the way that the function is divided into different specialized units, and the relationships between them. We listed several types of units often found within purchasing, and this list is continuing to expand

- There are many ways of organizing the units within purchasing, with the two main options having a vertical or horizontal focus. In practice, most organizations use some combination of these, with a trend towards more cross-functional operations encouraging horizontal forms

- Both centralized and decentralized purchasing has benefits, and the usual option is to use some combination of the two in a hybrid organization. The choice of functions and purchases to centralize depends on many factors, including size, geographical diversity, management culture and so on

- Teams are often used for purchasing projects and they can give good results. However, they are not necessarily the best option and there can be major hurdles to overcome

DISCUSSION QUESTIONS

1 Do you think that designing an organizational structure is easy? Is it easy to implement a new design?

2 Where might purchasing fit within an organizational hierarchy? Why is this position important?

3 What factors increase the importance of purchasing within an organizational hierarchy?

4 Why do purchasing staff specialize? In what areas might they specialize?

5 What exactly do the purchasing research staff do?

6 Discuss the differences between different levels of decisions in purchasing. Give some examples of tasks at each level.

7 Why might strategic purchasing managers be physically separated from operational staff?

8 Compare a vertical and horizontal organizational structure. What is the logic behind a vertical structure? What is the logic behind a horizontal structure?

9 Discuss the main benefits of centralized purchasing. Now discuss the main benefits of decentralized purchasing. Which is likely to be the most efficient?

10 What factors influence a firm to centralize or decentralize its purchasing authority?

11 Suppose that you are the CPO for a company with worldwide production and buying locations. How would you design an organizational structure for purchasing?

12 Discuss the advantages of using a cross-functional team to evaluate and select suppliers.

13 Why are teams useful for purchasing projects? Are there any barriers to using teams?

REFERENCES

Bloom H. and Nardone J. (1984) Organizational level of the purchasing function, *International Journal of Purchasing and Materials Management*, 20(2), p 16.

Champoux, J. (1999) Organization behaviour: essential tenets for a new millennium, Cincinnati, OH: South-Western.

Fearon, H. (1988) Organizational relationships in purchasing, *Journal of Purchasing and Materials Management*, 24(4), p 7.

Giunipero, L., and Handfield, R. (2004) Purchasing education and training II, Tempe, AZ: Centre for Advanced Purchasing Studies.

Hackman R. (1987) The design of work teams, in Handbook of Organizational Behavior, Englewood Cliffs, NJ: Prentice Hall, pp 315–342.

Hofstede G. H. (1984) Culture's consequences: differences in work-related values, Newbury Park, CA: Sage.

Johnson F. and Leenders M. (2007) Supply leadership changes, Tempe, AZ: Centre for Advanced Purchasing Studies.

Johnson F., Leenders M. and Fearon H. (2006) Supply's growing status and influence: a sixteen-year perspective, *Journal of Supply Chain Management*, 42(2), p 33.

Trent R. J. (2003) Procurement and supply management organizational design survey, Bethlehem, PA: Research White Paper, Lehigh University.

Trent, R. J. (2004) The use of organizational design features in purchasing and supply management, *Journal of Supply Chain Management*, 40(3), p 4.

Waters D. (2003) Inventory control and management (second edition), John Wiley and Sons, Chichester, West Sussex: John Wiley.

FURTHER READING

Anderson J. A. (2002) Organizational design: two lessons to learn before reorganizing, *International Journal of Organization Theory and Behavior*, 5(3–4), p 343.

Fearon H. and Leenders M. (1996) Purchasing's organizational roles and responsibilities, Tempe, AZ: Centre for Advanced Purchasing Studies.

Flood P., MacCurtain S. and West M. (2001) Effective top management teams, Dublin: Blackhall Publishing.

Johnson P. F., Klassen R. D., Leenders M. R. and Fearon H. E. (2002) Determinants of purchasing team usage in the supply chain, *Journal of Operations Management*, 20(1), pp 77–89.

Johnson P.F., Leenders M. and Fearon H. (2006) Supply's growing status and influence, *Journal of Supply Chain Management*, 42, pp 38–48.

Leenders M. R. and Johnson P. F. (2002) Major changes in supply chain responsibilities, Tempe, AZ: Centre for Advanced Purchasing Studies.

McDonough E. F. (2000) An investigation of factors contributing to the success of cross-functional teams, *Journal of Product Innovation Management*, 17(3), p 221.

Sweeney E. (2007) Perspectives on supply chain management and logistics; creating competitive organizations in the 21st century, Dublin: Blackhall Publishing.

Walter D. and Buchanan J. (2001) The new economy, new opportunities, and new structures, Management Decision, 39(10), pp 818–834.

CASE STUDY

Communidat-Schlatzberger AG

A recent meeting of the Purchasing Committee of Communidad-Schlatzberger ag discussed the role of cross-functional teams and the problems of getting them to work properly. Two members of the committee were particularly vocal, and the following script gives an impression of their views.

Carl: At one of our team meetings last week we were talking about a design issue and had to keep calling a supplier about some technical details. Eventually, someone said that it would be much simpler if we had the supplier with us during the meeting. We thought about it for a minute, and then the team leader simply vetoed the idea. His reason was that bringing a supplier into team meetings would expose us to too much risk. He said it would be like playing poker while showing all your cards to the other players.

Anna: So you made decisions with only part of the information – and the supplier was sitting in his office with everything that you needed to know. This reminds me of a meeting last week of our supplier selection team. Our team selected the best supplier, but when we presented our decision to the purchasing director he didn't look at all pleased. Later word came down through our team leader that we should have chosen the runner-up supplier.

Carl: Why wasn't the director pleased with the team's decision?

Anna: The runner-up is the existing supplier. Last year we switched one contract to a new supplier and things didn't go well. The supplier selection team were all corporate staff, and the users were plant people who had worked happily with the previous supplier. The first time that something went wrong, the plant people told the corporate staff to fix it since they had chosen the supplier. Now whenever there is a problem, it is the corporate staff's fault and they have to fix it.

Carl: So the corporate team has taken some of the work from plant staff who can now focus on things that really improve local operations. What's their problem?

Anna: How often does your team meet?

Carl: To be honest, I'm not sure that it meets often enough. We don't seem to have the same enthusiasm that we had when we started a year and a half ago. We used to meet monthly, then it became every other month, now it's quarterly. Maybe it is because some of our members have to fly in, so a 1-day team meeting takes them 2 or 3 days. I also hear there are questions about travel expenses. But even the local members don't seem as committed as they used to be. Perhaps our team is too big. We have 12 members and its difficult to co-ordinate everything and get agreement.

Anna: My boss was telling me the other day that one of his committees has only three members and he gets swamped by all the things he has to do.

Carl: At least he must know the rest of the team – our team keeps on changing and I don't know some of the people. And we rarely seem to get any excitement or create the synergy that cross-functional teams are supposed to produce.

Anna: You're lucky. We had a meeting the other day where the marketing rep and the finance rep started shouting and saying nasty things to each other. The rest of us didn't know what was happening and we just sat there – and then people started to take sides and things went from bad to worse.

Carl: What did the team leader do while this was happening?

Anna: She just sat there and let them get on with it. Sometimes I wonder what qualified her to be a team leader. I don't think that she has any training – but I guess the executives think that anyone can lead a team.

Carl: I suppose we could ask what qualified us to be team members? I certainly didn't get any training or preparation.

Anna: Speak for yourself – I play for the local football team!

Carl: I often wonder why we have teams at all. We only seem to make the same decisions that individuals used to make, but now instead of one person taking an hour to make a decision, it takes 12 of us a whole day to come to the same conclusion. And we certainly don't seem to be innovative or anything.

Anna: Do you get reviewed to say how well the team is performing?

Carl: Maybe we would if we had some measurable goals. When it's time for our annual reports half the team doesn't even mention that they are members, and the other half gives a small acknowledgment. Then their bosses don't recognize their efforts.

Anna: Is that a problem?

Carl: Well the functional managers don't know what happens in the team. Last quarter, three members put a lot of effort into a joint task, but their managers gave them completely different ratings for the same job!

Anna: Well 3 weeks ago we were having a team meeting when our engineering rep, got a call on his telephone. His manager called to tell him to get back to engineering fast because they 'needed him there to do some real work'.

Carl: Presumably the manager thought that purchasing should get on with buying things and leave him to engineer!

Questions

- Review this conversation and list the issues that could affect a team's performance. How would you set about overcoming the related problems?

- Which of the issues do you think could have most impact on team performance?

- What other problems are there with team work that was not raised in the discussion?

CHAPTER 5
PURCHASING
INTEGRATION

LEARNING OBJECTIVES
After reading this chapter you should be able to:

- Understand the concept organizational integration

- Appreciate the benefits of integration

- Discuss ways for purchasing to increase internal integration

- Discuss the aims and organization of external integration

- Consider the organizational changes that come with integration

- Discuss the role of cross-functional teams in purchasing

- Discuss the ways that supply management can work with other functions during
  new product development and order fulfilment

MEANING OF INTEGRATION

In the last chapter we saw how an organization consists of different units that do specialized jobs. The organizational structure defines these units, the jobs they do and the relationships between them. But the key point is that all of the different units must work together to achieve common goals. When a company wants to reduce operating costs, all divisions of the company have to co-operate to make real progress. This is the concept that underpins strategic alignment.

Purchasing has to work closely with other groups both within their organization and outside it. Sometimes they work so closely that it becomes difficult to separate their activities, and they effectively become integrated into a single purchasing effort. This chapter shows how such integration is an increasingly important aspect of purchasing.

Definition

Integration
Is the process of bringing together different groups, functions or organizations, to work together on common business related assignments.

Integration of purchasing means that it works seamlessly with other bodies, both within an organization and outside it.

The idea behind integration is that people come together to work on a common problem. We know that 'two heads are better than one' when it comes to solving problems, but in business the idea of bringing different people together to solve a common problem has often been missed. Here we discuss some of the benefits that come from having a range of different people, from different backgrounds and with different viewpoints working to make their organizations more effective and efficient.

A study of senior executives showed that integration is at the heart of logistics development (Giunipero, 2004). When asked about the skills needed for supply chain management they identified **relationship management**.

Relationship management
Consists of all the activities that organizations use to enhance relations with other parties – including the ability to act ethically, listen effectively, communicate and use creative problem solving.

Forms of integration

Integration can occur in many forms. It can occur within functions, such as integrated sourcing or new product development teams. It can also occur through cross-functional and cross-location teams, where people from different business units are brought together. These initiatives aim at getting people within the same organization working together, to give *internal integration*. Extending this idea gives cross-organizational teams, with members from suppliers, customers and other outside bodies – giving *external integration.*

Integration brings together people with different backgrounds, aims, opinions, knowledge, etc., and this is always going to be difficult. However, it can bring considerable benefits as they all provide:

Information

- About their markets
- About their own plans and requirements

Knowledge and expertise

- Product knowledge and technology
- Process knowledge and understanding of how it works

Business advantages

- Favourable cost and efficient services that can benefit customers

- Economies of scale, which can reduce costs

Different perspective on an issue

- Which encourages a team to look at a problem from a new perspective

Of course, having diverse teams work together is not the only way of achieving integration. When a customer gives their opinion to a supplier they are to some extent integrating their ideas. Some of the different ways that purchasing can achieve integration include:

- Cross-functional or cross-organizational committees to share ideas and management

- Cross-functional or cross-organizational teams that actually work together

- Information sharing, including aspects of e-business, EDI, the internet, videoconferencing, etc.

- Shared performance measures and targets that move towards agreed goals

- Process-focus with everyone focussing on the common process of delivering products to satisfy final customers

- Co-location, with suppliers and customers working together in the same location

- Buyer and supplier councils that give input and guidance to a steering committee

The starting point for virtually all purchasing integration initiatives is to have the purchasing function working more closely with other parts of their own firm – giving internal integration.

LEARNING FROM PRACTICE

Boeing 787 Dreamliner

In 2007 Boeing announced that its new wide-body jet, the 787 Dreamliner, would be delayed by at least 6 months. This was a blow to the company's plans to give global suppliers a greater role in building their airplanes and sharing the associated risks. In return for greater initial investment and sharing the development costs, suppliers get guaranteed orders for major sections of the airplane.

The benefits of this arrangement is that Boeing reduced its development costs by billions of dollars, and the efficiency of their own – and suppliers' – operations mean that a finished plane can be assembled in as little as 3 days. On the other hand, Boeing has less control over day-to-day operations. For instance, they were affected by upstream problems in a supply chain that resulted in a shortage of titanium and aluminium fasteners that hold airplanes together. Such problems were so severe that after the ceremony to unveil the first Dreamliner, the plane had to be largely disassembled as suppliers had not installed wiring or other components needed to make the systems work.

It was evident that outsourcing jobs to suppliers had considerable benefits – but also problems that would take some time to overcome.

Source: Lunsford J.L. (2007) Boeing delays 787 by 6 months as suppliers in new role fall behind, *Wall Street Journal*, 11 October, 2007, p A1.

INTERNAL INTEGRATION

Purchasing must communicate with a number of other functions (as illustrated in Figure 5.1). These linkages become even stronger and more important as the role of purchasing continues to develop.

Internal integration means that purchasing develops its internal links with other functions and business units. To develop these links successfully, purchasing staff must have at least a working knowledge of the work done in different departments – and conversely other departments should see what purchasing does. This is fairly obvious, and you would hope that a buyer of, say, chemicals would know something about the chemicals' properties, what they are for and what users want them for. But even this level of collaboration can be difficult as it needs people with skills in both procurement and the other functions. To improve internal integration, purchasing usually has to develop its links with the following functions.

Operations. Purchasing plays a leading role in supporting operations in its job of making the organization's products. Because the links between operations and

FIGURE 5.1 Communications with purchasing

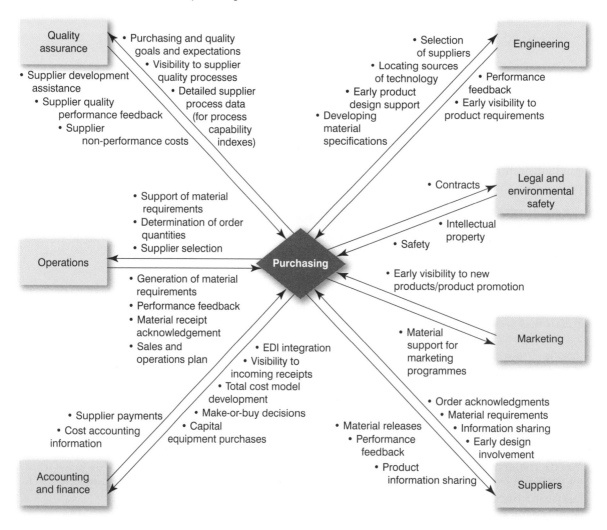

purchasing have to be so close, purchasing often report directly to operations management in the organizational structure. A major link between operations and purchasing is through their strategies, which must be closely aligned and may be developed jointly. These links must also be maintained at a tactical level. For instance, an operations production plan might show production levels over the next year, and this specifies the materials needed and their arrival schedule to be organized by procurement. Purchasing and operations must clearly work together at all levels, and this encourages many firms to 'co-locate' purchasing staff, which means that they physically work in operations facilities to respond quickly to needs.

Quality management. The quality of materials brought into an organization depends directly on procurement, so there is a clear link between the purchasing and quality management functions. This link has become more important in recent years as organizations have put more emphasis on product quality through programmes like Total Quality Management. Firms are also outsourcing more of their component and service needs, so purchasing must work closely with quality management to make sure that the extended supply base performs as expected. Joint projects involving the two functions might include supplier selection and evaluation, supplier quality training, process capability studies and corrective action planning.

Design. The design of new products, or changes to existing ones, is a central function in most organizations. In manufacturing it is often described as engineering. The link between purchasing and design is clearly important, and we have already mentioned the benefits of having purchasing involved early in the design process. Specific links between the two functions occur when design wants purchasing to identify the most technically capable supplier of an item, or to make sure that a supplier meets design's quality and delivery targets. Also, design want purchasing to identify sources of new technology that can be integrated into new products, and to encourage the supplier to offer innovative ideas. In practice, stronger links between purchasing and design can be formed in several ways. For instance, designers and buyers can work together on product development or supplier selection teams, or purchasing can co-locate a buyer within the design group, who can talk directly with product and process designers and respond quickly to their ides. Another option is a liaison group that co-ordinates communications and makes sure that each function is aware of what the other is doing. Thus, the two functions can hold regular meetings to report on items of mutual concern. A final option is for purchasing to have a policy of recruiting staff with strong technical backgrounds, who can work well with their design counterparts.

Accounting and finance. Although purchasing is responsible for acquiring materials, it is accounting and finance that set budgets and administer payments. So there must be clear communications between the two functions, largely concerned with the flow of money and accounting information. Increasingly, this is organized electronically through EDI and EFT. For example, purchasing may transmit a material releases to a supplier, with details automatically passed to the accounting system. When the material arrives, the material control system updates purchasing files (noting the materials are no longer on-order or in-transit), stock records (adding material to the available inventory) and accounts (updating the accounts payable). The two functions work closely together and they must share essential information – but they do need somewhat different kinds of data. Purchasing is more concerned with physical movements of materials and availability; accounting is more concerned with the flow of money and payments.

Marketing and sales. Purchasing is concerned with moving materials into an organization, while marketing and sales are more concerned with moving products out to customers. But they are still connected, as many ideas for new products and materials come from marketing when they return comments from customers. Also, marketing develops sales forecasts that convert into production plans and material requirements.

Legal. When purchasing signs a supply contract or purchase order it makes a legal agreement with the suppliers. The details of such agreements have to be written by lawyers, and this needs close co-operation between the two functions. In practice, standard terms are used for most contracts, so most time is spent on exceptional items or resolving disputes when things go wrong. Other points of contact refer red to include patent ownership, intellectual property, copyright, terms in new-product development, risk assessment, product liability claims, anti-competitive practices, escape clauses in long-term contracts – and any other legal issues.

Environmental management, health, and safety. Purchasing have a responsibility to ensure that the materials they buy meet all health and safety regulations – and,

LEARNING FROM PRACTICE

D^2C

When companies want to increase the amount of integration, they often face practical difficulties – such as incompatible systems or lack of suitable communication. Specialized software companies provide tools to help with such problems. D^2C is one such company. Its main products help overcome communication difficulties between inter-company teams working on new product development projects. These projects typically need efficient, safe and open communications between suppliers, clients, construction companies, engineering companies, architects, real estate companies, property managers, marketing specialists and finance companies. This needs a collaborative environment and D^2C provides solutions that typically allow managers to:

- Work and interact with colleagues around the world
- Take part in decision-making away from their desk
- Monitor the progress of projects and keep in touch with events as they happen
- Keep business partners up-to-date with progress and information
- Promote a knowledge-sharing culture
- Remotely access, store, search, retrieve and handle any type of file in a unique electronic library
- Share information with partners and make new staff instantly more productive

- Route essential information to the right people
- Assemble and work with a virtual project team
- Assist audits by automatically recording the movement of information and work
- Control the routing of transactional data, such as purchase orders, requisitions, timesheets, etc.

To achieve these functions, D^2C have developed a series of collaboration tools with a secure, web-based infrastructure that provides:

- An information store for all documents, files and digital assets that need to be shared by a team
- Workflow functionality to track tasks, decisions, events, contracts, variations – and the issuing and tracking of relevant documents
- Discussions, bulletin boards and email stores– that can trap and record the history of interactions in the team
- Procedures for managing contracts, costs, budgets and a full e-tendering process
- Project and programme collaboration, with an extranet and document store that manages all of the documents, drawings and other file types that need to be shared

Source: Based on www.d2c.org.uk

increasingly, that they do not cause environmental damage. Also, they have to ensure that suppliers, in their own operations, are using safe methods and are complying with relevant laws.

EXTERNAL INTEGRATION

Purchasing commonly presents the external face of an organization to suppliers, and it also serves as a primary vehicle for integration with external suppliers and other stakeholders.

Purchasing's external links

External integration means that purchasing has to create and maintain links with stakeholder groups outside the firm. These links work alongside its internal links to other functions. It is important to remember that purchasing's main external links may be with suppliers, but it has to work with many other organizations, illustrated in the following list.

Suppliers. Purchasing's primary external links are with suppliers. They are responsible for selecting the best supplier for a particular transaction, and then maintaining open communications to discuss anything that might concern the purchase agreement.

Government. Purchasing sometimes maintains links with governments at different levels. For example, purchasing may arrange for services to be delivered by governments, check on current health and safety regulations, look into government grants and aid, check environmental legislation, discuss international trade conditions or negotiate international counter-trade agreements.

Local communities. Because purchasing controls a large budget, it can affect certain social goals. These goals include sourcing from local suppliers, awarding business to specific types of suppliers and establishing ethical business practices. To ensure that these aims are met, purchasing has to have clear links to the local community and its various leaders.

Collaborative buyer-seller relationships

External integration can be achieved through various types of co-operation, and with suppliers this is generally referred to as **buyer-seller collaboration**. Most buyers and sellers recognize the need for collaboration as the best way of improving costs, quality, delivery, time and other measures of performance.

> **Buyer-seller Collaboration**
> Is the process by which two parties adopt a high level of purposeful co-operation to maintain a trading relationship over time.

The relationship is bilateral, which means that both parties have the power to shape its nature and future direction. Mutual commitment and balanced power are key features – commitment so that both parties keep the relationship working over time, and balance to give mutual benefits. This collaboration is often described as *supplier relationship management* (SRM), but some people say that there is an essential difference as SRM is a one way arrangement where buying firms manage their supply base. It stops using poor or marginal suppliers, and then develops the remainder through some form of collaborative relationship.

The following characteristics define a collaborative buyer-seller relationship:

- A limited number of suppliers – often one – for each purchased item
- Long-term contracts with agreed performance targets

- Mutual benefits and sharing of rewards

- Joint efforts to improve supplier performance across critical performance areas

- Joint efforts to resolve disputes

- Open exchange of information – including information about new products, supplier costs, production schedules and forecasts for purchased items

- A credible commitment to work together during difficult times – which means that neither party returns to old practices at the first sign of trouble

- A commitment to high quality, defect-free products with design specifications that the supplier's process is capable of meeting

Figure 5.2 compares the characteristics of traditional and collaborative buyer-seller relationships. An important point here is that no amount of collaboration can completely eliminate conflict – which is an inevitable part of trade. However, collaboration should always include a mechanisms for managing conflicts.

Advantages buyer-seller collaboration

A firm can gain many advantages from closer relationships with suppliers, and the following list mentions some of the most common (Spekman, 1988). These emerge from a smoother, more efficient flow of materials that gives better customer satisfaction.

Trust. This refers to the belief that the other party will act fairly and not take advantage of a situation. This is an essential part of any long-term relationship and it means, for example, that a seller can share cost data with a buyer without worrying about any harmful consequences. It leads to joint efforts to reduce costs, input from suppliers early in the design of new products, sharing of sensitive information and a whole series of other benefits.

Long-term contracts. After evaluating suppliers, the best can be courted in closer relationships and rewarded with longer-term contracts. Purchasers and sellers both

FIGURE 5.2 Characteristics of buyer/seller relationships

	Traditional approach	Collaborative approach
Suppliers	Multiple sources played off against each other	One of a few preferred suppliers for each major item
Cost sharing	Buyer takes all cost savings; supplier hides cost savings	Win-win shared rewards
Joint improvement efforts	Little or none	Joint improvement driven by mutual interdependence
Dispute resolution	Buyer unilaterally resolves disputes	Existence of conflict-resolution mechanisms
Communication	Minimal or two-way exchange of information	Open and complex exchange of imformation
Marketplace adjustments	Buyer determines response to changing conditions	Buyer and seller work together to adapt to a changing marketplace
Quality	Buyer inspects at receipt	Designed into the product

get benefits from these. Suppliers have long-term business which allows them to invest in new processes and equipment, ease scheduling, give more reliable supplies and so on; buyers have guaranteed supplies with agreed terms, joint improvements to give lower costs and improve performance, risk sharing, access to new technology, etc.

Shared information. One of the easiest ways of collaborating is through shared information, typically through an EDI link or website. This allows both buyers and sellers to base their decisions on accurate data about costs, supplies, forecasts, demands, etc.

More efficient operations. If a supplier knows the long-term demand for items, it can schedule operations more efficiently to meet these and it can recognize potential problems with schedules or supplies well in advance and take action to avoid them. The result if more efficient, lower cost and easier operations.

Faster response. Working with routine contacts – often with automated procedures – suppliers can respond quickly to any changes in circumstances. This can translate into a competitive advantage from more flexible operations.

Lower costs. When information is freely shared, both organizations can design operations that are best suited to the long-term requirements. This means that they can increase overall efficiency and reduce operating costs.

Higher customer satisfaction. This is achieved by the more efficient flows of materials, more reliable operations that match customer demands, lower costs, fewer problems, closer communications and so on.

Evolving from adversarial to collaborative relationships

Most organizations recognize the benefits of collaborative relationships and have moved some way in this direction. In particular, they have moved from traditional adversarial, arm's-length relationships towards one of mutual trust and commitment. This move generally occurs in four phases.

Phase 1 – Distrust. Which is the traditional adversarial relationship, where each party views the other with minimal trust or respect. Each thinks that it can only benefit at the other's expense, so relations are often confrontational and even hostile. Multiple sourcing, competitive bidding and short-term contracts are the characteristic purchasing policies. Buyers quickly replace suppliers who do not meet their expectations – and suppliers divert materials when they get better offers. Relationships are summarized as short-term and antagonistic.

Phase 2 – Suspicion. Multiple sourcing is still used to give a level of safety and control. Although the relationship remains at arm's-length, a history of trading is building-up and there is the beginning of a working relationship. There is increasing stability as buyers reduce their searches for better options and suppliers maintain their product range. Relationships are summarized as competitive and adversarial.

Phase 3 – Co-operation. Purchasers recognize the advantages of maintaining a smaller supply base and developing closer relationships with them. This encourages joint efforts to reduce costs and improve services, particularly through shorter lead times and more flexible responses to demands. The firms are beginning to work towards common goals, and buyers are more aware of the benefits of supplier input during product design. Relationships are summarized as co-operative.

Phase 4 – Trust. Both parties commit to working together and emphasize strategies for improving performance. Purchasing has chosen a supplier that supports the firm's objectives, and it nurtures the relationship. Trust and information sharing are widespread, with both parties focussing on ways to improve quality, costs and service. The seller effectively becomes an extension of the purchaser's organization. Relationships are summarized as collaborative.

It difficult to move through all of these phases, and most firms stop somewhere on the way. The majority of major companies are probably around phase 3. Companies that are in globally competitive industries, such as cars and electronics equipment, tend to have made more progress through these phases than firms in less competitive industries.

A critical step in the move towards closer collaboration is to start with a focus on the final product that is to be delivered, and not some abstract concept that cannot be translated into enough short-term benefits to sustain the initiative. Then a useful approach is (Waters, 2009):

- Specify a desired outcome at the business unit level (such as administrative cost savings, supply continuity, process improvement, access to new technology or process innovation)

- Let the business outcome drive the relationship by initiating projects that focus on achieving the outcome

- The overall relationship then emerges from various individual relationships, each of which is aiming to produce a specified result

- The benefits from these relationships appear across the business

Obstacles to buyer-seller collaboration

There are clearly considerable benefits to collaboration, but a number of obstacles can hinder or prevent its introduction. The most significant barriers to overcome include the following.

Confidentiality. The need for confidentiality about financial, product and process information is the most frequently cited reason for not developing closer supplier relationships. Confidentiality is a concern in many relationships. Purchasing managers are understandably reluctant to share critical information with suppliers who may also be selling to competitors; suppliers are reluctant to share information with buyers who may be working with competing suppliers When information is spread more widely there is always a greater chance that it will fall into the wrong hands. Also, conditions may change so that a buyer may stop buying a part and switch to making it internally – and then selling it in direct competition with their previous supplier (but the trend towards outsourcing makes this less likely).

Limited interest by suppliers. Closer relationships do not interest all suppliers, and many think that their share of any benefits is not worth the necessary investment. A dominant buyer might be able to exert some influence, but when suppliers have more power in a relationship – particularly when there is a monopoly or oligopoly of supply – there is little that a purchaser can do.

Legal barriers. In some industries, there are legal constraints on the type of relationship that is possible, such as government restrictions that force their own

LEARNING FROM PRACTICE

HaKaPac

Source: Based on Harkenman K. (2009) Integration or bust, HaKaPac, Copenhagen.

HaKaPac buys materials from many suppliers, but it wanted to develop closer relations with a few key ones. Although senior managers described this as one of their strategic aims, there seemed little enthusiasm among lower managers. An investigation soon showed that they were not aware of the potential benefits, and were happy to continue working as usual. So the company prepared documents to explicitly give the case for closer integration, especially listing:

- A statement of the goals of the integration programme, with criteria for success to be achieved within a realistic schedule
- Specific benefits to both HaKaPac and its suppliers
- The costs of adopting new ways of working, along with the time and resource invested in the programme
- A comparison of the overall costs and benefits, with net benefits accumulating over time
- Discussion of soft benefits that cannot be quantified
- Statistical information to support closer integration
- Case studies of integration from other companies

Their efforts seemed to work, and HaKaPac's integration programme became a model for other companies. Some of the key points that they learnt were:

- Different stages of collaboration need different people, skills, levels of investment and attention; the people needed to start the effort may not be the best ones to nurture, manage and sustain it
- Recruit from the supplier's business. The best supplier relationship managers are those who have worked in the business, understand the day-to-day pressures and share the same culture
- Monitor internal and external conditions, and establish mechanisms to adjust roles, measures, methods and deliverables
- Schedule regular meetings between stakeholders to assess performance and make necessary adjustments
- Keep commitment – or else the initiative will fail and all the work done on it will be wasted

departments to use competitive tenders. Anti-competition laws can also restrict closer relationships in some circumstance (a theme that we return to in chapter 14).

Resistance to change. Although people usually say that they enjoy the challenges of change, the reality is that most people like the familiarity of current operations. Most purchasing staff are familiar with an arm's-length approach and a shift toward a more trusting approach is not easy. Resistance to change is a powerful force that takes time, patience and training to overcome – and firms that use traditional practices may simply not have the skills or knowledge to invest.

ORGANIZING FOR INTEGRATION

The traditional model for a purchasing organizational structure has a set of units, each working more or less separately and working towards its own aims. The resulting hierarchical structure, divided into distinct functions with the consequent 'silo mentality', does not help co-operation. The need to share information and integrate actions across functions and organizations needs another structure. In particular, it needs executives in senior positions who can co-ordinate various supply chain functions to give an efficient flow of materials from suppliers through to customers. It also opens new career paths for staff, giving the opportunity to develop new, multi-functional skills.

This move towards greater integration has forced organizations to modify their organizational structures. Initially, organizations might have had distinct departments with names like 'Purchasing', 'Material Management', 'Warehousing', 'Physical distribution' and so on. Then with internal integration, departments with aligned interested merged until the standard pattern had three consolidated groups:

- *Procurement,* to manage the acquisition of materials to the point where they were delivered at an organization

- *Materials management,* to look after the movement of materials through operations within the organization

- *Physical distribution,* to move finished products out to customers

Many organizations stopped at this point, and in 1988 (Fearon, 1988) showed that 70 per cent of US companies used versions of this model. Over the following years firms increasingly combined these three functions into the co-ordinated function of logistics. Then over the past decade or so firms have increasingly recognized that other functions, such as information management and accounting, are important to the physical flow of goods. Adding these functions into the core of logistics has increased internal integration

More sophisticated information systems have improved information flows, giving 'visibility' across supply chain, which means that each member can see what is happening at other points in the chain. Then each member can co-ordinate and schedule its operations more efficiently, giving smooth and reliable flows of materials, smooth production, lower inventory levels, higher productivity, lower overheads, shorter cycle times, lower costs and so on. Frederick Smith, the chairman of FedEx, summarized this integrate view by commenting that 'Information about the package is more important than the package itself.'

Closer relationships between members of the supply chain gave external integration, and some people thought that it would be better to describe the associated function as supply chain management. This is really a semantic point, but it has helped raise the perceived importance of purchasing within an supply management hierarchy. Figure 5.3 illustrates a possible structure for such supply chain management (Waters, 2009), but obviously there are many variations on this.

CROSS-FUNCTIONAL SOURCING TEAMS

Cross-functional sourcing teams
Consist of people from different functions – and increasingly different organizations – brought together to achieve purchasing-related tasks. The tasks can be specific (such as product design or supplier selection) or broad (such as reducing unit costs or improving quality).

The essence of integration is that it promotes cross-functional and cross-organizational communication, co-ordination and collaboration. To support this effort, cross-functional sourcing teams have become increasingly important.

When working properly a cross-functional sourcing team can bring together knowledge, experience, skills and resources needed to work on joint problems – something that is difficult with rigid organizational structures. However, you should always remember that there is nothing implicitly good or bad about teams, and they can give poor results as well as good ones.

Figure 5.4 shows a classification of cross-functional sourcing teams according to their type of assignment (finite or continuous) and the member's commitment (full-time or part-time). Some firms use full-time sourcing teams, but they are usually part-time, and most work on continuous assignments – working in the bottom

FIGURE 5.3 Example of a functional organization structure

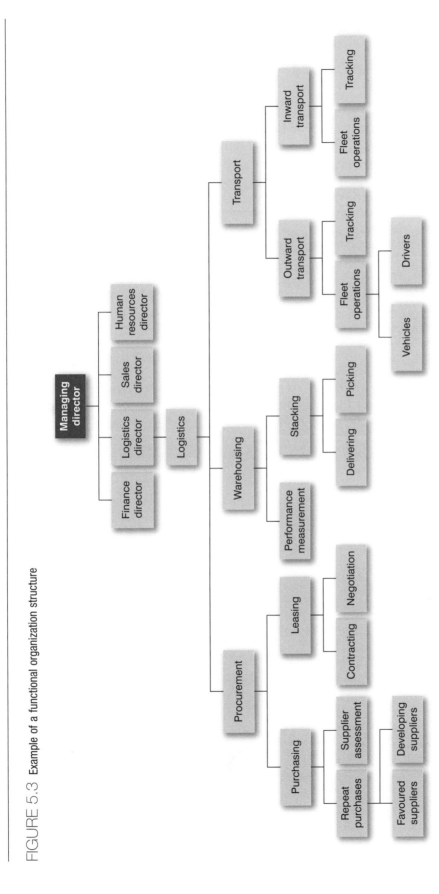

LEARNING FROM PRACTICE

BMP Ltd

BMP Ltd make mechanical parts for domestic electrical equipment assemblers in central Europe. In 2009 they analysed the effects of closer supplier collaboration in a project that was due to start later that year. In particular, they considered supply chain responsiveness, reliability and total cost for a component that they supplied to a major car assembly plant. Ironically, BMP had a close relationship with this customer, but not with its own suppliers.

This component involved several layers in the supply chain, and BMP were keen to see what improvements they could reasonably make to the supply chain. One of their own suppliers assisted by sharing detailed information on its forecasts of future conditions. This specified lead times of 12 days, with value-added time of 47 mins, and €500,000 of stocks of work in progress. The supplier felt that with closer collaboration, they could achieve a lead time of 5.5 days and €100,000 in stock, with the same amount of value-added time. This improvement was achieved by better planning and co-ordination allowing a flexible response to BMP's demands.

This initial analysis was optimistic, but a number of questions remained. Are the results from this single supplier typical for all BMP's other suppliers, and can they transfer the improved methods to other components? The company also identified some barriers to progress, including a lack of agreed performance measures, some unsatisfactory suppliers and a process for sharing the benefits of collaboration (where they were aware of the dangers of negotiations degenerating into arguments over 'who owns the savings').

Collaboration could bring even more benefits if upstream tiers of suppliers can be brought in at an early stage, but this increases the practical difficulties. Also, as more companies become involved it becomes increasingly likely that some will not want to be involved – but if BMP can overcome such difficulties, even to a limited extent, it seems as if they can get significant benefits.

Source: Based on Scarborough J. (2009) Supply chain optimisation, Operations Management Conference, Vienna.

FIGURE 5.4

Different types of sourcing teams

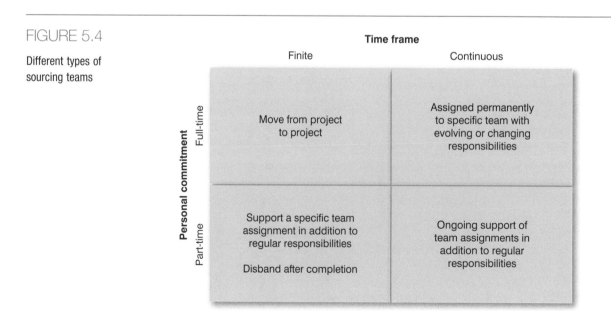

right-hand quadrant of Figure 5.4. But this presents special challenges, particularly getting commitment from team members who have other responsibilities.

Benefits from cross-functional teams

We have already discussed the general benefits of closer collaboration, and teams add some others, including the following.

Shorter time to complete a task. Teams often need less time to solve a problem or complete an assigned task than individuals. When individuals work on tasks, there is often duplicated effort, and even work in single-function groups can take a relatively long time. Cross-functional teams allow members to reduce duplication, reach agreement faster, get broad support for the findings and implement them quickly.

More innovation. Teams encourage more innovative products and processes that are essential to long-term success. Research suggests that teams with few formal rules and procedures, along with informal organizational structures, develop more innovative ideas (Russell, 1990).

Joint ownership of decisions. Through team interaction, members begin to understand each other's requirements and constraints, and they develop joint solutions that different units can support. Once a team makes a decision, the buy-in from all members makes it easier to implement.

Enhanced communications between functions and organizations. Cross-functional teams can help reduce communication barriers because members are in direct contact with each other – and with members of their respective organizations.

Realizing synergies by combining individuals and functions. Teams bring together individuals with different perspectives and expertise. The synergies of team work can generate new and creative ways to look at a situation, approach a task and solve a problem – giving better solutions than individuals or departments acting alone.

Better identification and resolution of problems. Teams with diverse knowledge and skills can quickly identify the underlying causes of a problem. This early identification and correction of problems reduces their impact – and the joint ownership of problems and responsibility for their solution reduces the chance that people will look around for someone to blame.

Drawbacks with cross-functional teams

Cross-functional sourcing teams do not guarantee a successful project. The team approach needs careful management, open exchange of information between members, motivated members, clearly understood and agreed goals, effective leaders and adequate resources. When any of these requirements are missing the teams can work poorly, with possible shortcomings including the following.

Team process loss. Process loss occurs when a team does not tackle its task in the best or most efficient way, or members do not use their resources to create a successful outcome (Steiner, 1972). Then the net benefits from the group are less than the expected benefits from its members working individually. Process loss means that the gains from team interaction are less than the costs of achieving them.

Negative effects on individual members. Even when the team is successful, there can be negative effects on individual members. These might arise when pressure is put on members to support a majority position that an individual does not agree with. An example has an engineer who is pressured by other team members to select the lowest-price supplier, even though the engineer knows that a higher-priced supplier would give better quality. Also, there are the usual problems with teams, where some individuals feel stifled in a team setting or may not interact well with other team members.

Poor team decisions. Cross-functional teams do not necessarily make good decisions – and they can make very poor ones. This effect has been described as *Groupthink,* which is the tendency of a rational team to arrive at a bad decision, despite the availability of information and better alternatives. A major problem is that individuals in a cohesive group strive for consensus, and to achieve this they suppress their own views and objections (Janis, 1982).

When to form a cross-functional team

Cross-functional teams need resources, and as these are constrained there is inevitably a limit on the number of teams that an organization can establish. Clearly, purchasing should not use a team for every decision it faces, as many decisions simply do not need a team approach. The basic, and obvious, principle is that teams should only be used when there are benefits from having people of different backgrounds working on a common problem.

More specifically, teams are most useful for tasks that are complex and large-scale, such as new product development, locating a new production facility, developing a procurement strategy or establishing a new business unit. These tasks are so large and complex that one person or function cannot really complete the assignment.

A firm may also use a team for tackling smaller problems where one person or department could arrive at a solution, but a team is likely to give a better one. For example, purchasing may be able to evaluate and select the supplier for an item, but a better result could come from a team with diverse experience and members who can view the problem from a number of perspectives.

A third type of task for teams is one that directly affects a firm's competitiveness, such as negotiations with a joint venture partner. Cross-functional teams can also be useful when no single function has the resources needed to solve a particular problem that has a broader impact.

Improving sourcing team effectiveness

Managers often ask basic questions about sourcing teams, and here look at six of the most common.

Question 1: What is involved in cross-functional team planning?

Extensive planning is needed before a team can start an assignment. If this planning is ignored, there is less chance that it will succeed in its task. Some issues that should be considered in planning include the following.

Selecting a task. Because of their limited resources, organizations should use teams selectively. Sourcing teams should work only on tasks that are important to an organization's success, have significant size, are complex, benefit from team members with a variety of skills, give an outcome with a significant impact and so on.

Selecting team members and leaders. One of the crucial planning issues is the selection of the right members, who should:

- Understand the team's task and aims
- Have knowledge and skills relevant to the task
- Have time to commit to the team
- Can work with other members of the team
- Can assume an organizational rather than strict functional perspective

Training. Working with a team needs a different set of skills from traditional work. Organizations must consider carefully the training needed by sourcing team members. This includes training in project management, conflict resolution, consensus decision making, group problem solving, goal setting and effective communication skills.

Resources. The types of resources available to teams make a major difference to team performance (Monczka and Trent, 1993). We can describe 10 categories of resources needed by a team, listed in Figure 5.5 (Peters and O'Connor, 1980). The resources that are most likely to affect a team's performance are (in order of importance) supplier participation, services and help from others, time availability and budgetary support.

Others. Other planning issues include the level of team authority, the types and frequency of team evaluations and rewards and the physical location of team members.

Question 2: Does senior management practice subtle control over sourcing teams?

Senior managers clearly have the authority to exercize direct control over a team, and can in the extreme simply disband it. But another issue involves subtle control over sourcing teams. This means that managers do not dictate team activities, but instead they take more restrained actions to increase the chances of a successful outcome. Types of subtle control include:

- Authorizing, or prohibiting, the creation and actions of a sourcing team
- Selecting the team's task, and the limits of its activities
- Establishing broad objectives (while the team itself later establishes specific targets)
- Selecting the team leader and members
- Requiring performance updates at regular intervals or at key milestones (as no team wants to report that they have made no progress)
- Conducting performance reviews and holding teams accountable for performance outcomes

Senior managers do not get involved in a team's day-to-day activities, but they must still work to ensure continuing progress.

FIGURE 5.5 **Team resource requirements**

1   **Supplier participation**

The degree to which suppliers directly support completion of the team's assignments when their involvement is needed.

2   **Required services and help from others**

Services and help required from others external to the team to perform its assignment.

3   **Time availability**

The amount of time that can be devoted by all team members to the team's assignment.

4   **Budgetary support**

Financial resources needed to perform the team's assignment.

5   **Materials and supplies**

The routine items that are required to perform the team's assignment.

6   **Team member task preparation**

Personal preparation and experience of team members, through previous education, formal training and relevant job experience.

7   **Work environment**

Physical aspects of the immediate work environment of the team, with characteristics that facilitate rather than interfere with team performance.

8   **Executive management commitment**

Overall level of support that executive management gives to the cross-functional team process.

9   **Job-related information**

Information, including data and reports, from multiple sources needed to support the team performance.

10   **Tools and equipment**

Specific tools, equipment and technology needed to perform the team's assignment.

Question 3: Do team members get recognized and rewarded?

There should be a direct link between rewards and individual team member's effort, and also between rewards and overall team performance. Unfortunately, many organizations fail to recognize the time and effort that members must commit to sourcing teams, and this lack of recognition means that members put most of their effort into non-team work.

While there is no simple answer to questions about recognition and rewards, we can give some guidelines. Firstly, team membership should be included as part of an individual's performance review. This sends a message that membership is valued and recognized by the organization. Secondly, along with an evaluation of the entire team's performance, management should consider assessing each individual's contribution to the team. This helps ensure that non-participating members do not benefit unfairly from the efforts of those who actually contribute. The rewards can appear in several ways including:

- Promotion to a more senior position within the organization
- Annual merit pay rises
- Monetary bonuses and other one-off cash awards
- Non-monetary rewards, such as corporate benefits and invitations to social events
- Recognition, such as mention in a company newsletter or achievement notices

Rewards offer an opportunity to reinforce desired activity and behaviour – and the old motto remains true that 'What gets rewarded gets done.'

Question 4: Are the right individuals chosen to be team leaders?

The effectiveness of a team leader is one of the strongest factors in team success. Most sourcing teams have leaders selected by senior managers, and Zenger *et al.* (1994) reports that:

- Most organizations find that they should give more attention, training and support to their team leaders
- Almost immediately after becoming a team leader, people realize that they need a new set of skills
- Even when there is shared team leadership among members, the team as a whole still reports to someone who needs team-leadership skills
- Overly structured and authoritarian team leaders significantly decrease the chances of team success
- Team leaders should be coaches and facilitators rather than dictators of action

An effective team leader has to satisfy a demanding set of responsibilities, and in reality, few people have the necessary qualifications, experience, skills and training. To help select appropriate leaders, managers should:

- Evaluate a team leader's performance, concentrating on their strengths and weaknesses
- Rank team leaders, which is useful when considering future leadership roles
- Provide feedback about improvement, with training that is targeted to the specific needs of the leader
- Allow individual leaders, teams and organizations to take corrective action as required

Question 5: Do sourcing teams effectively establish goals?

Although senior managers set the overall aims of sourcing teams, the teams themselves establish goals that focus on their end results. Establishing effective goals is important for several reasons. Firstly, it sets out exactly what the team wants to do, and by implication how it will do it, and what it will not do. The teams can use these goals to measure their progress, give feedback, see how well they are performing and allocating rewards for effort. Teams should set goals that are challenging rather than easy – 'demanding but attainable'.

A well-defined goal is specific, refers to results and includes a timetable, so a goal of 'reducing material costs by 5 per cent next year' is more effective than a goal of 'improving procedures'. Three steps are useful in defining goals:

1   Describe the team's assignment, saying exactly what job it was meant to complete and use this to define broad aims. (For example, optimizing the supply base and reducing the number of suppliers.)

2   Assess the team's ability to achieve these aims and then focus on the areas where they can have most impact and are most likely to succeed. (For example, concentrating purchases of a key item with two suppliers.)

3   Define specific goals related to the chosen aims. (For instance, selecting the two best suppliers for an item and signing new contrats within 3 months.)

Question 6: Are key suppliers part of the sourcing team?

Having supplier input to sourcing team decisions gives benefits including (Monczka and Trent, 1994):

● Teams that include suppliers are generally considered more effective than teams that do not include them

● Teams that include suppliers put more effort into team assignments

● Higher quality information is exchanged between the team and key suppliers

● There is more support from suppliers in achieving the team's goals

LEARNING FROM PRACTICE

Toyota

On July 19, 2007, Toyota temporarily closed its production facilities in Japan. This was due entirely to the shutdown of one of its suppliers, Tokyo-based Riken Corp, which supplies engine parts to several global car makers. The problem was that an earthquake of magnitude 6.8 had damaged Riken's main production plant, leaving Toyota no choice but to cease production at all 12 of its domestic plants for at least three shifts.

Despite using lean operations – and being a leading developer of stockless, just-in-time production – Toyota's plants had stocks of parts that allowed them to keep working for several days after the earthquake.

The disruption of supplies from Riken also affected several other car makers. Mitsubishi, Japan's 4th largest car maker, suspended production for at least 3 days at three of its major car assembly plants. The company sent 40 of its engineers to the Riken plant to help get it up and running again. Suzuki suffered from a production loss of about 10,000 cars and 5,000 motorcycles because of a temporary shutdown at five domestic plants. Fuji Heavy Industries, which makes the Subaru brand of vehicles, halted production at five plants. Honda and Nissan, also depend on Riken for engine parts, and were affected.

The widespread impact shows how many car assembly plants rely on a few suppliers for crucial parts of their product. Riken is Japan's biggest maker of piston rings and of seal rings, providing parts for more than half the cars built in Japan and about 20 per cent of cars worldwide, including vehicles from Ford, BMW and Volkswagen.

Source: Chozick A. (2007) Japan's car makers stall after quake hits supplier, Wall Street Journal, 19 July, p A3.

- There are fewer problems co-ordinating work and interactions between the team and key suppliers

- Suppliers make greater contributions across many performance areas, including ideas for cost reduction, quality improvement, process improvement, material-ordering procedures and faster delivery times

INTEGRATING FUNCTIONS INTO NEW PRODUCT DEVELOPMENT

Purchasing can play a key role in new product development. As a member of a new product development team, purchasing sees new product requirements early, and this allows buyers to contribute directly to the design and specification of material requirements. Also, as the main contact with suppliers, purchasing can bring suppliers into the design process, as well as checking their capabilities to deliver required materials.

FIGURE 5.6 Practices that distinguish 'the best' buyers

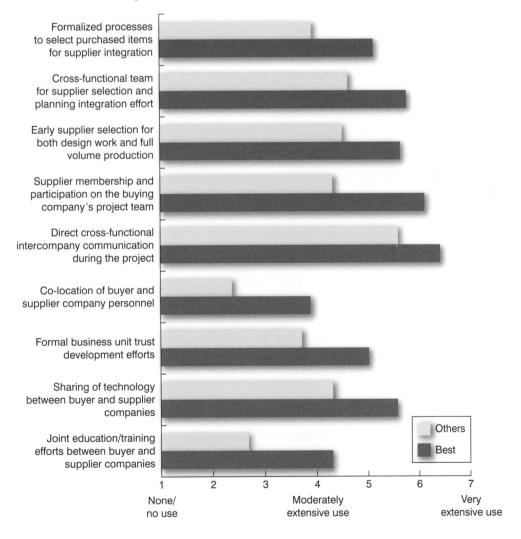

Common themes of successful supplier integration

Factors that lead to successful involvement of suppliers in new product development are shown in Figure 5.6 (Monczka *et al.*, 2000). This shows the difference on nine measures between 'the best' buyers and average performers.

1   **Formal process for selecting items for supplier integration** Purchasing's early involvement allows it to determine the materials needed for a new product, and it can recommend substitutes for high-cost materials or those whose price is volatile, suggest standard items wherever possible and assess longer term materials trends. Purchasing should always monitor supply markets and anticipate changes to provide up to date information. For example, it should routinely forecast long-term availability and prices of key items. It should also monitor technological innovations that affect materials or make substitute materials attractive. Based on this information it can contribute information about materials and the ones that would benefit from sourcing teams.

2   **Cross-functional teams for supplier selection and integration** The evaluation and selection of suppliers is a major part of purchasing's work, for which it ultimately retains responsibility, regardless of the selection procedure used. However, the actual supplier assessment can be done by a sourcing team who can use their various experiences. The analysis of materials to be acquired allows purchasing to anticipate product requirements earlier and identify the most capable suppliers. Then the team can do a systematic assessment of these potential suppliers, using both hard performance data and the subjective opinions of a cross-functional team. This data should be added to an assessment model that answers questions like:

   ● What is the likelihood that a supplier can deliver the materials needed to bring the product to market?

   ● On a range of factors, how does this supplier compare with other potential suppliers?

   ● What are the risks associated with using this supplier, and how can they be mitigated?

   ● At what point can we reverse a decision to use this supplier, and what would be the reasons for doing this?

   ● What are the contingency plans if problems occur?

3   **Early supplier selection** Supplier selection is often done before a new item is actually designed or reaches production. Once the team have an idea of the materials needed they can effectively start supplier selection. The use of a team can often help eliminate one source of frustration for purchasing, which is the lack of time available to evaluate, select and develop suppliers. A team has greater resources and can consider the following elements in considering new suppliers to enter the purchasing process:

   ● *Targets.* Is the supplier capable of hitting targets for cost, quality, technical performance, lead time, delivery quantities and other performance criteria?

   ● *Timing.* Will the supplier be able to meet production deadlines?

   ● *Production.* Will the supplier be able to increase their capacity and production fast enough to meet the projected demands?

   ● *Innovation.* Does the supplier have the required technical expertise and facilities to develop an adequate design, make it and solve problems when they occur?

- *Training.* Do the supplier's key staff have the skills needed to start and maintain the required operations, or is there adequate training?

- *Resource commitment.* If the supplier is deficient in any areas, is management willing to commit resources to remedy the problem?

4 **Supplier participation in new product development teams** Bringing suppliers into the product development process is more than sharing information. It also includes a sharing of ideas, willingness to invest in a new product and some form of commitment to its success. The benefits of supplier involvement in design – maybe as members of the new product development team – include gaining a supplier's insight into the design process, comparison of required production against a existing capabilities, comparison of alternative materials and allowing a supplier to begin pre-production work early.

   If given the opportunity, a supplier can bring a fresh perspective and new ideas to the development process, and have a major impact on the timing and success of a new product. The type of involvement can vary (as shown in Figure 5.7). At one extreme (sometimes called 'white box' design) the supplier is given complete designs and told to make the materials from them. At a more involved level (sometimes called 'grey box' design) the supplier's and buyer's designers work together to jointly design items. At the highest level of supplier involvement ('black box' design) suppliers are given functional requirements and asked to supply products that meet these requirements.

5 **Direct cross-functional inter-company communication.** The early stages of developing an integrated team are the most tentative, and they can have the most significant impact. Usually the initial meetings do not discuss specific products or projects, but they consider the potential for working relationships among the members. When there are shared views about products, close links may be formed; but often there is little common ground and the team member may simply not be able to work productively with each other.

   Common technology often influences the details of relationships between team members, at a basic level defining the patterns of communication. This affects routine communications, typically allowing team members to monitor the schedule of activities and to make sure that it is actually achieved. If a supplier cannot meet a delivery,

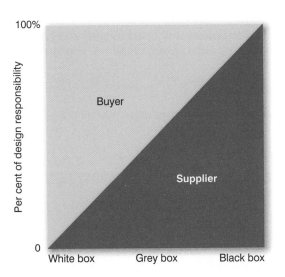

FIGURE 5.7

Extent of supplier involvement in design

purchasing should look for ways of rescheduling it or negotiating alternative plans. The sourcing team will define a set of milestones for their work, with good communications ensuring that they can all monitor progress. This prevents nasty surprizes from finding that a supplier has suddenly fall behind schedule.

6 **Co-location of buyer and supplier staff** The physical co-location of a supplier's staff in a buying organization has increasingly become a normal part of product development. Some manufacturing companies have a 'guest engineer' programme that invites key suppliers to have an engineer work in their company for a short time. This allows the trading partners to quickly agree design specifications and assign responsibilities for development. Alternatively, a buying company might co-locate staff to work with a supplier, with the same results – closer co-operation either throughout the whole project, or during critical stages.

Certain types of suppliers are more likely to use the physical co-location of staff in development teams. For instance, computer manufacturers work with rapidly changing technology and need particularly close contacts with suppliers to assess the continuing stream of new products. Suppliers of critical, non-standard items are more likely to use co-location of staff – while suppliers of non-critical, standard items will be less closely involved.

7 **Business unit trust** Sharing information is an essential part of integration, and it helps avoid unwelcome surprises during a project. This sharing of information is only possible when purchasing select capable and trustworthy suppliers. This element of trust is essential, as when an organization discusses a proposed new product with a supplier, it must be prepared to pass across enough information for the supplier to make its decisions and plans. This information flow is not in one direction, and suppliers have to pass back information about their production processes and capabilities, costs, schedules, capacity and other details. So both buyer and supplier have to exchange sensitive information, and pass it to the product development team. To ensure the necessary level of trust, all parties might have to sign an appropriate non-disclosure or confidentiality agreement.

8 **Sharing of technology** Close relationships are often easiest when organizations have a shared view of technology and its use. This means that technology strategies should be largely aligned for organizations participating in the development team. This is sometimes described as a *technology roadmap* which loosely refers to the type of technological products and specifications that an organization intends to use in the future. Some companies define their technology roadmaps in terms of products they are planning on developing over the next decade, while others consider a horizon of 50 years or more. The exact form of a technology roadmap varies, but it is typically defined in the following terms:

● Projected performance specifications for a type of product (for example, memory size, speed or weight)

● An intention to use a new material or component (for example, a new chemical or information channel)

● Use of a new process (for example, e-business or lean operations)

● Development of a new product to meet specific customer requirements (for example, new features in mobile phones)

● Integration of several complementary technologies to give a radical new product (for example, combining computer, television, telephone and cable technology)

9 **Joint education and training** It is difficult for many new product developers to achieve any significant level of integration because of:

LEARNING FROM PRACTICE

Source: McCormack K., Cavanagh P.H. and Handfield R. (2003) Foothills drilling team white paper, Suncor Energy, Calgary, Alberta.

Suncor Energy

Suncor Energy is a diversified oil and gas company based in Calgary, Alberta. Successful exploration and drilling relies on a co-operative effort from many suppliers and contractors. As part of the company's strategic supplier relationship programme it formed the Suncor Foothills Drilling-Asset Team. This includes people from Suncor's drilling department, the Foothills Asset Team, contractors and suppliers.

Drilling trial wells is a very cyclical and somewhat secretive business, with most of the actual drilling outsourced to specialized service providers. To drill a well needs materials from about 20 different suppliers. Often the staffing of a drilling project is determined by who is currently available, and the secrecy means that there is little information for planning, forecasting and workload levelling. The information used by the supplier is often changed at short notice, or is simply wrong. Changes in timing and design can affect each supplier significantly.

The administrative issues come in addition to the technical difficulties of drilling deep sour gas wells in hostile environments. Suncor's team typically drills around ten wells a year in the foothills of the Canadian Rocky Mountains, as deep as 6,400 m, with horizontal sections close to 2,000 m. Drilling in this mountainous region needs special expertise, with standard techniques adapted to very challenging conditions.

Poor drilling methods can give safety concerns, higher costs and lower capital returns. Even when drilling techniques are good, the complexities of local conditions give significant variations in timing that can affect the whole supply chain. To overcome these problems, Suncor developed integrated operations, effectively creating a single team with a single centre and aligned ideas. This integration is based on the Foothills Drilling-Asset Team, and includes contractors and other operators. There is now a high level of trust, with the key service providers and different groups from Suncor working together as though they are a single company with one set of objectives. This brings a number of benefits including a reduction of 18 per cent in drilling costs ($1.4 million a well), a reduction of 42 per cent in planning time (now 5 months), a reduction of 20 per cent in drilling time, a success rate of more than 80 per cent of wells drilled, a tripling of production from Foothills over a 5 year periods – and the Foothills Drilling-Asset Team has become one of the industry's preferred employers.

- Unwillingness of internal design teams to hand over any responsibility to outside functions or organizations
- Concerns over sharing proprietary information
- Lack of business processes to support integration
- Business cultures that are too far apart
- Lack of suitable working partners

Overcoming such problems may need education and training to reinforce the benefits of integration – as well as giving assurances that confidentiality agreements are in place. Internal design teams especially must realize that they are not relinquishing their authority over design, but that others are giving an additional viewpoint that will lead to a better product.

Supplier integration into customer order fulfilment

We have focussed on the integration of suppliers into the process of new product development, but many companies extend this involvement into order fulfilment. In

Order fulfilment
All the activities that combine to satisfy a customer's order.

its broad sense, order fulfilment includes all the activities from taking a customer's order through to delivering the finished product. Suppliers can give significant benefits in this process through, for instance, suggestion programmes, buyer-seller improvement teams and on-site supplier representatives.

Supplier suggestion programmes. Suppliers can be a valuable source of ideas for process improvement, and firms that do not tap into their suppliers' suggestions are missing out on a valuable source of expertise. Their suggestions can be collected through a website, emails, formal meetings, supplier conferences or some other mechanism. Typically, a supplier submits a suggestion in a standard format that identifies the nature of the improvement, the areas it affects, estimated savings and business unit that develops it. The suggestion then goes through a formal review, which may:

- Assess the suggested action's feasibility

- Estimate the resources needed to implement it

- Estimate the potential savings and benefits

- Make a decision on whether to proceed with the suggestion or not

- Give feedback to the supplier

Supplier suggestion programmes are more successful when they include several elements. Firstly, savings from the suggestion are not kept by the buying firm, but are shared according to a predetermined formula, typically 50/50. This encourages suppliers to offer further suggestions in the future. Secondly, the suggestion should focus on real cost reductions and not simply cut the supplier's margins. Thirdly, buying firms should give prompt feedback about suggestion, and also implement good suggestions promptly. This sends a clear message that suppliers' ideas are taken seriously.

Buyer-seller improvement teams. More firms are involving suppliers in various improvement teams (Monczka and Trent, 1993). This brings the usual benefits of multi-organizational teams, with suppliers providing cost reduction ideas, quality improvement ideas, actions to improve material delivery, suggestions to improve a process and its technology, greater satisfaction with the flow of information between the team and key suppliers, broader support for the team's goals and so on.

On-site supplier representative. Many firms are encouraging suppliers to provide a permanent on-site representative who can help improve customer order fulfilment. The idea behind this initiative (which has developed from the ideas of vendor managed inventory) is that a knowledgeable person can assist with managing the supply and stock of delivered materials, give technical support, answer specific questions about materials, assist in using the materials – and generally be available to solve any problems with the materials. In practice, on-site supplier representatives are most commonly used for spare parts, maintenance parts, waste management, printing services, computer equipment and software, health and safety equipment, process control equipment, production parts and transportation services.

On-site representatives can be placed in a number of functional areas:

- *Purchasing,* where the representatives can process purchase orders to their company using their knowledge of the systems

- *Sales,* where they can do some of the routine tasks of sales staff, such as selling directly to internal customers

- *Design,* where they can work on-site to give support in the design of products
- *Transport,* where they can control and co-ordinate all inbound and outbound transport

Both buyers and sellers benefit from on-site representatives (as shown in Figure 5.8). These benefits include:

- Greater customer-supplier co-ordination and integration
- Supplier staff give support and information to the purchaser
- Supplier staff do various buying and planning activities, freeing buyers to do other activities
- Suppliers get better understanding of customer needs and access to new designs
- Better planning and more efficient operations
- Fewer schedule and design changes
- Lower transaction costs
- Lower stock levels

		Customer wins with:			
		Consignment inventory	Direct floor stocking	Releases from rolling forecast	Resident at customer
Supplier wins with:	More business	X	X		X
	Access to new designs				X
	Stabilized production	X	X	X	
	Fewer transactions	X	X	X	
	Quicker payments	X			
	Less selling expense	X	X		X
	Assured sales		X	X	X
	Access to information earlier			X	X

FIGURE 5.8

Benefits from on-site supplier representatives

LEARNING FROM PRACTICE

Motorola

Customer-focussed supply chains that can link the various members are likely to gain a competitive advantage. Supply chain integration with agreement on goals, business strategies, and information transparency can have significant impacts on capacity investment, inventories, design, responsiveness, and support of a firm's worldwide product/service development, operations and sourcing. An example of this effect is given by Motorola.

In 2005, Motorola started the task of linking the various elements that make its worldwide supply chains. The objectives were improved costs, cash flows and customer service. Lower costs would enable competitive pricing; improved cash flows would enhance business investment; better customer service would give better customer retention.

The challenge was significant, as Motorola has sales in virtually every corner of the world and suppliers in 47 countries – and the six business divisions did little sharing of resources or facilities. To transform these diverse operations into an integrated new structure needed alignment of product designs, procurement, manufacturing, logistics and customer service. The following six key steps were used to achieve the changes:

1 Identify best-in-class processes for duplication throughout the company.

2 Develop a supply base of the best size and improve working relationships with key suppliers.

3 Establish clear supplier quality expectations and give performance feedback.

4 Establish effective and efficient manufacturing and logistics operations.

5 Focus IT improvement projects to maximize the impact across all business units.

6 Create an action-oriented and results-driven culture.

The results of the transformation were dramatic and by 2007 included:

- Teams identified best practices and the highest-priority ones were implemented worldwide

- Business units worked collaboratively to solicit quotes and award business

- Suppliers were required to develop 'quality renewal plans' to continue working with the company, and Motorola returned performance data to suppliers

- Consolidating facilities reduced the area occupied by manufacturing and distribution operations by 40 per cent

- Ninety per cent of IT spending was on systems that were common to all business units

- Defects from suppliers were reduced by 50 per cent; on-time deliveries to customers rose from 85 to 92 per cent, manufacturing efficiency rose by 40 per cent, and stock turnover increased by 18 per cent

Source: Cook J.A. (2007) Metamorphosis of a supply chain, CSCMP Supply Chain Quarterly, 2007, pp 34–38.

CHAPTER REVIEW

- Integration is the process of bringing together different groups, functions, or organizations, to work together on common business related assignments. Purchasing always works closely with other groups, and should work towards closer integration

- Integration can be achieved in many ways, ranging from joint meeting to combined information systems. This can bring considerable benefits in terms of cost, lead time, quality and so on. Barriers, characterized as 'silo mentality' can make these difficult to achieve

- Internal integration means that purchasing works closely with other functions within its organization, notably operations, quality management, design, accounting, marketing, legal and safety departments. Such collaboration means that purchasing staff must develop a working knowledge of methods used in these departments

- External integration is largely – but not exclusively – based on collaboration between buyers and sellers. There are numerous benefits from this collaboration, ranging from lower costs to more flexible response. However, there can be barriers to achieving these benefits

- Integration needs a different type of organizational structure that moves away from the traditional 'silos'. This has an integrated function that coordinates the work or purchasing with other functions and organizations within the supply chain

- Cross-functional – or cross-organizational – teams are an important way of improving integration. They get people from different backgrounds to work together on a common problem. The results can give significant benefits, as well as some problems

- Organizations increasingly use teams to streamline and improve new product development

- Purchasing has a key role to play on these teams, selecting suppliers, advising product designers, negotiating contracts – and generally liaising with different parties throughout the process

- Procurement works best when it is integrated with other functions and organizations. Some organizations look to integrate order fulfilment, which includes all the processes from taking customer order through to delivering the final product

DISCUSSION QUESTIONS

1 What exactly is 'integration' and what benefits does it bring?

2 Describe the different types of integration for purchasing.

3 What types of information might purchasing share with other internal and external functions?

4 What are the barriers to integration? How can they be overcome?

5 Describe the traditional model of buyer-seller relationships. How does this differ from a collaborative model? How can purchasing move from the traditional model to a collaborative one?

6 Cross-functional sourcing teams which include members from suppliers are, on average, more successful than teams that do not include suppliers. Why?

7 Are there any problem of using cross-functional teams?

8 Why is setting goals so important to the success of a sourcing team? What is the role of the team leader when setting goals?

9 Relatively few people have the qualifications, experience or training to become effective sourcing team leaders. Do you think this is true?

10 Discuss the factors that encourage the early integration of purchasing into new product development. How is this integration achieved?

11 What types of information can a supplier provide that are useful during new-product development?

12 How much contribution can suppliers make to the design of materials for new product development?

13 What criteria determine whether a supplier should be involved in a new-product development effort?

REFERENCES

Fearon H. (1988) Organizational relationships in purchasing, *Journal of Purchasing and Materials Management*, 24(4): 7.

Giunipero L. (2004) Purchasing education and training, Tempe, AZ: Centre for Advanced Purchasing Studies.

Janis I. L. (1982) Groupthink: psychological studies of policy decisions and fiascoes, Boston: Houghton Mifflin.

Monczka R. M. and Trent R. J. (1993) Cross-functional sourcing team effectiveness, Tempe, AZ: Centre for Advanced Purchasing Studies.

Monczka R. M. and Trent R. J. (1994) Effective cross-functional sourcing teams: critical success factors, *International Journal of Purchasing and Materials Management*, 30(4): 7–8.

Monczka R., Handfield R., Ragatz G., Frayer D. and Scannell T. (2000) Supplier integration into new product/process development: best practices, Milwaukee, WI: ASQ Press.

Peters L. H. and O'Connor E. J. (1980) Situational constraints and work outcomes: the influences of a frequently overlooked construct, *Academy of Management Review*, 5(3): 391–397.

Russell R. D. (1990) Innovation in organizations: toward an integrated model, *Review of Business* 12(2): 19.

Smityh M. and Zsidisin G. (2002) Early supplier involvement at MDR, Practix, 5(4): 5.

Spekman R. E. (1988) Strategic supplier selection: understanding long-term buyer relationships, *Business Horizons* 31(4): 76.

Steiner D. (1972) Group process and productivity, New York: Academic Press.

Waters D. (2009) Supply chain management: an introduction to logistics (2nd edition), Basingstoke, Hampshire: Palgrave Macmillan.

Zenger J., Musselwhite, E., Hurson, K. and Perrin, C. (1994) Leading teams: mastering the new role, Irwin, IL.

FURTHER READING

Cousins P., Handfield R., Lawson B., and Peterson, K. (2006) Creating supply chain relational capital: the impact of formal and informal socialization processes, *Journal of Operations Management*, 24(6): 851–864.

Handfield R. and Bechtel C. (2001) The role of trust and relationship structure in improving supply chain responsiveness, *Industrial Marketing Management*, 31: 1–16.

Handfield, R., Ragatz, G., Monczka, R., and Peterson, K. (1999) Involving suppliers in new product development, *California Management Review*, 42(1): 59–82.

Handfield R., Ragatz G. and Peterson K. (2003) A model of supplier integration into new product development, *Journal of Product Innovation Management*, 20(4): 284–299.

Monczka R., Frayer D., Handfield R., Ragatz G. and Scannell T. (2000) Supplier integration into new product/process development: best practices, Milwaukee, WI: ASQ Quality Press.

Monczka R. M. and Trent, R. J. (1994) Cross-functional sourcing team effectiveness: critical success factors, *International Journal of Supply Management and Materials Management*, Fall, pp 2–11.

Trent R. J. (1996) Understanding and evaluating cross-functional sourcing team leadership, *International Journal of Supply Management and Materials Management*, Fall, pp 29–36.

Trent R. J. (1998) Individual and collective team effort: a vital part of sourcing team success, *International Journal of Supply Management and Materials Management*, Fall, pp 46–54.

Ward N., Handfield R. and Cousins, P. (2007) Stepping up on SRM, CPO Agenda, Summer, pp 42–47.

CASE STUDY

Maber-Reinhoff Corporation

Maber-Reinhoff is a supplier of components in the aerospace industry, providing vital technology for civilian and military aircraft. The industry is driven by costs – but more importantly, reliability, safety and quality. Their components need extensive research and development, leading to a continuing stream of new products.

Maber-Reinhoff is largely driven by its engineers, and they have successfully implemented an 'early supplier involvement' (ESI) initiative which has the engineers working in conjunction with their purchasing departments and key suppliers. This initiative started with a proposal and support from upper management,

but the initial work gave substantial benefits and design engineers now routinely seek ESI support at the concept stage of product design. Initially, two pilot projects were run using ESI, and the results were so encouraging that the procedures were incorporated into normal working policies. The full ESI process consists of the steps shown in Figure 5.9 (Smityh and Zsidisin, 2002).

The full value of ESI is only realized when it starts at the earliest possible stage of product development, and benefits are considerably reduced if it is delayed for any reason. Another important observation is that the returns of ESI depend upon a productive

FIGURE 5.9 Good practice process at Maber-Reinhoff

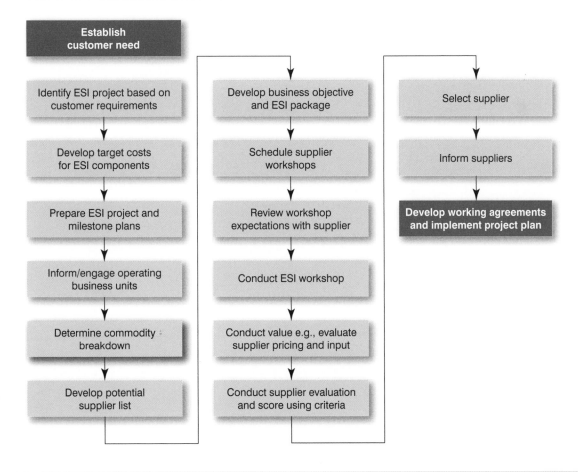

relationship with selected suppliers. The company has found that the effort needed to globally source materials from the best suppliers is well-rewarded, because these leading suppliers are better prepared for close business relationships and to provide the expertise that design collaboration needs.

For its part, Maber-Reinhoff believes that it must openly and honestly share information with trading partners, as the only way of building a relationship and ensuring success. This honesty and openness must extend to both internal and external partners, as any misleading or hidden agendas can harm projects that would otherwise bee successful.

Maber-Reinhoff develops aggressive cost targets for each of its major components, and suppliers make significant strides toward meeting these. For instance, in one project ESI gave an overall reduction of 40 per cent of unit cost in a market that is very cost sensitive, allowing the company to capture significant market share. In another project where it is a subcontractor, the company had a target cost reduction of 34 per cent, but the ESI initiative actually achieved a 37 per cent reduction.

Questions

● Review Maber-Reinhoff's process for ESI and discuss any elements that you think could be improved

● What are the potential risks for Maber-Reinhoff of using ESI?

● How are these risks minimized? Do you think that the benefits outweigh these risks?

CHAPTER 6
PURCHASING POLICIES

LEARNING OBJECTIVES   After reading this chapter you should be able to:

- Understand the role of purchasing policies

- Appreciate the reasons why purchasing policies are important

- Review different types of purchasing policies

- Discuss policies for the role of purchasing, conduct of purchasing staff, buyer-seller relationships, operational issues and social objectives

- Describe the role of purchasing procedures

IMPORTANCE OF POLICIES

Policies
Provide rules or guidance that staff should follow when doing certain activities. They put constraints on staff behaviour. They show how the purchasing function will work to achieve its strategic aims.

A policy refers to the set of purposes, principles and – particularly – rules that guide the work of an organization (Klein and Murphy, 1973). It includes all the directives, both explicit and implied, that describe the aims of an organization, and gives guidelines for how people will act to accomplish the aims. For instance, a company might have a policy of buying 40 per cent of products from local producers, or a policy of buying from 'green' suppliers.

Policies are sometimes described as *rules of action,* which describe procedures, rules and regulations that must be followed for purchases. These are usually written explicitly in a formal document, but may also be unwritten or informal policies that have developed over time and eventually become part of the organizational culture.

A key point is that policies do not just appear, but they have to be carefully designed. Typically, policies start with broad principles, perhaps suggesting that 'employees must behave ethically'. Then more details are added to show exactly what this means, perhaps saying that employees should not accept any kind of gift from a supplier. The level of detail that policies are expanded into is a decision for managers – but whatever they decide, the resulting policies must be monitored and adjusted over time to allow for changes in the business environment and internal operations.

Advantages and disadvantages of policies

Policies give an opportunity to define and clarify senior management aims and describe how they will be achieved. So the fundamental purpose of policies is to allow senior manager to communicate their views and standards throughout their organization. A series of high-level policy statements provide broad guidance to employees at all levels.

Another advantage of policies is that they create a framework for consistent decision making and action. An effective policy defines the rules and procedures that apply to all employees, so it ensures that everyone within an organization acts in a manner that is consistent with senior management's expectations.

LEARNING FROM PRACTICE

Swissengerhoff

Franco Zoallo was driving past the Swissengerhoff facility in Zurich when he remembered a question that he wanted to ask one of their sales staff about a purchase that his company would probably be making. Rather than go back to his office, Franco went in and asked the receptionists if the sales people he had been talking to could answer his question, which would only take a few minutes. The receptionists apologized, but explained that it was a company policy not to allow sales staff to meet anyone who did not have a prior appointment. Franco asked if he could make an appointment to see the sales staff now, but was told that things did not work like that. Instead the receptionists pointed out a paragraph in the company's policy manual which said:

'*Policy:* Sales staff are not allowed to see visitors who have not made a prior appointment.
Reason: To allow sales staff to prepare for meetings and collect relevant information and to improve staff work schedules.'

Franco asked if the receptionists could make an exception, but was told, 'We don't have the authority to override company policies – and there would be no point in having policies if we ignored them.'

Source: Based on de Broglie G. (2009) Policies and politeness, National OM Conference, Zurich.

There are also potential disadvantages with using policies. For instance, there is the problem of implementation, where it can be difficult to communicate and enforce common standards throughout large organizations. A broad policy of 'treating customers courteously' is easy to define in a remote office, but is harder to control in circumstances of stress in every location.

Another consideration is that employees might view policies as a substitute for effective management. Policy statements are guidelines that outline senior management's belief or position on a topic, but they are not meant to give a recipe of instructions that describe what staff should do in any specific conditions. Suppose you get angry when something goes wrong in a shop, and ask to see the manager. If you are told, 'It is not our policy to let customers speak with managers,' you will get even more angry. This may be a policy, but good management would suggest ignoring it and tying to placate a customer, who may have a real cause to complain and constructive suggestions for solving a problem. This raises the question of just how rigid or flexible a policy should be. Is it better to give a detailed list of procedures that must always be followed in specified conditions (of the type you would expect to see in the armed services) or would less specific guidelines and suggestions be better? There is no answer to this, but the solution is a matter of management decision and depends on many factors, including prevailing management style and culture.

Another problem is that policies can restrict flexibility and innovation. If a policy describes exactly how staff must act, they cannot vary this even when they see better alternatives and when conditions change slightly, employees may still be restrained by previous policies, even when a more flexible approach would be better. For instance, a policy of using express mail to post a catalogue of products to all customers might become too rigid when customers have access to a company website.

A final warning is that the number and scope of policies should be controlled. Too many, especially when accompanied by cumbersome procedures, can become a burden that encumbers operations rather than helps them.

What makes for an effective policy?

Several features are needed to make a policy effective. The first is that they describe positive actions – giving guidance for the way that things should be done. They should give enough detail to guide behaviour in a certain direction, but they should not be so detailed that they actually discourage people from using them. For example, a policy might guide employers to be friendly towards customers, but it does not normally need to go into the details of how customers should be greeted. So an effective policy is relevant to organizational aims, should describe procedures and it should avoid trivial or unimportant issues.

Often the way that a policy is stated is important. They should be concise (or else nobody will read them) and unambiguous (so that no-one can be in any doubt as to the policy's intent and direction). Policies that are unclear or can be interpreted in different ways will inevitably lead to inconsistent behaviour. And people simply ignore policies that are difficult to understand.

Another characteristic of effective policies is that they are timely and current, which means that there are periodic reviews – typically every year or so – to maintain clarity and their ability to deliver desired aims.

To summarize, effective policies should be:

● Action oriented, meaning that they describe the way to do something

● Guiding people towards desired behaviour

- Relevant to aims and current operations

- Concise

- Clear, unambiguous and easily understood

- Timely and up-to-date

As with all decisions, they only become useful when implemented, so there must be procedures to enforce policies. It is one of management's responsibilities to train employees in the use of policies, and to retrain them when there are any problems.

LEARNING FROM PRACTICE

Redstone

Redstone is an IT and communications company that provides services to organizations in the UK and Ireland. It is 'committed to being the partner of choice for IT and Communication solutions'. With more than a thousand employees, it has a turnover of £200 million a year.

The company has a formal purchasing policy which provides flexible and practical guidelines for the purchasing of goods and services. The group finance director is responsible for regular reviews of the policy, which has two main parts that cover legal requirements and good practices.

1   Statutory policies – cover things that must be done to comply with UK and EU laws and regulations. These include:

- *Safety,* which 'is our primary concern when procuring goods and services'. The Health and Safety at Work Act 1974, together with other safety legislation, imposes duties upon all aspects of purchasing

- *Legislation.* The purchasing process is governed, or affected, by various UK and EU legislation

- *Environment.* The provision of goods and services must be undertaken in accordance Redstone's Corporate Social Responsibility Policy, Environmental Policy and corporate objectives

- *Corporate social responsibility.* The company is committed to operating in a socially responsible manner. Its suppliers must comply with all

relevant legislation and international standards relating to trading policy, child and forced labour, health and safety of workers, non-discrimination, employment law, human rights and bribery and corruption

2   Good practice policies – describe the standards that Redstone adopts itself and expects from its suppliers.

- Redstone's ethical purchasing policy is based on its aim of purchasing goods and services that are produced and delivered under conditions that do not involve abuse or exploitation and which have the least negative impact on the environment

- The company insists on the following code of conduct for all members of their supply chains:

  ○ Employment should be freely chosen

  ○ There is freedom of association and the right to collective bargaining

  ○ Working conditions should be safe and hygienic

  ○ There should be no exploitation of children

  ○ Living wages should be paid

  ○ Working hours should not be excessive

  ○ Discrimination should not be practiced

  ○ Regular employment should be provided

- Redstone have a framework of delegated authorities that define who is authorized to buy items within specified financial limits

Source: Based on www.redstone.co.uk

○ The company uses standard and explicit terms and conditions for purchases

A summary of the broad purchasing policy says that Redstone will:

- Only source products from suitably approved suppliers

- Ensure that there are appropriately experienced and qualified people managing the procurement process

- Ensure that the scope of the procurement process is clearly defined

- Ensure all individuals involved in procurement work to high ethical standards

- Procurement staff must declare in writing any actual or potential conflict of interest and must not:

  ○ Use their position of authority for personal gain

  ○ Divulge confidential or sensitive information to any unauthorized persons

  ○ Accept gifts unless of a token value

  ○ Accept hospitality which may be deemed to have influenced a business decision

POLICIES TO PROVIDE GUIDANCE AND DIRECTION

Senior purchasing managers develop policies to provide guidance and support for all purchasing staff. These policies start with general outlines that clarify management's position on a subject, and they are expanded into more detail about actual activities. There are many different types of purchasing policies, and each organization designs ones that meet their own specific requirements. Nonetheless, there are common patterns and most policies fall into one of five categories that define:

1   The role of purchasing.

2   The conduct of purchasing staff.

3   Buyer-seller relationships.

4   Operational issues.

5   Social objectives.

Policies that define the role of purchasing

This set of policies answers the broad question of 'What does purchasing do?' – and the associated question of, What does it not do?' Policies generally review the objectives of the purchasing function and define the responsibilities of people working at different levels, with typical issues covered including the following.

Origin and scope of purchasing authority. Everyone within an organization must be aware of purchasing's authority to conduct business and to represent organizational interests. This authority comes from senior managers, who may also detail the authority of purchasing to delegate certain tasks to other departments or functions.

The key element of this part of a policy is that it identifies the areas where purchasing does and does not have authority. For instance, the policy may say that all purchases of spare parts must be done by the purchasing department, but they are not be responsible for buying properties, medicines, or other areas where they do not have expertise.

Objectives of the purchasing function. Having decided where purchasing has authority, the next issue is what it should achieve. We know that this is defined in the supply strategy, and now the results can be summarized in the purchasing policy.

Policies typically review broad objectives and principles guiding the purchasing process. For example, a company might describe its purchasing objectives and principles as:

- To select suppliers that meet purchase and performance requirements

- To purchase goods and services that comply with internal customer specifications and quality standards

- To promote buyer-seller relations and to encourage supplier contribution

- To treat all suppliers fairly and ethically

- To work closely with other departments within the company

- To conduct purchasing operations so they enhance community and employee relations

- To support all corporate aims and strategies

- To maintain a qualified purchasing staff and to develop their professional capabilities

These are broad objectives, but they serve a useful role in formally stating purchasing's commitment to effective and efficient operations. They are also important in leading to more detailed policies for purchasing.

Corporate purchasing office responsibilities. As we saw in chapter 4, a large and diverse corporation can have several autonomous purchasing departments, each working within its own division. Then the corporation can maintain a central or corporate purchasing office to co-ordinate the activities of these separate units and provide central services. This policy defines the role of the corporate purchasing office and its relationships with the other purchasing units at business, divisional and plant levels. The corporate purchasing office gives guidance on how corporate purchasing staff:

- Carry out executive policies

- Develop purchasing policies and procedures that support purchasing operations at all levels

- Co-ordinate the operations of different purchasing units

- Evaluate the performance of purchasing units

- Provide expert support to purchasing units, typically in global sourcing, contract negotiations, systems development or other specialized areas

- Perform all the other tasks typically assigned to corporate support staff

Figure 6.1 suggests a format for a policy setting corporate purchasing office responsibilities.

Policies defining the conduct of purchasing staff

These policies outline management's commitment to ethical and honest behaviour while guiding staff who face difficult situations, such as business practices that are technically legal but are potentially unethical or questionable. Purchasing managers must develop policies that provide guidance in these grey areas, as purchasing staff act as legal representatives of their firms and they must uphold the highest standards.

FIGURE 6.1 Example of corporate purchasing policy

ABC Technologies purchasing policy

Applies to: Corporate purchasing staff
              Divisional purchasing units

Date: 1-1-01

Subject: Corporate purchasing office responsibilities

This policy outlines the responsibilities and authority of the corporate purchasing office and staff and its relationship to division purchasing and buying units.

ABC Technologies is organized on a functional basis, with decentralized divisional operations. Its corporate policy is to devolve responsibility and delegate authority for operational matters to divisional management. All responsibilities not delegated to divisional management remain the responsibilities of the corporate staff.

Purchasing is devolved to buying units within each division, but corporate staff retain responsibility for the following functions:

- Ensuring that each division and buying unit adheres to corporate purchasing policies

- Developing functional purchasing policies and procedures to support efficient and effective purchasing operations throughout the company

- Co-ordinating strategy development between divisional purchasing and other buying units to improve company-wide efficiencies and reduce duplicated effort

- Developing systems to evaluate company-wide purchasing operations and performance

- Providing expert support to buying units throughout the company

- Taking responsibility for (a) tasks typically associated with corporate support staff and (b) tasks not directly devolved to buying units

This policy reaffirms the autonomy of the divisions and their buying units to conduct operational purchasing duties. It also reaffirms the company's commitment to efficient company-wide purchasing operations through strong corporate support staff.

Ethics. These policies outline management's commitment to ethical and honest behaviour – and they guide people who are for some reason placed in a difficult situation. For instance, few people would notice if a sales representative buys a potential customer a cup of coffee during their discussions; but suppose that they also bought dinner at the end of the day, and then included a trip to the theatre and maybe a follow-up discussion in a holiday resort? The purchasing policy should give guidance on how staff should react, particularly in grey areas. A starting point is to emphasize that purchasing staff act as legal agents and representatives, so they must uphold the highest standards. We return to this question of ethics in chapter 14.

Reciprocal purchases. Another concern is reciprocal purchase agreements, where customers put pressure on suppliers to buy their own products as a condition of securing a contract. For instance, a software supplier agrees to buy hardware, provided the hardware supplier buys some amount of software. Managers often have specific policies to prevent this kind of trading and ensure that their employees do not:

● Give preference to suppliers that purchase from the buyer's organization

● Expect suppliers to purchase the buying company's products as a condition of securing a purchase contract

● Look favourably on competitive bids from suppliers that purchase the buyer's products

Contacts and visits to suppliers. Most firms give explicit guidance on who should visit or make other contacts with suppliers and potential suppliers. If people from other departments visit suppliers, and can undermine purchasing's authority as the principal commercial contact and organizations want to avoid situations where suppliers have to interpret statements from a range of different departments, each of whom states their own requirements. On a practical level, it is in no-ones interest to have suppliers snowed-under with a burden of unnecessary visits and contacts.

Former employees representing suppliers. Occasionally, an employee will leave a firm and start working for a supplier. This is a concern because the former employee has knowledge about business plans or other confidential information that might give an unfair advantage over other suppliers. Such use of inside knowledge is generally regarded as unethical, or even illegal. One way around the issue is to establish a policy prohibiting business transactions with suppliers that employ former employees known to have inside or confidential information. This exclusion can range from a period of a few months to several years, depending on the employee and the situation. Another option is to insert a clause in an employee's employment contract that prohibits them from working with a competitor or a supplier for a specified time.

Reporting of irregular business dealings with suppliers. These policies establish a mechanism for buyers or other employees to report irregular business dealings. Examples of irregular dealings include bribes, cronyism, accepting late bids, owning a stake in a supplier's company, insider knowledge – and other behaviour that is unacceptable. The policy can specify the procedure for reporting irregularities, safeguards to protect the person making the report and the need to report suspected irregularities as soon as possible. This policy sends the message that management will not tolerate any kind of irregular business practice by employees.

Policies defining buyer-seller relationships

There are many types of policies that cover the complex area of buyer-seller relationships.

Supplier relations. These policies acknowledge that the relationship between buyers and sellers can be critical for trading success. If there is a breakdown in the relationship neither side can benefit, so policies aim at developing and maintaining supportive business relationships. These are based on mutual trust and respect, and they generally include statements about:

● Treating suppliers fairly and with integrity

● Supporting and developing those suppliers that work to improve quality, delivery, cost or other performance criteria

LEARNING FROM PRACTICE

AECI

Source: Based on www.aeci.co.za

AECI is a specialty goods and services group of companies based in South Africa. It has the broad aim of providing 'value-adding solutions to customers through science, technology and industry knowledge'. Like most other companies it has a strict policy about conflicts of interest. Here the policy is also needed to comply with South Africa's Companies Act and is a requirement for listing on the Johannesburg Stock Exchange.

The conflict of interest policy is designed to assist a responsible person in identifying situations that could present potential conflicts of interest, and to give procedures for dealing with them. In this context a responsible person' is any officer, director, employee of the company and their close family members. A potential conflict could arise whenever 'the responsible person has an interest in, or connection with, an organization with which AECI transacted or might transact business (or with individuals associated with such an organization) or has an interest in an unrelated business that does not necessarily transacted or intend transacting business with AECI, and where that interest is of such a nature that it might influence the independent judgement of the responsible person or distract them from devoting their full-time efforts during business hours towards the business of AECI'.

Typically, potential conflicts of interest arise in the selection and use of consultants or other professional advisors; the selection or supervision of contractors, suppliers or vendors; the sale of products; the purchase of materials, supplies and equipment; and the investment and borrowing of funds.

The policy gives some specific practices that are not allowed, including accepting gifts (with more than a token value) from anyone where the gift is given because of the responsible person's relationship with AECI, accepting cash gifts in any form, excessive entertainment, a loan, financial benefits, any gift that needs a return favour, illegal gifts, anything that violates AECI's commitment to mutual respect or other favours from individuals who seek to do business with AECI.

- Providing prompt payment to suppliers
- Encouraging suppliers to submit innovative ideas with joint sharing of benefits
- Developing open communication channels
- Telling suppliers why they did not win a purchase contract
- Establishing a fair process to award purchase contracts

Qualification and supplier selection. Buyers need guidance about the performance criteria that will be used to evaluate their bid for a particular contract. If a contract is to be awarded for low price rather than, say, fast delivery, they need to know this before submitting their quotation. This policy describes the criteria used to evaluate and select suppliers, which may include:

- Price or total cost of ownership
- Product quality
- Delivery performance
- Financial health of supplier

- Technology and technical competence

- Management of second tier suppliers

- Management skills and experience

- Ability of suppliers to work well with the customer

- Potential for innovation

This policy may also outline management's position on factors like single and multiple sourcing, and the use of longer-term purchase agreements. It may also acknowledge purchasing's need to rely on other people to evaluate technical or financial criteria during the supplier selection process.

Principles for awarding purchase contracts. The process for selecting and awarding purchase contracts is a central part of purchasing, and we return to the theme in chapter 7. It is important to have a standard set of policies for managing the award of contracts so that the process is clearly fair and gives the best overall results. Policies in this area cover issues such as:

- The limits on a particular buyer's authority to award a contract, typically specified in terms of the contract cost

- Circumstances where a competitive bid process is and is not used

- Conditions outlining the way that competitive bids are managed

- Process for analyzing and comparing competitive bids

- Conditions in which bids will be awarded to suppliers who do not offer the lowest bid

- Events that will lead to a second or further round of bidding

- Guidelines for the way that negotiations of contracts are performed

Difficulties at suppliers. An organization may experience severe difficulties if the supply of critical materials is disrupted by some kind of problem at the supplier. For instance, a fire or industrial action at a supplier may make it difficult for a firm to continue working, particularly if they use just-in-time operations. To deal with such situations, firms can define policies about risks and how to mitigate their effects. For instance, if there is industrial action at a supplier, can an organization legally gain access to the stocks already in place – or should it quickly look for alternative sources?

Other policies dealing with buyer-seller relations. Many other policies might be relevant depending on circumstances. For example, organizations sometimes have to be careful about using information given by suppliers who are interested in working with them. Then a policy may state that the buyer accepts unsolicited proposals from suppliers only on a non-confidential basis. Or another policy might clarify an organization's position about suppliers' involvement in new product design. In particular, they may request specific targets for reducing costs in the early phases of new-product design, or giving guidance about the extent of their financial obligation to suppliers. At a basic level, the policies may specify the extent of supplier involvement in the whole process of new product design – as well as the types of non-disclosure agreements used, the criteria for sharing patents, and other joint issues.

LEARNING FROM PRACTICE

Gap Inc.

Gap Inc. is an international retailer with more than 3,000 stores that specialize in clothing and accessories. They have strong policies of social responsibility that, 'go beyond the basics of ethical business practices, and embrace our responsibilities to people and to the planet'. These policies extend to the plants run by suppliers, where the company does not accept unsavoury practices, including excessive overtime, low wages and fining workers who wanted to leave their jobs.

In 2005 Gap reported the findings of 92 inspectors, who scrutinized almost all of the 2,672 factories approved to manufacture their clothes. As a result of this, the company severed ties with 70 factories, rejected 15 per cent of the new factories seeking to make its clothes in 2004 – but continued to buy from hundreds of overseas factories that reputedly mistreated its workers. Gap products were made at 423 factories in China, but somewhere between 25 and 50 per cent of these did not fully comply with local labour laws, and 10 to 25 per cent of them pay below the minimum wage. In the Persian Gulf, Gap uses 29 factories, but more than half of these imposed working weeks of more than 60 hours.

By publicly acknowledging problems at suppliers' factories – often characterized as 'sweatshops' – Gap hopes that its entire industry will look for reforms and establish more rigorous standards to improve the working conditions. They say that, 'The more open and honest we can be about conditions and challenges, the more helpful we can be in addressing them.'

Policies defining operational issues

The broadest of the five types of purchasing policy includes all the different policies that give guidance for all aspects of normal purchasing operations. For instance, how do staff deal with poor quality products or late deliveries? These come in such a variety of forms that we cannot do more than mention a few common themes.

Hazardous materials. Hazardous materials are those that potentially harm health or the environment, and the handling of some of these is inherently risky, such as radioactive substances, corrosive chemicals, blue asbestos, inflammable fuels and so on. Most countries have strict laws that govern the way that hazardous materials are handled, moved, stored and disposed of. There are also international agreements, notably the Basel Convention (2009) which came into effect in 1992 and prescribes international restrictions on the way that hazardous materials are dealt with. As there is a general trend towards increasing environmental concern, these policies will inevitably become more severe.

Another trend is the requirement for organizations to be ISO 14000 certified, which defines procedures for aspects of environmental management (ISO, 2009). ISO 14000 certification requires companies to establish an environmental management system which (Melnyk, 1999):

- Creates a broad environmental policy

- Sets appropriate objectives and targets for environmental management

- Designs and implements a programme to achieve these objectives

- Monitors and measures the effectiveness of these programmes

- Monitors and measures the effectiveness of general environmental management activities within the firm

It is clearly important for purchasing to be involved in any environmental management scheme because they are responsible for acquiring and probably disposing of hazardous materials. Companies that routinely use or produce hazardous materials need a policy that outlines in detail the way that it is handled. Policies here ensure that purchasing only select those suppliers that conform to all legal and regulatory requirements. Then before awarding a contract, some policies require that the supplier provide:

- Evidence of valid permits and licences

- Specification of the types of hazardous waste services the supplier is licenced to provide

- Evidence of safeguards to prevent accidents, along with contingency plans if a hazardous event occurs

- Details of the specific process used to control hazardous material once it leaves a buyer's facilities

- Evidence of satisfactory supplier's liability insurance

- Evidence that any waste disposal uses properly certified sites

Supplier responsibility for defective material. Sometimes – but hopefully rarely – materials are delivered that are in some way defective. These policies define the actions that are needed to remedy this, specifically for replacing materials, ensuring better performance in the future and recovering costs that should be born by the supplier. These costs include material rework, repackaging for return to supplier, additional material-handling, return shipping, lost or delayed production and so on. Organizations using just-in-time operations are particularly vulnerable to material quality, so they usually have strict policies for charges arising from supply problems.

Purchased item comparisons. This policy gives guidelines for the continual evaluation of purchased items. It checks that quality and delivery requirements are being met, and suggests periodic evaluation of suppliers to ensure that they still give the best value. Essentially the policy compares the supply of purchased products with plans and possible alternatives. When firms use competitive bidding, purchased item comparisons generally mean requesting new bids from a shortlist of other qualified suppliers. Then the policy says how often management should run competitive comparisons, and the general procedure for conducting them. For items on longer-term purchase contracts, purchased item comparisons may involve benchmarking against leading competitors.

Other operating policies. Purchasing can use many other operating policies, including those for:

- Ensuring compliance with all relevant national and international laws and regulations

- Restricting departments other than purchasing from selecting suppliers

- The proper disposal of waste

- Purchasing's legal right to terminate a purchase contract

- Using emergency orders and premium transportation rates

- Supplier-requested changes in contract terms and conditions

- Ensuring commercial confidentiality
- Supplier use of trademarks, copyright and patented items

Policies defining social objectives

It is in the long-term interests of most organizations to support certain broad social objectives that go beyond immediate commercial returns – and, of course, there are many organizations, like charities and governments, that have social rather than commercial missions. Some common social objectives include developing local sources of supply, encouraging firms that have strong environmental protection policies and awarding business to firms with specialized minority interests. In this way, purchasing's actions help develop a role of good corporate citizenship.

Environmental issues. We said about hazardous materials that it is increasingly common for organizations to set policies for aspects of environmental management, and that these are often required by law. Materials need not be hazardous to need considerate handling, such as the recycling of paper, plastics and metals. Policies in this area include the use of recycled material, proper disposal of waste, air pollution, carbon dioxide emissions, reusing materials and so on. Organizations use policies to define their, and their supplier's compliance with environmental laws, regulations and guidelines.

LEARNING FROM PRACTICE

Sony Corporation

Sony has put a lot of effort into developing environmentally sound purchasing policies. As they say, 'Sony sees global environmental conservation as one of the most critical issues for mankind in the 21st century. Sony, as a good corporate citizen, has therefore established the Sony Environmental Vision to form the basis for aggressive actions to conserve the environment and create a sustainable society.'

Work on the Corporation's 'Green Procurement Operations' was implemented in 1998, and developed over the following years into broader green policies. Sony works with countless global suppliers, whose environmental performance they closely monitor from acquisition of raw material through to final shipment. In 2001, they designated suppliers who co-operated in the production of environmentally-sensitive products and reached specified standard as 'Green Partners'. They then established Green Partner Standards which aimed at encouraging suppliers to introduce Green Partner environmental

management systems and further improved their performance.

Environmental impact studies are emphasized in all new product development, with suppliers involved at an early stage and made aware of updates to policies that make certain materials and processes inappropriate. To ensure their standards are met, Sony spends a lot of time running audits of suppliers' operations that monitor:

- The supplier's stance on environmental matters
- Volumes of harmful substances used in making products
- Use of recyclable materials
- Frameworks for quality maintenance, packing and distribution
- Reuse and recycling of packaging materials, moulds, equipment and other items
- Management of upstream suppliers
- A range of other factors

Source: Based on Procurement Centre (2005) Sony green partner activities, Sony Corporation, Tokyo; Sroufe R., Handfield R. and Walton S. (2004) Green purchasing commodity strategies, business and the environment; www.sony.net

Supporting diversity in suppliers. There are many variations on these policies, but they essentially say that all suppliers should receive a fair and equal opportunity to participate in a purchasing process. However, sometimes there are policies that give some suppliers a positive advantage, such as those who employ or are run by certain types of people. For instance, changing demographics mean that the features of a population might change, and this should be reflected in the workforce – so policies may state an organization's attitude towards employing people from diverse backgrounds, and its requirements that suppliers adopt similar policies.

We could continue with the list of policies, but there is a huge number of areas that we could mention. However, the message is clear, that policies are set by higher management to show how the organization will behave in a variety of circumstances – they clarify management's position on a topic, give guidance to people responsible for carrying out the policy, allow consistent actions by employees and generally give guidelines for the way that purchasing should be done.

PURCHASING PROCEDURES

Procedures
Are the operating instructions that detail the tasks done in purchasing.

Procedure manual
Is a how-to manual, describing how to do various jobs.

Those policies that describe how activities should be performed are often separated into a set of **procedures**, collected into a procedures manual.

The purpose of procedures

A **procedure manual** is clearly related to a policy manual, but it is generally more detailed and extensive. In essence a policy manual gives the broad picture of what is wanted and the context, while the procedures manual adds details to show exactly how each activity is done. You can imagine this in a company that uses power tools, where a policy might say that, 'Power tools should always be used in a safe way and with due concern for the operators and those around them.' A procedures manual could go into more detail of exactly what is to be done, perhaps starting with, 'Before turning on the power tool read the manufacturers instructions for its use. Then make sure that you are wearing the correct safety clothing.'

A large purchasing department may have hundreds of procedures giving the details of the ways of dealing with many different situations. Every organization develops a unique set of operating instructions that meet its own specific requirements. We cannot give more than a brief review of such procedures, but can outline some common themes.

A procedure manual serves a number of purposes. The obvious one is that it is a reference guide for purchasing staff. For new staff it is especially valuable with its explanations of how to do various tasks. For experienced staff, it gives clarification of potentially uncertain areas, or it simply reinforces knowledge about different topics.

The second purpose of the manual is that it gives consistency by describing the formal steps that everyone should use to perform a task. These procedures should be well-tested and provide the best way of doing each task. The methods should correspond to industry best practices and might be found through benchmarking comparisons with leading firms.

Wherever possible, purchasing should aim at simplifying procedures. Then the manual should give a concise, accurate and complete set of operating instructions. Precision is important, as a procedure that gives too much detail or has too many steps is likely to be ineffective – and often ignored. Managers should continually review the manuals to look for improvements that reflect current best practices. This updating is especially relevant with the growth of e-procurement and other efficient processes.

Figure 6.2 shows an outline of one purchasing procedure for a large company. This procedure shows what purchasing should do when faced with the problem of an engineering department that specifies a supplier. This is always a difficult problem as engineering needs are often different to commercial ones – so purchasing has to evaluate the reasons for using the specified supplier, the benefits, alternative suppliers and possible conflicts of interests.

Types of purchasing procedure

Procedures can cover just about any task or area of purchasing. For instance, there can be special procedures to deal with dangerous goods, deliveries that are late, emergency orders, high value items, repeat orders and so on. However, most purchasing procedures cover actions in the following areas.

The purchasing process. In chapter 2 we described the purchasing cycle which starts when internal customers recognize a need for some materials and ends with a review of the procurement process and measurement of performance. Procedures document the proper way to do all of the steps and options in the purchasing process.

The proper use of purchasing forms. Purchasing typically uses many different forms. Historically these were actual paper forms, but they are increasingly electronic ones that are generated automatically, or at least partially automatically. The procedures manual includes a description of the proper way to use each form, the meaning of each information field on the form and a description of its proper handling and storage. Handling and storage is largely automated, but policies are still needed to specify the location of data, time it is stored, access and necessary approvals for uses.

Design of legal contracts. Purchase contracts are legal documents that can cover many topics. Not surprisingly, they can be very long – and for major projects they are extremely long and complicated! Most organizations have specific procedures for writing contracts with suppliers, and purchasing staff have to be familiar with these procedures and follow them carefully. Some of the topics discussed in legal contract procedures include:

- Basic contract principles
- Features of a standard purchase contract
- Execution and administration of agreements
- Essential elements of the contract
- Compliance with contract terms and performance assessment
- Formal competitive contracting procedures
- Contract development process
- Examples of sample agreements
- Legal definitions
- Use of formal contract clauses

FIGURE 6.2 Example of purchasing procedures

ABC Technologies

Purchasing procedure manual

Subject: Sourcing requests from engineering

I. Introduction

This procedure outlines the steps to follow when purchasing receives a material request from engineering with a specified supplier form attached. Processing a specified supplier request differs from routine purchasing and a request with a suggested or preferred supplier. The purpose of this procedure is to evaluate engineering's source request in a fair, timely and thorough manner.

II. Related policy

Purchasing policies require purchasing units to obtain materials, components and other items that meet the delivery, quality, lowest total cost and other competitive requirements of the company. Restricting this requirement can have a serious impact on purchasing's ability to perform its duties. However, under certain conditions departments other than purchasing may specify or request a particular supplier.

III. Responsibility

When a buyer receives a specified supplier form from engineering, they must pass it to their direct purchasing manager. This manager has the responsibility of evaluating the circumstances and acting in accordance with the following procedure.

IV. Procedure

1   Upon receipt of a specified supplier form from engineering, a purchasing manager verifies that each section of the form is properly completed.

2   The purchasing manager must verify that the requested item is not currently an actively purchased item. If the item is currently purchased, purchasing must inform engineering of this.

3   For items not currently purchased, the purchasing manager must evaluate engineering's reasons for specifying a particular source for the item. If these reasons are found not to reflect acceptable purchasing or market principles, purchasing may identify and evaluate other equally qualified suppliers.

4   If engineering's supplier request is accepted, the purchasing manager signs the specified supplier form and processes the purchase order.

5   Rejected requests are sent back to engineering with reasons. Then purchasing will work with engineering to identify sources that satisfy engineering's technical requirements and also meet the commercial requirements of the company.

6   To promote close working relations between purchasing and engineering, purchasing will respond to specified supplier requests within a reasonable time.

The procedures involved in designing legal purchase agreements are detailed and complicated, so purchasing often needs specialized staff to deal with the legal intricacies.

Operating procedures. These are the instruction for completing a broad range of operations, from receiving a request to purchase materials, through to accepting delivery. A procedure can be developed for any operations, and it describes a series of coherent steps that defined the 'best' way of doing the operations. You can get an idea of the type of topics covered by operating procedures from the following list which are used by a major manufacturer:

- Control of information sent to suppliers
- Storage of purchasing documents
- Process of supplier qualification
- Use of purchasing computer systems
- Analysis of competitive quotations
- Use of single source selection
- Requirements for order pricing and analysis
- Analysing total cost of ownership
- Acceptable cost reduction techniques
- Intra-company transactions
- Processing and handling of over-shipments
- Supplier acknowledgment of purchase orders
- Treatment of defective materials
- Removal of company-owned resources from suppliers

LEARNING FROM PRACTICE

Hansraj Bharadwaj

Hansraj Bharadwaj is the trading name of an electrical goods wholesaler based in Delhi. The company has an ordering system that is partly automated and partly manual. Procedures for both of these are defined in a formal Procedures Manual. This is a bulky document that covers most common situations. In particular, operating procedures are designed for all of the following eight step procurement process. This starts with a user identifying a need for materials (step 1 and 2), moves through supplier selection (steps 2 to 4) and then arranges the purchase (steps 4 to 8). The whole procedure finishes when materials are delivered and

paid for. This procedure is illustrated in Figure 6.3, and is based on a series of key documents (which are underlined in the following description).

1 *A user department:*
   - Identifies a need for purchased materials
   - Prepares specifications to describe the details
   - Checks departmental budgets and get clearance to purchase
   - Prepares and sends a purchase request to procurement

2 *Then procurement:*

- Receive, verify and check the purchase request
- Examine the material requested, looking at current stocks, alternative products, make-or-buy options, etc. – and after discussions with the user department confirm the decision to purchase
- Form a long list and then a short list of possible suppliers, from regular suppliers, lists of preferred suppliers or those known to meet requirements
- Send a request for quotations to this short list

3 *Then each supplier:*

- Examines the request for quotations
- Checks the customer's status, credit, etc.
- Sees how it could best satisfy the order
- Sends a quotation back to the organization, giving details of products, prices and conditions

4 *Then procurement:*

- Examine the quotations and do commercial evaluations
- Discuss technical aspects with the user department
- Check budget details and clearance to purchase
- Choose the best supplier, based on the details supplied

- Discuss, negotiate and finalize terms and conditions with the supplier
- Issue a purchase order for the materials (with terms and conditions attached)

5 *Then the chosen supplier:*

- Receives, acknowledges and processes the purchase order
- Organizes all operations needed to supply the materials
- Ships materials together with a shipping advice
- Sends an invoice

6 *Then procurement:*

- Acknowledge the delivery
- Do any necessary follow-up and expediting
- Receive, inspect and accept the materials
- Notify the user department of materials received

7 *Then the user department*

- Receives and checks the materials
- Authorizes transfer from budgets
- Update inventory records
- Uses the materials as needed

8 *Then* procurement

- Arrange payment of the supplier's invoice

FIGURE 6.3 Steps in Hansraj Bharadwaj's procurement process

User department	Procurement	Suppliers
1. Identify need Requests purchase →	2. Receive request process Request quotations →	3. Receive request process
	4. Receive quotation ← Discuss and process	Send quotation
Discuss ────→	Send purchase order →	5. Receive order process Ship goods and
	6. Receive and check ←	invoice
7. Receive and check ← Authorize payment →	Transfer 8. Arrange payment ────→	Receive payment

CHAPTER REVIEW

- Policies provide rules or guidance that staff should follow when doing certain activities. They put constraints on staff behaviour. They show how an organization will work towards its strategic aims

- Purchasing policies are guidelines for the behaviour of purchasing staff. They describe procedures and guidelines for accomplishing the supply strategy. These policies should be phrased in terms that are rigid enough to control actions, but broad enough to allow people to use their discretion

- Well-formulated policies support efficient, effective and consistent purchasing operations. On the other hand, policies that are out-of-date, too detailed, irrelevant to current issues, unclear or too vague will not help purchasing

- Each organization defines its own purchasing policies to deal with its own unique circumstances.

Nonetheless, there are general patterns that identify five major types of policy that refer to the broad role of purchasing. Specifically, these cover the conduct of purchasing staff, buyer-seller relationships, operational issues and social objectives. The policies for each of these come in many forms and cover many issues

- As the function of purchasing evolves, senior managers must continually revisit their purchasing policies, to make sure that they are keeping up with current practices

- Policies set the broad picture for purchasing, but more details of how to actually do every task are given in procedures. These are collected in a procedures manual which forms a 'how-to' manual for a purchasing department

DISCUSSION QUESTIONS

1 What exactly is a policy? Why are purchasing policies important?

2 Is a policy really a recipe for doing a job? If it is, how does this affect skilled employees who really should know how to do jobs?

3 Write a brief policy statement about the need for using more diverse suppliers. What features should you include in such a policy statement?

4 Why is it important to have a policy that outlines the origin and scope of purchasing authority? What might happen if there is no such policy?

5 Why should managers periodically review their purchasing policies? What are the consequences if they omit these reviews? How often do you think they consider minor and major updates?

6 What are the benefits of a comprehensive policy manual? What might such a manual contain?

7 Is it possible for a policy manual to be too detailed and comprehensive?

8 What do you understand by ethics? Why is the purchasing profession particularly sensitive about this topic?

9 Describe some ethical dilemmas that a purchasing department might meet in its normal activities.

10 Find an example of a company's code of practice for purchasing. Review its contents and give examples of behaviour that would violate elements of this code.

11 Do external groups affect purchasing policies? Give an example to support your views.

12 The chapter listed a number of operational procedures. Describe three additional areas that might benefit from written procedures.

REFERENCES

Basel Convention. (2009) The control of transboundary movements of hazardous wastes and their disposal, Basel Convention, Geneva.

ISO. (2009) ISO 14000 Environmental management, International Standards Organization, Geneva.

Klein W. H. and Murphy D. C. (1973) Policy: concepts in organizational guidance, Boston, MA: Little Brown.

Melnyk S. (1999) ISO 14000: assessing its impact on corporate effectiveness and efficiencies, National Association of Purchasing Management, Tempe, AZ.

FURTHER READING

Baumer D. L. and Poindexter J. C. (2002) Cyberlaw and e-commerce, New York: McGraw-Hill.

Baumer D. L. and Poindexter J. C. (2004) Legal environment of business in the information Age, New York: McGraw-Hill.

Centre for Advanced Purchasing Studies. (1999) ISO 14000: Assessing Its Impact on Corporate Effectiveness and Efficiencies, Tempe, AZ: CAPS Research.

Duerden J. (1995) 'Walking the walk' on global ethics, *Directors and Boards*, 19(3): 42–45.

Handfield R. and Baumer D. (2006) Conflict of interest in purchasing management, *Journal of Supply Chain Management*, 42(3): 41–50.

Ireland J. (1998) Purchasing policies and procedures, *Supply Management*, May 21.

Maignan I. (2002) Managing socially-responsible buying: how to integrate non-economic criteria into the purchasing process, *European Management Journal*, 20(6): 641–648.

Murray J. E. (2003) When you get what you bargained for—but don't, *Purchasing*, 132(4): 26–27.

National Association of Purchasing Management. (1995) Ethics policy statements for purchasing, supply and material management: examples of policies and procedures, National Association of Purchasing Management, Tempe, AZ.

Quayle M. (2002) Purchasing policy in Switzerland: an empirical study of sourcing decisions, *Thunderbird International Business Review*, 44(2): 205–236.

CASE STUDY

Danisco Sugar

Danisco is one of the world's leading food ingredients companies with more than 7,000 staff and a presence in more than 40 countries. Among its activities, it is the world's largest producer of the artificial sweetener xylitol, half of ice creams include their ingredients and they are the world's second largest producer of cheese and yoghurt cultures.

Until 2009 Danisco Sugar was a key part of the group, producing a million tonnes of sugar a year in Northern Europe. Then the division was sold to the Nordzucker Group, under the name of Nordic Sugar. Daniso Sugar's general purchasing policy laid down rules for all its purchasing activities, with the aim of ensuring that purchasing gave the best possible support to the strategy of Danisco Sugar and the Danisco Group. The policy is quite long, but you can get a feel for its role from the following review of 19 principles.

Responsibility

1. Purchasing has overall responsibility for all purchasing (apart from purchase of sugar beet) at Danisco Sugar in Denmark, Sweden and Germany. Purchasing is responsible for using processes that are up-to-date, ethical and environmentally sound. On occasions, Purchasing may delegate decisions to other departments, but it retains responsibility for coordinating the purchase of major items across divisional boundaries of the Danisco Group.

2. Purchasing activities are organized in a central department (Purchasing) – and to a lesser extent in some other central departments and in some local organizations, according to rules drawn up by Purchasing. The authority to carry out purchasing includes responsibility for its correct performance, including compliance with the purchasing policy.

Basic principles

3. All employees who work in purchasing will work with honesty, credibility and professionalism. They will refuse financial inducements, and apply fair and honest negotiation techniques.

4. Purchasers will not have any other motive to use a particular supplier other than serving the best interests of Danisco Sugar, and purchasers will have no connections with the supplier.

5. Danisco Sugar will defray all the expenses of their employees' visits to suppliers, in order to avoid any dependence on the supplier.

6. Purchasing activities will be governed by a broad view, and in addition to price they will consider factors like quality, environmental impact, delivery, supplier reliability, service, total lifetime costs, capital commitment and payment terms.

Suppliers

7. Purchasers and others involved in purchasing may not inform any third party of competing prices and other conditions.

8. Compliance with the purchasing policy will give a uniform code of conduct that will enhance the company's external image.

9. Suppliers will be selected on a professional business basis, to ensure sound competition, and according to their ability to fulfil the company's expectations of timely, safe, correct, service-oriented delivery on competitive terms.

10. Good relations and co-operation with suppliers will be fostered over extended periods. But the supply base cannot be static, and the company is always looking for competent new suppliers.

11. When a supplier has been selected, Purchasing will look for opportunities to use them to consolidate purchases from other companies in the Danisco Group.

Purchasing

12. Purchasing should be co-ordinated across all areas where this is financially beneficial.

13. Some purchasing may be placed with local suppliers, when this is appropriate and does not lose the benefits of co-ordination.

14. Purchasing will be conducted by staff who have the necessary training, experience and instruction in company rules to give them appropriate knowledge of the purchasing area.

15. Purchasers should make continuous efforts to reduce the number of suppliers.

16. When the company acquire materials from only a single supplier, there must always be a separate risk evaluation.

17. Standardization is encouraged to rationalize purchasing and capital expenditure.

18. Administrative support systems for purchasing, especially IT systems, must be designed to support safe, up-to-date and optimized trade with suppliers, to enhance efficiency in administrative procedures, to ensure uniform, correct and rapid reporting and to provide the necessary information to all employees.

Environmental issues

19. Danisco Sugar's employees must always make it clear to suppliers that the company gives high priority to the environment in its purchasing. The company will take into account impacts on the environment and give priority to sustainable resources, recycling and low energy consumption.

Questions

- How do you think Danisko Sugar set about designing their policies?

- Are you surprized by any of the points mentioned? What changes or other policies would you expect to see?

- How would these policies affect suppliers?

- Is the change of ownership likely to have any effects on these policies?

Source: Based on www.danisco.com; www.nordicsugar.com

CHAPTER 7
CHOOSING A SUPPLIER

LEARNING OBJECTIVES   After reading this chapter you should be able to:

- Discuss the choice between insourcing and outsourcing

- Review the factors to consider when deciding whether to insource or outsource

- Describe a seven-step process for evaluating and selecting suppliers

- Understand the information needed about potential suppliers and its sources

- List important criteria that affect the choice of a supplier

- Know how to construct and use supplier scorecards

- Discuss ways of reducing the time needed for supplier evaluation

OUTSOURCING OR INSOURCING

An important decision, which can have serious long-term effects, is whether to make some material such as a particular component, assembly, process, or service or whether to buy it from an outside supplier. This choice is characterized as a 'make or buy' decisions, with the associated alternatives of **insourcing** or **outsourcing**.

In this form, the decision to outsource seems tactical or even operations based. However, it is more far reaching than this, and reflects a strategic decision to focus on core operations and move the supply to outside experts. Outsourcing is a positive, long-term decision that reinforces a business strategy. For instance, a business strategy based on consolidation and vertical integration would encourage insourcing; one based on core capabilities and global sourcing would encourage outsourcing.

Insourcing-outsourcing decision process

Purchasing managers have to use a variety of knowledge for the insourcing-outsourcing decision. Their essential approach is to analyse and compare the benefits of insourcing and outsourcing, and a typical process for this has three steps.

Step 1: Strategy alignment – sees how the insourcing-outsourcing decision fits into an organization's strategic plans. The concern is strategic alignment, where any long-term procurement plans have to fit in with business – and functional – strategies. For example, if a production department has a strategy of technological strength that includes the design of state-of-the-art products, then it might be in the best position to make specialized components internally. Procurement should

---

Insourcing

Means that an organization internally makes a particular material that it needs for its operations.

Outsourcing

Means that it buys the material from an external supplier.

LEARNING FROM PRACTICE

The Rising Sun

Jose Esperanza is the owner of The Rising Sun Restaurant in Cantalajara, Mexico. This is a busy family restaurant that tries to give reasonable food to a large number of clients, at a reasonable price. Unfortunately, in 2009 several of the long-standing kitchen staff left to start their own restaurant in a neighbouring town. Jose started to look for new staff, but this proved surprisingly difficult. There were few suitable people in Cantalajara looking for kitchen work, and those who were looking wanted to work in the more expensive, higher status restaurants – and they wanted correspondingly high wages.

Jose considered another option. A company in Leon produced high quality commercial pre-prepared meals. Jose could use these frozen meals as the basis of The Rising Sun's menu, with only the finishing and presentation done within the restaurant. This would mean that he could offer a wider menu, employ less skilled kitchen staff (losing most of the chefs), keep his prices low and still offer food that his customers would appreciate.

The customers' reaction would be uncertain, but most budget restaurants with extensive menus use pre-prepared meals. Jose knew that several restaurants near to him already used frozen meals, and this was particularly common over the border in American TexMex restaurants. Effectively, these companies had made a strategic decision to outsource the preparation of their meals, rather than use their own facilities.

include this information when they design, and align, their purchasing strategy. Specifically, procurement should look for answers to some key questions:

- What are the current – and likely future – business and functional strategies?

- How are these supported by internal sourcing of materials?

- How might external suppliers help achieve the strategies?

- What is the supply chain likely to look like in 5-years time?

- What plans is the organization pursuing for changing technology?

The sourcing decision is important because it affects costs, but it also defines the boundaries that an organization draws around its operations. Organizations are likely to keep operations internal that they consider part of their core activities, while they are more likely to outsource activities that they consider more peripheral. So the outsourcing decision depends on the business strategy, and its definition of core activities. Prahalad and Hamel (1990) define core capabilities as the key activities that an organization does particularly well, and which give it some kind of competitive advantage. These appear as distinctive capabilities (Waters, 2006), which are the activities that an organization does better than its competitors, and which differentiate its products. In these terms, managers have to ask whether the supply of some material is an integral part of an organization's core capabilities. When a particular item is closely aligned with a firm's core capabilities, managers are more likely to source it internally; when an item is not closely aligned with a core capability, it might make more sense to outsource it.

Another strategic question concerns the process used, and particularly the level of technology. Welch and Nayak (1992) described a strategic sourcing model (summarized in Figure 7.1) which considers a firm's process technology with its competitors', the maturity of industry technology, and the significance of the technology for competitive advantage. There are several outcomes within this framework. When the competitive advantage provided by technology is low, a firm is likely to outsource

Core capability
Key activity that an organisation does particularly well.

Distinctive capability
Activities that an organisation does so well that it gains a competitive advantage.

FIGURE 7.1 Strategic sourcing model

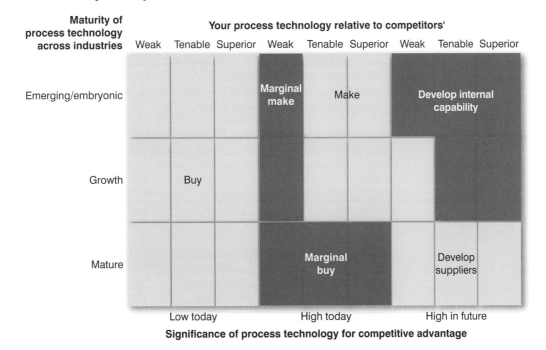

Significance of process technology for competitive advantage

materials and focus its own resources on high-value-added activities. A 'marginal buy' comes with mature technologies that provide significant competitive advantage, yet are better developed in other industries. Here the firm should consider acquiring the necessary technology itself. When technology provides a competitive advantage but it is not yet mature, a firm should start building the technology into a future competency, and when technology may give a future advantage but it is still at an emerging stage, it should be nurtured through research and development.

Step 2: Analysing alternatives to see which gives the best value. The strategies designed by senior managers set the context for outsourcing, but cost is often a primary driver. Manufacturing is outsourced to China, information processing to India, clothing manufacture to Indonesia, because firms find it cheaper to do this. But managers have to go beyond the obvious costs (such as purchase price, direct labour and raw materials) and also consider the indirect costs (unused equipment, spare capacity, lower productivity, loss of jobs, industrial relations problems, etc). Figure 7.2 gives a list of some of these important costs.

All the costs have to be weighed against future savings, with a template for a typical comparison shown in Figure 7.3 (Cavinato, 1988).

Identifying the costs involved in these decisions is often difficult. In principle, suppliers quote a price, but other costs have to be added, such as stocks and administration. Figure 7.2 illustrates a general form for internal costs, where there are three main categories:

- *Variable costs,* which are directly associated with the product and vary with the level of production

- *Fixed costs* that are directly attributable to production, but they do not change with the level of production (at least in the short term)

- *All of the other overheads* that are not included in running a facility, such as head office costs, communication costs, etc.

One further consideration for the total cost of internal operations is deciding whether to add some profit to the in-house production. To give an accurate view of

FIGURE 7.2

Costs to include with outsourcing decisions

Total variable cost elements		
• Direct materials	• Direct labour	• Inbound freight
• Variable fringes	• Variable overhead	• Supplies
• Expensed tooling	• Variable overtime premiums	
Total fixed cost elements		
• Total variable costs	• Fixed overhead costs	• Rent/building payments
• Fees	• Property taxes	• Support staff salaries
• Research and development	• Advertising	• Utilities
• Indirect labour and fringe benefits	• Indirect materials costs	• Maintenance
Full operating costs		
• Total production costs	• Executive salaries	• Corporate administration
• Depreciation	• Transfer pricing	• Commercial expenses
• Expensed tooling		

FIGURE 7.3

Template for comparing costs

1. Insourcing		2. Outsourcing	
Operating expenses:		Purchase costs	
Direct labour		Inbound freight/delivery	
Direct materials		Space	
Inbound freight		Administrative costs of control, contact with supplier	
Facilities		Continuing investment	
Depreciation		Costs of inventories	
Overhead		Working capital costs	
Direct management costs		Total outsource costs (2)	
Cost of inventories			
Working capital costs		Net savings (1) minus (2)	
		Less: taxes on savings	
Total insourcing costs (1)		Net after-tax savings (3)	

internal costs, the internal transfer price really should include the same profit as when it is sold to outside customers. However, many firms are hesitant to do this as it gives a bias towards outsourcing. This suggests a grey area for the insourcing-outsourcing decision, which asks which costs should be included in the analyses? The total variable cost is usually included as it is fairly readily found and varies with the level of production. It is more difficult to say which fixed costs should be included as these are less obvious and difficult to assign to specific products. For example, how much of a company's head office administration can be attributed to the production of a particular item – when this is unlikely to change regardless of whether the item is made internally? The timeframe considered is also important here, as a decision for a relatively short term might be based on only the variable costs and a small part of the fixed operating costs; while a decision for the longer-term might include all relevant costs, including some level of profit.

The proper allocation of overheads is not easy, but it can dramatically affect the final decision. But for this important decision managers should also consider a variety of other factors that go beyond costs, such as a supplier's competency, quality, delivery time, technology, responsiveness, reliability and continuous improvement (as suggested in Figure 7.4). These factors are often forgotten in the drive for immediate cost reductions, and organizations that impulsively outsource key operations can suddenly find that they have lost a core capability, and the supplier cannot deliver acceptable performance.

Step 3: Implementing the decision to start the actual sourcing. This relies on three critical activities which must be done well.

- *Effective supplier selection.* A formal selection process should be used to choose the best supplier(s) for particular materials, which we consider in the rest of the chapter

- *Information sharing.* Both technical and business information must be shared with the outsourced supplier

- *Resource allocation.* Allocating enough resources to give trouble-free sourcing and solve problems as they appear

FIGURE 7.4

Advantages of insourcing
and outsourcing

Insourcing	
Advantages	**Disadvantages**
• Higher degree of control over inputs • Visibility over the process increased • Economies of scale/scope	• High volumes required • High investment needed • Dedicated equipment has limited uses • Problems with supply chain integration
Outsourcing	
Advantages	**Disadvantages**
• Greater flexibility • Lower investment risk • Improved cash flow • Lower potential labour costs	• Possibility of choosing wrong supplier • Loss of control over process • Long lead times/capacity shortages • 'Hollowing out' of the corporation

LEARNING FROM PRACTICE

Eaton Corporation

Eaton Corporation is a diversified power management company – which means that it makes a wide range of products that can be classified as electrical, hydraulic, aerospace, truck and automotive. They employ 75,000 people, with sales of more than $15 billion, and operations in more than 150 countries.

In 2007 they won the US Purchasing Medal of Excellence. Their 3500 strong supply chain team has run a variety of initiatives for supplier selection, including:

● A supply chain data warehouse that integrates data from all the company's Enterprise Resource Planning (ERP) systems to create a single repository of critical data

● A goal of reducing the supply base by 50 per cent in the period to 2010

● A 50 per cent reduction over 3 years in the number of defective parts delivered, in part by eliminating poor-performing suppliers

● Major savings and better communications between functions by using special commodity teams. For instance, the electronics team reduced its supplier base from 127 to 5 key firms and reduced associated costs by 12 per cent a year; the packaging team consolidated 175 suppliers to one, with savings of 12 per cent a year

● A 10 per cent reduction in the cost of delivering small packages in North American by moving 95 per cent of shipments to a single company

● Partnering with five logistics suppliers across the globe for raw materials and finished goods shipments has given 6 per cent savings a year since 2005

● Expanding globalization of material sources

● Software for improving communication with suppliers and other business groups

● State-of-the-art training, called the Supply Chain Functional Excellence Programme

These initiatives begin with Eaton's rigorous process to find suppliers whose business practices match their own. In a process that can last for more than a year, Eaton rigorously analyse the quality, efficiency, business practices, ethics, environmental record and potential of prospective suppliers. A key point is the supplier's willingness to work closely with Eaton.

Internally, Eaton's purchasing co-operate with virtually every function, including finance, IT, human resources, legal and ethics – which both gives savings and boosts procurement's presence. Externally, it encourages collaboration between Eaton's engineers and its customers. And a company cannot be successful without innovation, so Eaton encourages – and even expects – its suppliers to be innovative. This means bringing them in at the earliest stages of the design process so that they clearly understand the product and its requirements.

Source: Teague P.E. (2007) Eaton wins purchasing's medal of professional excellence. *Purchasing*, 13 September; www.eaton.com

SUPPLIER EVALUATION AND SELECTION

For those items that they decide to outsource, managers now have to find suitable suppliers. This means that they have to identify potential suppliers, evaluate them, narrow the list down to a reasonable shortlist and identify the best supplier for a particular order. This is widely considered to be one of the most important processes that organizations perform. It may still involve competitive bidding, which is the traditional process of getting bids from a shortlist of about four potential suppliers and awarding the contract to the lowest price. But procurement departments have now developed a broader range of options, and they put significant resources into evaluating suppliers' capabilities across many different areas. A good decision at this point can reduce or prevent a host of problems, especially as firms are reducing their supply base and signing long-term agreements with the few remaining suppliers.

The aim of supplier selection is, obviously, to choose the best supplier for a particular item, and this means ensuring a reliable supply, with reasonable terms, low risk – and maximizing overall value to the purchaser. Unfortunately, there is no single best way of ensuring this, and each organization uses its own approach, that is tailored to its specific needs.

The amount of effort put into selection should generally relate to the importance of the materials. For many small, standard items, this means that the choice of supplier is relatively unimportant. But expensive items need an extensive evaluation process and a major commitment of resources. Figure 7.5 shows the seven key steps in a typical process for this.

Recognize the need for supplier selection

It seems obvious, but the first step of the evaluation and selection process is to recognize that there actually is a need. Perhaps purchasing staff are working with a new product development team and they recognize the need for future purchases.

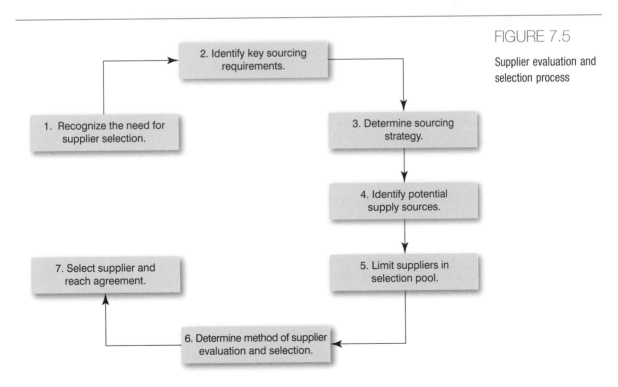

FIGURE 7.5

Supplier evaluation and selection process

Then they start the evaluation process with some tentative enquiries based on pre-liminary specifications for materials, but without specific details. The initial moves become firmer as more detailed requirements emerge.

In practice, the recognition that buyers need to evaluate suppliers occurs in many different ways, with the most common listed in Figure 7.6. Purchasing groups are increasingly proactive in supplier selection, anticipating needs rather than waiting until they are approached by users. For instance, they may have a list of pre-approved or preferred suppliers for many types of materials, and this significantly reduces the lead time before orders actually begin to arrive.

Identify key sourcing requirements

Again it may seem obvious, but throughout the evaluation process, purchasing staff have to keep in mind what they are trying to do. They are acquiring materials, but have to meet specific requirements that are set by users and indirectly by other members of the supply chain. For example, a company that makes chocolate has to buy milk, and buyers must ensure that it is delivered with perfect quality, as quickly as possible, with specified fat content – and maybe meet other requirements such as produced by organic farmers. A buyer of petrol is probably more interested in price and long-term stability of costs, and so on. We return to this discussion of different types of requirement later in the chapter.

Determine sourcing strategy

In chapter 3 we saw how a purchasing strategy sets the long-term context for procurement. For example, a strategy of developing more strategic alliances will mean that buyers look for long-term trading partners. Some key strategic decisions that affect the choice of supplier include:

- The choice of single or multiple suppliers

- Short-term or long-term contracts

FIGURE 7.6 **Starting the process of supplier evaluation and selection**

- During new product development
- Due to poor performance of existing suppliers (either internal or external)
- At the end of a contract
- When buying new equipment
- When expanding into new markets or products
- When internal users submit requisitions for new goods or services
- When performing market tests
- When meeting countertrade requirements
- During outsourcing and re-engineering analyses
- When consolidating volumes across a business
- When conducting a reverse auction
- When current suppliers have insufficient capacity
- When reducing the size of the supply base

- Supplier's desire to develop a working partnership rather than arm's-length relations
- Using suppliers that can provide design support rather than those that cannot customize designs
- Full-service or restricted service suppliers
- The choice of local, domestic, foreign or global suppliers

The requirements often change in the shorter term because of prevailing market conditions, changed user preferences, adjusted corporate goals and so on. So the strategy and subsequent policy choices have to be carefully re-evaluated when choosing a supplier.

Identify potential supply sources

This step identifies a long list of firms that can actually deliver our requirements. Buyers can use a number of sources to develop this initial long list. These range from a quick search of company websites through to a long and detailed search for companies that can design and make specialized products. So a basic question asks how much effort should be put into this initial search – too much effort and expensive resources are being wasted; too little effort and good potential suppliers might be missed. Some important factors here include how well existing suppliers of similar products perform, the strategic importance of an item and its technical complexity. A rule of thumb for determining the effort to put into supplier selection might start by comparing the efficiency of current suppliers and the strategic strategic importance of an item, as shown in Figure 7.7.

The following list gives the most widely-used sources of information about potential suppliers.

Current suppliers. An obvious option is to use existing suppliers who perform well for a new purchase. Current suppliers may be on a list of preferred suppliers, which means that they consistently meet the buyers' requirements. Using a current supplier

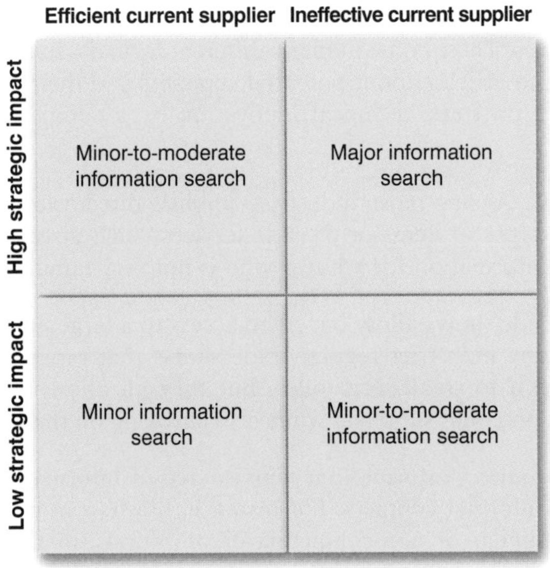

	Efficient current supplier	Ineffective current supplier
High strategic impact	Minor-to-moderate information search	Major information search
Low strategic impact	Minor information search	Minor-to-moderate information search

FIGURE 7.7

Effort needed for information collection

means that buyers do not have to develop and maintain relations with an additional supplier – and doing business with a familiar supplier reduces the time and effort needed to evaluate their capabilities. On the negative side, existing suppliers may not always give the best long-term results, and without some kind of comparison, buyers cannot tell whether better suppliers are available. For this reason, most organizations continuously scan information to identify potential new sources of supply.

Sales representatives and agents. All purchasers receive marketing information from sales representatives, and these can be a valuable source of information for new items. Even when there is no immediate need for a supplier's services, buyers can file the information for future reference.

Internet searches. Most sellers have websites as part of their marketing effort, and buyers can get a lot of information from a simple search of potential sources. Other websites give reviews, comparisons, comments, analyses, case studies, listings and all sorts other information that can help in finding and evaluating potential suppliers.

Commercial databases. Many commercial databases give details of firms that can supply and support different kinds of products. These are particularly useful for industries where technology changes rapidly – for example, NCR's database of 30,000 companies serving the computer industry. Some of these databases are private, but specialized companies maintain other databases that can be purchased.

Experience. Experienced purchasing staff usually have a wide knowledge of potential suppliers. A buyer may have worked within an industry for many years and may be familiar with the main suppliers and their characteristics. This is the main argument against rotating buyers between types of purchases, as they may lose the expertise built-up over many years.

Internal sources. Large organizations have different business units, each of which may have its own purchasing operation. So a valuable source of information is other units within the same organization. This exchange of information can occur through informal meetings, formal team sessions, purchasing newsletters, an internal database and so on.

Trade and industry journals. Most industries have some groups that publish journals and magazines. These come in many different formats, but they usually include advertisements and articles about potential suppliers and their products. Typically, the articles focus on some technical innovation by a company, or report on its operations.

Trade directories. Again, most industries publish directories of companies that produce specific types of items or provide services. Such directories are a valuable source of initial information for a buyer who is not very familiar with an industry.

Trade shows. Trade shows allow buyers to access to a large number of suppliers in a short time. Many industries regular trade shows that range from huge international events down to small local ones. But they all allow buyers to collect information about potential suppliers while also checking on the latest developments.

Second-hand or indirect information. This source of information includes a wide range of largely informal contacts. For instance, buyers can get information from other buyers in similar or non-competing organizations, or they may develop informal networks for passing on information.

Limit suppliers in the selection pool

After collecting information about potential suppliers, purchasing staff have to sift through it, analyse it, consolidate it and present it in a form that allows them to make informed decisions. This can be a major task, depending on the number of suppliers and the information collected. For example, a company looking for transport to deliver finished products to customers may have a choice of several hundred alternative suppliers, with a considerable amount of information published on each. A large amount of information can be a useful starting point, but buyers have to go through it and start eliminating those suppliers that are unlikely, for some reason, to give the best results. In other words, having created a long list of potential suppliers, buyers have to eliminate the weakest until they are left with a strong shortlist. The final supplier is chosen from this shortlist.

In practice, buyers generally start with a broad sweep of the long list to quickly eliminate the worst performers – and they continue iteratively removing the weakest, until they are left with a manageable short-list of potential suppliers. The implication is that these remaining firms possess entry qualifiers that put them on the shortlist and allow them to proceed to the next stage of evaluation. Howard (1998) suggests that entry qualifiers include financial strength, appropriate business strategy, strong supportive management, proven manufacturing capability and design capability. In practice there are many reasons for accepting some firms and eliminating others, and some factors that might influence the decision include the following.

Entry qualifiers
Features that are needed to add a potential supplier to a shortlist.

Buying directly from a manufacturer or through a distributor. You would imagine that the lowest price should be available from an original manufacturer. This avoids the costs of wholesalers and other intermediaries, as well as their profit margins. However, many manufacturers cannot – or choose not to – handle the intricate transactions that accompany direct sales to customers. Also, customers are requiring more services from their suppliers, perhaps including vendor managed inventory and product customization. Factors like this often make the use of some value-adding intermediary a more attractive option. This final choice is usually based on four criteria: the size of the purchase, the manufacturer's policies about direct sales, storage space available at the buyer's facility, and the additional services required.

Local, national, international or global suppliers. The choice here is largely between international suppliers who can generally offer the best price and technical service, and local suppliers who are more responsive to small deliveries and frequent changes in orders. Just-in-time systems favour local suppliers, and this also allows buyers to support the local economy and build community goodwill. International suppliers can sometimes give dramatic price reductions, but these have to be balanced by higher transport costs, stocks, communication problems and general levels of risk.

Large or small suppliers. Buyers generally focus on a supplier's capability to do the job regardless of its size, but this is sometimes a serious concern. For instance, if there could be a sudden increase in demand, then a large firm may be in a better position to provide the extra capacity. Thus, a buying firm might want to reduce its supply base by consolidating orders, but this means that suppliers must have a wide variety of products – suggesting that they are large. Again, a buyer may not want a seller to become dependent on its business, so it will have a policy of ensuring that its purchases never represent more than a certain percentage (perhaps 35–45 per cent) of a supplier's total business. Such policies favour large firms, but buyers may also have policies of building diversity into the supply base, and deliberately dealing with small suppliers.

Multiple or single sourcing. When a number of different suppliers can supply a product, buyers have to decide how many of them to use? Should it use several to spread business and allow alternative sources if one supplier gets into difficulties. Or should it identify the single best supplier and develop a long-term partnership with them. The trend is to reduce the supply base, which brings benefits but also increases inherent risks. The answer to this question usually needs guidance from business strategies which define the broad shape of the supply base.

Acceptable financial risk. Purchasers should be aware, at least to some extent, of the financial condition of prospective suppliers. A supplier that is in a poor financial condition might see these problems grow and affect either with its current operations or with its ability to meet future orders. Buyers should do an initial financial analysis at this stage to get a feel for the overall financial health of the supplier – and this is followed by a more comprehensive analysis for final supplier evaluation.

Availability of supplier performance. A prospective supplier may have an established performance record with an organization, perhaps through previous purchases or orders from other parts of the organization. Based on this prior experience, buyers may consider a supplier for a new item – or if there were problems they may eliminate the supplier from further consideration.

Evaluation of supplier-provided information. Buyers often request specific information from potential suppliers, typically collected by a preliminary questionnaire to ask about the suppliers' type of business, ownership, costs, process technology, quality, market share, reliability and any other important area. Buyers can use the returns to screen suppliers and assess their likely capabilities.

Determine the method of supplier selection

The last stage has created a shortlist, typically of four or five potential suppliers, and now buyers must decide how to evaluate these. The remaining firms may appear equally qualified, so buyers have to look at the alternatives in more detail. For this they can use supplier-provided information, supplier visits, preferred supplier lists and third-party information.

Supplier-provided information. Buyers can get detailed information from suppliers, largely through their requests for quotations. This information used to focus on product description and supply, which was the main concern in purchasing decisions. Now buyers want more details of operations to evaluate suppliers, and they increasingly request a detailed cost breakdown of the price they quote, including detailed costs of labour, materials, overheads and profit.

Supplier visits. A visit by a cross-functional team to a supplier's facilities is often the most efficient way of getting an overall view of the supplier and its likely performance. Site visits are expensive and take a lot of time, and buyers have to balance their desire to collect as much information as possible with the supplier's need to maintain commercial confidentiality. Figure 7.8 shows some kinds of information that buyers should consider during a site visit.

Use of preferred suppliers. Purchasers can reward their best suppliers by creating lists of preferred supplier who consistently meets stringent performance criteria. This greatly simplifies the supplier evaluation process, as a buyer only has to refer to the purchasing database to see if there is a current supplier that can deliver the required items. Buyers can also use a preferred supplier list as an incentive for

FIGURE 7.8 **Key information to be collected during a supplier visit**

- Management capability
- Quality management
- Familiarity with levels of technology
- Planning and scheduling effectiveness
- Financial strength
- Personnel relations
- E-business capabilities
- Sophistication and efficiency of operations
- ISO certifications
- Skills, knowledge and experience of staff
- Evidence of good management and housekeeping
- Types of inventory and related systems
- Nature of the receiving, stores and shipping areas
- Environmental practices
- Employee employment contracts
- Any significant changes planned or expected
- Contact details for key decision makers

existing suppliers to improve their performance and get on the list. A variation on this has pre-qualified suppliers, who are not currently delivering to the organization, but they have been assessed to make sure that they could perform well.

External or third-party information. This is all the other information that is available about a potential supplier. For example, TQM insists that suppliers meet the same quality standards as buyers, and this generates streams of related information flowing through the supply chain. Other organizations may tap into this to get information about each firm. In the late 1990s Mattel had a problem with lead paint on toys, and other companies noted the effects and improved the third-party quality audits of potential suppliers (Casey *et al.*, 2007).

Select supplier and reach agreement

The final step of the evaluation process is to select the supplier and sign a contract. The activities needed for this step vary widely with the item purchased. For routine items, it may simply mean sending a supplier a standard purchase order. For a major purchase, the process can be much more complex, and still need detailed negotiations to agree specific details.

SUPPLIER EVALUATION CRITERIA

In the last section we reviewed the need for purchasers to evaluate potential suppliers to get onto the long list, then get onto the shortlist and then to be selected as the supplier of choice. Each of these reviews includes multiple criteria, with each

LEARNING FROM PRACTICE

Versteg-Schmindhof

Versteg Schmindhof offers advice on supply chain management to companies in Northern Europe. They have developed a checklist of features that identify a good supplier, based on the earlier list of Schorr (1998). A part of this checklist suggests that a good supplier:

- Uses TQM to ensures that its products have high quality, with an aim of zero defects

- Invests in new product development, to give a continuing stream of products that satisfy customer demands

- Makes delivery performance a priority, working with purchasers to improve reliability and reduce lead times

- Is willing to make frequent deliveries to point-of-use areas at a purchaser's facility

- Works with customers to find ways of improving their trading relationships and sharing mutual benefits

- Is flexible and responsive to purchasers' needs, with qualified, experienced and accessible people look after purchasers' accounts

- Shares information with purchasers about capability, workload, schedules, upstream suppliers and other requested data

- Invests in process improvement, taking a long-term view and always searching for better ways of working

- Is financially secure

Source: Based on Schorr J. (1998) Purchasing in the 21st century, John Wiley and Sons, New York; company promotional material.

organization – and possibly each purchase – defining its own criteria, and the weight given to each. For instance, purchasers in a just-in-time assembly plant will give high priority to suppliers who can deliver high quality products with short lead times; in a high-technology manufacturer, buyers will emphasize a supplier's technological capabilities or commitment to research and development.

In practice, most organizations start by rating suppliers on three primary criteria – price, quality and delivery. But this is only a starting point and buyers also have to look at other capabilities. The following list suggests the range of criteria that they might consider.

Management capability

Assessing a potential supplier's management capability is a difficult, but important, step. After all, management runs the business and makes the decisions that affect its operations, products, competitiveness and general performance. A buyer might ask specific questions about:

- Management's mission and long-term strategic planning

- Understanding of strategic supply management

- Investment in research and development, and whether this is enough to sustain growth

- Commitment to TQM and continuous improvement

- Turnover rates of managers and other employees

- The experience and knowledge of key people

- Training and development programmes

- The overall commitment to customer service

- Success at maintaining long-term relations with customers

- History of industrial relations

It is difficult to judge such factors from a brief visit or analysis of available data, but buyers should attempt to get a realistic view of the overall capabilities of management.

Employee capabilities

This looks at the people who are not described as managers, but who work on the supplier's process. Then buyers might consider factors like:

- The extent to which employees are committed to supplying high quality products

- Their views and response to continuous improvement

- Overall skills and abilities of the workforce

- Employee-management relations

- Worker flexibility

- Employee morale and turnover

Financial stability

Procurement managers should assess a potential supplier's financial circumstances. Some purchasers view the financial assessment as a screening process that must be passed before a more detailed evaluation can begin. Buyers may be tempted to give an order to a company that has financial problems as a way of giving it business and return it to stability. But the reality is that a supplier in poor financial condition increases risks. Firstly, there is the risk that the supplier will go out of business and discontinue supplies. Secondly, suppliers that are in poor financial condition may not have the resources to invest in plant, equipment or research that is needed to improve products and processes. Thirdly, the supplier may become too financially dependent on a single purchaser. Finally is the risk that financial weakness is a sign of underlying problems, such as poor customer satisfaction, or inefficient operations.

Sometimes, there are genuine reasons for buying from a supplier that has a weak financial position. For instance, the supplier might be the only source of some item, or it may have invested heavily in a technologically advanced product that is now ready for delivery, or it may offer good terms in a bid to generate cash. So buyers must balance the benefits with the risks.

Buyers can take a range of different financial ratios to check that a supplier can make necessary investments, pay its bills and continue to meet financial obligations. A lot of this information is given in annual reports or trading updates. Figure 7.9 reviews some common ratios that can suggest a supplier's financial health.

Costs

The financial analysis extends to detailed costs, including the total costs, direct labour costs, material costs, operating costs, indirect costs and general overheads. Understanding these costs helps a buyer see how efficiently a supplier can produce an item, and it also helps identify areas where costs can be reduced.

FIGURE 7.9 Interpreting key financial ratios

Ratios	Interpretation
Liquidity	
Current ratio = Current assets/Current liabilities	Should be over 1.0, but look at industry average; high – may mean poor asset management.
Quick ratio = (Cash + Receivables)/Current liabilities	At least 0.8 if supplier sells on credit; low – may mean cash flow problems; high – may mean poor asset management.
Activity	
Inventory turnover = Costs of goods sold/Inventory	Compare industry average; low – problems with slow inventory, which may hurt cash flow.
Fixed asset turnover = Sales/Fixed assets	Compare industry average; too low may mean supplier is not using fixed assets efficiently or effectively.
Total asset turnoer = Sales/Total assets	Compare industry average; too low may mean supplier is not using its total assets efficiently or effectively.
Days payments outstanding = (Payments due × 365)/Annual sales	Compare industry average, or a value of 45–50; too high hurts cash flow; too low may mean credit policies to customers are too restrictive.
Profitability	
Net profit margin = Profit after taxes/Sales	Represents after-tax return; compare industry average.
Return on assets = Profit after taxes/Total assets	Compare industry average; represents the return the company earns on everything it owns.
Return on equity = Profit after taxes/Equity	The higher the better; the return on the shareholders' investment in the business.
Debt	
Debt to equity = Total liabilities/Equity	Compare industry average; over 3 means highly leveraged.
Current debt to equity = Current liabilities/Equity	Over 1 is risky unless industry average is over 1; when ratio is high, supplier may be unable to pay lenders.
Interest coverage = (Pretax Inc. + Int. Exp.)/Int. Exp.	Should be over 3; higher is better; low may mean supplier is having difficulty paying creditors.

Collecting this information can be difficult, either because suppliers do not have such detailed cost information in the format required, or else because they view the data as confidential. This means that suppliers often use reverse pricing models that take the final price of an item and estimate the breakdown of different cost components (we discuss this in chapter 10).

Quality management

A key factor of supplier evaluation is their ability to deliver products of uniformly high quality. For this, buyers evaluate not only the obvious topics associated with quality (definitions of quality, management commitment, number of defects, variability, process control, etc) but also safety, training, maintenance of facilities and equipment, quality circles, continuous improvement and anything else that can affect quality.

An important point is that buyers working in organizations that are registered for ISO 9000 – the International Standards Organization quality management standards – have to work with suppliers who share the same dedication to quality. Generally, firms that have this ISO certification prefer to work with suppliers who also have it (which we discuss in chapter 11).

Process design and technology

Different types of operations used to supply products have strengths and weaknesses that buyers must be aware of. For instance, an automated production process should have few problems making large numbers of fault-free, standard items – but it may not be very good for making a few, tailored ones.

Buyers should take a broad view of the process and include all of the activities, technology, design, methods and equipment used to supply a product. Their evaluation should include current capabilities, and capital equipment plans, research and development and strategy that will affect future capabilities. When organizations try to reduce the time needed to develop new products by having qualified suppliers design some of the parts, they have to include their design capability in any assessment.

Production scheduling and control systems

Production scheduling is concerned with the timing of operations in a supplier's process. Some suppliers use efficient schedules that reduce costs and improve delivery, such as those derived from material requirements planning or just-in-time operations. But other suppliers use ad hoc arrangements that give variable results. Buyers should check how schedules are designed, and how well they achieve stated targets. Included in this assessment of schedules is the availability of capacity and how efficiently it is used. Companies that want to source high volumes of product will clearly want to know that a supplier has enough useable capacity.

Environmental regulation compliance

All organizations are increasingly aware of the necessity to protect the environment from needless damage. Virtually all countries have laws for controlling air pollution, dumping waste, recycling industrial materials, polluting waterways and so on. Purchasers certainly do not want to be associated with firms that have a record of environmental damage – because of adverse publicity, potential liability – or because it is unethical. Supplier's ability to comply with environmental regulations is becoming increasingly important, with the most common environmental requirements including:

● Disclosure of past environmental law violations

● Procedures for hazardous and toxic waste management

● Recycling policies and management

● Measures to reduce waste

● ISO 14000 certification

- Control of ozone-depleting substances

- Carbon dioxide emissions

Green operations are not a drain on resources, but can give substantial benefits. For example, DuPont's environmental program began by cutting greenhouse gas emissions at its factories by 72 per cent, an initiative that saved $3 billion in energy costs. Now the company views its environmental policies as a key element in increasing revenue (Seegers *et al.*, 2007).

E-commerce capability

The ability to communicate electronically is an essential requirement for suppliers. In the past, this was largely achieved by EDI, but most firms now use the internet for their B2B transactions. But apart from the basic systems for managing e-business, buyers should also look at other aspects of IT. For instance, how sophisticated is a supplier's computer-aided design (CAD) capability, and can it be integrated with the buyer's systems? Does the supplier use RFID? Do staff use the latest mobile phone technology? When a supplier is using the latest methods and technology, it is reasonable assurance that it can develop new e-commerce technologies in the future.

Supplier's sourcing policies

Supply chain visibility means that buyer's interests do not end at suppliers, but they extend backwards to upstream members of the supply chain. A supplier can not reliably deliver materials unless its own suppliers are also reliable. Buyers cannot investigate all members of a supply chain, but there are ways of obtaining information about the performance of second and even third tier suppliers. For instance, when a company evaluates the sourcing strategies of a supplier, it can directly ask for information about the performance of its second tier suppliers. Of course, when the supplier evaluates the sourcing strategies of a second tier supplier it can get information about third tier suppliers, and so on back through the supply chain. In practice, investigations into extended supply chain are both difficult and time-consuming, so relatively few firms invest the necessary effort. Those firms that are willing to invest to gain a better understanding of their second and third tier suppliers can use this information to gain a competitive advantage.

Potential for longer-term relationship

A supplier's willingness to move beyond a traditional purchasing relationship can be a key part of the evaluation process. Spekman (1988) suggested a number of questions that buyers should ask for this, including the following.

- Has the supplier indicated a willingness or commitment to a longer-term relationship?

- Is the supplier willing to commit resources to develop this relationship?

- How early in the product design stage is the supplier willing or able to participate?

- What does the supplier bring that is unique?

- Is the supplier committed to understanding the customer's problems and joint efforts to solve them?

- Is the supplier interested in improving operations and coming forward with innovations?

- Will there be free and open exchange of information between the two firms?

- How much planning is the supplier willing to share?

- Is the need for confidential treatment of information taken seriously?

- What is the general level of compatibility between the two parties?

- How well does the supplier know the customer's industry and business?

- Is the supplier willing to commit capacity exclusively to the customer's needs?

SUPPLIER SCORECARDS

Having identified key factors in the choice of supplier, organizations need a structured way of evaluating the alternatives. This can be relatively easy with quantitative factors (such as costs and on-time delivery rates), but becomes more difficult with qualitative factors (such as management stability and trustworthiness).

A **supplier scorecard** can help with these analyses. These list the selection criteria, give a weight to each that shows its relative importance, and then buyers assign an actual score to show how well a supplier performs in that criterion. The scores can be based on quantitative data, or they can be qualitative figures agreed by the buyers. Figure 7.10 shows a seven step process for creating a scorecard.

A scorecard of this type should have certain characteristics. Firstly, it should be comprehensive and include all the performance criteria that buyers think are important. Secondly, it should be as objective as possible, which means that it is better to use quantitative data or to assign some kind of meaning to each value. Thirdly, criteria and their measurement should be reliable, which means that different people reviewing the same situation will arrive at the same conclusion. Fourthly, the scorecard should be flexible enough to use for a range of different circumstances.

Supplier scorecard
Review of a supplier's performance in different areas.

LEARNING FROM PRACTICE

Dun and Bradstreet

Imagine that you work for a small company that does not have the resources to do extensive analysis of suppliers. Or perhaps you have to make a relatively minor purchase that does not justify a major search. You do not want to use an untried supplier because the risk of the unknown is simply too great. So how do you get information easily and quickly about potential suppliers?

One answer is to use an external party to collect and present relevant information. To make this easier, several companies already have the information and make it available to subscribers. Dun & Bradstreet is 'the world's leading source of business information', and it has detailed information about virtually all companies. Their website has specific types of information – including reports for supply management and procurement. Buyers can purchase supplier evaluation reports for any of the 150 million worldwide businesses contained in Dun and Bradstreet's databases.

These databases allow purchasers to compile reports on many different aspects of suppliers, including a business overview, history, operations, payment information, risk assessment, financial information, payment speed, ISO 9000 certification and so on.

Source: www.dnb.co.uk

FIGURE 7.10

Building a supplier
scorecard

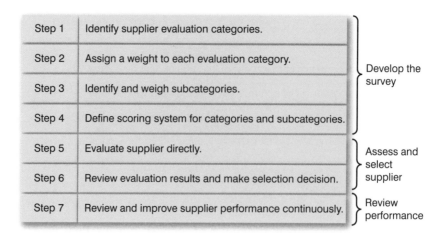

Step 1	Identify supplier evaluation categories.
Step 2	Assign a weight to each evaluation category.
Step 3	Identify and weigh subcategories.
Step 4	Define scoring system for categories and subcategories.
Step 5	Evaluate supplier directly.
Step 6	Review evaluation results and make selection decision.
Step 7	Review and improve supplier performance continuously.

Steps 1–4: Develop the survey

Steps 5–6: Assess and select supplier

Step 7: Review performance

This really means that buyers can adjust the performance criteria and weights assigned to each to reflect different situations. A final characteristic of the scorecard is that it should be easy for everyone involved to understand, use and interpret the results.

Step 1: Identify supplier evaluation categories

The first step in designing a supplier scorecard is deciding the factors or categories to include. We saw in the last section that there can be many of these. But to illustrate the principles we assume that a purchaser decides the important factors are quality, management capability, financial condition, supplier cost structure, expected delivery performance, technological capability, systems capability and a general category of miscellaneous performance factors.

Step 2: Assign a weight to each evaluation category

Buyers give each category a weight that reflects its relative importance. This weight is typically in a range of 1 to 10 – or some other agreed scale. Figure 7.11 shows the weights assigned to each category in our sample scorecard. The first category of Quality systems has a total weight of 20, which means that it is considered four times as important as Information Systems capability, which has a total weight of 5.

Step 3: Identify and give weights to subcategories

This breaks the scores given to each category in step 2, down into more detailed subcategories. For example, the quality systems category is broken down into subcategories of process and control systems, total quality commitment and parts per million defect performance. Buyers have to agree the weights given to each subcategory, with the sum of weights given to subcategories equal the total weight of the category (as illustrated in Figure 7.11).

FIGURE 7.11 Example of a supplier scorecard

	Weight	Subweight	Score (5 Point scale)	Weighted score	
1. Quality systems	20				
Process control systems		5	4	4.0	
Total quality commitment		8	4	6.4	
Parts-per-million defect performance		7	5	7.0	
					17.4
2. Management capability	10				
Management/labour relations		5	4	4.0	
Management capability		5	4	4.0	
					8.0
3. Financial condition	10				
Debt structure		5	3	3.0	
Turnover ratios		5	4	4.0	
					7.0
4. Cost structure	15				
Costs relative to industry		5	5	5.0	
Understanding of costs		5	4	4.0	
Cost control/reduction efforts		5	5	5.0	
					14.0
5. Delivery performance	15				
Performance to promise		5	3	3.0	
Lead-time requirements		5	3	3.0	
Responsiveness		5	3	3.0	
					9.0
6. Technical/process capability	15				
Product innovation		5	4	4.0	
Process innovation		5	5	5.0	
Research and development		5	5	5.0	
					14.0
7. Information systems capability	5				
EDI capability		3	5	3.0	
Computer-Aided Design/Computer-Aided Manufacturing (CAD/CAM)		2	0	0	
					3.0
8. General	10				
Support of minority suppliers		2	3	1.2	
Environmental compliance		3	5	3.0	
Supplier's supply base management		5	4	4.0	
					8.2
			Total weighted score		80.6

Step 4: Define a scoring system for categories and subcategories

Step 4 gives an actual score that a supplier achieves in each performance category. Typically, buyers use a 5-point scale to assess actual performance, with a score of 1 being the worst and 5 being the best. These scores may be subjective, but it is better to use quantitative values, or scores with specific meanings. Then a score of, say, 3 means that the supplier has met some standard of performance. Other scales might be more appropriate, such as a 2-point scale for a performance standard that is either achieved or not, or a 10-point scale where 1 = poor, 3 = weak, 5 = marginal, 7 = qualified and 10 = outstanding. A 4-point scale is often used, based on the terminology of quality management, with:

1 *Major non-conformance to requirements* – absence or complete failure of operations, which mean that the supplier is unlikely to make a satisfactory delivery.

2 *Minor non-conformance* – operations that are less obviously defective, but judgment and experience suggests that they are variable and unlikely to provide satisfactory delivery.

3 *Conformity* – with no problems identified and operations reaching the required level to give reliable deliveries.

4 *Adequacy* – where operations meet or exceed all requirements, ensuring continuing satisfactory – or even superior –performance.

The benefit of this approach is that it takes criteria that are highly subjective and develops a quantitative scale for them. In particular, different people working independently should give the same score for a specific level of performance.

Step 5: Evaluate supplier directly

This step has buyers visiting a supplier to perform the evaluation. A typical site visit might take a day – or several days for more significant purchases. This alone, together with travel time and subsequent analysis of results, means that organizations cannot afford to consider too many suppliers in its shortlist, and it must carefully select those that are serious contenders.

Often a cross-functional team performs the evaluation, allowing team members with different knowledge to focus on specific features. Then the calculations for Figure 7.11 start with the category of Quality Systems, which gets the following scores:

● *Process control systems:* scores 4 points out of a possible 5 points. The sub-weight is 5, so the weighted score is (4/5) × 5 = 4.0

● *Total quality commitment:* scores 4 points out of 5. The sub-weight is 8, so the weighted score is (4/5) × 8 = 6.4

● *Defect performance:* scores 5 points out of 5. The sub-weight is 7, so the weighted score is (5/5) × 7 = 7.0

● *Total points for the category* = 4.0 + 6.4 + 7.0 = 17.4, or 87 per cent of the possible 20 points

The total score for this supplier is 80.6. The next step is for buyers to compare the scores of different suppliers competing for the same purchase contract, and identify the best. Alternatively, purchasers could set minimum acceptable standards for suppliers, and delete any that do not qualify. In the example here, the supplier performs well in most categories except delivery performance (9 out of 15 possible points). Purchasers must decide if this is acceptable, correctable or if the supplier simply cannot give a satisfactory performance.

Step 6: Review evaluation results and make a selection

At some point, buyers must decide whether to recommend or reject each supplier. As no supplier is likely to be perfect, this usually means assessing the shortcomings and the extent to which these might affect performance. Then buyers make their decision. This may be a simple accept or reject, but it can be more complicated. For instance, several suppliers may all perform similarly, and then more discussions are needed before a final choice. Or there may be different degrees of problem, some of which can easily be overcome once they are identified. For example, Alcoa defines the difference between a performance problem (which is 'a discrepancy, non-conformance or missing requirement that will have a significant negative impact on an important area of concern in an audit statement') and a deficiency (which is 'a minor departure from an intended level of performance, or a non-conformance that is easily resolved and does not materially affect the required output') (Alcoa, 2009). This shows that an important outcome from this step is identification of areas that a supplier might improve.

The supplier scorecard gives useful information for supplier evaluation, but there are other issues to consider, such as the relative size of a supplier or their view on social issues:

- **Relative size.** An organization may deliberately choose suppliers that are relatively small, as they can exert greater influence – especially when the organization has a large share of the supplier's total business. You can imagine the benefits of this when a small company wants to introduce just-in-time operations, but cannot persuade its suppliers to change their practices as it does not have enough influence over them. On the other hand, some organizations prefer to work with larger suppliers as they feel that this is more likely to give continuing, guaranteed deliveries

- **Use of global suppliers.** The decision to switch to global sourcing has important consequences. For instance, global sourcing is generally more complicated than domestic buying, so the evaluation and selection process has to be more rigorous. And the lead times needed for deliveries from remote suppliers can become prohibitive – especially for just-in-time operations

- **Competitors as suppliers.** Another important issue can be the extent to which a buyer is willing to purchase some materials from a direct competitor. Purchasing from competitors has the disadvantages of limiting the amount of information shared, and not allowing close working relationships or mutual commitment

- **Countertrade requirements.** This is a broad area where a buyer and seller have a partial exchange of products. These can be organized as straightforward cash transactions, or they can become exchanges when, for example, a hardware manufacturer sends some products to a software company in exchange for certain programs. The desirability or otherwise of such arrangements can clearly affect the choice of supplier

- **Social objectives.** Many purchasers want to do more business with suppliers who are pursuing objectives that go beyond short-term profits. For example, many firms buy Fair Trade products or environmentally friendly products as a way of supporting these initiatives. This is an aspect of procurement that is growing in importance

Of course, all of these can be included in a well-designed scorecard. Whatever route is chosen, buyers now have objective information which they can use to compare suppliers. The final step is to make a selection. The buyer or team who evaluate suppliers may have the authority to make the final choice of supplier – or they may present their findings and recommendations to a manager or committee who has final authority. The authority for this varies from organization to organization.

Step 7: Review and improve supplier performance

When all the relevant factors have been considered and a supplier has been selected, it is time to sign a contract and start trading. But the supplier must then continue to deliver satisfactory service and meet the buyers' requirements. So the emphasis moves from an initial evaluation and selection of suppliers, to evidence of continued good performance and improvement. We discuss this in chapter 9.

REDUCING THE TIME FOR SUPPLIER EVALUATION

Competitive pressures are constantly forcing organizations to work more quickly, reducing lead times and developing new products faster. For instance, in the 1970s car makers were taking as long as 60 months to design and bring a new car to market, but this dropped steadily, with a current target of 18 months. Associated processes, such as supplier evaluation and selection, must also be done faster – as too long spent on this preparatory decision, will inevitably delay the arrival of materials and hence the delivery of products to customers.

There are two ways that procurement can speed-up its evaluation process. Firstly, it can find new ways of doing the process, making it smoother and shorter. For

LEARNING FROM PRACTICE

H.B. Fuller

H.B. Fuller is an international manufacturer of chemical products for a variety of industries. With a net revenue of $1.5 billion, it has operations in 36 countries and customers in more than 100.

First-hand information gained from supplier visits plays a large part in narrowing the corporation's supply base. For instance, the Latin America sourcing manager Roy Calderón tours supplier plants whenever possible and talks to the supplier's staff. He says that his first job is to try to understand the logistical and manufacturing capabilities of a supplier, as well as their quality assurance process and systems. What he sees at a supplier's plant helps him determine how much H.B. Fuller can expect from that supplier. Calderón also assesses the production staff, saying that 'Morale and work environment is hard to put into fixed numbers or dollars, but it needs to be part of a supplier's intelligence profile.' If the workers seem to be

proud of their work, it's more likely that supplier will give consistently high-quality products.

Calderón also explores the plant's infrastructure, particularly looking for signs that might signal future problems. For example, if a machine looks like it might wear out or if the plant seems like it is falling apart, he takes notice. He also inspects the speed at which operations work as an indicator of a supplier's health. If a supplier is too busy and overloaded, it might not be responsive enough to any order changes; if it is too relaxed, it might not be economically viable for much longer. Neither extreme is encouraging. Some suppliers might want to keep Calderón in management offices, but he insists on the broader picture. 'If all I see are fancy offices and the suppliers aren't willing to show me their manufacturing process and let me talk to their employees, that's a big question mark,' he says.

Source: Varmazis M. (2007) How to narrow your supply list, *Purchasing*, 17 July; www.hbfuller.com

instance, it might use a specialized unit that is experienced in supplier selection and can do the procedures faster. The second way is to become increasingly proactive, anticipating the need for supplier selection before it formally appears. For instance, it can pre-qualify potential suppliers to identify sources that can be called upon at short notice.

The challenge is to shorten the process for evaluating suppliers, while still arriving at effective decisions. There are several tools that can help with this, as suggested by the following list.

Map the current supplier evaluation and selection process

Process mapping is used to identify all the steps, activities, times and costs involved in a process. It shows the activities involved and the relationships between them. Once we understand the current process, we can look for improvements, identifying the parts that are less efficient and might usefully be improved. There are several different formats for process maps (Waters, 2002) and they should be the first step in finding improvements.

Integrate with internal customers

The need to anticipate rather than react to an immediate need for supplier evaluation means that buyers must work closely with internal customers. This can be achieved in a variety of ways, perhaps with purchasing moving physically closer to operations or product design to get an early insight into future requirements. Purchasing's aim should be an integrated and seamless series of transactions from an initial recognition that materials will be needed through to settlement of the account.

Data warehouse with supplier information

A data warehouse is a large and easy to access store of data and information. An organizational data warehouse can quickly supply information about potential suppliers, performance of current suppliers, details of contracts, expiration dates of contracts, forecasts of demand for purchased items and any other information that supports a faster selection process. External data warehouses, like those provided by Dun and Bradstreet, can give even more information about most potential suppliers.

Electronic tools

IT providers have developed a host of tools to improve the evaluation and selection process. As the simplest level, e-learning scorecards can be used during initial visits to suppliers, and these manage the scoring of supplier performance and recommend a quick 'yes or no' decision (Hartley, 2000). A host of more sophisticated models are available to assess suppliers, typically based on mathematical analyses that identify 'optimal' suppliers. A benefit of these models is that they can be linked to communications systems to collect information and produce results very quickly.

Third-party support

We have already mentioned that third party or external sources of supplier data can significantly reduce the time and effort needed for analysis. The internet is the main source of huge amounts of such data, especially online directories, potential suppliers, industry analysts and reviews. As always, buyers have to be particularly careful about the reliability of these online sources.

Preferred supplier list

Many firms create a list of their best-performing suppliers, who consistently deliver the best services and products. A variation on this is to pre-qualify suppliers who do not currently deliver to the organization, but investigations show that they could provide a good service. Then, rather than searching for a supplier from scratch, buyers can start by looking to see if there is a suitable supplier on their list of preferred suppliers or pre-qualified suppliers.

New organizational design

Organizations are increasingly using commodity or supply teams to manage important purchases. These teams have a detailed knowledge of families of purchased items – and they can use this specialized knowledge to find improvements in purchasing their commodity. Many firms also use a lead buyer, usually for items that are not critical enough for a commodity team. Then the lead buyer is responsible for managing – and improving – the buying process.

Standard contracts

There is still a tendency, especially in firms with a large legal department, to write a new contract for each purchase. But most contracts cover similar ground and the alternative is to use standard contracts that can be adjusted during negotiations. The role of the legal department now changes from writing new contracts, to reviewing changes to the standard contract.

LEARNING FROM PRACTICE

Buying information technology

Using the wrong supplier for IT products can create problems that last for years. The rate of technological change can make even the best products obsolete within months, and it is usually difficult to switch quickly to a new supplier and ensure compatible systems. The initial choice of supplier is clearly important, and experts offer some sound suggestions.

- Do not rely on a single supplier. Too many firms try to source all their IT requirements from one or two big suppliers. A better approach is to build a network of suppliers that includes smaller firms that use promising emerging technologies

- Make sure you and the supplier are moving in the same direction, with both organizations working towards common platforms, technologies, capabilities, features and functions that are compatible

- Choose the best suppliers that strengthen your ability to add value to products. Do not choose suppliers simply because they offer a good purchase price

- Be a big fish in a little pond. Sourcing from the biggest supplier might bring a good purchase price but limits your influence. A smaller supplier may be more innovative and flexible

- Understand how your suppliers are using the internet to add value to the products they develop, manufacture, service or distribute

Source: Based on Editorial (1998) Tips on supplier evaluation, InfoWorld, 26 October, 1998, p 72.

CHAPTER REVIEW

- The choice between outsourcing and insourcing a particular item is a basic question facing organizations' concerns. The choice is based on the business strategy which defines the type of activities that the organization will perform. To put it simply, if a firm is better at buying than it is at making, it is more likely to outsource the production of materials

- The choice between insourcing and outsourcing can significantly affect costs and the effectiveness of operations. Managers should use a formal procedure for determining those items that should be outsourced. We outlined a standard procedure with three steps

- For materials that are outsourced, managers have to identify the best suppliers. This is one of the most important functions of purchasing, and when it is done well procurement lay the foundations for successful supplier performance

- Organizations need a formal procedure for evaluating suppliers. Unfortunately, there is no simple process for this, but every organization develops its own approach. These are generally based on seven steps that start with the recognition that a supplier has to be selected, and ends with the actual selection and award of a contract

- Buyers assess suppliers before putting them on a long list, before moving them to a shortlist and then when selecting the winner. They can use many different criteria in these assessments. We reviewed a number of these ranging from management capability through to delivery reliability

- A scorecard is a useful way of organizing a detailed comparison of suppliers capabilities. This identifies key factors in the decision, and by giving each a score, identifies the supplier with the best overall performance. There are many variations on this theme

- Competition is forcing organizations to work more quickly, and this needs faster associated services, including procurement. Specifically, buyers should look for ways of reducing the time taken to assess and select suppliers. A range of tools can help with this

DISCUSSION QUESTIONS

1 If Company A outsources some activities to Company B, then Company B will expect to make a profit from doing the activities. Why does Company A not do the activities itself and keep the profit?

2 What activities would you expect to see most commonly outsourced?

3 Why do organizations commit extensive resources to the evaluation of suppliers before selecting one?

4 Discuss the ways that purchasing may become aware of the need to evaluate and select a supplier.

5 What sources of information are available to buyers when they start looking at potential sources of supply? When do you think it is appropriate to use each of the sources?

6 Describe in detail the procedure that you would use to evaluate and select a supplier.

7 When a buying team visit a potential supplier, what evidence might they find that managers are not forward-looking or that the company might not perform well?

8 Why are suppliers sometimes reluctant to share cost information with buyers, particularly during the early part of a buyer-seller relationship?

9 What issues should purchasing address when deciding whether a supplier is a candidate for a longer-term relationship?

10 Describe the features and use of supplier scorecards.

11 What are the advantages of assigning numerical scores to the factors in a supplier scorecard?

12 If a supplier has some are as of weak performance, when would it be better to find ways of overcoming this weakness, rather than using another supplier?

13 When might a purchaser select a supplier that is having financial difficulties?

14 Why should the time taken to evaluate and select suppliers decrease? What methods have the greatest impact on reducing supplier selection time?

REFERENCES

Alcoa (2009) Supplier Certification Guidelines, Pittsburgh, PA: Alcoa.

Casey N., Zamiska N., and Pasztor A. (2007) Mattel seeks to placate China with apology on toys, *Wall Street Journal*, September 22, pp A1, A7.

Cavinato J. (1988) How to calculate the cost of outsourcing, Distribution, January, pp 72–76.

Hartley D. (2000) Looking for a supplier? Use the e-learning scorecard, *Training and Development*, 54: 26.

Howard A. (1998) Valued judgments, *Supply Management*, 17: 37–38.

Prahalad K. and Hamel G. (1990) The core competencies of the corporation, Harvard Business Review, May–June. pp 79–91.

Schorr J. (1998) Purchasing in the 21st century, New York: John Wiley and Sons.

Seegers L., Handfield R. and Melynk S. (2007) Green movement turns mainstream for corporate America, Environmental Leader, website at www.environmentalleader.com

Spekman R. E. (1988) Strategic supplier selection: understanding long-term buyer relationships, Business Horizons, pp 80–81.

Waters D. (2002) Operations management (2nd edition), London: FT Prentice Hall.

Waters D. (2006) Operations strategy, London: Thomson Learning.

Welch J.A. and Nayak P.R. (1992) Strategic sourcing, a progressive approach to the make-buy decision, *Academy of Management Executives*, 6(1): 23–31.

FURTHER READING

Carbone J. (1999) Evaluation programs determine top suppliers, *Purchasing*, 127(8): 31–35.

Carter R. (1995) The seven c's of effective supplier valuation, Purchasing and Supply Management, pp 44–46.

Choi T. Y. and Hartley J. L. (1996) An exploration of supplier selection practices across the supply chain, *Journal of Operations Management*, 14:333–343.

Desai M. P. (1996) Implementing a supplier scorecard program, *Quality Progress*, 29(2):73–76.

Ellram L. M. (1991) A managerial guideline for the development and implementation of purchasing partnerships, *International Journal of Purchasing and Materials Management*, 27(3):2–9.

Gottfredson M., Puryear R. and Phillips S. (2005) Strategic sourcing: from periphery to the core, *Harvard Business Review*, 83(2):132–139.

Gustin C. M., Daugherty P. J. and Ellinger A. E. (1997) Supplier selection decisions in systems/software purchases, *Journal of Supply Chain Management*, 33(4):41–46.

Przirembel J. L. (1997) How to conduct supplier surveys and audits, West Palm Beach, FL: PT Publications.

Schorr J. (1998) Purchasing in the 21st Century, New York: John Wiley and Sons.

Woods J. A. (editor) (2000) The Purchasing and Supply Yearbook: (2000 edition) New York: McGraw-Hill.

CASE STUDY

Simon and Singh

Jacques Pascalle is a purchasing manager at Simon and Singh, a consumer food products company located in the UK. He recently attended a seminar that discussed current issues in sourcing and supply chain management. In one session, a speaker presented the results of a study which suggested that the concept-to-customer cycle time for new products was getting shorter by an average of 50 per cent every 5 years. Obviously, some industries had far less reduction, but others had rates of change that were even faster.

The speaker used the car industry as an example. In the 1980s the three big US manufacturers – GM, Ford and Chrysler – took 5 years to design and produce a new car. By the early 1990s this had declined to 4 years and by the mid-1990s the target was a cycle time of 3 years. However, the US companies had been left behind by Japanese companies who by this time had reduced development time to 2 years. In 2002 the Wall Street Journal quoted the CEO of Honda as saying that his company needed to reduce development times to 18 months. The seminar speaker made the obvious point that such reductions in the major process of new product development also needed the equivalent reductions in the sub-processes that support it – including procurement.

Jacques considered these comments and came to two conclusions. First, there were the same pressures to speed up new product development in the food products industry as in the motor industry. These pressures probably arrived later, but they were no less intense, and the life cycles of Simon and Singh's products were continually getting shorter. In some ways the pressures were even more pressing, as the barriers to new entrants to the industry were lower, and firms needed to be very flexible and responsive to customer needs. Second, Jacques realized that many supplier evaluation and selection decisions were associated with new product development. As his company reduced the product development cycle times, it would also need to reduce the time taken to evaluate and select suppliers.

Jacques began to wonder how he could reduce the time taken to select the company's suppliers by 30 per cent, 40 per cent or even 50 per cent. He started by drawing diagrams – or process charts – of the supplier evaluation and selection process and then looked for ways of improving the core operations.

Questions

- Why should companies spend time and resources to evaluate and select suppliers? When are such decisions needed?

- What is forcing companies to reduce the time it takes to develop new products?

- Describe in detail the process that a company can follow when evaluating, selecting and negotiating supply contracts. What kind of charts can be used to describe this process?

- Discuss ways of reducing the time taken to evaluate, select and negotiate agreements with suppliers

CHAPTER 8
GLOBAL SOURCING

LEARNING OBJECTIVES After reading this chapter you should be able to:

- Understand the movement towards global trade

- Describe the features of worldwide sourcing

- List reasons why firms use worldwide sourcing, and the barriers they face

- Identify the total costs of international purchasing

- Understand the type of issues that arise when firms move towards international purchasing

- Understand the features of global sourcing

- Discuss the factors that can achieve successful global sourcing

GLOBAL OPERATIONS

One of the dominant themes of business is the growth of globalization and the way that it is changing trading patterns. Organizations increasingly look for global opportunities, viewing the world as a single market around which they can freely move. The importance of this trend for purchasing is that the best suppliers need not come from the same country or region, but can be located anywhere in the world.

For many years manufacturers have looked for low-cost centres to supply components, but in recent years there has been a flood of companies purchasing goods from foreign suppliers. This has obviously benefited China, which has become 'the factory of the world', but many other countries export manufactured goods as a way of increasing their Gross Domestic Products (GDPs). The outsourcing of services has also grown, with India as the leader, employing millions of people in call centres, software development, IT and communications.

The obvious attraction of importing materials from low-cost areas is the price advantage, but it might also ensure access to scarce resources, give high quality, use new innovative products and ease expansion into new markets. This last point is important, as globalization allows new sources of supply and also new markets. The principle is that low cost countries start by supplying profitable exports, which create local wealth and consequently increase demand for imports. You can see this effect in the increasingly affluent Chinese and Indian middle classes who are buying goods that range from L'Oréal cosmetics through Glenfiddich whisky and on to BMW cars.

There are always imbalances in international trade. In 2007, the US exported $1,163 billion of merchandize, but imported $2,020 billion, while China exported $1,218 billion and imported $956 billion (World Trade Organization, 2009). Of course, the real picture is more complicated than this, with some industrialized countries like Germany and Japan exporting much more than they import – and some developing countries like South Africa and Vietnam importing more than they export.

LEARNING FROM PRACTICE

Global steel production

Globalization is changing the structure of many markets. For instance, Bethlehem Steel was once the second largest steel producer in the USA, but it went bankrupt in 2001. Its remaining assets were sold to International Steel Group in 2003, which merged with Mittal Steel in 2005, which merged with Arcelor in 2006. The resulting company, ArcelorMittal, is the world's largest producer of steel, with roots in India and its current headquarters in Luxembourg. This is a familiar story in steel with, for example, 90 per cent of British steel companies nationalized in 1967 to form British Steel Corporation, which was privatized in 1988 and merged with Koninklijke Hoovogovens in 1999 to form Corus Steel. In 2007, Corus was taken over by Tata Steel of India, to form the world's 6th largest steel producer. Such convoluted histories explain why, for example, the largest steel mill built in the USA for more than 40 years – costing more than €3 billion – was built by Germany's Thyssen Krupp (World Steel Association, 2009; www.thyssenkrupp.com).

International operations

Organizations adopt many different structures for their international operations, with the most common described as (Waters, 2008):

1   *National companies* – which only work within their home country. If they want to trade in international markets, they work through some kind of third party.

2   *International companies* – which have facilities in different countries, but they are centred on one home country. The headquarters (and often the main operations) are located in this home country from where all the subsidiaries are controlled.

3   *Multi-national companies* – where a conglomerate has more loosely linked, largely independent companies working in different countries. This arrangement is often described as a multi-domestic organization, with no rigid control from a central headquarters, and separate divisions having flexibility to adjust operations to local needs.

4   *Global companies* – see the world as a single market, moving materials anywhere in the world, and using the best locations for any operations. The feature of global organizations is that all activities are managed as if they occur in a single market. For example, Coca-Cola make the same products around the world, with global operations co-ordinated to meet local demands as efficiently as possible.

Levitt (1983) summarizes the difference between multi-nationals and global companies by saying that, 'The multi-national corporation operates in a number of countries and adjusts its products and prices in each - at high relative costs. The global corporation operates with resolute certainty - at low relative costs - as if the entire world (or major regions of it) were a single entity; it sells the same things in the same way everywhere.'

These descriptions suggest that firms choose a single best organization and use it for all their operations, but in reality they have to be flexible enough to respond to local conditions, practices and demands. Then a company might work 'globally' in Europe and 'internationally' in Africa. Such flexible structures are sometimes described as 'trans-national'.

Worldwide purchasing

Because of its role in acquiring materials, purchasing has a key role in international trade. Again, people suggest different names for different types of sourcing, but three common options:

1   *Domestic purchasing* – the most straightforward transaction with an organization buying materials from suppliers working in the same country.

2   *International purchasing* – where a buyer is located in a different country to the supplier. This is usually more complex than a domestic purchase, and buyers must deal with more demanding negotiations, longer lead times, more complex laws and regulations, currency fluctuations, varying requirements and a host of other variables such as language and time differences.

3   *Global sourcing* – which can be viewed as an extension to international purchasing that takes a more integrated view of global activities. This means that it has a broader scope, is more complex – and generally integrates the supply of items, operations, designs, technologies and other aspects of supply across worldwide locations.

Worldwide sourcing and global sourcing
Refers to any purchase where the supplier and buyer are in different countries.

These terms are often little more than convenient labels, so we will use the general terms **worldwide sourcing** and **global sourcing** for any international purchases.

LEARNING FROM PRACTICE

Worldwide sourcing

Leontiades (1985) notes that, 'One of the most important phenomena of the 20th century has been the international expansion of industry. Today, virtually all major firms have a significant and growing presence in business outside their country of origin.' Figure 8.1 shows the growing value of world exports of manufactured goods since 1995. Some of this growth is due to rising prices, but Figure 8.2 shows how the total volume of goods exported has risen since 1963. This rise is steeper than the growth of GDP, suggesting that a higher proportion of goods are being traded internationally.

In 2008, many national economies went into recession, and countries that had become used to continuing growth suddenly went into decline. But this was not universal. For example, China still maintained a growth in GDP that was relatively close to its 10 per cent average in recent years, largely fuelled by exports that had quadrupled during the previous 7 years. Figure 8.3 shows the value of exports that three major developing economies (Brazil, China and India) sent to each geographical region in 2007. The bulk of these exports were in goods. Although the service sector adds about two-thirds of value added to global production, its share of world trade is below 20 per cent. Not surprisingly, trade in service is increasing quickly and although this is still dominated by Europe (48 per cent of world trade), Asia (24 per cent) and North America (15 per cent) the major growth areas are again led by India and China.

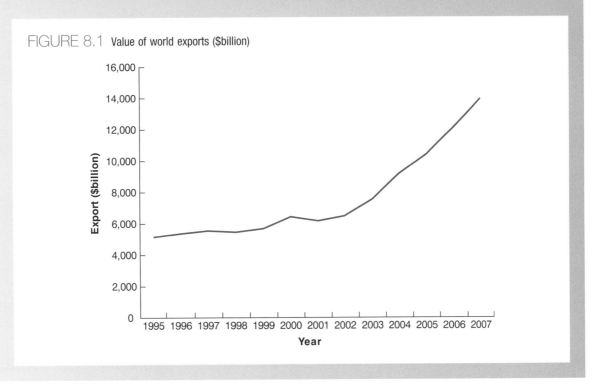

FIGURE 8.1 Value of world exports ($billion)

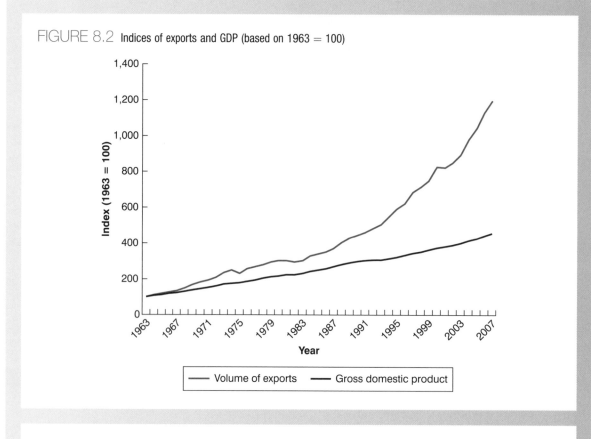

FIGURE 8.2 Indices of exports and GDP (based on 1963 = 100)

FIGURE 8.3 Exports of major developing economies ($billion in 2007)

	Brazil	China	India
Africa	9	37	13
Asia	26	521	46
Commonwealth of independent states	4	8	2
Europe	43	264	34
Middle East	6	44	25
North America	32	264	22
South and Central America	38	39	4

Source: Based on World Trade Organization (2009) International trade statistics, WTO, Geneva; www.wto.org, May 2009; IMF (2009) World economic outlook, International Monetary Fund, Washington.

WORLDWIDE SOURCING

Reasons for worldwide sourcing

People have suggested a number of reasons for increasing worldwide trade over the past 20 years or so. For instance, the end of the Cold War and economic reforms led to easier trade with developing markets in Russia, Eastern Europe and China. At the same time, trade restrictions were reduced, partly as a result of the General Agreement on Tariffs and Trade (GATT) signed in Uruguay. Free-trade areas have grown in importance, including the EU, North America Free Trade Association (NAFTA), Association of South-East Asian Nations (ASEAN), Mercosur in South America and the African Union.

In reality, these factors encouraged international trade, but did not give reasons for actually doing it. Here the dominant factor has been cost, where it is simply cheaper to buy an item from a distant supplier in a low-cost area, than to buy the same item in a nearby high cost area. But there are other reasons for worldwide sourcing, as suggested in the following list. The overriding concept is that by operating globally a firm can use all available resources and strive to become the best in the world, and not just the best in their particular country.

Lower cost. When assessing the costs of sourcing internationally, buyers have to look beyond the unit price and include all relevant costs including transport, risk, quality, delivery, insurance and so on. But even when these are included, firms still report prices that are 20 to 30 per cent lower, because of:

- Lower labour rates
- Different productivity levels
- Lower profit margins
- Favourable currency exchange rates
- Lower cost of raw materials and other inputs
- Government subsidies

Access to product and process technology. New technology solutions are developed throughout the world, such as electronic components developed in Taiwan and South Korea. Organizations that want access to the most advanced technology have no choice but to source materials through international trade.

Quality. Ensuring high quality used to be a stumbling block for worldwide sourcing, with a low price often associated with low quality. But efficient operations, along with developments in quality management, mean that high quality products can be guaranteed in most areas. Total quality management has become such an accepted part of good management that producers in many countries work to the same standards that guarantee the combination of low costs and high quality.

Access to limited sources. There are often relatively few sources of items. For instance, if you want to buy platinum, there are relatively few mines and you have to buy internationally (usually, of course, working through intermediaries). You can also see this effect for manufactured goods or services, where market forces have concentrated supply into a few hands. For instance, there is only a handful of major computer chip manufacturers, and international mobile phone operators. To have access to a limited number of suppliers, purchasing has to work anywhere in the world.

Competition for domestic suppliers. Competitive forces generally maintain price and service levels within many industries, and then a company can use worldwide sourcing to introduce competition for domestic suppliers. For instance, a company based in Belgium might feel that domestic freight transport is becoming less efficient, and consider Dutch transport companies as a way of encouraging improved domestic performance.

Following the buying patterns of competitors. One firm will often imitate the action of competitors, either informally by spotting a business opportunity, or by more formal benchmarking and industry standards. To put it simply, firms try to duplicate factors that contribute to their competitors' success – and this may include sourcing from the same suppliers or countries. To be more positive, firms believe that if they do not follow the successful practices of their competitors' they will be at a disadvantage. This is probably the least-mentioned reason for worldwide sourcing, because few firms want to admit that they are reacting simply to copy the practices of competitors.

Establish a presence in a foreign market. It makes good economic and political sense for organizations to create a presence by buying in markets where they are planning to sell. This develops goodwill in the country and helps gain product acceptance, while developing business relationships that will help an expanded marketing presence.

Barriers to worldwide sourcing

Firms with little or no international experience often face obstacles when they begin worldwide sourcing. These include:

Lack of knowledge and skills in global sourcing. This typically includes a lack of information about potential suppliers, and a lack of familiarity with procedures and documentation needed to complete a purchase. Typically, buyers might want to use worldwide sourcing, but simply not know how to contact trustworthy suppliers. Even when they have identified a supplier and agreed terms they still need letters of credit, multiple bills of lading, dock receipts, import licences, certificates of origin, inspection certificates, certificates of insurance coverage, packing lists and commercial invoices.

Resistance to change. Most people prefer to keep working with established routines, rather than introduce new and untried ideas. So it is understandable that buyers are reluctant to transfer business from familiar, domestic sources to unknown foreign ones. Even when there are clear benefits with worldwide sourcing, reluctant staff can find reasons for sticking to the established way.

Different business customs, language and culture. When buyers meet and negotiate with international suppliers, they need a working knowledge of the customs and culture of the suppliers' country. Differences can lead to misunderstandings, make even the simplest interactions difficult and cause problems in building relationships.

Longer lead times. Almost by definition, worldwide sourcing means that materials have to travel further, and this inevitably takes longer. The longer lead times mean that accurate demand forecasts and reliable transport become critical. In general, international sourcing considerably raises the levels of logistical, political and financial risk (Waters, 2008).

Currency fluctuations. The exchange rates of currencies change continuously, and this can have a significant impact on the price paid for an item. Buyers have to understand the options for minimizing the effects of these variations (which we describe later in the chapter).

Lack of senior management support. Like any major initiative, worldwide sourcing will fail unless top management gives its clear support. Managers must send the message that going international is an important step in using the best suppliers and remaining competitive.

Higher risks. Worldwide sourcing inevitably includes a range of higher risks, some of which are due to more complex operations (extended supply chains, more

Source: Handfield R. and Krause D. (1999) Think globally, source locally, *Supply Chain Management Review*, Winter, pp 36–49; www.sony.com

LEARNING FROM PRACTICE

Sony Corporation

The increase in global trade means that countless organizations are facing a similar problem. They are expanding production facilities or distribution networks in a new country, and must develop local sources of supply, either to meet domestic content regulations or to minimize transportation costs.

Sony have a global procurement strategy of buying local materials whenever possible, and producing in those countries where the company's products are sold. Sony plants in Europe source about 90 per cent of their needs locally; in Asia, it obtains 30 to 50 per cent of materials locally. When production expands into a new area, Sony develops local suppliers whenever possible. If no suitable local supplier exists, the company may negotiate with a Japanese supplier to set up local production in the new country of operation. Although Sony does not contribute capital to suppliers setting-up these production facilities, it will help with training of staff at new locations. As a last resort, Sony may negotiate with Japanese suppliers to ship parts to the new production facilities.

complicated transport, intermodal journeys, etc), some are caused by natural events (earthquakes, typhoons, etc), some are caused by human behaviour (political instability, wars, piracy, etc).

The usual way of overcoming these barriers is through education and training. This can generate support for the process of working globally, as well as overcoming the anxiety associated with change. Publicizing success stories can also show the benefits that worldwide purchasing gives. At a practical level, e-business, improved websites, joint computer-aided design systems, email, sophisticated telephone and tracking systems that monitor the movement of materials can reduce the communication barriers.

COSTS OF INTERNATIONAL PURCHASING

Before moving to international purchasing, buyers must examine the additional costs involved. There are certain common costs for a purchase whether it is from a domestic or foreign producer, but there are inevitably some additional costs with foreign purchases. When price is a major factor, buyers must compare the total cost of ownership from a foreign supplier with the total cost from a domestic one. Figure 8.4 reviews the various charges of international purchasing (Monczka and Giunipero, 1990).

Common costs

Certain costs are common to both domestic and foreign purchases. Although these are incurred for both types of purchases, they are certainly not equal. For example, there is always a delivery charge, but this is likely to be considerably higher for imported materials than locally sourced ones. The two main common costs are:

● *Purchase price,* including quantity discounts, minimum quantities, the effect of emergency orders and any surcharges and extras specified by the supplier

● *Transport costs,* including packaging, insurance, mode of transport, routes taken and the effect of buying at the 'factory gate' rather than having the supplier organize transport

FIGURE 8.4 **Elements of the total cost for international sourcing**

Unit Price

- Basic purchase price together with quantity discounts, minimum purchase orders, shipping efficiency and surcharges
- Prices for emergency shipments and smaller-than-planned quantities

Packaging

- This can be a hidden cost that may be expensive for goods that need special protection, long distances and multiple handlings
- Consult a packaging supplier or specialist for methods to minimize the cost for international shipments

Inflation

- With prices generally rising over time, it is important to see how long a quoted price is valid, and how the effects of inflation are added
- Consider the components of inflation, ensuring that price increases are not hidden in other costs

Transport

- Obtain assistance from logistics people who have expertise in international transportation
- Consider consolidation of shipments with other corporations from the same geographical area
- Use multi-national carriers or brokers to manage shipments and costs
- Use the supplier as a source of information about freight operators

Customs duty

- Duties may be paid any time a shipment crosses international frontiers, and these can vary widely with change at short notice
- Customs brokers give assistance with transactions and, for example, Items that fall into more than one duty classification

Insurance

- Varies widely with the type of item and the transport details
- Check existing insurance cover and do not pay for extra that may be already in place for international transactions
- Not normally included in ocean shipment prices, as special marine insurance is needed

Payment terms

- Foreign suppliers often give better terms than domestic suppliers
- If dealing with intermediaries, their payment may become due on shipment

Additional fees and commissions

- Check with suppliers, customs broker, transportation operators and others about what other costs may be incurred and who is responsible for paying them

- Check who pays if the shipment is delayed. For instance, if it is held at the port of entry because of faulty documentation, who pays the additional storage fee?

Port, terminal and transhipment centre handling fees

- Ports and container terminals charge handling fees for unloading cargo, administration and general use of the port

- Intermodal transport changes between modes of transport or operators at transhipment centres. What are the associated charges?

Agent and broker fees

- Customs brokers and other agents may charge a flat charge for each transaction, or a percentage of the value of items moved

Taxes

- Consider any additional taxes that may be paid

Communication costs

- Higher costs of telephone, travel, mail, emails, etc.

Payment and currency fees

- Payments of bank transactions, including money transfers, bills of exchange, money clearing, etc.

- Charges for exchanging currencies

- Financial arrangements including hedging and forward contracts

Inventory carrying costs

- More stock will be held because of longer lead times

- Costs include the usual inventory ones including opportunity costs, insurance, storage, obsolescence, loss, taxes, etc.

International transaction costs

International purchasing changes the nature of costs, and buyers clearly need to analyse these carefully, or they will get misleading results. One cost that can rise significantly is due to packaging, where longer distances and increased handling mean that more protection is needed. Each item entering a country is subject to a customs duty that varies widely for seemingly small differences in items. A knowledgeable customs broker may reduce the amount of duty paid, as well as speeding shipments through customs.

Other costs include port and terminal handling fees. Depending on the terms of the purchase contract, a purchaser can expect charges for unloading of cargo, administration and general use of a terminal, and there may be additional broker and agent fees. Insurance can also be more expensive, as ocean carrier liability is generally limited and extra cover is needed for broader risks.

A practical detail for international purchases is that a supplier may request a letter of credit with a first purchase. Letters of credit are issued by the purchaser's bank working in conjunction with another bank in the seller's country, and they assure the seller that the necessary funds are available.

Currency risk

A major concern with international purchasing is managing the risk associated with currency fluctuations. Currency values change quickly and this can quickly lead to a significant new cost – or, of course, a gain.

International buyers have to track the movements of currencies to identify long-term trends and revized sourcing opportunities. They also have to monitor suppliers' practices, as they often protect themselves against fluctuating currencies by adding a premium to their quoted price. It is better for buyers to avoid uncertainty from fluctuating currencies and they can take several measures to mitigate the effects. The obvious starting point is to agree payment in a currency that has a relatively stable value – traditionally US dollars, but possibly the Euro, Yen or Pound. However, this is only a partial solution, as the buyer now has to buy the chosen stable currency, and the local currency may still fluctuate against this.

A generally better option is for trading partners to agree a price, and then share the risks from currency fluctuations between them. In the example above, the European company found that it had to pay an additional €11,111 for equipment bought from the USA, and an equal sharing of risk would mean that each partner contributed €5,555 to this. The benefit of this approach is its basic equity, and the fact that suppliers do not have to add risk allowances to their price. There is also some flexibility, as partners may not choose to share risks equally, but one can accept a greater share in return for higher potential returns.

WORKED EXAMPLE

A European company buys equipment from a US supplier in June. The purchase price is agreed at US $100,000 to be paid on delivery in November. In June the exchange rate is €1 equals US$1. How would the costs be affected if the Euro weakens, or strengthens by 10 per cent by November?

Solution

If the Euro is 10 per cent weaker by November, €1 equals US$ 0.90. Now the European company has to find US$100,000 to buy the equipment, but instead of costing €100,000 it now costs US$100,000 /0.9 or €111,111. If the purchaser has not protected itself from fluctuating currencies, the equipment would cost €11,111 more than originally planned.

If the Euro had strengthened by 10 per cent by November, €1 equals US$1.1. Now the purchase only costs US$100,000 / 1.1 = €90,909, saving the buyer €9,091.

Another option is to use currency adjustment clauses, where both parties agree that payment occurs as long as exchange rates do not fluctuate outside an agreed range. If exchange rates move outside the agreed range, the parties renegotiate terms. This gives some mutual protection as both partners know, within fixed limits, what the payment will be.

In practice, there are two variations on currency adjustment clauses:

● *Delivery-triggered clauses,* stipulate that partners will review conditions just before a delivery to verify that exchange rates are still within the agreed range – and if they are outside this range either partner can ask to renegotiate the contract price

● *Time-triggered clauses,* stipulate that both partners review a contract at specified intervals to monitor the effect of fluctuating exchange rates. Then they renegotiate terms whenever the rate falls outside the agreed range

Moving to more sophisticated options, currency hedging involves buying the necessary amount of currency with a futures contract – which means paying a fixed amount for the currency at a specified point in the future. At that specified point, the futures contract transfers currency to the buyer at the fixed rate, and the buyer transfers the same amount out to the supplier. In the example above, the European buyer could take out a futures exchange contract with a finance company in June that would effectively say, 'We will buy $100,000 from you in November and pay €100,000'. It is the job of the finance company to assume the risks – effectively removing them from both trading partners – and earn an arrangement fee.

More sophisticated approaches to currency risk management need considerable financial expertise, found in the finance departments of globally trading companies.

LEARNING FROM PRACTICE

Costs of Sourcing in China

The trend for firms to source products from China shows no signs of slowing down. But the experience of many is that the cost savings they initially expected may be reduced by hidden costs. A study of more than 150 executives – three quarters of whom outsource at least one function in China – highlights some important points.

Many of the issues raised by the executives were cultural and extend into normal business practices – so managers from other countries should be familiar with these norms before entering any serious negotiations. Neglecting this is a recipe for much higher costs or outright failure. For example, it is important to determine the nature of the relationship that will develop. This can range from a simple agreement for standard items to a very involved partnership for critical items. However, the type of contract is often coupled to reciprocal obligations, such as an agreement to buy one item from a Chinese supplier being coupled to a future order for other items.

When a firm is considering outsourcing operations to China, the current process should already be stable and working at a competitive level. It is not a good idea to outsource a process that already has problems, because a Chinese company may lack the experience and skills to solve the problem. If a process does not work in one environment, then it is foolish to imagine that moving it to another will automatically remove the problems.

Most executives reported that the transition to international sourcing involves a considerable commitment of both people and time. A rule of thumb was that it took twice as long as originally estimated to reach a steady state of performance. A way of reducing this time is to learn from the experiences of other firms that have moved to China to see how they have succeeded. Another comment was the importance of actually visiting the site where operations are to be performed. Then managers can verify the existing experience, skills, knowledge and turnover rate of employees.

Hidden costs can add 15–25 per cent to the quoted unit price. These hidden costs include higher shipping costs (10–15 per cent), warranty costs (4–7 per cent), and travel and co-ordination costs (1–3 per cent). A significant problem is that intellectual property laws are not consistently enforced and firms must have procedures for protecting their patents and copyright. Also, there are other effects, such as widely varying labour costs, which are generally increasing because of growing demand.

To summarize, any move towards sourcing from China needs a clear strategy that includes a budget for contingencies, an understanding of the culture, allowance for hidden costs and risks and site visits to clearly communicate expectations and required improvements.

Source: Householder B. (2005) The challenges and hidden costs of outsourcing, Presentation to PRTM Group, Waltham, MA, November.

MOVING FROM DOMESTIC TO INTERNATIONAL PURCHASING

One view is that organizations generally move from domestic to international purchasing either because suitable domestic supplier no longer exist, or because they have to keep up with competitors who are gaining an advantage through their international purchasing. The suggestion is that this is a reactive move, with firms responding to pressures rather than proactively adopting worldwide sourcing as a way of improving performance. Other pressures that may drive firms towards international purchasing include events in the supply market (such as a disrupted supply of materials), rapidly changing currency exchange rates, a declining domestic supply base, inflation within the home market and the sudden growth of global competitors. Whatever the reason for working internationally, purchasing departments now have to consider issues that were not needed for domestic sourcing – or the issues are now much more significant than they used to be.

Information about worldwide sources

After making the decision to purchase internationally, a firm must choose the best supplier. We discussed the procedure for this in the last chapter. But with international operations there are more factors to consider. The first is how to collect and evaluate information on potential suppliers, or identify intermediaries who can help with this. This step alone can be challenging to a company that has no international experience. In the last chapter we suggested collecting data from current suppliers, sales representatives, experience, internal sources and so on. Firms can use the same sources for international suppliers, but they are likely to be more varied and remote. The most useful sources of information for international trade probably include the following.

Internet. An obvious first step is to search for useful websites. Of course, there are the usual problems, and a basic search for 'chemical suppliers' might give millions of matches, only a handful of which are useful. But the greater concern is that most sites are maintained by companies, who always give a flattering view of their capabilities – there is no real indication of how well a supplier actually performs, or even if they are honest traders. Of course, there are many sites that give reviews, comparisons and comments on suppliers and these are generally the most useful sources.

Government agencies. Governments invariably have departments to encourage trade and enforce some control over companies. These can also give advice about potential suppliers. They will not usually recommend specific companies, but they may give useful information about industries, trading standards, regulations, export licences, duties and so on. As well as working within their own countries, government agencies often support offices – or trade consulates – at key locations in foreign markets.

Industrial directories. Hundreds of industrial directories of international suppliers are available, and these give a lot of basic information. Some examples include:

- The World Marketing Directory is published by Dun & Bradstreet and covers 50,000 businesses in all industries that have an interest in foreign trade

- Marconi's International Register details 45,000 firms that work internationally

- ABC Europe Production covers 130,000 European manufacturers that export products

International trade shows. These regular shows are often a good way to collect information about many suppliers in a specific industry at one time. Trade shows occur throughout the world for practically every industry – with well-known ones including motor shows, computer exhibitions, book fairs and ideal homes.

Third-party support. External experts are available to provide assistance with most aspects of international sourcing. Agents or brokers act as intermediaries between buyers and sellers to do some of the necessary transactions. For instance, when a firm does not have enough information about suppliers in a particular region, an agent can help identify and evaluate local sources. And an independent agent, working on commission, can act as purchasing representatives in a foreign country, typically doing the administration, managing transactions and handling paperwork. These experts usually offer advice in a specific area or within a certain geographical area.

Full service trading companies. These are intermediary companies that offer a full range of services to complete the transactions of international purchasing. For instance, they can handle the finances, issuing letters of credit and paying brokers, customs charges, dock fees, insurance, ocean carriers and inland transport companies. In practice, these companies can do everything from finding qualified suppliers, evaluating them, doing product quality audits, negotiating contracts, managing logistics, inspecting shipments, expediting and everything else to arrange delivery to buyers. Using a full-service trading company can give lower total costs and smoother flows of materials than a series of distinct firms, each of which handles one aspect of the purchase.

Supplier selection issues

After collecting information about international sources, the next task is to select a supplier. This process is essentially the same as that described for domestic suppliers in the last chapter, which means that foreign suppliers must have the same – or in some cases even more rigorous – performance evaluation. It is important to remember that a foreign company will not necessarily work in the same way as a domestic supplier, so it is important for suppliers to ask questions like:

- Is there a significant difference in total cost between domestic suppliers and foreign sources?

- Will foreign suppliers maintain the price differences over time?

- What is the effect of longer material supply chains and increased average stock levels?

- What are the supplier's technical and quality capabilities?

- Can the supplier assist with new designs?

- How good is the product quality, and what systems does the supplier have to protect this?

- Can the supplier guarantee reliable deliveries?

- What is the delivery lead time?

- Can we develop a longer-term relationship with this supplier?

- Is the supplier generally trustworthy?

- Are patents, proprietary technology and information safe with a supplier?

- What legal system does the supplier work within?

- What are the supplier's payment terms?

- How does the supplier manage currency exchange issues?

To get more information about such issues, buyers will often use a small trial orders to see how the supplier performs. Then they may continue with domestic suppliers until they are confident that a foreign source can actually deliver the materials needed.

Cultural differences

A major barrier to international sourcing is the cultural differences between countries.

For supply managers, two important factors in **culture** are summarized as *values* and *behaviour*. Here values consider the ways that people think and the importance that they give to various qualities; behaviour considers attitudes and describes the way that people act. Understanding these two factors, and cultural differences in general, can improve buyers' effectiveness in international business. This seems obvious, but many people are unaware of the subtleties of cultural differences, and this can give unwelcome surprizes. At a trivial level, some gestures are very insulting in some cultures, but completely meaningless in others. At a deeper level, standard procedures for negotiation and contracting are distinctly different in Asia, Europe and the USA. And there are different views about the dividing line between genuine consultancy fees and bribes.

Cultural differences also appear in language and communication, with Locke offering some basic advice (Locke, 1996):

- If suppliers are working in their second language, the buyer should be responsible for preventing communication problems

- Always speak slowly, use communication graphics and eliminate jargon, slang and metaphors from your language

- Bring an interpreter to all but the most informal meetings – and allow time for the interpreters to clarify issues and vocabulary

- Document, in writing, the conclusions and decisions made in a meeting before adjourning

Culture

Is a very complex idea, but it includes all the understandings that govern human interaction in a particular society. It includes a mixture of language, values, attitudes, customs, social institutions, education, religion and so on.

Logistical Issues

Managers should not underestimate the effects of extended supply chains, with high stocks of materials, longer lead times, and slower reactions to problems or changes. Lead times are likely to be longer than for domestic suppliers, but they can be much longer than anticipated when, for instance, a country does not have a well-developed transport infrastructure. We have mentioned trade with China, which has less paved roads and railways than European countries, but far easier transport than, say, Botswana. Such lack of infrastructure gives higher logistics costs and less reliable deliveries. A rule of thumb might suggest that logistics costs amount to 15 per cent of production costs in industrialized countries, but this might be more than 25 per cent in developing countries (Hickey, 2003).

An extensive array of shipping terms also makes international purchases more complex. Now *incoterms* are internationally recognized standard definitions maintained by the International Chamber of Commerce (2009) that describe the responsibilities of a buyer and seller in a commercial transaction. In particular, these define the point at which a buyer takes ownership of a delivery, and the responsibility for various aspects of transport (summarized in Figure 8.5). For historical reasons, these are often phrased in terms of ships moving materials from ports, but they apply more generally to any mode of transport.

Legal issues

Each country has its own legal system, which might be based on common (case) law, or code (civil) law. These have widely different features for purchasing and contracting. In general, countries with case laws have longer and more complicated purchase contracts than countries with code laws. A classic example had IBM working under common law in the USA, with a standard contract form more than 40 pages long (they later reduced this to around six pages).

Countries often have complex legislation to give buyers protection and fair treatment, but these are inconsistent unless co-ordinated by international agreements, such as those applying within the EU. Many countries have few laws for consumer protection, with no effective protection to protect intellectual property. Buyers should do a thorough check of the legal systems in which suppliers work before releasing designs or other proprietary information. Also, buyers and sellers doing business across international borders have to agree – preferably in the contract – about the laws that apply to their business.

In practice, international contracts become easier when the supplier's country follows the United Nations Convention on Contracts for the International Sale of Goods (CISG) (United Nations, 1980). This took effect in 1988 with the purpose of facilitating international trade by removing legislative barriers and introducing unified sales laws. Unless parties have agreed to the contrary, CISG applies to sales of goods contracts between parties with places of business in the 'contracting states'. Here the 'contracting states' are the 71 countries (to 2009) that have ratified the CISG. In the same way, the 153 countries that are part of the World Trade Organization are expected to follow certain basic international trade practices.

Organizational issues

An important question for meeting a company's growing worldwide sourcing requirements is whether to retain purchasing close to operations, or whether to open local offices nearer to suppliers. We discussed this question in chapter 4, and here the main consideration is whether to open international purchasing offices (IPOs) in selected areas around the world. These offices are largely staffed by foreign nationals, who are familiar with local conditions and usually report directly to a corporate procurement office. Clearly, larger firms have more resources and are more likely to have IPOs than smaller, where they have various roles (as suggested in Figure 8.6).

The increase in international purchasing in recent years has lead to an increase in IPOs. Firms are using them to provide broad operational support from the development phase through to contract management. Specific IPO activities included facilitating import and export procedures, resolving quality and delivery problems and measuring supplier performance.

FIGURE 8.5 International Chamber of Commerce Incoterms

Service	EXW Ex works	FCA Free carrier	FAS Free alongside ship	FOB Free onboard vessel	CFR Cost and freight	CIF Cost insurance and freight	CPT Carriage paid	CIP Carriage insurance paid	DAF Delivered at frontier	DES Delivered ex ship	DEQ Delivered ex quay duty unpaid	DDU Delivered duty unpaid	DDP Delivered duty paid
Warehouse storage	Seller	Seller	Seller	Seller	Seller	Seller	Seller	Seller	Seller	Seller	Seller	Seller	Seller
Warehouse labour	Seller	Seller	Seller	Seller	Seller	Seller	Seller	Seller	Seller	Seller	Seller	Seller	Seller
Export packing	Seller	Seller	Seller	Seller	Seller	Seller	Seller	Seller	Seller	Seller	Seller	Seller	Seller
Loading charges	Buyer	Seller	Seller	Seller	Seller	Seller	Seller	Seller	Seller	Seller	Seller	Seller	Seller
Inland freight	Buyer	Buyer/Seller	Seller	Seller	Seller	Seller	Seller	Seller	Seller	Seller	Seller	Seller	Seller
Terminal charges	Buyer	Buyer	Seller	Seller	Seller	Seller	Seller	Seller	Seller	Seller	Seller	Seller	Seller
Forwarder's fees	Buyer	Buyer	Buyer	Buyer	Seller	Seller	Seller	Seller	Seller	Seller	Seller	Seller	Seller
Loading on vessel	Buyer	Buyer	Buyer	Seller	Seller	Seller	Seller	Seller	Seller	Seller	Seller	Seller	Seller
Ocean/air freight	Buyer	Buyer	Buyer	Buyer	Seller	Seller	Seller	Seller	Seller	Seller	Seller	Seller	Seller
Charges on arrival at destination	Buyer	Buyer	Buyer	Buyer	Buyer	Buyer	Seller	Seller	Buyer	Buyer	Seller	Seller	Seller
Duty, taxes, and customs clearance	Buyer	Buyer	Buyer	Buyer	Buyer	Buyer	Buyer	Buyer	Buyer	Buyer	Buyer	Buyer	Seller
Delivery to destination	Buyer	Buyer	Buyer	Buyer	Buyer	Buyer	Buyer	Buyer	Buyer	Buyer	Buyer	Seller	Seller

FIGURE 8.6

Role of international
purchasing office

| Identify potential suppliers
Solicit quotes or proposals
Expedite and trace shipments
Negotiate supply contracts
Obtain product samples | Manage technical and commercial concerns
Represent the buying firm to suppliers
Manage countertrade requirements
Perform supplier site visits |

North America —

— Europe

South America —

— Asia Pacific

Another organizational issue concerns the structure of the overall purchasing effort. In chapter 4 we suggested that maintaining central control over the strategic elements of global sourcing increase the likelihood that it will be a success. This is true even when firms decentralize operational activities. Then Figure 8.7 shows a structure that contains elements of centralized and decentralized decision making. In particular,

FIGURE 8.7 Decentralized purchasing with centralized international purchasing

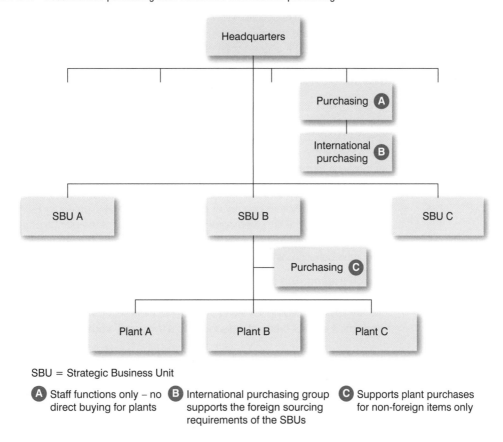

SBU = Strategic Business Unit

A Staff functions only – no direct buying for plants

B International purchasing group supports the foreign sourcing requirements of the SBUs

C Supports plant purchases for non-foreign items only

decentralized purchasing at the business level organizes domestic sourcing, while a centralized office manages the international requirements of different business units.

Countertrade requirements

We have already mentioned countertrade agreements, whereby a buyer and seller have at least a partial exchange of goods for products. This exchange can involve a complete trade of goods for goods, or it can involve some payment in cash.

A country can impose countertrade demands for a number of reasons, the most obvious being that it simply does not have enough hard currency to purchase imported goods. Another reason for countertrade is that it gives a means of selling products in markets to which a company would otherwise have no access. Then a country wishing to sell its products in global markets may use the expertise of multinationals to arrange marketing of the products.

Countertrade demands generally occur for expensive items, such as military equipment or aeroplanes. They also occur when a country's products are available from many other sources, and there is no way to differentiate them. In practice, several different forms of countertrade have evolved, with five dominant types.

1   **Barter.** This is the basic form of trade, which has a straightforward exchange of some products for others, and no exchange of money. It needs trading parties to enter into a single contract, which describes a specific transaction, and covers a short time. Despite its apparent simplicity, barter is one of the least-practiced forms of countertrade.

2   **Counterpurchase.** This requires a supplier to purchase a specified amount of products from the country that purchased its products. The amount of counterpurchase is generally somewhere between 10 per cent and 80 per cent of the value of sales, and is occasionally more than 100 per cent. The essential feature of counterpurchase is that a company buys products that are unrelated to its primary business. Typically it is given a list of acceptable products that can be used for countertrade and has to decide which of them to buy. Then it has to market these or pass them to a third party, both of which add complexity and cost to the transaction.

3   **Offset.** These agreements are closely related to counterpurchase, and they also require a supplier to purchase products of some agreed value from the country over a specified period. However, offset agreements allow a firm to buy any products from companies in the country. So the supplier usually buys items that are directly related to its business requirements, particularly raw materials, parts and components.

4   **Buy-back.** This is also described as compensation trading, and it occurs when a firm builds a plant in another country or provides a service, equipment or technology to support a plant. The firm then agrees to take a portion of the plant's output as payment. Countries that lack hard currencies for payment but are rich in natural resources benefit most from this type of arrangement.

5   **Switch trading.** This involves a third-party trader who sells earned counterpurchase credits. Switch trading occurs when a supplier agrees to accept products from a buying country as partial payment instead of cash. But if the supplier does not actually want the products, it can sell them, at a discount, to a third-party trader who then markets them.

Purchasing's role in countertrade is not usually as visible as marketing's, which is largely responsible for negotiating such agreements. Instead, purchasing is largely reactive, identifying supply sources that will help satisfy countertrade requirements, negotiating terms, managing agreements, determining the market value of countertrade products, selecting appropriate products for countertrade and so on.

LEARNING FROM PRACTICE

Meredith & Guys Ltd.

Meredith & Guys Limited (MG) is an industrial electronics company based in Western Europe. During the 1990s it enjoyed the expansion of EU industry, but in the early 21st century its profit margins were declining because of intense global competition. It also had a mature product line (with some major products now approaching 20-years-old) and was in danger of losing market share to new competitors and technologies. With some difficulty, the company decided to make changes and be more responsive to new demands from the market. In particular, MG decided to redesign its sourcing. The company organizes supply management into three distinct groups: raw materials purchasing, indirect purchasing and finished goods purchasing. Each group was persuaded to develop innovative approaches to worldwide sourcing.

Raw materials purchasing – is responsible for the materials that are needed directly for production. As part of its global procurement strategy, the raw materials group focusses on (1) identifying and qualifying sources worldwide and (2) aggregating orders to give more influence over suppliers.

A major change in raw materials procurement has technical people, operations and procurement working together worldwide to continually refine their needs for components. This cross-functional approach, which is co-ordinated at the corporate level, looks for new sources and tradeoffs which give the lowest overall total cost. A second major change emphasized the global strategy, with product leaders in different sites being responsible for worldwide requirements of items. This provides an individual who is responsible for a procurement area and becomes the resident expert, supported by local staff at each plant.

Indirect purchasing – is loosely responsible for acquiring those items that are not considered raw materials. Even though MG had manufacturing plants in the UK, Italy, Czech Republic, Canada, Mexico and China, previous sourcing initiatives for indirect purchases had focussed on Western Europe. A major initiative – described as Global Vision – now moved towards global sourcing. This has project teams systematically review MG's worldwide indirect spending with a goal of reducing cost by 7 to 15 per cent a year. The cross-functional project teams are guided by an executive steering committee, each member of which is responsible for a number of specific projects. The main functions of the project teams are to:

- Develop a sourcing strategy
- Analyse the industry and identify buyer and seller strengths and weaknesses
- Define improvement goals
- Identify potential suppliers
- Forward and analyse supplier proposals
- Determine the criteria for supplier selection
- Select suppliers

Contract purchasing – long ago MG realized that it could not deal internally with all aspects of its 20 to 40 new-product launches a year, so it uses contract purchasing to buy finished products from suppliers. Most of these products are self-contained electronic components, which are relabelled and sold on by MG. These components are outsourced to take advantage of suppliers technological and manufacturing expertise, as well as their intellectual property.

Several years ago MG formed a contract manufacturing organization with primary responsibility for outsourcing. This group is now responsible for identifying and qualifying outsourcing partners, ensuring product quality and working with contract manufacturers during new-product development. The contract manufacturing organization also has responsibility for two international purchasing offices (IPOs), which identify potential contract manufacturers and suppliers for specific products. The IPOs also support the raw materials and indirect purchasing groups.

MG shows how a company faced with new competitive threats and declining markets can use procurement to help it move towards a prospering global enterprize. It also illustrates that there is not a single approach to this, but three procurement groups can each use a different approach to help achieve corporate objectives.

Source: Company documents and publicity.

MOVING FROM INTERNATIONAL PURCHASING TO GLOBAL SOURCING

Moving to international purchasing is an important strategic step, but it is not the end of progress. Organizations might recognize even more untapped benefits and look for further international co-operation. This can move them towards global sourcing, which is achieved in a series of steps. Figure 8.8 shows five stages in this progression from domestic purchasing through international purchasing and then on to global sourcing.

Level I has firms only purchasing domestically. Although they only buy from local suppliers, these might include global companies that have a significant local presence and facilities. When the constraints of working at Level I become too severe, or organizations recognize that they may benefit from broader sourcing, they move on to Level II which includes basic international purchasing. This is usually a reactive move where firms respond to cost or competitive pressures, and the result is ad-hoc procedures with no co-ordination across purchases of different products, suppliers or from different buying locations.

As international sourcing becomes more ingrained in operations, organizations recognize that it can bring significant improvements and it becomes a part of their supply strategies. This gives Level III, where firms have properly designed and executed worldwide sourcing strategies. However, these strategies still do not give a purchasing process that is well co-ordinated across products, buying locations or suppliers. Progress towards this comes with Level IV, which now includes the integration and co-ordination of sourcing operations across worldwide locations. This represents a sophisticated level of strategic development that includes:

● Worldwide information systems

● Staff with sophisticated knowledge and skills

FIGURE 8.8 Levels of worldwide sourcing

			Current	Expected 3–5 years	Expected change
	Level I	• Engage in domestic purchasing only	13.4%	7.8%	−42%
International purchasing	Level II	• Engage in international purchasing as needed	21.3%	7.8%	−63%
	Level III	• International purchasing as part of sourcing strategy	31%	14.3%	−54%
Global sourcing	Level IV	• Integration and co-ordination of global sourcing strategies across worldwide buying locations	18.1%	15.6%	−14%
	Level V	• Integration and co-ordination of global sourcing strategies with other functional groups	16.1%	54.5%	+238%

% = Per cent of companies indicating a particular level
N = 169

- Extensive mechanisms for co-ordination

- An organizational structure that promotes central co-ordination of global activities

- Leadership that endorses a global approach to sourcing

At this level, purchasing still co-ordinates activities at different locations rather than across different functions. For instance, there might be global co-ordination of fuel supplies to all operations, but this might not be co-ordinated with the supplies of other commodities. This comes with level V, where organizations have full integration and co-ordination of products, processes, designs, technologies and suppliers across all their worldwide operations. This level of integration needs very sophisticated operations that include the worldwide control of product design, development, production, logistics, procurement and all other functions. At present, very few organizations can claim to be near to this.

Factors that encourage success in global sourcing

Many different factors can assist a successful move towards global sourcing, with the following list giving those that are considered most significant (illustrated in Figure 8.9) Monczka *et al.*, (2006).

A well-defined approach to global sourcing. This is a critical factor for success. Some organizations try to use their existing operations, based on a particular item or geographical area, and then used it for global sourcing, but this does not recognize the essential differences of global sourcing. For example, the existing operations might give inappropriate weights to certain factors – perhaps giving less weight than necessary to supply chain risk or total costs. A process specifically designed to implement global sourcing helps overcome many of the inherent differences met when working around the world.

Centrally co-ordinated decision making. Maintaining central control and leadership over activities that are strategic in nature increases the probability of successful global sourcing. The benefits of this include:

- Standardization and consistency in the sourcing process

- Early supplier involvement

- Better long-term supplier relationships

- Greater stakeholder satisfaction with sourcing

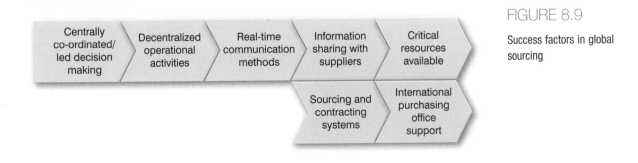

FIGURE 8.9

Success factors in global sourcing

Decentralized operational activities. Firms that decentralize global sourcing operations are likely to have lower total costs, better inventory management and improved performance. Decentralized operation typically include:

- Issuing orders and material releases to suppliers
- Expediting orders when necessary
- Resolving performance problems
- Planning stock levels
- Developing and implementing logistics plans

Real-time communications. It is hard to imagine a successful global sourcing effort without access to reliable and timely information. This information might include lists of purchased goods and services, details of existing and potential suppliers, existing contracts, reports on supplier capabilities and performance, volumes by purchase type and location, prices and conditions and so on. The information must be supplied by a global information system, with related data warehouses. In reality, many firms do not have the IT capabilities to provide such systems. They may have evolved from distinct units or grown by mergers and acquisitions, but the result is a range of legacy systems and processes that are difficult to integrate. Firms clearly have to spend time and money to standardize their systems.

Information sharing with suppliers. Successful global sourcing requires both access to critical information – and the willingness to share that information with suppliers around the world. Firms that share information with their most important suppliers generally get lower purchase prices and cost. The most relevant information to share includes details about supplier quality, delivery, cycle time and flexibility. A second type of information concerns broader factors, such as suppliers' technological sophistication, future capital plans and product variety data.

Availability of critical resources. Resources that affect global success include budget support for travel, access to qualified personnel, time for staff to develop global strategies and systems that ensure the ready availability of information and data. Time is one of the most important resources, with teams that have time to pursue their agenda generally more effective than those that are too rushed.

Sourcing and contracting systems. The most important way to ensure access to information is to develop technology systems that make critical information available on a worldwide basis. Firms with systems that provide access to relevant information are more likely to reduce costs and improve global sourcing. Examples of the features and the information they provide include a worldwide database of purchased goods and services, contract management, supplier assessment, analyses of worldwide product usage and cost analyses.

International purchasing office support. IPOs give a higher level of support to global sourcing through access to product and process technology, reduced cycle times, increased responsiveness and so on. Additionally, IPOs can provide operational support from initial negotiations through contract management.

One clear message from these success factors is that it is essential to have the right qualified staff to support global sourcing. The knowledge and skills needed for global sourcing are different from those needed for domestic purchasing and they include financial knowledge, an understanding of worldwide supply markets, the ability to negotiate globally, legal knowledge, effective communication, an understanding of global strategy, working effectively with people from other cultures and so on (Giunipero, 2000). The other underlying message is importance of efficient worldwide communications. There are obvious problems with global communications, such as limited face-to-face meetings. Sophisticated systems allow electronic communications – or virtual meetings – but even then differences in languages, business practices, culture, laws, etc raise problems for clear communications. Some ways of reducing these include regular review meetings, virtual meetings, conference calls, effective use of organizational websites net-meetings, intranets, joint training sessions, co-location of functional staff and so on.

LEARNING FROM PRACTICE

Rosschmann Grebar

Rosschmann Grebar is an industrial chemical company with headquarters in Switzerland and operations in many areas, particularly South America and South East Asia. Over many years of global sourcing it has refined the following process:

Step 1 *Identify global sourcing opportunities*

An executive steering committee and global sourcing executive ask:

- Which operations have the most pressing needs to reduce costs?
- What major items does the company currently buy?
- How are these items currently specified and sourced?
- How much effort would it take to create a set of specifications?
- What benefits would global sourcing bring?

Step 2 *Establish global sourcing development teams*

The executive steering committee forms cross-functional teams with worldwide members to develop the global opportunities.

Step 3 *Propose a global strategy*

Project teams have responsibility for proposing a global strategy. For this, teams validate the original assumptions underlying the project, verify current volumes and expected savings, assess global suppliers, evaluate the current set of product specifications and propose a global strategy for sourcing materials.

Step 4 *Develop a request for proposal*

Teams develop a RFP to send to selected suppliers and invite them to submit bids for supplying materials.

Step 5 *Release RFPs to suppliers*

The team sends RFPs to an average of five suppliers for a normal item (but fewer than this for specialized items, and more for some commodities). Project teams are responsible for answering any queries from suppliers and any other follow-up.

Step 6 *Evaluate bids and proposals*

The team do a commercial and technical evaluation of the bids returned by suppliers. Project teams get suppliers' best and final offers and then conduct site visits and collect any further information.

Step 7 *Negotiate with suppliers*

A smaller part of the team negotiates with suppliers to finalize contract details. These negotiations are usually fairly brief, but for complex issues they may last up to 3 days, and even longer if it is difficult to agree price and service targets. They usually occur at a convenient Rosschmann Grebar plant.

Step 8 *Award the contract*

Information about the awarded contract is circulated through the company's email and intranet. The steering committee calculates expected savings and maintains the agreements in a corporate database.

Step 9 *Implement contract and manage supplier relations*

This loads global agreements into the corporate system, and then monitors relations and transactions with the supplier. It also manages any transition from old practices to new ones.

Source: Company records.

Benefits of global sourcing

We have described the benefits of international purchasing, and global sourcing generally extends these. A survey of purchasing managers (Monczka *et al.*, 2006) reveals some interesting differences between the perceived benefits of international purchasing and global sourcing. Figure 8.10 summarizes the 10 most common benefits for each. Interestingly, managers named a total of 16 benefits, and the average rating from all of these is 30 per cent higher for global sourcing than for international purchasing.

FIGURE 8.10   Comparing the benefits of international and global sourcing

(a) Benefits of international purchasing

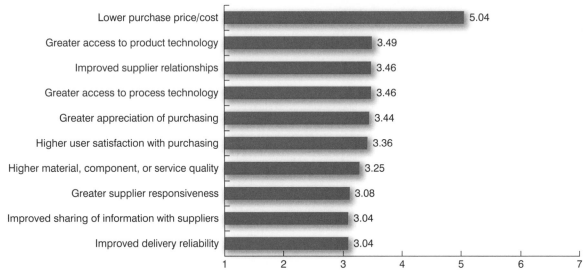

(b) Benefits of global sourcing

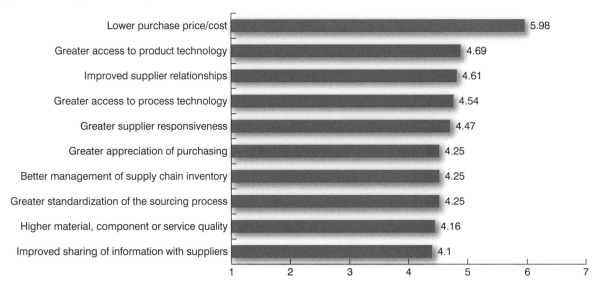

1 = not realized, 4 = moderately realized, 7 = extremely realized
Average across 16 benefits = 4.23/7
N = 52

The leading benefit of worldwide sourcing is the lower purchase price. This is particularly noticeable with international buying, but as firms move towards global sourcing other types of benefits become more apparent. In particular, greater access to product and process technology becomes easier, a result that is particularly important the dynamic companies that are most likely to adopt global sourcing. Better management of supply chain stock is also a major benefit that comes from global sourcing, and this is important as firms move towards integrated logistics and tighter control over stocks.

Source: Monczka R. M., Trent R. J. and Peterson K. J. (2006) Effective global sourcing and supply for superior results, Centre for Advanced Purchasing Studies, Tempe, AZ; www.airproducts.com; www.airproducts.co.uk

LEARNING FROM PRACTICE

Air Products

Air Products is a global supplier of industrial gasses and chemicals, with operations in more than 40 countries and annual revenue of $10 billion. In 1999, an internal study concluded that the company would have to lower operating costs by 30 per cent to remain globally competitive. The problem was that industrial buyers were increasingly viewing the company's products as standard commodities and low-cost competitors were emerging in Asia. One way of helping to achieve these lower costs and improving performance was global sourcing.

Historically, engineering customers would specify materials and order them through regional design and procurement centres. This gave a highly customized design and procurement. But there was little co-ordination between different divisions of the company, say, between its North American and European units. Then the new competitive pressures encouraged the company to co-ordinate design and sourcing activities across its worldwide locations, and this led to the development of a global engineering and procurement process.

The design of each new facility now involves an extensive analysis to identify areas of commonality, standardization and synergy in procurement and design. Cross-functional teams, with members from around the world, work together to develop common design specifications and contracts that satisfy each centre's needs. After 5 years of global sourcing experience and with more than 100 global agreements in place, Air Products has achieved an average cost reduction of 20 per cent compared with regional sourcing and design. In addition, work at worldwide design and procurement centres is more closely aligned with sourcing strategies and the broader company's business strategy. The integrated global sourcing gives a new source of competitiveness to a company working in a mature industry.

CHAPTER REVIEW

- One of the main features of business in recent years has been the growth in international trade. This is likely to continue, meaning that successful firms must have an increasingly global perspective

- Buyers should look for materials from the best global suppliers, rather than their traditional local

sources. There are significant benefits from purchasing worldwide. The most obvious are lower costs, but other benefits range from access to new technology through to higher guaranteed quality

- There can be drawbacks and problems with worldwide sourcing. These can become fairly obvious (when, say, hidden costs emerge) or they can be less obvious (such as different cultural views of business relations). To overcome such problems, firms need staff who are familiar with the intricacies of global purchasing

● Costs are the main driver for worldwide sourcing, so buyers have to examine the total cost of ownership carefully. There are two types of costs – some are always incurred for purchases (notably the unit price and transport), other are additional costs of international transactions (such as customs duty and currency exchange)

● A first step towards global sourcing has firms move from domestic to international sourcing. This raises many issues, including sources of information, supplier selection, cultural differences, legal issues, logistical issues, organization and so on. On occasions, countertrade agreements have a significant impact

● International purchasing is an important move, but it is not the end of the journey. Organizations can move towards the integrated process described as global sourcing. This integrates and co-ordinates all the activities of acquiring materials from suppliers throughout the world

● In practice, firms work at five levels of worldwide sourcing, starting with local purchasing and ending with integrated global sourcing. Few firms have actually reached this final phase

● There are considerable benefits to global sourcing, but they are difficult to achieve

DISCUSSION QUESTIONS

1 How does globalization affect industrialized countries? How does this compare with its affects on developing countries?

2 The BRIC countries of Brazil, Russia, India and China are seen as 'hot spots' of globalization. What does this mean? What problems might there be in sourcing from these countries?

3 Why do companies use worldwide sourcing?

4 What are the barriers to worldwide sourcing? How can firms overcome these?

5 Many companies have moved to worldwide sourcing on a reactive rather than proactive basis. What does this mean and what are the consequences?

6 Leading companies should develop staff who have global perspectives. What does this mean and is it true? Does it apply to organizations of all sizes?

7 Discuss some of the sources of information a buyer can use to identify potential foreign sources of supply.

8 How would the process for sourcing machine parts globally differ from the process for sourcing them from domestic suppliers?

9 Why would a company use third-party agents to help with worldwide sourcing?

10 What are the advantages of establishing an international purchasing office? What services would such an office provide?

11 How do international purchasing and global sourcing differ? Do you think the differences are meaningful?

12 What factors might differentiate successful from less-successful efforts at global sourcing?

13 Why is countertrade used? What different forms are available, and which of these are the most flexible?

REFERENCES

Giunipero L.C. (2000) A skills-based analysis of the world class purchaser, Tempe, AZ: Centre for Advanced Purchasing Studies.

Hickey K. (2003) Chinese puzzle, Traffic World, September 15.

International Chamber of Commerce. (2009) Incoterms, Paris: ICC.

Leontiades J.E. (1985) Multi-national business strategy, Lexington, MA: D.C. Health & Co.

Levitt T. (1983) The Globalization of Markets, Harvard Business Review, May/June.

Locke D. (1996) Global supply management, Boston, MA: McGraw-Hill.

Monczka R.M. and Giunipero L.C. (1990) Purchasing internationally: concepts and principles, Chelsea, MI: Bookcrafters.

Monczka R. M., Trent R. J. and Peterson K. J. (2006) Effective global sourcing and supply for superior results, Tempe, AZ: CAPS Research.

United Nations (1980) United Nations Convention on Contracts for the International Sale of Goods, United Nations, Vienna and website at www.un.org

Waters D. (2008) Supply chain management (2nd edition), Basingstoke, Hampshire: Palgrave Macmillan.

Waters D. (2008) Supply chain risk management, London: Kogan Page.

Website at www.thyssenkrupp.com (2009)

World Steel Association. (2009) Top steel producers, Brussels: WSA.

World Trade organization. (2009) International trade statistics, Geneva: WTO.

FURTHER READING

Bozarth C., Handfield R. and Das A. (1998) Stages of global sourcing evolution: an exploratory study, *Journal of Operations Management*, 16: 241–255.

Fraering M. and Prasad S. (1999) International sourcing and logistics: an integrated model, *Logistics Information Management*, 12(6): 451.

Kaufmann L. and Carter C. R. (2006) International supply relationships and non-financial performance: a comparison of U.S. and German practices, *Journal of Operations Management*, 24: 653–675.

Monczka R. M. Trent, R. J. and Petersen K. J. (2008) Getting on track to better global sourcing, *Supply Chain Management Review*, March.

Murray J. Y. (2001) Strategic alliance-based global sourcing strategy for competitive advantage: a conceptual framework and research propositions, *Journal of International Marketing*, 9(4): 30–58.

Petersen K. J., Frayer D. J. and Scannel T. V. (2006) An empirical investigation of global sourcing strategy effectiveness, *Journal of Supply Chain Management*, 36(2): 29–38.

Rexha N. and Miyamoto T. (2000) International sourcing: an Australian perspective, *Journal of Supply Chain Management*, 36(1): 27–34.

Samli A. C., Browning J. M. and Busbia C. (1998) The status of global sourcing as a critical tool of strategic planning, *Journal of Business Research*, 43(3): 177–187.

Trent R. J. and Monczka R. M. (2007) Achieving excellence in global sourcing, *Sloan Management Review*, Fall, pp 24–32.

Waters D. (2007) Global logistics: new directions in supply chain management, London: Kogan Page.

CASE STUDY

Latvico Hanks

Astrid Zandersons is a chief buyer at Latvico Hanks, an Eastern European producer of sub-assemblies for the automotive market. A production manager approached her to get a fast response for an order for cable harnesses (which are strings of wires that are bound together so that they can easily be fitted into equipment). Astrid sent out a request for quotations to three regular suppliers and two new ones. Unfortunately, only two of these replied with an interest in quoting the business.

The harnesses must be pre-packaged in 50cm×30cm×15cm cartons, each of which weighs around 5kg. The estimated demand for the harnesses is 5,000 units a month. Both suppliers will incur some costs to retool for this harness.

Quotation 1

The first quotation received is from a supplier in Poland. This quotation was delivered in person, by a sales agent and an engineering representative. The sales agent told Astrid that engineering would be happy to work closely with Latvico Hanks to develop the unit and would welcome discussions on ways of reducing costs. They would be interested in future business that would lead to a long-term relationship. The quotation included a unit price, and additional costs for tooling, packaging and shipping. The company needs no special warehousing and would guarantee daily deliveries from its manufacturing site directly to Latvico Hanks' assembly operations.

Quoted costs:

- Unit price = €30
- Packing costs = €0.75 per unit
- Tooling = €6,000 one-time fixed charge
- Freight cost = €5.20 for 50 kg

Quotation 2

The second quotation received is from a supplier in Guangdong Province, China. This supplier must pack the harnesses in a container and ship via rail to the port of Shanghai, then by container ship to Hamburg and by road to Latvico Hanks' plant. The quoted unit price does not include international shipping, for which the buyer must pay.

Quoted costs:

- Unit price = $19.50
- Shipping lead time = 8 weeks
- Tooling = $3,000

In addition to the supplier's quotation, Astrid must consider a number of additional factors for the Chinese quotation:

- Each monthly shipment needs three 40-foot containers
- Packing costs for containerization add $2 a unit
- Cost of inland transportation to Shanghai port add $200 a container
- Freight forwarder's fee are $100 per shipment (to prepare a letter of credit, documentation, etc.)
- Cost of ocean transport is $4,000 a container. This has risen significantly in recent years due to a shortage of ocean freight capacity
- Marine insurance is $0.50 per $100 of shipment
- Hamburg port handling charges are $1,200 per container. This fee has also risen considerably this year, due to increased security
- Customs duty is 5 per cent of unit cost
- Customs broker fees are $300 a shipment
- Transport from Hamburg to Latvico Hanks' plant costs $18.60 for 50 kg
- Extra warehousing is needed for at least 4 weeks of stock at Latvico Hanks to allow for uncertainty in lead time. This costs $25.00 a cubic metre a month

- Accounting conventions set a notional cost of 15 per cent of the value held a year for all stocks

- Currency hedging and brokers fees cost $400 a shipment

- Additional administrative time to deal with international shipping is estimated to take 4 hours a shipment at a cost of $25 an hour

- At least two 5-day visits a year are needed to China to meet suppliers and give updates on performance and shipping. Estimated costs of these are $20,000 a year

Both suppliers have agreed either to pay any additional costs and then send an invoice to Latvico Hanks, or else to include them in a revized delivered unit price. Astrid knows that the cable harness is a standard product that is unlikely to change during the next 3 years, but which could become a regular purchase for many years. But there are also rumours about the next generation of automobile electronics that will reduce the need for cumbersome cable harnesses.

Questions

- Find the total cost per unit of buying the cable harnesses from each supplier.

- Based on the information available, which supplier would you recommend?

- What other issues besides cost should be considered?

- How might the procurement process be improved and simplified?

CHAPTER 9
SUPPLIER MANAGEMENT AND DEVELOPMENT

LEARNING OBJECTIVES After reading this chapter you should be able to:

- Recognize the importance of measuring supplier performance

- Discuss types of supplier measures

- Understand the concept of supply base optimization and rationalization

- Describe ways of optimizing a supply base

- Understand the role of supplier management and development

- Describe an approach to initiating a supplier development programme

- Discuss barriers to supplier development and ways of overcoming them

SUPPLIER PERFORMANCE MEASUREMENT

The last two chapters have looked at decisions about the choice of suppliers. In this chapter we move on to the next stage and measure the performance of these firms when they are in the supply base. Then we want to find ways of improving performance. This is an increasingly important topic, as organizations recognize that to be successful they have to manage resources efficiently across a network of supply chain partners (Minahan and Vigoroso, 2002). This whole area is loosely described as supplier management and development.

What to measure

It is no surprize that purchasing managers want to improve the performance of their suppliers, but an underlying assumption is that there is some means of measuring their performance. The old truism says, 'What you can't measure, you can't manage.' Without effective measurements to monitor performance, buyers cannot really know how well their suppliers are doing, or whether they are satisfying their contractual obligations. So purchasing managers needs to define appropriate measure of supplier performance, and then design systems to collect and analyse the necessary data. The resulting supplier measurement system is a critical element of sourcing, and its end result is a report card to say how well suppliers are performing.

Organizations face several key decisions when developing a supplier measurement system, with the obvious one asking what to measure. Managers will usually have a series of factors they consider important and want to measure, so the next decisions concerns the relative weight given to each. For instance, one company may decide that punctual delivery is the vital factor, while another considers this less important than delivered cost. In practice, the most common measures concern:

Delivery performance. Purchase orders and material releases sent to suppliers include all the relevant information about deliveries, including quantities, lead times and due dates. A routine task for buyers is to see how well a supplier actually meets these conditions.

Cost performance. Buyers want their suppliers to give the best available costs, preferably with price reductions over time. In practice, there are a number of ways that cost performance can be measured, with the most common monitoring delivered real price after adjustment for inflation. Other methods compare a supplier's prices against other sources within the same industry, or against a baseline, target price or accepted norm.

Quality performance. Products should be delivered in perfect condition, so buyers need measures of quality. The usual measures look for comparisons of the latest performance with agreed standards, previous performance, industry norms or some other figures.

An obvious problem is that not all of these measures – or the many other factors that are important for assessing performance – are actually measurable. Firms can measure the proportion of deliveries that are late, but they cannot give a convincing measure of, say, technical ability, or closeness of relationships. Figure 9.1 gives a summary of some important, but non-quantifiable, factors. However, buyers can still assign a surrogate measure to these by giving a score or rating to each factor. Typically, buyers use a scale of 1 to 5, with performance judged as somewhere on

Supplier management and development Includes an array of actions taken to measure, manage and continually improve performance of the supply base.

FIGURE 9.1

Examples of qualitative factors in supplier performance

Factor	Description
Ability to solve problems	Supplier's attentiveness to problem resolution
Technical ability	Supplier's manufacturing ability compared with other industry suppliers
Reporting progress	Supplier's ongoing reporting of existing problems and recognizing and communicating potential problems
Corrective action	Supplier's solution of problems and timely response to requests for corrective actions, including requests for changes
Cost-reduction ideas	Supplier's willingness to help find ways to reduce total purchase cost
New-product support	Supplier's ability to help reduce new-product development time and cost, and their ability to help with this
Buyer/seller compatibility	Subjective rating of how well a buying firm and a supplier work together

this scale. This is the effect that you see when questionnaires ask 'On a scale of 1 to 5, how strongly do you agree with the following comment, when:

- 1 means you strongly agree

- 2 means you agree

- 3 means that you neither agree nor disagree

- 4 means that you disagree

- 5 means that you strongly disagree'

The result is not really an objective measure, but at least it puts an opinion on a more reliable basis. The result is a surrogate measure that can be analysed and give useful findings – provided that you remember the limitations of the basic data.

A benefit of these surrogate measures is that buyers can incorporate them into a scoring model, which is a standard way of giving a structured view of essentially subjective data. Scoring models need the following five steps (Waters, 2009):

Step 1. Decide on the most important performance factors

Step 2. Give each factor a weight that shows its importance; these weights are typically fractions that add upto one

Step 3. Consider each supplier in turn; give each factor a score, typically out of 5 or 10, to show how it actually performs

Step 4. Multiply each score by its weight, and add these to get a total score for the supplier

Step 5. Find the highest total score, discuss the result and make decisions

As you can see, this is another version of the supplier scorecard that we described in chapter 7.

Source: Based on Richmond E. (2009) Supplier assessment, Richmond, Parkes and Wright, London.

LEARNING FROM PRACTICE

Wroxham-Penhal

Wroxham-Penhal is a wholesaler of stationery who stock almost 100,000 items from 10,000 suppliers. They take the management of their supply base very seriously, and have a large programme of supplier development. At the heart of this system is a series of measures for supplier performance, and we can illustrate a part of one of these by looking at an associated scoring model. The following table shows six factors for five possible suppliers of an item. The purchasing committee assign weights to each factor, and then scores for each up to a maximum of 10.

Factor	Weight	A	B	C	D	E
Reliability	0.1	9	6	10	7	5
Lead time	0.15	6	5	7	3	5
Price	0.3	6	8	7	9	9
Quality	0.3	7	6	8	6	5
Systems	0.1	8	9	6	8	7
Flexibility	0.05	7	4	6	8	9
Total weighted score	1.0	6.85	6.65	7.45	6.85	6.6

The weighted scores are found by multiplying the actual score by the weight, and then the total weighted score for each supplier is found by adding these. For example, the total weighted score for supplier A is:

$$(0.1 \times 9) + (0.15 \times 6) + (0.3 \times 6) + (0.3 \times 7)$$
$$+ (0.1 \times 8) + (0.05 \times 7) = 6.85$$

The best supplier is the one with the highest total weighted score, and this limited amount of information suggests that supplier C is the best – but this is clearly only a starting point for detailed analysis and discussion.

Reporting frequency

An important issue for supplier performance is the frequency of reporting. This does not just mean how often a report is prepared by the buyer (which is often virtually continuous) but also how often information is fed back to the supplier. A guideline says that buyers should be told immediately of any severe delivery problems, and get a daily summary of normal activities. These daily reports can be consolidated into weekly, monthly, quarterly and annual reviews. Managers then have to decided which reports should routinely be sent to suppliers. Often this feedback is done every month or quarter, with more formal face-to-face meetings at least annually. These formal meetings can review actual performance, monitor changes, discuss targets, identify potential improvements and so on. When a supplier's performance fails to meet an agreed standard, they should be told quickly, with special reports and meetings. As a matter of principle, any problems with poor supplier performance must be addressed as soon as they are recognized to avoid escalating financial and operational problems.

Uses of measurement data

Buyers can use the data gathered from its measurement system in a number of ways. To start with, they can identify suppliers that are not meeting performing targets, and can highlight areas that need improvement. Then remedial action can be taken to raise performance back to acceptable levels, or to find new suppliers. At the other 'end of the scale, measurement systems also identify superior performance, and helps identify preferred suppliers and those that will qualify for longer-term partnerships.

Another key task of measurement data is that it helps with supply base rationalization, as it identifies the worst performing suppliers, and those that are not improving. These are likely to be removed from the supply base, while better performers get more business. So supplier performance data also helps with setting future purchase volumes, and reinforces the incentive for suppliers to meet or exceed buyers' expectations.

Supplier measurement techniques

All supplier measurement systems have elements of subjectivity that rely on management opinion. Even the most automated system needs subjective decisions about the data to analyse, measures to use, performance categories to include, weight given to different categories, frequency of reporting, how to use the performance data and so on. We have already seen how scoring models – along with other analyses – can add a quantitative view of qualitative data. Now we mention three common techniques for evaluating supplier performance, each of which differs in its ease of use, level of subjectivity, required resources and implementation cost. Figure 9.2 shows a comparison of the advantages and disadvantages of the three techniques.

1 **Categorical technique.** A categorical approach takes some aspect of performance, say lead time, and defines a set of categories for performance. For instance, a typical

FIGURE 9.2

Comparison of supplier measurement and evaluation systems

System	Advantages	Disadvantages	Users
Categorical	Easy to implement Needs minimal data Different people contribute Good for firms with limited resources Low cost	Least reliable Less frequent evaluations Most subjective Usually manual	Smaller firms Firms that are developing a new evaluation system
Scoring model	Flexibility Gives supplier ranking Moderate costs Quantitative and qualitative factors combined into a single system	Subjective inputs Depends on the criteria and weights Tends to focus on a few criteria	Most firms
Cost-based	Gives a total cost approach Specific areas of non-performance identified Objective supplier ranking Greatest potential for long-range improvement	Based on accounting conventions Most complex Higher costs	Larger firms Firms with a large supply base

rating describes performance as excellent, good, fair or poor and buyers decide which category a supplier fits into. This is the easiest measurement system, and it is also the most subjective. It is easy to use and relatively inexpensive, so is common in even the smallest organizations.

The drawbacks of categorical techniques are that they give only a limited structure to measures, and they do not really give a clear view of performance. They rely on some subjective input, so tend to be slower than automated methods, with less frequent reporting. The reliability of the categorical method is also the lowest of the three techniques, and there is often significant variance in the subjective ratings.

2 **Scoring model.** This technique overcomes some of the subjectivity of the categorical technique by calculating a weighted score for different performance categories. This technique is more reliable than categorical techniques, and it still has moderate implementation costs. It is also flexible as buyers can change both the categories included and the weights assigned to each. These two factors are the key elements of scoring models, and although they are subjective decisions, managers can get a consensus through careful planning and involvement of different people. Ideally, a distinct meaning should be attached to each score, along the lines of, 'A lead time between 1 and 2 weeks, means a score of 2.'

Figure 9.3 gives a sample scoring model based on a 5-point scale, where 5 represents the best possible performance. In practice, more complicated scales are generally used.

3 **Cost-based techniques.** The most thorough and least subjective of the three techniques is based on costs. This approach seeks to find the total cost of doing business with a supplier, recognizing that the lowest purchase price is not always the lowest total cost of acquisition. In particular, this technique collects data from the buying firm's information system and then analyses the total costs, especially the

Performance category	Weight	Score*	Weighted score
Delivery			
On time	0.10	4	0.4
Quantity	0.10	3	0.3
Quality			
Inbound shipment quality	0.25	4	1.0
Quality improvement	0.10	4	0.4
Cost competitiveness			
Comparison with other suppliers	0.15	2	0.3
Cost-reduction ideas submitted	0.10	3	0.3
Service factors			
Problem resolution ability	0.05	4	0.20
Technical ability	0.05	5	0.25
Corrective action response	0.05	3	0.15
New-product development support	0.05	5	0.25
Total rating	1.00		3.55

*1 = Poor, 3 = Average, 5 = Excellent

FIGURE 9.3

Example of a scoring model for supplier evaluation

extra costs that occur whenever a supplier fails to perform as expected. The usual format for these measures is based on a supplier performance index (SPI).

$$SPI = \frac{\text{total purchase costs} + \text{non-performance cost}}{\text{total purchase costs}}$$

This index has a value of 1.0 when everything goes well, and increases when problems appear. Then the total cost is found by multiplying the price paid for each item and multiplying by this index. Figure 9.4 illustrates this calculation by comparing the total cost of ownership for three suppliers of two items (Monczka and Trecha, 1988). Notice that the lowest-price supplier, BC Techtronics, is not the lowest-total-cost supplier when the costs of non-performance are included.

It can be difficult to calculate the SPI, and Figure 9.5 suggests the type of approach. This summarizes the total number of times something goes wrong – described as the

---

FIGURE 9.4

Example of a cost-based supplier comparison

Commodity: Integrated circuit

Part number	Supplier	Unit price	SPI	Total cost
04279884	Advanced Systems	$3.12	1.20	$3.74*
	BC Techtronics	$3.01	1.45	$4.36
	Micro Circuit	$3.10	1.30	$4.03
04341998	Advanced Systems	$5.75	1.20	$6.90*
	BC Techtronics	$5.40	1.45	$7.83
	Micro Circuit	$5.55	1.30	$7.21

* Lowest total cost for item (total cost = unit price × SPI).

FIGURE 9.5

Example of a supplier performance report

Supplier: Advanced Systems
Commodity: Integrated circuit
Total part numbers in commodity: 2
A. Total purchase dollars this quarter: $5,231.67

Non-performance costs

Event	Number of occurrences	Average cost per occurrence	Extended cost
Late delivery	5	$150	$750
Return to supplier	2	$45	$90
Scrap labour costs	3	$30	$90
Material rework cost	1	$100	$100
B. Total non-performance costs			$1,030
C. Purchase + non-performance cost		(Line A + B)	$6,261.67
D. Supplier performance index		(Line C/A)	1.20

number of non-performance occurrences – and the cost of each, as identified by the buyer. Then lines C and D give the figures needed to calculate the SPI.

The costs of non-performance may be difficult to find, as traditional cost accounting does not separate such data. The average cost of a late delivery may vary widely, depending on its impact on customers, potential lost sales, rescheduling operations, shutdown costs, penalties, revized stock levels and so on. Organizations get around this difficulty by assigning an agreed standard charge. This is useful for comparisons, but does not necessarily reflect the true cost of a late delivery. However, if we assign notional costs to certain events, we can also assign them for other qualitative factors to give a fuller picture of supplier performance. For example, buyers might assign a notional cost when a supplier's administrative system becomes dated, or their internet site is not very good.

Another problem is that the SPI sometimes gives an incomplete or misleading picture. For example, imagine a supplier that delivers €100,000 of material, with one late delivery charged at €5,000. The supplier has an SPI of (100,000 + 5,000) / 100,000, or 1.05. Now imagine a second supplier that delivers only €30,000 of material and has one late delivery also charged at €5,000. This supplier has an SPI of (30,000 + 5,000) / 30,000, or 1.17. The first supplier is considered much more favourably than the second, even though both suppliers breached requirements to the same extent – and you might even consider the second supplier as better as their

WORKED EXAMPLE

A company has information for three suppliers – A, B and C – for one quarter. The average cost of a delivery is €2,500, and each company incurred a single charge for late delivery of €4,000.

	SUPPLIER A	SUPPLIER B	SUPPLIER C
Deliveries in quarter	20 lots @ €500 each	20 lots @ €1,000 each	20 lots @ €10,000
Total value of shipments	€10,000	€20,000	€200,000
Average delivery cost	€500	€1,000	€10,000
Non-conformance charges	Late delivery €4,000	Late delivery €4,000	Late delivery €4,000
SPI for the quarter	(10,000 + 4,000)/ 10,000 = 1.40	(20,000 + 4,000)/ 20,000 = 1.20	(200,000 + 4,000) / 200,000 = 1.02
Average cost of a delivery from all suppliers	€2,500	€2,500	€2,500
Q calculation	500/2,500 = 0.2	1,000/2,500 = 0.4	10,000/2,500 = 4

Notice that the SPI values for the three suppliers are all different, even though each had the same non-conformance charges. In particular, supplier C has the highest value deliveries, and consequently the lowest SPI. The basic SPI values can be adjusted by including the factor Q to give:

$$\text{Adjusted SPI} = \frac{\text{Cost of material} + \text{Non-conformance costs} \times Q}{\text{Cost of material}}$$

Then the revized SPIs give a fairer comparison:

- Supplier A: 10,000 + (4,000 × 0 .2) / 10,000 = 1.08
- Supplier B: 20,000 + (4,000 × 0 .4) / 20,000 = 1.08
- Supplier C: 200,000 + (4,000 × 4) / 200,000 = 1.08

delay affected a smaller value of materials. A way of preventing smaller suppliers being treated more severely is to use a normalization adjustment (Q), where:

$$Q = \frac{\text{average cost of a delivery of materials from an individual supplier}}{\text{average cost of a delivery of items from all suppliers}}$$

Multiplying non-conformance costs by this factor eliminates the bias in favour of the larger supplier.

LEARNING FROM PRACTICE

FedEx Corporation

FedEx is a global leader in package delivery and has built a reputation for reliable, on-time service. Throughout its history, FedEx has focussed on operational excellence and the ability to consistently pick up, sort and deliver packages on time to their final destination. In recent years, the package delivery industry has become highly competitive as new companies have entered the market. Emails have introduced a different kind of competition as people simply attach files to electronic messages instead of sending paper copies.

FedEx purchases billions of dollars of goods and services annually, making supply management a major value-adding activity. Its choice of suppliers greatly affects costs and the company's ability to serve its customers. For instance, a supplier of aircraft spare parts that misses a delivery affects FedEx's ability to keep its planes flying safely and on time. To help with its supplier management, the company has created a detailed scorecard to evaluate supplier performance. This scorecard establishes a level of uniformity among the diverse supply management groups at FedEx, as buyers maintain scorecards for the suppliers that they are responsible for. Then completed scorecards are put onto company databases, so that they can be reviewed and analysed.

Figure 9.6 gives an example of FedEx's supplier scorecard template. This allows buyers to choose the categories and sub-categories of performance factors to include and to adjust the weights given to each so that they reflect the unique needs of a purchase agreement. The system gives substantial flexibility, but there are constraints. For example, the performance category titled Diverse Supplier Development must be included in each evaluation. More specifically, each sub-category must be scored on a scale of zero to 5, and it is assigned an individual weight, with the scores for each category adding to 100. The score for each category is multiplied by the category weight, and all of these weighted scores are added to arrive at a performance level ranging from 0 to 500. Then FedEx describe suppliers as:

- ≤ 300   Needs special attention
- 300–349   Bronze standard
- 350–399   Silver standard
- 400–449   Gold standard
- 450–500   Platinum standard

A detailed user's manual gives guidance for completing the scorecard. For instance, scores for on-time delivery are typically based on:

Percentage of on-time deliveries	≤60	60–69	70–79	80–89	90–94	95–100
Score	0	1	2	3	4	5

The scores only give partial information, and buyers must talk with everyone involved to get a fuller picture of each supplier's performance. The results include some qualitative judgments, and suppliers may question parts of their score. This is considered a positive aspect of the system as it encourages communication between FedEx and its suppliers.

Source: Based on www.fedex.com

FIGURE 9.6 FedEx supplier scorecard

Supplier number	Eval. period: From
FSC code	To
Supplier name	Date:
Address	FedEx rep:
	Manager:
Representative	Department:

Category	Weight	Score	Total
1. On-time delivery performance 6 mths 3 mths 1 mth No. of on-time deliveries Total deliveries Pct. on-time (100–95% = 5, 94–90 = 4, 89–80 = 3, 79–70 = 2, 69–60 = 1, less than 60 = 0)	25		
2. Cycle time improvement (Yes/No)	5		

3. Quality
A. Discrepancy rate
   No. of problem receipts
   Total receipts
   Discrepancy rate (rec.)
   No. of problem invoices
   Total invoices
   Discrepancy rate (inv.)
   Total discrepancy rate
(0–1% = 5, 2–3 = 4, 4–6 = 3, 7–9 = 2, 10–12 = 1, greater than 12 = 0)
B. MTBF
C. Bad from stock
D. No. of customer/quality complaints
E. No. of warranty claims
F. Turn time on warranty claims
G. Certification (yes/no)
(Average score for quality)
	10		

4. Service A. Flexibility B. Customer service responsiveness C. Operational compatibility/coverage/accessibility D. Sales person product knowledge E. Sales person knowledge of FedEx F. Post sales support G. Technology upgrades/enhancements (Average score for service)	15		
5. Financial stability (measured by D&B)	5		
6. Cost A. Price competitiveness B. Cost trends C. Add-ons D. Frequency/value of cost-reduction ideas E. Supplier savings sharing F. Gratis service (no incremental costs) G. FedEx cost of quality (or benefit) (Average score for cost)	20		
7. Diverse supplier development (DSD) — contact DSD for scoring A. Direct reporting B. Indirect tier reporting (completed by DSD & Prime) C. Use of local suppliers (Average score for DSD)	10		
8. Optional or supplier/Product specific A. B. C. (Average score for optional)	10		
9. Total score	100		

Scoring scale: 5 = Excellent, 4 = Above average, 3 = Average, 2 = Below average, 1 = Poor, 0 = Unacceptable
Performance level: 500–450 = Platinum, 449–400 = Gold, 399–350 = Silver, 349–300 = Bronze, <300

CREATING A MANAGEABLE SUPPLY BASE

Supply base optimization
Ensures that only the most capable, best performing suppliers are maintained in the supply base.

Supply base rationalization
Removes those suppliers that are unwilling or incapable of achieving specified performance objectives.

The measurement of supplier performance helps with a key question for supplier management, which asks about the optimal number of suppliers that an organization should maintain. This is the basis of **supply base optimization,** which is the continuous process that maintains the supply base efficiently. People use this term in different ways, but essentially it sets a best number of suppliers, selects this number of the best performing suppliers and then develops the remainder to give continuing improvements. The removal of worse performing suppliers is referred to as **supply base rationalization.**

Current trends are towards fewer suppliers who deliver more materials with long-term arrangements, so rationalization generally looks to remove the weakest and smallest suppliers. However, this is not always the best answer, and the key to optimization is to determine the best number of suppliers. For instance, you can imagine a European fashion store that buys most of its garments from manufacturers in the Far East, but the extended supply chains increase variability in lead time and general levels of risk. To overcome these effects, the store uses other European suppliers that can react quickly to changing demand; when a delivery is delayed from, say, Bangladesh, an Italian supplier steps in to meet demand at short notice. The net result is more suppliers – but more efficient logistics.

Advantages of an optimized supply base

With supply base optimization a firm maintains and develops the best suppliers, which by definition are those that add most value to the relationship. Removing the worst performers gives real improvements in cost, quality, delivery, available technology, information flows and every other measure. The following list give some idea of the associated benefits.

Easier administration. With fewer suppliers, buyers can focus on developing closer relationships with a smaller core of remaining ones. Administrative tasks include contacting suppliers about product design, discussing material specifications, agreeing quality and other requirements, negotiating terms and conditions, visiting and evaluating supplier operations, providing feedback on performance, working to overcome problems, passing on information about changing requirements, transmitting material releases and a host of other activities. These all have associated costs, time and effort – so the administrative overheads of maintaining a small supply base of the best, say, 50 suppliers is far less than the cost of a diverse group of, say, 1,000. The interactions with better suppliers are more likely to focus on performance improvement and adding value rather than solving problems that have arisen.

Use of full-service suppliers. With fewer suppliers, those remaining are generally larger firms that can offer a broad range of value-adding services. In the same way that airlines are described as 'budget' or 'full service' we can describe these firms that offer a range of opportunities as 'full-service suppliers'. They typically offer services for research and development, design, testing, production, information processing, inventory management, financial control transport and so on. In the extreme a supplier can do complete design and build work, with the buyer outsourcing manufacturing.

The motor industry gives many examples of full-service suppliers. For example, all vehicles have extensive electrical wiring systems. Traditionally, car makers designed each individual wiring harness internally and sent the design specifications to suppliers for a competitive bidding process. Then it was common for a company to have 10 different suppliers delivering parts of a wiring system for a single vehicle. Supply base optimization moved to a single supplier who was contracted to design and produce the complete wiring system. Because of the full-service supplier's expertise, they can design the wiring system at the same time as the main car design, reduce concept-to-customer development time, give lower costs, guarantee quality and give a more reliable service.

Reduction of risk. The reason why organizations traditionally preferred more suppliers was to spread the risks and reduce the chance of any damaging failure. If one supplier hit financial problems then buyers could switch orders to another. Here risk is the chance of any unexpected event in the supply chains that might disrupt material deliveries. This includes financial problems at a supplier, poor quality, late deliveries, accidents, natural disasters, industrial action and so on (Waters, 2007). Multiple sourcing allows other suppliers to take the place of one that hits troubles, so it seems illogical to say that using fewer suppliers can actually reduce risk to the supply base. But the argument is that by carefully selecting a few suppliers, and developing close working relationships with them, supply risk can actually decrease. Having more suppliers increases the amount of variability – fewer suppliers give better average performance and consistency.

Lower total cost. Procurement managers have to consider all factors and choose an optimal number of suppliers. Their choice depends on individual circumstances, but opinions have evolved in recent years. In particular, buyers recognized that with more suppliers:

- Acquisition costs increase because of duplicated orders to different suppliers, repeated administration, variation in products, variable quality, different delivery procedures, little incentive for suppliers to improve products or deliveries, etc.

- Supply costs increase because of smaller orders given to each supplier, short-term purchase contracts, smaller deliveries, repeated administrative tasks, etc. – and these were passed on in higher prices

The conclusion, then, is that economies of scale mean that the lowest production, distribution and operating costs come when a few suppliers receive bigger orders.

Risks of maintaining fewer suppliers

Not even the most pessimistic buyer would argue in favour of multiple suppliers for every item they purchase. When they choose the number of suppliers, buyers generally want to maintain a limited number of qualified suppliers, believing that buying from a range of suppliers promotes a healthy level of competition. However, other managers believe that close relationships with a single source delivers better cost and quality over the life of a product.

Managers who prefer working with more suppliers, point out the inherent risks of reducing the supply base. The following list illustrates the most significant of these.

Supplier dependency. Some managers fear that a supplier can become too dependent on a single buyer. When a buyer combines its total purchases for an item with a single supplier, then large suppliers can absorb the work. But smaller suppliers have limited capacity and they may need to eliminate some existing customers to meet the requirements of the larger customer. Then the supplier may become too dependent on a single buyer for its financial well-being. If, for some reason, the buyer no longer wants a particular item, or changes mean that the supplier cannot meet new requirements, then the overly dependent supplier's future must be in doubt. It is not in the long-term interests of customers to see a healthy supplier go out of business, so questions of their financial viability are important.

Absence of competition. When all buyers in a market reduce their supply base, there is an inevitable reduction in the number of suppliers serving the market. Hopefully, it is the weakest suppliers who leave and move into other areas where they can be more successful. But the remaining market has fewer suppliers and is – by definition – less competitive. Then buyers lose the benefits of a competitive marketplace, and suppliers gain in power and may take advantage of their position to unduly raise prices and become complacent about performance. The more difficult and expensive it is to change suppliers, the more likely this is to happen. On the other hand, managers might argue that careful supplier selection and the use of equitable contracts should stop suppliers taking advantage of such circumstances.

Supply disruption. As we mentioned before, one of the problems with single sourcing is the increased risk of supply disruption. There are many examples of this (Waters, 2007) such as the 1999 earthquake in Taiwan that caused computer chip plants to shut down for several days, with output reduced for several weeks. Customers reacted by hoarding chips and reducing their production of finished goods, while suppliers not affected by the quake increased their prices. The resulting disruptions caused a ripple throughout the electronics industry (Robinson, 1999). Likewise, fires, acts of nature, production problems, poor quality, industrial action – or a whole host of other factors can disrupt the smooth flow of materials. Buyers can minimize risk by sourcing from several suppliers – or by using a single supplier with multiple production facilities. For example, Dell Computers use multiple sourcing from manufactures in Asia for key components, and if supply from one facility is disrupted, Dell can quickly shift its sourcing to another facility from the same supplier or to a different supplier (Friedman, 2006).

Another way of reducing the risk of supply disruption is to use suppliers with multiple capabilities—the practice of cross-sourcing. This means that for each item there is a primary supplier and a back-up secondary one, which is the primary supplier of other items. When problems occur with a primary supplier the secondary supplier takes over.

Overaggressive supply reduction. Buyers can move too aggressively when rationalizing the supply base, and try to work with too few suppliers. When this happens, the remaining suppliers may not have enough capacity to meet purchase requirements, or to respond to changing conditions and demands. For example, a leading manufacturer of hand tools had reduced the number of suppliers of rechargeable nickel-cadmium batteries that were used in its products. But when the manufacturer introduced a new range of products, the battery suppliers did not have enough capacity to meet the new demands. The hand-tool manufacturer had to quickly qualify new sources and expand its supply base.

Formal approaches to supply base rationalization

Having decided to optimize – or realistically rationalize – the supply base, there are several possible approaches, with Bhote (1989) describing a framework with three primary elements:

1 Initial reduction of current suppliers.

2 Select finalist suppliers.

3 Select partnership suppliers.

Within this framework, there are several common approaches to rationalizing the supply base.

Eighty-twenty rule. This is based on Pareto's law, which in this context says that 80 per cent of problems come from 20 per cent of suppliers, in the way that 80 per cent of problems with quality typically come from 20 per cent of suppliers. These poorly performing suppliers should be the first to consider for elimination. In the same way, 80 per cent of purchases come from 20 per cent of core suppliers, so the other suppliers deliver relatively few products and should be considered for elimination. Quality and order size are only two possible criteria for considering supplier elimination, and other factors include the usual range of reliability problems, lead time, cost, quality and so on.

Organizations often use the eighty-twenty rule when they want a rapid reduction in the number of suppliers. But it has the disadvantage of identifying suppliers who are very capable, but fail because they only receive small orders. The best suppliers need not be the ones that receive the largest orders – and the worst suppliers are not necessarily the ones that fail some arbitrary measure.

'Improve or else' approach. This gives all suppliers, regardless of their performance history, a chance to remain in the supply base. It tells them that they have a specified period in which to meet new performance requirements – and that those which fall short of expectations may soon be removed from the supply base. This dramatic approach can force rapid performance improvements, but it can also be a heavy-handed way of dealing with suppliers. There are notorious examples of its effects, such as the decree by General Motors in 1992 that all suppliers should reduce their prices by 3 to 22 per cent or risk losing their existing contracts (Greenwald, 1992).

Triage approach. This evaluates the performance of suppliers and puts each into one of three categories. The first category, and generally the largest, contains suppliers that are marginal performers or incapable of meeting performance requirements. Buyers target these suppliers for immediate removal from the supply base. The second category contains suppliers that do not consistently meet all requirements, but they seem capable of improvement. The most promising of these are chosen for supplier assistance and development. The third category contains the high-quality, capable suppliers that perform very well and do not need further improvement. These suppliers are candidates for more collaborative relationships, which typically offer long-term contracts in return for continuous improvement. Figure 9.7 illustrates one company's triage approach to supplier reduction. This company describes the three categories as unacceptable performers, suppliers that meet minimum requirements but are not world class and world-class performers worthy of closer relationships.

Competency staircase approach. This requires suppliers to successfully navigate a succession of performance hurdles in order to remain in the supply base. The first hurdle is typically a basic quality standard; the second might be an ability to meet product technical specifications; then subsequent hurdles might include sustained production competence, delivery capability, willingness to share information, capacity, lead time, physical proximity to the buyer and so on. Each hurdle eliminates some suppliers, and brings the remaining ones a step closer to the ultimate goal of remaining in the buyer's supply base.

In practice, there is a variety of approaches to supply base rationalization and we can only mention a sample of these. An organization need not use these methods in

FIGURE 9.7

Supply base optimization
and development

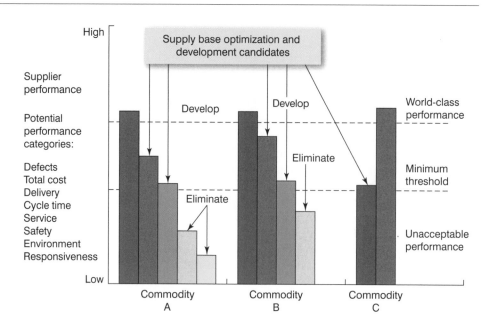

isolation, but it can combine several into an overall approach. Remember that it does not have to limit its evaluation to suppliers currently in the supply base, but it should always remain open to the possibility of adding new suppliers when this makes good business sense.

Supply base optimization – and rationalization – is a critical first step in effective supply management. It is difficult to manage a large number of suppliers as efficiently as a small core group. This is the reason why almost half of companies responding to a US survey in 2000 had recently reduced their supply base by 20 per cent, and almost 15 per cent of companies reduced their supply base by 20–60 per cent (Reese, 2000).

LEARNING FROM PRACTICE

McDonald's

In 2006 McDonald's wanted to improve supplier performance, so they introduced a supplier relationship management (SRM) process for their global purchases of technology. This 'requires dedicated supply managers, effective processes to create standardized best practices and tools to track and evaluate the results'. Their process started with effective performance measurement and then made decisions about suppliers based on these measures. Their experience suggests four prime measures that organizations should consider in their supplier performance management systems.

1   Day-to-day tactical measures such as quality, service, responsiveness and delivery performance.

2   Measures of contract management, making sure that previously agreed contractual arrangements are followed.

3   Measures of financial management, including checks on invoices and payments to track deliveries and payments.

4   Buyer-supplier relationship and the level of two-way communication between the parties.

Source: Forrest W. (2006) McDonald's applies SRM strategy to global technology buy, Purchasing, 135 (12), 16–17.

SUPPLIER DEVELOPMENT

Supplier development is generally considered to have started in Toyota, Nissan and Honda in the 1930s. Certainly by 1939 Toyota's Purchasing Rules discussed the need to treat suppliers as an integral part of the company, and to work together to improve their collective performance (Sako, 2004). The rest of the world was somewhat slow to take up supplier development (Lamming. 1993), but by 2003 the United Nations had produced its own guide that is designed to improve the skills, capacities and competitiveness of industrial purchasing (de Crombrugghe and Le Coq, 2003). This describes supplier development, which consists of all the activities done by a buyer to improve a supplier's performance.

Organizations can perform a variety of activities to improve supplier performance, including sharing technology, providing incentives for better performance, encouraging competition among suppliers, providing necessary capital, involving suppliers in product design, training, joint process improvement teams and so on. Perhaps the most challenging route to supplier development has staff from a buying company working directly in a supplier's operations. Not only must internal management be convinced that investing resources in an outside supplier's operation is worthwhile, but the supplier must also be convinced it is in its own best interests to accept the placement. Gaining a supplier's acceptance is particularly difficult, as they usually assume that buyers only want to find a way of translating all cost saving into lower prices. Even when there is a mutual understanding of the importance of supplier development, both parties still need to allocate the necessary resources.

> **Supplier development**
> Includes any activity undertaken by a buyer to improve a supplier's performance or capabilities to meet the buyer's short and long-term supply needs.

Process for supplier development

Figure 9.8 shows a generic procedure for initiating supplier development (Handfield *et al.*, 1998). Many organizations have successfully introduced the first four stages of this, but there has been less success with the last four stages.

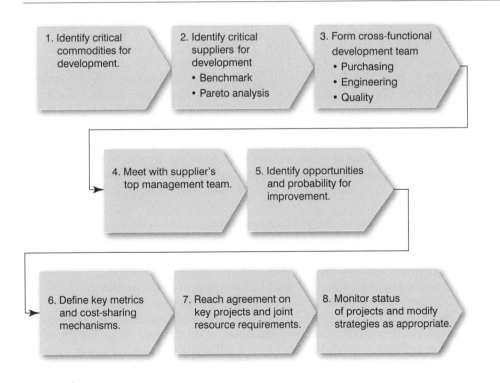

FIGURE 9.8

Process for implementing supplier development

1. Identify critical commodities for development.

2. Identify critical suppliers for development
   • Benchmark
   • Pareto analysis

3. Form cross-functional development team
   • Purchasing
   • Engineering
   • Quality

4. Meet with supplier's top management team.

5. Identify opportunities and probability for improvement.

6. Define key metrics and cost-sharing mechanisms.

7. Reach agreement on key projects and joint resource requirements.

8. Monitor status of projects and modify strategies as appropriate.

Step 1   Identify critical commodities for development

Not all organizations need to pursue supplier development. For instance, an organization's existing supplier selection processes may lead it to work with the best suppliers available, or its external purchases may only be a very small proportion to total costs. So supply managers must analyse their own circumstances to see whether they need to use supplier development at all. Specifically, they need to assess all suppliers' performance to identify specific items that need attention. For this they should ask the following questions, where frequent answer of 'yes' suggest a need for supplier development (Hahn *et al.*, 1990).

- Do purchased materials account for more than 50 per cent of product value?
- Is the supplier an existing or potential source of competitive advantage?
- Do you currently purchase, or do you plan to purchase, on the basis of total cost rather than initial purchase price?
- Can existing suppliers meet your competitive needs 5 years from now?
- Do you need suppliers to be more responsive to your needs?
- Are you willing and able to become more responsive to your suppliers' needs?
- Do you plan to treat suppliers as partners in your business?
- Do you plan to develop and maintain open and trusting relations with suppliers?

If the answers to such questions suggest that it is worth putting resources into supplier development, an executive committee should then decide where to focus the effort. For this they can look at the relative importance of all purchased materials, and define a portfolio of critical materials where supplier development will give tangible benefits.

Step 2   Identify critical suppliers for development

Having identified the items for which supplier development is beneficial, the next step is to identify those suppliers that should be targeted for development. The usual approach for this is based on a routine analysis of supplier performance, such as those suggested in the last section. For instance, Figure 9.7 illustrates one result of triage used to rank suppliers. Those failing to meet predetermined minimum performance standards are candidates for elimination from the supply base. But if one of these suppliers makes a unique and essential product – or there is some other factor that makes it difficult to replace – the supplier should be considered for development. At the other end of the spectrum are the best suppliers who are already performing well and they do not need any further development. In between these two are those suppliers that meet minimum requirements but do not give the best performance, and these are the most likely candidates for development.

Step 3   Form cross-functional development team

Firms cannot just approach suppliers and ask for improved performance, but first they have to have their own policies and procedures working properly. This needs a cross-functional consensus to support the development initiative. Procurement managers always emphasize that supply base improvement begins from within through a firm's own activities – so the buying company must have its own house in order before expecting commitment and co-operation from suppliers. The precise function of the development team is described by its charter, which the members must define and which gives details of how it will work and what it has to achieve.

Step 4   Meet with supplier's top management team

Once the development team's charter is established and an appropriate supplier has been identified for improvement, the team should meet the supplier's top management to discuss the programme. Their aim is to establish three building blocks:

- *Strategic alignment,* which requires an alignment between the firms of strategy, aims, operations, technology, communications and operations in general

- *Measurement,* requires an objective, accurate and timely assessment of the results wanted from the development programme, and progress towards these goals

- *Professionalism,* which can be demonstrated by approaching the supplier's top management with a solid and mutually beneficial business case for improvement. A professional approach by all parties helps to establish a positive tone, reinforce collaboration, foster two-way communication and develop mutual trust

Step 5   Identify opportunities and probability for improvement

At meetings with supplier's senior management, supply managers should discuss areas for improvement. In particular, they should take a long-term view of supply base development and agree on those areas that give greatest opportunities for improvement, and which will probably give the greatest returns. Bearing in mind the aim of supply chain management to deliver products through to final customers, these discussions are usually driven by final customer requirements and expectations.

Step 6   Define key metrics and cost-sharing mechanisms

Having identified general areas that have potential for improvement, the next step is to add details and define more specific development projects. This step defines projects, considers their feasibility, examines the ROI, assigns priorities and so on. The buyer and supplier jointly determine whether the opportunities are realistic and achievable, and for those projects that are beneficial they establish measures and improvement goals. Crucially, the buyer and seller must also agree on how to divide the costs and benefits from a project. A common arrangement shares rewards equally, but the actual calculations must take into account each party's investment and commitment.

Step 7   Reach agreement on key projects and joint resource requirements

After identifying the specific projects to pursue and the expected gains, each party must identify the resources needed to carry out the project and make the commitment to employ them. As usual, these resources can include a range of money, time, information, facilities systems and so on. The parties also have to agree the specific performance standards that will confirm the project's success, and show that these resources have been used efficiently. The best approach to this is not to define a single overall target, but a series of realistic and visible milestones that are reached over time. Agreements between the parties should specify the role of each in achieving these milestones, particularly which is responsible for each activity, and the manner and timing for deploying agreed resources.

Step 8   Monitor status of projects and modify strategies as appropriate

Assigning the resources for projects effectively implements them and starts the actions for achieving improvements. Then progress must be monitored to make sure that the project proceeds as expected. This needs an effective two-way exchange of information to maintain momentum, showing visible milestones and their

LEARNING FROM PRACTICE

Raytheon

Raytheon in a leader in the defence and aerospace industries, with 73,000 employees and an income of more than $23 billion. They appointed Shelley Stewart as a supply manager, and he introduced or expanded various initiatives, including:

- Introduction of a single process for strategic sourcing across all Raytheon businesses
- Company-wide deployment of a process for sourcing indirect materials using teams
- Application of Raytheon's Six Sigma quality initiative to the company's supplier development
- Company-wide adoption of the aerospace and defence industries' e-procurement exchange, Exostar, as well as FreeMarkets' reverse auction
- Creation of a leadership development programme

- Enhancement of the company's supplier diversity programmes

In keeping with Raytheon's corporate goals, Stewart's organization is applying Six Sigma quality approaches to the company's supplier development activities. He has also assembled a network of Raytheon Six Sigma champions to work directly with suppliers. The Raytheon process for supplier development has six steps:

1 Identify supplier candidates for projects.
2 Define objectives and resources.
3 Baseline the opportunities and rank.
4 Analyse selected opportunities.
5 Implement projects.
6 Document and realize improvements.

Source: Avery S. (2001) Linking supply chains saves Raytheon $400 million, Purchasing, 23 August; www.raytheon.com

achievement, describing progress and creating new or revised objectives based on actual progress. Details of the original project will generally be modified over time as things move on, perhaps changing the goals and milestones, using different resources, adjusting responsibilities, refocussing priorities and so on.

OVERCOMING THE BARRIERS TO SUPPLIER DEVELOPMENT

Not all supplier development projects are successful. Figure 9.9 shows the results of one study which suggests that significant benefits can be achieved (Krause, 1997), but there is no guarantee that such benefits are inevitable. On the contrary, there are often barriers and challenges that make it very difficult to get any benefits at all.

FIGURE 9.9

Benefits from supplier development programmes

Criteria	Before supplier development	After supplier development
Incoming defects	11.65%	5.45%
Percentage of on-time delivery	79.85%	91.02%
Cycle time (from order placement to receipt)	35.74 days	23.44 days
Percentage of orders received complete	85.47%	93.33%

Organizations can use a variety of methods to overcome such barriers, and these fall into three main categories:

Direct-involvement activities – a hands-on approach where firms send their own staff to assist at suppliers. Buyer's representatives are directly involved in supplier activities, correcting faults, identifying and solving problems and generally improving performance. For example, a buyer might assign a process engineers to the supplier's facility to assist in physically rearranging and rescheduling equipment to be more efficient.

Incentives and rewards – where buyers offer suppliers incentives to encourage improvements, largely through their own efforts. For example, a buyer might agree to increase future order volumes if the supplier can reduce its lead time within a specified period.

Warnings and penalties – when direct help and incentives do not work, buyers may threaten future sanctions unless a supplier's performance improves in a specified way. For example, a company might withhold future business from a supplier whose performance is deemed unacceptable or where there is a lack of improvement. Often the warnings are more subtle, and buyers may simply point out the mechanisms of a competitive market to pose a threat.

Organizations generally use some combination of these three methods to drive supplier improvement. The combination can be used to overcome most barriers, which generally fall into three categories:

- Buyer-specific barriers

- Buyer-supplier interface barriers

- Supplier-specific barriers

Buyer-specific barriers

A buying firm will not have any kind of supplier development programme unless senior management recognizes the need and the benefits it can bring. If supply managers have not already optimized their supply base, they are likely to be working with too many suppliers, and the volume of purchases from each make it difficult to justify the investment in development. This suggests the first type of barrier to overcome, which is inadequate supply base optimization, uncertainty in top-level support – and any of the following problems within a buying organization.

Purchase volumes do not justify the investment in development. The solution here starts with a review of the supply base to see if it is too big. Removing smaller suppliers will increase average order size, as well as giving economies of scale and scope. A more detailed study considers the benefits of single sourcing. Such arguments lead the Daewoo Corporation, for example, to use single-sourcing wherever possible, relying on two or more suppliers only when there are high levels of risk in the supply chain.

A different approach standardizes parts across several products, so that fewer items are needed, again increasing the average order size for the remaining ones. For example, IBM's Networking Hardware Division produces customized networking equipment and is constantly striving to increase its use of standardized parts. Currently, over 50 per cent of purchased components for major hardware projects contain unique items. When IBM staff believe that customized components give a market advantage, they will continue to use them. However, standardization remains an important way reducing the supply base and allowing supplier development.

There are no immediate benefits to the buyer. The solution is to look for a stream of continuing, small benefits rather than a single dramatic improvement – looking for continuous improvement rather than re-engineering. Varity Perkins, a manufacturer of diesel engines, recognized the benefits of this when its initial supplier development efforts seemed unsuccessful. This lowered expectations and dampened enthusiasm for development efforts, but managers soon realized that they were trying to accomplish too much in a short time. So the company focussed on a smaller group of suppliers and used continuous improvement to make a series of small gains. Over time the incremental improvements combined to give significant benefits and renewed interest in the development process.

An item is not important enough to justify the development effort. The solution is to take a longer-term view, and consider the accumulated benefits over time, which may be substantial. We learn from Total Quality Management that performance does not just depend on the most expensive items, but on every person, part and activity involved in its supply. Even the smallest item can help achieve major benefits.

Lack of executive support within the buying organization. Senior managers will naturally support supplier development when they become convinced that it will improve the firm's overall performance. So the solution here is to establish, evaluate and prove the benefits. A starting point is to calculate the proportion of costs that go to suppliers, and when the figure approaches 80 per cent, it is easy to convince them that an improvement can give significant benefits. For companies that spend less on materials, the argument is more difficult, but it can still be convincing. Proving a direct link between better supplier management and improved organizational performance needs purchasing managers to document, analyse and highlight the potential benefits. These are usually so clear that they should convince the internal sceptics.

Buyer-supplier interface barriers

Barriers to supplier development can also originate at the interface between the buyer and supplier, largely caused by problems in communication, alignment of organizational cultures, and trust. A reluctance to share sensitive information by either the buyer or supplier is generally seen as the most significant barriers of this type.

There are problems with buyer-suppliers relations. A common way of solving this problem is to appoint a 'supplier ombudsman', who is an independent third party who can investigate and sort-out problems and liaize between the two parties. For example, Honda often appoint a supplier ombudsmen who deals with the 'soft side' of relations – primarily human resource issues not usually associated with cost, quality or delivery. Because the supplier ombudsman is not directly involved in contract negotiations or fulfilment, suppliers are much more willing to talk openly with them. Then a supplier might approach the ombudsman with a problem that emerges from poor communication or misunderstanding, the ombudsman lets the customer know about the problems, and leads efforts to sort things out. It takes time to build trust between a buyer and a supplier, and an ombudsman can smooth interactions during the formative period.

Confidentiality inhibits information sharing on costs and operations. Organizations are understandably reluctant to share commercially sensitive information, particularly in highly competitive industries. But this is essential if buyers and suppliers are to work closely together. One way of overcoming this barrier is to use non-disclosure agreements, explicitly prohibiting a trading partner from passing on information to a third party, A variation on this theme is an exclusivity agreement, where a supplier provides a product to only one buyer and is, therefore, less likely to pass information inadvertently to a competitor. Such arrangements are especially useful for technologically advanced products that contribute to the buyer's competitiveness.

Supplier does not trust the buying organization. This is a fundamental problem, and the way to overcome it is to spell out every aspect of transactions in a formal contract. We mentioned Varity Perkins above, and they believe that the only way to discuss development with a supplier is with a properly written agreement between the parties. Some supply managers feel that this is excessive and they prefer to get started with an informal agreement – but Varity Perkins believe that a clear contract is needed right from the start, and especially with new suppliers. In one instance, it took the company 8 months to convince a supplier to consider a development project, largely because the supplier had worked on a similar project with another company that had failed to give any improvements. In this case, the problem of trust was compounded by Varity Perkins' previous arm's-length relationships with suppliers, exemplified by their frequent changes of suppliers to get the lowest prices. The company has moved to change this perception by implementing a new supply management philosophy that emphasizes collaboration with suppliers.

Organizational cultures are poorly aligned. Global operations mean that there can be major differences between business cultures. One solution is to adapt to local conditions, but there are few things more difficult than changing an ingrained culture, so this step can be very difficult. When setting up an assembly plant in South Carolina, BMW quickly realized it would have to change its approach to supplier development. In Germany the company uses a consulting approach, which involves analysing suppliers' processes and showing how they can be improved. This works well in mature relationships, where the supplier understands clearly what the customer wants. But suppliers in the USA did not have such mature relations with BMW and they often had difficulty understanding what was required in terms of quality and continuous improvement. The result was strained relationships, with BMW spending a lot of time explaining its expectations to suppliers. Eventually, they published a Supplier Partnership Manual that clearly described expectations and supplier responsibilities.

Suppliers do not give enough inducements to participate. There are essentially two ways of overcoming this barrier. The first is to have incentives explicitly included in the design of the improvement programme. For example, Laughfarsch assemble electronic control systems, and before they grew into a major corporation, suppliers had little incentive to join them in development programmes. So Laughfarsch emphasized that a supplier's parts could become designed into its products, making them an essential part of the delivered product. This formed a strong link with suppliers and increased the chance of future business.

An alternative approach gives direct financial incentives to participate. For example, Hyundai rates supplier performance from 1 (highest) to 4 (lowest). Class 1 suppliers receive cash immediately on their invoices; Class 2 suppliers receive payment in 30 days; Class 3 suppliers receive payment in 60 days; and Class 4 suppliers receive no new business. Because suppliers know how Hyundai evaluates their performance, they can take the steps necessary to ensure higher levels of performance.

Supplier-specific barriers

Suppliers can fail to recognize the benefits of supplier development, largely because they see improvement projects as an attempt to reduce prices. This means that their senior management may not be fully committed to the joint effort. This lack of commitment can mean that the programmes are so starved of resources that they never generate feasible ideas for improvement – or it can mean that the ideas developed are never implemented. Or a third type of failure implements the new practices, but gives no monitoring, control or follow-up to maintain the initiative, and the supplier's performance reverts back to its previous level.

Lack of commitment on the part of supplier's management. The way around this is to only consider development projects with suppliers that show commitment – and to question whether the others should stay in the supply base. For example, John Deere's managers say that they will not consider a development project with any supplier unless the supplier's management demonstrates full commitment to the process. To get this commitment, purchasing managers from the company arrange an initial meeting with a supplier's top local management, and they presents details of the scope and impact of project as well as the likely resources needed and benefits. When suppliers' senior management see the potential benefits and agree to participate in principle, a joint team adds details to the project, examining the operations, goals, resources, work to be done, responsibilities, costs, benefits, etc. John Deere typically allows the supplier to recover initial investment in the project, and then they share future savings, usually through a lower purchase price. An equitable sharing of benefits encourages suppliers to take part in development projects – and success stories from other suppliers demonstrate the viability of the development process.

Supplier's management agrees to improvements but fails to implement the proposals. A way to solve this problem is to have some kind of supplier champion who works for the supplier and is responsible for ensuring that they meet their agreements. For instance, JCI, a manufacturer of motor components, noticed that many of their suppliers failed to implement procedures that ensured they delivered the qualities required by JCI's own customers. To overcome this, JCI initiated a Supplier Champions Programme, which finds exactly what suppliers need to do to implement an improvement project, and they make sure that all the necessary resources are available. The programme also designates a Supplier Champion, who is a key supplier employee who understands JCI's expectations and ensures that actions identified in the supplier's operations are actually performed.

Supplier lacks resources to implement solutions. Overcoming this barrier generally needs direct support. In other words, the purchaser supplies the resources needed, either accepting the costs as part of its operating costs, or else somehow arranging for repayment and compensation. For example, Honda has invested a significant amount of resources in its supplier support infrastructure, and can provide resources when needed. When a small supplier did not have the capacity to keep up with requested volume, its product quality declined. Honda stationed four of its staff at the supplier for 10 months at no charge, with additional services offered when they were needed. As a result, the supplier improved its performance and now is a well-established supplier.

Suppliers are not convinced that development will give them benefits. The solution to this is to give suppliers detailed information about operations and performance. Varity Perkins used to send a quarterly report to suppliers summarizing their quality, delivery and price performance. The company did not actually use the results, so suppliers did not take them seriously. Then Varity Perkins revamped their supplier evaluation system to show the impact of supplier performance on their operations and highlight areas for improvement. Since then on-time delivery has improved to 90 per cent and the measurement system has become the foundation for the company's supplier development programme.

Supplier lacks employee skills to implement solutions. Many firms, particularly smaller ones, simply lack the internal skills needed to implement improvement ideas. For example, if a project suggests a new approach to product quality, a small company may not have the internal skills to introduce it. But a large buyer can invest in supplier training centres and arrange the necessary training. When Ford first introduced Total Quality Management, it trained tens of thousands of its suppliers' staff. In the same way, JCI and Hyundai established training centres for internal staff, suppliers and customers.

An alternative solution has a buyer providing staff who are already trained. For example, Hyundai recognizes that small suppliers cannot consistently recruit and retain highly skilled engineers and other critical employees, so it selects engineers from its own operations to spend time at suppliers' facilities. The engineers are co-located with their supplier counterparts, doing a range of work that passes on their knowledge.

Supplier lacks required information system. This used to be a more pressing problem, but technology has made sophisticated information systems available to even the smallest company. A more serious issue is getting compatibility between systems in different organizations, or different parts of the same organization. This can need substantial investment in IT support. For example, NCR manufacture banking machines, and an important focus of their supplier development programme is to get its suppliers to invest in compatible EDI systems – and they offer support to suppliers that do not have sufficient resources of their own.

Lessons learned from supplier development

Many of the barriers to supplier development are interrelated, and when a company works toward solving one problem, it also makes progress toward solving others. We can use this observation to focus on three themes for supplier development successes:

1　Managerial attitudes are a common and difficult barrier to overcome. Supplier development can only succeed when it has management support, and when this is absent there can be no progress. However, all problems have a solution, and organizations can take steps to get positive management support. This is often as simple as education – showing that the projects give real savings that are readily achievable, and that they do not drain resources that could be better used elsewhere.

2　Ensuring a competitive advantage from procurement needs a strategic approach that aligns purchasing aims with broader business objectives. A strong procurement mission statement helps promote this strategic emphasis and alignment. For instance, a European component manufacturer has a procurement mission statement that says, 'We are committed to procure goods and services in a way that delivers our aims of becoming the most successful component business in the world.' The company pursues this mission through:

● Development of a high quality supplier base

● Obtaining the highest-quality, most cost-effective materials in a timely manner

● Establishing long-term relationships with suppliers that strive for continuous improvement in all areas

3 Supplier development depends on careful management of the relations between trading partners. Strengthening relationships between buyers and sellers develops mutual trust and understanding, thereby making the entire supply chain stronger and more competitive. Ideally, supplier development will reinforce the message that both buyers and suppliers have the same overall aim, which is a successful trading relationship that leads to final customer satisfaction.

Pursuing supplier development is neither quick nor easy. It relies on co-operation, but suppliers are sometimes not willing to accept outside help, either because they do not see the benefits of improving their performance, or else because they do not want to accept outside help. Successful development needs vision, commitment, open communication and equitable sharing of costs and benefits. The long-term objective is to transform the supply base in such a way that continuous improvement becomes an integral part of each supplier's culture. Such joint accomplishments are achieved over time, and only by those firms that are patient and tenacious enough to make supplier development an important part of their management processes.

LEARNING FROM PRACTICE

Choudray, Larisot Freres

Choudray, Larisot Freres is the consulting arm of an international baking corporation, with headquarters in Paris. It specializes in giving advice to companies and governments on how to implement supplier development programmes. For this, they have developed a list of activities that give practical help with supplier development, and which are used by the most successful organizations. For example, they found that supplier training was the most frequently used tool, and this had most impact on a project's success. The following set of activities for improvement, listed in order of popularity, is based on findings of the US Air Force.

1 Supplier training, typically arranged by a major customer.

2 Supplier performance measurement and rating.

3 Making customer technical expertise available to suppliers.

4 Integrated customer and supplier teams to solve problems and improve performance.

5 Supplier focus groups and suggestion programmes.

6 Supplier continuous improvement programmes.

7 Use of financial incentives, such as volume discounts in prices.

8 Structured methodology for problem solving.

9 Compatible and integrated technology.

10 Development of a supplier's capability prior to outsourcing.

Source: Based on Larisot J. (2009) Supplier development, presentation to IMF, Paris; Editorial (1999) Air Force pushes its supplier development programme forward, Purchasing, 6 May, 1999, pp 34–37.

CHAPTER REVIEW

- The last chapters discussed the evaluation of supplier before their selection; this chapter discussed the continuing performance of suppliers who are in the supply base. This topic is described as supplier management and development

- Supplier management and development takes the view that buyers no longer simply buy materials, but they manage supplier relationships

- Supplier management includes an array of actions to manage and improve the performance of the supply base. This means that it must include measures of performance. There are many possible measures of performance, and different analyses

- Performance measurement is an important element of supply base optimization. Here optimization means using the right number of the best suppliers; rationalization means removing weaker firms from the supply base. Several types of benefit emerge from an optimized supply base

- The current trend is to use fewer suppliers, so these have to be carefully selected and managed. Nonetheless, there are risks associated with reducing the supply base

- Supplier development describes all the activities done by a buyer to improve a supplier's performance. We described an eight step procedure for implementing a programme of supplier development. This starts by assessing the need for supplier development and ends with its implementation

- Not all supplier development programmes work, primarily because there are barriers to effective implementation. We described these barriers as buyer-specific barriers, buyer-supplier interface barriers or supplier-specific barriers. These come in many forms, but there are a variety of ways of overcoming them and achieving the benefits of improved supplier performance

DISCUSSION QUESTIONS

1 Commentators say that few firms have adequate systems for measuring supplier performance. Why do you think this is?

2 What are the benefits of using a supplier measurement system?

3 What is a Supplier Performance Index? What are the benefits and problems of calculating and using an SPI?

4 Why do supplier management and development programmes lead to a smaller supply base?

5 What is an optimized supply base? What is the role of rationalization?

6 Why might buyers use multiple suppliers for an item?

7 What is a full-service supplier? What would you expect them to do, and what are the benefits of using full-service suppliers?

8 Many companies use websites to publish performance information. What are the benefits of this to both buyers and suppliers?

9 Review the different types of supplier development and support that a firm can offer. Which are the most common?

10 How would you introduce supplier development?

11 Purchasing manager often say, 'We shouldn't have to spend money on supplier development – we are not in business to train suppliers and do their job for them.' How would you respond to such a statement?

12 What do you think is the most difficult barrier to supplier development to overcome?

13 A senior executive in the motor industry once said that, 'Only about one in five supplier development efforts are 100 per cent successful.' What do you think makes successful supplier development so difficult?

REFERENCES

Bhote K. R. (1989) Strategic supply management: a blueprint for revitalizing the manufacturer-supplier partnership, New York: AMACOM.

de Crombrugghe A. and Le Coq G. (2003) Guide to supplier development, United Nations Industrial Development Organization, Vienna.

Friedman T. L. (2006) The world is flat, Release 2.0, Farrar, New York: Straus and Giroux.

Greenwald J. (1992) What went wrong? Everything at once, Time, November 9, and website at www.time.com

Hahn C. K., Watts C. A. and Kim K. Y. (1990) The supplier development program: a conceptual model, *International Journal of Purchasing and Materials Management*, 26(2): 2–7.

Handfield R., Krause, D., Scannell T. and Monczka R. (1998) An empirical investigation of supplier development: reactive and strategic processes, *Journal of Operations Management*, 17(1): 39–58.

Krause D. R. (1997) Supplier development: current practices and outcomes, *International Journal of Purchasing and Material Management*, 33(2): 12–19.

Lamming R. (1993) Beyond partnership: strategies for innovation and lean supply, London: Prentice Hall.

Minahan T. and Vigoroso M. (2002) The supplier performance measurement benchmarking report, and website at www.aberdeen.com

Monczka R. M. and Trecha S. J. (1988) Cost-based supplier performance evaluation, *Journal of Purchasing and Materials Management*, Spring, pp 1–4.

Reese A. (2000) E-procurement takes on the untamed supply chain, iSource, November.

Robinson S. (1999) Taiwan's chip plants left idle by earthquake, New York Times, September 22.

Sako M. (2004) Supplier development at Honda, Nissan and Toyota: comparative case studies of organizational capability enhancement, Industrial and Corporate Change, 13(2): 281–308.

Waters D. (2007) Supply chain risk management, London: Kogan Page.

Waters D (2009) Supply chain management (2nd edition), Basingstoke, Hampshire: Palgrave Macmillan.

FURTHER READING

Bolstorff P. and Rosenbaum R. (2007) Supply chain excellence: a handbook for dramatic improvement using the SCOR model (2nd edition), New York: AMACOM.

Davenport T. H. and Harris J. G. (2007) Competing on analytics: the new science of winning, Boston, MA: Harvard Business School Press.

Dunn S. C. and Young R. R. (2004) Supplier assistance within supplier development initiatives, *Journal of Supply Chain Management*, 40(3): 19–29.

Forker L. B., Ruch W. A. and Hershauer J. C. (1999) Examining supplier improvement efforts from both sides, *Journal of Supply Chain Management*, 35(3): 40–50.

Handfield R. B., Krause D. R., Scannell T. V. and Monczka R. M. (2000) Avoid the pitfalls in supplier development, Sloan Management Review, 41(2): 37–49.

Hartley J. and Jones G. (1997) Process oriented supplier development: building the capability for change, *International Journal of Purchasing and Materials Management*, 33(3): 24–29.

Humphreys P. K., Li W. L. and Chan L. Y. (2004) The impact of supplier development on buyer-supplier performance, Omega: *The International Journal of Management Science*, 32(2): 131–143.

Krause D. R. and Ellram L. M. (1997) Success factors in supplier development, *International Journal of Physical Distribution and Logistics Management*, 27(1): 39–52.

Krause D. R., Handfield R. B. and Tyler B. B. (2007) The relationship between supplier development, commitment, social capital accumulation and performance improvement, *Journal of Operations Management*, 25(2): 528–545.

Krause D. R. and Scannell T. V. (2002) Supplier development practices: product and service based industry comparisons, *Journal of Supply Chain Management*, 38(2): 13–22.

Li W.-L., Humphreys P., Chan L. Y. and Kumaraswamy M. (2003) Predicting purchasing performance: the role of supplier development programs, *Journal of Materials Processing Technology*, 138(1–3): 243–249.

Liker J. K., and Choi T. Y. (2004) Building deep supplier relationships, Harvard Business Review, 83(1): 104–113.

Nelson D., Moody P. E. and Stegner J. R. (2005) The incredible payback: innovative solutions that deliver extraordinary results, New York: AMACOM.

Robitaille D. (2007) Managing supplier-related processes, Chico, CA: Paton Professional.

Rogers P. A. (2005) Optimizing supplier management and why co-dependency equals mutual success, *Journal of Facilities Management*, 4(1): 40–50.

Sánchez-Rodríguez C., Hemsworth, D. and Martínez-Lorente A. R. (2005) The effect of supplier development initiatives on purchasing performance: a structural model, Supply Chain Management, 10(3–4): 289–301.

Teague P. E. (2007) How to improve supplier performance, Purchasing, 136(4): 31–32.

Theodorakioglou Y., Gotzamani K. and Tsiolvas G. (2006) Supplier management and its relationship to buyers' quality management, Supply Chain Management, 11(2): 148–159.

Wagner S. M. (2006) Supplier development practices: an exploratory study, European Journal of Marketing, 40(5–6): 554–571.

CASE STUDY

Incellor Steel

Encellor Steel is a large producer of steel with plants in Eastern Europe and Asia. It recently decided to re-negotiate the energy supplies for one group of businesses, to see how new energy providers that had entered the market after deregulation compared with existing suppliers. Up to this point, each steel plant had a separate contract with a local energy provider.

A strategy development team included managers from operations, finance, property maintenance, engineering and purchasing. This team considered the group energy use, did background research, identified potential suppliers and sent an initial Request For Interest to a number of companies. They identified four potential suppliers, who were interviewed to discuss their proposals for reducing the company's cost. This included the current supplier (Company A) and three new suppliers.

Company A

Company A was the first company to respond, it submitted the best initial response and continued to improve it as the selection process moved forward. All of the information requested was provided promptly and in an organized way and was accompanied by relevant information about the company and its performance. Some elements of the offer were:

- A comprehensive energy analysis of the group with recommendations on how to improve energy efficiency

- A pricing schedule that depends on the group's energy usage

- A 'net 30 days' payment term with a 0.3 per cent discount if payment is made within 10 days

- Access to a diverse group of energy service companies

- The company's extensive experience with both the energy market and Incellor's operations

The existing contact person from Company A answered all of Incellor's questions and was very helpful throughout the process. During the meeting the prices for Incellor's smaller accounts were also discussed.

Company B

Company B had not initially been contacted, but they wrote to ask if they could receive the Request For Interest and be included. At first, it seemed doubtful that they would be competitive, but they actually gave one of the most impressive responses. They offered competitive pricing and a network that spans the area of Incellor's group operations. However, they are energy wholesalers and do not have any of their own electricity generation. While this is not a limiting factor, it did cause some concern. The company has some large accounts and a positive track record, but nothing that could really compete with the history that Incellor had developed with Company A.

Company B discussed the option for short-term fixed pricing (3 or 6 months) that could be adjusted to reflect the market for the remainder of the contract. And they discussed longer-term contracts such as 12 or 24 months, where their prices were lower than Company A's. There were also discussions about sharing the effects of changes in market price, even if Incellor agreed a fixed price.

Company B's representative was very knowledgeable and helpful throughout the sourcing process. The company seemed to understand the market, have innovative ideas and be prepared to work in new ways to ensure customer satisfaction.

Company C

Company C did not complete the Request For Interest but instead submitted the information they thought Incellor should have. They answered some of Incellor's questions, but sent a standard packet of information to supplement it.

Company C was competing on price, where its original submission was lowest, but it was unwilling to negotiate away from the original offer. This suggested that changes in energy market prices could remove their main advantage. Although Company C was a relatively small supplier, it was a member of a major international corporation that had a long history of successful energy supply. Their parent company had extensive generation capacity and could guarantee supply.

Two representatives from Company C visited Incellor to explain the benefits of choosing them. While both seemed knowledgeable, they appeared more interested in putting on a show than in answering any direct questions.

Company D

Company D was originally expected to be a leading contender, but its proposal was disappointing. While they were able to offer almost everything that Incellor wanted from an electric company, their prices were the highest. Their quotes were based on prevailing market prices, and uncertainty in short-term supply had caused these to rise to levels that Incellor would be unwilling to pay over the long term.

Company D did not really want to bid for Incellor's smaller accounts because they would be uneconomic.

They gave the impression that almost everything was negotiable, and even if Incellor did not offer them a contract now, they would like to develop a good relationship for possible future business.

Questions

- What would be the next steps in choosing a supplier? What specific information would you need about each company in the shortlist?

- With tahis limited amount of information, which supplier seems most likely to win a contract? What are the risks and benefits associated with this choice?

- After winning the contract, the company has to work with Incellor. How do you think that they should develop their working relationship?

- What factors would be important in assessing an energy supplier's performance?

CHAPTER 10
COST MANAGEMENT

LEARNING OBJECTIVES After reading this chapter you should be able to:

- Appreciate the role of cost management and pricing in procurement

- List factors that affect the price of an item

- Understand the approach of market-driven pricing and describe a number of different models

- Describe the idea of cost-based pricing and reverse price analysis

- Calculate a total cost of ownership

- Discuss collaborative approaches to cost management

- Describe the approach of value analysis

A STRUCTURED APPROACH TO COST REDUCTION

Reducing operating costs is an almost universal aim of managers, and paying less for the procurement of goods and services has become an attractive option to achieve this. It is still a largely untapped area for giving major improvements in financial performance. An underlying problem is that many firms do not design good purchasing strategies, and the result is a limited focus on the long term with few linkages to the business strategy. Sometimes this limited strategic view is caused by the purchasing department's lack of awareness or concern for broad company strategies; at other times, purchasing has simply not been included in the strategy development process. These are symptoms of senior management's continuing failure to recognize the strategic importance of procurement and its contribution to business strategy.

Adding value

The driving force behind global competition is to provide customer value. Here, value is defined as the ratio of benefit that a customer receives over the cost they pay.

$$\text{Value} = \frac{\text{Perceived benefits of an item}}{\text{Price paid}}$$

Value
Ratio of perceived benefits to price paid for an item.

The problem with this equation is that the benefits are largely qualitative with no simple measures – for instance, how could you measure the benefit of buying a theatre ticket? Nonetheless, purchasing clearly has a major impact on the value added by materials entering an organization. This impact appears in their acquisition of materials that add more value, and their ability to pay less for these. To put it simply, purchasing affects the price paid for an item, hence the perceived value to customers of the firm's products, then customer satisfaction with the product – and finally to competitive position and business performance.

Here we concentrate on purchasing's role in setting the price of an item, where their fundamental aim is to pay a fair and reasonable amount. In essence, they can do a detailed analysis of costs incurred by a supplier, and compare this with the price it charges. This seems simple, but is actually difficult for most buyers as they need commercially sensitive information. An alternative is to simply check the prevailing price asked by competing firms in a free market. This brings its own difficulties, but it suggests that there are two approach, which we can characterize as cost analysis and price analysis.

Cost analysis
Considers each individual element of cost (material, wages, energy, overheads, profit, etc.) that together add up to the final price.

Price analysis focusses on a seller's price with no consideration of the production cost, and sees how this compares with the prices from competing suppliers; cost analysis finds how suppliers arrive at their selling price. A cost analysis is more rigorous, and when it identifies the cost to produce an item, it should be easier for a buyer and seller to agree a fair and reasonable price – and they can jointly develop plans for future cost reductions.

Price analysis
Is the process of comparing a supplier's prices with external price benchmarks.

Cost reduction

All members of a supply chain have the same overall aim, which is to deliver a product that satisfies final customers. This means that organizations within the same supply chain should work together to achieve this goal, and this means taking a supply chain perspective (illustrated in Figure 10.1) rather than a narrow organizational one.

Traditionally, firms focussed their efforts on reducing costs by internal initiatives. There are many ways of doing this, including value analysis (VA), process

FIGURE 10.1

Cost management
approach

Supply chain strategic cost management

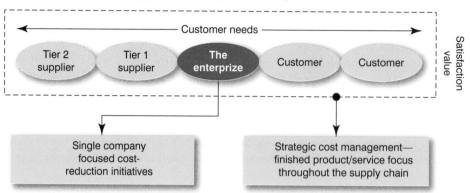

improvement, standardization, automation, better financing and so on. These internal approaches are still very effective and they are easiest to introduce – but their impact on overall costs is not as great as it used to be. We could say that the major sources of internal cost reduction have already been found, and firms are now looking for smaller adjustments. But another factor is the increase in outsourcing, which means that the cost of products is more dependent on the prices charged by external suppliers. As supplier prices become critical, it means that organizations can only make an impact on cost reductions by working with both upstream and downstream members of their supply chains. Collaboration is the only way of getting significant benefits. Examples of such joint initiatives include team-based value-engineering, supplier development, continuous improvement, cross-enterprize cost reduction projects, brainstorming efforts for new products, supplier suggestion programmes and supply chain redesigns (illustrated in Figure 10.2). Such projects need both parties committed to cost reduction methods that go far beyond simple haggling over prices.

One common pattern has the type of cost management initiative varying according to the stage of a product in its life cycle (as shown in Figure 10.3). In the initial concept and development stages, purchasing acts proactively to establish cost targets (which we discuss later in the chapter). Other approaches to cost reduction at this stage include quality function deployment, and technology sharing.

As a product is launched onto the market, supplier integration, standardization, value engineering and design for manufacturing can reduce costs. During the product's mature stage, purchasing adopts traditional cost reduction approaches, including competitive bidding, negotiation, VA, volume consolidation, service contracts focussing on savings and linking longer-term pricing to extended contracts. Then when the product reaches the end of its life, purchasing looks at the value of environmental initiatives to remanufacture, recycle or refurbish products that are becoming obsolete. An example of this occurs when printer manufacturers develop new methods that allow customers to recycle empty ink cartridges, which are then refurbished and used again.

The greatest benefits come when purchasing is involved early in new product development, and then it can make decisions early enough to consider effects over the product's whole life. When purchasing is involved later in product development, efforts to reduce costs have less impact because the major decisions about the types of materials, choice of suppliers and procurement procedures have already been made. Calabrese (2,000) describes this effect by saying, 'In the past, we allowed engineering to determine the specifications, the materials and the supplier. In fact, the supplier already produced the first prototype! That's when they decided to call in purchasing

FIGURE 10.2 Cost management processes

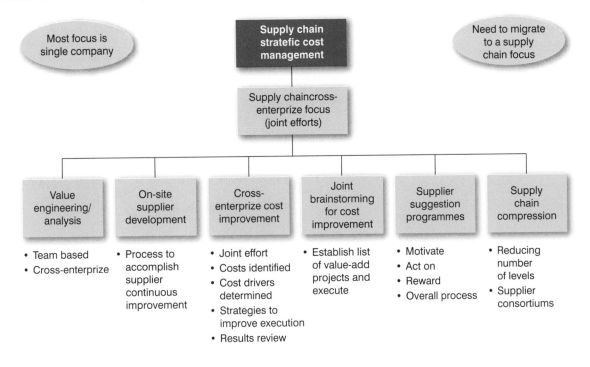

FIGURE 10.3 Managing life cycle costs

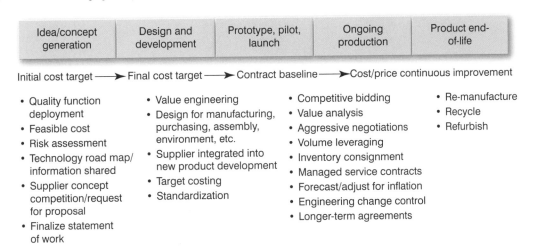

to develop the contract. How much leverage do you have in convincing the supplier to reduce costs when the supplier already knows they are guaranteed the business, and they have already sunk money into a fixed design and tooling for the product?'

Focussing effort

Organizations usually have alternative plans to reduce their costs, and they have to prioritize efforts. Figure 10.4 shows a structured framework for this, which considers the combination of value and number of suppliers. Low-value, standard items – characterized as generics – have a competitive market with many potential suppliers

FIGURE 10.4

Framework for cost reduction

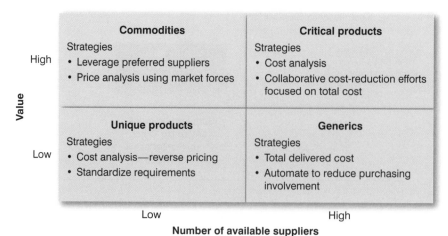

Value

High

Commodities

Strategies
- Leverage preferred suppliers
- Price analysis using market forces

Critical products

Strategies
- Cost analysis
- Collaborative cost-reduction efforts focused on total cost

Low

Unique products

Strategies
- Cost analysis—reverse pricing
- Standardize requirements

Generics

Strategies
- Total delivered cost
- Automate to reduce purchasing involvement

Low   High

Number of available suppliers

who emphasize total delivered price. There is no need to spend time on a detailed cost analysis for these, as it would not be worth the effort. Instead, they can be ordered directly through repeat blanket orders, supplier catalogues or e-procurement.

In this sense, commodities typically have a higher value, but there is still a competitive market – with typical items including computers and communications technology. These items can be sourced through traditional bidding processes, with price analysis to ensure a competitive price in a free market. Greater standardization in many types of product, means that items once considered as critical are moving into this quadrant.

LEARNING FROM PRACTICE

Southwest Airlines

The surge in oil prices in 2007 had an impact on many industries, including airlines whose fuel costs make up a significant part of operating costs. But in this period, Southwest Airlines was able to use its advance purchasing of fuel to gain a significant advantage. It had agreed fuel purchases years in advance as a hedge against higher prices. When oil went to $150 a barrel, most of the airline industry faced a huge rise in costs. But Southwest's long-term contracts allowed it to buy most fuel through to 2009 at prices based on $51 a barrel.

By 2007 Southwest had long-term contracts in place which included options that allowed – but did not require – it to buy fuel at certain prices. During the first 9 months of 2007, these hedging arrangements cost $42 million. This expenditure was questioned at the time, when higher oil prices seemed unlikely, but they became a good investment when oil prices rose

sharply. The price of oil fell in 2008–2009, but Southwest's hedging could have saved it more than $2 billion.

Other airlines were more affected by oil prices rises, with many report increasing losses in 2008 despite rising fares. American Airlines estimated that its annual fuel costs rise by $80 million for every dollar increase in a barrel of oil. While other airlines introduced a series of fare increases and fuel surcharges, Southwest's average ticket price rose by only 62 cents over the year.

A key question is whether Southwest can turn an obviously temporary advantage into a continuing long-term edge. It has relatively modest plans to raise revenues, and its costs will inevitably rise again. However, it has already gained a major benefit in an industry that was in turmoil with more than 70 bankruptcies in 2008.

Source: Bailey J. (2007) An airline shrugs at oil prices, New York Times, November 29, p C1; Bowker J. (2008) Airline bankruptcies set to double, Reuters, 19 October, www.uk.reuters.com

Unique products give a different challenge as the value is still low, but buyers strive to reduce costs when there are few available suppliers. Examples of such items include spare parts for machines, specialized fasteners, bulk chemicals and so on. For such items, purchasers are especially keen to identify suppliers that are charging too high a price and negotiate new terms. 'Reverse price analysis' (described later in the chapter) can identify excessive prices that can be reduced through standardization of requirements, or negotiations with problematic suppliers. In effect, the aim is to move items from the unique quadrant to the generic quadrant.

The major thrust of a buyer's efforts to reduce costs should be on critical items, where there are relatively few suppliers but the items are higher value. Managers should spend time exploring opportunities for VA, sharing cost savings, collaborative efforts to identify cost drivers, supplier integration early in the product development cycle and other approaches to reduce delivered costs.

PRICE ANALYSIS

To understand the factors that affect prices, we have to do a market analysis – which means identifying the primary forces that set prices and causes them to change. In the classic economic supply and demand model illustrated in Figure 10.5, prices are largely driven by competition. The principle is that a high price for a product means that more suppliers want to sell it, but fewer customers want to buy it: a low product price means that more customers want to buy it, but there are fewer suppliers willing to try and make a profit.

A compromize price is reached which generally satisfies both customers and suppliers, and then there is some equilibrium with supply more or less matching demand. When demand exceeds supply (to the left of the graph in Figure 10.5) there is a seller's market. This suggests that the price is low and you would expect the price to rise and supply to fall until equilibrium is regained. Alternatively, new suppliers will enter the market to meet the excess demand and maintain the low price – assuming that new suppliers can work with the low price and still make a profit. When supply exceeds demand (to the right of the graph) there is a buyer's market. This suggests that the price is high and you would expect it to fall or prices to fall until equilibrium is regained. Alternatively, some existing suppliers will leave the market and maintain the high price – but this assumes that they have a reason to stop selling a product which appears to be over-priced. In practice, it is usually much easier to adjust the price than the supply, so this is the dominant mechanism.

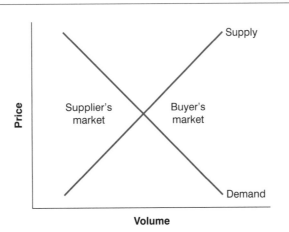

FIGURE 10.5

Market forces setting a price

Thus, global competitiveness creates more choice for consumers, and generally shifts market power away from the producer and towards the purchaser.

Apart from this general principle of economics, other factors affect the price, including the market structure, economic conditions and pricing strategies.

Market structure

Market conditions clearly have a major impact on price, but it can be difficult to identify the specific factors that have greatest effect. The market environment generally consists of a number of competitors offering similar products, the amount of similarity (or underlying differences) between their products, and any barriers for new competitors to enter the market. You can imagine these conditions as a spectrum. At one end of the spectrum is a monopoly, where there is only one supplier for a given item. An example of this is the pharmaceutical industry, where a company does the research and development on a new drug, and then a patent gives it exclusive rights to the drug for 7 years. This supplier can effectively dictate terms and has to be constrained by other means, usually anti-monopoly legislation.

At the other end of the spectrum is perfect competition, in which there are many suppliers for identical products with minimal barriers for new suppliers to enter the market. Our pharmaceutical example moves in this direction when the patent expires and generic manufacturers can copy the drug's formulation, enter the market, increase supply and drive down costs.

This model assumes that price is solely set by the forces of supply and demand, with no single seller controlling enough of the market to affect the market price. If a seller reduces its price with the hope of increasing sales and getting more influence in the market, a perfect market responds and the supplier simply reduces its long-term revenue. This picture of a perfect market is a gross simplification, that is never really achieved. One common compromise structure has a few large competitors that dominate the market and form an oligopoly. Examples of oligopolies include aeroplane making, banks, the steel industry, computer chips and car makers. In their markets, these major competitors interact, with the market and pricing strategies of each directly influence the others. One firm may become a price leader that raises or lowers prices to suit its own aims, and all other firms then have to review their prices and options. If all other firms follow the leader, they may create new market conditions – but if they do not follow, the price leader might be forced to reverse its change.

Economic conditions

General economic conditions determine whether a market favours sellers or buyers. When the economy is buoyant, demand for products is strong – but at least in the short-term producers are working at full capacity and supply is tight. Strong demand and constrained supply together form pricing conditions that favour sellers. Alternatively, when the economy is weak, demand is depressed and producers are working with low capacity utilization. Low demand and excess capacity means that customers can negotiate good terms.

The macroeconomy also has more subtle influences on prices. For example, the level of interest rates influences the cost of capital, and hence suppliers' internal rates of return and their attitudes towards investments. Similarly, the relative strength of currencies influences the real price of international purchases. Tight labour markets can also increase costs, leading to higher purchase prices.

The message is that purchasing managers should keep a watch on economic conditions and identify the factors that affect the supply and demand for their products. This can help set realistic budgets for purchases and gives valuable information for price negotiations.

Pricing strategy of the seller

Suppliers have different strategies that affect the price of their products. For instance, some producers have a low cost strategy and build lean operations that guarantee the lowest prices. Others have high service strategies that come with higher costs. The underlying premise is that organizations offer similar items at different prices, largely as a result of their strategies and means of adding value. For instance, both economy and full service airlines will transport you between two points, but at widely different conditions – and prices.

To remain in business, suppliers must cover all their costs, but the price charged often bears little relationship to the costs actually incurred. This seems strange, but pricing policies are often based on factors other than costs. For instance, a seller may quote an unusually low price to win a contract, with the intention of raising the price once it drives competition from the marketplace. Or a seller may sense that it has some advantage over a purchaser and exploit its position by charging an excessively high price. For example, a customer that needs an emergency delivery of spare parts is usually willing to pay way above the market price and, of course, many suppliers have simply not done the analyses needed to identify accurate costs, so they base prices on competitors' prices or 'what the market will bear'.

To get a clear picture of prices, buyers should ask several questions about a seller's pricing strategy, including:

- Does the seller have a long-term pricing strategy, or does it set prices in response to short-term pressures?

- Is the seller a price leader (who sets new pricing levels in the market) or a price follower (only matching the prices charged by competitors)?

- Is the seller trying to build entry barriers to other competitors by establishing a low price initially, then preparing to raise prices in the future?

- Is the seller using cost-based pricing (which calculates a price based on actual costs) or market-based pricing (matching prevailing prices in the market)?

MARKET-DRIVEN PRICING MODELS

We have mentioned the general principle of market-driven pricing models, where a supplier sets its price based on prevailing market conditions. Typically, a supplier matches the prices charged by its main competitors, but there are variations on this theme (Bendorf, 2002).

Price volume model

With a price volume model, a supplier analyses the market to find the combination of unit price and number of sales that maximizes its profit. This analysis is based on the assumption that:

1 Lowering the unit price will result in more units being sold, and

2 Higher volumes of sales will spread the overheads and indirect cost over more units, therefore increasing the average profit per unit.

An example of this model appears when suppliers offer price discounts for larger orders – which you can see in supermarkets that have special offers for larger quantities. In response, companies can combine their requirements across separate operating units to get lower prices – in the same way that shopping co-operatives combine the needs of several families to get the discounts from bulk purchases.

A major benefit of a reduced supply base is the lower price that comes from offering suppliers higher volumes of business. But both customers and suppliers have to be careful. From the customer's point of view, a quantity discount may reduce the purchase costs, but it increases other costs, particularly associated with higher stock levels. And there can be other costs of financing, obsolescence, insurance, ware-housing and so on. From the supplier's point of view, there comes a point below which there are no more benefits, and they might be working at a loss – so they cannot be too generous with discounts.

Market share model

Here pricing is based on the assumption that long-term profitability depends on the market share obtained by the supplier. This approach – which is also called 'pene-tration pricing' – is an aggressive approach for efficient producers. Then a supplier is willing to accept lower profit margins, or even a loss, in the short term, assuming that this will attract customers from other suppliers. In the long term the supplier is aiming for substantially higher sales that give economies of scale and prove most profitable.

Market share pricing can lead to faster market penetration, but we have to give a word of caution. Buyers have to ensure that a supplier offers a low price because it has efficient operations and is willing to accept a low profit margin while it builds market share – not because it is dumping products onto the market as a means of driving out competition, with the intention of raising prices later to much higher levels.

Market skimming model

This model is designed to trap unwary buyers who do not realize the true value of an item and lack knowledge, experience or sophistication to negotiate a reasonable market price. The price is set to earn a high profit on each transaction, with buyers persuaded to pay more than is necessary. You often see examples of this when suppliers bypass designated purchasing procedures and use maverick selling to deal directly with users.

Purchasing managers should always reduce the potential impact of this pricing model by analysing market costs, prices and value – and then ensuring that any higher price is justified by additional benefits.

Revenue pricing model

When there are downturns in market demand, suppliers often resort to a revenue pricing model. This sets a price that is high enough to cover current operating costs, but not necessarily make a profit or even make a reasonable contribution to over-heads. Suppliers using this strategy are typically concerned about cash generation, capacity utilization, retaining a skilled workforce during market slowdowns – and they are willing to reduce their prices until market conditions improve. In these conditions firms are tempted to offer inferior products or worse service as a way of reducing costs, but this can cause long-term harm to a business. The essence of revenue pricing is that it offers the same product at a temporarily lower price.

Promotional pricing model

The traditional view of promotional pricing is that it offers a short-term discount to introduce a new product to the market, and once customers are aware of its benefits the promotional price is raised to a normal level. More generally, a promotional pricing model sets prices for each part of a package to raise revenue from the overall product package, rather than to make each part profitable. For example, mobile phones are sold below cost price as an inducement to buy the annual service contract; and computer printers are sold at low prices because customers have to continue buying highly profitable ink cartridges. Total cost of ownership is discussed later in the chapter, and this should avoid the potentially damaging impacts of suppliers using this model.

Competition pricing model

This model focusses on the price that is offered – or is expected – by a supplier's competitors. Then the price offered is essentially the highest reasonable price that is still below the price offered by competitors. This is the policy used by many shops who guarantee that you cannot buy the same item cheaper at another local shop. It it also the thinking behind reverse auctions, where customers advertize on the internet that they want a product, and suppliers are invited to submit their competing bids.

Cash discounts

This seems like an administrative arrangement, where suppliers offer incentives, typically to encourage customers to pay invoices promptly. A common arrangement has a supplier offering a discounts for payment within a certain period, such as an electricity supplier specifying full payment within 30 days of receiving an invoice, but offering a discount of 2 per cent for invoices paid within 10 days.

This is a simpler and more flexible variation of the price volume model, but there are still other costs to consider. Specifically, the discount must be so high that purchasers cannot earn more by using the money for other purposes – in other words, the cash discount is higher than the opportunity cost of not taking the discount.

Using the producer price index

Organizations monitor prevailing market prices and base their own process on this. This is particularly prevalent when price is largely a function of supply and demand, such as steel, paper, plastic and other types of bulk commodities. Then managers have to decide a price that is fair in current market conditions, and for this they can monitor price changes using an external index. These indices are widely available from governments or industry institutions, such as the Pink Sheets giving commodity prices published by the World Bank (World Bank Prospects, 2009).

A typical index tracks price movements from week to week, and shows the price as a percentage of the price in a base week. For example, an item might cost €10 in the first week of a cycle, €11 in the second week and €9 in the third week, so the indices would be 100 (for the base week), 110 for the second week (11/10 × 100) and 90 for the third week (9/10 × 100). Converting prices into a standard form allows buyers to compare prices offered by different suppliers, prices at different times, prices charged for different materials and see whether price increases are reasonable. Some firms explicitly try to beat price inflation, which means that the prices they pay rise less than the producer price index.

A real benefit of price indices is that they allow comparisons between different commodities. For example, three sourcing teams might have the following results for the past year:

Oil products Team:	15 per cent cost increase
Components Team:	10 per cent cost increase
Services Team:	2 per cent cost increase

At first glance, it seems that the Services Team did best because they have the lowest cost increase. However, comparing these results with product price indices could give a different picture. The Components Team might have performed worse that the market where general prices have only risen by 6 per cent, while the Services Team may have performed in-line with broad market increases, and the Oil Products Team could have contained price rises to 15 per cent when market prices for oil products have risen by 25 per cent.

When the prices paid by a company are less than the related producer price index, it can translate this into lower costs to get a competitive advantage (as shown in Figure 10.6). However, firms should be careful when comparing their own prices with broader industry standards. To start with, buyers should ensure that they are using the right index and that it has a strong correlation with the item being purchased. Then they should ask specific questions:

- Do prevailing conditions make a price charged for an item seem fair and reasonable at the time?

- Have conditions (such as delivery requirements) changed over time?

- How does the price change with order quantity or other conditions?

- Was the supplier the only available source or were there competitors?

- Are the index comparisons driving purchasing strategies?

LEARNING FROM PRACTICE

JB Canswell

JB Canswell assembles components for office equipment. Part of its core business is to buy printed circuits from suppliers in Europe and sell the finished components through long-term contracts to manufacturers. For one circuit it has noticed that the average price paid in the quarter ending in April 2009 was €52.50 a unit, while the average price paid in the following quarter was €53.20 a unit. This was an increase of $(53.20 - 52.50) / 52.50 = 1.33$ per cent

At the same time, the producer price index for printed circuits rose from 127.2 to 127.5, giving a rise of $(127.5 - 127.2) / 127.2 = 0.2$ per cent. So the prices paid by JB Canswell had risen by 1.33 per cent during a period when broad industry prices had risen by 0.2 per cent. This suggests that the company should investigate, question its suppliers about their recent price increase and negotiate a better deal for the future.

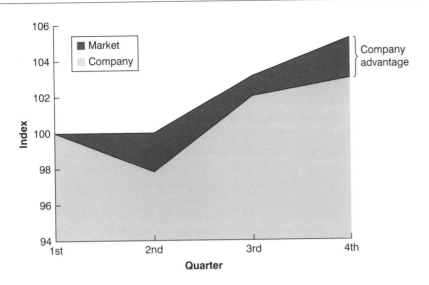

FIGURE 10.6

Actual price change vs market index

LEARNING FROM PRACTICE

Maytag Corporation

Maytag is part of the Whirlpool Corporation, whose sales of $20 billion a year make it a leader in the global domestic appliance industry. One of Maytag's leading products is a dishwasher, which is assembled in Jackson, Tennessee.

For a long time, bulky appliances like dishwashers were insulated from competition from imports because of the cost of transport. As Maytag's managers explain, 'Big boxes of air are expensive to ship across the ocean.' However, competition increased when low-cost production in some areas more than offset the higher transport costs. This meant that Maytag had to find ways of competing against China's Haier, Korea's LG Electronics and other imports. It found that the policy of sourcing major components globally and assembling them nearer their main US markets works well. It gains the benefits of low-cost operations, has reasonable transport costs, keeps assembly near to final customers and avoids the dramatic step of moving production away from its home base.

Maytag buys motors in China – from a plant owned by GE – because the design is standardized and China offers the lowest price. Then the company buy wire harnesses in Mexico. This gives the benefits of relatively low prices with flexibility – as the design is less stable and is different in each dishwasher model, so sudden shifts in demand would make it difficult to get supplies from farther away. This solution has evolved over time and at one point subassembly work (essentially putting pumps and motors together in one piece with cables and connectors) was done in Reynosa, Mexico. But eventually it grew more cost-effective to do the work in Tennessee, using a simpler design and less-expensive parts imported from China.

Maytag not only monitor their own material costs, but dissect competitors' appliances to determine the cost of every component. For instance, whenever a competitor introduces a new model, Maytag buys one and takes it to Jackson where they dismantle it. Then engineers examine each component to see how and where it was made, and how much it would cost.

There are still some parts that Maytag will not source globally, such as patented components whose design they particularly want to protect. Sometimes Maytag's approach simply cannot compete with imports. For example, profit margins on refrigerators with the freezer on top became so small that Maytag decided to stop making them itself and buy them from Daewoo Electronics in Korea, where they are re-branded and sold under the Maytag name.

Source: Aeppel T. (2003) Three countries, one dishwasher, Wall Street Journal, 6 October, p B1; www.maytag.com; www.whirlpoolcorp.com

The aim here is to make sure that comparisons with a broad index are meaningful, and that they give reasonable guidance for a specific purchase.

COST-BASED PRICING MODELS

An alternative to market-pricing is based on costs incurred and highlights opportunities for reductions. Figure 10.7 shows the separate elements that make up the price of an item. Essentially, the supplier's costs include materials and labour (which together form the operating costs), plus overheads, general and administrative expenses (which set the total production cost) plus profit margin (which then sets the price charged).

Clearly, when purchasers define the specifications for a tailored product, they have an inevitable impact on the price they pay – which is one of the reason why buyers should try to use industry standards parts whenever possible. In cost analysis, the buyer performs a detailed analysis of these different elements and identifies the forces that are driving change (Bendorf, 2002). Again, there are several models for such analyses.

Cost mark-up pricing model

This is the basic model in which a supplier simply takes its estimate of costs and adds a percentage mark-up to get a desired profit.

$$\text{Price} = \text{costs percentage mark-up}$$

This mark-up may be added only to the direct costs of production (the direct costs of materials and labour) in which case it would have to cover both profit and all overheads of operating the business. However, when the mark-up is applied to the total cost (including indirect costs of general expenses, administration and sales) the mark-up is solely profit. For example, a supplier that wants a 20 per cent profit margin for an item that costs a total of £50 to make would add a 20 per cent mark-up and quote a price of (£50 × 120 per cent =) £60. If the £50 is only direct costs, and accountants estimate the indirect costs are a further 30 per cent of this, the quoted price becomes (£50 × 130 per cent × 120 per cent =) £78.

FIGURE 10.7

Components of price

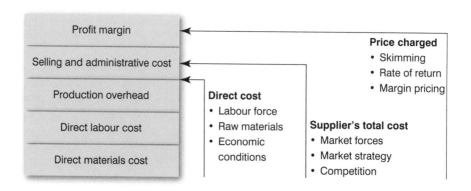

Margin pricing model

This is a variation on the mark-up pricing model, but instead of using a fixed percentage mark-up to cost suppliers set a price that will give a predetermined profit margin. The profit margin is a percentage of selling price, so:

$$\text{Price} \quad (1 - \text{profit margin}) = \text{cost}$$
$$\text{Or:} \quad \text{Price} = \text{cost}/(1 - \text{profit margin})$$

For example, if the supplier above wants to work with a profit margin of 20 per cent, its price is:

$$\text{Price} = £50/(1 - 0.2) = £62.50$$

Rate-of-return pricing model

Here the price is set by adding a profit that is based on achieving a specific rate of return on the financial investment – rather than an addition to the cost. For example, a supplier might decide to make 4,000 units of an item and spend £300,000 on research and development, design, testing, etc. If the supplier wants a rate of return of 20 per cent on investment, this means $(300,000 \times 0,2) / 4,000$ for each unit made. Then with a production cost is £50 a unit, the selling price is:

$$\text{Price} = \text{cost} + (\text{investment rate-of-return})/\text{number of units made}$$
$$= 50 + (300,000 \times 0.2)/4,000$$
$$= £65.$$

Estimating supplier costs using reverse price analysis

It is often useful for a buyer to analyse the costs of its suppliers, to see if these are reasonable and identify places for improvement. However, the ability to do such a cost analysis depends on the quality and availability of information provided by the supplier. If a buyer and seller have a close working relationship, they may exchange information relatively freely – but a more distant relationship is more difficult. So the obvious approach of asking a seller to give a detailed break-down of production costs when they submit a purchase quotation has mixed success. And buyers must always consider the reliability of such data.

A different approach for buyers is called reverse price analysis (sometimes loosely called 'should cost' analysis). This breaks down a quoted price into its components of materials, labour, overheads and profit. In the long run, a price must covers all of these costs, so a purchaser can analyse the details to make sure that all the elements seem reasonable, that they are assigned in an appropriate way and that the final price is acceptable. When suppliers do not provide this information, purchasers have to use their own estimates of what it should cost to produce an item, or use historical information or review the seller's publications to identify key data. For this last option, purchasing managers have to review a firm's published accounts to see what information they give – suggesting that it works best with publicly traded, small suppliers that make a limited product range. Although the accounts can give useful general information about costs – such as overheads and profit margins – they rarely give enough information about specific products. Also, it is more difficult with private companies that do not publish such information – or with larger companies that merge it with the costs of many other activities.

Despite the difficulties, a reverse price analysis can often estimate a supplier's costs from publicly available information. Imagine an organization that is buying a

Reverse price analysis
Considers components of price to check a quoted value.

product for the first time without any experience of what a fair price might be. Because they are busy and have little time, or they do not have experience with the analytical tools, many purchasing managers will simply make an informed judgement about whether a quoted price seems reasonable. However, it may be worth the effort of doing some additional research. For instance, suppose that an item has a quoted price of €20 a unit. Managers can start by considering the amount of this that goes towards profit – and the amount spent on sales, general costs and administrative (SGA). For publicly traded companies, these can be estimated from their published accounts; for private companies buyers may have to use industry norms that are published by various agencies, or search through the internet to find relevant information. Although these figures are rough estimates, they give a reasonable starting point for estimates. Figure 10.8 illustrates this calculation using estimates from industry standards for profit and SGA costs.

The next step is to consider the labour and material components of price. Material costs can often be estimated by consulting engineers or other people with relevant experience. They assess the materials needed, and prevailing market prices and in Figure 10.8 these were estimated at $4. Again, to find out how much labour is needed we can ask experienced people to give informed estimates, or we can use industry standards, such as the US Annual Survey of Manufacturers (Department of Commerce, 2009). These figures show the industry norms for standard industry classifications, often phrased in terms of a 'materials-to-labour' ratio. So having estimated the cost of materials, we can use this to estimate the labour costs. In our example, the ratio of materials to labour is 1.333, which comes from industry standards, suggesting a direct-labour cost of (4 / 1.333 =) $3.

After subtracting the estimates for profit, overheads, materials and labour from the price, the remaining portion of cost is described as an operations burden, overheads or additional costs. Now the purchaser has to decide whether $10 is a reasonable amount of additional cost on an item with a price of $20. The overheads are typically expressed as a percentage of labour costs. For labour-intensive industries, the ratio can be as low as 150 per cent; for capital-intensive industries, it can be as high as 600 per cent. In our example, the overheads are (10 / 3 × 100 =) 333 per cent of labour costs.

The cost analysis is only an approximation, but it should give reasonable guidelines that are good enough for purchasers to start negotiations with a supplier. These negotiations might home-in on the supplier's actual costs and how it relates to the price – and they should consider the following factors that might lead to cost reductions.

FIGURE 10.8

Example of reverse price analysis

Hypothetical price	$20		
Profit and SGA costs at 15 per cent	$3		
Subtotal		$17	
Direct material		$4	
Subtotal			$13
Direct labour			$3
Operating burden			$10

- **Facilities utilization.** Additional business for a supplier can affect their operating efficiency and consequent costs. Will additional volume allow economies of scale and reduce costs? Or are facilities already working at full capacity with new business increasing costs through overtime payments, etc.?

- **Process capability.** Do the projected purchases match a supplier's process – for instance, it may be inefficient to buy small amounts from a supplier that usually works with long production runs to minimize costs. On the other hand, suppliers specializing in smaller batches cannot easily accommodate large volumes in longer production runs. Buyers should also see whether facilities are state-of-the-art or outdated, whether they are efficient, make high quality products and so on

- **Learning-curve effects.** A learning-curve shows the effects of experience, with greater numbers of repetitions reducing the time needed for each unit. They also allow a seller to reduce its unit cost with long-term repetitive production of an item

- **The supplier's workforce.** A supplier's workforce clearly affects costs, through their skill levels, productivity, motivation, awareness of quality and so on. When visiting a supplier's facility, purchasers should take the time to talk to employees about quality and other work-related items, as this can give valuable insights

- **Management capability.** Management skills affect costs by their design of efficient operations, assigning resources to improvement programmes, managing quality, introducing technology, using financial resources well and a host of other ways. The effects are both tangible and intangible, and ultimately every cost element is a direct result of management capability

- **Purchasing efficiency.** Suppliers face many of the same uncertainties and forces with their own purchases as their customers do – so visits to suppliers should also monitor the ways that they meet their own requirements

Break-even analysis

Break-even analyses look at the costs and revenues of an item to identify the point where revenue equals expenditure. In other words, the point where all fixed costs are covered and firms begin to make an overall profit from the item. In practice, organizations perform break-even analysis at different organizational levels. At the corporate level, top management uses them as a strategic planning tool, perhaps considering the sales of a product to see whether it is worth opening new facilities to enter new markets. At a business level managers can use them to evaluate new product options. For example, a brewery can estimate expected profit or loss over a range of beer sales. At a lower level, the analysis can see how the break-even point moves after introducing cost-cutting measures.

Purchasing managers use break-even analysis to:

1   See whether a target purchase price gives a reasonable profit to a supplier.

2   Analyse a supplier's costs, as break-even analyses needs estimates of production costs.

3   Do sensitivity analyses by assessing the effect on a supplier of different mixes of purchase volumes and purchase prices.

4   Prepare for negotiation, as break-even analyses allow a purchaser to anticipate a seller's pricing strategy.

Break-even analyses allow a purchaser to identify the relationships between cost, volume and profit, generally assuming that (Waters, 2002):

1 Costs and revenues associated with a product are known with reasonable accuracy.

2 Costs can be defined as either fixed (the constant overheads that do not vary with production level) or variable (which are directly proportional to production level).

3 Fixed costs remain constant over the period and volumes considered.

4 Variable costs are directly proportional to production level (although this is not always true).

5 Revenues are directly proportional to the volume of sales (so the graph has a rising total revenue line beginning at the origin).

6 Break-even analyses consider total costs rather than average costs (but they often use the average selling price of an item to find the total revenue).

As we have mentioned, there can be problems getting reliable figures, particularly when fixed costs are shared between departments or products, and it is difficult to apportion these fairly. You can imagine this with a company making two products, A and B, and dividing the fixed costs equally between them. If the company stops making product B, then all the fixed costs transfer to product A, which becomes more expensive. Effectively, the costs of product A have increased, even though there has been no change to the product itself or the process used to make it.

The break-even point gives a broad picture for a purchase decision, but it can rarely be relied on for detailed figures. And it only considers quantitative factors, while managers must consider all relevant qualitative information before making any decisions.

LEARNING FROM PRACTICE

Gupta-Hussein

Figure 10.9 shows the break-even graph that Gupta-Hussein drew for a major item from one of their suppliers. Because the company did the calculation for a supplier it did not have access to precise data, so it estimated reasonable values. Their aim was to check that the supplier made a reasonable return based on their anticipated demand for 9,000 units at the stated purchase price.

Figure 10.9 shows that the supplier's break-even point is:

$$\text{Income} = \text{costs}$$
$$PD = VD + F$$
$$10 \times D = 6 \times D + 30,000$$
$$\text{Or:} \quad D = 7,500 \text{ units}$$

The supplier needs to sell at least 7,500 units to avoid a loss, and then the profit is:

$$\text{Profit} = \text{Income} - \text{costs}$$
$$= PD - VD - F$$

With expected sales of 9,000 units we have:
Where:

P = average purchase price	= €10 per unit
D = demand for units	= 9,000 units
V = variable cost per unit	= €6 per unit
F = fixed cost of producing the item	= €30,000

Giving an expected profit of:

$$\text{Profit} = PD - VD - F$$
$$= 10 \times 9,000 - 6 \times 9,000 - 30,000$$
$$= €6,000$$

Assuming the data are reasonably accurate, the supplier earns a profit of €6,000 on sales of (10 × 9,000 =) €90,000. Whether this is an acceptable return depends on prevailing conditions and negotiated terms. If the analysis suggested that the supplier would expect a loss, then Gupta-Hussein must consider several questions:

● Are the cost and volume estimates accurate?

● Is the target purchase price too optimistic and puts an unreasonable strain on the supplier?

● Are the supplier's costs reasonable compared with other firms in the industry?

● If the cost, volume and target price are reasonable, is this the right supplier to produce this item?

● Will direct assistance help reduce costs to the supplier?

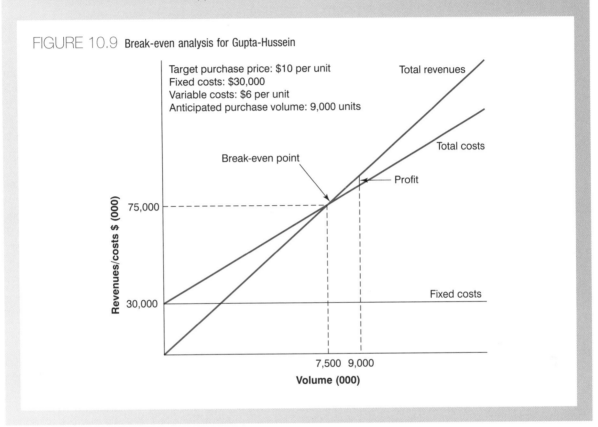

FIGURE 10.9 Break-even analysis for Gupta-Hussein

Target purchase price: $10 per unit
Fixed costs: $30,000
Variable costs: $6 per unit
Anticipated purchase volume: 9,000 units

TOTAL COST OF OWNERSHIP (TCO)

Total cost of ownership (TCO)
Is defined as the present value of all costs associated with a product that are incurred over its expected life.

To find the TCO buyers identify costs beyond the standard unit price, transport and delivery – and they consider all the costs associated with a product during its life.

Most firms go beyond the basic unit price and delivery costs when they consider purchase decisions, but there is wide disagreement about the actual components to include. These cost components can be classified in four broad categories (Menezes, 2001):

● *Purchase price* – the basic amount paid to the supplier for the product

● *Acquisition costs* – all other costs associated with bringing the product to the customer's location, including administration, transport, packaging, insurance and taxes

● *Usage costs* – including all the costs of using the product through its expected life. The usage cost of capital equipment might include installation, operator training, warranty, maintenance, capital, depreciation, spares, downtime and so on. For raw materials the usage costs includes the costs of converting materials into finished products and then supporting it through its usable life. For services, the usage costs include all the costs of performing the service that are not included in the purchase price

- *End-of-life costs.* These include all costs that are incurred when an item reaches the end of its usable life. In the simplest case, this equals the cost of disposing of an item, minus any residual resale or scrap value. Examples of end-of-life costs are recycling charges, disposal, clean-up, project termination costs and so on

Building a total cost of ownership model

It is not easy to build a TCO model as it requires input from different parts of an organization – and a thorough understanding of operations throughout an item's entire life cycle. Collecting this data needs the following steps:

Step 1. Build a process map describing all activities from the time a need for an item is identified all the way through to the end of its life cycle.

Step 2. Using the process map as a guide, identify all the sub-costs that make up each TCO category – in other words, the cost elements that combine to give the costs of each category.

Step 3. Determine how each cost element identified in step 2 is to be measured. For example, step 2 might identify the costs of sourcing labour as one of the elements in acquisition costs; then step 3 determines that this should be measured from the hourly rate of the individuals performing the sourcing and the amount of time they spend on the sourcing.

Step 4. Gather data and calculate costs for each of the measures identified in step 3. This is the most difficult and time-consuming step and can require information from various sources including interviews, surveys, accounting systems and other internal databases.

Step 5. Develop a timetable of costs for the full length of the life cycle. This involves placing each cost element measured in step 4 into its appropriate time period, and then adding the total cost for each time period.

Step 6. Discount costs to present value. Amounts of money have different values at different point in the future, so a cost of £100 now has a different value to £100 spent 10 years in the future. The reasons for this include inflation, opportunity costs, interest payments and other financial adjustments. To get around problems of comparing different amounts of money at different points in time, we generally calculate a present value for all amounts – described as discounting to present values. Then the total cost of ownership is equal to the sum of present values for each time period.

Important factors to consider when building a total cost of ownership model

The key factor with TCO is clearly to include all costs. It is easy to forget some of these, such as the opportunity costs, which is the benefit lost by choosing one alternative for spending money rather than another. For instance, if you buy a car you cannot also go on holiday, so the opportunity cost is the benefit that you would have gained by going on holiday. This is an additional cost that must be considered in a purchase, and it typically includes lost sales, lost productivity and downtime.

The reminder to include all costs is only one factor to consider for a TCO model, and others include:

- Include all costs, with the best estimates of values available; remember, especially with global sourcing, hidden costs such as risks in extended supply chains

- Building a TCO model can be costly and time-intensive activity, so they should only be considered for larger purchases

- Get senior management support, as this makes data collection much easier, especially when working with different parts of an organization

- Work as a team, as this will greatly reduce the time needed for data collection

LEARNING FROM PRACTICE

Example of a TCO model

Supply manager Joe Smith is considering the purchase of 1,000 desktop PCs for his company. The life cycle is 3 years and the company discounts future values by 12 per cent a year. Joe has calculated the TCO for one of the purchase options as shown in Figure 10.10.

Using these elements, Figure 10.11 shows the calculation for the total cost of ownership. This shows that the service costs such as equipment support and network support are highest, and the supply manager should explore the possibilities of reducing them. This may present difficulties as these are typically the most profitable area for the supplier.

FIGURE 10.10 TCO calculation for one purchase option

Cost elements	Cost measures
Purchase price (step 1):	
• Equipment (step 2)	Supplier quote: $1,200 per PC (steps 3 and 4)
• Software licence A	Supplier quote: $300 per PC
• Software licence B	Supplier quote: $100 per PC
• Software licence C	Supplier quote: $50 per PC
Acquisition cost:	
• Sourcing	2 FTE @ $85K and $170K for 2 months
• Administration	1 PO @ $150, 12 invoices @ $40 each
Usage costs:	
• Installation	$700 per PC (PC move, install, network)
• Equipment support	$120 per month per PC—supplier quote
• Network support	$100 per month—supplier quote
• Warranty	$120 per PC for a 3-year warranty
• Opportunity cost–lost productivity	Downtime 15 hours per PC per year @ $30 per hour
End-of-Life:	
• Salvage value	$36 per PC

FIGURE 10.11 Total cost of ownership calculation

Cost elements	Present	Year 1 (step 5)	Year 2	Year 3
Purchase price:				
Equipment	$1,200,000			
Software licence A	$300,000			
Software licence B	$100,000			
Software licence C	$50,000			
Acquisition cost:				
Sourcing	$42,500			
Administration	$150	$480	$480	$480
Usage costs:				
Opportunity cost—lost productivity		$450,000	$450,000	$450,000
Installation	$700,000			
Equipment support		$1,440,000	$1,440,000	$1,440,000
Network support		$1,200,000	$1,200,000	$1,200,000
Warranty	$120,000			
End-of-life costs:				
Salvage value				($36,000)
Total	$2,512,650	$3,090,480	$3,090,480	$3,054,480
Present values discounted by 12 per cent a year (step 6)	$2,512,650	$2,759,799	$2,463,113	$2,174,790

- Focus on the biggest costs first, and remember that spending time on the smallest cost elements is unnecessary and will only delay the decision

- Make sure to obtain a realistic estimate of the life cycle, as a life cycle that is too short or too long could give a wrong decision

- A TCO model is a powerful aid to making the right decision for a purchase, at least from a cost perspective

COLLABORATIVE APPROACHES TO COST MANAGEMENT

Purchasing managers have learned that the most effective way to reduce the costs of purchases is not usually through price haggling, but by effective collaboration. When people from both the supplier and the buyer put their heads together they can find innovative ways to reduce costs and gain mutual benefits. Two of the most

Source: Based on Mannheim S. (2009) Company reports, SMS, Berlin.

LEARNING FROM PRACTICE

Sacha Mannheim

Sacha Mannheim was evaluating two alternative machines. Alternative A was priced at €100,000, while B was priced at €125,000. The lead time for Machine A was 90 days, and Machine B was 30 days; so the usage costs for A should include the lost revenue that would have been generated during the extra (90 − 30 =) 60 days that Machine B would be available. This extra revenue is an opportunity cost for choosing Machine A, and when it is included, Machine B became the better alternative, despite its higher price.

In another example, Sacha Mannheim decided to purchase Machine Y instead of Machine X. However, their analysis was based on price and omitted the opportunity cost from the difference in capacity of the two machines. In practice, Machine X was capable of producing 10 per cent more units than Machine Y. If demand rose, Machine Y would be unable to meet the increase and a new machine would be needed, while Machine X could have coped for some time.

common approaches to collaborative cost management are target pricing and cost-savings sharing.

Target pricing

Target pricing is used in the early stages of new product development to establish a contract price. Japanese manufacturers refined target pricing during the 1980s, in an effort to counteract the rising value of the Yen and motivate engineers to select designs that could be produced at a low cost. Their idea was that the cost of a new product is not a consequence of its design and production process, but rather is an input to the design. Then the challenge is to design a product with the required functionality and quality that keeps within this prescribed price and gives a reasonable profit. For instance, with a new type of computer the development team may work with marketing to determine a target price that fits the computer's target market segment. Then the product is disaggregated into major systems, such as the CPU, motherboard, memory – and based on the overall target cost, each major element is set its own target cost. Then disassembly continues with increasing detail until managers identify individual components and assign target costs. The target cost for each item is the price that a purchaser hopes to obtain from a supplier (assuming the item is externally sourced, or else it sets the maximum cost of internal production).

Traditional pricing may use the costs as a starting point, saying:

$$\text{Selling price} = \text{total item costs} + \text{profit}$$

Target pricing turns this the other way around and says that an item's allowable cost is a function of what a market segment is willing to pay:

$$\text{Allowable total cost of items} = \text{selling price} - \text{profit}$$

At the start of negotiations a supplier's current price is probably greater than the target price set by the buyer. Then the gap between the two must be reduced by a collaborative effort – perhaps using methods like value engineering, quality function deployment, design for manufacturing, standardization, waste elimination and so on. Of course, this assumes a reasonable target price, and targets that are too aggressive may simply be unachievable, no supplier will deliver them and the failed negotiations may create ill-will. On the other hand, a target price that is too low is easily achievable and the buyer may lose its competitive position.

Honda has played a leading role in developing target pricing, breaking target costs down to the level of individual components. Then suppliers are asked to provide a detailed breakdown of their own costs, including raw materials, labour, tooling, packaging, delivery, administration and other expenses. This breakdown is helpful in suggesting areas for improvement (Krause and Handfield, 1999).

Once an organization has established a target price with a supplier for, say, the first year of a contract, it should look for ways of reducing this over the life of the product. Sharing cost savings is a way of encouraging both sides to look for these reductions. But they should bear in mind the cardinal rule that the target cost must never be violated. This means that even when either side find a way to improve the functionality of an item, they cannot introduce the improvement until they can offset any additional cost.

Cost-savings sharing

As its name suggests, cost-savings sharing assumes that any benefits gained from improved operations are shared between buyers and suppliers. This differs from traditional procedures in several ways. Firstly, shared cost-saving requires both sides to agree the cost of producing an item, and this needs an open exchange of information. Secondly, profit is a function of the suppliers' investment committed to an item, and their requirements for a reasonable return on this investment. So profit is a ROI and not a direct function of cost, typically phrased as a percentage of selling price. This gives suppliers greater incentives to invest in continuous improvements, knowing that they will benefit from any cost savings achieved (rather than simply lowering their selling price and profit).

Another feature of cost-savings sharing is the financial incentives offered to sellers for improvements above and beyond those agreed in the purchase contract. Again, this differs from traditional pricing where one party – usually the buyer – seeks to capture all the savings made from suppliers' improvements.

Prerequisites for target pricing and cost-savings sharing

To use target pricing and cost-savings sharing, there must be joint agreement on a supplier's full costs. As well as the detailed costs, both parties must agree product volumes, quality levels, productivity, capacity requirements, assets used, ROI needed, profit margins and other basic production information. They must also agree on the point in time when mutual sharing of cost savings takes place, as well as the formula used to share the rewards. These shared savings occur from both improvements agreed in the purchase contract, and from savings achieved above and beyond these levels.

Clearly, this approach needs high degrees of trust, information sharing and joint problem solving. The process will fail if one partner tries to take advantage of the other or violates the confidentiality of information. There must also be a willingness to provide the resources to resolve any problems that arise.

Another key prerequisite is the ability to manage risks associated with target pricing, perhaps arising from volume variability. The volume of trade clearly affects cost levels, so both parties must carefully manage the impact of any changes from planned volumes. Higher than projected volumes will generally allow a supplier to get greater economies of scale and lower unit costs – but these lower costs are not the result of any recognized improvement in the supplier's performance, so need careful consideration. On the other hand, lower than projected volumes can raise a supplier's average costs, even when it works as efficiently as expected.

You can see that this kind of collaborative approach is not suitable for all items. Many items are too cheap or unimportant to warrant the complex analysis. The prices may simply be defined by prevailing market conditions, so these approaches are not generally used for items that are readily available from multiple sources, standardized rather than customized and heavily influenced by the forces of supply and demand. In general, a cost-based approach is feasible for complex items, customized and relatively expensive, where the seller contributes high added value to an item, it contributes specialized expertize.

LEARNING FROM PRACTICE

An example of target pricing and cost-savings sharing

Although actual target and cost-savings sharing agreements can be lengthy and complex, the following example demonstrates the underlying principles.

This example is based on real conditions that occurred between a car assembly plant and a first tier supplier.

FIGURE 10.12 Key date for the pricing example

First-year target price: $61.00	
Negotiated or analysed cost	
Material	€ 20 per unit
Labour	€ 8.50 per unit
Overheads	200% of direct labour
Scrap rate	10%
Selling, general, and administrative expense rate	10% of manufacturing cost
Effective volume range	125,000 units per year ± 10%
Projected product life	2 years
Agreed ROI	30%

		Year 1	Year 2
Supplier investment	€ 3 million	€ 2 million	
Total supplier investment	€ 5 million		
Supplier improvement commitment			
Direct labour	10% reduction annually		
Scrap rate	50% reduction annually		
Improvements additional to agreed-upon performance improvements: shared 50/50			

Purchasers are looking for a designed component that is put into their company's final product. The selling price of the product has been determined through discussions with marketing, and this figure has been broken down into a cost for each component. For one component, the company and a supplier have agreed a target price of €61 for the first year.

Cost savings sharing assumes that the buyer and seller work together to identify the most efficient processes for the component. The approach does not reward inefficient practices, and it assumes that engineers at the buying company are flexible enough to modify product specifications when beneficial. Then the supplier's costs and required ROI form the basis for a fair and competitive price. Both parties agree to this collaborative approach because they have already developed a close working relationship, supported by the sharing of detailed cost data.

Figure 10.12 gives details of the costs and investment data needed for a cost based purchase contract. Then Figure 10.13 gives details of the costs and subsequent price of the component for the 2 years of the contract. Data for year 1 include the information derived in Figure 10.12, and then data for year 2 assume that the following events affected the selling price at the beginning of the year:

- Raw material costs rise by 4 per cent due to inflation
- A joint VA team identifies a substitute material that reduces material costs by €1.50 a unit
- Labour rates increase by 3 per cent due to a contractual increase at the supplier
- The supplier meets the agreed improvement targets for reduced scrap and improved labour productivity

Then the year 2 data include:

- The supplier receives 50 per cent of the €1.50 material cost reduction identified by the VA team

FIGURE 10.13 Cost and profit breakdown for the pricing example

	Year 1	Year 2	
Materials	€20.00	€19.24	Materials reduction of €1.50 plus an increase of 4 per cent, giving (20.00 − 1.50) × 1.04 = €19.24
Labour	8.50	7.88	Reduction of 10 per cent for the contractual target and the increase of 3 per cent, giving €8.50 × 0.9 × 1.03 = €7.88
Overheads (200 per cent labour)	17.00	15.76	
Total materials, labour and overheads	€45.50	€42.88	
Scrap (10 per cent of production)	4.55	2.14	Scrap reduced from 10 to 5 per cent for the contractual target, giving costs of €42.88 × 0.05 = €2.14
Manufacturing cost	€50.05	€45.02	
Selling, general and administrative expenses (10 per cent of sales)	5.00	4.50	
Total cost	€55.05	€49.52	
Profit (at agreed rate of 30 per cent ROI)	6.00	6.75	Includes €0.75 share for joint material reduction, giving €6 + (€1.50/2) = €6.75
Selling price	€61.50	€56.27	New selling price after year 1 events

- The profit for year 2 includes the supplier's share of the material cost reduction
- The selling price at the start of year 2 becomes €56.27

By focussing on joint and continuous improvement, the purchase price was reduced at a time when material and labour costs were both increasing.

VALUE ANALYSIS

Value analysis examines all the parts of a product to make sure that it fulfils its intended function at the lowest total cost. Typically, it examines all the components to see if any can be replaced by lower-cost alternatives. Value analysis is primarily applied to existing products, and the equivalent process for new products is described as value engineering. Then value engineering is more proactive, while VA reacts to existing conditions. However, the underlying principles are the same and we can describe them both under the umbrella of VA. Although VA is traditionally used for tangible goods, there is no reason why the same methods cannot be used for services.

As we saw earlier, value is defined as the perceived benefit from a product divided by its total cost:

$$\text{Value} = \frac{\text{Perceived benefit}}{\text{Cost}}$$

Then VA looks for ways of maximizing this value – which means increasing the perceived benefits of an item without increasing its price, or reducing its costs while giving the same benefits. For example, a cable television service can increase the value of its service by reducing the price it charges, or increasing the number of channels it offers.

Value analysis and value engineering
Check that a product reaches specifications at the lowest overall cost.

Who is involved in value analysis?

Value analysis crosses the boundaries of many functions, but because procurement is responsible for acquiring the chosen materials it should take an active role. A common approach starts with the creation of a multi-functional VA team with members from:

Executive management to provide overall guidance and support for the VA process and allocate necessary resources.

Suppliers because much of the VA is concerned with purchased materials, it is sensible to request input from suppliers. They can propose alternative products, variations (such as standard items or new materials), insights learnt from other firms, and they can design lower-cost production methods.

Purchasing often takes a primary role in VA because of their job of liazing with suppliers and acquiring materials.

Product design evaluate any proposed changes to the design of an item. They also help define product functions, establish quality and performance standards and evaluate the effect of VA changes on other parts of a product.

Marketing provides information about the impact that VA changes may have on customers.

Operations managers are responsible for producing the products, and they can propose better ways of using items.

Process design can contribute extensively, particularly when discussing alternative ways of producing and delivering a product.

Quality management can assess the impact of proposed changes on quality.

This team can then ask a number of questions to identify opportunities increasing value:

- Does the use of this product contribute value to our customers?

- Is the cost of the final product proportionate to its usefulness?

- Are there additional uses for this product?

- Does the product need all its features or internal parts?

- Are design or quality specifications excessive for customer requirements?

- Is it possible to reduce the product weight or physical features?

- Are alternative products available?

- Is there a better production method for the product?

- Would cheaper materials work just as well as more expensive ones?

- Can a lower-cost standard part replace a custom-made one?

- Are we using the best equipment for making the product?

- Can an alternative supplier provide equivalent materials at lower prices?

- Are competitors buying materials at lower prices?

- Is it possible to use less packaging?

- Is the item classified properly to get the lowest transportation rates?

- If we are making an item internally, can we buy it for less (and vice versa)?

In practice, the most common areas for VA improvement include modifying product design and material specifications, using standard components to replace customized ones, substituting higher cost materials by cheaper ones, reducing the number of parts that a product contains and developing better production methods.

The value analysis process

Value analysis projects usually follow a standard approach that starts with identifying a product as a VA candidate, and then progress through the following five stages.

1   **Gather information.** During this stage, all relevant details about a product are collected. These include current sales, trends, supplier performance, costs, price, customers requirements, competition, design, quantity estimates, production analyses and so on. An important element here is to agree about an items intended functions for

customers. For this, VA teams should ask questions along the lines of, 'What does this product do for the customer?' and 'Why does a customer buy this product?' In this stage it is important to get a clear understanding of a product's functions to form the basis of following stages.

2   **Speculate.** This stage calls for creative thinking on the part of the VA team to develop as many improvement ideas as possible. Brainstorming is an ideal way of generating ideas without making initial judgments on particular suggestions. After this stage the team has a list of ideas that might be used to improve value.

3   **Analyse.** This stage critically evaluates the different ideas put forward during the speculation phase. Analysis can take many forms including feasibility studies and cost/benefit analyses. The result of this stage is a prioritized list of ideas that satisfy the original goals of the VA, and which should be considered for implementation. By this stage the VA has moved on from generalities to a specific list of options.

4   **Recommend and execute.** The VA team now considers the list of options and must make their final decisions. This stage passes recommendations back to senior managers who make the decisions. When a VA team receives approval to go ahead with an idea, it has to work on its implementation, which usually needs support from a range of outside people. To make things run smoothly, the team must design an implementation plan with timings, budgets and responsibilities.

5   **Summarize and follow-up.** After implementing the approved ideas, the VA team has to follow up and monitor performance to make sure that predicted improvements have actually materialized. During this stage the team checks the gains achieved by VA, and makes any necessary adjustments.

CHAPTER REVIEW

- Organizations compete by adding value to products. This value is essentially the perceived benefits of a product divided by the price charged. Procurement has a major impact on value, through its effects on both benefits and price

- Purchasing managers have to focus value, and their major effort is in cost reduction. This means that they find ways of acquiring materials at the lowest reasonable cost. Their overall approach depends on the type of items bought

- The laws of supply and demand set the context for pricing policies, but there are several other factors, such as the structure of the market, economic conditions and business strategies

- There are two broad approaches to pricing, based on either price or cost analysis

- Market-driven pricing bases the price charged for an item on prevailing market conditions. There are several models for this based on price volume relationships, market share, market skimming, revenue pricing, promotional pricing, competition pricing and cash discounts

- Cost analyses use the production cost of an item to set a price. There are several variations on this idea – along with reverse price analysis – to estimate the costs incurred by a supplier. These costs can be used in further analyses, typically finding a supplier's break-even point and expected profit

- The total cost of ownership gives a broader view of costs, identifying all components for purchase, acquisition, usage and disposal

● Purchasers and suppliers can get more, shared benefits from collaboration. Two specific ways of identifying and sharing benefits use target pricing and cost-savings sharing

● Value analysis is a procedure for examining all elements of a particular product to make sure that

it fulfils its intended function at the lowest total cost. For this it has to increase perceived value, or reduce costs, to maximize overall value

DISCUSSION QUESTIONS

1 Why should a buyer consider the cost of making an item internally instead of simply finding the prevailing purchase price? Is this true for all types of products?

2 List some of the reasons that suppliers are reluctant to share detailed cost information. What can purchasers do to overcome this reluctance?

3 Is it true that low international labour rates mean that global sourcing is always the cheapest option? What other information has to be considered?

4 Discuss the different pricing policies that a seller can adopt, along with their key features.

5 Find some examples of suppliers that are currently using a price volume model, market share model, competition pricing model and revenue pricing model.

6 What types of cost and price information are available on the internet? Is this information reliable?

7 Under what conditions does a buyer have more power than a seller? When does a seller have more power than a buyer?

8 How is the price of an item established with a cost analysis? What makes target pricing an attractive option?

9 What is the total cost of ownership? Describe the main difficulties that must be overcome when using a total cost system?

10 What happens if a supplier cannot meet a purchaser's initial target price?

11 If a buyer and seller do not have a close working relationship, how can a buyer obtain relevant cost data?

12 Discuss the concept of value as it relates to VA. Why might a company use VA?

13 If you were the leader of a VA team, how would you identify opportunities to increase product value?

REFERENCES

Bendorf R. (2002) Supplier pricing models, Inside Supply Management, May, pp 18–19.

Calabrese J. (2000) R. Handfield personal interview with the General Motors Vice President of Advanced Purchasing, August 16.

Department of Commerce. (2009) Annual Survey of Manufacturers, Washington, DC: US Department of Commerce, and website at www.census.gov/prod/www/abs/industry.html

Krause D. and Handfield R. (1999) Developing a world class supply base, Tempe, AZ: Centre for Advanced Purchasing Studies.

Menezes S. (2001) Calculating the total cost of ownership, Purchasing Today, January, pp 28–32.

Waters D. (2002) Operations management (2nd edition), Harlow, Essex: Pearson Education.

World Bank Prospects (2009) Commodity price data (Pink sheets), Washington, DC: World Bank, and website at www.worldbank.org/prospects

FURTHER READING

Bendorf R. (2002) Supplier pricing models, Inside Supply Management, May, pp 18–19.

Degraeve Z. and Roodhooft F. (1999) Effectively selecting suppliers using total cost of ownership, *Journal of Supply Chain Management*, 35(1): 5.

Dubois A. (2003) Strategic cost management across boundaries of firms, Industrial Marketing Management and website at www.elsevier.org

Ellram L. (1996) A structured method for applying purchasing cost management tools, *International Journal of Purchasing and Materials Management*, 32(1): 11–19.

Ellram L. (2002) Supply management's involvement in the target costing process, *European Journal of Purchasing and Supply Management*, 8(4): 235–244.

Ferrin B. and Plank R. E. (2002) Total cost of ownership models: an exploration study, *Journal of Supply Chain Management*, 38(3): 18–12.

Hartley J. (2000) Collaborative value analysis: experiences from the automotive industry, *Journal of Supply Chain Management*, 36(4): 27–32.

Lockamy A. and Smith W. I. (2000) Target costing for supply chain management: criteria and selection, *Industrial Management and Data Systems*, 100(5): 210–218.

Newman R. and McKeller J. R. (1995) Target pricing: a challenge for purchasing, *International Journal of Purchasing and Materials Management*, 31(3): 3, 12–20.

Shank J. K. (1999) Case study: target costing as a strategic tool, *Sloan Management Review*, 41(1): 73–83.

Stundza T. (2000) Focus Is on total cost of ownership, Purchasing, March 2, p 34.

CASE STUDY

Compulink Electrical

Companies recognize that costs are effectively designed into their products from the outset. The total cost of ownership over a product's life cycle is an important factor for Compulink Electrical, a large manufacturer of computer systems. They recognize that successful order fulfilment starts with early decisions about product design. To help with this they use a procedure for product design that implicitly involves both 'the voice of the factory' (VOF) and 'the voice of the customer'. This was an idea that originated with upper management, effectively giving individuals a place in a team structure. The structure of the teams and ways that people communicate their ideas varies by product and by team.

An operations manager explained his views. 'We were continually involved in negotiations about features that marketing wanted to add to our products. Most of the requests they wanted had to be justified and brought in front of the VOF team. This typically fought against any decisions that would add complexity to the process or make the product more complicated.'

The VOF teams tell people who are not familiar with manufacturing the type of problems they face. These comments are particularly useful in planning and pre-production tests, where the VOF reports on problems encountered with plans and assembly, and request that these issues be considered by the design team. The VOF teams present their arguments to design teams at regular meetings, and the two are connected during the entire project.

An initial concern from the VOF was the need for involvement of different business functions in the early stages of product design, and their observation that in practice this was a rarity. Then problems with, say costing, only appeared when a significant amount of preparation and early work has already been done on a product. Now a target cost procedure is used to provide cost targets for the various groups involved. This aligned R&D, operations and marketing with supply chain managers in finding ways to achieve those target costs at the component and finished product levels. At the component level these four major groups would take their respective expertize – perhaps doing some value engineering, market analysis, supplier surveys, etc, – and agree target costs and ideas for how this could be achieved.

The operations manager gave an example of how this works. 'Proliferation of part numbers was a recurring issue, with new parts and components continually being introduced. So we introduced a requirement to carry over old parts into new products, which involved minor adjustments to designs. New design guidelines called for at least 50 per cent of existing parts in new products, so R&D, operations and purchasing get together to decide which parts would be carried over. First R&D make recommendations, then operations checked that these would work and the investment needed, then procurement check to see if the parts would be available for another 4 years. At the same time, marketing check the impact on customer demands.'

The input of marketing is particularly important in balancing the desirability of introducing new parts with the perceived benefits to customers. The operations manager explained that, 'If there are specific marketing features that are suggested, the decision goes one of two ways. But if a senior marketing executive insist that the product has to have some feature, no-one is likely to oppose it too aggressively, even when other team members do not like it. More positively, approval is likely to be agreed when marketing have suggested a minor adjustment, written a business case, identified the number of extra that will be sold, calculate margins and so on.'

Questions

- What costs are generally involved in decisions about new product development?

- What arguments are typically put forward by marketing for increasing the complexity of a product by adding new features and options?

- What arguments are typically put forward by operations and the Voice of the Factory for simplifying products?

- What key elements in a decision support tool would help resolve this issue? Where would the data for building this decision support tool come from?

CHAPTER 11
QUALITY
MANAGEMENT

After reading this chapter you should be able to:

● Define quality and the broader aims of quality management

● Appreciate the importance of supplier quality and the factors that influence it

● Describe the principles of Total Quality Management

● List the steps needed to implement Total Quality Management

● Understand the principles of Six Sigma quality

● Discuss the benefits of ISO 9000 certification

OVERVIEW OF QUALITY MANAGEMENT

In the last chapter we looked at the costs of materials. We often assume that higher quality products inevitably come at a higher cost, so in this chapter we are going to investigate this relationship and see if buyers really do have to balance cost and quality. A starting point for this asks exactly what we mean by quality.

Quality
In its broadest sense, is the ability of a product to meet – and preferably exceed – customer expectations.

Defining quality

A basic problem with quality is that it is difficult to define. We all think that we recognize high quality when we see it, but the problem is that we use different criteria and have different expectations. When you listen to some music, eat food or look at a painting someone will think it has very high quality, while someone else will think it has very low quality. The problem is that there are many aspects of quality, and when you buy a computer you may judge its quality by its speed, weight, memory, sound quality, weight, colour, cost, ease of use, technical support, durability and so on. Some of these can be measured, but many are a matter of personal preference. As a result, it is impossible to define a simple measure for overall quality (Waters, 2002).

We can start considering quality by suggesting that the item has high quality if it achieves the aims it was designed for. When a customer finds that a pen writes properly, we can say that it has fundamentally high quality. This idea of quality as a measure of how well a product meets customer requirements is the approach of several pioneers of quality management. For instance, Juran (1988) defined quality in terms of its fitness for use; Crosby (1979) defined it in terms of conformance to requirements. However, some people went further and said that a product is only really high quality when it exceeds customer expectations, in the way that you are happy when a train journey takes 45 minutes rather than the advertised hour. In this light, Feigenbaum considers quality in terms of the combination of goods and services that will meet or exceed customer expectations (Feigenbaum, 1983).

A problem with such views is that customer expectations are dynamic and constantly changing – and actions taken by competitors can change user's expectations. For example, a customer may be satisfied with a 3-day package delivery service until another company offers a 2-day service at the same price. Changes introduced by competitors can dramatically redefine the standards that customers expect, and their views of quality. For instance, when an internet service provider increases the speed of its connections, other providers have to offer a similar service or accept that customers will view them as lower quality.

Supplier quality
Represents the ability of a supplier to deliver products that consistently meet or exceed current and future customer expectations or requirements in critical performance areas.

The challenge for organizations is to analyse customer expectations and translate them into viable products. Then they have to transmit the subsequent requirements to organizations upstream in the supply chain. In this way, all suppliers are involved in quality management, and we develop the idea of supplier quality.

There are three parts to this definition:

1   *Consistently meet or exceed customer expectations or requirements.* This means that suppliers deliver products that customers are happy with, in each and every delivery. They guarantee that their deliveries are not inconsistent, their goods are not faulty, and their service is good.

2   *Current and future customers.* Suppliers must deliver products that satisfy existing customers who are becoming increasingly demanding. They must also anticipate

and satisfy future customer requirements, which suggests that they must be able to generate continuous improvements.

3 *Critical performance areas.* Supplier quality does not refer only to the physical attributes of a product, but it must satisfy buyer's expectations in many diverse areas, including product delivery, conformance to specifications, after-sales support, technology, features, cost and many others.

Remember that the products delivered by suppliers are not simple goods or services, but they are inevitably a complex combination of the two. This means that suppliers must take a broad view of quality that includes many different factors – and they should make every aspect of the purchase successful. They cannot focus only on physical goods, but must include services and the supporting systems and processes that create the overall output. When you buy a new phone you want the actual phone to work, but you also want it delivered quickly, at reasonable price, sold by helpful sales people, with no mistakes in the bill or receipts, with sensible packaging and so on.

Part of purchasing's role in quality management involves being a good customer. It is difficult to maintain a trusting and collaborative relationship and to receive high-quality service when there are strained relationships with suppliers. So buyers should learn how to work well with suppliers and become preferred customers by understanding what suppliers appreciate in a buyer-seller relationship. For instance, suppliers want a minimum number of changes to product design once their operations begin, information about future purchase volumes, early access to new product requirements, adequate lead times, ethical treatment from buyers, accurate information and timely payment of invoices. The message is that supplier quality does not just mean that suppliers bend over backwards to meet the demands of their challenging customers, but that both parties should work together to get mutually satisfactory – or high-quality – results.

Why be concerned with supplier quality?

There are several reasons why all members of a supply chain should be concerned with quality, based on the joint aim of getting customer satisfaction. After all, if high quality means that customers are satisfied, then low quality products mean that they are not satisfied.

Consequences of poor quality. Customers want the product they pay for, and if there is any problem with quality they are not happy with the result. As you know, when you buy new clothes, you expect them be in perfect condition and exactly as described by the salesperson. If this is not the case you may return them, ask for a replacement, complain, tell people about your experiences and not buy anything else from the shop. The problem is that all of these consequences of poor quality have direct costs for both the supplier and the purchaser. This is a general result, that any lapse in product quality is likely to have extra costs, more work and sour relations between trading partners.

Reliance on suppliers. When an organization want to pass on high-quality products to its customers, it needs to buy high-quality items from its suppliers. It is a simplification, but managers often emphasize their requirements from suppliers in terms of product quality and delivery (Trent and Monczka, 1998). Firms have to rely on their suppliers, particularly those using just-in-time operations, high technology components, single sourcing, specialized expertize, strategic alliances and any other factor that reduces the number of potential suppliers. This dependence makes firms more vulnerable to the quality of supply. You can imagine this with a manufacturer that uses just-in-time operations and buys a particular part from a preferred supplier. If one delivery of the part is late or contains a defect, it immediately stops the manufacturer's operations – and relations with the supplier inevitably deteriorate. But all organizations rely to some extent on their suppliers, and if one supplier does not deliver acceptable materials, then the customer will start looking for another that will.

Supplier impact on quality. Crosby estimated that suppliers are responsible for 50 per cent of a firm's product quality problems (Crosby, 1979). As more than half of a typical firm's expenditure goes on purchased goods and services – and this approaches 100 per cent for some types of manufacturer – it is not surprising that they are concerned with the quality of the items they buy. A firm that focusses only on its own internal quality can fail to recognize the underlying root causes – which may be items bought in from suppliers. Poor supplier quality can comprehensively undermine any attempt by a firm to improve its product quality.

Continuous improvement. Most firms aim for continuous improvement in all aspects of their operations, and one way they can achieve this is through effective quality management. Firms compete by improving their quality, and it follows that any firm that does not respond by continuous improvement will get left behind. The speed of these improvements depends on a firm's industry and how well its current performance compares with competitors. Companies in high-technology industries face intense competitive pressure and they have to look for new perfect quality levels to remain competitive; any firm that does not achieve this extremely high quality has to make dramatic improvements or else lose out to more successful competitors. Other industries, such as furniture making, face a slower and less dramatic rate of change. But regardless of their industry, all organizations face competition and experience at least some pressure from customers to achieve continuous quality improvement.

Outsourcing. This is a clearly increasing trend, with firms outsourcing their non-core activities and putting more reliance on suppliers. For example, Dell Computers is primarily an assembler of equipment that purchases most of its PC components (monitors, hard drives, keyboards, microprocessors, power units and so on) from external suppliers. The larger the proportion of the final product that comes from suppliers, the greater the impact they have on overall product quality.

LEARNING FROM PRACTICE

Mattel Inc.

With a turnover of $5 billion a year, Mattel is one of the world's leaders in the design, manufacture and marketing of toys, including many household names. In 2007, the company was hit by a problem with suppliers that turned into a public relations nightmare. Some toys purchased from Chinese manufacturers were found to be decorated with paint that contained high levels of lead. This is widely banned because of its harmful effects, potentially causing learning and behavioural problems in children. Some of the suspect Mattel toys had paint with lead content of more than 180 times the legal limits in international markets.

Source: A sampling of Wall Street Journal and New York Times from August and September 2007; www.mattel.com; www.bbc.com

Within a short period, Mattel identified 20 million toys at risk worldwide, and had three separate recalls (including 600,000 Barbie dolls).

Mattel's problems started when it started outsourcing manufacturing to low-cost areas. They had a long-term supplier based in Hong Kong, but this company then sub-contracted work to another company that did not use Mattel-approved paint.

The results of these incidents have been far reaching. The subsequent public outcry forced many companies to look more carefully at their outsourced manufacturing, and other products with high levels of lead paint began to appear, such as ceramic dishes, cookware and various PVC products. The owner of one of the Chinese manufacturing facilities involved committed suicide. Mattel founded a new corporate responsibility unit, which led an internal investigation. National governments have encouraged the Chinese government to strengthen its regulations and enforcement (recognizing that local governments within China have a history of avoiding national policies that negatively affect their local economies). Enterprizing companies have started to market home lead test kits for worried parents. Companies outsourcing manufacturing in China have increasingly monitored operations and moved employees to local factories. Countless lawsuits were taken out against Mattel, which also won a 'bad product' award in 2007. Needless to say, their sales, profits and share price all suffered.

The important question here asks 'Who is really to blame for the quality problems?' Almost invariably, the final buyers of these products blame the company whose name is on the label and the distributor because, from their perspective, these share responsibility for safety. However, external suppliers actually made the toys so they should accept some portion of the blame. Certainly it is impossible for any producer to make a high-quality product when the inputs received from its suppliers are flawed.

Perhaps the main lesson from this experience is that the more dispersed the global supply chain is, the more buyers must strive to ensure that quality and safety standards are upheld. Perhaps the manufacturers of these unsafe toys focussed too much on the design, assembly and cost rather than quality. Certainly, customers put such emphasis on the quality of products that they are unwilling to forgive this kind of failure.

PURCHASING'S ROLE IN MANAGING SUPPLIER QUALITY

Procurement managers play a leading role in managing quality from external suppliers. A number of factors influence the amount of attention that they should commit to this.

The ability of a supplier to affect the overall quality of a buyer's products. Some suppliers deliver items that are critical to a firm's success; if these items are in any way defective the firm cannot hope to make acceptable products. Buyers must clearly manage the suppliers of these critical items more intensively than those providing lower-value, standardized or easy-to-obtain items.

The resources available to support supplier quality management. Firms with limited resources and minimal expertize in quality management must carefully decide where to allocate their resources. This decision will have a considerable influence over the effectiveness of the firm's quality management efforts.

The ability of a buying firm to practice world-class quality. A buying firm can help its suppliers understand quality management concepts only after it has understood these concepts itself. It follows that it is much easier for a leading quality firm to encourage quality management in suppliers.

A supplier's willingness to work jointly to improve quality. Not all suppliers are willing to work closely and collaboratively with a buyer. Instead, some suppliers

LEARNING FROM PRACTICE

Firestone Tyres

In 2001, a survey reported that component makers were cutting corners in response to car assembly plants' demands for lower prices. Only 20 per cent of 261 suppliers reported that they were actively improving quality. This can lead to disagreements about the causes of problems when things go wrong. In the previous year, the US National Highway Traffic Safety Administration had contacted both Ford and Firestone about the apparently high incidence of Firestone tyre failures in Ford Explorers, Mercury Mountaineers and Mazda Navajos. There were no obvious causes, but the two parties started to blame each other. Ford said that the quality of tyres could not be relied upon as other tyre suppliers gave no problems; Firestone said that Ford had problems with vehicle stability and then recommended using a tyre pressure that was below the designed specifications. Many tests, recalls and

lawsuits were inconclusive. Nonetheless, relations between the two companies deteriorated to the extent that Firestone said that it would no longer supply tyres to Ford, ending a century-long trading relationship.

There is no doubt that when suppliers are pressurized to reduce their prices and cut costs they may be tempted with shortcuts that affect quality. But higher quality does not really mean higher costs, and surveys by Industry Week suggest that higher quality comes from reducing scrap and waste rather than increasing costs. Many companies understand how to both lower operating costs while continuously improving quality. For example, Toyota expects an annual reduction in costs from its suppliers, but still maintains its reputation for high product quality. It achieves this by working with suppliers to identify ways of jointly reducing costs.

Source: Based on Reid R.D. (2002) Purchaser and supplier quality, quality progress, August; Bartholomew D. (2001) Cost vs. quality, Industry Week, 250(12), 34–41; American Society for Quality at www.asq.org; www.industryweek.com

prefer a traditional purchasing relationship, characterized by limited interaction and involvement and a more hand's-off style. Others will enthusiastically embrace a long-term, collaborative partnership – and it is easier to develop quality management with these.

A supplier's current quality level. This affects the amount and type of work needed by a buying firm to ensure high supplier quality. If the supplier is already working at world-class levels, it needs less attention; if its products are currently less than satisfactory, more work is needed.

A buyer's ability to collect and analyse quality-related data. Purchasing needs an effective system to monitor and collect information about how well a supplier is meeting quality goals. For most firms, this means some links between the supplier's and the purchaser's information system to automatically collect and analyse quality data. In principle this might seem straightforward, but in practice it can prove more difficult.

Total Quality Management
Has the whole organization working together to guarantee, and systematically improve, quality.

TOTAL QUALITY MANAGEMENT

To put it simply, **Total Quality Management** requires everybody in an organization to work towards achieving high quality. The aim of TQM is to satisfy customers by making products with zero defects. This is the only real way of ensuring value in a supply chain, feeds benefits down to customers, and purchasing staff at all levels must understand and commit themselves to the principles of TQM.

TQM has expanded from its basic ideas to form one of the most robust and powerful business philosophies. It changes the way that people within an organization work, and their broad aims and beliefs. A key element of TQM is that suppliers must deliver materials of perfect quality – meaning that they also adopt the principles of TQM, spreading the ideas throughout entire supply chains. Initially, this formed a barrier as some firms were reluctant to change their existing practices, but this situation has changed as the principles of TQM are becoming almost universally accepted. Those suppliers that do not use it to some extent find it increasingly difficult to compete.

Deming's 14 principles

Edwards Deming is widely described as the father of the modern quality movement, and his views on TQM can be summarized as follows (Deming, 1986):

- Variation is the primary source of poor quality

- Reducing variation and improving quality is a never-ending cycle of design, production and delivery, followed by surveying customers –then starting all over again

- Quality is everyone's responsibility, but senior managers are ultimately accountable for quality management

- Interacting parts of a system must be managed together as a whole, not separately

- Psychology helps managers understand their employees and customers, as well as interactions between people

- Intrinsic motivation is more powerful than extrinsic motivation

- Predictions must be grounded in theory that helps to understand cause-and-effect relationships

These ideas form the basis of a movement that has taken quality from a limited technical issue to a broad management philosophy. Deming summarized the context for this move in a comprehensive set of 14 principles (Deming, 1986). These do not prescribe specific actions and programmes for management to follow, but they set the context which TQM needs to succeed. The important point about these principles is that they are not a menu for quality improvement from which managers can pick only those points they like, but they form a complementary set of components that are essential for to implement a TQM culture.

Principle 1. Create a quality vision and demonstrate commitment. The top managers in an organization are responsible for its long-term direction, so they should take a lead in quality management and include quality an important strategic issue. They should focus the whole organization on delivering high quality products that satisfy customers, and commit the resources needed to achieve this.

Principle 2. Learn the new philosophy. Quality management must be understood by everyone in the organization, and it appears in everything the organization does. The important point is that people should refuse to accept the customary levels of mistakes, delays, defects and errors – but should instead work to overcome them and produce perfect quality.

Principle 3. Understand inspection. Inspecting products to find defects is the traditional way of controlling quality, with the underlying belief that defects are inevitable and must be inspected out of the process. However, the proper way to deal with defects is to build quality into products, so that defects never occur in the first place. This means that everyone within the organization understands the variation in a process and how it affects quality – and they should work to reduce its effects.

Principle 4. Stop making purchases based purely on price. Finding the lowest purchase price of an item may be good in the short run for a procurement department, but it may increase longer costs somewhere else in the process, perhaps by more scrap, defects, warranty claims and so on. The focus should be on reducing the total costs, not just purchase price, and this inevitably considers the product quality.

Principle 5. Improve constantly and forever. If the firm does not change – and specifically improve its product quality – it will be overtaken by more flexible competitors. So continuous improvement – often described by the Japanese term **kaizen** – must be an implicit part of all operations. There is always room for improvement, and everyone in the organization must continuously look for ways of reducing variation, reducing costs, making things faster, being more innovative and so on.

Principle 6. Institute training for all employees. It is very important that employees and suppliers have all the knowledge, skills and tools they need to do their jobs efficiently and effectively. Well-developed and targeted training can enhance quality and productivity – as well as improving morale. For quality, specific training should include diagnostic and analytic tools, decision making and problem-solving.

Principle 7. Institute quality leadership. Managers have traditionally emphasized the direction and control of people under their control – effectively telling them what to do, and then making sure that they do it. This is an inefficient approach, and a better option is to guide and coach employees, giving them incentives to improve their skills and find new, more efficient ways of working. This is the basis of organizational leadership through a motivated and empowered workforce.

Principle 8. Drive out fear. There are many types of fear in a workplace: employees may be afraid to make a mistake and be reprimanded for it; most people fear changes that will alter their routines and jobs; they fear failure so they do not want to try anything new; they fear losing their job when sales fall; managers fear losing control over their departments; departments fear releasing too much information, and so on. But organizations must change, so they have to develop a culture that accepts new ways of working and drives out all the related fears. This is best achieved by open and honest two-way communication which eliminates fear and encourages people to experiment, try new ideas, exchange information, collaborate and all the other activities that eventually lead to higher quality and greater productivity.

Principle 9. Break down barriers. Most organizations have structures that put people into distinct departments, with most interactions kept within the department and crossing few boundaries. This encourages the 'silo' effect, where ideas are not exchanged and departments become introspective, focussing on their own activities rather than taking a broad view of the whole organization working to solve problems. These barriers between departments and groups should be broken down, so that everyone works together to achieve customer satisfaction.

Principle 10. Eliminate exhortations. Slogans, signs and posters are meant to change people's behaviour and encourage them to work in some preferred way. But they are seldom effective and signs that exhort people to 'Do it right the first time' or produce 'Zero defects' simply do not work. Firstly, they assume that quality problems are due to human behaviour and they can be solved by exhorting people to somehow work better. In reality most quality issues are set at the design stage (for both product and process) and few depend on people's motivation. The designed-in quality is the responsibility of managers not workers. Secondly, the signs give no advice about what people should actually do or how they should do it better.

Principle 11. Eliminate arbitrary quotas. Managers almost invariably set numerical goals for operations, but these may be arbitrary and not properly justified. People exhorted to achieve the quotas often have no control over operations, which might respond to customer demand for products, economic conditions, capacity and so on. Then employees may be set a target of 'improving production by 5 per cent this year' but with no justification of the figure, suggestion of how to achieve it or even control over the process. These goals do not give incentives to improve quality, but encourage short-cuts. Why would someone stop to adjust a piece of equipment that is increasing product variability if this means that they would miss their production quota? Such goals generally focus on the short-term, while quality improvement must take a longer-term perspective.

Principle 12. Remove barriers to pride in workmanship. Often employees are treated as little more than a resource – an interchangeable part of the production process. Performance appraisal systems in most organizations encourage this view, as they do not value individual skills or pride in workmanship, but they reward gross production and promote quantity over quality. When given the proper climate in which to work, most people want to do a good job. Unfortunately, the evaluation and reward systems in many companies do not stimulate this kind of culture that allows people to take pride in their efforts. We reward doctors by the number of patients they see, but not the quality of care they give; we give sales people a commission based on sales value, but not their customer relations; and so on.

Principle 13. Encourage education and self-improvement. Training is generally targeted at learning specific tasks or skills that are needed to do a job: education and self-improvement are broader and concerned more with improving people's quality of life. Organizations that invest in education and self-improvement generally find that their employees are more highly motivated, and they bring additional benefits to both their work and their individual lifestyle.

Principle 14. Take action. Top management must initiate and invest in these principles to improve quality, and then broaden organizational performance. But the principles must be implemented throughout the entire organization, and for this they need grassroots support. So everybody must embrace these 14 principles, understand their aims, and work towards their goals. The key for success is to maintain momentum for TQM over the long term.

LEARNING FROM PRACTICE

Sony Corporation

In August 2006 it was noticed that six cases had been reported of laptop computers overheating, and even bursting into flames. The common feature was that the laptops contained batteries that were made by Sony. Millions of the lithium-ion batteries had been sold, as they were widely used by manufacturers of computers. Only a handful of them had any problems, but Sony immediately investigated the defects. It emerged that when the batteries were made, the tiny rolls of metal that make up the cells were crimped, and microscopic shards of metal could be released into the battery. These could cause a short circuit, which in turn could cause overheating.

In the first morning after the news was reported, Dell received 100,000 phone calls and their website had 23 million visits. Even though the risks were very small, they were clearly too great for computer manufacturers to ignore. Dell started by recalling 4.1 million batteries and replacing them, with Apple recalling another 1.9 million. Lenovo, which took over IBM's PC business, recalled half a million ThinkPads, along with Fujitsu, Toshiba and other manufacturers. In total, it is estimated that Sony had to replace over 9.6 million batteries, raising its costs by $429 million, and doing considerable harm to its image as a high quality manufacturer.

Source: Based on Associated Press (2006) Recall of Sony laptop batteries grows, *The Boston Globe*, October 5 ; Aughton S. (2006) IBM and Lenovo recall 'fire hazard' Sony laptop batteries, *PCPro* 29 September.

IMPLEMENTING TOTAL QUALITY MANAGEMENT

Deming's 14 principles summarize the TQM philosophy and from this we can derive eight core activities needed to implement it (shown in Figure 11.1) (Trent, 2001).

Define quality in terms of customers and their requirements

One of the main causes of poor supplier quality is faulty communications and the resulting misunderstanding of specifications, expectations, requirements, terms and so on. Buyers must work closely with internal customers to provide clear specifications and unambiguous performance requirements for materials – along with any

FIGURE 11.1 Eight key principles of Total Quality Management

1. Define quality in terms of customers and their requirements.

2. Pursue quality from suppliers.

3. Stress objective rather than subjective analysis.

4. Emphasize prevention rather than detection of defects.

5. Focus on process rather than output.

6. Strive for zero defects.

7. Establish continuous improvement as a way of life.

8. Make quality everyone's responsibility.

other information that might affect their purchased quality. Not surprisingly, incomplete or inaccurate development and communication of specifications has a disproportionate effect on supplier quality.

A rule of thumb suggests that more than half of quality problems with suppliers are caused by poor specifications, for which the buying organization is largely responsible. Specifications are typically vague and arbitrary, and are often designed by product development teams without enough input from suppliers. Then suppliers receive requests to tender for items that they have seldom been consulted about, and they are afraid to question specifications for fear of losing the business (Evans and Lindsay, 2008). So the first cure for poor supplier quality is to eliminate fickle specifications by having suppliers involved earlier in the development process.

Building a clear understanding of a buyer's expectations and requirements needs two elements. The first is the ability of buyers to work with users and identify, clearly define, quantify and specify its technical and sourcing requirements. The second element is the purchaser's ability to communicate these requirements to suppliers. Only when these two elements are in place can both parties understand the requirements. Figure 11.2 gives an example of the sort of document that can effectively communicate a purchaser's expectations to a supplier.

Pursue quality from suppliers

As a product moves through its supply chain, each activity in turn adds value – but it can also be a point where faults or defects are introduced. Pursuing quality from

FIGURE 11.2 A typical statement of responsibility

The following details specify the responsibilities of XYZ Company project team and ABC supplier during the design and development of light truck.

Responsibility	XYZ project team	ABC supplier
Agree on performance targets for product cost, weight, quality and improvement.	X	X
Work directly with XYZ project team to meet product performance target levels.	X	X
Provide design support for component requirements.		X
Develop total project timing requirements.	X	
Provide build schedules as needed.	X	
Support vehicle launch at assembly plant.	X	X
Report project status to executive steering committee.	X	
Attain manufacturing feasibility sign-off.	X	
Provide technical/engineering project support.	X	X
Develop final product concept.	X	
Provide prototype parts according to agreed-upon schedule.		X
Identify critical and significant product characteristics.	X	X
Prepare final detail drawings and transmit to XYZ.		X
Provide material and product test results.	X	X

suppliers means that an organization extends its own quality concerns backwards in the supply chain to ensure that its suppliers are also concerned with quality and only deliver high quality materials. Because of its key role in managing external sourcing and acquiring materials, procurement can have a major effect on overall product quality.

Because suppliers have a significant role in product quality, it makes sense to include quality considerations when choosing them. Also, when items are delivered, procurement can monitor quality and ensure that agreed standards are being met. In other words, by choosing the right suppliers and then monitoring performance, purchasing can ensure that high quality is maintained. They can do this through personal visits, monitoring systems, automatic data transfer and all the other means of monitoring supplier performance. One option is to use a supplier certification programme, which is a formal procedure for verifying (usually through an intensive cross-functional site audit) that a supplier's processes and methods can be relied on to produce consistently high quality products. Certification usually includes a number of analyses to guarantee that no defective items leave the supplier's facility. This approach where one organization certifies the quality of its suppliers has been replaced by the more general ISO 9000 standards (which we mention later).

The idea of having suppliers guarantee the quality of their products reinforces the idea that they should be involved in design decisions at an early stage. Then they can use their expertize and experience to influence designs and give better quality – perhaps by suggesting ways of simplifying a product, using alternative materials, standardizing components, anticipating problems, improving tolerances and so on.

Stress objective rather than subjective analysis

One of the keys for achieving total quality is to use objective checks on performance. This seems obvious, but many organizations have not developed sufficiently objective or rigorous measures for their supplier performance – either for selection or for post-selection evaluation. There may be many reasons for this, but a leading one suggests that senior managers still have not recognized the importance of external suppliers to quality.

Measuring supplier quality is important because the results allow procurement to develop a list of preferred suppliers for future business, to identify opportunities for performance improvement, to give feedback about changed operations and future development, to track the results from improvement initiatives and so on.

Emphasize prevention rather than detection of defects

Defect prevention involves any procedure that avoids a fault being introduced to a product. In principle, a fault can be introduced at every point in a process, and prevention is needed at every point to guarantee a perfect product. This is the basis of quality at source. This means that people working at each point in the process ensure that they do their own operations properly and do not add any defects. When this is repeated at every step in the process, the result is a final product that is free of defects. This replaces the traditional approach, where defects are introduced at various points in the process, but they are not detected until further through the process, usually at quality control inspections. So TQM changes the emphasis from accepting that faults are added to products and using inspections to find them, to ensuring that operations are done properly with no faults added, and inspections confirm that there really are no faults.

Defect preventive can take many forms, but its key feature stresses the need for consistency and reduced variation in the process. From procurement's viewpoint this means a rigorous approach to supplier selection and evaluation, ensuring that suppliers have the required systems, processes and methods in place to prevent defects. In practice, organizations can save a lot of effort by insisting that their suppliers have ISO 9000 certification, as this ensures that they use suitable procedures for quality management.

Focus on process rather than output

One of the most dramatic differences between traditional quality control and TQM thinking is the shift from a product orientation to a process one. This means that TQM focusses on the processes that creates products, rather than on individual units. The argument for this is that high quality processes create high quality products, so it makes sense to look at the process of creation and design operations that avoid defects.

Imagine a company that awards business on the basis of competitive bids and some samples of products. Realistically, a supplier will provide a small number of samples, and buyers examine these to see whether they meet requirements. This gives a product focus, with buyers making decisions based on a small sample of products, with less emphasis on the process that produced them. Then the company has to ask:

- Would any supplier knowingly send a poor sample?

- How many parts did the supplier produce to get an acceptable sample?

- Are the samples representative of the process operating under normal conditions?

- Did the supplier use the same process, methods and materials that it will use during normal production, or was the sample made under controlled laboratory conditions?

- Did the supplier actually produce the sample, or did a subcontractor?

- Do samples tell the buyer enough about the supplier's capacity or process capability?

An emphasis on process rather than finished product requires a supplier to provide evidence of their **process capability** on a continuing and regular basis. Thus, every time a supplier modifies a process, it needs a new capability study to satisfy customers so that it can continue to give satisfactory performance.

To be considered 'capable' some measurable features in every unit produced must reach specified quality levels. Traditionally, this means that the measurements must fall between upper and lower limits. Perhaps a bus journey is expected to take about 20 minutes, and it is considered acceptable if it takes between 18 and 22 minutes. This is based on the assumption that there is always some unavoidable variation in a process, and it has to be controlled rather than eliminated. Specifically, we assume that the output is normally distributed, which gives the useful property that 99.73 per cent of all observations of process output are within three standard deviations of the process mean. So a process that is stable and in control will produce virtually all of its output within these tolerance limits (as shown in Figure 11.3).

To check the capability of a process, purchasers have to run a process capability study. This is designed to provide information about the performance of the process under stable operating conditions when there are no special conditions or causes of variation. Then a process capability study can:

- Show whether the process is capable of achieving the specified quality standards

Process capability
Is the ability of a process to generate outputs that meet specifications and customer requirements.

FIGURE 11.3

Traditional view of
acceptable performance

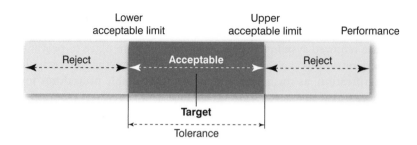

- Provide objective evidence of process performance
- Prioritize potential quality improvement projects

Strive for zero defects

TQM argues that the only acceptable quality target is zero defects, which means that all units conform to requirements. Taguchi argued that any deviation from this target carries some level of cost, perhaps measured by customer dissatisfaction or loss due to scrap and reworking (Taguchi, 1986).

The main mechanism for perfect quality has TQM introducing quality at source. Then each element in the process only passes forward units that it knows to be of perfect quality. However, there are other ways of moving towards the aim of zero defects, such as a well-designed supplier selection process that means a firm will only do business with suppliers that also strive for zero defects. This move is usually associated with supply base optimization, which is the process of determining the right mix and number of suppliers for a given purchase (described in chapter 9).

This aim for zero defects is the key point of TQM, and we can demonstrate its importance by considering the costs associated with quality which we can classify as either control or failure costs (Foster, 2007).

- **Control costs** are the costs incurred to monitor quality, measure performance and make improvements. There are two types of control costs, which are described as appraisal and prevention. Appraisal costs include the direct costs of measuring quality, specifically doing the checks that measure quality and ensure that it is reaching required standards. This is the area that is traditionally described as quality control and includes all the inspections, statistical testing, supplier audits and other types of monitoring. Prevention costs cover all the activities needed to ensure that defects are not made in the first place. These include introduction of quality management programmes, quality planning, training, setting-up of specialized facilities, maintaining related systems and so on

- **Failure costs** are incurred when things go wrong and defects are actually made. There are two types of failure cost – for internal and external failure. Internal failure costs occur when the defect is found within the organization, and covers things like testing, scrap, reworking, extra inspections, process downtime, etc. External failure costs occur when a product is actually delivered to a customer who then finds the fault. These include warranty costs, repair or replacement of defective units, hassle for managers, lawsuits and loss of customer goodwill

Traditional accounting systems rarely give a clear picture about these quality costs, as they are included in different categories and spread over different departments. Many quality-related costs, such as training, are somewhat subjective and not easily identified. Nonetheless, there is agreement that the costs can be

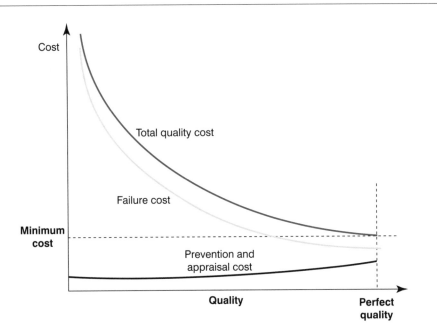

FIGURE 11.4

The lowest overall costs
come with perfect quality

surprisingly high, particularly the costs of external failure. If you plot the individual costs against quality, the control costs generally rise with increasing quality while the failure costs generally fall (as shown in Figure 11.4). Adding the four elements to give a total cost of quality gives a curve that falls with increasing quality; in other words the lowest costs come with perfect quality. This is the rationale for TQM – that lowest costs, and other measures of performance, occur when no defects are produced. This is also the reason why quality management is so important for every organization.

Establish continuous improvement as a way of life

All organizations continually look for improvements, but the feature of TQM is that this is more focussed and is a systematic and remorseless search. In practice, there is a variety of ways to make supplier improvement part of the organizational culture. One of these is to routinely use supplier measurement systems to raise performance targets whenever they succeed at achieving current targets and are willing to look for further improvements.

Value analysis, described in the last chapter, is another way of pursuing continuous improvement. This has the organization systematically studying every element of product design to ensure that it fulfils its designed function at the lowest possible cost. Suppliers that are an active part of value analysis can routinely submit ideas for improving quality through improved materials and processes. Purchasing managers can also offer rewards to encourage a supplier to improve performance – with Figure 11.5 illustrating the type of rewards that are available.

On a broader front, larger firms have become increasingly willing to invest in improved supplier performance, typically through training of suppliers. Then they expect tier one suppliers to support the quality efforts of tier two suppliers, and so on back through the supply chain.

Apart from ad hoc arrangement, firms can use a more formal arrangement to systematically search for improvements. One of the best known of these is the 'plan-

FIGURE 11.5 **Types of incentive for supplier quality improvement**

- Award longer-term purchase contracts.
- Offer a greater share of the purchaser's total volume.
- Share the savings and benefits from supplier-initiated improvements.
- Provide suppliers with access to new technology.
- Provide early information about new business opportunities and product development plans.
- Invite suppliers to participate early in new product and process development projects.
- Allow suppliers to use the purchaser's supply agreements to obtain favourable prices for its own supplies.
- Create a preferred list of suppliers that are offered first opportunity for new business.
- Invite suppliers to participate in executive buyer-supplier councils.
- Publicly recognize superior suppliers, perhaps by 'supplier of the year' awards.

do-check-act cycle' where a team of people systematically go through an organization to find improvements using the cycle (Waters, 2002):

Plan – looking at the existing operations, collecting information, discussing alternatives and suggesting a plan for improvements

Do – where the plan is implemented, and data is collected on performance

Check – which analyses the performance data to see if the expected improvements actually appeared

Act – if there are real improvements, the new operations are made permanent, but if there are no improvements, lessons are learnt and the new operations are not adopted

The team is continuously looking for improvements, and at this point they return to the beginning of the cycle, and start looking for more improvements.

A variation on this theme is associated with Six Sigma operations (which we discuss later) and describes the systematic search for improvements in terms of a cycle to 'define, measure, analyse, improve and control' (shown in Figure 11.6).

Make quality everyone's responsibility

The essential feature of TQM is that everyone within an organization is responsible for the ultimate quality of their products. This needs a change in culture and new types of operations, which can only be achieved with considerable education and retraining. TQM can only be achieved when this principle is extended back through tiers of suppliers in the supply chain. Now an important question asks how everyone involved can align their own views of quality and those of suppliers.

Physically co-locating staff with suppliers is one powerful way to spread the message that quality is everyone's responsibility – and at the same time improve buyer-supplier communication. This is clearly a difficult step, but it can be achieved. For example, Volkswagen built a truck assembly plant in Brazil with seven suppliers located within the assembly facility. These suppliers produce components and subassemblies in the Volkswagen facility using their own equipment, with their own workforce.

Six Sigma supplier quality

Obviously, the principles of TQM only give the expected benefits when they are properly implemented. When it became popular in the 1980s, many firms told their

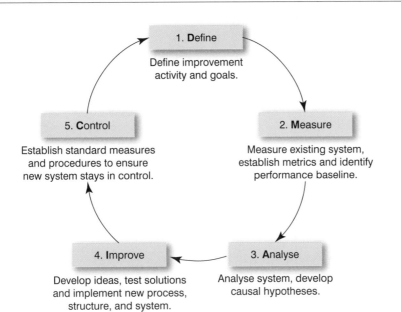

FIGURE 11.6

Performance improvement model

employees about the principles involved without committing the resources needed to change the corporate culture. Often they believed that taking some steps in the direction of improved quality was good enough – so it is not surprising that they failed to make the kind of improvements that they anticipated. As a result, many firms became disillusioned about quality programmes, and few were enthusiastic enough to extend their internal TQM efforts out to their suppliers.

However, things changed and TQM has now moved on from being a means of getting a competitive advantage to being a requirement of business. New methods have been introduced to streamline the implementation of TQM, and make it easier to use. These did not change the principles underlying TQM, but they gave new models and practical procedures. One of these methods is described as **Six Sigma**, which Pyzdek (2000) described as, 'A rigorous, focussed and highly effective implementation of proven quality principles and techniques. Incorporating elements from the work of many quality pioneers, Six Sigma aims for virtually error-free business performance.'

Six Sigma
An approach and set of methods used in quality management.

Sigma, the Greek letter σ, is used by statisticians to measure the standard deviation in a set of data, and here it describes the variability and hence quality of a supplier's performance. We know that all processes have some variation, with actual performance generally following a normal distribution about the target mean. Quality management tries to reduce this variation as much as possible. If we specify a maximum and minimum performance level, some variations will inevitably be outside these limits (as shown in Figure 11.7). But when the variability is reduced, the number of units lying outside the limits will be lower.

Historically, companies set targets and then reduced variation until the limits were three standard deviations away from the mean, meaning that 99.73 per cent of units were acceptable. Of course, this still left 0.27 per cent – or 2,700 parts per million – outside the specifications and of poor quality. Many organizations found this unsatisfactory, and Motorola is generally credited with coining the term Six Sigma quality to define an improved level of performance. Specifically, it means that variation is reduced to the point where the acceptable limits are six standard deviations away from the mean. Actually, it is a bit more complicated than this, but Six Sigma generally described as producing fewer than 3.4 defective units per million. Although this seems like very high quality, it is increasingly seen as the level that is

FIGURE 11.7

The effect of reducing
variation

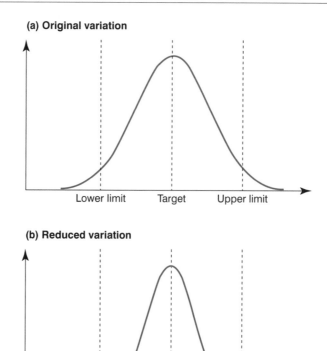

(a) Original variation

Lower limit   Target   Upper limit

(b) Reduced variation

Lower limit   Target   Upper limit

necessary to remain competitive. Also, remember than when a aeroplane contains several million parts it is reassuring that so few are likely to be defective.

Apart from allowing competitiveness, Six Sigma has the advantage of reducing costs – in line with the belief that higher quality leads to lower costs. Suppliers operating at 3 or 4 sigma quality seem to spend 25 per cent of their revenues fixing problems; those working at Six Sigma reduce this to 5 per cent of revenues.

Six Sigma quality has been the basis of a drive to take the complexity out of TQM. Proponents say that TQM became too complicated and includes more than 400 different tools and methods, while Six Sigma concentrates on a smaller set of proven methods. On the other hand, opponents say that Six Sigma is only a different name for the central theme of TQM.

LEARNING FROM PRACTICE

Zamnat Resources Ltd

Zamnat Resources (ZR) is a producer of copper and other metals in Southern Africa. It has developed an audit system to certify that its suppliers satisfy the company's quality expectations. Primary goals of the audit are to help with a decision about supplier quality certification, and to encourage ZR suppliers to achieve continuous quality improvement.

ZR's supplier certification process assesses supplier quality management and systems rather than individual products, and it actively helps suppliers make

Source: Based on Richmond D. (2008) Supplier certification, *SOORS Conference,* Johannesburg.

substantial quality improvements. The process cen-tres on a formal audit of suppliers' operations, but before this, a trial audit is done to minimize possible surprizes and give suppliers a fair chance to prepare and make adjustments before the formal audit. The whole audit process has six steps.

Step 1. *Meet and plan.* When ZR identifies the suppliers that it plans to evaluate, they organize a series of meetings with the suppliers' management team. This reviews their aims and makes sure that both sides agree common aims and the steps to achieve these.

Step 2. *Supplier's self-survey.* Each supplier is encouraged to do a survey themselves to measure their likely performance in ZR's formal survey, and sort out any initial problems in quality management, quality measurement, safety and training and facilities. This survey helps to identify and focus on the areas with which ZR is most concerned.

Step 3. *Initial improvements.* ZR and the supplier use the results of the supplier's self-survey to identify specific strengths and weaknesses. Where there are weaknesses, ZR expects them to be strengthened, and if necessary assigns a team to work with the supplier.

Step 4. *Trial audit.* ZR conducts a trial audit once the supplier has implemented an initial improvements. The trial audit serves two purposes. Firstly, it shows the status of the supplier's quality and improvement efforts.

Secondly, it prepares the supplier for the formal audit that will follow.

Step 5. *Formal audit.* The formal audit includes information from two separate sources. Firstly, each ZR department that has direct contact with a supplier gives its own evaluation of their performance. This evaluation considers material quality, delivery, administration, marketing services, disputes resolution and after-sales service. Secondly, a multi-functional team from ZR visit the supplier to do the bulk of the audit using a standard corporate survey format. This includes assessment of quality management, quality measurement, safety and training, and facilities. When a supplier reaches a minimum standard in every factor it can become a certified supplier – so the audit team's recommendations can be certification, certification after corrective action or no certification.

Step 6. *Recommendation review.* A review committee considers the recommendation of the audit team, together with all other available information, to reach a final decision. There are five options here, each of which means different types of trading interactions with ZR. In decreasing level of performance:

i.   Supplier of excellence.
ii. Preferred supplier.
iii. Certified supplier.
iv. Can be certified after corrective action.
v.   No certification.

ISO CERTIFICATION

Organizations can use their own supplier certification process to ensure that suppliers reach certain standards – or they may assume that a supplier that is certified by another customer will reach acceptable standards. Using such standards can focus on the desired mix of factors, but it inevitably has a lot of duplication as many customers might certify a particular supplier. To avoid this, supply managers turned to established benchmarks, and the universal standard for quality management is ISO 9000 (ISO, 2009). The International Standards Organization introduced this family of standards in 1987 and they have been regularly updated ever since. Companies that do not have the necessary resources for their own certification scheme, or who see no point in duplicating internationally accepted work, accept ISO 9001 certification as evidence of a supplier's quality management. By 2009 more than a million companies in 175 countries had been certified as reaching the ISO 9001 standard.

ISO 9000 Standards

ISO 9000 consists of several standards concerned with process quality. It recognizes that the process is the critical element in determining product quality, so it defined procedures to ensure that processes can deliver high-quality products. Specifically, an audit is carried out by independent assessors to see whether a firm meets required standards for certification. Meeting these standards is not easy, but it has become recognized as a minimum requirement for competing globally.

The focus of the standards on process rather than products themselves is important. For example, if a company says that it will make tubes with a diameter of 10 cm, then ISO 9000 describes management procedures for ensuring that the tubes is reliably close to this target – but it does not say whether that target is reasonable or whether it would have been better to make tubes with a diameter of 12 cm.

The ISO 9000 family of standards is regularly reviewed and the 2008 version described procedures for meeting customer quality requirements, applicable regulatory requirements, enhanced customer satisfaction and continual improvement. ISO 9001 is the main standard which describes the requirements of a quality management system, while ISO 9004 offers guidance for quality improvement (Drickhamer, 2001).

The standards are based on eight quality management principles:

1 *Customer focus* – as organizations should understand current and future customer needs and strive to exceed their expectations.

2 Leadership – to establish purpose and direction. Leaders should create an environment where people can support and help achieve the organization's objectives.

3 *Involvement of people* – including full involvement of employees at all levels to enhance quality performance.

4 *Process approach* – which considers processes rather than outputs as the way to achieve desired results.

5 *System approach to management* – identifying, understanding and managing interrelated operations as an integrated system.

LEARNING FROM PRACTICE

The Malcolm Baldrige National Quality Award

In the 1980s, US companies were falling behind in quality management and President Reagan initiated the Malcolm Baldrige National Quality Award as a means of encouraging quality improvement. The awards are based on a standard set of criteria in seven categories (listed in Figure 11.8). Many companies now use these as a basis for their own quality management systems, and some managers believe they give a more comprehensive view than ISO 9000.

You can see from Figure 11.8 that an organization can score a maximum of 1,000 points for the seven categories of leadership, strategic planning, customer and market focus, information and analysis, human resource focus, process management and business results. Continuous improvement is a basic requirement in each, and firms must show how they plan to improve in each area. Successful companies score 700 points or more, and demonstrate balanced and superior performance across each category. It can take a company 8 to 10 years to develop a quality system that is likely to win the annual award.

Source: Based on US National Institute of Standards and Technology at www.quality.nist.gov; Handfield R., and Ghosh S. (1994) Creating a total quality culture through organizational change. *Journal of International Marketing*, 2(4), pp 15–30.

FIGURE 11.8 Template for Malcolm Baldridge National Quality Award

Score summary worksheet — Business criteria

Examiner name _____ Application number _____

Summary of criteria items	Total points possible **A**	Per cent score 0–100% (stage 1–10% units) **B**	Score (A x B) **C**
1 Leadership			
1.1 Organizational leadership	85	_____ %	_____
1.2 Public responsibility and citizenship	40	_____ %	_____
Category total:	125		_____ SUM C
2 Strategic planning			
2.1 Strategy development	40	_____ %	_____
2.2 Strategy deployment	45	_____ %	_____
Category total:	85		_____ SUM C
3 Customer and market focus			
3.1 Customer and market knowledge	40	_____ %	_____
3.2 Customer satisfaction and relationships	45	_____ %	_____
Category total:	85		_____ SUM C
4 Information and analysis			
4.1 Measurement of organizational performance	40	_____ %	_____
4.2 Analysis of organizational performance	45	_____ %	_____
Category total:	85		_____ SUM C
5 Human resource focus			
5.1 Work systems	35	_____ %	_____
5.2 Employee education, training and development	25	_____ %	_____
5.3 Employee well-being and satisfaction	25	_____ %	_____
Category total:	85		_____ SUM C
6 Process management			
6.1 Product and service processes	55	_____ %	_____
6.2 Support processes	15	_____ %	_____
6.3 Supplier and partnering processes	15	_____ %	_____
Category total:	85		_____ SUM C
7 Business results			
7.1 Customer-focussed results	115	_____ %	_____
7.2 Financial and market results	115	_____ %	_____
7.3 Human resource results	80	_____ %	_____
7.4 Supplier and partner results	25	_____ %	_____
7.5 Organizational effectiveness results	115	_____ %	_____
Category total:	450		_____ SUM C
Grand total (D)	1,000		══════ D

6 *Continual improvement* – which should become a permanent organizational objective.

7 *Factual approach to decision making* – using objective analyses and decisions.

8 *Mutually beneficial supplier relationships* – recognizing that an organization and its suppliers are interdependent, and co-operation creates shared value.

It is in the best interests of suppliers to pursue ISO 9000 certification as a way of both improving quality and ensuring customers of their commitment and capabilities – and certification is increasingly a prerequisite for doing business, particularly with customers that are certified. Thus, buyers benefit from using certified suppliers, primarily because they do not have to develop and conduct their own checks on supplier quality.

ISO 14000 Standards

A related set of standards are the ISO 14000 standards which are designed to promote environmental protection and management. When organizations include environmental standards in their definition of quality, these give a way of analysing and documenting a supplier's environmental impact. The standards cover a broad range of environmental disciplines, ranging from an environmental management system to auditing, labelling, and product standards. Benefits achieved through ISO 14000 certification include fewer pollutants generated, improved treatment of waste, reduced liability, improved regulatory compliance, better public and community relations and lowered insurance premiums (Swift *et al.*, 1998).

Like TQM, the basis of ISO 14000 is that better performance can reduce costs, in this case through improved resource management and lower waste. Again, many buying firms now require their suppliers to become ISO 14000 certified.

CHAPTER REVIEW

- All organizations survive through their ability to design, produce and supply high-quality products. This means that all organizations should be concerned with the quality of products they supply

- It is difficult to define quality, as it depends on so many factors. The current view is that high quality is defined as meeting and preferably exceeding customer expectations

- Without high-quality products, customers are not satisfied, and companies cannot expect to compete against more obliging competitors. To supply high-quality products to its customers, an organization has to buy high-quality items from its own suppliers. This idea of supplier quality is a key element in quality management

- The principle of TQM is that everyone within an organization is responsible for quality. This view has developed into a much broader management philosophy. Deming outlined the core of this in his '14 Principles'

- The introduction of TQM is difficult and involves fundamental changes to an organization and its culture. We described eight factors that are important in achieving this transformation, including striving for zero defects, introducing quality at source and making quality everyone's responsibility

- TQM involves major changes that are not easy to implement. Some forms have looked for short cuts which give unreliable results. However, others have developed simplified procedures and rules that can bring benefits. Six Sigma is one of these, that describes a process for moving towards quality targets of 3.4 faults per million units

- Organizations often audit their suppliers quality and certificate successful ones. However, this duplicates effort and does not give standard measures of performance. A better approach is to use standard procedures, with ISO 9000 being the universally accepted standard for quality management

DISCUSSION QUESTIONS

1 What exactly is quality?

2 Why should a buyer be concerned with supplier quality management?

3 Why is it important for a buyer to be a good customer? How can this be achieved?

4 'Supply management not only buys materials from suppliers, but it also buys a supplier's performance capability.' What does this mean?

5 Do all suppliers have an equal impact on product quality? Discuss the factors that affect a supplier's impact on a firm's final product quality.

6 How can early supplier involvement in product design contribute to higher levels of quality?

7 Discuss the role of Deming's 14 Principles in managing supplier quality.

8 Why did many TQM initiatives in the 1970s and 1980s not succeed as well as expected?

9 Some managers argue that suppliers should not be rewarded for doing something that is already expected (such as providing products with perfect quality or continuously improving quality). Do you agree with this?

10 Discuss the benefits to a supplier of achieving ISO 9000 certification. How do these compare with the benefits of a buying company using its own certification?

11 What is meant by Six Sigma quality?

12 What principles of TQM does a well-developed supplier evaluation and selection process satisfy?

13 Describe the various classifications of quality costs.

REFERENCES

Crosby P. B (1979) Quality is free, New York: McGraw Hill.

Deming W. E. (1986) Out of the crisis, Cambridge MA: MIT Press.

Drickhamer D. (2001) Standards shake-up, Industry Week, March 5, pp 37–40.

Evans J. R. and Lindsay W. M. (2008) Managing for quality and performance excellence (7th edition), Mason, OH: South-Western.

Feigenbaum A. V. (1983) Total quality control (3rd edition), New York: McGraw-Hill.

Foster S. T. (2007) Managing quality: integrating the supply chain (3rd edition), Upper Saddle River, NJ: Prentice Hall.

Juran J. M. (1988) Juran on planning for quality, New York: The Free Press.

Pyzdek T. (2000) The Six Sigma revolution, and website at www.pyzdek.com/six-sigma-revolution.htm

ISO (2009) Quality management, International Standards Organization, Geneva and website at www.iso.org

Swift J. A., Ross J. E. and Omachonu V. K. (1998) Principles of total quality (2nd edition), Boca Raton, FL: St. Lucie Press.

Taguchi G. (1986) Introduction to quality engineering, Asian Productivity Association, Tokyo.

Trent G. J. (2001) Linking TQM to SCM, Supply Chain Management Review, 2001, 5(3): 71.

Trent R. J. and Monczka R. M. (1998) Purchasing and supply management: trends and changes throughout the 1990s, International Journal of Purchasing and Materials Management, pp 2–11.

Waters D. (2002) Operations management (2nd edition), Harlow,' Essex: Pearson Education.

FURTHER READING

Columbus L. (2007) Quality partnerships with your customers, Quality Digest, pp 44–48.

Crosby P. B. (1996) Quality is still free: making quality certain in uncertain times, New York: McGraw-Hill.

Dasgupta T. (2003) Using the Six-Sigma metric to improve the performance of a supply chain, *Total Quality Management and Business Excellence*, 14(3): 355–366.

Deming W.E. (1986) Out of the crisis, Cambridge, MA: MIT Press.

Evans J. R. and Lindsay W. M. (2008) Managing for quality and performance excellence (7th edition), Mason, OH: South-Western.

Foster S. T. (2007) Managing quality: integrating the supply chain (3rd edition), Upper Saddle River NJ: Pearson Education.

Gould R. A. et al (2006) Quality management, In: Cavinato J. L., Flynn A. E. and Kauffman R. G. (editors), The supply management handbook, New York: McGraw-Hill.

Juran J. M. (1999) Juran's quality handbook (5th edition), New York: McGraw-Hill.

Maass R., Brown J. O. and Bossert J. L. (1999) Supplier certification: a continuous improvement strategy, Milwaukee, WI: ASQ Quality Press.

Merrill P. (1997) Do it right the second time: benchmarking best practices in the quality change process, Portland, OR: Productivity Press.

Nelson D., Mayo R. and Moody P. E. (1998) Powered by Honda: developing excellence in the global enterprize, New York: John Wiley & Sons.

Pande P. S., Neuman R. P. and Cavanaugh R. R. (2000) , The Six Sigma way, New York: McGraw-Hill.

Reid D. R. (2002) Purchaser and supplier quality, *Quality Progress*, 35(8): 81–85.

Smith B. (2003) Lean and Six Sigma – a one-two punch, *Quality Progress*, 36(4): 37–42.

Smith L. (2006) Quality around the world, Quality Digest, June, pp 41–47.

Stundza T. (2007) Assured quality critical in global sourcing, *Purchasing*, 136(11): 32.

Taguchi G. and Clausing D. (1990) Robust quality, Harvard Business Review, January–February.

Trent R. J. (1999) Achieving world-class supplier quality, *Total Quality Management*, 10(6): 927–939.

Zhu K., Zhang R. Q. and Tsung F. (2007) Pushing quality improvement along supply chains, *Management Science*, 53(3): 421–436.

CASE STUDY

Integrated Devices

Bill Edwards is a quality engineer assigned to the Injected Moulding Commodity Team at Integrated Devices. The commodity team is responsible for evaluating, selecting and negotiating agreements with plastic-injected moulding suppliers. It is also responsible for improving the quality of services and raw material that Integrated Devices buy from its suppliers. Bill's role starts after supplier selection and involves working directly with suppliers that require training or technical assistance with quality management and improvement.

The company spends about 70 per cent of its revenue on purchased goods and services, so suppliers have a major impact on product quality. Recently Bill received a call about a recurring manufacturing problem at Integrated Devices' Plant No. 3. The plant buyer said the plant is experiencing some quality variability with a key plastic-injected moulding component supplied by Trexler Plastics. The component is sometimes too short or too long to fit properly with other components in the finished product. Although the unit cost of the component is only €1.55, these quality issues are creating production problems that far exceed the component's purchase price.

The local buyer announced he was having difficulty resolving the problem and asked for support from the corporate commodity team. He said, 'The corporate team selected this supplier, so the least you can do is to help us solve the problems it is creating.' This comment surprised Bill, but it soon became clear that staff from the plant resented not being able to select their own suppliers. Bill went back and reviewed the corporate team's decision to select a single supplier for an entire family of plastic-injected mouldings. He found that Trexler had quoted the lowest price for components and had provided samples that passed Integrated Devices' engineering tests.

After investigating the problem during a tense meeting with plant staff, Bill recognized that he would have to visit Trexler and work with their process engineers to look at the operations that caused the component variability. However, when he arrived at Trexler, Bill learned that they did not have a dedicated process engineer. One engineer, Steve Smith, was responsible for plant layout, process, quality and industrial engineering. Steve had been hired 2 months previously and was still becoming familiar with Trexler's procedures. When Bill asked to review the supplier's quality control procedures, Steve had to ask several people before he could locate them.

Bill decided that his next step should be to understand the process for producing the component, so he asked Steve for some output data. Steve explained they did not routinely collect data for process capability or statistical control. But there is an inspector who examines every finished unit to determine if it should be shipped to the customer. However, Steve added that sometimes, 'Things don't seem to be working properly' with production equipment.

Bill explained the basics of process capability to Steve, and then asked him to collect data from the components process. In particular, he requested periodic measurements of samples from the process so they could do some statistical analyses. He returned 3 days later to examine this data (shown in Figure 11.9). Bill did some initial calculations with this data and examined the training and quality control procedures at Trexler. He realized that he had some serious work ahead of him.

FIGURE 11.9 Data for the production of plastic-moulded component

Component: #03217666							
Description: Bracket							
Design specification: 4 ± 0.06 inches							
4.01	4.02	4.00	3.99	3.98	4.00	4.00	4.03
4.04	4.02	4.07	3.95	3.98	4.01	4.03	4.00
4.00	3.96	3.94	3.98	3.99	4.02	4.01	4.00
4.05	3.98	3.97	4.03	4.07	4.04	4.02	4.01
3.99	3.96	4.00	4.00	4.01	4.02	4.02	4.01
3.98	3.99	3.94	3.93	4.00	4.02	4.00	3.97
3.99	4.02	4.04	4.00	3.96	3.97	4.00	4.01

Questions

- What information can you get from the limited amount of data collected?

- The local buyer at Integrated Devices did not seem pleased that a corporate team selected the supplier. Why?

- Is quality a major concern for Trexler? How are their quality management systems working?

- When evaluating supplier quality, why is it important to focus on the process that produces the material rather than on the material itself?

- What is the likelihood that Bill will resolve the problems with this component. If Integrated Devices decides to continue using Trexler as a supplier, what must each company do to improve quality?

CHAPTER 12
NEGOTIATION

LEARNING OBJECTIVES   After reading this chapter you should be able to:

- Discuss the general features of negotiations

- Understand why and how purchasing negotiations are undertaken

- Discuss the importance of planning the negotiation process

- Appreciate the different sources of power in negotiations

- Describe a formal approach to planning negotiations

- Understand the role of concessions during negotiations

- Describe a range of tactics that are used to reach agreement in negotiations

- Discuss the concept of win-win negotiations

- Recognize the subtleties and complexities of global negotiations

WHAT IS NEGOTIATION?

Negotiation

Is a process of formal communication, either face-to-face or electronically, where two or more people come together to seek mutual agreement about an issue or issues.

Everyone negotiates something every day, whether it is dealing with other drivers at road junctions or discussing the price of acquiring a company. As such, **negotiation** is a highly complex and dynamic process. It is one of the most important activities performed by procurement managers, who continually negotiate terms with their suppliers. Procurement is certainly not the only group in an organization that negotiates, but they may be the most consistent users as negotiation is a vital part of every sourcing process.

We all have a general idea of what negotiations are, as they are the discussions that we have with other people to seek agreement about some topic. There are many formal definitions along the lines of, 'A negotiation is an interactive communication process that may take place whenever we want something from someone else or another person wants something from us (Shell, 2006).' 'Negotiation is the process of communicating back and forth for the purpose of reaching a joint agreement about differing needs or ideas (Acuff, 1997).' 'Negotiation is a decision-making process by which two or more people agree how to allocate scarce resources (Thompson, 2005).' 'Negotiating is the end game of the sales process (McCormack, 1995).'

Negotiation process

The negotiation process involves the management of time, information and power between individuals and organizations. Each party wants something that the other party has, and recognizes that a process of compromise and concession is needed for the exchange to take place. With standard purchasing a seller has a product and wants money; a buyer has money and wants the product; negotiations are needed to arrange the exchange on mutually agreeable terms.

It often seems like organizations are negotiating, but you have to remember that the process actually involves relationships between people. It involves each party trying to persuade the other party to do something that is in its best interest. The process involves skills that individuals, with the proper training and experience, can learn and improve. Good negotiators are not born; they hone the necessary skills through planning and practice.

BATNA

Is the best outcome one party can get without negotiations.

A starting point for negotiations is the **best alternative to a negotiated agreement** (BATNA), which is also known as the negotiator's bottom line or reservation point. This is the return that one party will get if they do not negotiate. It follows that if negotiations are not achieving this minimum return, it is best for the party to walk away from the table and implement their next-best option (Fisher *et al.*, 1991). Each negotiator has a BATNA, but they should not reveal this to the other party, or else it becomes a target and the final settlement is unlikely to move far above that point. All negotiated settlements are ultimately judged in the light of the other viable alternatives, or the amount of movement away from BATNA.

Position

Is the stated demand that is placed on the table by a negotiator.

Another key concept is a negotiator's **position**, which we can define as their opening offer, and which represents their ideal outcome.

During negotiations a party will start by stating a position and will aim at reaching an agreement somewhere between this and the BATNA. Another element to consider is the negotiator's interest, which is the unspoken motivation or reason that underlies a negotiation position. Usually the negotiator's interests are never stated, either because they are not germane to the stated position, or because they may be based on a complex mixture of personal and business preferences. Sharing the interest behind a position may cause a negotiator's power to shift towards the other party, followed by a less-than-desired outcome. So a successful negotiator must identify the other party's interests through a series of open-ended, probing questions – as reaching an agreement depends on meeting the other party's underlying interests, and not necessarily their stated position (Fisher *et al.*, 1991).

An astute negotiator must also be able to distinguish between the other party's needs and wants. Needs are those outcomes that a negotiator must have in order to reach a successful outcome; wants are those outcomes that a negotiator would like to have. This means that wants can be exchanged as concessions to the other party during a negotiation because they are not critical to achieving a successful conclusion. When negotiators do their initial planning they have to classify all potential issues into needs and wants, thereby setting priorities and listing outcomes that must be achieved and those that can be exchanged. This mention of planning is important, as before they start work negotiators have to:

1   Know exactly what you want;

2   Find out what the other party wants and make them feel heard;

3   Propose action in such a way that both parties can accept it (Anderson, 1994).

Step 1 determines and formalizes the negotiators' goals and being specific and writing these down helps them remain focussed on their priorities. Writing down the goals also allows negotiators to refer back to them during the course of discussions, when it is easy to be distracted by the other negotiators' tactics and the pace of progress. The more clearly negotiators define their priorities, the more likely they are to achieve them in the final agreement.

Step 2 tries to determine what the other negotiators are likely to need and want. It is difficult to develop common ground in the negotiation without knowing exactly what the other party wants, so ask specifically, 'What does the other party need or

Source: Based on Scarborough J. (2008) Negotiating success, Purchasing Practice, 2 (4), pp 17–25; Ciancareili A. (1999) Strategic negotiating goes far beyond best price, Purchasing, 25 March.

LEARNING FROM PRACTICE

Haas Chetchem and American Airines

The Purchasing Director of Haas Chetchem is old enough to remember when the sign of a good purchasing negotiator was someone who could get a rock-bottom price from suppliers. He often saw good companies driven into financial difficulties by purchasers who saw a weakness and persuaded suppliers to deliver on terms that were unsustainable. Once he saw a buyer offer a major contract to a small company who overextended their finances to increase capacity – and then the buyer cancelled the order, but bought materials cheaply in the following bankruptcy sale.

Today the Purchasing Director realizes that not all negotiations focus on price or reward aggressive positions. Getting the best price may be a good indicator

of effectiveness, but it is not necessarily the best option for long-term success. For some materials it is essential to get good prices, but for others it is less important. The vice president of purchasing with American Airlines recognizes this and says, 'Win-win negotiations are conducted in long-term relationships with suppliers. In these cases it is important that the supplier and American Airlines feel they are getting a good deal because the plan is to work together for a long while.' He continues by saying that 'Principle-based negotiating is used in a single-source situation or alliance where the two parties begin the negotiation by agreeing to certain principles, such as how the companies plan to grow together.'

want?' – and delve into their likely positions to find their underlying interests. An obvious point here is that negotiators cannot assume the other parties think the same way they do, so they should start with some open-ended, probing questions to identify their needs and wants. They should also make the other party feel heard so that there can be a clear exchange of ideas. This will allow progress to step 3, where mutually acceptable terms are first proposed and then agreed.

NEGOTIATION FRAMEWORK

A good way to approach a buyer-supplier negotiation is through an interactive, give-and-take process that involves five phases (shown in Figure 12.1):

1   Identify or anticipate a purchase requirement.

2   Determine if negotiation is required.

3   Plan for the negotiation.

4   Conduct the negotiation.

5   Execute the agreement.

FIGURE 12.1 Five phases of a negotiation process

Identify or anticipate a purchase requirement	Determine if negotiation is required	Plan for the negotiation	Conduct the negotiation	Execute the agreement
1	2	3	4	5
• Purchase requisitions	• Is bid process inadequate?	• Identify participants	• Perform fact finding	• Provide performance feedback
• Inventory counts	• Are many non-price issues involved?	• Develop objectives	• Recess or caucus as necessary	• Build on the success of the negotiation
• Reorder point systems	• Is contract large?	• Analyse strengths and weaknesses	• Work to narrow differences	
• New product development	• Are technical requirements complex?	• Gather information	• Manage time pressures	
• New facilities	• Does contract involve plant and equipment?	• Recognize counterpart's needs	• Maintain informal atmosphere	
	• Does contract involve a partnership?	• Identify facts and issues	• Summarize progress periodically	
	• Will supplier perform value-added activities?	• Establish positions	• Employ tactics	
	• Will there be high risk and uncertainty?	• Develop strategies and tactics	• Keep relationships positive	
		• Brief personnel		
		• Practice the negotiation		

Identify or anticipate a purchase requirement

A purchasing process begins when someone within a firm identifies or anticipates a requirement to purchase materials. For existing items, it may not be necessary to identify a supplier and negotiate terms, as an agreement is already in place. But whenever there are new requirements – perhaps identified by a new product development team – they need new contracts. So whenever there are new items, new suppliers or new contracts with existing items, purchasing managers have to negotiate terms.

Determine if negotiation is required

Not all purchases need extensive negotiations. Competitive bidding often needs little follow-up, particularly for items that are low value, widely available commodities or have pre-existing standards. On the other hand, negotiations are more common for larger purchases, when issues other than price are important or when competitive bidding does not satisfy the buyer's requirements. More specifically, negotiations with suppliers are needed when:

- *The total contract value is large,* supply managers often negotiate very large contracts, and any weakness on the part of a supplier performance can cause severe problems

- *The purchase involves complex technical requirements,* perhaps including product and process specifications that are still evolving

- *The purchase involves expensive plant and equipment,* with suppliers customizing capital purchases to meet a buyer's needs

- *The agreement involves a special or collaborative relationship,* addressing issues beyond a conventional purchase agreement. For example, the two parties may discuss the joint development of new technology with the sharing of R&D efforts

- *The supplier will perform important value-added activities,* buyers are increasingly asking suppliers to perform activities such as product design, testing, packaging and inventory management – which need significant negotiations

We have mentioned price negotiations, but there are many other factors and buyers may need to negotiate:

- Price

- Payment terms and currency issues

- Delivery schedules and lead times

- Product quality levels

- Warranties and replacements

- Performance measures

- Non-performance penalties and performance incentives

- Improvement requirements in products and processes

- Technological support and assistance

- Contract volumes

- Capacity commitments

- Mode of transport and selection of carriers

- Special packaging and shipping

- Liability for loss and damage

- Schedules for progress payments

- Contract length and renewal

- Resources used for developing closer relationships

- Information to be collected and shared

- Protection of proprietary information

- Ownership of intellectual property

- Spare parts, after-sales service and other support

- Supplier's allowable costs

- Dispute resolution mechanisms

This list, although lengthy, is by no means exhaustive and represents only a portion of the topics that negotiators can address.

An important question for negotiations is how information technology – such as electronic communications and internet-based reverse auctions – can change the need to negotiate. For instance, reverse auctions have clearly reduced the need for face-to-face negotiations between buyers and sellers. However, the type of items acquired through reverse auctions – usually standard commodities with moderate cost – would probably not warrant significant negotiations in the first place. For items that are critical to the buyer or involve significant non-price issues, it is unlikely that buyers and sellers will stop face-to-face negotiation.

Plan for the negotiation

Many buyer-supplier negotiations are relatively straightforward, but they still need some basic preparation and planning. Sometimes the negotiations are particularly complex and these need months of thorough preparation. Regardless of the scale, buyers who take the time to prepare for negotiations usually get better outcomes than those who rush through inadequate plans.

We have just said that new technology is reducing the need for face-to face negotiations. It is a very attractive alternative to the international travel that is an inherent part of global sourcing – with globalization itself raising a host of new negotiation challenges. It also changes the way that managers plan for and conduct negotiations. For instance, the internet allows buyers to negotiate a broad range of issues with suppliers, regardless of their physical location. At a basic level, a buyer sends an electronic template for a request for quotation (RFQ) to selected suppliers, and they return the completed form with relevant details (Waxer, 2001). At a more sophisticated level, trading partners can discuss details at virtual meetings, or e-meetings. These bring obvious benefits, but they still do not replace the need for face-to-face discussions as an efficient way of forming relationships.

Apart from the technology, effective planning also needs decisions about:

- The nature and purpose of the negotiations

- Needs, wants and their priorities

- Aims and interests

- Opening bids

- The other party, including their personality, experience, style, etc.

- Responses, including issues that may be raised and reactions

- Defining protocols – where and when the negotiation occur, who is present, what the agenda is, how long talks will last and so on (Lewicki *et al.*, 2006)

Apparently small details, such as deciding where to negotiate, can be an important factor of planning. A home location can give a real advantage to a negotiator, particularly during international negotiations. There is general agreement that the most successful outcomes need an informal atmosphere to build trusting relationships and long-term commitment – with excessive formality constraining all parties and restricting the free exchange of ideas.

Conduct the negotiation

Negotiations should only begin when both the supplier and the buyer feel confident about their level of planning and preparation. However, there are always deadlines to meet, and these bring pressures to initiate, conduct and conclude negotiations within a reasonable time.

It is during the negotiation that both parties play out the tactics that they have prepared, and use their skills to achieve a desired end. Then face-to-face negotiations often move through four phases:

1 **Fact finding and information sharing.** This part of the process helps clarify and confirm information provided by the buyer and seller.

2 **Recess.** This allows each party the opportunity to reassess relative strengths and weaknesses, review and revise objectives and positions and organize the negotiation agenda.

3 **Narrowing of differences.** This typically includes the offering of proposals and counter-proposals and exchanging concessions.

4 **Agreeing terms.** Reaching an agreed position that is acceptable to both sides, concluding the negotiations and establishing any follow-up activities.

Experience suggests that successful negotiators display certain behaviours during discussions. For example, they are willing to compromise and revise their goals, particularly when new information challenges their initial position. They also view each issue independently, without linking it to any other issues. This is important as negotiators that link issues into a predetermined sequence risk undermining an entire negotiation when they cannot reach agreement on a single issue within the whole package. Effective negotiators also establish lower and upper ranges for each major issue rather than a single, rigid position that limits the number of viable options and is more likely to create an impasse.

It also seems that effective negotiators explore more options, and develop more common ground, rather than focussing on the differences. For this reason, it is a good idea to summarize positions and points of agreement throughout negotiations, as this helps reduce misunderstanding while keeping track of progress. It may also help to have dedicated note-taker to record what was said, who said it, what the reaction was and what the areas of agreement were.

LEARNING FROM PRACTICE

Murray Pardoe Limited

The Purchasing Director of Murray Pardoe Limited has spent many years improving the performance of their procurement department. His primary aim has been to increase the ROI for the company, which has meant increasing returns while simultaneously reducing the value of assets. In practice, stocks are one of the company's biggest assets, and the value of holdings has been considerably reduced in recent years. To achieve this, the purchasing department negotiated longer-term contracts with consignment inventory to replace short-term, ad hoc arrangements with suppliers. (Consignment inventory involves deferring payment for an item until an internal customer actually uses it, and passing some responsibility for stock back to suppliers.)

Murray Pardoe is organized into four divisions, each of which used to be responsible for its own purchasing. Now the Purchasing Director works with each division to develop and negotiate corporate contracts. For this the corporate function identifies items for long-term contracts, looks for opportunities to standardize materials, analyses potential suppliers, creates benchmark prices to compare with final prices, calculates annual demand and represents the interests of each division during negotiations with suppliers. Before negotiations start, there is a period of preparation during which each division can present its specific needs, define the purchasing options they prefer and list any issues they would like to see addressed. The preparation period allows divisions to agree their requirements with the corporate function, which can then define its requirements and see how best to achieve these.

The new systems automated much of the material movement and control, along with associated administration and information flows. It also increased the use of the internet for negotiations with global suppliers. Almost 85 per cent of purchases are now covered by long-term agreements; while stock levels have fallen by 40 per cent and associated costs by 50 per cent.

Source: Based on Richmond D. (2008) Negotiation practice, Purchasing Practice, 2 (2), pp 45–53.

Effective negotiators also make fewer irritating comments about the other party, give fewer reasons to support their position (as too many supporting reasons can dilute an argument), and make fewer counter-proposals (as this would suggest that they are compromising too much or offering too many concessions).

Execute the agreement

Reaching agreement is not the end of the negotiation process – but rather it represents the beginning of the contract's execution. An important part of executing a negotiated agreement is adding the terms to a contract so that others become are aware of its contents. Then during the life of the agreement each party should do what they agreed, and they should build on the success of their agreement to lay the foundations for more work in the future.

NEGOTIATION PLANNING

Planning
In the context of negotiations planning leads to a method or scheme.

In the last section we said that planning is an essential part of the negotiation process – and it is generally considered the single most important factor for success. There are many negotiators that fail simply because the participants have not properly prepared.

At least 90 per cent of successful outcomes of any negotiation are achieved by effective planning (Lewicki *et al.*, 2006). Preparing at the last minute is a sure recipe for failure, especially when the other person is far better prepared – and being clever at thinking on your feet is never enough to reach a successful conclusion. Planning is a proactive process that consists of the following nine steps.

Develop specific objectives

The first step of negotiation planning involves developing specific goals and objectives for the negotiation. In principle, an objective is a broad aspiration to work towards, while a goal is a more limited, measurable target. Then an objective of sourcing negotiations might be to reach a long-term agreement for purchasing a particular product, while a goal is to arrange a delivery next week within a specified price range.

Neither buyers nor sellers would commit resources if they thought that negotiations would fail, so at the start both parties must believe that they can eventually reach an agreement. This may refer to many factors, including a fair and reasonable price, required lead time, improved quality levels or increase the level of collaboration. Not all objectives are equally important, so negotiators must set the importance of each and prioritize them – specifically into 'must have' and 'would like to have' objectives, corresponding to needs and wants respectively.

Analyse each party's strengths and weaknesses

Successful negotiators have to understand their counterparts, meaning that they should know what is important to them, their personality, methods, knowledge and skills, objectives and so on. It also means that when buyers negotiate with a supplier for the first time, they must commit the necessary time and energy to get a clear picture of them.

The message is that when buyers prepare for negotiations they need to understand both the issues to be negotiated, and the other party they are negotiating with – including their strengths and weaknesses. This understanding can greatly influence the tactics used at the bargaining table. This is an important point as buyers often feel that they have an advantage, simply because they are the ones that will pay the bill. But negotiation is a joint venture and neither side can assume that it has power or influence over the other. Often a supplier holds power over a buyer – perhaps because of its financial size, full order book, list of satisfied customers, reputation, economic climate, lack of competition and so on.

Gather relevant information

When buyers seek to understand suppliers – and their own – requirements, they need timely and accurate information. Collecting this need not be difficult, particularly when buyers and sellers have previously worked together and negotiated purchasing contracts. Then, the buyers will already have answers to a number of important questions. Did the negotiations go well? Were both parties satisfied with the outcome? What were the areas of disagreement? Are the same negotiating teams used? What are the supplier's main issues? What are the important issues to us? Can the rules of negotiation be changed?

Such basic data is easy to find for repeat negotiations, but is more difficult with a new supplier. One possible source is to contact other buyers who have experience with the supplier – or buyers can search the internet for reports on the supplier and their methods of working. Other published sources of information include trade journals, business publications, trade associations, government reports, annual reports, financial evaluations (such as Dun & Bradstreet reports), commercial databases and inquiries directly to the supplier's employees.

Recognize your counterpart's needs

Buyers and sellers are in many ways mirror images of each other, but they both share a common interest in reaching an acceptable agreement. While buyers gather information about suppliers, it is important to identify key issues that are critical to the supplier. For example, a supplier may want to maintain or increase its market share and output volume, so receiving the entire purchase contract, rather than only a portion, may be an important objective.

The issues that are critical to a supplier are unlikely to be the same as those that are most critical to a buyer. When one party has a requirement that is relatively unimportant to the other, then they are more likely to reach agreement. For example, a supplier's production schedules may require it to produce a buyer's products late in the day with delivery during the evening. If a buyer has an evening work crew that can receive late deliveries, it can easily satisfy the supplier's requirement. In return, the buyer may now expect the supplier to be more accommodating on issues that it considers more important. Give and take is a core aspect to negotiation, and neither party should expect to prevail on all issues. This is why it is important for buyers to do their preparation and identify ranges of acceptable outcomes for each issue, setting priorities for the inevitable concessions and trade-offs.

Identify facts and issues

For planning it is important to differentiate facts from issues – and the two parties should quickly agree on what is a fact rather than an issue. A fact is a reality or truth that the parties can state and verify. In negotiation, facts are not open to debate. For instance, it may be a fact that a buyer wants to purchase a piece of equipment; there is no negotiating about whether the buyer actually wants the piece of equipment (although the specific type of equipment may be less certain).

Issues, on the other hand, are topics to be resolved during the negotiation. Part of the planning process requires all critical issues to be identified so that each party knows what has to be resolved during the negotiations. This may seem a clear distinction, but this is not necessarily so. When a person visits a garage selling new cars a salesperson may assume it to be a fact that the person wants to buy a new car – but this might really be an issue that has to be agreed during negotiations.

Establish a position on each issue

Parties to a negotiation should establish positions that give flexibility. This usually means a range of positions – perhaps with a minimum acceptable position (or BATNA), a maximum or ideal outcome, and a most likely position for agreement somewhere between these. For instance, when the issue is price, a seller may have a minimum acceptable price that it is willing to accept, generally around the cost of making the product plus some contributions to profit. Any price lower than this minimum means that there can be no deal, or at best an unacceptable outcome to the supplier. At the other extreme is a realistic maximum price that the market will support. Somewhere between these two extremes is a reasonable target price that the seller is looking for. At the same time, the buyer has a maximum price that it is willing to offer, generally its overall evaluation of the product, a low target price that it would ideally like, and between these a reasonable offer price that it would be willing to work with. When the buyer's and seller's price ranges overlap they can reach agreement in the bargaining or settlement zone (Lewicki *et al.*, 2006). The bargaining zone represents the heart of the negotiation process, as any proposal outside this range is likely to be rejected by one of the parties.

Figure 12.2 illustrates a settlement zone for a price–based negotiation. In example A, there is no overlap of the ranges, so parties will probably not reach agreement unless one modifies their original position. In example B, the two positions overlap, with the buyer willing to pay up to £11.45 a unit and the supplier willing to sell as low as £11.15 a unit. The two parties should reach an agreement somewhere between those two figures. As a bargaining tactic, the buyer is likely to open with an offer of something less than £11.00, while the seller is likely to suggest a price of more than £11.50 – and they will probably compromise around £11.30.

Several factors influence a decision for one side to modify or even abandon their original position, including their desire for the contract, new information that challenges the accuracy and credibility of the original position or a major concession that leads the other party to modify its position on another issue.

Develop the negotiation tactics

Negotiation tactics refer to the overall approach used to reach an agreement. They include the broader questions of who, what, where, when and how to negotiate. Then there are the range of more detailed arts and skills that negotiators employ as a means of accomplishing their objectives. (We discuss these later in the chapter.)

Brief other personnel

Purchasing negotiations usually affect other parts of an organization, so the negotiators should brief these internal stakeholders and ensure that they are aware of – and in agreement with – the objectives of the negotiation. This briefing should review the major issues of the negotiations and the organization's positions on these issues. Briefing internal stakeholders before negotiations helps eliminate unwanted surprises later. It also encourages stakeholder support for the negotiation process, and ensures that the outcomes are implemented as agreed.

FIGURE 12.2

Negotiating ranges for a purchase price

LEARNING FROM PRACTICE

E-procurement

The number of people buying online continues to grow, so certain changes are inevitable for purchasing staff who have traditionally succeeded through their face-to-face people skills. Khamil Chekan, a purchasing specialist working for JJK Managemant Consultants in Ankara, Turkey says that, 'A strong negotiator often gets a good deal for the short term, but today we are looking at the long term and rapidly changing market conditions. It is no longer enough to develop face-to-face and negotiating skills, when more negotiations are being done online or using electronic communications. Today purchasers have to be familiar with the latest technology and keep up with global market changes.'

Despite the growth of e-procurement, it is unlikely that it will completely replace face-to-face negotiation in the near future. Emery Zobro, president of the John Michael Personnel Group in Chattanooga, TN, is confident that, while the requirements of supply management will change over time, certain qualities will survive the growth of e-procurement. He says that, 'In 5 years a person who hasn't established a track record with e-commerce and e-procurement will definitely be left behind.' Nevertheless, he remains firmly convinced that 'Buying things over the computer will never take the place of one-on-one negotiations.'

Source: Francis D. (2000) The decline of the Negotiator?, Purchasing, 129 (3), 160; personal interviews.

Practice the negotiation

Experienced negotiators often rehearse before starting formal negotiations, especially if they involve a major expenditure or are critical to the organization's success. One way of arranging this practice is to hold a mock or simulated negotiation. Then some staff from within the organization take the role of the supplier, playing devil's advocate and raising questions and issues that the buyer had not originally considered.

Another option is to conduct a mock negotiation which involves role-playing, with buyers taking the suppliers' role. This allows them to learn more about the suppliers' position, giving valuable insight into their expected needs and wants.

The outcome of negotiation is an agreed position that both sides are happy to work with. It is in neither parties' interest to create ill-feeling and discontent. Effective planning means that buyers achieve an agreement that is more valuable than ones available to their competitors.

POWER IN NEGOTIATION

An important aspect of negotiation is the analysis of relative power of each party, where power is the ability to influence another person or organization. Company A has power over company B when it can get B to do something that directly benefits A. Power can be both good and bad, so in itself it possesses neither a positive nor a negative connotation. It is how the power is used that gives it a particular perception. Within negotiation, the use of power by both parties can dramatically influence the outcome and even result in a stalemate.

Both individuals and organizations bring different sources of power to the negotiation table; some of these are detrimental to a continued relationship, while others are beneficial. It is important for negotiators to understand the advantages and disadvantages of using each source of power, and the effects that it will have on the relationship between parties.

Sources of negotiation power

The power exercized by individuals or organizations generally comes from six sources – informational, reward, coercive, legitimate, expert and referent (French and Raven, 1959).

1. **Informational power.** Ready access to relevant and useful information is generally the most common source of power in negotiations. It relies on one party influencing the other by presenting facts, data and persuasive arguments – sharing information to support one viewpoint and to challenge the other. However, the effective use of information does not necessarily mean open and complete sharing. One party will generally present only favourable information that supports its position, while the other party presents only negative information to refute a position. You have to be careful here, as this kind of manipulation of information to increase power and control options available to the other party, can soon become unethical.

2. **Reward power.** This occurs when one party is able to offer something of perceived value to the other party, such as a purchase contract or access to a new source of technology. Use of rewards is a more direct way of exerting control over negotiation than the more subtle informational power. The basis of reward power is the belief that individuals respond and behave appropriately when in return for valued rewards. However, this comes with the risk that one party may learn to respond positively only when offered rewards.

3. **Coercive power.** Coercive power is the mirror of reward power, and gives a different aspect of the same effect. If one party can give the other party something of value (reward power), then it can also take it away (coercive power). Coercive power is essentially the ability to punish the other party for non-performance. The punishments are usually financial, though they can include other factors such as reputation or morale. Repeated use of coercive power will inevitably have a damaging effect on business relationships. There is a strong likelihood that if power shifts, there will be retaliation. For example, buyers generally have power over suppliers in times of economic depression, and they might use coercion to get good deals by threatening to move their business to other firms. But during economic recovery, power can move to supplier who may retaliate against coercive buyers by negotiating large price increases, reducing service quality or even disrupting their supply.

4. **Legitimate power.** The job position that an individual holds – rather than the individual himself or herself – is the source of legitimate power. Examples of individuals with legitimate power include parents, managers, police and political officeholders. In sourcing, buyers may have legitimate power by their job as senior managers, legally representing a prominent organization, and possessing the authority to negotiate major contracts.

5. **Expert power.** This is really a special form of informational power, which involves the development and retention of a major body of knowledge. Informational power exists when someone has thoroughly researched and prepared for a negotiation; expertise goes beyond this, and an expert is recognized as having accumulated and mastered knowledge about a particular subject, often with verifiable credentials to document that mastery. Expert power can influence negotiations by reducing the chance that the other party will successfully refute the expert's opinions – or will even attempt to challenge them.

6 **Referent power.** This is based on the attractiveness of a negotiator that emerges from a range of personal qualities, such as personality, physical appearance, honesty, charisma, friendliness and sensitivity. In this source of power, an individual has some personal qualities that are attractive to the other parties – and then the other parties want the individual to look favourably upon them. Referent power is most successful in negotiations when the person with power is fully aware of their position.

Parties in negotiations generally apply all types of power to their advantage, but they must be careful not to abuse their power, or else they damage relationships, invite retaliation and diminish the value of the power. In most negotiations, the sources of power that are most effective are legitimate, informational and expert. These allow parties to maintain a positive relationship after reaching agreement, while reward and coercive powers are less likely to encourage long-term relationships. Referent power is largely used to reinforce the other sources, making them stronger and more effective.

CONCESSIONS

A fundamental part of all negotiations is the offering and exchange of concessions – or movement away from a position that offers something of value to the other party. For example, a buyer's willingness to pay a price of €8.50 a unit instead of €8.25 is a concession that favours the supplier. Effective negotiators like to offer concessions that have little value to themselves in exchange for concessions by the other party that do have value. To make the negotiations work, each party must recognize that the give and take of concessions is a normal and necessary part of any negotiations.

The general format for negotiations has each side stating their opening position, and then making concessions until they reach a final agreement. Each side clearly wants to minimize the amount they concede on each issue, so they aim at exchanging concessions and gaining a corresponding value in return. A key point is not to give away any concession without getting something of equal or greater value in return. Concessions are a key element in negotiations, with the amount of preparation and the relative power of each party influencing how much, how often and when each party concedes a positions.

Without this kind of trading in concessions, most negotiations will simply fail to reach an agreement. However, a deadlock does not necessarily mean that the negotiations failed. The parties could be so far apart in their positions that an agreement was never likely, and then it may be better not to reach an agreement than to accept a poor one. This is why negotiators must establish a BATNA before the negotiations begin, and not agree to anything that gives returns inferior to this.

The manner in which a negotiator approaches concessions can have a significant effect on the outcome – as well as the cost and duration of negotiations. A buyer who opens the negotiation with a low initial offer followed by relatively small concessions is signalling a reluctance to be flexible, making it difficult to reach agreement. Conversely, a co-operative opening position followed by relatively strong concessions shows a willingness to be flexible and to reach agreement.

Hendon, Roy and Ahmed offered the following 12 guidelines for making successful concessions (Hendon *et al.*, 2003):

1 Give yourself enough room to make concessions.

2 Try to get the other parties to start revealing their needs and objectives first.

3 Be the first to concede on a minor issue but not the first to concede on a major issue.

4 Make unimportant concessions and portray them as more valuable than they are.

5 Make the other party work hard for every concession you make.

6 Use trade-offs to obtain something for every concession you make.

7 Generally concede slowly and give a little with each concession.

8 Do not reveal your deadline to the other party.

9 Occasionally say 'no' to the other party.

10 Be careful trying to take back concessions, even in tentative negotiations.

11 Keep a record of concessions made in the negotiation and try to identify a pattern.

12 Do not concede too often, too soon or too much.

Some negotiators try a completely inflexible approach, where they open by stating their best and final offer, and then are not prepared to make any concessions. This approach generally creates unrealistic expectations, because negotiators invariably expect concessions to follow. When these fail to materialize, the other side can become angry or believe that its counterpart is not bargaining in good faith. This approach is now generally described as bad-faith or no-concession bargaining, and it commonly ends in deadlock without agreement.

LEARNING FROM PRACTICE

Volvo Trucks

Volvo Trucks is the world's second largest manufacturer of heavy duty trucks, with the group including Mack, Renault and UD trucks. The company makes 100,000 units a year in 15 countries, but faces intense pressure on prices, particularly since the global decline in sales during 2008–2009. This put pressure on the company to improve the management of material costs, including better global procurement.

The Volvo approach to global sourcing has nine steps, and part of its benefit is the discipline built into each step. Cross-functional sourcing teams follow the process as they develop and negotiate global procurement contracts, even for contracts that the sourcing teams see as regional rather than global. Figure 12.3 outlines the Volvo nine-step global sourcing process. Steps 1–5 involve strategy development, while Steps 6–9 involve strategy implementation.

Step 1. *Select global sourcing projects.* An executive steering committee is responsible for selecting sourcing projects and identifying the cost savings expected from each. The steering committee plays a vital role in maintaining the intensity of the sourcing process.

Step 2. *Launch the project.* This forms a sourcing team, with members selected because of their familiarity with the items under review. The team develops a list of deliverables, schedules and expected milestones. It also collects and analyses related data, with various tools used to support these analyses.

Step 3. *Develop the sourcing project.* The sourcing team identifies potential worldwide suppliers and sends them a request for information, which is a generic questionnaire that asks about sales, production capacity, quality certification, familiarity with the truck business and major customers. Replies allow the team to home-in on a short list of suppliers – and they also give an opportunity to standardize designs and specifications.

FIGURE 12.3 Volvo's nine step global sourcing process

Step 1	Select global sourcing projects
Step 2	Launch the project
Step 3	Develop the sourcing project
Step 4	Develop requests for proposals
Step 5	Recommend strategy and negotiate with suppliers
Step 6	Certify suppliers
Step 7	Formalize the sourcing contract
Step 8	Sample testing and approval
Step 9	Production readiness

Step 4. *Develop requests for proposals.* This step develops and sends requests for proposals to the suppliers identified in Step 3. Suppliers typically need 6 weeks to analyse the RFPs and return their proposals. The sourcing team analyse the details, define the criteria used to assess each supplier and then agree on their choice of a recommended supplier.

Step 5. *Recommend strategy and negotiate with suppliers.* The sourcing team recommends to an executive committee the selected supplier, along with a purchasing strategy, schedule and expected savings. Then it prepares for negotiations, followed by face-to-face discussions with the supplier. Specifically, the team shows the supplier the global sourcing process, emphasizing that they are only making recommendations. Before negotiations begin in earnest, the team receive feedback, which allows them to revise their proposals. A lead negotiator is appointed to head talks and the sourcing team leader's role begins to diminish.

Step 6. *Certify suppliers.* Purchasing and engineering groups receive the sourcing team's recommendation and results from negotiations. Functional directors begin budgeting expected savings in their financial plans. The output from Step 6 is a certification by functional groups, accepting the recommended supplier.

Step 7. *Formalize the sourcing contract* Here the lead negotiator follows the process until the contract is completed. With the help of the legal department, a buyer writes a contract using a standard template. The contracts, which are typically 2 to 3 years in duration, normally include productivity improvement requirements to offset material cost increases and encourage technical advances by the supplier.

Step 8. *Sample testing and approval* This assesses any samples provided by the supplier. The production facilities prepare initial sample inspection reports, and the lead negotiator designs a plan to support production.

Step 9. *Production readiness.* This final step is the pilot production stage, where the supplier typically sends enough materials to allow a trial production run.

TRYING TO REACH AGREEMENT

We have already mentioned that negotiators design tactics, which are the actions they take to gain concessions, change the other party's position or influence others to achieve their objectives. Effectively, tactics consist of all the means used to persuade other parties to endorse a certain position or agree to a preferred outcome. As both sides are using their own tactics, a negotiator must learn to recognize the tactics a counterpart is using, and perhaps mitigate their effects.

Some tactics used by negotiators are little more than ploys or tricks to get the other party to agree to an issue without question. However, there are many legitimate and ethical tactics that can persuade other parties to endorse a particular idea. The following list gives only a small sample of these:

Attractive initial offer – which usually involves a seller offering an unusually good deal to win a buyer's business. Once a buyer makes a commitment to a seller, it becomes more difficult to switch to another supplier. The obvious problem is that terms may be less favourable after the initial purchase.

Honesty and openness – where parties with a close working relationship have a level of mutual trust that promotes free and open sharing of information. The objective of this tactic is to make each party aware of the relevant information needed to create a mutually acceptable agreement.

Questions – allowing open-ended questions to serve a dual purpose. Firstly, shrewd questions can reveal new information about the interests underlying the other party's stated position. Secondly, questions provide a period of relief or reflection as the other party takes time to consider an answer.

Interlude – which involves a break from negotiations. Parties might need to process new information, take a short break or take a longer recess if negotiations are not going well. Negotiators might feel they are making too many concessions and need to break the pattern.

Trial balloon – where a negotiator takes a new direction and might ask, 'If I can persuade my manager to endorse this option, would you go along with it?' Trial balloons are tests of acceptability for a new idea. The other party's reaction shows whether the parties should pursue the idea further.

Price increase – where sellers argue that, if a buyer does not agree to a certain price or condition, the price will soon increase. A well-informed and adequately prepared negotiator can tell the difference between a real price change and a misleading tactic used by the seller.

Unattractive opening offer – which involves taking an abnormally high initial position on an issue, such as a seller opening with an extremely high selling price. The underlying logic is that, once one party makes a significant concession from the extreme position, the new position may appear more acceptable. It also attempts to shift the bargaining zone in one party's favour.

Best and final offer – which often signals the end of a negotiation on a given issue. The caveat is that the person making the best and final offer must be prepared to actually end discussions if the other party does not accept it. When negotiators offer a best and final offer, and then quickly amend it, they lose credibility and this tactic loses its effectiveness.

Silence – which involves not immediately responding when the other party makes an offer, in the hope that an awkward silence will encourage further offers or concessions. We have a natural tendency to fill-in gaps in a conversation, so silences can be an effective way of eliciting a response. And when one party makes a point that weakens the other's position, it may be better to remain silent than to admit the weakness.

Planned concessions – to influence the other party's behaviour. The use of a concessions signals that it is now the other party's turn to reciprocate and make its own concession on an important issue. There is a natural tendency for a party to respond in kind when receiving a concession.

Venue – with some negotiators insisting on meeting in a location that is more favourable to them. One party may have to travel a great distance, face the sun or sit in an uncomfortable chair in an effort to create stress. The choice of venue can also affect whether a negotiator can get up and leave the negotiation at a critical time.

There are literally hundreds of such negotiating tactics, and according to Cialdini (2001) they can be classified into six categories that reflect fundamental principles of human behaviour:

1 **Reciprocation.** Virtually every human society adheres to the principle of reciprocation. This means that when somebody gives us something, we feel an obligation to give them something back of equal or greater value. In negotiations, this creates an obligation to return something when the other party offers a concession. Effective negotiators understand this principle and generally follow a planned pattern of concession exchange. An important point with this, is that it is not really essential for a negotiator to respond when they have been asked to make an important concession.

2 **Consistency.** People prefer to be consistent in their beliefs and actions. In a negotiation, if we can get others to agree to something, then not following through with other agreements would be inconsistent and irrational – which is behaviour that they would seek to avoid. Skilled negotiators also understand that, after people agree to something, they feel better about the decision than before they agreed. When they have made a small commitment, it becomes easier to use consistency as an argument for requesting larger commitments later.

3 **Social proof.** According to this principle, we look to the behaviour of others to determine what is desirable, appropriate and correct[8]. This principle often works against negotiators who look to others for guidance on behaviour. For example, a seller may state that a well-respected company uses its product, thereby providing social proof of the value of the purchase.

4 **Liking.** This principle states that we work well and are more agreeable with people we like or who are like us. Effective negotiators, therefore, should take time to get to know their counterparts, knowing that desired concessions are more likely when there is some level of familiarity.

5 **Authority.** This principle states that we are more likely to accept the positions, arguments and direction from recognized authority figures – as we see them as having legitimate power. In negotiations, a senior sales executive may be able to significantly influence an inexperienced buyer, simply because of their implied authority and position in the organization.

6 **Scarcity.** Sellers learn early in their career the powerful influence that scarcity – or even the perception of possible scarcity – can have on a buyer. Nobody wants to run even the slightest risk of closing a plant because there will be a shortage of some key material next month. So purchasers are encouraged to buy larger orders than are actually needed. The same argument applies to price increases, where buyers are encouraged to act before a price increase takes effect.

In practice, all negotiations are in some ways unique, and a tactic that works well during one negotiation may not be successful in another, even with the same negotiators. This means that effective negotiators must be willing to quickly modify tactics that are not proving effective, and prepare themselves with responses to tactics that may be used against them. Tactics are most effective when the other party is unprepared, stressed, under severe time deadlines, inexperienced, fatigued or uninterested.

Win-win negotiations

Many traditional purchasing managers believe that the primary aim of negotiations is to win at the expense of suppliers. This is a win-lose negotiation where one party can only win at the expense of the other. Win-lose negotiation – also known as a zero-sum game – means that two parties are competing for a fixed pot of money or benefits, and that when one party gains, the other must lose the same amount. For instance, an increase in the purchase price benefits the seller, and increases the buyer's costs by the same amount.

The inevitable competition in a win-lose negotiation means that parties rarely want to co-operate with each other. But this means that they may be losing potential benefits that are not available to competitors. This is recognized in win-win negotiations which look for simultaneous gains to both parties.

Win-win negotiations seeks to expand the overall value of benefits from negotiations. Then co-operation gives greater rewards, and both parties benefit more than they would by selfishly seeking their own ends. The parties still negotiate, but they do so determine how to achieve and then divide the greater returns. For example, increasing the amount purchased can give lower prices – benefiting both parties. Co-operation to reduce duplication and waste, or assistance in developing new technology or improved product design gives benefits to both negotiators and all other members of the supply chain. Figure 12.4 suggests some of the key differences between win-lose and win-win negotiation.

The fundamental question of win-win negotiations is how the buyer and seller, through collaborative negotiations, can expand the benefits available. There are essentially five different methods that can achieve this (Lewicki *et al.*, 2006):

1 **Expand the pie.** Working closely together, the parties identify creative ways to create more benefits, expand available resources or generate new value. For example, a seller can create new value by offering a buyer early access to new technology that it can include in its own new products. If the market approves of the new product, sales will increase and the supplier will receive larger purchase orders. Both parties are better off.

2 **Logroll.** This means that the parties identify more than one issue where they disagree – and then they trade-off these issues so that each party has a top-priority issue satisfied, while making concessions in a lower priority issue.

3 **Non-specific compensation.** This means that one party achieves their objective on an issue, while the other receives something else of value as a reward for agreement. This approach works only when the compensating party knows what is valuable to the other party, and makes a reasonable offer for agreement.

Characteristics of win-lose negotiation	Characteristics of win-win negotiation
• Assume rigid negotiating positions. • Compete over a fixed amount of value. • Practice strict use of power by one party over another. • Pursue adversarial relationships.	• Understand each other's needs and wants. • Focus on common rather than personal interests. • Conduct joint efforts to solve problems and develop creative solutions that provide additional value. • Engage in open sharing of information.

FIGURE 12.4

Comparison of win-lose and win-win negotiations

4   **Cut costs.** With cost cutting, the buyer gets a lower price, as the parties have work jointly to reduce the seller's costs, or the transaction costs of doing business. These cost reductions are greater than the price reductions, so the buyer gets a low price, while the seller becomes more competitive through reduced costs.

5   **Find a bridge solution.** Bridging involves inventing new options that have not been considered before, but which satisfy each party's needs. Bridging solutions are unlikely to completely satisfy either party, but they are usually acceptable to each side.

INTERNATIONAL NEGOTIATION

The continuing growth of global sourcing and international business in general has dramatically increased the need to negotiate efficiently across cultures. Many companies have built truly global supply chains, such as Dell which assembles parts from around the world into its computers. They use multiple suppliers located in different countries for different parts of their computer systems, and if a particular supplier is unable to meet current demand, Dell can shift its sourcing to another supplier in another part of the world (Friedman, 2006). For instance, they can shift sources of Intel microprocessors between factories in the Philippines, Costa Rica, Malaysia or China.

Negotiations with global suppliers take on added complexity when the parties have different languages, customs, laws and cultures. The preparation for negotiations with a supplier from another country takes substantially more time and effort to allow for translation, travel and other foreign business requirements. Negotiators have to do their normal planning and preparation, but also additional work to understand the customs and traditions of their counterpart.

At the heart of the difficulties are the impacts of different cultures, which can be strong enough to cause a 'culture shock' (Martin *et al.*, 2003). This occurs when negotiators are immersed in a place where their established norms no longer apply – and their existing values, beliefs, rules and behaviour are not relevant. Emotions run high, and negotiators may initially feel anxiety, disorientation and confusion. Needless to say, this substantially reduces the likelihood that they will achieve their desired results.

Various barriers can dramatically affect the conduct of international negotiations (Min and Galle, 1993). In order of importance, these obstacles include miscommunication due to language differences, time limitations, cultural differences and limited authority of the international negotiator. It is easy to both misunderstand, and not be understood. During international negotiations, an interpreter might translate the words yet not convey the full significance of unspoken actions, signals and customs that are invisible to the foreign negotiator. Even when using the same language, words may have completely different meanings in different countries – in the way that 'cheap' can mean low cost, good value, low quality or a range of other subtle differences.

Some companies develop guidelines of prevailing characteristics of negotiators from different countries (Morrison *et al.*, 1994). Understanding these profiles might be useful for developing negotiation tactics or understanding the tactics that the other party may use. But they are inevitably based on stereotypes and oversimplifications of different cultures. There is so much variation between people in any single culture that the guidelines can only give very broad advice – perhaps along the lines of, 'it is considered impolite to show someone the sole of your shoe' or 'this gesture is considered very impolite'.

Impact of the internet on negotiations

Use of information technology, particularly the internet, email and instant messaging, can dramatically change the nature of a negotiation. Electronic negotiations tend to equalize the interactions between the parties because normal visual cues and sources of power are not as evident. The cues of status disappear, negotiators are largely anonymous, social norms and behaviours are more difficult to recognize, and voice inflections, which add significant meaning to words, do not exist electronically. The whole spectrum of non-verbal communication is missing from electronic negotiations, and this can make considerable differences to tactics and results.

Research suggests that negotiators communicating electronically adopt a different persona than they do face-to-face. Specifically, e-negotiators engage in more risky behaviours, ask fewer questions, make more assumptions – and are more aggressive in their demands, threats and take-it-or-leave-it ultimatums. They also feel less accountable for the outcome of negotiations because of the lack of connection with their distant counterparts, and the more adversarial 'us-versus-them' mentality.

The overall message is that negotiators who work face-to-face are more likely to reach agreement and avoid impasse than their electronic counterparts. However, time constraints and high travel costs mean that some negotiations, particularly for global sourcing, must be done at a distance. The usual way to overcome the problems with distant negotiations is to have an initial face-to-face meeting to set the scene and build some kind of relationship, followed by electronic negotiations to sort out the details. If a face-to-face meeting is impractical, there are some benefits from telephone conference calls, a videoconference or e-meeting.

LEARNING FROM PRACTICE

Federal Express

Mike Babineaux, of FedEx's Strategic Sourcing and Supply Centre of Excellence, offers good advice for buyers who negotiate internationally. He warns that, 'Every person who negotiates with other cultures must be aware of the serious and costly mistakes and misunderstandings in business practices that are caused by cultural differences.'

Nations may appear to be changing and moving towards common understandings – but these changes are largely superficial, and fundamentals of culture evolve at a much slower pace. Babineaux gives an example from communication where, 'Americans tend to speak directly and openly. They want the truth, and they want it now. They are suspicious when they think someone is being evasive.' Unfortunately, this direct style of negotiation is not appreciated in many cultures, and is often considered very impolite. An open person may be seen as weak, directness may come across as abrupt and written contracts may imply that a person's word is not good. Babineaux explains that any negotiator is likely, 'To be on a different wavelength than the foreigner because our style of communication is very different from others.' In the end, he says, 'Negotiators who have the greatest success in doing business around the world are those who have learned to have a credible appreciation and understanding of those with whom they do business.'

Source: Mazel J. (2000) Five negotiation experts reveal their secrets to supplier management, Institute of Management and Administration, Newark, NJ; www.ioma.com

CHAPTER REVIEW

- Negotiation is a process of formal communication, either face-to-face or electronically, where two or more people come together to seek mutual agreement about an issue or issues

- An organization's success is partly due to its skills in negotiation, and these skills are often concentrated in the procurement function. Skilled negotiators share common traits, which come with study, practice and training

- A formal negotiation process has five steps that starts with the recognition of a need to purchase and ends with implementation of the agreement

- Planning and preparation are an essential part of negotiations, and can be the single most important factor for success. We described a nine step process for planning, which started with developing specific objectives and goes through to practicing the negotiations

- Power refers to the ability of one party in a negotiation to influence the actions of the other party. There are six main sources of power – informational, reward, coercive, legitimate, expert and referent

- Concessions are a central part of negotiations, with both sides stating initial positions and then offering concessions until they reach agreement

- Negotiators design tactics to show how they will conduct the negotiations. Many different tactics are available, ranging from an attractive initial offer through to silence. These tactics can be divided into six broad categories that reflect fundamental principles of human behaviour

- Negotiations are traditionally viewed as win-lose situations, where one party can only win at the expense of the other. In reality, there are methods of co-operating that can increase the overall benefits so that both sides gain in a win-win situation

- Global sourcing means that more negotiations have to be done internationally. These can be very difficult, especially to overcome cultural differences, and negotiators have to put a lot more effort into preparation and planning

DISCUSSION QUESTIONS

1 Why are negotiations such an important part of the purchasing process?

2 Will electronic purchasing through the internet decrease the need for negotiation between buyers and sellers?

3 Sellers can try to avoid negotiation by saying, 'This is what I have to offer. These are my price and conditions. Take them or leave them.' What are the benefits and risks of this approach?

4 Discuss the resources needed for effective negotiation planning and execution.

5 Discuss the concept of BATNA and explain how a buyer can use it effectively to plan a negotiation.

6 The parties to a sourcing negotiation can discuss many issues besides price. Choose five of these issues and explain why it is important to the buyer and seller, and what they may try to achieve.

7 Discuss the skills and knowledge that successful negotiators need.

8 What information should a buyer collect about a supplier before entering negotiations?

9 What types of tactics are available to negotiators?

10 Give some examples of tactics that might be considered unethical.

11 What are the most important sources of power in a buyer-seller negotiation?

12 Why are concessions important during a sourcing negotiation? How do negotiating parties demonstrate their willingness to compromize?

13 Discuss the differences between win-win negotiations and win-lose ones.

14 What problems might you meet when negotiating with global suppliers?

REFERENCES

Acuff R. L. (1997) How to negotiate anything with anyone anywhere around the world, New York: AMACOM.

Anderson K. (1994) Getting what you want: how to reach agreement and resolve conflict every time, New York: Plume.

Cialdini R. B. (2001) Influence science and practice (4th edition), Boston, MA: Allyn and Bacon.

Fisher R., Ury W. and Bruce Patton. (1991) Getting to yes: negotiating agreement without giving in, London: Penguin Books.

French and Raven. (1959) The bases of social power, Ann Arbor, MI: University of Michigan Press.

Friedman T. L. (2006) the world is flat: a brief history of the twenty-first century, Release 2.0, Farrar, New York: Straus and Giroux.

Hendon D.W., Roy M.H. and Ahmed Z.U. (2003) Negotiation concession patterns: a multicountry, multiperiod study, *American Business Review*, 21: 75–83.

Lewicki R. J., Saunders D. M. and Barry B. (2006) Negotiation (5th edition), Irwin, New York: McGraw-Hill.

Martin D., Mayfield J., Mayfield M. and Herbig P. (2003) International negotiations: an entirely different animal, In: Lewicki R. J., Saunders D. M., Minton J. W. and Barry B. (editors), Negotiation: readings, exercizes, and cases (4th edition), Irwin, New York: McGraw-Hill.

McCormack M. H. (1995) On negotiating, Los Angeles: Dove Books.

Min H. and Galle W. (1993) International negotiation strategies of US purchasing professionals, *International Journal of Purchasing and Materials Management*, 29(3): 46.

Morrison T., Conaway W. A. and Borden G. A. (1994) Kiss, bow, or shake hands: how to do business in sixty countries, Holbrooke, MA: Adams Media Corporation.

Shell G. R. (2006) Bargaining for advantage: negotiation strategies for reasonable people (2nd edition), London: Penguin Books.

Thompson L. (2005) The mind and heart of the negotiator (3rd edition), Harlow, Essex: Pearson Education.

Waxer C. (2001) e-Negotiations are in, price-only e-auctions are out, iSource, June, pp 73–76.

FURTHER READING

Burr A. M. (2001) Ethics in negotiation: does getting to yes require candour? *Dispute Resolution Journal*, 56(2): 8–15.

Cialdini R. B. (2001) Influence: science and practice (4th edition), Boston, MA: Allyn and Bacon.

Corvette B. A. B. (2007) Conflict management: a practical guide to developing negotiation strategies, Upper Saddle River, NJ: Prentice Hall Pearson.

Gelfand M. J. and Brett J. M. (editors) (2004) The handbook of negotiation and culture, Palo Alto, CA: Stanford University Press.

Ghauri P. N. and Usunier J.-C. (editors) (1996) International Business Negotiations, Oxford: Pergamon Press.

Hendon D.W., Hendon R. A.. and Herbig P. (1998) Negotiating across cultures, *Security Management*, 42(11): 25–28.

Hunt P. (2000) Making a good deal, *Supply Management*, October 5, pp 37–39.

Lewicki R. J., Saunders, D. M. and Barry B. (2006) Negotiation (5th edition), Irwin, New York: McGraw-Hill.

Lewicki R. J., Saunders D. M., Minton, J. W. and Barry B. (2003) Negotiation: readings, exercizes and cases (4th edition), Irwin, New York: McGraw-Hill.

Lytle A. L., Brett J. M. and Shapiro D. L. (1999) The strategic use of interests, rights and power to resolve disputes, *Negotiation Journal*, 15(1): 31–51.

McRae B. (1998) Negotiating and influencing skills: the art of creating and claiming value, Thousand Oaks, CA: Sage.

Miller P. and Kelle P. (1998) Quantitative support for buyer-supplier negotiation in just-in-time purchasing, *International Journal of Purchasing and Materials Management*, 34(2): 25–31.

Mintu-Wimsatt A. (2002) Personality and negotiation style: the moderating effects of cultural content, *Thunderbird International Business Review*, 44(6): 729–748.

Mortensen K. W. (2004) Maximum influence: the 12 universal laws of power persuasion, New York: AMACOM.

Shell G. R. (2006) Bargaining for advantage: negotiation strategies for reasonable people (2nd edition), London: Penguin Books.

Thompson L. (2005) The mind and heart of the negotiator (3rd edition), Upper Saddle River, NJ: Pearson Education.

Watkins M. (2002) Breakthrough business negotiations: a toolbox for managers, San Francisco, CA: Jossey-Bass.

CASE STUDY

Porto

Competitive pressures mean that computer manufacturers are constantly looking for ways to reduce costs. They compete fiercely for contracts by meeting the technology, quality and price requirements of customers – but profit margins and ROI targets are always under pressure.

In their drive to continuously improve quality and reduce costs, manufacturers typically have long-term relationships with their suppliers, and only sign contracts with high-quality suppliers. Porto is a major hardware company, which has initiated a supplier development programme that looks for continual improvements to efficiency and productivity as a way of reducing material costs over the foreseeable future. Porto also expects its suppliers to share cost-saving ideas whenever possible. But cost is not the only factor in supplier development, and in a volatile industry new technology, capacity, reliability and other factors can become critical.

The high-technology industry is characterized by high-fixed costs, largely due to research and development, but also because of large investments in plant and equipment. However, low variable production costs, and high volumes mean that profits can still be high.

Porto currently requires an electronic component called 'New Prod' which is part of a recently designed product. Their estimated initial demand for New Prod is 200,000 units with additional orders likely in the future, at times determined by final customer demand. For the New Prod component, Porto feels there are five to eight highly competitive suppliers, each of whom is capable of producing the item. These suppliers are located around the world. Porto sent a request for quotations to these suppliers and after a preliminary analysis decided to pursue discussions with Technotronics, which is based in South Korea, but with production facilities in China and the Philippines.

Porto has a team of experienced procurement negotiators who must plan and prepare for the initial contacts with Technotronics. Then, assuming that the initial meetings go well, they must prepare for more detailed negotiations. There initial step is to define the best negotiation tactics.

Questions

- Assume that you work in the purchasing department of Porto. How would you set about preparing for the negotiations with Technotronics?

- What specific information would you need? What other help would you want? Where would you find it?

- Discuss the types of negotiation strategy that you might consider

CHAPTER 13
CONTRACT
MANAGEMENT

LEARNING OBJECTIVES After reading this chapter you should be able to:

- Appreciate the importance of purchase contracts

- Review the contents of contracts

- Describe different types of contracts and their use

- Understand the benefits and drawbacks of long-term contracts

- Recognize that different types of contracts are used for non-traditional purchases

- Discuss alternatives for resolving contractual disputes

CONTRACTS

Global sourcing inevitably leads people to make risky deals. The reality is that they make promises they cannot keep, sign contracts without reading them, agree to terms they do not understand, make risky assumptions, make unreasonable demands, assume that the terms of one market are acceptable in another and do not recognize cultural differences. These do not mean that managers are going around with their eyes closed or are trying to be awkward, but they are simply consequences of extremely complex global operations. It is virtually impossible for managers working in one area to understand all the subtleties of working in another. The terms of an agreement are specified in a contract, and managing contracts in a global environment is a major source of problems for procurement (Handfield, 2005).

Contracts are legally binding documents (Law and Smullen, 2008), but each depends on the legal system in the country in which it applies. There are some broad agreements in international contract law, but there are also fundamental differences. Among these differences is the relative importance of legislation, where in some areas it is simply not worth taking legal action against firms that seem to have breached the terms of a contract. Such uncertainty encourages firms to be proactive and spend more time on the initial contracting stages so that they understand clearly stakeholders' requirements and expectations.

This design of contracts is difficult, but Brown (1950) notes that, 'It usually costs less to avoid getting into trouble than to pay for getting out of trouble.' In other words, it is better to spend time on planning, preparation, discussing expectations, negotiating terms, exploring options and have contingencies in place – rather than fight a lawsuit when things go wrong. Despite the logic of this argument, firms continue to fight lawsuits and spend extraordinary amounts on legal dispute (we discuss alternatives in the next chapter).

It is essential for procurement managers to understand the legal considerations underpinning business transactions, and to develop the skills needed to manage these on a day-to-day basis. The key point is that when a contract has been negotiated and signed, the real work begins. From the moment of signing, it is the procurement manager's responsibility to ensure that all of the terms and conditions of the agreement are met – and if the terms are breached it is the procurement manager's responsibility to resolve the ensuing conflict.

In a perfect world, there would be no need for contracts as all deals would be sealed with a handshake. However, in reality contracts are important elements in buyer-supplier relationships, where they explicitly define the roles and responsibilities of each party. They establish the conditions under which two parties agree to conduct business, they define the type of relationship and they pave the way for ensuring that both parties come away with mutual benefits.

Contract
Is a legally binding agreement that is the result of an offer and acceptance, with an agreed consideration.

Elements of a contract

There are significant differences in the wording and details of contracts used by purchasing managers – particularly in different countries – but we can give some guidelines for the contents, which generally follow a common pattern. This standard pattern is established by a firm's legal department, and it is modified for different types of suppliers, products and conditions.

A contract typically begins by reviewing the parties who will be engaged in the contract. Following this introduction, there is a set of numbered sections called clauses, which describe the activities covered by the contract and conditions that the parties agree to follow. These clauses usually refer to a series of schedules that are

Clauses and schedules
Important elements in a contract.

contained in appendices at the end of the contract, and which provide specific details for the clauses, such as the operations to be used, a statement of work, how to calculate measures, heath and safety requirements, pricing schedules and any other important details.

A typical contract has three main sections:

- Introduction
- Clauses
- Schedules

LEARNING FROM PRACTICE

Contract contents

We can illustrate the structure of a typical contract with the following template for a purchasing contract between two companies. Bear in mind that there are major variations on this, and each country will have its own standards.

Introduction

This agreement is made between

1 ABC (add the buyer's name and address) and
2 XYZ (add the seller's name and address)

on the (add the date)

Clauses

1 *Definitions:* for all the important terms contained within the contract. These might include definitions of products and terms such as raw materials, purchase orders, on-time delivery and price. These often seem obvious, but it is essential for everyone to understand – and agree – exactly what each term means in the contract right from the start of negotiations.

2 *Scope of the agreement:* says exactly what is covered by the contract, and might include the geographical limits, validity of prior contracts, preferential treatment by the supplier and related elements.

3 *Purchase orders:* outlines the relationship between the contract and any other purchase orders issued by the company.

4 *Supply and delivery:* specifies the terms for delivery of the products. For instance, it might stipulate a 10-day lead time, and say what happens if the supplier does not deliver in time.

5 *Specifications, quality, and health, safety, environment:* describes method of manufacture and quality requirements for products. This point might also include a series of measures to ensure safe working conditions, protect public health and the environment.

6 *Payment:* specifies the price and method of payment, defining any adjustments for exchange rates, inflation, etc.

7 *Liability:* describes the responsibilities and procedures if something goes wrong and there are injuries or damage. This can be a contentious clause, especially for products that are considered dangerous.

8 *Force majeure or acts of god:* describes what happens if there are unforeseen events such as earthquakes, hurricanes or war that prevent a supplier fulfilling its obligations.

9 *Effective date and termination:* states when the contract becomes effective, when it terminates and possible extensions. It also stipulates when either party can terminate the contract, and how much notice they must give.

10 *Intellectual property:* states who owns any patents and copyright that emerges from the agreement.

11 *Assignment and contracting:* stipulates whether the supplier can assign its rights described in the agreement to another party, and whether subcontracting is permitted.

12 *Technology improvements:* if the buyer becomes aware of any technology or cost improvements, this section specifies how they can share this information with the supplier, and what the supplier should do in response.

13 *Favoured customer status:* states whether the buyer can expect to receive preferential status over the supplier's other customers.

14 *Confidentiality:* ensures that all IT, etc. shared by the parties remains confidential and is not passed to other parties.

15 *Statistics:* provides guidelines about the type of reporting statistics and measures that must be provided.

16 *Key performance indicators and compensation:* provides specific details on how performance will be measured and if any compensation will be awarded if predefined levels are not met.

17 *Notices:* establishes where bills, invoices and other documents should be sent, as well as the key contact person at the buying and selling companies.

18 *Severability:* describes what happens if a portion of the contract becomes void or is unenforceable, and which legal jurisdiction will resolve differences.

19 *Third-party rights:* stipulates that any benefits attributed to a third party (other than the buyer and supplier) identified in the contract must be enforced. For example, when a bank handles financial transactions, its charges must be paid.

20 *Free trade areas:* identifies any free trade issues and benefits.

21 *General:* contains any other general business principles.

22 *Governing law:* stipulates the legal jurisdiction under which any disputes will be settled. It may also stipulate the use of arbitration or other forms of conflict resolution (described later in the chapter).

23 Signatures: including the signature, titles, dates and witnesses of authorized people who sign the contract.

Schedules

Schedule 1: Product/process/service specifications, statement of work or scope of work
Schedule 2: Prices and price adjustment mechanisms
Schedule 3: Health, safety and environment guidelines and requirements
Schedule 4: Packaging materials
Schedule 5: Approved method of manufacture, delivery or service deployment
Schedule 6: Delivery targets and lead times
Schedule 7: Supplier's hours of operation
Schedule 8: Storage and inventory control
Schedule 9: Quality assurance manual
Schedule 10: Loss allowance calculations and throughput allowances.

How to write a contract

Most organizations have standard contract formats, with each new contract using this standard template, with modifications to fit specific requirements. This minimizes the amount of administration for a new contract, but there is a danger in blindly assuming that what has worked in the past will inevitably be appropriate for the future. However, a standard template is certainly the best way of drafting a new contract, along with samples of past contracts for similar circumstances. These have generally been designed by legal departments, with different forms for different types of routine purchases. To ensure that the template is appropriate, purchasers must ensure that it (Hancock, 1987):

● Identifies clearly what is being bought and the cost

● Specifies how the purchased item is going to be shipped and delivered

● Says how the items will be installed (if this is part of the contract)

● Details exactly how and when the purchaser will accept the products

- Describes the guarantees and warranties

- Spells out remedies, including consequences of late deliveries, quality problems, damages, etc.

- Includes standard terms and conditions for purchase agreements

After signing a contract, both sides hope that everything will run smoothly and deliver the agreed materials, but in practice there are often problems and disagreements. In practice, the schedules and their technical details are the source of most disputes. However, procurement staff must pay attention to clauses about (Baumer and Poindexter, 2004):

- *Integration clauses* – which effectively say that, 'This is the entire agreement' meaning that additions or modifications can be made.

- *Forum* – if there is a dispute, where would arbitration for resolving the dispute take place?

- *Choice of law* – the jurisdiction that will be used to resolve a dispute.

- *Payment* – what currency will be used to make payments?

LEARNING FROM PRACTICE

Intuit

Intuit is a provider of small business and personal finance software such as Quicken and QuickBooks. In 2004, it decided that overall performance would be improved by routing all purchasing contracts through the procurement department. There, four contract managers were assigned to specific business units to provide a single point of contact.

To provide consistency and ensure the coverage of all key issues, Intuit developed a standard Master Service Agreement (MSA) that is used for all call centre contracts. This MSA contains the standard terms for Intuit agreements, with key elements including:

1 Services to be performed by the supplier with reference to the statement of work.

2 Intuit's obligations, which provide the supplier with licences and training for software they will support during the provision of services, along with any other obligations.

3 Business turndown/upturn and disaster recovery, which describes responses to any significant change in business, and defines contingency plans in case there is a disaster.

4 Compensation and payment terms, including early payment discount, process for disputed invoices and maintaining financial records.

5 Quality management and sharing of opportunities for mutual gains.

6 Term, expected duration and events that would terminate the agreement prematurely.

7 Ownership, which outlines the property rights of all software, works from the agreement and other materials.

Other terms include confidential information, representation and warranties, indemnification, insurance, limitation of liability and dispute resolution.

Attachments to the MSA generally include a statement of work, privacy requirements, security requirements, reimbursement/expendable items and amendments to the statement of work. A risk and reward clause is also included that identifies expected performance levels: if suppliers exceed expectations on key performance measures they receive additional payments; if they fall short of requirements their payments may be adjusted.

Source: Based on Ellram L. and Tate W. (2004) Managing and controlling the services supply chain at Intuit, Practix, CAPS Research, August; www.capsresearch.org

- *Language* – the official language to be used in the contract (as translations are never exact).

- *Force majeure* – what happens when events take place that make performance as agreed impossible?

TYPES OF CONTRACTS

Purchasing contracts can be classified into different ways, but as most include some kind of pricing mechanism we use this to define some basic types. Figure 13.1 shows a classification of contracts according to the pricing mechanism used.

Fixed-price contracts

These assume that a simple fixed price is agreed for a product or piece of work. There are actually several variations of this.

Firm fixed price. Is the basic contractual pricing arrangement, where the price stated in the contract does not change, regardless of changing economic conditions, industry competition, quantities supplied, market prices or other factor. Fixed-price

---

FIGURE 13.1 Types of pricing mechanism for contracts

Type of contract	Description	Buyer risk	Supplier risk
Firm fixed price	Price stated in the agreement does not change, regardless of any type of environmental change.	Low ↑	High ↑
Fixed price with escalation	Base prices can increase or decrease based on specific identifiable changes in material prices.		
Fixed price with re-determination	Initial target price based on base-guess estimates of labour and material then renegotiated once a specific level or volume of production is reached.		
Fixed price with incentives	Initial target price based on best-guess estimates of labour and materials, then cost saving due to supplier initiatives are shared at a predetermined rate for a designated time period.		
Cost plus incentive fee	Base price is based on allowable supplier costs, and any cost savings are shared between the buyer and supplier based on a predetermined rate for a designated time period.		
Cost sharing	Actual allowable costs are shared between parties on a predetermined percentage basis and may include cost productivity improvement goals.		
Time and materials contract	Supplier is paid for all labour and materials according to a specified labour, overhead, profit and material rate.		
Cost plus fixed fee	Supplier receives reimbursement for all allowable costs up to a predetermined amount, plus a fixed fee, which is the percentage of the targeted cost of the goods or service.	↓ High	↓ Low

contracts are the easiest to manage because there is no need for auditing or additional input from either side.

When the market price of purchased materials rises above the stated contract price, the seller bears the financial loss; and when the market price falls below the stated contract price, the purchaser bears the loss. There is some uncertainty even with fixed prices, so it is important for purchasing staff to understand market conditions before signing a fixed-price contract.

Fixed-price contract with escalation. If an item is to be supplied over a longer period, such as raw materials for a continuing process, there is a strong likelihood that inflation will raise costs. Then parties may include an escalation clause in the basic contract, which either increases – or sometime decreases – the base price depending on prevailing conditions. The price changes are generally linked to a third-party index, such as a government producer price index for a specific material. If this index rises by, say two points then the price charged also rises by 2 per cent. This mechanism gives protection to the supplier, while the purchaser may benefit from improved performance and price reductions.

Fixed-price contract with re-determination. When the parties cannot predict accurate labour or material costs and quantities to be used – perhaps because of new products, unproven technology or uncertain conditions – they can use a fixed-price contract with re-determination. This means that they negotiate an initial target price based on their best estimates of costs and volumes. Once this volume has been reached, the two parties review conditions and redetermine a revized price. Depending on circumstances, the redetermined price may be applied only to following production, or it may be applied retrospectively to all or part of the previous production.

Fixed-price contract with incentives. This is similar to the fixed-price contract with re-determination except that any cost-savings during the contract are shared. If the supplier can demonstrate real cost savings through improved operations, the savings from the initial price targets are shared between the supplier and the purchaser at a predetermined rate. This type of contract is again used when parties cannot arrive at a firm price before delivery, typically for items with high unit costs and long lead times.

Cost-based contracts

When costs are less certain, it is better for contracts to include some mechanism for dealing with this wider variation – and this is the purpose of cost-based contracts. By relating prices to actual costs, these reduce the risk to suppliers, and they can also give lower overall costs to the purchaser. The two parties must agree about the costs to be included in the calculation, and it is important for these to be carefully monitored and controlled.

Cost-based contracts are generally used for goods or services that are expensive, complex and important to the purchasing party – or when there is considerable uncertainty about material and labour material costs. They are generally less favourable to the buyer because the threat of financial risk is transferred to them from the seller. There is also less incentive for suppliers to improve their operations and reduce the price to the purchaser. In fact, there is an incentive, at least in the short run, for suppliers to be inefficient, thereby raising unit costs and subsequent prices and profits.

Again there are several variations on cost-based contracts. To be effective, they should include incentives for process improvements that drive down costs during the life of the contract.

Cost plus fixed-fee contract. This is the basic form of cost-based contract, where the supplier gets reimbursed for all of its allowable costs up to a predetermined maximum, and then adds a fixed fee to give the final price. This fee may be a stated amount, but it is typically a percentage of the total cost of items being purchased. Although suppliers are guaranteed a profit margin, there is little incentive for them to improve operations and reduce costs. Purchasers have to be careful about the scale and type of costs that are included. Governments are often criticized for using these contracts and allowing excessive profits for common items at the expense of taxpayers.

Time and materials contract. This type of contract is generally used in plant and equipment maintenance agreements, where the supplier cannot determine accurate repair costs in advance. The contract spells out the appropriate labour rate, plus an overhead and profit, giving a price paid for resources actually used. A maximum value is usually set to costs, but the purchaser has little real control over the price. Needless to say, the actual work done and associated expenses should be carefully audited over the life of the contract.

Cost-sharing contract. These typically set a basic price for an item, and then any allowable extra coast or benefits incurred are shared between the parties on a predetermined basis. This is useful when, say, raw material costs are rising, and the contract shows these extra costs are shared between the parties. This mechanism can avoid problems with widely varying prices, but it needs a firm set of operating guidelines to spell out the parties' roles and responsibilities.

Cost plus incentive fee. This is similar to the cost plus fixed-fee contract, except that the base price varies with the supplier's performance. In other words, if the supplier is able to improve efficiency and reduce its costs, then the two parties share the savings at a predetermined rate.

WORKED EXAMPLE

A supplier spends €100 making an item. If the buyer's contract gives a fixed fee of 10 per cent of costs, what would be the supplier's profit? What would happen if the supplier reduced its costs to €90? How does this compare with a cost plus incentive fee contract with shared benefits?

Solution

With a cost plus fixed fee contract the price would be 100 × 1.1 = €110 and the supplier makes a profit of €10. Next year the costs reduce to €90, so the price is €99 and the supplier's profit is €9. By increasing efficiency the supplier has lowered its profits.

With a cost plus incentive fee, the cost reductions of €10 would be shared between the parties, giving the supplier 99 + 5 = €104. So the suppliers profit rises to 9 + 5 = €14 and the buyers costs fall by 110 − 104 = €6.

Considerations when selecting contract types

The most important factors to consider when negotiating with a supplier over contract type are shown in Figure 13.2.

Market uncertainty. Fixed-price contracts are decreasingly appropriate with rising uncertainty in market prices. Any uncertainty in costs increases risks with fixed price contracts, and the same argument also applies with unstable currency exchange rates, and uncertainty in general.

Long-term agreements. The longer the term of a purchase agreement, the less likely that fixed-price contracts will be acceptable to a supplier. For ongoing purchase arrangements, suppliers generally prefer fixed price with escalation or any of the cost-based contracts. For short-term contracts, and with stable conditions, fixed and fixed price with re-determination are most common.

Degree of trust between buyer and seller. If the relationship between buyer and seller has existed for some time, it should give some level of trust, allowing agreement over costs and cost-based agreements.

Process or technology uncertainty. With high levels of process or technological uncertainty, fixed-price contracts are less desirable for the seller. Then cost-based contracts may be preferable, with incentives to adjust the price according to the efforts of the supplier.

Supplier's ability to impact costs. Often a supplier has little control over its own costs, particularly when its material purchases form the greater part of its operating costs. However, they may be able to reduce costs through continuous improvement, and then an incentive-based contract may benefit both parties.

Total value of the purchase. As the total value of a contract increases, purchasers should put more effort into effective pricing mechanisms with incentives, and they should carefully consider each factor in Figure 13.2 over the lifetime of the contract. They should remember that both parties in a contract must benefit – but not necessarily to the same extent.

FIGURE 13.2   Desirability of using types of contract

Environmental condition	Fixed-price contract	Incentive contract	Cost-based contract
High market uncertainty	Low ←	Desirability of use	→ High
Long-term agreements	Low ←		→ High
High degree of trust between buyer and seller	Low ←		→ High
High process/technology uncertainty	Low ←		→ High
Supplier's ability to affect costs	Low ←		→ High
High value purchase	Low ←		→ High

LONG-TERM CONTRACTS

A common method of classifying contracts considers the time over which they are effective.

- *Spot contracts* are for one-off purchases where there is no intention of developing a longer relationship with the supplier

- *Short-term contracts* are for routine purchases over a relatively limited time, typically one year or less

- *Long-term contracts* are for purchases on a continuing basis for a long period typically several years, or even indefinitely

Long-term contracts involve greater commitments into the future, so they need to be developed more carefully. At least in the initial stages this often means a more formal procedure, especially if partners are moving beyond 'preferred supplier' and corresponding 'preferred customer' status and on towards partnerships and strategic alliances (Waters, 2006). This can be a difficult move, so we should start by asking the likely benefits.

Benefits of long-term contracts

All interactions between buyers and sellers are governed by their contract, so each party would expect a greater level of commitment from the other in a long-term contract. This commitment alone should make trading easier, and administration becomes routine as a level of trust grows between the trading partners. It also allows projects to create joint value, with the sharing of information, risk, schedules, costs, needs and even resources. The main reasons why both buyers and suppliers would consider a long-term contract are summarized in Figure 13.3.

Assurance of supply. From a buyer's perspective, the most compelling reason to consider a long-term contract is usually to guarantee interrupted supplies of materials. By committing to a clearly defined and mutually beneficial long-term agreement, buyers can reasonably assure themselves of a continuing supply. This is particularly important if the material bought is subject to wide variations in quality, price, availability or delivery.

Access to supplier technology. Long-term contracts can help buyers gain exclusive access to a supplier's proprietary technology. Not only can a buyer use this to gain a

Potential advantages	Potential disadvantages
Assurance of supply	Supplier opportunism
Access to supplier technology	Selecting the wrong supplier
Access to cost/price information	Supplier volume uncertainty
Consolidating orders to get quantity discounts, economies of scale, etc.	Supplier forgoes other business
Supplier receives better information for planning	Buyer is unreasonable

FIGURE 13.3

Advantages and disadvantages of long-term contracts

competitive advantage, but it might use an exclusivity agreement to block competitors' access to the technology. This can give a significant advantage, at least until other suppliers start offering equivalent products. Tying up a supplier in the introductory stage of a new product forces competitors to spend time and effort searching for a comparable product either from other suppliers or developed internally. However, buyers must be careful to choose suppliers with the most promising new products, otherwise they may lose any competitive advantage by locking themselves into a long-term agreement with a supplier delivering the wrong technology.

Access to cost/price information. A long-term contract generally allows a buyer more access to cost information from the supplier. Then they have an incentive to work together, making the necessary investments to improve and expand their joint operations. Long-term contracts usually include incentives that reward the supplier for improving performance, and at the same time sharing some of the savings with the buyer. Joint buyer-seller teams may work together to improve processes and divide the resulting savings (not necessarily 50/50).

Consolidating orders. With long-term contracts a buyer can often drive the supplier toward more performance improvements, using the influence that comes from larger orders. Long-term contracts with incentives are based on the notion that they allow purchase volumes to increase, allowing suppliers to get economies of scale and lower unit costs. Then long-term contracts give opportunities for productivity improvement with sharing of benefits.

Supplier receives better information for planning. The stability that a long-term contract brings means that a supplier gets better information about future demands, which in turn helps its production planning, and hence improves efficiency and materials planning. With less uncertainty in production schedules, the supplier's purchasing departments can buy material in larger quantities, thereby getting volume discounts. Detailed projections of volumes and delivery dates allow the supplier to budget the flow of funds and investments it needs, giving lower financial costs. The supplier can also get lower administrative costs, as procedures become routine, there is no duplication of administration of smaller contracts and less effort is spent on finding new business.

Risks of long-term contracts

Buyers and sellers must consider a number of risks when deciding whether a long-term contract is necessary or even desirable. For this, they should consider the following factors.

Supplier opportunism. This asks whether a supplier is likely to take advantage of the purchaser – or vice versa. From the buyer's perspective, the major risk is that a supplier becomes too complacent and loses motivation to maintain or improve performance. Performance deterioration can appear in a variety of ways, including higher price, falling quality, less reliable delivery, lagging technology and increased lead times. It is important for buyers to build appropriate incentives into long-term contracts to ensure that suppliers continue to perform as expected over the term of the agreement.

Selecting the wrong supplier. An obvious risk with long-term contracts is the possibility that a buyer does not recognize or choose the best available supplier. A buyer has to do the necessary research to analyse a supplier's past performance, capabilities, financial health, stability, use of technology and commitment to the relationship. Only when the results of these analyses are positive should they consider forming a long-term relationship. Once such an agreement is signed, it is much more difficult and expensive to switch to another supplier.

Supplier volume uncertainty. A successful long-term contract meets the needs of both parties, and this generally includes a certain volume of trade. Unfortunately, there is always some uncertainty in this volume, particularly when dealing with a new product or a new customer. Then there are good reasons why the expected volume of trade never materializes and both partners lose out. Possible reasons for this include forecasting errors, lack of customer sales for the product, competition in the marketplace and other environmental considerations such as government regulation.

Supplier forgoes other business. Agreeing to a long-term contract with an exclusivity agreement that prohibits the supplier from selling an item to other buyers could lock it out of profitable opportunities. Also, when a firm agrees to supply a particular customer's needs, limited capacity might prevent it from taking on more profitable business with other customers.

Buyer is unreasonable. The supplier must also consider the risk that the buyer will make unreasonable demands once the contract is signed. Perhaps the buyer will make unreasonable delivery requirements that were not explicitly stated in the agreement, and issues like this generally give higher costs that the supplier may or may not be able to recover.

Contingency elements of long-term contracts

Reasonable long-term contracts should contain elements that allow for contingencies, such as the following.

Initial price. A buyer must determine an acceptable initial price, especially if this price is fixed over the course of a long-term contract. Even when there is some mechanism for adjusting the price, this is usually based on the initial price – typically increasing it by a percentage determined by prevailing rate of inflation. Then an initial price that is too high will cause all following prices to be even higher. In this context, buyers should recognize that some suppliers front-load their initial price by including excess profits, and this inflates all future prices. Likewise, if the initial price is too low, the supplier has no incentive to perform as expected because all future prices will also be too low. In an extreme, suppliers will deliberately underperform as a way of terminating the contract.

Price-adjustment mechanisms. Designing an appropriate price-adjustment mechanism is also a key consideration. If future price adjustments are linked to an outside index or the price of a related product, then care should be taken in selecting a reasonable comparison. A poor choice can result in unacceptable prices, or unreasonable variations, over the term of the agreement.

Supplier performance improvements. Buyers should include specific supplier performance improvements in long-term contracts. This needs extensive research into the supplier's capabilities and past performance – and into the types and levels of risks involved. However, such continuing improvement is one of the most significant benefits of long-term agreements.

Evergreen clauses. This concerns the decision of whether a long-term contract should be written for a specific period, say 3 years, or whether it should be a series of shorter rolling contracts with an evergreen clause. An evergreen clause assumes that a contract is renewed, usually every year, unless the supplier is told otherwise. An effective evergreen clause is based on regular joint reviews, and should incorporate systems to reward the supplier for acceptable performance, or take action when specified targets are not met.

Penalty and escape clauses. A penalty clause allows the buyer (usually) or the supplier (less commonly) to take action when the other party fails to live up to contractual requirements. The penalty might be a formal request for corrective action, reduce payments, charges for lost time and expenses or in the extreme termination of the contract. Termination – through an escape clause – usually comes after calls for corrective actions from the supplier.

Penalty clauses state that the buyer must notify the supplier within a specified time period that performance has not met expectations. The supplier has a certain time to take corrective action. If it succeeds in reaching targets, the trading relationship continues, possibly until another review; if the supplier fails to reach targets, the buyer can impose penalties or terminate the contract. Negotiating such contingency plans may prolong the initial discussions, but they may prove invaluable when problems occur.

LEARNING FROM PRACTICE

Hoffmann-La Roche

Hoffmann-La Roche is one of the world's major health companies with headquarters in Switzerland and sales of 36 billion Swiss Francs. One of its divisions is Roche Diagnostics (RD), which makes a range of products for clinical use and research.

In 2003, a small team of contracts managers in RD were struggling to keep pace with company growth and the increasing complexity of industry pricing schemes. Whenever problems arose, they deployed resources to find an immediate solution, but the result was a fragmented organization, spread over different business groups and with significant variations. Contract administration was a transactional job, doing tasks required in the short term, with limited sharing of information, little consolidation to highlight trends and issues and few opportunities to look for improvements. It became increasingly clear that short-term fixes were no longer enough, and more serious attention was needed.

Analysis soon revealed some consequences of the current, fragmented, largely manual systems. These included a heavy administrative burden both within the company and for their customers' procurement groups, time-consuming financial control and billing and inconsistent contracting policies and practices. Initial moves to improve things focussed on acquiring new software – as RD's problems were clearly not unique, there is likely to be standard applications to tackle them. The investigating team found some software, but they were not cheap. More importantly, the team soon realized that they lacked expertise in the area and had no real knowledge of contracting best practices.

Real progress was not easy, and it really started when an Executive Steering Committee agreed a mission: 'Roche Diagnostics' Contracting will deliver industry-leading contract life cycle management that creates a competitive advantage and ensures quality, driving sustainable market share, sales and profitability.' Then came an effective contracting strategy along with consistent processes – and the support of internal stakeholders, including Marketing, Legal,

Source: Based on www.roche.com; www.iaccm.com

Pricing, Regulatory, Sales, Credit and Human Resources.

In 2004 RD discussed their work with the International Association for Contract and Commercial Management (IACCM) who had published a study of best practices in contracting and the top 10 areas for companies to focus on. RD had already been working in some of these areas, and now they had external benchmarks to work with.

Initially, the Sales groups were reluctant to agree on any centralization or rationalization, fearing that it would reduce their flexibility and responsiveness to customer needs. It was important to show that centralization did not mean more bureaucracy or a rigid, rules-based mentality. There were also questions about who should be in overall charge of contract management, with the decision eventually going to Finance because of their process focus and ability to understand risk and opportunity trade-offs.

Three years later the re-engineering had made substantial progress on five of the top 10 areas identified by IACCM. These include close alignment with product life cycle management; development of an electronic contracting strategy; proactive change management; and strategically aligned measurements and reporting. But senior management identified seven areas where they still needed to make progress:

1 Earlier realization of business benefits.

2 Improved or advanced cash flow.

3 More efficient operations.

4 More effective control over contracts.

5 Improved customer/partner relationships.

6 Better communication and information flow.

7 Improved employee morale.

NON-TRADITIONAL CONTRACTING

For most of their purchases firms use standard contracts, but there are some purchases that usually need a different kind of contract, and we can describe these as non-traditional contracts. We can illustrate these by the special requirements of buying information systems, consultants and service providers.

Systems outsourcing contracts

Systems outsourcing contracts get subcontractors to do a firm's Information Processing. A subcontractor provides the systems to allow organizations access to efficient computer networks and software, without the problems of either buying or running them.

This is a major issue for many companies, where both legal and purchasing managers should discuss this major commitment. Unfortunately, IT departments often sign the agreements, based on a technical evaluation and with little input from other departments. You can imagine a technologically advanced system that does not give the reliable service needed to run an e-business. The organization is left paying to maintain, repair and develop an unsatisfactory system for many years. Before committing to an outsourcing contract, buyers should consider the time covered by the agreement, the effect of company growth or decline, data security, control of costs and control of information flows. There are also a number of specific issues for IT contracting, including the following.

Changing conditions. One of the leading causes for failure of outsourced information processing is that firms become locked into systems and prices that do not allow for changing circumstances. Examples of such changes include dramatic shifts in user demand patterns, dramatically reduced costs for services provided and leaps in software and hardware technology.

Level of service. The extent that a subcontractor becomes involved in the buying firm's operation is described by three levels of service:

1 *Turnkey,* where the buyer essentially turns over the entire system to a subcontractor at a given point in time. Then the service provider performs all of the agreed functions for the buying organization.

2 *Modular,* the service provider only does a small number of functions for the buyer, who continues to do the remaining IT functions internally. Over time, as trust grows, the service provider may take over more services from the client.

3 *Shared,* where the service provider and the client share resources and operational control over the outsourced service.

Price. There is often uncertainty in future IT needs, so buyers generally negotiate a fixed, all-inclusive fee instead of a flexible pricing mechanizm that may not reflect changing business conditions. Assuming that future requirements will change, purchasers should consider carefully how contract prices are set to reflect these changes. They should also audit work done to ensure that work performed is billed at the appropriate rate.

Performance criteria. It is often difficult to measure the performance of IT operations, but a contract should at least specify the overall business requirements. Beyond this, buyers should design measures for evaluating the service provider. Both parties must understand the specifications and measurements defining how the outsourcing system is expected to perform. The more specific a purchaser can be in providing clear goals and objectives, the less likely it is that misunderstandings and conflicts will occur.

Conversion. Outsourced IT contracts should provide a conversion plan that details the steps taken to convert from an in-house system to an outsourced one. Again, the more specific a purchaser can be with this information, the less likely it is that problems will occur. Buyers should also be clear how technological changes will be handled, as updates to systems can be expensive and time-consuming. It is the joint responsibility of the purchasing manager and the supplier to ensure that the technology provided remains up to date and can deal with future needs (Wetherbe, 1991).

Other service outsourcing contracts. The use of outsourcing contracts is by no means limited to information processing, and it is used for a wide variety of tasks. Among the most common of these are facility management, legal services, research and development, logistics and material handling, order entry and customer service operations, accounting and audit services. This list is continually expanding, with outsourcing representing one of the most significant business trends over recent years.

Consulting contracts

Consultants can play a valuable role in decisions, by giving an objective point of view and expertise that is not available internally. An important point to remember when hiring outside consultants is that they are acting as the purchasing firm's agent, not its employee. This distinction can be important, for instance with intellectual property developed during a project, whose ownership is retained by an agent but is passed to the organization from an employee. Any different arrangements have to be agreed in the contract. Another aspect of this is 'residuals', which are new intellectual property (including tools, methodologies and knowledge) developed as the result of interactions between an organization and the consultant. Companies often impose specific conditions in a contract requiring that they retain ownership of any residuals, thereby preventing the consultant from taking this knowledge and selling it to a competitor.

Consultants typically consider the following six goals when negotiating a contract for their service (Samelson and Levitt, 1982):

- Avoidance of misunderstanding
- Maintenance of working independence and freedom
- Assurance of work
- Assurance of payment
- Avoidance of liability
- Prevention of litigation

From a consultant's point of view, the most important clause of a contract is probably the assurance of payment. This typically involves a down payment of up to a third of the total amount, with a range of options for paying the balance, including by percentage of work finished, or time elapsed.

Another concern is the possibility of lawsuits, with contracts written by consultants seeking to minimize their exposure to liability and subsequent litigation. Clauses in the contract should spell out exactly what the consultant is and is not liable for. In practice, the two main causes of litigation between consultants and their clients are:

1 The belief on the purchaser's part that the consulting work was not completed in full, within a reasonable time or properly.

2 The consultants' belief that they have not received the entire fee that they believe is due and proper.

Contracts describing the details of what consultants will do are essential, along with comprehensive payment clauses and an arbitration agreement that allows disputes can be resolved quickly (Shenson, 1990). The arbitration agreement is particularly interesting as it suggests that consultants are more likely to use arbitrators to solve disputes rather than lawsuits (as we see later in the chapter).

To summarize, it is essential for purchasing to develop a standard contract template for all consulting and professional services. This standard contract gives visibility of a company's policies for all potential consultants, and it is often presented for downloading from a company's website. Before this is signed, the entire scope of the project should be defined, with the various elements of the consulting project scope included as clauses in the contract. These should include deliverables, deadlines, budget and so on. If a company uses an incentive system to reward or penalize consultants, this should also be built into the contract.

Construction contracts

Typical construction contracts have a purchaser – or owner of the new facilities – seeking bids from four or five contractors. Then a common sequence of events starts with the purchaser determining a shortlist of preferred contractor bidders. The

LEARNING FROM PRACTICE

Best Practices in Consulting Contracts

A benchmarking study of how different companies manage professional services and consulting contracts was performed by a team from the Supply Chain Resource Cooperative. The study found that 66 per cent of the participating companies used some sort of standard contractual agreement, form, policy or process for the procurement of professional services. All of the companies that use a standard contract indicated that every element of the agreement is useful.

None of the participating companies used a different contract when procuring professional services for the first time. While 66 per cent of the survey respondents indicated that their company's procurement contract did not change when urgency becomes an issue (for example, a company might use a unique process when acquiring immediate services versus those services that are not required until some time in the future).

Then 66 per cent of the survey respondents had incentives to ensure compliance with their company's formal contract requirements (for example, incentives to use preferred suppliers). Also, 66 per cent of the participating companies used a formal pricing method (for example, job-specific price list, price scale or hourly rate) for the procurement of professional services.

bidders are then contacted before distributing a bid package to ensure that they are interested in submitting a bid for the project. After distributing the bid requests, the purchaser usually holds a pre-bid meeting with interested bidders to answer any questions about the initial bid documents. All further questions are then submitted to the purchaser in writing to prevent any misunderstanding.

All final bid submissions should consider the project duration, as purchasers usually require all bids to break the total price into different costs by type, phase and location. The purchaser should also give guidance on how bidders should deal with overheads. In general, these are divided into categories based on the chosen method of cost allocation, with common categories including payroll taxes, insurance premiums, field project overheads and home office overheads.

Safety requirements are always an important aspect of construction contracts, and to ensure that a bidder has a satisfactory safety performance, buyers should (MacCollum, 1990):

1   Make a thorough review of each bidder's written safety plan.

2   Before the final selection, consider each bidder's previous injury record to see whether there are too many injuries of a particular type, suggesting that some area of safety needs improving. Check with government and other sources to see if there have been any recent mention of the bidder in injury claims. Check with regulators to see whether the contractor has failed to complete work safely and in a timely manner.

3   Make a site visit to projects on which bidders are currently working to see firsthand the day-to-day quality and functioning of their safety programmes. And check in detail the references given by past clients.

The aim here is to determine whether senior managers in the bidding company have established systems for ensuring safe working conditions. Only when top management include safety as an organizational goal does everyone else in the company take it seriously. A buyer of construction services who adopts a 'hands-off' policy may be surprized after an accident to find that they can still be held responsible; an old saying says that the only way to avoid liability for accidents is to ensure that no accidents happen (Singer, 1990).

Once a construction contract has been signed and the work is underway, a regular cost summary should be used to monitor the contractor's progress. By checking actual costs, managers can compare these with original plans and estimate likely future costs. Needless to say, any claims presented by the contractor must be carefully scrutinized, as they may refer to planned expenditure rather than costs actually incurred.

Purchasers can reduce the chances of claims from a contractor in a number of ways. Firstly, they can ensure that the schedule of work is realistic and allows for unforeseeable delays that are beyond the control of either the contractor or the buyer. Secondly, the buyer should provide clear specifications that define exactly what is to be built. Thirdly, designs should be kept up-to-date, reflecting every change as it occurs. If such actions fail and the contractor still makes a claim against the purchaser, the purchaser should collect at least the following information:

- A breakdown of the claim by cost, divided into the greatest possible number of elements

- A detailed outline of the derivation of all hourly rates, equipment costs, overheads and profit

- The underlying assumptions on which the claim is based to help ensure that the claim is not inflated

Contracts for construction projects usually include penalty clauses to avoid delays in completion. Technically, penalty clauses may have some other name, such as 'liquidated damages clauses', as lawsuits in some jurisdictions have decided that penalty clauses are not enforceable.

Other types of contracts

Many other kinds of contracts can need special attention, including the following.

Purchasing agreements. Which are agreements that group similar items together for procurement to reduce the amount of paperwork for repetitive small orders. Purchasing agreements also increase the buyer's negotiating power by creating larger orders. There are a number of variations of purchasing agreements:

- **Annual contracts,** which cover purchases for the next year, after which they may or may not come up for renewal

- **National contracts,** specify that the purchaser will buy, overall, a certain amount of materials during the period of the agreement

- **Corporate agreements,** specify that all business units within a corporation must buy from a specific supplier during the term of the agreement

- **National buying agreements,** non-binding agreements on either the purchaser or the supplier; typically giving discounts to corporate buyers based on the total volume bought by the corporation as a whole, rather than for any individual order

- **Blanket orders,** cover low-cost items (such as office supplies) that allow a series of purchases under the same purchase order, thereby minimizing repetitive paperwork in the purchasing department

- **Pricing agreements,** occur when a buyer is allowed to automatically discount the purchase price published in a catalogue by a negotiated percentage

- **Open-ended orders,** are similar to blanket orders but allow the addition of items not originally included in the blanket order; and they may allow the original purchase order to be extended for a longer term

Online catalogues and e-commerce contracts. Which are increasingly used for standard purchases. Most organizations have turned to e-commerce for at least some of their orders as a way of reducing administrative overheads. A simple version of this has online catalogues that allow users to buy directly from websites through blanket orders and national contracts.

Despite the obvious benefits from e-procurement, there are still concerns of security and lack of control that buyers must consider (Hancock, 1987):

- **Security.** Despite continuing improvements in security, there is no such thing as a completely safe website. There is always the danger that someone will tap into messages at some point on their journey and make illegal use of the information – typically raiding bank accounts

- **Parity between electronic and paper records.** In some areas there is still some uncertainty in the way that electronic documents are treated, and in some jurisdictions they do not yet have the same status as their paper equivalents

- **Enforceability of boxtop agreements and licences.** Often, buyers have to agree to conditions, the details of which are enclosed appended to the products they buy. For instance, computer software is downloaded, at the same time as details of the licence agreement, or goods are delivered with the purchase agreement in the box. Such conditions are not apparent to purchasers at the time of purchase

- **Attribution procedures.** With electronic purchases, a vendor needs some secure mechanisms to ensure that an order received is legitimate, and that payment will be received (usually through a credit card). With e-business there is still a large element of trust, as both sides struggle for ways of validating transactions

- **Digital signatures.** With paper contracts, signatures are used to uniquely identify the parties to a contract. Electronic signatures can be used in the same way, but many legislatures are looking for ways of finding acceptable substitutes

LEARNING FROM PRACTICE

Leaking capacitors

Aluminium electrolytic capacitors are components that smooth out the power supply to computer chips. They are used in computer motherboards, but throughout 2002 suppliers were noticing that some units were breaking open and failing. Motherboard and PC makers stopped using the faulty parts. But such problems are largely hidden as the parts may fail over a period of several months. It became clear that a faulty electrolyte was to blame for the burst capacitors. The question is, 'Where did it come from and which manufacturers used it?'

Japanese sources initially claimed that major Taiwanese capacitor firms, including the market leaders, Lelon Electronics Corporation and Luxon Electronics Corporation, had turned out faulty products. But both companies denied the accusations. Most of the leaking capacitors seemed to be labelled 'Tayeh', which is not a brand affiliated with known capacitor makers. Others were unmarked. However, some had the trademarks of Taiwanese companies including Jackcon Capacitor Electronics Co. (Taipei). Jackcon claimed that they had been out of the

Source: Based on IEEE Spectrum News and Analysis; www.spectrum.ieee.org

market for 2 years, but remained confident in the quality of its products which were independently tested, and blamed any problems on motherboard design.

The origins of the capacitor problems seem to be more obscure. According to a source in Taiwan, a scientist stole the formula for an electrolyte from his employer in Japan and began using it himself at the Chinese branch of a Taiwanese electrolyte manufacturer. Someone then sold the formula to an electrolyte maker in Taiwan, which began producing it and selling it to unknown capacitor firms. Unfortunately, the formula proved to be incomplete and lacked some additives, so capacitors made from it became unstable when charged, generating hydrogen gas, bursting and letting the electrolyte leak onto the circuit board. Tests showed that the capacitors'

expected lifetimes were less than half of the 4000 hours they were rated for.

Computer manufacturers assemble parts from their component suppliers, and they usually specify a list of trusted second tier suppliers for materials. It might be that in an effort to cut costs, some component suppliers used materials from sources that were not on an approved list. This would clearly be in default of their contractual terms.

Taiwanese capacitor manufacturers have vigorously denied using any bad materials, but there are concerns as they produce 30 per cent of the world's total capacitors. Japanese computer companies threatened to boycott manufacturers who have any contact with suspect suppliers. Taiwanese capacitor makers are trying to shore up relations with their customers, and even talks of a general recall.

SETTLING CONTRACTUAL DISPUTES

All contracts, no matter how carefully prepared and worded, can be subject to some form of dispute or disagreement. It is virtually impossible to negotiate a contract that covers every possible contingency. Probably the most common source of disputes is the interpretation of terms and conditions. Not surprisingly, the more complex the nature of the contract, the broader the scope, and the greater the costs, the more likely it is that a dispute will occur.

Purchasing managers must be aware of the possibility of disputes and include mechanisms for resolving any problems that actually arise. The traditional mechanism for resolving contract disputes is to take legal action under commercial law. Then an impartial judge acts under the relevant jurisdiction to hear the facts of the case and render a decision in favour of one party or the other. Because of the uncertainty, cost and time needed to settle a dispute in almost every judicial system, buyers and sellers usually prefer to avoid litigation and deal with disagreements in other ways. Taking legal action over a dispute should be viewed as a last resort, not an automatic choice. Figure 13.4 lists some alternatives to legal action.

Non-legal actions

These are the methods of settling buyer-seller disputes that do not go to a trial. Such methods have become more popular in recent years, but their use depends on the jurisdiction in which the contract operates. Although they come in many forms, they have the following general characteristics (Singer, 1990):

- They exist somewhere between the extreme options of doing nothing and taking legal action
- They are less formal and generally more private than ritualized courtroom confrontation
- They allow firms with disputes to have more active participation and control over the processes for solving their problems

FIGURE 13.4

Means of settling
contractual disputes

Action	Description
Legal action	File a lawsuit in a relevant court
Non-legal actions	
i. Arbitration	Use of an impartial third party to settle a contractual dispute
ii. Mediation	Intervention by a third party to promote settlement, reconciliation or compromise between parties involved in a contractual dispute
iii. Minitrial	An exchange of information between managers in each organisation, followed by negotiation between executives from each organisation
iv. Rent-a-judge	A neutral party conducts a 'trial' between the parties and is responsible for the final judgment
v. Dispute prevention	A progressive schedule of negotiation, mediation, arbitration and legal proceedings agreed to in the contract

- Most of the methods have been developed in the private sector, but courts and other agencies have begun to adopt some of the methods

The simplest way of resolving a contractual disagreement is straightforward, face-to-face negotiation between the two parties. Other factors surrounding the dispute can be brought into consideration by the parties, even though these factors are not directly involved in the dispute. For example, if a buyer and seller disagree on the interpretation of a contract's terms for delivery, they might be able to compromise by adjusting other conditions such as price or scheduling.

The option of face-to-face discussions is exhausted when both parties recognize that they are unlikely ever to agree on a solution by themselves. At this point both parties probably have an emotional reaction to their lack of success, such as frustration, disappointment and anger. This reaction may then prevent further rational analysis of the disagreement, and it becomes very difficult to negotiate without assistance from outside parties – perhaps using arbitration.

Arbitration

Arbitration

Is 'the submission of a disagreement to one or more impartial persons with the understanding that the parties will abide by the arbitrator's decision'.

The use of an outside arbitrator, or third party, to help settle a dispute is becoming increasingly popular.

When properly designed, **arbitration** (Coulson, 1982) can protect the interests of both parties to a dispute, generally giving a reasonable solution, relatively inexpensively, quickly and in private. This is such a popular option that many purchasing managers routinely include an arbitration clause in the terms and conditions. This typically spells out the types of disputes for which arbitration will be considered and how the parties will choose an arbitrator. It is important to ensure that the arbitrator's opinion is binding on both parties, or else it could be a pointless exercize. Such planning for potential disputes and their resolution is an efficient way of ensuring that problems do not escalate, and a minor disagreement does not grow quickly into expensive legal action.

Purchasing managers who want to use arbitration should understand several points. The main one is that they should be sure – after consulting with legal advisors – that the ruling of an arbitrator will be legally binding. Some jurisdictions do not recognize the process of arbitration, and others do not accept that it is legally binding. Before arbitration can even be considered, both parties must recognize the implications of binding arbitration and explicitly accept its use in their documentation.

Other forms of conflict resolution

A number of other types of conflict resolution are available, with a popular option being **mediation**. An arbitrator is essentially a judge who compares the case of each party, but is more actively involved in searching for a solution and promoting reconciliation, settlement and compromize. This is also a mediator's role, as they listen to the facts presented by both parties, rule on the appropriateness of evidence, bring the sides closer together, look for new solutions and try to get agreement on a solution that reconciles the interests of both parties. However, the key difference is that arbitration is binding on both parties, while mediation is not binding and the parties preserve their rights to make a final decision themselves. Effectively the mediator brings both sides together, but they are responsible for making their own agreement.

Mediation, minitrial, rent-a-judge, dispute prevention
Methods of conflict resolution

A third mechanism for dispute resolution is called a **minitrial**. In fact, it is not a trial at all but a form of presentation, involving an exchange of information between the disputing organizations. Once managers hear both sides of the presentation, they attempt to resolve the dispute through negotiation with their counterparts. Because minitrials are generally more complicated than other forms of negotiation, they are typically used when the dispute is significant and highly complex. One of the benefits of such a process is that it turns a potential legal conflict into a business decision and promotes a continuing relationship between the parties.

Another related mechanism is loosely called **rent-a-judge**, which is the process by which a pending lawsuit is referred to as a private, neutral party. The neutral party (perhaps a retired judge agreed by both parties) conducts a 'trial' as though it were conducted in a real court. This suggests the outcome that would be achieved in a real trial, but with far less cost, time and effort. If one or both of the parties is dissatisfied with the rent-a-judge decision, they can proceed to the normal legal channels.

Another alternative that is gaining in popularity is **dispute prevention**, which is a key element of collaborative business relationships such as long-term contracts, partnerships and strategic alliances. When parties initially design a contract they include specific processes to prevent disputes from escalating. These processes typically involve a progressive schedule of negotiation, mediation and arbitration followed by litigation as a last resort. By working closely together in the mechanics of dispute resolution, both sides appreciate what is involved – and are more likely to reach an early settlement.

Choice of approach

A number of factors can be important in the choice of dispute-resolution mechanism.

Type of relationship. Usually the main consideration is the type of relationship between the disputing parties. When this relationship is ongoing and expected to continue for the foreseeable future, they naturally prefer to resolve disputes through less aggressive means that will hopefully preserve their business relationship.

Type of outcome wanted. If buyers want to establish a precedent to govern their actions in future disputes as well as the one at hand, they may look for a more formal, binding process.

Amount of direct involvement of the parties. Here more active participation generally giving a more equitable and harmonious resolution, rather than involving combative lawyers.

Level of emotion. If levels of anger and frustration are high, the total cost of litigation can be considerably more than originally anticipated. The harsh experience of a prolonged court battle has convinced many potential litigants to consider less costly alternatives.

Speed. The importance of speed in obtaining a resolution can be a key factor in determining the best option, with the alternatives to court action much faster at getting results. Time pressures may also encourage disputing parties to be more creative and understanding in reaching a resolution.

Cost. Taking legal action is always expensive and should only be used as a last resort. There is essentially a direct relationship between the time needed to settle a dispute and the cost involved, so the quicker methods generally come at lower cost.

Information required. The closer the parties come to having the courts settle their dispute, the more formal the information requirements. Thus, with trials, the information becomes public, while neither party wants adverse publicity or disclosure of sensitive commercial information. Strict rules of evidence in lawsuits may make it difficult to introduce some relevant facts, and the credibility of experts and other witnesses becomes more difficult to maintain.

LEARNING FROM PRACTICE

Online dispute resolution

As with other aspects of the internet, the growth and rate of innovation in online dispute resolution (ODR) has been rapid. These individual sites (none of which we either recommend or do not recommend) come in many forms. For example, Cybersettle.com, is an online mechanism for settling disputes, particularly those that involve insurance companies. Not surprisingly, other companies are offering variations on this site for both mediation and arbitration services. For instance, mediation websites include Online Mediation (www.onlineresolution.com) and MediationNow (www.mediationnow.com). Online arbitration services include Online Resolution-Arbitration (www.onlinesolution.com/index-ow.cfm). According to the latter's website, 'Online Arbitration is similar to traditional arbitration, except that all communications take place online. The Online Arbitrator appointed for your case will be an experienced professional, who knows the subject area of your dispute.'

One advantage of ODR is that using a computer link, rather than personal appearances reduces the costs of attending negotiations – but they lose the benefits of face-to-face interactions. It is important to bear in mind that most mechanisms for resolving disputes online are unfamiliar to many businesses. For ODR to serve as an effective mechanism, both parties must agree to use it, even though they are likely to be unfamiliar with the process and are likely to be very cautious about its use. In order for the results to be enforceable, the prevailing legal system must accept the concept of ODR.

Source: Baumer D.L. and Poindexter J.C. (2004) Legal environment of business in the information age. McGraw-Hill/Irwin,New York.

CHAPTER REVIEW

- Contracts are an important element of buyer-supplier relationships. They are legally enforceable documents that define the roles and responsibilities of each party. Managing contracts in a global environment is a major concern for purchasing

- Contracts appear in many different forms, depending on the types of organization, legal systems, culture, etc. Nonetheless, there are some standard features of purchasing contracts, and they generally consist of three parts – an introduction, clauses and schedules

- There are several classifications for contracts. A useful one describes the mechanism for setting the price. Fixed-price contracts are more useful for stable conditions where they tend to pass risks to the supplier; cost-based contracts are more useful with uncertainty, where they tend to pass risks to the buyer. Both sides have to consider many factors before deciding on the most appropriate type

- Another classification considers the time covered by a contract. These range from spot contracts, through medium term and on to permanent agreements. There can be considerable benefits to both buyers and sellers in developing close working relationships over a long period. These can appear as partnerships and strategic alliances

- As well as standard purchasing contracts, organizations inevitably use specialized contracts for specific functions. For instance, they may have special contracts for outsourcing IT systems, consulting contracts, construction contracts and so on

- Unfortunately, disagreements and disputes are a common part of contract management. When two parties cannot agree – usually about the meaning of conditions – they can take legal action to resolve the issue. However, this should be the last resort, as there are other faster, easier and cheaper alternatives. These include negotiation arbitration, mediation, minitrial and so on

DISCUSSION QUESTIONS

1 What is the purpose of purchasing contracts? What might they typically contain (give examples to support your ideas)?

2 What parts of a contract are purchasing managers likely to spend most time negotiating?

3 What are the dangers of taking an old contract and changing the name of the supplier for a new 3-year contract with a different supplier?

4 Give some examples of price indices that can be used to track commodity prices such as steel or copper. How might these be included in purchasing contracts?

5 What are the risks to buyers in each type of contract (fixed-price, cost-based, etc.)?

6 What are the risks to suppliers in each type of contracts (fixed-price, cost-based, etc.)?

7 Certain industries face constantly changing technologies, short product life cycles, many small suppliers and demanding customers. Under these conditions, what type of contract would you recommend for a critical component supplier?

8 Under what conditions are short-term contracts preferable to long-term ones?

9 Suppose you are the manager of a consulting firm installing a major new system for a customer. What key elements would you want to include in a contract?

10 Which types of firms are most suited to using turnkey contracts for subcontracted information processing?

11 Why do firms try to avoid litigation in settling contract disputes? How do they do this?

12 What are the implications of e-commerce on enforcing contracts?

13 What are the specific problems with writing and enforcing international contracts?

REFERENCES

Baumer D. L. and Poindexter J. C. (2004) Legal environment of business in the information age, Irwin, New York: McGraw-Hill.

Brown L. (1950) Manual of preventive law, New York: Prentice Hall.

Coulson R. (1982) Business arbitration: what you need to know (2nd edition), New York: American Arbitration Association.

Hancock W. A. (editor) (1987) The law of purchasing (2nd edition), Chesterland, OH: Business Laws.

Handfield R. B. (2005) Legal and regulatory requirements in the emergent global supply chain, white paper, Supply Chain Resource Cooperative, Chapel Hill, NC: North Carolina State University and website at www.scm.ncsu.edu

Law J. and Smullen J. (2008) Dictionary of finance and banking, Oxford: Oxford University Press.

MacCollum D. V. (1990) Construction safety planning, New York: Van Nostrand Reinhold.

Samelson N. M. and Levitt R. E. (1982) Owner's guidelines for selecting safe contractors, ASCE National Spring Convention Proceedings, April 26–30, pp 617–623.

Shenson H. L. (1990) The contract and fee-setting guide for consultants and professionals, New York: John Wiley and Sons.

Singer L. R. (1990) Settling disputes: conflict resolution in business, families, and the legal system, Boulder, CO: Westview Press.

Waters D. (2006) Operations strategy, London: Thomson Learning.

Wetherbe J. C. (1991) Executive information requirements: getting it right, *MIS Quarterly*, 15(1): 51–65.

FURTHER READING

Baumer D. L. and Poindexter J. C. (2004) Legal environment of business in the information age, Irwin, New York: McGraw-Hill.

Behn R. D. (1999) Strategies for avoiding pitfalls of performance contracting, Public Productivity and Management Review, June, pp 470–490.

Buvik A. (1998) The effect of manufacturing technology on purchase contracts, *International Journal of Purchasing and Materials Management*, Fall, pp 21–28.

Cummins T. (2007) Contracting excellence, November, website at www.iaccm.com

Emiliani M. L. and Stec D. J. (2001) Online reverse auction purchasing contracts, *Supply Chain Management*, 6(3–4): 101–105.

Fisher R. X. (2000) Checklist for a good contract for IT purchases, Health Management Technology, March, pp 14–17.

Gordon S. B. (1998) Performance incentive contracting: using the purchasing process to find money rather than spend it, Government Finance Review, August, pp 33–37.

MacCollum D. V. (1990) Construction safety planning, New York: Van Nostrand Reinhold.

Maughan A. (2003) Crash-proof contracts, *Supply Management*, 8(1): 37.

Murray J. (2001) Contract modifications can lead to problems, *Purchasing*, 130(5): 20–22.

Rohleder S. (1999) Contracting for the best results, *Government Executive*, September, p 72.

Tuttle A. (2001) Becoming a single source, *Industrial Distribution*, 90(9): 47–49.

Werner C. (1998) Contract compliance: a double-edged sword for most suppliers, Health Industry Today, May, pp 1–2.

CASE STUDY

Negotiated terms focus on failure

Each year, the International Association for Contract and Commercial Management (IACCM) collects data from more than 500 international organizations, representing several thousand contract negotiators. Their questionnaire asks members about the terms and conditions they negotiate most frequently (shown in Figure 13.5). The data tells us where time is spent; it reflects changing issues and concerns; and it also reveals much about the ways companies behave and the value they place on trading relationships. After analysing the 2006 survey, the CEO wrote a blog to show his disappointment in the results:

> *'The results for 2006 indicate many opportunities for rethinking the role of contracting in shaping relationships, supporting brand image and as tools for sophisticated risk management – as opposed to blunt instruments for risk allocation. This report highlights the results and suggests new approaches that could result in significant business benefits.'*

There are new tools available for improving contract management, with many authorities emphasizing the importance of 'quality of interactions' in defining a company's image and reputation. Senior managers are increasingly aware of the direct link between style of contract management and business success. But the blog continues:

> *'For all the talk about a changing environment, this year's top ten frequently negotiated terms shows no sign that it has affected the behaviour or attitudes of those charged with responsibility for setting policy or leading negotiations.'*

The disappointing aspect of the survey was that despite all the changes in procurement, when it came to the crunch organizations were still negotiating over the same ideas – limitations of liability, levels of indemnity, control of intellectual property, rights to terminate, liquidated damages for performance failure, etc.

FIGURE 13.5 IACCM Top 30 frequently negotiated terms

	Term
1	Limitation of liability
2	Indemnification
3	Intellectual property
4	Price/charge/price changes
5	Termination (cause/convenience)
6	Warranty
7	Confidential information/data protection
8	Delivery/acceptance
9	Payment
10	Liquidated damages
11	Service levels
12	Insurance
13	Performance bonds/guarantees/undertakings
14	Applicable law/jurisdiction
15	Rights of use
16	Assignment/transfer
17	Dispute resolution
18	Audits/benchmarking
19	Invoices/late payment
20	Most favoured client
21	Freight/Shipping
22	Business continuity/disaster recovery
23	Entirety of agreement
24	Security
25	Enterprize definition/future acquisitions/divestiture
26	Non-solicitation of employees
27	Force majeure
28	Export/import regulations
29	Product substitution
30	Escrow

These are often called 'value reduction' terms because they contribute little to a trading relationship or the likelihood of its success – but they distract from activities that could positively add value such as increasing collaboration, sharing information, risk management and so on.

Managers seem to be aware of their options, but they are not using them. They declare a strategy of partnerships to add value – but actually reinforce messages of control, cost reduction, standardization and risk avoidance. They highlight the need to be flexible, adaptive and agile – yet they introduce software tools and measurement systems that enforce compliance and inhibit change.

The IACCM had hoped for more changes to negotiation that would move towards a more collaborative framework for business relationships, such as change management, business continuity and relationship reviews. Arguably, the only clause that forms part of good corporate governance is dispute resolution.

Many clauses raise questions. For instance, as international trade mushrooms, legal systems are ill-equipped to manage trading disputes, and arguments over governing law and jurisdiction are common. There appears to be evidence that some jurisdictions favour national companies with court decisions that are weighed against foreign litigants – so why would any company want to lose the advantage of home jurisdiction?

Another example which wastes time is in the area of liquidated damages. A lot of effort is put into these, but then organizations have no mechanism to monitor performance, or they consistently choose not to enforce the terms because 'it would damage our relationship'.

Perhaps the conclusion from the survey is that companies that really want to focus on customer value should study the list and consider new terms and conditions that might offer real differentiation.

Questions

- There is never enough time to discuss all the terms in a contract? Do you think this is true, and if it is what are the consequences?

- Do you agree that limitation of liability, indemnification and intellectual property clauses, etc. are 'value reduction' clauses? What are the implications if negotiations focus primarily on these?

- What would be alternative value-adding clauses? What would be the benefits of focussing on these?

Source: Based on Cummins T. (2007) The top ten most frequently negotiated terms reveal continued focus on failure; www.tcummins.wordpress.com; www.iaccm.com

CHAPTER 14
PURCHASING LAW AND ETHICS

LEARNING OBJECTIVES   After reading this chapter you should be able to:

- Appreciate the type of legal and regulatory constraints that apply to purchasing

- Understand the work of buyers as agents for their organization

- Understand the essential elements of contract law

- Consider the issues around contract cancellation

- Appreciate the international nature of contract law

- Understand the importance of ethical behaviour in purchasing

- Discuss different types of unethical behaviour and the associated risks

- Appreciate the increased role of corporate social responsibility

LEGAL AUTHORITY

As we saw in the last chapter, the whole process of purchasing is encased in laws and regulations, so it is essential for procurement managers to understand the legal framework in which they work. However, an obvious problem is that every country, and even every region, has its own laws. For instance, a company working in Edinburgh has to comply with laws passed by the EU, UK and Scottish governments (as well as local trading regulations); a company working in Seville, has to comply with the same EU laws, but slightly different laws passed by the Spanish and Andalusian governments (as well as other local regulations). These laws have to work within the broader context of international trade regulations, treaties and agreements. It is clearly impossible to give a detailed description of all the laws that might face a purchasing manager, but there are general patterns and similarities in many laws.

The majority of purchasing laws come in three types:

1 *Contract law,* that creates legal rights between trading parties and defines the nature of agreements that are enforceable.

2 *Agency law,* deals with the role of managers as representatives acting on behalf of their organization.

3 *Consumers protection,* defining rights that customers should expect when making a purchase.

Purchasing managers generally deal with the first two of these, and especially contract law which we will discuss in more detail. Consumer protection is largely concerned with purchases by final customers. Then it is reasonable for purchasers to assume that something they buy is of good quality and fit for the purpose for which it is intended – and that they will be protected from unscrupulous traders. You might argue that if customers are cheated by a company, they will not do any repeat business, but this is a simplistic view. When you buy pills for a headache, you expect them to contain the chemicals stated, and to actually cure a headache. But as an individual, you cannot really test either of these propositions. So consumer protection laws give purchasers some basic rights.

Agency laws

Principal

Is the corresponding person or entity for whom agents carry out their authority.

Agent

Is a person or entity who has been authorized to act on behalf of some other person or entity.

Agency laws are concerned with governing the relationship of **principals** and **agents**.

We can think of a purchasing manager acting as an agent who has been authorized to make purchases on behalf of their organization as the principal. The purchasing manager has broad authority to negotiate prices, terms and conditions – and a supplier dealing with such an agent has a right to rely on the individual's integrity and rigour in performing their duties. It is important for purchasing managers to understand their role as agents of their organization, acknowledging their power to do business with trading partners, being careful not to exceed their responsibilities and working in a legal and ethical manner.

Purchasing managers generally have final authority over procurement decisions within their firms. These decisions may be reached after extended internal discussions within multi-functional sourcing team, but in the end someone has to sign the contract. Purchasing managers act as general agents with legal authority to make purchases. However, it is in their own self-interest to ensure that everyone is aware that their actions are on behalf of their organization. This is the reason that contracts are generally signed in a way that demonstrates the agency relationship, typically including phrases like (Hancock, 1989):

'Signed by [buyer's name] on behalf of [buyer's company's name]'

The relationship between a purchasing agent and an organization is created when the organization hires an individual to do its purchasing. Then it provides a job description which is an agreement that sets the buyer's authority. Buyers have the right to require clear and unequivocal instructions from their employer (actually senior management representing the organization) about the scope of their work, authority, work to be done and expectations of performance.

At the same time, purchasing staff have a duty to act in the best interests of their employer. This means that they do the work prescribed by their organization, in the manner expected. When they carry out these duties in a loyal, honest, ethical and conscientious manner, their obligations to the employers are fulfilled.

Sometimes a buyer's authority is not obvious, and there can be a misunderstanding about actual and apparent authority. Actual authority stems from an organization appointing an agent with specified authority, instructions and job description. These documents define the parameters under which buyers work. Apparent authority is that level of authority that the seller perceives as being available to the buyer, generally suggested by the amount of authority possessed by other purchasing managers in similar positions within the same industry.

Personal liability

Buyers are agents who are responsible for acting in the best interests of their employer. Of course, this does not mean that they are immune from making genuine mistakes. There are several ways in which purchasing staff can be held personally liable for the consequences of their actions, even when they supposedly follow organizational guidelines.

When buyers, in carrying out their normal duties, exceed their actual (but not apparent) authority, the employer is still generally responsible for fulfilling the contract. But they may take legal action against the buyers personally.

When buyers exceeding both actual and apparent authority, and they perform some damaging or illegal act without the authority of their firm, they can be held personally liable (as shown in Figure 14.1). This personal liability can occur even when buyers believe (incorrectly) that they possess the authority and think that they are working to benefit their organization.

LEARNING FROM PRACTICE

Legal Disputes

During an interview, one executive from a major international company said:

'We have a legal counsel to avoid litigation. We will do everything possible to stay out of the court systems, because it always costs money. We do not want to be involved in appearances of the big bad Fortune 100 company versus the little supplier. Ethically we seek to do the right thing. We will settle and go to extremes to stay out of the press.'

Source: Based on Handfield R.B. (2005) Legal and regulatory requirements in the emergent global supply chain, white paper, Supply Chain Resource Cooperative, North Carolina State University, Chapel Hill, NC; www.scm.ncsu.edu

FIGURE 14.1

Actual and apparent
authority

Actual authority
(what the agent is authorized to buy)

	Within	Exceed
Within	OK	Employer responsible for performance of contract
Exceed	Not relevant	Purchasing manager liable (dire consequences)

Apparent authority
(what the seller perceives)

Some activities that could lead to personal liability for buyers include (Cavinato, 1984):

- Deception for personal gain while acting as an agent for the principal firm (which includes taking bribes)

- Violating the lawful protection of items owned by others, such as patent infringement

- Use or misuse of proprietary information

- Violation of anti-monopoly laws

- Unlawful transportation of hazardous materials and toxic waste

These activities are related to another important aspect of purchasing law – ethical behaviour, which we discuss later.

CONTRACT LAW

Contract law defines the legal framework in which procurement works, and is a part of commercial law (as opposed to criminal law) (Scheuing, 1989).

Elements of a contract

We all agree to do things every day, but few of these agreements are actually contracts.

An example of a **contract** occurs when Paul offers to drive Jasmine to the supermarket and says, 'I will drive you to the supermarket to buy your shopping for £10.' Jasmine agrees to the offer. This shows the essential characteristics of a contract:

1   *Offer* – Paul offers to do a specified action of driving Jasmine to the supermarket.

2   *Acceptance* – Jasmine agrees to the offer.

Commercial law
Is that 'body of [the] law that refers to how business firms (parties) enter into contracts with each other, execute contracts and remedy problems that arise in the process'.

Contract
Is a legally enforceable agreement between two or more parties to do specified actions in return for some consideration.

3   *Consideration* – the £10 payment.

If any one of these elements is lacking, then an enforceable contract does not exist. The contract is completed after the journey is made and paid for.

Offer

An offer is a proposal or expression by one person that he or she is willing to do something for certain terms. For example:

> Chris goes into Rashi's Wholesale Video Store and says to Rashi, 'I want to buy 1000 DVDs of the Harry Potter movie. I will pay you €15 for each DVD.'

Chris has made an offer (to purchase a specific movie) in specific volumes (1000 units) at a specific price (€15,000). This constitutes a valid offer. It is a fixed offer, which is somewhat different to a conditional offer that includes extra criteria which must be met. For example, a conditional offer adds a deadline that must be met:

> Chris goes into Rashi's Wholesale Video Store and says, 'I want to buy 1000 DVDs of the Harry Potter movie from you. I will pay you €15 for each DVD if you deliver them to my shop on 1st February, 2012.'

Acceptance

Legally, a contract does not exist until the offer is formally accepted. The offer and acceptance should generally match, but this does not always happen and an acceptance can have additional terms. These additional terms become part of the contract unless the buyer objects within a reasonable time. In the example above, Rashi can make an unconditional acceptance to Chris's offer, or a conditional acceptance, perhaps saying, 'I accept your offer provided that you pay me a week in advance.'

Assuming the offer and acceptance match, there is an agreement leading to a contract. If they do not match there is likely to be some negotiation: an offer, to which someone responds with a counter offer rather than an acceptance, and this generally needs the offer to be restated. This procedure continues until both sides reach an agreement, bringing together an offer and acceptance.

Depending on prevailing laws, both the offer and acceptance can be in any reasonable medium, but they are usually written in formal documents. However the acceptance may be more flexible and can even be implied from the delivery of products. For instance, if someone advertizes that they cut your hair for £10, sitting down in their shop and letting them start is a sign that you have accepted their offer. In practice, purchase orders typically contain a description of the procedures for acceptance of the offer. In practice, most suppliers accept customer orders using their own standard documents, and these contain language and terms that are different from the customer's original purchase order. When this happens, the supplier's terms are automatically incorporated into the final contract unless:

1   The supplier's terms materially alter the original terms of the offer, or

2   The buyer lets the supplier know that it does not agree to the acceptance terms, or

3   The purchase order explicitly states that no alteration of terms can be made.

When the terms of the buyer's purchase order and the supplier's acceptance conflict, some renegotiation is needed before final agreement.

Offer
Acceptance and consideration –key elements for a contract.

Consideration

Consideration is the formal term for something of value that is transferred between parties. In a contract both parties give something of value to the other – sellers give up ownership of their products, while buyers transfer some of their money. In the example above, Chris's consideration included the €15 paid for each DVD, while Rashid's consideration included ownership of the DVDs.

Three other elements are generally assumed in contract law:

1　*Competent parties* – which means that the parties to a legally enforceable contract must have full authority and capacity to make the agreement, either through being principals or their agents.

2　*Mutual assent* – which means that the use of any type of force or coercion to reach an agreement is not acceptable. Both parties must enter into the agreement of their own free will.

3　*Legal subject matter* – which means that a contract can only cover legal activities. If an agreement is made to do an illegal act, the resulting contract is void. If executing the contract depends on the performance of some illegal act, then it is also void.

Is a purchase order a contract?

In chapter 2 we summarized the purchasing process (summarized in Figure 14.2) which leads to a purchase order and award of a contract. The process starts with a quotation (an RFQ), sent by the buyer to the supplier, which contains:

● Description, specifications and end use of the product

● Quantity and conditions of product delivery

● Standard terms and conditions of the transaction

FIGURE 14.2

The contracting process

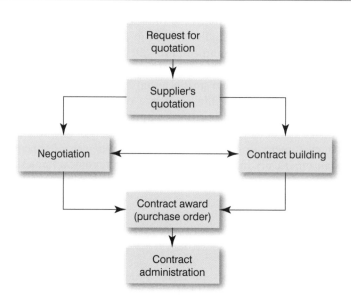

- With a competitive bid, a description of the manner and time in which the bids will be evaluated

- Any other service or legal considerations

- Any other relevant details for the RFQ

The RFQ is not an offer but is a request for price and availability. The supplier will generally respond to the RFQ with a quotation – essentially an offer to sell – which may initiate further discussion and negotiations. Eventually, these lead to a purchase order – which is the basis of the contract and contains all the agreed points.

Generally a purchase order is an offer to buy, and when accepted it becomes a contract. However, in different circumstance a purchase order can be an offer, acceptance or counter offer. It is an offer when it is sent directly to a seller stating that it wants to buy certain materials. It is an acceptance when it agrees to a seller's stated quotation. It is a counter offer when it is sent in response to a quotation, but changes some of the terms (such as delivery quantity or packaging).

Purchase orders – and subsequent contract – contain many elements, perhaps including:

- Material specifications

- Prices and quantities (including taxes)

- Buyer's right of inspection and rejection

- Right to make specification or design changes

- Conduct over patents and copyrights

- Supplier's right to assign the contract to a third party

- Instructions concerning risk and loss

- Statement of credit and payment terms

- Packing and preparation

- Tracking and identification systems

- Warranties and guarantees

- Shipment quantities and dates

- Assignment of seller's rights

- Dispute and arbitration procedures

- Rights to cancel unshipped portion

Standard terms and conditions are often pre-printed on the back of purchase orders, and these are intended to give a measure of protection for the purchaser. Similarly, the seller often has standard terms and conditions pre-printed on the back of their acceptance forms, to give themselves a measure of protection. Unfortunately, the wording on purchase order and sales documents often conflict, so it is important to know exactly which terms are in effect. Many purchase orders are placed over the telephone, in person and through the internet, so purchasing managers must be aware of the potential pitfalls of such contracts. However, the underlying principle is that a contract is really a relationship between the parties involved, and the written contract is only evidence of the existence of this relationship. A written contract describes the relationship, and it supersedes all previous verbal agreements. This is why when you

LEARNING FROM PRACTICE

Amanthang Services

Amanthang Services (AS) make electronic sub-assemblies for manufacturers, often of military equipment. In turn, they purchase components from many manufacturers and distributors. For one major contract, AS sent out RFQs for a number of components, and one contract was awarded to a distributor of integrated circuits (ICs). In essence, AS agreed to buy all of the ICs needed during the contract period from the distributor.

After 9 months the distributor noticed that the quantities of ICs bought had dropped dramatically. They sent an email to AS's supply manager saying that hardly any ICs had been purchased during the past 6 weeks. The supply manager's email reply was that, 'A competitor is supplying the same ICs, with the same specifications, at less than half of your price. If you can meet the price, we will continue doing business; otherwise we can no longer work with you.'

The distributor agreed that new technology and suppressed demand had lowered market prices, but earlier in the year AS had agreed to purchase all the ICs at a higher price. Subsequent meetings failed to produce a satisfactory agreement and the parties agreed to binding arbitration. Here, AS argued that the contract only represented an agreement to purchase as many or as few ICs as it needed, and the

distributor was obligated to supply the circuits as needed. Because AS now had enough circuits from other suppliers, it did not need any more. The distributor argued that AS was committed to buying all ICs from it at the agreed price. Any purchases from an outside source violated the spirit and terms of the contract.

The arbitrator ruled that a price drop was not sufficient reason to circumvent the terms of the contract. First, the contract was voluntarily made by competent parties. There was no indication of undue pressure or that one of the parties was forced to accept the terms. Thus, the contract was not 'unconscionable'. Second, a needs contract should be given its literal interpretation. In this case, AS must purchase any ICs it needs from the distributor named in the contract – and it clearly needed the circuits it purchased from competitors. It is unfortunate for the buyer that the market price dropped – but if the price had risen, the distributor would have had to supply the circuits at the lower price. These are hazards of the marketplace that are faced by both buyers and sellers. AS was directed to purchase the entire quantity of ICs it had contracted for from the distributor, along with all future needs over the remainder of the contract period.

Source: Based on Richmond D. (2008) Arbitration in practice, RPW, Johannesburg.

buy a car a salesperson may describe the virtues of a particular car while walking around the garage, but when you review the written contract these features are not in writing – and this means that they do not apply.

CANCELLATION OF ORDERS AND BREACH OF CONTRACT

A good contract will protect the interests and rights of both buyer and seller – and the contractual obligations are equally binding on both parties. This means that people cannot go around arbitrarily cancelling or defaulting on their contracts. However, there are circumstances in which one of the parties can justifiably seek to cancel a contract. For instance, a supplier may fail to perform in the agreed manner, and a buyer must review the contract to see what actions it can take.

Cancellation of orders

There are three types of contract cancellations:

1   **Cancellation for default** – follows a failure of one of the parties to live up to the terms and conditions of the contract. For instance, suppliers can breach the terms of a contract by late deliveries, poor quality, damaged goods, failing to meet product specifications or otherwise failing to perform in accordance with the contract provisions. At the same time, buyers can breach the terms of a contract by late or non-payment and changing specifications. In these cases the injured side may seek to cancel the contract and seek compensation for damage. In the last chapter we saw that it is more effective to reach agreement for damages through negotiation rather than litigation.

2   **Cancellation for the convenience of the purchaser** – perhaps because anticipated demand for the buyer's products did not materialize. But if the buyer agrees to make certain purchases, it is liable for any damage to the supplier for cancellation. A general rule is that a supplier should not be forced to incur any loss due to the purchaser's default.

3   **Cancellation by mutual consent** – that cancellation of a contract does not automatically lead to legal action, as both parties can agree to a termination, effectively creating another contract that nullifies the first. If there is no loss, a supplier will often accept a purchaser's cancellation in good faith as a normal risk of doing business. Even when suppliers have already purchased materials to fulfil the contract, both parties can normally reach a mutually agreeable resolution, preferably through negotiation rather than litigation.

Breach of contract

A **breach of contract** occurs when either a buyer or seller fails to perform the obligations described in their contract without a valid or legal justification. Such a breach may entitle the injured party to certain remedies or damages.

In the example above, Chris and Rashid's Wholesale Video Store have a valid contract, with Chris promising to buy 1000 DVDs for €15 each, and Rashid promising to deliver them to Chris's shop on 1st February. If Rashid does not show up with the delivery he may be liable for breach of contract. A warning here is that buyers should not routinely tolerate suppliers that breach purchase conditions. For instance, if a purchaser routinely accepts late deliveries from a supplier, this may become part of normal trading and it effectively waives their rights to on-time deliveries in the future. To regain these rights, the buyer may have to give explicit written notice requiring the supplier to provide the agreed service, and they must allow a reasonable time to meet the new delivery requirements.

Breach of contract
Occurs when one party does not act as agreed in a contract.

Damages

Damages are based on the idea that a party who is damaged by a breach of contract must receive damages that bring them back to the position they would have been in if the breach had not occurred. This seems reasonable, but it can be very difficult to assess the actual damage suffered. To avoid this, organizations often include a termination or liquidated damages clause in a contract to specify the mechanism for calculating damages. For instance, they may specify damages for late delivery as the value of items when they were due to arrive minus their value at the time they actually arrived. Incidental damages might include expenses reasonably incurred in inspection, return transport and the care of goods rejected by a purchaser.

Damages include either actual damages (which include losses that are real or known, or can be reasonably estimated), as well as punitive damages (extra money as a punishment for the defendant's bad behaviour). In contract law, punitive damages are rare, so buyers essentially meet three types of actual damages:

- *Restitution* – money the buyer actually paid to the supplier in connection with the contract

- *Reliance* – money the buyer lost because they were relying on the contract, depending on the supplier to live up to their obligations

- *Expectancy* – money the buyer was hoping to gain from the contract in the future

Back at Rashid's Wholesale Video Store, suppose that Chris had given Rashid €2,000 as a down payment on the delivery of DVDs, and had spent €5,000 building new shelves to display the DVDs, and expected to make a profit of €20,000 from selling or renting the DVDs to customers. When Rashid did not deliver the DVDs, Chris could sue for breach of contract and might expect €2000 in restitution damages for loss of the down payment, €5000 in reliance damages for the shelves and €20,000 in expectancy damages for the loss of profits, making a total of €27,000. Of course, to collect damages a firm must produce credible evidence of its costs, and this is particularly difficult to loss of expected profits. In this case, Chris's loss of €20,000 profit might be questionable. It would be rare to recover €27,000 on a contract where real costs were only €7000, and judges might ask why Chris did not buy the DVDs from another supplier.

Sometimes, in spite of the best efforts of buyers and sellers, honest mistakes occur in contracts. Then both sides should consider the circumstances to check whether the contract is still valid. Generally, honest mistakes will not make a contract void, and parties can rely on negotiations – and if necessary contract law – to solve any resulting disputes.

Acceptance and rejection of products

A common cause of damages has purchasers who consider materials to be in some way defective and only accept part of a delivery and reject the remainder, or they reject an entire shipment. When buyers reject a delivery for non-conformance, they have to notify the supplier within a reasonable time, explicitly stating the reasons for rejecting the delivery, and saying that they supplier has breached its contract.

This decision to accept or reject materials is critical, as the supplier's rights increase and the purchaser's rights decrease when a delivery is accepted – specifically, purchasers may not be able to return them and cannot normally withhold payment. The implication is that buyers have a right to inspect materials before actually accepting them, but once accepted they have made a formal decision and ownership is transferred. Usually there are no rituals or formalities to transfer ownership, and any words or acts by a purchaser to indicate its intention of accepting a delivery is enough to effect the transfer. Unfortunately, this means that the transfer is often unclear, so to avoid potential problems, buyers can take formal steps to manage the acceptance process (Hancock, 1989).

- Include in receipts for products a statement along the lines of 'Received subject to inspection, counting and testing'

- Include in purchase orders a statement that All receipts for materials delivered will be subject to inspection, counting and testing'

- Specifically state in purchase orders what is a reasonable time for this inspection and acceptance

- Inspect all delivered materials as quickly as possible, preferably immediately after delivery

- For materials that are not inspected until they are used, use a stock rotation system to ensure that older deliveries are used first (first-in-first-out)

- Set up an internal reporting system to ensure that defects are reported to the purchasing department within a reasonable time so that they can consider remedies

- For items like production equipment include a statement in purchase orders that Acceptance will not be made until the equipment has been installed, tested and run satisfactorily for a certain period

- Carefully define the acceptance criteria for computer hardware and software, and notify the supplier of the specific process used for tests

Of course, there are some latent defects that cannot be discovered during an inspection, and then buyers can report defects as soon as they are discovered and expect a remedy. In certain circumstances, particularly when there are severe latent defects or when an inspection could not take place for some valid reasons, a purchaser can revoke an earlier acceptance of delivered products and look for damages.

Source: Editorial (1991) UCC article 2 quiz, Purchasing Management of Silicon Valley Newsletter, April.

LEARNING FROM PRACTICE

You be the judge

Question 1. The Mark Anthony Pet Shop writes to Cleopatra, stating, 'Dear Cleo: A once-in-a-lifetime opportunity for you. We just received a shipment of Asps. They are healthy, friendly, love kids and make great watch-snakes. As a preferred customer you can receive one for $50. Please respond quickly by email.' Cleo sent a letter in the post and awaited delivery. Is Cleo's acceptance valid?

Question 2. The Voyager Ports Steamship Line contracts to buy 50 of the 25-person-capacity lifeboats from Robinson Crusoe's Lifeboat Company. Crusoe ships the 15-person lifeboats instead of the 25-person ones. Could there be a contract under these conditions?

Question 3. Amanda, a buyer for ABC, orders 100,000 RAM devices for delivery on 1st June. On 10th May the seller advizes Amanda there will be no shipment on 1st June because of production problems. What are Amanda's alternatives?

Answers

Question 1. Cleo's acceptance is not valid because Mark Anthony specifically and unambiguously asked for an email. Acceptance through any reasonable means is normally valid, but suppliers can restrict the means of acceptance.

Question 2. There is a contract only if Voyager Ports Steamship accepts the non-conforming boats. They could do this by: (1) notifying Crusoe that it will take the boats even though they do not conform to specifications; (2) failing to inspect the boats within a reasonable time; and (3) implicitly accepting ownership by attaching the lifeboats to their ships.

Questin 3. This is a breach of contract, and jurisdictions typically respond by allowing ABC to go into the market and buy goods needed to replace those not delivered. Then ABC can recover from the seller the difference between the contract price and price they actually paid, plus any additional expenses.

INTERNATIONAL LAWS

We have described some general principles of contract law, but cannot go into more details as these depend on the jurisdiction and legal systems in place. Even within a single market, such as the EU, there are wide variations in contract law. To simplify international trade, the EU has attempted to unify these laws, but this is a protracted and difficult project. The European Commission (2009) acknowledges that, 'The exchange of goods and services is governed by contract law. Problems in relation to using, agreeing, interpreting and applying contracts in cross-border transactions may therefore affect the smooth functioning of the internal market.' They are taking steps to overcome these problems, moving from specific measures and towards harmonized national laws. 'To date, the European Commision legislator has aimed to address problems in contracting in the Internal market by adopting measures relating to specific contracts or sectors. This sector-specific approach has, however, not been able to solve a number of problems. The European Parliament and Council have consistently affirmed the need for greater coherence in order to ensure the proper functioning of the internal market (European Commision, 2009).'

The USA had a similar problem, as each state enacts its own contract laws, but since the 1950s the federal government developed a Universal Commercial Code (UCC). This does not actually define a contract law as such, but it is a gap-filler that comes into play when the parties themselves do not supply a contract term, or when the term is left open. For example, if nothing is said in a sales contract about delivery, then under the UCC goods are considered delivered when a buyer receives them at the seller's establishment. Similarly, under the UCC if nothing different is said in a sales contract, payment is due at the time of delivery of goods. In general, the terms dictated by the UCC are applicable unless the parties agree to something else (which they generally do) (Baumer and Poindexter, 2004).

The problem with agreements like the European Contract Law and UCC is that they only apply to internal trades and outside fixed boundaries. The United Nations has tried to get even broader agreements, in particular with its Convention on (CISG) (United Nations, 1980). The goal of this convention is to reduce the uncertainty in contracts among international traders who may not understand or accept one another's laws. This in turn should reduce the costs of international transactions and promote more efficient world trade. The first draft of the convention was completed by the United Nations Commission on International Trade Law at the Vienna Conference in 1980 and has since been ratified by more than seventy countries that account for 75 per cent of world trade (United Nations, 2009). The treaty represents a major effort at unification of international trade law across economic, legal, developmental and political barriers. But it is not without problems, firstly as not all countries have signed the treaty. Perhaps more fundamentally, there is no international court with jurisdiction over disputes arising from the treaty, and its long term success depends on the extent to the which disputes can be resolved in national courts.

The consolidation of different contract laws is based on the premise that there are some common underlying principles of trade, good practice and acceptable standards that transcend national boundaries. A successful international treaty has to cover areas like how a contract is formed, what are the risks and how are they shared, how products are moved and delivered, how a contract is satisfied, what happens when things go wrong and so on. The following sections illustrate some of the principles that have to be addressed by international treaties.

Buyers' and seller's rights

Generally sellers expect rights, including:

● Ownership of products that are properly supplied but not paid for by the prospective purchaser

● Recourse to legal action against a buyer who refuses to pay for products that have been properly supplied

● Compensation for additional expenses that are incurred by a buyer's wrongful conduct

● Recovery of reasonable expenses when forced to resell products to another buyer

At the same time, buyers expect rights that include:

● Rejection of defective products that the seller cannot make right within a reasonable time

● Recourse to legal action for breach of contract by the supplier

● Recourse to legal action to force a seller to deliver items that have been properly paid for

● Recovery of reasonable expenses when forced to buy replacement items from another supplier

● Recovery of expenses caused by a breach of warranty by the supplier

Warranties

Warranties ensure that a buyer can rely on delivered products to be in a satisfactory condition. In a basic form, a warranty is, 'A promise or representation made by the seller, which, if necessary, can be legally enforced (Stockton and Miller, 1992).' In practice, there are two main types of warranty:

Warranty
Assurance that materials are delivered in condition agreed.

Explicit warranty is any fact or promise made by the seller which relates to the items purchased, and which becomes part of the contract. These may be presented in descriptions of goods, published specifications, contents of advertisements, statements made by salespeople and so on. For example, imagine Bob's Flour Mill agreeing to deliver to Michel's Bakery a shipment of Grade A flour, and giving a sample of flour and a written statement of its quality. Michel buys some flour, but when it arrives it is not Grade A and has been contaminated by insects. Here, Michel has an explicit warranty – both verbal and written – and in virtually every legal system can take action against Bob for failing to meet the terms of the contract.

Implied warranty which deals with the concept of fitness for use and merchantability. These concepts are also part of a contract even though they are not written down. The implied warranty of fitness for use means that the seller is aware of the purpose for which products are required, and the buyer has a right to rely on the seller's judgment to furnish suitable products. For example, Michel goes to buy an industrial air-conditioning unit for the bakery and approaches Monique's Air-Conditioning Company. Michel describes the size of the bakery, the amount of heat produced by machinery, how cool the facility has to remain and so on. Monique recommends some equipment, and Michel buys it. But the machinery turns out to be inadequate and cannot keep the bakery cool enough. In this case, there was an implicit warranty that the air conditioner would be able to do the job for which it was bought. Monique knew the job it was needed for, and in most jurisdictions has broken an implicit warranty. An implicit warranty essentially says that products are of merchantable quality and fit for the purpose intended.

Buyers may also meet two other types of warranty. *Warranty of title* means that a seller actually owns the materials it is selling and that they are not really owned by someone else or are stolen. This seems clear, but we have mentioned that there is no ceremony to transfer ownership, and at certain points there may be some doubt. When there are any doubts about the legitimate owner of materials, buyers need to ensure that a supplier really has the right to sell it.

Warranty of infringement refers to the supplier's guarantee that items being sold do not illegally infringe another party's patents or copyright. When patent owners identify an infringement, they can take legal action to prevent further use of an item – and this might disrupt another firm's operations. This can be so damaging that most purchasing agreements contain an appropriate patent indemnification clause.

Transport terms and risk of loss

Transport terms and documentation can be very important to a purchase, but they are often overlooked in contracts. Transport documents are used to govern, direct, control and provide information about shipments as they are moved through supply chains (Waters, 2009). These documents are notoriously complicated, and they come in many formats.

A **bill of lading** is the most common shipping document and it describes the origin of the shipment, provides specific directions for the carrier, gives transportation contract terms and functions as a receipt for the shipment. In some circumstances, the bill of lading may also serve as a certificate of ownership. It contains basic information like:

Bill of lading, freight bill, delivery terms
Types of documents needed for material delivery.

- The name and address of the consignor and consignee
- Routing instructions for the carrier
- A description of the goods being transported
- The number of items
- The rate for goods being shipped

A **freight bill** serves as the carrier's invoice for the freight charges of a particular shipment. **Delivery terms** describe who is responsible for choosing a carrier and paying the freight bill, and the method in which the title of goods passes from the supplier to the purchaser. The most common term in delivery terms is 'free-on-board' (FOB) (free on board) which refers to the historical practice of transferring the ownership of goods when they were put on a ship for overseas trade. Now terms like 'FOB shipping point' show that the purchaser is responsible for transport and assumes ownership at the supplier's premises. 'FOB destination' says that the supplier is responsible for transport, with the purchaser assuming ownership when delivered. The FOB term also defines who is responsible for filing any claims for damage on the journey, as the party who owns the materials is responsible for filing any claim. CIF (cost, insurance and freight) is similar to FOB, and means that the contract price includes transport and insurance.

Usually, a loss of goods during shipment results in a claim against the carrier. But there can be disagreement about who is responsible for certain losses. To avoid this, buyers should clearly specify delivery terms in the purchase contract, giving as much detail as possible.

Patents and intellectual property

As suppliers become increasingly integrated into new product development, intellectual property agreements are becoming more common. National and international laws give protection of intellectual property, typified by the USA where, 'Congress shall have the power … to promote the progress of science and useful arts, by securing for limited times to authors and inventors the exclusive right to their respective writings and discoveries (Kintner and Lahr, 1975).'

There are three kinds of intellectual property – patents, copyrights and trade secrets. Patents allow an owner exclusive rights to make, use and sell an invention for the life of the patent, which is usually around 20 years from the date of filing a claim with a Patent Office. At the end of this period the patent expires and anyone else can use it. Patent laws tend to be national, so inventors have to patent their products in each country where they want protection.

Not all patent infringements are deliberate, and many firms protect themselves from inadvertent patent infringement by including a clause in their contracts. This clause might typically include:

● An indemnification, which seeks the supplier's assurances that materials being bought do not infringe any other party's patents

● A requirement that the supplier defend any patent infringement lawsuit itself

● The right to have the purchaser's own lawyers involved in defence of any lawsuit

Copyright law is designed to give protection for anyone who creates original written work such as books, software, songs and films. Copyright generally lasts for an extended period, such as the life of the author plus 50 years. Unlike patent laws it is automatic and does not require the authors to make a formal application. It is not necessary for the author to place any legend or indication on the protected material – as copyright is automatically assumed.

Trade secrets are a very broad category of intellectual property. Virtually any information believed to be confidential and important to an organization can be considered as a trade secret, including formulae, suppliers, customer lists, costs, operations, training programmes and so on. Trade secret laws tend to be less prescriptive than patent and copyright laws, with an aim of protecting ideas that would not otherwise have legal protection. This information is:

● Economically valuable

● Not generally known

● Kept as a secret

This is a much vaguer area, and difficult to enforce. For instance, stock exchanges are generally covered by laws prohibiting insider trading, but successful prosecutions are very rare. Often courts take the view that organizations should protect

FIGURE 14.3 Non-disclosure agreement

Re: Non-disclosure agreement

In conjunction with recent discussions, it is anticipated in the future that our Company will disclose to your company or your company will observe, or come in contact with, certain confidential information that is the property of our Company. This information will include, without limitation, certain proprietary items related to our Company's know-how, processes, machinery and manufacturing aspects of our Company's business.

It is our understanding that except as specifically authorized in writing by our Company, your company shall not disclose to any party any confidential information disclosed by our Company to your company or that your company observes or comes in contact with, or any marketing, financial, or technical information developed or generated by your company for our Company. Your company shall neither use nor furnish to any party any equipment or material embodying or made by the use of such information. However:

1   Should any of the aforesaid information be published or otherwise made available to the public through sources that are entitled to disclose it, and should your company demonstrate to our Company that it has obtained this information from a source available to the public, then your company shall be free to disclose said information to any party.

2   Your company understands that nothing herein shall be seen as granting any right or licence under any patents, trademarks and copyrights of our Company.

their own trade secrets by limited access and other security measures. The argument is that if someone unauthorized gets access to information, then it has not been protected properly, so by definition cannot be secret. This argument is not always convincing as trading partners have to exchange a lot of information as part of their normal business dealings, and although it is shared it may also be considered secret. Both parties must know which information is proprietary and must be kept confidential, and for this they use a formal non-disclosure agreement (with part of an agreement shown in Figure 14.3).

A problem with intellectual property laws is that some countries do not have relevant laws. In recent years, the World Trade Organization has been trying to standardize laws and introduce more rigorous protection. However, there are still problems with monitoring actions and making sure that treaties are being enforced. It is fair to say that theft of intellectual property remains a serious problem around the world.

LEARNING FROM PRACTICE

Callaway

Most of the golf clubs that you are likely to see in shops are made in China, in an area just north of Hong Kong. But alongside legitimate manufacturing there are often shady operations that are involved in counterfeiting. The owners either do not know that they are doing anything illegal, or do not care. In 2003, one such operation was investigated by Callaway, a leading international manufacturer of high quality clubs.

Callaway suspected Lily Wan, a Chinese businesswoman, and her firm Hong Kong Cedar

Source: Based on Swift E.M. and Yaeger D. (2003) Pssst...wanna buy some clubs?', *Sports Illustrated*, 22 September.

International, of shipping counterfeit Callaways to Europe. A private investigator learned that Wan would attend the Professional Golfers Association meeting in Orlando, and set a trap by pretending to be an executive interested in placing an order. Wan arrived and laid down on a coffee table a counterfeit of a Callaway ERCII driver, a Great Big Bertha II and a Steelhead X-15 iron. Stu Harrington, Callaway's security director, said that, 'The Great Big Bertha was a very, very impressive copy.' Wan quoted a price of $33 for the golf club head. A generic graphite shaft might cost another $6, a grip 50 cents, so for a total outlay of $39.50 they had a first-rate copy of a club that retails for $499.

The investigators identified themselves to Wan who 'insisted she'd done nothing wrong'. In the end, they let her go and she left. Trafficking in counterfeit goods is a crime, but successful prosecutions are infrequent. The feeling was that 2-years ago Wan might have been prosecuted, but US law enforcement was focussing on other issues. Having given a warning it was assumed that Wan would not return. However, at the same meeting in Orlando, another person was seen to collect a lot of information and photographs about a particular club. As the investigator commented, 'Everyone knew what he was doing.'

PURCHASING ETHICS

Ethics is concerned with appropriate actions, and behaving in a manner that goes beyond legal requirements, and is also fair and acceptable.

In a business setting, ethical behaviour is the use of recognized social principles involving justice and fairness throughout a business relationship. Ethical buyers treat suppliers in a just, decent, fair, honest and fitting manner – and they follow practices viewed as acceptable by those within the profession as well as the community (Haynes and Helms, 1991; Page, 1986).

Three rules are at the heart of ethical behaviour.

Ethics
Are the set of moral principles or values guiding our behaviour.

1 Buyers must work for their organization's benefit, rather than for personal gain at the expense of the organization. Specifically, ethical buyers do not accept outside gifts or favours, are not influenced by the unethical practices of some salespeople and do not have personal financial arrangements with suppliers.

2 Buyers must act ethically toward suppliers and potential suppliers, treating them professionally and with respect.

3 Buyers must uphold the ethical standards defined by their profession, generally included in the code of conduct of appropriate purchasing associations.

Purchasing staff – more than any other group within a firm – experience enormous pressure to act in unethical ways. There are several reasons for this. Firstly, purchasing controls large sums of money, and buyers responsible for a major contract can meet sellers who are willing to use any means of gaining a competitive advantage. Secondly, is the pressure put on many salespeople by their own company's aggressive sales targets, making them more likely to resort to questionable sales practices.

Risks of unethical behaviour

Perhaps the greatest concern for a buyer who acts unethically is that they are also acting illegally. For example, in most countries a government buyer who accepts payment from a defence contractor has clearly committed an act that is both unethical and illegal. Both the buyer and their employer risk prosecution.

With a more limited perspective, unethical behaviour also risks a buyer's professional reputation. Sellers quickly become aware of buyers who are open to offers 'on the side' and once a buyer earns this reputation it is difficult to change it. Perhaps the most immediate concern for buyers is that their own management will discover their lack of ethics and terminate their employment. Buyers carry their professional reputations throughout their career, so this can be a serious blow – especially if their company decides to pursue some kind of legal claim. So the more pressing consequences of unethical behaviour include unemployment, personal bankruptcy and jail.

A final risk of unethical behaviour is to a firm's reputation. A buyer who makes purchase decisions based on factors other than legitimate business criteria risks the reputation of the entire firm. For example, the quality of a company's own products may suffer if a buyer accepts sub-standard materials from a supplier that offered outside inducements.

Of course, with global sourcing buyers sometimes encounter behaviour that they believe to be unethical, but the local culture accepts. For instance, in some areas personal gifts are seen as a polite accompaniment to business transactions, eventually giving a routine source of extra income. However, global firms are increasingly adopting an unequivocal zero-tolerance stance toward any form of bribery – even when this means sacrificing short-term profitability to maintain a global reputation of integrity and honesty. Accepting a supplier's outside gifts and favours in exchange for special treatment is a form of corruption, and successful firms do not have to practice such unethical behaviour to win contracts.

Types of unethical purchasing behaviour

The line between ethical and unethical behaviour is often difficult to define – and difficult to keep to. For instance, suppose that a buyer has the highest ethical standards, but works for a manager who asks them to do something they feel is unethical. A manager may tell a buyer to award a contract because of their personal friendship with a supplier. Does the buyer simply award the contract as directed by the manager, and ignore their own values? Or does the buyer refuse to award the contract, thereby challenging the authority of a manager and jeopardizing their career? The answer is that they refuse to award the contract and report the manager to higher management – but this illustrates the way that individuals can be pressurized to behave in ways that conflict with their values.

Different people, organizations and cultures see ethics in different ways, but there is widespread agreement that certain behaviour is unethical. Most organizations have guidelines that formally prohibit certain actions including the following.

Reciprocity – which insists that potential suppliers will only be considered if they buy products from the organization (Parker *et al.*, 1982). In simple terms, it is a purchasing arrangement that dictates 'I'll buy from you only if you buy from me.' Reciprocal purchasing is considered unethical, and even illegal, but this does not mean that a customer is prohibited from becoming a supplier. It means that buyers must use legitimate performance criteria to evaluate their capability – and not award business solely as a condition of winning other sales contracts.

Personal buying – which occurs when someone gets their employer to buy materials for their personal use. For instance, a company can purchase safety shoes and special tools required by employees for their work – but it should not buy computers for use at home. As you can imagine, this is a grey area for many firms. A company buys a manager a computer for her office, but not one for her home; but what happens when she sometimes works from home and needs a computer there? A buyer who is given a request for personal buying should determine the legal status of the request and then carefully check the firm's ethical policies.

Accepting supplier favours – with accepting gifts and favours from suppliers as probably the most common ethical infraction. Such gifts can affect a buyer's judgment to evaluate and select the most capable suppliers, but policies are often confusing. At what point does a supplier's gift become more than a friendly show of appreciation and start to influence a buyer's decisions? Most firms address this issue in their ethics policy by specifying exactly what a buyer may accept from a supplier.

Financial conflicts of interest – when a buyer awards business to a supplier because the buyer, or the buyer's family, have a direct financial interest in the supplier. This is considered a seriously unethical practice, and is one reason why many companies require employees to give details of their investments in outside companies.

Sharp practices – which is any misrepresentation by a buyer that falls just short of actual fraud (Haynes and Helm, 1991). Sharp practice occurs whenever a buyer begins to work in an underhanded manner, including:

- **Deliberate use of misinformation,** when a buyer knowingly deceives a supplier to gain some advantage. For example, requesting quotations on inflated volumes and then placing smaller orders at the reduced price

- **Exaggerating problems,** perhaps when a buyer exaggerates the size of a problem caused by the supplier to extract a larger penalty or concession

- **Requesting bids from unqualified suppliers,** with the sole purpose of driving a qualified supplier's price lower

- **Gaining information unfairly** through deception

- **Sharing information on competitive quotations,** as the competitive bid process requires some confidentiality, and buyers who share information about supplier quotations abuse the process

- **Not compensating a supplier** for design or other work. Buyers often request design and cost-savings assistance from suppliers, and they should offer fair compensation for these efforts

- **Taking unfair advantage of a supplier's financial situation,** when a buyer who knowingly pressures a financially troubled supplier into quoting a lower price pushes the supplier in even further financial jeopardy

- **Lying or misleading,** with anything other than the truth forming a sharp practice

Influence

Influence is the power to sway other people's thinking or actions by means of argument, example or force of personality. Obviously, suppliers want to influence procurement into buying their products – whilst buyers have to resist the effects of influence and ensure that they continue to work objectively (Adler *et al.*, 2007).

Influence in the supply chain comes in many forms. Some persuade suppliers to adopt new ideas and share information; these are positive influences and add value to decisions. But other influences include inappropriate sharing of confidential information and accepting gifts; these are negative influences that detract from the quality of decisions. A survey by the Institute for Supply Management's Ethical

LEARNING FROM PRACTICE

Eaton Corporation

When Eaton Corporation Chairman and CEO Alexander Cutler addressed the winners of the company's Supplier Excellence Awards, he thanked the winners and explained the company's goals. These did not include price reductions, but instead talked about values. 'We want to be the most admired company in our markets through supply chain performance,' he told the attendees. 'Have the right ethics and the right business practices and you'll attract the best people and suppliers who'll produce the best results.'

The company has an ombudsman for ethics, whom employees or anyone else can meet. It publishes an ethics guide that goes to all employees to help them understand Eaton's expectations and their responsibilities. The company does not hesitate to stop doing business with suppliers whose business practices are not up to its own high standards, regardless of their quality or prices.

Cutler specifically mentioned several examples that had arisen. He said, 'We had an issue many years ago where we were doing some advanced product development work for a significant global customer. There were established timetables for development, testing and shipment, and our customer was expecting the fully-tested product to be shipped at the end of a particular quarter. When it came to the end of that quarter, not all of the testing had been accomplished. Two senior operating managers in the USA falsified the test results and thereby misrepresented the product's readiness for shipment. Both signed the reports willingly. Upon investigation, we learned that they felt they should do this in order to meet the targeted shipment timetables, because they thought this was what both Eaton and the customer wanted. Yet clearly this was a violation of Eaton's quality and ethics policies. We terminated the two managers.'

He continued, 'We will not tolerate any compromise of our standards for quality. Nor will we knowingly violate any laws or regulations in any country. At Eaton, we do not practice what I call 'geographic' ethics. We have one set of ethics worldwide. If the laws and regulations of a given country differ from our own company standards, we comply with whatever requirement represents the higher standard of behaviour in that situation. Several years ago we had a facility that encountered piracy of our technology, theft of other intellectual property and the sale of our products into grey markets. Additionally, local businessmen made copycat versions of Eaton products and threatened to label them with Eaton brand names unless we paid them not to. The local government repeatedly approached us for payments, without which it would not pursue or prosecute these matters. It became clear that we were not going to be able to do business in an environment where the ethics of local officials were so different from our own. So we abandoned the facility and our business in that country, at a not-insignificant cost.'

He quotes another example of conflicts of interest, 'Eaton had a plant manager in China, a Chinese national, who fell foul of our prohibition against conflicts of interest. Although his actions may have been acceptable to some in that country, they were not acceptable to Eaton. He replaced the supplier that was providing a commodity to our plant with a supplier in which his wife had a financial interest. It was quite clear that his decision had not been based on quality or price issues with the previous supplier. Until then, we had been very pleased with this executive's performance. He was a highly valued employee in whom we'd invested considerable training, including almost 4 years of cumulative operations experience in the USA and China. Despite our investment in this employee, we had to let him go. We simply could not allow this action to stand or to appear to be endorsed when it was so clearly a violation of our conflict-of-interest standards.'

Source: Cutler S. (2003) Eaton Today, August, Chairman's Column, One-to-One; Teague P.E. (2007) Eaton wins purchasing's Medal of Professional Excellence, Purchasing, 13 September.

Standards Committee showed that purchasing managers were concerned by the effects of influence (ISM, 2008). Inappropriate preference for suppliers was a concern of 34 per cent of respondents, while politics inappropriately influencing sourcing decisions was a concern to 46 per cent of respondents (as shown in Figure 14.4)

Influence issues	No influence	Influence
There are instances where your organization gave inappropriate preference to suppliers in sourcing decisions.	66%	34%
There are examples in your organisation where politics inappropriately influenced sourcing decisions.	54%	46%
Gifts or entertainment inappropriately influenced sourcing decisions in your function.	93%	7%
Meals with suppliers influenced sourcing decisions in your function.	94%	6%
Others outside of your function have received gifts or entertainment from suppliers outside of your organisation's policy.	55%	45%

FIGURE 14.4

Concerns over influences affecting purchasing

Although only a few purchasing managers were concerned about gifts influencing sourcing decisions within their function, 45 per cent of respondents indicated that individuals outside of their function were influenced by such gifts from suppliers.

The Institute for Supply Management is clear in its view of influence, which it states as follows:

'Nothing can undermine respect for the purchasing profession more than improper action on the part of its members with regard to gifts, gratuities or favours. People engaged in purchasing should not accept from any supplier or prospective supplier any money, gift or favour that might influence, or be suspected of influencing, their buying decisions. We must decline to accept or must return any such gift or favour offered to us or members of our immediate family.'

Supporting ethical behaviour

A firm can take many actions to make sure its employees conduct business in an ethical manner. The following list summarizes some of these.

Developing a code of ethics. Adopting a formal ethics policy helps define and deter potentially unethical behaviour; conversely, firms without formal ethical policies behave in less ethical ways, such as disclosing supplier bid prices to other suppliers (Forker and Janson, 1990). In essence, a formal ethics policy helps define the boundaries of ethical behaviour.

Top-management commitment. Senior management sets the ethical code of behaviour within a firm. The behaviour of top executives sends a message about whether unethical behaviour is tolerated.

Closer buyer-seller relationships. Dealing with a smaller supply base probably does more to promote ethical purchasing than any other action. Firms are increasingly using buying teams to evaluate potential suppliers, and using a team to check a small number of supplier's capabilities limits the opportunity for unethical behaviour.

Ethical training. New buyers generally attend a training programme before starting their duties, and these usually include purchasing ethics. Such programmes give an opportunity to educate a new buyer about a firm's commitment to the highest ethical standards.

LEARNING FROM PRACTICE

Institute for Supply Management

The Institute for Supply Management (ISM) is a major organization representing the purchasing profession. It recognizes that, 'It is necessary for all of us to exercize a strict rule of personal conduct to insure that relations of a compromising nature, or even the appearance of such relations, be scrupulously avoided.'

Since 1959 ISM has adopted standards of conduct which serves as a guide for members. These specify three guiding principles of: '(1) integrity in your decisions and actions, (2) value for your employer and (3) loyalty to your profession'. From these principles ISM derived its Principles and Standards of Ethical Supply Management Conduct (ISM, 2008).

1 **Perceived impropriety.** Prevent the intent and appearance of unethical or compromising conduct in relationships, actions and communications.

2 **Conflicts of interest.** Ensure that any personal, business or other activity does not conflict with the lawful interests of your employer.

3 **Issues of influence.** Avoid behaviours or actions that may negatively influence, or appear to influence, supply management decisions.

4 **Responsibilities to your employer.** Uphold fiduciary and other responsibilities using reasonable care and granted authority to deliver value to your employer.

5 **Supplier and customer relationships.** Promote positive supplier and customer relationships.

6 **Sustainability and social responsibility.** Champion social responsibility and sustainability practices in supply management.

7 **Confidential and proprietary information.** Protect confidential and proprietary information.

8 **Reciprocity.** Avoid improper reciprocal agreements.

9 **Applicable laws, regulations and trade agreements.** Know and obey the letter and spirit of laws, regulations and trade agreements applicable to supply management.

10 **Professional Competence.** Develop skills, expand knowledge and conduct business that demonstrates competence and promotes the supply management profession.

Source: Based on .

Developing consistent behaviour. Confusion about proper behaviour can arise when different functions have their own ethical standards. A firm that prohibits its purchasing staff from accepting gifts from suppliers, but allows its marketing department to distribute gifts to its customers is not acting consistently. When different standards apply within a single firm, it becomes easier to slip to the lowest standards.

Internal reporting of unethical behaviour. Senior managers should create an atmosphere that supports the reporting of unethical behaviour. A buyer should be able to approach management about an ethical impropriety with confidence that they will correct the problem. A buying firm should also encourage suppliers to report instances of unethical behaviour by anyone within the firm.

Preventive measures. One common tactic is to rotate buyers among different items or commodities, thus preventing them from becoming too comfortable with any particular group of suppliers. This seems strange as buyers should develop expertise in their purchased items and suppliers, but it is often a good idea to rotate staff every few years.

Limited authority to purchase This limits a buyer's authority to buy without higher-level approval. For example, a firm's policy may limit a buyer's authority for awarding contracts to £20,000, and anything more than this needing a manager's signature.

Corporate social responsibility

Corporate social responsibility is based on the idea that organizations have an obligation to society that extends beyond compliance with regulations, and should consider the broader effects of their actions.

Social responsibility extends the ideas of ethical behaviour and has become a central part of organizational work, and a core element of purchasing. As such, the Institute for Supply Management (ISM, 2008) has developed a guide for managers, describing policies for the areas of: (1) community (2) diversity (3) environment (4) ethics (5) financial responsibility (6) human rights and (7) safety (shown in Figure 14.5).

We can illustrate some ideas of social responsibility by reference to environmental concerns. Here the broad green movement has had considerable influence, and firms

Social responsibility
Is a set of corporate policies, procedures and resulting behaviour designed to benefit the workplace and, by extension, the individual, the organization and the community.

FIGURE 14.5 Areas for corporate social responsibility (in alphabetical order)

Community

1 Provide support and add value to your communities and those in your supply chain.

2 Encourage members of your supply chain to add value in their communities.

Diversity

1 Proactively promote purchasing from, and the development of, socially diverse suppliers.

2 Encourage diversity within your own organization.

3 Proactively promote diverse employment practices throughout the supply chain.

Environment

1 Encourage your own organization and others to be proactive in examining opportunities to be environmentally responsible within their supply chains either 'upstream' or 'downstream'.

2 Encourage the environmental responsibility of your suppliers.

3 Encourage the development and diffusion of environmentally friendly practices and products throughout your organization.

Ethics

1 Be aware of ISM's Principles and Standards of Ethical Supply Management Conduct.

2 Abide by your organization's code of conduct.

Financial responsibility

1 Become knowledgeable of, and follow, applicable financial standards and requirements.

2 Apply sound financial practices and ensure transparency in financial dealings.

3 Actively promote and practice responsible financial behaviour throughout the supply chain.

FIGURE 14.5 (Continued)

Human rights

1   Treat people with dignity and respect.

2   Support and respect the protection of international human rights within the organization's sphere of influence.

3   Encourage your organization and its supply chains to avoid complicity in human or employment rights abuses.

Safety

1   Promote a safe environment for each employee in your organization and supply chain. (Each organization is responsible for defining 'safe' within its organization.)

2   Support the continuous development and diffusion of safety practices throughout your organization and the supply chain.

are increasingly aware of the need to reduce their impact on the environment. For example, General Electric's campaign of 'eco-imagination' was expected to sell $14 billion of environmentally friendly products in 2007, rising by another 10 per cent in 2008. The company has also reduced harmful gas emissions by 4 per cent in 2 years (Kranhold, 2007). Even the car industry, historically not a leader in environmental protection, is spending millions of pounds on reducing fuel consumption, electric and hybrid cars, alternative fuels, new engine technology and so on (Blumenstein, 2007).

As firms are themselves looking more carefully at the environmental impact of their operations, buyers are pressing their suppliers for greater environmental

LEARNING FROM PRACTICE

S.C. Johnson

S.C. Johnson works to improve the environmental impact of the raw materials it purchases. To support their green efforts, the company developed 'Greenlist' as an environmental classification that rates ingredients on between four and seven relevant criteria such as biodegradability and aquatic toxicity. Scoring ranges from 3 (the best) to 0 (where ingredients are only used with special permission, and a substitute must be found). The results of their effort have been very successful, including:

- Elimination of thousands of tonnes of 0 rated materials

- Use of materials rated as 2 and 3 increased by more than 13 thousand tonnes

- Phased out chlorine-based external packaging

- Phased out the use of bleached paperboard, which uses chlorine as a bleaching agent

S.C. Johnson believes it must still work closely with organizations that have varying priorities, but it has found widespread support for its Greenlist and objectives in its disparate suppliers. There is genuine enthusiasm for helping the company meet its objectives, and their successes would not have been possible without the active collaboration of suppliers – and without a clear process to guide collaboration.

Source: Based on Johnson S. and Long D. (2006) The greening of the supply chain, Supply Chain Management Review, May–June 2006, pp 36–40.

efforts. You can see the effects in, for example, the Carbon Disclosure Project which records the carbon footprint of almost 2000 companies around the world (CDP, 2009) (where carbon footprints are estimates of the amount of carbon dioxide emitted by firms in producing and distributing their products). As firms include their upstream suppliers in a more comprehensive carbon footprint, the results give a more complete picture of emissions. For instance, Cadbury calculate the total amount of carbon released in making a chocolate bar from the farm through the factory and on to the retail shop that finally sells it. Some people suggest that in the future food labels could contain a carbon footprint number along with the calories and ingredients (Spencer, 2007). Wal-Mart recognized this need to include the whole supply chain in their sustainability strategy, with a vice president remarking, 'We recognized early on that we had to look at the entire value chain. If we had focussed on just our own operations, we would have limited ourselves to 10 per cent of our effect on the environment and eliminated 90 per cent of the opportunity that's out there (Plambeck, 2007).'

CHAPTER REVIEW

- Purchasing managers work in an area that is surrounded by complex laws and regulations. These laws are different in every jurisdiction, so we can only describe some of their general features.

- Purchasing managers act as agents for their organizations. Both agents and principles have legal responsibilities and authorities. Exceeding these can leave both open to legal action, including personal liability of the buyer.

- Contract law defines the terms under which buyers and sellers conduct their business. The three essential parts of a legally enforceable contract are offer, acceptance and consideration.

- Contracts are in place to protect both parties. Unfortunately, there are often disagreements about terms and conditions. Purchasing managers must be aware of the potential pitfalls in standard legal terminology and must work to avoid such disputes. When disputes occur, it is always better to try and solve them through negotiation rather than lawsuits.

- . There are valid conditions under which contracts can be cancelled. These are classified as cancellation for default, for convenience of the purchaser or by mutual consent. When one party suffers harm because the other party cancels a contract, they may be awarded damages.

- Every jurisdiction has its own contract laws. Attempts have been made to standardize these, particularly through the United Nations Convention on Contracts for the International Sale of Goods. Such treaties are based on common elements in trade – such as buyer and seller rights, warranties and transport risks. Understandably, such treaties need a lot of time and effort to get working properly.

- Ethics are the set of moral principles or values guiding our behaviour. In a business setting, ethical behaviour is the use of accepted social principles of fairness and justice during a business relationship.

- Many types of activity are considered unethical – ranging from personal buying through to financial conflicts of interest. These can damage both individual buyers and their organization. Most organizations deal with these with a formal ethical policy for their buyers.

- Corporate social responsibility is based on the idea that organizations have an obligation to society that extends beyond compliance with regulations and considers the broader effects of their actions. As more organizations adopt corporate responsibility, they typically adopt policies with concern for community, diversity, environment, ethics, financial responsibility, human rights and safety.

DISCUSSION QUESTIONS

1 Why is it important for purchasing managers to understand legal issues? Is this the job of lawyers?

2 What does the term 'agent' mean? Under what conditions can purchasing agents be held personally responsible for abusing their position?

3 Suppose you arrive at a verbal agreement with someone about the price of purchasing their car. Under what conditions have you reached an enforceable contract?

4 A seller verbally tells you that his cleaning product can remove any stain from a kitchen work surface. Later you find that this is not true, and the cleaning product does not work very well at removing certain stains. Do you have a legal claim against the seller? What type of damages might you be entitled to?

5 Suppose you sign a contract to buy $15 000 worth of components. You tell the supplier that you are only authorized to sign contracts for $10 000 without approval from your boss, but the supplier agrees anyway. Later, you find out that you only need $8000 worth of components. What is your legal position?

6 Suppose that a supplier gives you a price on a contract and then later says that he mistakenly

wrote down the wrong price. What would you do?

7 If you write a contract that contains clauses about transport requirements, and the supplier agrees to it but later claims that it is not acceptable, who do you think has the stronger case?

8 Discuss the concept of ethics. Why is the purchasing function particularly sensitive to this topic?

9 What are the different risks associated with unethical behaviour?

10 Discuss the types of issues that a buyer faces where the ethical perspective can be unclear.

11 Why is it important for a firm to have a written ethics policy? What is the importance of top management's commitment to the policy?

12 Imagine that you are a buyer for a major company, and the Chief Executive has strongly encouraged you to buy materials from a supplier that belongs to his club. How would you handle this?

13 Would you be more interested in working for an organization that supports environmentally friendly policies? Are there any negative aspects to working in this type of organization?

REFERENCES

Adler D., Baranowski J., Kalin L., Lallatin C., Smiley S., Turner G. and Sturzl S. (2007) Ethical behaviour: boundaries of influence, 92nd ISM International Conference Proceedings, May.

Baumer D. L. and Poindexter J. C. (2004) Legal environment of business in the information age, Irwin, New York: McGraw-Hill .

Blumenstein R. (2007) GM to invest in green technology in China, Wall Street Journal, October 30, p A10.

Cavinato J. L. (1984) Purchasing and materials management: integrative strategies, St. Paul, MN: West Publishing.

CDP (2009) Responding Companies 2008, Carbon Disclosure Project, London and website at www.cdproject.net

European Commission (2009) European Contract law, EU, Brussels, and website at www.ec.europa.eu

Forker L. B., and Janson R. L. (1990) Ethical practices in purchasing, International Journal of Purchasing and Materials Management, 26(1): 19–26.

Haynes P. J. and Helms M. M. (1991) An ethical framework for purchasing decisions, Management Decision, 29(1): 35

Hancock W. A. (editor) (1989) The law of purchasing (2nd edition), Chesterland, OH: Business Laws.

ISM (2008) Principles and standards of ethical supply management conduct, Institute for Supply Management, Tempe, AZ and website at www.ism.ws

ISM (2008) Principles of social responsibility, Institute for Supply Management, Tempe, AZ and website at www.ism.ws

Kintner E. W. and Lahr J. L. (1975) An intellectual property law primer, New York: Macmillan.

Kranhold K. (2007) GE's environment push hits business realities, Wall Street Journal, September 14, pp A1, A10.

Page H. (1986) More on ethics—helping your buyers, Purchasing World, 30(12): 60.

Parker R. C., Fordyce G. C. and Graham K. P. (1982) Ethics in purchasing, In: Farrell L.G. and Alijian L.A. (editors), Purchasing Handbook, New York: McGraw-Hill.

Plambeck E. L. (2007) The greening of Wal-Mart's supply chain, Supply Chain Management Review, July–August, p 19.

Scheuing E. E. (1989) Purchasing management, Englewood Cliffs, NJ: Prentice Hall.

Spencer J. (2007) Big firms press suppliers on climate, Wall Street Journal, October 9, p A7.

Stockton J. and Miller F. (1992) Sales and leases of goods in a nutshell (3rd edition), St. Paul, MN: West Publishing.

United Nations (1980) United Nations Convention on Contracts for the International Sale of Goods, UN, New York.

United Nations (2009) website at www.un.org

Waters D. (2009) Supply chain management, Basingstoke, Hampshire: Palgrave Macmillan.

FURTHER READING

Baumer D. L. and Poindexter J. C. (2002) Cyberlaw and e-commerce, New York: McGraw-Hill.

Baumer D. L. and Poindexter J. C. (2004) Legal environment of business in the information age, Irwin, New York: McGraw-Hill.

Carter C. R. (1998) Ethical issues in global buyer-supplier relationship, Center for Advanced Purchasing Studies, Tempe, FL.

Cavinato J. L., Flynn A. and Kauffman R. (2006) The supply management handbook, New York: McGraw-Hill.

Cooper R. W., Frank G. L. and Kemp R. A. (1997) The ethical environment facing the profession of purchasing and materials management, International Journal of Purchasing and Materials Management, 33(2):2–11.

Duerden J. (1995) 'Walking the walk' on global ethics, Directors and Boards, 19(3):42–45.

Gabriel H. (1994) Practitioner's guide to the Convention on Contracts for the International Sale of Goods (CISG) and the Uniform Commercial Code (UCC), New York: Oceana Publishing.

Griffiths M. and Griffiths I. (2002) Law for purchasing and supply, Harlow: Financial Times Prentice Hall.

Murray J. E. (2003) When you get what you bargained for – but do not, Purchasing, 132(4):26–27.

Schildhouse J. (2005) Corporate ethics: taking the high road, Inside Supply Management, March, pp 30–31.

Van Den Hendel J. (1995) Purchasing ethics: strain or strategy, Purchasing and Supply Management, Summer, pp 50–52.

Woods J. A. (editor) (2000) The purchasing and supply yearbook, New York: McGraw-Hill.

CASE STUDY

Ethical Issues

Case 1

Bernan Janz was just arriving back in his office when his wife called to say that she had been sent a parcel in the post. The parcel contained a clock, now sitting over their fireplace. Assuming that the clock was a present from a family member, Bernan asked who had sent it. His wife said that she did not recognize the name of Henry McEnroe. Bernan immediately told his wife that this was a supplier who had been trying win business with his company. They could not accept the clock, and she should repack it and return it. His wife was disappointed, and said that the clock was a present to her at their home address, and not to Bernan at his office.

Case 1 Questions

1   What should Bernan do about the clock?

2   Why do you think the supplier sent the clock to Bernan's home and addressed it to his wife?

3   Does the mere act of sending the clock to Bernan mean that M. McEnroe is unethical?

Case 2

Lisa Jennings thought that her company, Assurance Technologies, was at last about to win a major order from Sealgood Instruments. They were bidding for a contract worth at least $2.5 million a year, which would form a significant part of their annual sales of $30 million. Her team had spent hundreds of hours preparing the quotation and knew that they could meet Sealgood's requirements for quality, cost, delivery, part standardization and simplification. Lisa had never been more confident about a quotation meeting the demanding requirements of a potential customer. So she was disappointed when Troy Smyrna, the buyer at Sealgood Instruments responsible for awarding this contract, asked to discuss a concern. Troy informed Lisa that Assurance Technologies had indeed prepared a good quotation for the contract. However, when he visited Assurance's facility on a pre-qualifying visit, he was disturbed to see them using a significant amount of a competitor's products.

He felt uneasy about releasing plans and designs to a company that clearly had involvement with a competitor. When Lisa asked what Assurance could do to minimize his uneasiness, Troy replied that he would be happier if Assurance stopped using the competitor's equipment and replaced it with Sealgood's equipment. Lisa responded that this would mean replacing several hundred thousand dollars worth of equipment. Unfazed, Troy simply asked whether she wanted the business.

Case 2 Questions

1   Do you think the buyer at Sealgood Instruments, Troy Smyrna, is acting unethically?

2   What should Lisa do in this situation?

Case 3

Bjorg Gibson, the purchasing manager at Coastal Products, was reviewing the cost of packaging materials with Jeff Joyner. Bjorg was particularly disturbed by the amount spent on corrugated boxes purcha1sed from Southeastern Corrugated. Bjorg said, 'I don't like the salesman from that company. He loves to come around and tell us about his fancy car, house and holidays. He must be making too much money from us!' Jeff responded that he heard that Southeastern Corrugated were going to ask for a price increase to cover the rising costs of paper stock, and they would probably ask for more to cover rising overheads.

After the meeting, Bjorg decided that he was not going to allow the salesman to keep taking advantage of Coastal Products, so he called Jeff and told him that it was time to do some competitive tendering before Southeastern came in with a price increase. Jeff knew several companies that could be included in the bidding process, and these would probably give a lower price, partly because they used lower-grade boxes that would be good enough for Coastal Products' purposes. Jeff also explained that these suppliers were not really serious contenders for the business, but they would create competition. Bjorg told Jeff to make sure that the new suppliers knew that the price was going to be the determining factor in their quotation, and that Southeastern knew that these new suppliers were bidding for the contract.

Case 3 Questions

1 Is Bjorg Gibson acting legally and ethically?

2 If you were the Marketing Manager for Southeastern Corrugated what would you do when you received the request for quotation from Coastal Products?

Case 4

Sharon Gillespie, a new buyer at Visionex, was reviewing quotations for a tooling contract submitted by four suppliers. Her manager, Sean Cox, entered her office and asked how everything was progressing, who the interested suppliers were and whether she had made a decision. Sharon said that one supplier, Apex, appeared to fit exactly the requirements Visionex had specified in their RFQ. Later that day Sean again visited Sharon's office, said that he had done some research on the suppliers and felt that another supplier, Micron, appeared to have the best track record with Visionex. He pointed out Apex was a new supplier and there was some risk involved with that choice. Sean suggested that he would be happier if she selected Micron for the contract.

The next day Sharon was having lunch with another buyer, when she mentioned the conversation with Sean and her belief that Apex really was the best choice. The other buyer shook his head and said, 'I heard last week that Sean's brother-in-law is a new part owner of Micron. I was wondering how long it would be before he started steering business to them. He is not the straightest character, and remember that you are replacing a buyer who was sacked for not going along with one of Sean's previous preferred suppliers.'

Case 4 Questions

1 What do you think about financial conflicts of interest?

2 What should Sharon do in this situation?

CHAPTER 15
MANAGING SUPPLY CHAIN INVENTORY

LEARNING OBJECTIVES After reading this chapter you should be able to:

- Understand the purpose of stocks within a supply chain

- Describe the different types of inventory

- Discuss the costs and financial impact of holding stock

- List valid reasons for investing in stock

- Describe the features of just-in-time and lean operations

- Consider elements needed to create a lean supply chain

- Discuss ways of effectively managing stocks

- Appreciate the idea of a perfect customer order

SUPPLY CHAIN INVENTORY

Historically, organizations used to carry high stocks, which they almost viewed as a sign of wealth (Waters, 2003). However, this attitude changed many years ago when organizations learned that managing inventory efficiently and effectively is a key element in remaining competitive. Any excess stock raises costs with consequent effects on profit, sales, market share and overall performance. A more subtle problem is that high stock levels hide other problems, such as poor material quality, inaccurate forecasts of demand and unreliable suppliers. Rather than solve the underlying problems, firms found it easier to hide them under extra stocks.

The drive to reduce stocks has led to new methods of inventory management. These have led to considerable reductions in stock levels and consequent costs. But you should not forget that stocks actually serve a useful purpose, so our aim is to manage them, but not necessarily eliminate them.

The materials that an organization buys are delivered to the organization, but they are not usually used immediately. If a user has to have a particular item on Monday, they add a margin of safety and get it delivered the previous week. These materials are put into storage until they are needed, forming part of the organization's stocks.

Stocks
Which are also loosely described as inventories – are the stores of materials that an organization has acquired, but it is not ready to use.

Types of inventory

There are five categories of inventory (1) raw materials (2) work-in-progress (WIP) (3) finished goods (4) maintenance, repair and operating (MRO) supplies and (5) pipeline or in-transit stock.

1   **Raw materials inventory** – includes the items purchased from suppliers, or produced internally, which are waiting to be used in operations. Raw materials include components, bulk chemicals, petroleum, parts and anything else that is used in the operations to make a product.

2   **Work-in-progress inventor** – is the total stock that is held within operations. It is the incomplete products that have not yet been transformed into finished products and includes materials that are:

    — Waiting to move to the next operation
    — Actually being moved between operations
    — Waiting for the next operation to begin
    — Currently being worked on
    — Waiting because of a hold-up, perhaps caused by a bottleneck or machine breakdown.

    If WIP increases beyond a certain level, there may be a production delay or bottleneck, both of which are symptoms of inefficient operations, and may need a scheduler to reroute the flow of material around the hold-up. A rule of thumb suggests that only 25 per cent of WIP is actually being worked on, 40 per cent is in line waiting for further work to start, another 25 per cent is waiting to move on to the next operation and 5 per cent is actually being moved (Handfield, 1993).

3   **Finished goods inventory** – is completed products that are available for shipment or waiting for customer orders. A firm that produces items in anticipation of customer orders – make-to-stock operations – should monitor its stocks of finished goods closely. Rising levels of finished goods may signal a decrease in customer demand, while falling levels may suggest a rising customer demand.

Make-to-stock operations hold finished goods until new customer orders arrive, and then they can satisfy these orders very quickly. The alternative is make-to-order, where firms make products in response to actual customer orders. This gives very low stocks of finished goods, but longer delivery lead times.

4   **Maintenance, repair and operating supplies inventory** – includes all the items used to support operations, but which are not physically part of a finished product. They include the office supplies, machine spare parts, tools, computers, lubricants and other items that are needed for continuous operations.

5   **Pipeline/in-transit inventory** – is the stock that is actually moving out to a customer or is located somewhere in the distribution channels. Most consumable-goods inventory is either in transport moving through tiers of customers, or is on shop shelves waiting to be bought.

Inventory costs

The drawback of holding excess stock is the effect it has on a firm's working capital. All organizations need working capital, which represents the funds committed to operating a business, and this is spent on a variety of things, including the purchase of stock. Excess inventory ties up money that a firm could use more productively elsewhere. Buying and storing inventory incurs several costs, which can be surprisingly high.

Unit costs. The basic inventory cost, and easiest to measure, is the total cost of acquiring one unit of an item. The unit cost appears in several forms. Firstly, each item purchased from a supplier has a price, which is the unit cost that the firm pays to the supplier. Secondly, an item may be made internally, in which case the unit cost is the production cost. This is more difficult to calculate, as it has to cover direct materials used to make the item, labour cost, overheads, opportunity costs and so on.

Reorder cost. Include all the costs associated with the release of an order and accepting delivery of the materials. These costs may include the cost of generating and sending an order, transport, receipt, quality checks and any other costs connected with an order. If a firm makes an item itself, the ordering cost may include equipment setup costs, preparation, etc.

Holding costs. Consist of all the costs for holding and storing materials. There are quite a few elements in this, but we can summarize them in three main components:

- *Financial cost,* primarily for the capital tied-up, but also the opportunity cost (as money spent on inventory is not available for other uses). There may also be taxes and various other charges on the amount of stock held

- *Providing the storage,* providing a warehouse, racking, administration systems, etc.

- *Maintenance costs,* such as providing the right conditions, insurance, stock checks, along with obsolescence, deterioration, damage and loss

Holding costs are typically around 20 per cent of the value of the inventory, but varies widely with the cost of capital (illustrated in Figure 15.1) (Bowersox and Closs, 1996). It is calculated from:

$$\text{Total holding cost} = \text{average number of units held}$$
$$\times \text{ unit price} \times \text{holding cost a year}$$

FIGURE 15.1

Inventory carrying costs

Element	Average	Ranges
Capital cost	15.00%	8–40%
Taxes	1.00%	0.5–2%
Insurance	0.05%	0–2%
Obsolescence	1.20%	0.5–2%
Storage	2.00%	0–4%
Total	19.25%	9–50%

If a company averages 1000 units in stock, and the unit price is €2.00, and the annual holding cost is 25 per cent of value, the total carrying cost is (1000 × 2 × 0.25) = €500 a year.

Shortage costs. Are the costs of not having an item available when it is needed. For instance, if a customer wants a product from a shop, but the shop has run out of stock then the customer will go elsewhere. In the short term this means that the shop has a cost of lost custom, but in the longer term there are costs for lost future sales, and effects on their reputation for reliability. When manufacturers run out of raw materials there can be very high costs for shutting down production and operations come to a standstill. Shortage costs are usually very difficult to find accurately – but they are the reason for holding stock in the first place. Essentially, organizations are willing to incur the cost of holding stock to avoid the even higher costs of shortages (Waters, 2003).

It is often difficult to find the total costs associated with stocks. This is partly because little attention has historically been given to inventory costs, and partly because accounting systems do not separate out the individual components.

Asset or liability?

From an accounting perspective, inventory is considered a current asset (as shown in Figure 15.2). Then inventory is included in the same category as cash and market-able securities, which implies that there is actually something good about holding lots of stock.

As well as being an investment, it was argued that stocks were needed to provide customer service, and the savings from lower stock levels would be outweighed by the cost of lower customer service. But this view was based on the assumption that holding stock was virtually free, and when the true costs were recognized organizations immediately looked for ways of reducing them. For many years, reducing stock has been seen as a way of significantly improving corporate performance. Now financial analysts explain the major impact that committing funds to inventory has on cash flow, working capital requirements and profitability.

Figure 15.3 illustrates one way of translating the impact of improved inventory turns on ROI. In this example, two firms have almost identical performance, except that Firm B has half the amount of stock on its balance sheet as Firm A, and a slightly higher profit margin (resulting from the lower average holding costs that come with faster stock turnover). The calculations show that a doubling of

FIGURE 15.2

Example of a consolidated balance sheet

	2009	2009
Current assets		
Cash and cash equivalents	647595	408378
Marketable securities	242952	421111
Receivables	638974	632870
Inventories	917495	771233
Prepaid expenses	84588	70211
Total current assets	2531604	2303803
Investments and other assets		
To affiliates	205835	160455
Long-term marketable securities	770808	813631
Other assets	567350	403140
	1033378	1014400
Property, plant and equipment		
Agricultural processing	2275016	1724460
Transportation	4206090	4073470
	2695625	2131807
	€ 6260607	€ 5450010

FIGURE 15.3

Linking inventory management and financial performance

	Firm A (£ million)	Firm B (£ million)
Sales	£200	£200
Profit margin	6%	7%
Assets		
Cash	£10	£10
Securities	£15	£15
Receivables	£8	£8
Inventories	£20	£10
Plant and equipment	£75	£75
Total assets	**£128**	**£118**
Financial formulae:		

Inventory turns = Sales/Inventories
  £200/£20 = 10   £200/£10 = 20
Asset turnover = Sales/Total assets
  £200/£128 = 1.56   £200/£118 = 1.69
ROI = Profit margin × Asset turnover
  6% ×1.56 = 9.36%   7% ×1.69 = 11.55%

inventory turns, combined with consequent higher profit margins, increases ROI by almost 25 per cent, from 9.36 per cent to 11.55 per cent.

Lower stocks mean that materials move quickly through an organization. The speed of movement is measured by **inventory turns,** which are the number of times that stock turns over in a year. Generally, the higher this figure, the better the management of stocks (Waters, 2003).

Inventory turns = sales / average stock level

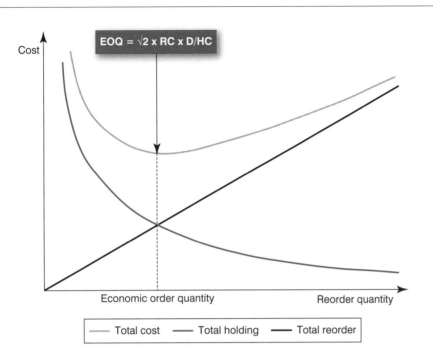

FIGURE 15.4

Optimal order size

Economic order quantity

A useful feature of the inventory costs is that they allow you to calculate an optimal size for purchases. The principle is that placing a large number of small orders gives low stock levels but high administrative costs; placing a few large orders gives high stock levels but low administrative costs. If we balance these two opposing forces, we can calculate an optimal order size, which is called the economic order quantity.

$$\text{Economic order quantity} = \sqrt{\frac{2 \times reorder\,cost \times demand}{holding\,cost}}$$

Orders of this size give the lowest costs (if we make a few assumptions); smaller orders cost more because of the high administration costs; larger orders give higher costs because of the higher stock levels (as illustrated in Figure 15.4).

We can also calculate the optimal costs from:

Total cost = purchase cost + variable cost
Purchase cost = demand × unit price
Variable cost = $\sqrt{(2 \times recorder\,cost \times holding\,cost \times demand)}$

WORKED EXAMPLE

The demand for an item is constant at 20 units a month. Unit cost is €50, the cost of processing an order and arranging delivery is €60 and the holding cost is €18 per unit a year. What are the economic order quantity, corresponding cycle length and costs?

Solution:

Listing the values we know in consistent units:

Demand $= 20 \times 12 = 240$ units a year
Unit cost $= €50$ per unit
Reorder cost $= €60$ an order
Holding cost $= €18$ per unit a year.

Then substituting in the standard equations gives:

Order size $= \sqrt{(2 \times 60 \times 240/18)} = 40$ units
Variable cost $= \sqrt{(2 \times 60 \times 18 \times 240)} = €720$ a year
Purchase cost $= 50 \times 240 = €12\,000$ a year
Total cost $= 12\,000 + 720 = €12\,720$ a year

We can find the cycle length by noting that we buy 40 units at a time, and the demand is 20 units a month, so each order will last 2 months, and we have to place six orders a year.

LEARNING FROM PRACTICE

Palladium

Small quantities of palladium are used in the manufacture of cars. The main source of palladium is Russia, which created chaos on the market by holding up deliveries, and delaying releases of the metal from its huge stockpile. At one point, concerns over secure supplies drove the price up from its normal cost of around $200 an ounce to nearly $1000. There is less than an ounce of palladium in most vehicles, where it is used in the catalytic converter, but this kind of price surge means that palladium is suddenly causing concern for car makers.

The demand for palladium rose when vehicle manufacturers looked for ways of reducing exhaust emissions and increasing fuel efficiency, and they found that replacing platinum in catalytic converters with palladium cleaned exhaust emissions sooner after starting the engine. There was also a price advantage, as the price of palladium had remained close to $200 an ounce, while platinum had jumped above $400. Economic principles suggest that higher demand for palladium should encourage producers to boost output, but geology makes palladium special. It occurs in small quantities with other metals, principally nickel in Russia and platinum in South Africa. So to get more palladium, producers would have to process large amounts of ore, and risk flooding the markets with nickel and platinum.

Buyers responded to the uncertain palladium supply in different ways. General Motors signed a 5-year supply deal with Stillwater Mining Company in Montana – the only major producer outside of Russia and South Africa, Ford secured its supply by signing long-term contracts with prices at near-record highs. Interestingly, engineering changes then reduced the amount of palladium needed in each vehicle, and Ford found itself with massive quantities of overpriced metal. In 2002, they announced a $1 billion write-off of the value of its palladium stockpile.

Source: White G.L. (2000) Unruly element: Russian manoeuvres are making palladium ever more precious, Wall Street Journal, 6 March, p A1; White G.L. (2002) How Ford's big batch of rare metal led to $1 billion write-off, Wall Street Journal, 6 February, p A1.

REASONS FOR HOLDING STOCK

Stocks play a key role in all organizations, where managers have to make some basic decisions. For instance, should they hold finished goods in store or use make-to-order operations; should they hold stocks of raw materials or buy from suppliers with short lead times? All such decisions lead to the underlying question of what items to hold in stock – and the answer is that items should only be held when the benefits exceed the costs. Beyond this bald statement, we can suggest some specific reasons for holding inventories, including the following:

Right reasons for holding stock

- *Support operations* – and avoid the effects of any disruption to supply. These may include raw materials, semi-finished goods, packaging, spare parts for equipment and so on, and their purpose is to ensure that operations always have materials to work with, even when there is some disruption to supply chains. This production inventory is a major investment, so firms develop ways to control and reduce stock levels, particularly work-in-progress. The need to support operations is always a primary reason for holding stock, but this does not mean excessive stock. In practice, managers have to balance the costs of holding excess stock with the risk from disruptions that come with lower stocks

- *Support facilities* – nearly every organization carries MRO supplies to support operations. The true cost of holding these often goes unnoticed because firms do not track them as intensely as production stock. Multiple or obsolete items can remain in stock for a long time unless proper tracking systems show that they are not being used. One option here is to put MRO in a special, central store where they can be more closely monitored. Another option is to outsource the management of these stocks to a full-service distributor who is then responsible for ensuring supplies of MRO items

- *Support customer services* – as many products (such as computers, appliances and cars) need suppliers to hold stocks of spare parts that can be shipped out to customers when there is a breakdown. These spare parts increase the likelihood of meeting customer service demands, but at the cost of a significant investment in stock. As breakdowns should be relatively rare, holding too many, unused spare parts can be a major waste – or a source of customer dissatisfaction if the stocks are too low

- *Hedge against marketplace uncertainty*. There is often considerable uncertainty in market conditions, particularly the availability of materials and the prevailing prices. When buyers anticipate materials shortages or price increases, they often make additional purchases to protect themselves against these effects. Increasing inventory levels to deal with a perceived threat can be a sensible response, at least in the short term. However, these actions are not without risks, as prices and supplies can fluctuate very quickly in a volatile market. Then organizations can find that they have excess stocks of materials that they bought at too high a price

- *Take advantage of order quantity discounts*. Suppliers often give quantity discounts to encourage larger orders. For instance, a buyer might order 2-months' supply of a product rather than the normal 1 month's in exchange for a 5 per cent discount in unit price. These discounts can be worthwhile as they give a lower average purchase price, but they may not translate into a lower overall cost. Larger orders mean higher stocks, and higher holding costs – and these can more than offset the gains from lower pries

Wrong reasons for holding stock

There are valid reasons for holding stock, but managers sometimes quote other reasons which are definitely not valid. Excess stocks usually appear to cover uncertainty and variability in the supply chain – perhaps caused by variable customer demand, forecast errors or supplier reliability. The real answer is not to hold more stocks to cover such uncertainty, but to eliminate the source of variability. If a supplier is unreliable, managers should work to improve supplies rather than hold stock to hide the effects (which is a theme that we return to later in the chapter). The following list gives some of the bad reasons for maintaining an investment in stocks.

Poor quality. Historically, product quality could not be guaranteed, and it was routine for organizations to buy more units than they actually needed to allow for the defective units that would inevitably be delivered. This obviously raised stock levels, but it was easier to hold extra stock than to solve the underlying problem of poor quality. However, high quality – based on the principles of TQM – has made this thinking obsolete, and there is no need to hold this extra stock. Organizations should be confident that their suppliers will solve any quality problems, and they need only order the amounts that they actually need.

Material yield. This is a term typically used for raw materials, where there is variation in the amount of a product that can be produced from a specified amount of input. For instance, a metal producer might expect to recover a certain weight of metal from a tonne of ore, but there is always some variability. Variable yield encourages organizations to increase their purchase quantities to guarantee the required production.

Unreliable supplier delivery. Suppliers that cannot meet delivery schedules create uncertainty. To compensate for this, supply chain managers usually increase safety stocks – while they should be helping suppliers become more reliable. The underlying problem may be a result of poor production scheduling at the supplier, accidents, delays at international customs, bad weather and many other unexpected problems. Purchasers themselves are sometimes partly to blame, as they give too little notice of orders, demand unrealistic lead times, change requirements at the last minute and so on.

Extended order times. A common procurement objective is to reduce the total lead time between recognizing a purchase is needed and the physical receipt of material. Lead times have tended to lengthen with the growth of global sourcing and their extended supply chains, and a common reaction has been to carry more stocks. The reasoning is based on the belief that it is more difficult to plan material requirements accurately over a long lead time, so higher stocks are needed to cover the increased uncertainty.

Inaccurate demand forecasts. Inaccurate forecasts are a common source of uncertainty, particularly in make-to-stock operations. Then firms use higher safety stocks to compensate for the uncertain demand. A confectioner found that there was an average error of 45 per cent in its monthly forecast demands, and held high stocks to cover the resulting uncertainty. A closer investigation revealed that the marketing department, which prepared the forecasts, found the task a nuisance that diverted them from their real jobs. Not surprisingly the forecasts were given low priority, inventory was severely misallocated across geographic locations and product lines, there were problems meeting delivery dates for key customer orders and the costs of stock were four times those of competitor.

Specifying custom items for standard applications. Buyers would like to buy industry-standard parts wherever possible, as long as they still meet the users' requirements. Customized parts are more expensive – because of the extra design, specialized production and smaller numbers – so using them when equivalent standard ones are available has two adverse effects. Firstly, there is the higher cost of keeping a certain number of more expensive items in stock; and secondly, is the duplication as each product needs its own stocks, rather than sharing an inventory of common materials.

LEARNING FROM PRACTICE

Bosch

The Bosch Group is a leading global supplier of technology and services, with sales of over €45 billion from its 300 subsidiaries. Its Automotive Technology Division makes a huge number of products for cars, with a corresponding number of bought parts. It is looking for greater standardization of these parts as a way of reducing its own and suppliers' significant investment in stocks.

To illustrate the scope of the problem, Bosch pointed out that they make 44 different heads for speed sensors on their anti-lock braking system. All of these sensors do essentially same job, and the amount of variation could be significantly reduced without affecting the products' functions. This would give economies of scale and lower operating costs. Increasing this type of parts standardization could cut typical production costs by 5–10 per cent, and up to 30 per cent for certain products.

This amount of teamwork between Bosch, its suppliers and OEMs (Original Equipment Manufacturers) needed to introduce the changes, is an important consideration. How effective purchasing is in working collaboratively with suppliers in the future could bring considerable competitive advantages to Bosch.

Extended material pipelines. Long supply chains connecting global operations give higher inventory levels. Greater distances mean that pipeline stocks are inevitably higher, shipments are more susceptible to delays, damage and loss and there is more uncertainty.

Inefficient operations. A supplier with inefficient operations must hold higher stocks of finished goods to compensate for poor quality or planning. Large amounts of WIP are often a sign of inefficient operations.

CREATING LEAN SUPPLY CHAINS

When firms move stocks so quickly that they essentially hold zero inventory, they are creating **lean** supply chains (Bozarth and Handfield, 2008). Shook (1998) defined **lean** as 'A philosophy that seeks to shorten the time between the customer order and the shipment to the customer by eliminating waste.' Womack and Jones (1996) argue that all activities associated with leanness attempt to achieve three objectives: flow, pull and striving for excellence. Here:

Flow means that inventory moves through a supply chain continuously with minimal queuing on activities that do not add value.

Pull means that customer orders trigger operations and pull materials through the supply chain (rather than having schedules for upstream activities driving the rate of production). This means that materials are only bought when a final customer buys a product, and this signals all upstream operations to move materials and make a replacement product.

Striving for excellence, means that supply chains must have efficient operations that remove all waste.

Lean operations essentially aim at removing all waste from operations – including resources, people, equipment, time, costs, materials – and all non-value adding activities. Elimination of all waste gives a very efficient supply chain that uses minimal resources. This idea of a lean supply chain has its origins in the JIT philosophy, which came to the fore in the early 1980s and has since been adopted to some extent by almost every major organization.

JIT operations have every activity done at exactly the right time (Waters, 2002). Materials arrive just as they are needed, products are delivered just as customers want them, equipment become free just as it is due to start a job and so on. This initial idea of not wasting time, has grown into a broad management philosophy of not wasting any resources Some of the key elements of JIT are to do work at the time it is needed, have materials delivered exactly as needed to eliminate stocks, have perfect quality with zero defects, make lead times as short as possible, reduce production batch sizes, look for continuous improvement and accomplish these activities at minimum cost.

Firms using JIT often gain remarkable improvements in productivity, inventory levels, quality and other measure of performance. There is an enormous amount of anecdotal evidence for this, which we can illustrate by an early comparison of the worlds largest car manufacturers in 1986. At this time Toyota's Takaoka facility used JIT while GM's Framingham plant did not (Womack *et al.*, 1991). The numbers shown in Figure 15.5 give an idea of the impact of JIT, as the Toyota plant needed fewer hours to make a car, much less inventory, lower operating costs, faster delivery time, better quality, lower overheads and so on. Not surprisingly, there has been an enormous movement to adopt JIT principles. The ability of JIT to do more work with fewer resources of every kind eventually grew into lean operations, with its aim of eliminating all forms of waste.

The lean perspective on waste

The essential element of the JIT philosophy is its never-ending effort to eliminate **waste**, which is defined as 'Any activity that does not add value to the goods or service in the eyes of the consumer (Cox and Blackstone, 2002).' Taiichi Ohno, a Toyota engineer and developer of their JIT systems, identified the following eight common sources of waste (Womack and Jones, 2003):

1   *Overproduction* – caused by inflexible or unreliable processes that cause organizations to produce goods before they are required.

2   *Waiting* – caused by inefficient layouts or an inability to match demand with output levels.

3   *Unnecessary transport* – moving goods more than necessary, thereby increasing costs and the risk of damage, but without adding value for the final customer.

4   *Inappropriate process* – using overly complex operations, when simpler, more efficient ones would do.

FIGURE 15.5

The performance advantage of a JIT plant in 1986

	GM Plant Framingham	TOYOTA Plant Takaoka
Assembly hours per vehicle	40.7 hours	16 hours
Defects per 100 vehicles	130 defects	45 defects
Average inventory levels	Two weeks	Two hours

5   *Unnecessary stocks* – held in response to uncertainty in quality, delivery lead times, demand, etc.

6   *Unnecessary or excess movement* – caused by poorly designed processes.

7   *Defects* – creating uncertainty in the process and robbing production of capacity by creating products that need rework or scrapping.

8   *Under-utilized employees* – not fully using the skills and decision-making capability of employees.

It might seem difficult to remove these wastes, but when organizations think critically about their processes they can make startling improvements. To put it simply, managers have to analyse their operations and find better ways of doing things. For instance, suppose that it takes an inspector at a factory 30 minutes to inspect an delivery of material. A traditional perspective would say that such inspections are a necessary and prudent business expense, and it would be an improvement if the inspection time could be reduced to 20 minutes. JIT sees any inspection as a waste of time, and a better approach would have suppliers using TQM to deliver materials of guaranteed perfect quality.

Lean perspective of inventory

A characteristic of the leanness is its emphasis on reducing – and preferably eliminating – all kinds of stock throughout the supply chain. This is because inventory is seen as wasteful in itself, and also because it hides other forms of waste and poor management practices.

To illustrate how inventory can hide problems, consider a simple facility consisting of three work centres (A, B and C), shown in Figure 15.6. The triangles represent stocks, and we assume that there is plenty of storage space for WIP between each centre. Look at Centre B and consider what happens if some equipment breaks down and reduces output. In the short run, only Centre B is affected. Centre A can continue to work normally and build higher stocks between A and B, and Centre C can continue working normally, using the existing stocks between B and C. Whatever the reason for the disruption in Centre B (perhaps broken equipment, employee illness, problems with quality, etc.) the stocks effectively insulate the

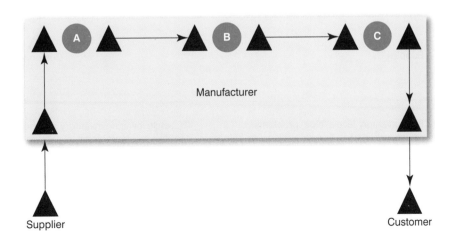

FIGURE 15.6

Inventory hiding inefficiency

problem and hides its effects. Customer service is maintained, but at a high cost of stocks.

If we take the same facility after JIT has been introduced, the work centres are moved physically close together to eliminate wasted movement and space where inventory could pile up. Set-up times have also been reduced, allowing the work centres to make only what is needed when it is needed (as shown in Figure 15.7).

Stocks of WIP between the work stations have been eliminated, and if equipment at Centre B breaks down everything stops, including shipments to the customer. Centre C has to stop because there is no inventory that it can work on, and Centre A has to stop because there is nowhere for it to put anything that it finishes. This seems rather drastic, but now there is a clear incentive to look at the equipment in Centre B, see why it broke down, and make sure that it does not break down again. JIT forces managers to solve the problem of unreliable equipment so that from now onwards operations will always continue smoothly.

Inventory in a supply chain is often compared to water in a river, with rocks presenting problems (shown in Figure 15.8). If the water (stock) is high enough, it covers all the rocks (which are problems like quality, equipment breakdowns, absenteeism, etc.), and everything appear to be running smoothly. JIT systematically remove the 'water' until the first 'rock' is exposed, thereby establishing the most urgent obstacle to work on. After resolving this problem, inventory levels are reduced further until another problem appears. This process continues until all forms of waste and uncertainty have been eliminated.

This is certainly not an easy approach to implement, as every time a process is working smoothly, managers change it to look for further improvements. This seems illogical to many people, but the long term benefits more than compensate for the short term pain.

FIGURE 15.7

Introducing JIT

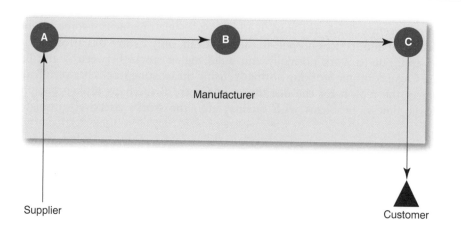

FIGURE 15.8

Effects of reducing stock levels to identify new problems

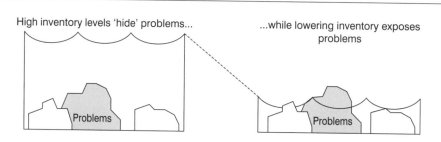

LEARNING FROM PRACTICE

Amazon.com

When they first started appearing in the late 1990s, web-based 'e-tailers' such as Amazon.com hoped to replace the 'bricks and mortar' of traditional retailing with the 'clicks' of online ordering. Rather than opening separate stores filled with expensive inventory, an e-tailer runs a single virtual store that serves customers around the globe. In particular, inventory is kept at a few key sites chosen to minimize costs and facilitate quick delivery to customers – with large facilities getting considerable economies of scale. In theory, e-tailers can add large numbers of new customers with little or no additional investment in inventory or facilities, unlike traditional retailers who have to add new stores to increase their customer base.

Figure 15.9 shows sales and inventory figures for Amazon for the years 1997 to 2006. The third column shows inventory turns, which is calculated as net sales/ending inventory. These results show some interesting points. In late 1999, Amazon learned that managing inventory can be a challenge even for e-tailers. This was the year the company expanded from books into new product lines, such as electronics and household goods. They had little experience with these and purchasing managers were faced with the question of how much stock to hold. Too little, and they risked losing orders and alienating customers; too much, and they could lock up the company's resources in unsold products.

When sales for 1999 were lower than expected Amazon's inventory levels rose dramatically and it became clear that they had overstocked. By the end of 1999, the inventory turnover was 7.4 – worse than the typical bricks-and-mortar retailer. After 1999, Amazon learnt its lesson and inventory turns rose again. For comparison, in 2006 WalMart, the world's biggest retailer, had 9.7 inventory turns.

FIGURE 15.9 Amazon.com financial results 1997–2006

Year	Net sales ($million)	Inventory ($million)	Inventory turns
1997	$148	$9	16.4
1998	$610	$30	20.3
1999	$1640	$221	7.4
2000	$2762	$175	15.8
2001	$3122	$143	21.8
2002	$3933	$202	19.5
2003	$5264	$294	17.9
2004	$6921	$480	14.4
2005	$8490	$566	15.0
2006	$10711	$877	12.0

Source: Bozarth C. and Handfield R. (2008); Operations and supply chain management (2nd edition). Prentice Hall, Upper Saddle River, NJ.

ASPECT OF LEAN OPERATIONS

Lean thinking has effects on all aspects of procurement, and we can illustrate these by reference to four of its elements – JIT production, JIT purchasing, JIT transport and kanban systems.

Just-in-time production

Lean production removes waste from the whole process of transforming raw materials and other inputs into finished goods that satisfy customer orders. Of course, lean operations come in many different forms, but common features include:

- Uniform throughput with stable and steady operations
- A pull of materials through the process triggered by actual customer orders
- Short equipment set-up time to allow flexible and responsive operations
- Perfect quality through TQM
- Continuous improvement to remove remaining waste
- Changing the layout of facilities to reduce movements
- Standard materials which are handled in reusable containers
- Product and process simplification
- Preventive maintenance to ensure facilities always work properly
- Flexible and multi-skilled workforce organized in teams
- Relevant and achievable performance measures
- Suppliers that can meet the demands of JIT, and who may be practising it themselves

These features help to ensure a smooth flow of materials, but some of them are difficult to achieve in practice. For example, reducing the time needed to set-up equipment between making different products means a shorter time when equipment is unavailable for productive work, increases flexibility, and raises productivity. It means replacing major set-ups, by minor, routine adjustments to equipment, and there are four approaches to this:

1. Efficient housekeeping, such as planning which product is to be made next, knowing exactly when the change will take place, and having the required tools and equipment ready before the change.

2. Analyse the way that the changes are made and find more efficient methods.

3. Eliminate changes as much as possible by scheduling production so that only minor adjustments are needed between each.

4. Purchase new equipment that is easier and quicker to change.

All of the features of JIT can be difficult to implement, so they need a concerted effort from everyone involved. For instance, JIT pulls a product through a process, with upstream work centres only delivering materials when asked by a work station that is ready to use it. This downstream work station gives some kind of visible signal such as a production card, empty container, empty designated floor space, electronic signal or some other message – and the upstream station sees this and makes the necessary delivry.

This is completely different to the traditional push system, where upstream work centres have their own production schedules and they produce material and then deliver them on to the stock of WIP in front of the next work centre in the supply chain. Usually this next centre is doing something else, working to its own pre-determined schedule, does not need the new material immediately and may be unaware that they are being delivered until they arrive. The result is varying stocks of WIP, and a series of unco-ordinated work centres, each of which is keeping to its own predetermined schedule. All of this is removed by JIT.

There are other effects of the smooth flows with JIT, such as the removal of space needed to keep stocks of WIP, so the work centres can be moved closer together to reduce movement.

Just-in-time purchasing

JIT operations demand new practices from procurement – which we can describe as JIT purchasing. Rather than buying large quantities of materials at well-spaced in-tervals, JIT needs small, frequent orders to meet immediate requirements. This small order size – typically enough for one day's needs or even a few hours – is the main difference with normal purchasing. Its features include:

- A commitment to zero defects by the buyer and seller
- Frequent shipment of small quantities of materials with short lead time and strict delivery performance standards
- Close and collaborative buyer-seller relationships
- Stable products and production schedules sent to suppliers some time in advance
- Extensive sharing of information between supply chain members
- Electronic data interchange and free flows of information with suppliers

JIT purchasing is not a series of techniques, but it applies the philosophy of leanness to procurement, eliminating any waste in the interactions between buyer and seller. As always, this seems like a simple idea, but it requires major and per-manent changes in the way that a firm conducts business. For instance, when JIT production removes stocks of raw materials, the aim is to actually eliminate them and not simply push them back to upstream suppliers. To achieve this, JIT pur-chasing needs a very close working relationship with trading partners across the supply chain.

It is always difficult to introduce JIT purchasing, and there are some specific barriers to overcome. These barriers include:

Dispersed supply base. Most purchasers have a geographically dispersed supply base, but JIT relies on frequent, reliable deliveries of small quantities from suppliers. It is difficult to achieve the required level of service from remote and distant sup-pliers – as greater distance often means greater variability in delivery performance. For this reason, JIT prefers to use suppliers that are physically close, often en-couraging suppliers to open facilities near to major operations.

Historic buyer-seller relationships. Buyers and sellers often lack the close co-op-erative relationship needed for JIT purchasing. JIT needs mutual trust and respect between parties rather than traditional adversarial relationships.

Number of suppliers. Some supply chains still have too many suppliers to support efficient JIT operations. Like other efficient purchasing strategies, JIT requires a smaller supply base to minimize interaction and communication costs.

Supplier quality. Some sellers simply have not achieved the levels of near-perfect quality required for JIT. A total commitment to product and delivery quality is a prerequisite for successful JIT implementation.

In practice, these – and many other barriers that can limit the use of JIT purchasing – are breaking down, as firms increasingly accept the principles of JIT as good management practice.

Just-in-time transport

JIT transport refers to the efficient movement of materials between the buyer and seller to support lean operations. This involves frequent deliveries – typically one a day, but often several a day – of smaller quantities directly to the point of use at the purchaser.

Lean transport has delivery vehicles picking up and delivering materials on a regular basis. Their journey is usually organized as a closed-loop to deliver materials to a purchaser, and then return to the supplier carrying packaging, containers and anything else to return. JIT prefers suppliers to be located near to operations, so this journey is short and can be repeated several times a day. Longer journeys might include movements between other members of the supply chain to increase the efficiency of transport vehicles.

Figure 15.10 compares traditional delivery with JIT. In a traditional system, the supplier and purchaser do not co-ordinate their material requirements or production schedules, and they keep a lot of stock in various stores. JIT transport delivers the materials pulled through the chain, moving materials from one production point to another.

JIT transport includes certain key requirements:

- Reduction in the number of transport operators, typically to a single efficient carrier in each region of operation

- Long-term contracts negotiated with carriers to give stability to the transport network

- Electronic tagging and EDI links between members of the supply chain to monitor and co-ordinate the movement of materials

- A closed-loop system, where vehicles pick up all items from suppliers and deliver to customers, returning with reusable packaging and containers

- Efficient handling of material, using state-of-the-art equipment and technology. This may include specialized vehicles to allow easy loading and unloading of smaller quantities. It may also include the extensive use of reusable packaging and containers

- Pick-up and delivery close to operations. Because excessive material handling and movement is wasteful, transport pick-up materials directly from a supplier's work station and delivers them close to the point where the material is actually used

Kanban
Is used to control operations by using containers, cards or visual cues to control the production and movement of materials through a supply chain.

Kanban systems

We have said that JIT needs some kind of signal to tell upstream work centres that it is time to send another delivery of materials. This signal comes in different forms, but is generally described by the original Japanese term of **kanban**.

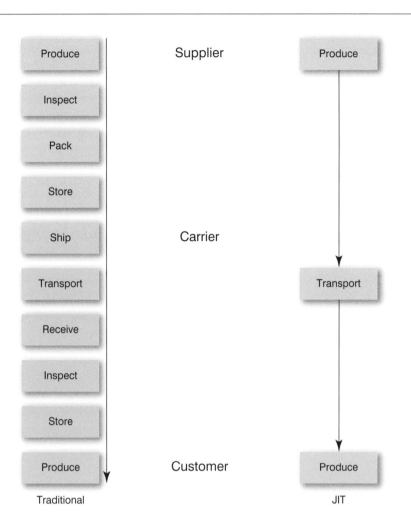

FIGURE 15.10

Comparing traditional
and JIT transport

LEARNING FROM PRACTICE

Relief operations

In October 2005 a huge earthquake hit Kashmir. A major international relief effort followed – including an experiment in fast delivery from the Pakistan Air Force base in Islamabad. Staff on loan from express-shipping company DHL improvized a method for quickly getting food and shelter to some of the hundreds of thousands of earthquake survivors camping on remote mountainsides where roads and airports are rare. Part of their solution was nicknamed 'speedball', where tents, food, water and other supplies were stuffed into the red polypropylene bags that DHL used to move loose cargo. Each bag held enough to keep seven people alive for 10 days, and they were tough enough to be tossed into helicopters and dropped out near rough landing strips in the hills. In 2 weeks 6000 of the bags were delivered.

This operation is one result of the global cargo industry's efforts to transform the notoriously inefficient supply chains for disaster relief. A loose-knit collection of companies is helping governments and private aid groups respond more effectively to major disasters. Their approach is to use the same basic inventory management and logistics methods that have revolutionized their own industry. Logistics companies are experts in squeezing inefficiencies out of operations, tracking packages, inventory control, transport and cramming lots of material into small spaces – exactly the skills that are needed in disaster relief supply chains.

Adrian van der Knapp, who co-ordinates emergency-relief operations for the United Nations and helps DHL get quick government authorization to go into disaster zones, says that, 'The most important thing in a sudden disaster is logistics.' After a disaster appeal, aid groups are often deluged with donated supplies, but then they struggle to get them to the point where they are needed.

Source: Simpson G.R. (2005) In year of disasters, lean emergency materials management brings order to the chaos of relief operations, Wall Street Journal, 22 November, p. A1

These systems have several key characteristics:

1   They are used to control the production and movement of materials by pulling materials through a supply chain.

2   They use some simple signalling mechanisms such as a card, empty container or even an empty space, to show when specific items should be produced and moved.

3   They can be used to synchronize activities within a single facility, or between different supply chain partners.

4   They are not planning tools, but control the flow of materials. Operations are ultimately controlled by the demands of final customers who initiate the whole movement of materials.

5   Some higher levels of planning must be done using, say, material requirements planning (which we meet later in the chapter). This gives a longer term view of requirements, while kanbans control the actual production and movement.

MANAGING INVENTORY INVESTMENT

Inventory management has a dual role in both providing service to customers, and forming part of an organization's assets. How managers view inventory depend on where they work in the supply chain. Financial planners tend to view inventory in terms of the costs reported in annual accounts, while supply chain managers view it in terms of units held and service levels achieved. Neither of these – or other alternative views – is inherently 'right', but they suggest that it is worth taking a broad view of inventory performance.

Managers often describe inventory performance in terms of the 'three Vs' – volume, velocity and value of inventory. Figure 15.11 summarizes this model, including key objectives, measures and examples of activities that relate to each factor.

Volume. Refers to the total amount of inventory that a firm owns at any given time. Volume measures include the number of items held, the number of units of each item, physical volume occupied, number of withdrawals, etc.

Velocity. Describes how quickly materials move through the supply chain. Velocity measures include number of units delivered, turnover, material throughput, inventory turns, order-to-cash time, etc.

Value. Refers to the total cost of stored inventory which is calculated from:

$$\text{Total value} = \Sigma(\text{volume} \times \text{unit cost})$$

FIGURE 15.11 'Three Vs' view of inventory performance

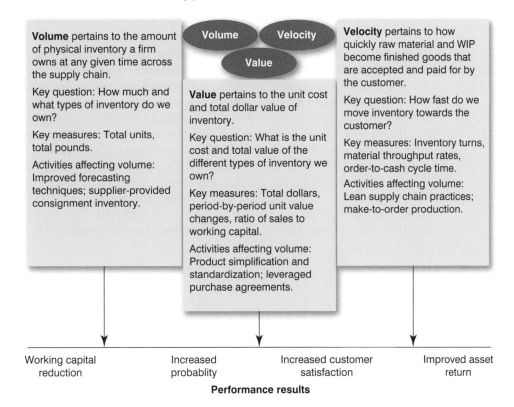

Volume pertains to the amount of physical inventory a firm owns at any given time across the supply chain.

Key question: How much and what types of inventory do we own?

Key measures: Total units, total pounds.

Activities affecting volume: Improved forecasting techniques; supplier-provided consignment inventory.

Value pertains to the unit cost and total dollar value of inventory.

Key question: What is the unit cost and total value of the different types of inventory we own?

Key measures: Total dollars, period-by-period unit value changes, ratio of sales to working capital.

Activities affecting volume: Product simplification and standardization; leveraged purchase agreements.

Velocity pertains to how quickly raw material and WIP become finished goods that are accepted and paid for by the customer.

Key question: How fast do we move inventory towards the customer?

Key measures: Inventory turns, material throughput rates, order-to-cash cycle time.

Activities affecting volume: Lean supply chain practices; make-to-order production.

| Working capital reduction | Increased probablity | Increased customer satisfaction | Improved asset return |

Performance results

These three factors are clearly related – and increasing velocity means that both volume and value decline. So managers must look for the best balance, but generally be aiming for higher velocity. The following sections review some concerns for these decisions.

Achieve perfect record integrity

A sensible place to begin the management of inventory is to make sure that there is agreement between:

- *Physical stocks* – the number of units actually held in stock, described as the physical material on hand (POH), and

- Notional stocks – the record of material on hand (ROH) held on the inventory records.

When these two match (POH = ROH) there is 'record integrity'; when they do not match (POH ≠ ROH) there is an error somewhere. This error might have been introduced by someone forgetting to record an issue or delivery of items, deterioration of items that can no longer be used, damage, theft and so on.

Hopefully, the errors in stocks are generally small, but the effects can be severe. When POH > ROH physical inventory exceeds the amount recorded – but the excess cannot be used or sold as nobody knows it exists. On the other hand, when POH < ROH records show 'phantom stock' which might be assigned to production or sold to a customer. When the item does not exist, there may be production disruptions and dissatisfied customers. Apart from the operational problems, there are also financial ones as the value is an intrinsic part of annual accounts.

Firms often compensate for any uncertainty – including possible errors in stock records – by holding extra stock. To reduce the wasted investment in unnecessary stocks, organizations should aim for perfect record integrity. Of course, an obvious problem is knowing how good record integrity actually is. The answer comes from having people physically count the stock (giving POH) and compare the results with records (ROH). This is a time-consuming process, so it cannot be done often. Many firms organize a continuing cycle of stock checks, where vulnerable items are checked relatively frequently, while less vulnerable ones are checked less frequently.

To maintain record integrity, managers have to identify the sources of errors and take actions to eliminate them. For this they need answers to a series of questions. Are the errors random or do they follow a systematic pattern? How severe are the differences between POH and ROH? Are proper receiving, storage and withdrawal procedures in place and being followed? Is theft a problem? Are suppliers delivering quantities that match orders and documentation? Are effective stock counting procedures used? Are scrap, damage and obsolescence accounted for correctly? Do employees properly move, handle and disburse material? The answers to such questions lay the foundations for effective procedures to avoid errors and ensure record integrity.

Improve product forecasting

One of the most important pieces of information for inventory management is the forecast of end customer demand. This effectively drives all activities within the supply chain, but many organizations still fail to recognize the effects of inaccurate forecasts. As always, managers react to uncertainty by keeping more stock, so when forecasts are poor, stock levels rise – and related costs rise, inventory is misallocated across locations and products, customer service is poor, assigned capacity does not match product demand, production schedules make the wrong products, safety stocks become excessive and so on. The clear message is that organizations which are serious about improving inventory management need reliable forecasts.

Standardize and simplify product design

Simplified designs need fewer parts than more complex ones, so they need fewer suppliers, fewer transactions to support the inventory, fewer items held in stock and lower inventory costs. The same arguments apply to standard items, where there are considerable benefits from having several products using the same readily available parts, rather than having each product use its own specially designed parts.

Sometimes greater standardization is surprisingly difficult, not because of the technical difficulties but because of prevailing organizational culture. Specifically, standardization suggests that a firm is making a strategic move away from customized products and towards standardized ones. For example, a heavy truck builder was simplifying its entire production by using more standard parts, and a manager described the changes as follows (Handfield *et al.*, 2006):

> 'We primarily engineer to order – but are moving more towards standardized options. We are making some components standard and are moving from 13 variations to three or four and are being pushed to do that by senior management. In the past, if the customer wanted it, we would put it on. The move towards standardization is a senior management decision.'

During product design is the best time to simplify and standardize, but later adjustments can improve the original designs. Standardization does not mean that every product is the same, as firms can still maintain a broad product range and – under certain circumstances – customize their offering. The following list suggests for maintaining a product range.

Establish premium pricing for customization. Many firms are reluctant to develop premium pricing options, but it can shape customer demand and generate extra revenue. There is a cost associated with complex, customized products – and customers should be prepared to offset this cost.

Establish geographic-specific options and standards. Firms can establish regional requirements based on local customer preferences, and they can design supply chains around these.

Maintain a database of options requested. Some firms have a policy of maintaining product complexity and diversity, in spite of the difficulties. The operations need particularly careful planning. One manager described this as follows (Handfield *et al.*, 2006):

> 'We track active options and customer-requested ones. We track usage, and if we have a group of options that has no usage over time, we will try to eliminate them from the available product offerings and get them out of the maintenance mode. On the other hand, if we have some customized options showing increasing usage, we will promote them . . . (and) . . . look closely at the design to see if it is designed for higher volume, to get some cost out of the process.'

Do not eliminate frequently requested options. It is important for a firm to maintain its product range and allow customer choice – particularly of its trademark items. This contradicts the argument for standardization, and reinforces the view that organizations must carefully consider decisions about standardization. Especially, they must be careful not to eliminate options that are critical to their product brand and market position.

Use business modelling tools to reduce complexity. Many standard business tools can help reduce complexity. For example, Dell uses a template of decision criteria against which product design decisions for new parts are measured (Handfield *et al.*, 2006):

1. Will components be sole, single or multi-sourced?

2. Does the design involve new technology and the associated risks?

3. Who are the manufacturers and who are the integrators for components?

4. Where are the suppliers located, and what is the logistics plan?

5. Where are these parts used in the industry today and could this change and affect future demand?

6. What are the expected costs?

7. What are the possible product developments and substitutes?

8. Are there any key alliances that need to be considered from suppliers or competitors?

9. Is there scope to use components from other product lines, or can this part be used in other products?

10. Can these parts be sold as after-market options or service parts?

Consolidate company-wide purchase volumes

The consolidation of purchases for common items across various locations – even on a global scale – is now an accepted part of good management (Trent and Monczka, 1998). The result is major cost reductions from large contracts that agree a lower unit prices – and this in turn significantly reduces the amount of capital committed to inventory.

Consolidation of purchases reduces transactions and enables other issues, such as consignment. This has a supplier placing items in a customer location without receiving payment until the buyer actually uses the items (Cox and Blackstone, 2002). You can imagine this in a bookshop, where publishers supply books but are only paid when customers buy them.

Use suppliers for on-site inventory management

Most organizations use specialized distributors to provide some of their material requirements. These distributors stock a full range of items from different manufacturers, which they can supply at very short notice – and are typically used for equipment spare parts. If a firm generates enough volume, the distributor may be willing to open some kind of presence in their facilities. In the simplest case, this might be a small stock of goods located in a warehouse, but it might include an employee to manage the inventory. These are increasingly common arrangements, with contracts stipulating that a distributor will stock a range of items and provide agreed levels of service – and in return the buyer will purchase exclusively from the distributor. Outsourcing these stocks reduces the buyer's administration of orders and need to manage certain items. This can be a significant benefit, particularly with MRO items that are often considered a nuisance because of their low value and disproportionate use of buyers' time.

Reduce delivery time from suppliers

Shortening the journey between suppliers and buyers reduces the amount of inventory in a system. When goods take 6 weeks to move from China, more pipeline stock is held in ships than would be needed for a 2-hour journey from a local supplier. So shorter journeys both reduce the total amount of pipeline stock held, and they increase flexibility by allowing frequent orders of small quantities.

Several actions can be taken to reduce delivery time, including:

- *Use of electronic communications* – which removes the paperwork, increases data accuracy and automates purchasing procedures, reducing the overall delivery time by 15 to 40 per cent

- *Supplier development support* – which means working directly with suppliers to improve performance, perhaps including buyers working at their facilities to speed order entry, production and delivery

- *Delivery time measurement* – as tracking the details of delivery times can identify areas of improvement. This encourages the use of performance measures that are based on time and speed of operations

- *Include second-tier and third-tier suppliers* – as the ability of a purchaser to reduce delivery time depends on its own capacity to get its materials delivered by second-tier suppliers. Buyers are increasingly concerned with activities two and three tiers away from them.

LEARNING FROM PRACTICE

Lockheed Martin Energy Systems

Lockheed Martin Energy Systems (LMES) has radically overhauled the management of its MRO stocks. There is a constant stream of requests to purchase the thousands of inexpensive MRO items that LMES stock. The company found it difficult to track stocks and usage, so they created an Accelerated Vendor Inventory Delivery (AVID) system. This links LMES electronically with a selected group of MRO distributors and allows users to order online from electronic catalogues (illustrated in Figure 15.12). A web-based version of AVID includes current suppliers and allows LMES to increase the number of electronic catalogues.

AVID allows users to purchase inexpensive off-the-shelf items with significantly lower transaction costs. In total, more than 3400 users can buy directly from 36 suppliers, with 225 000 transactions costing $55 million a year. Typical items bought include electrical items, laboratory supplies, building maintenance supplies, standard office equipment and office supplies.

The benefits AVID has brought include:

- JIT delivery for MRO items
- shorter total lead times
- no need to stock MRO items at the company's facilities
- drastically reduced inventory holding costs
- increased purchasing power with larger volumes bought from fewer suppliers
- streamlined channels of communication between LMES and suppliers
- improved quality of MRO items and reduced inventory obsolescence
- less paperwork and consequent increases in purchasing productivity

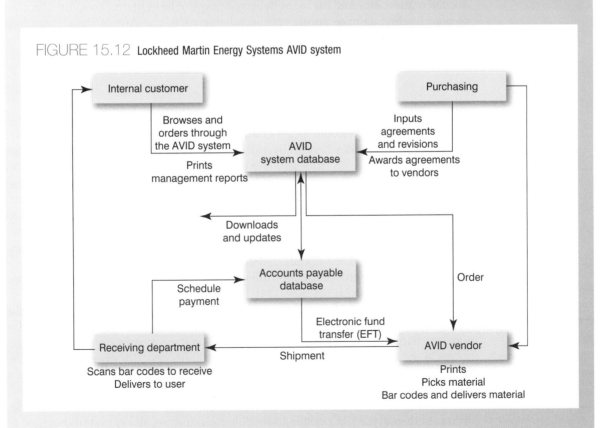

FIGURE 15.12 Lockheed Martin Energy Systems AVID system

- better material tracking through bar codes
- Improved accountability from both users and suppliers

LMES offers selected suppliers the opportunity to become the company's sole supplier for a wide range of items. In return, the company requires a price reduction on MRO items, 24-hour turnaround on regular replenishment orders, 2-hour emergency deliveries and no paperwork. In addition, suppliers must carry more stock to guarantee meeting company requirements, and meet other requirements for their warehousing operations, delivery capabilities, inventory management, financial strength and the ability to work with the AVID system.

Source: Interviews with company managers.

DELIVERING THE PERFECT CUSTOMER ORDER

When an organization matches its inventory policy to the deliveries from suppliers and demands of customers, it may be able to deliver the perfect customer order. Simply put, the perfect customer order is one that is delivered on time, accurately and in perfect condition. Hoffman says that, 'The perfect order metric is especially valuable because it is a comprehensive measure of demand-fulfilment capability and acts as a lightning rod for all the deficiencies in a company's operations' (Hoffman, 2003).

There are many reasons why an order is not delivered perfectly, some of which are related to stock management. For example, orders may be late because of shortages of stock, production problems, transport delays, accidents, industrial problems and so on. Then an order arriving at a customer may not meet specifications because it is the wrong product, wrong quantities, incorrect billing, missing documentation, etc. And the items delivered may not be in perfect condition because of poor quality, damage during transit, missing parts, etc. Any of these conditions give a less-than-perfect order. Managers take steps to overcome such problems, including the following suggestions.

Material requirements planning

We mentioned the economic order quantity as a way of finding the best order size. Methods like this work when the overall demand for an item is made up of a number of independent demands from separate customers. You can imagine this with sales of, say, bread in a supermarket, where overall demand emerges from the independent demands of lots of separate customers. However, there are many circumstances when demands are not independent, but are clearly related. For example, in a manufacturer of bicycles the demands for wheels and frames are not independent, but they are related through the production plans for finished bicycles. As the demand for wheels doubles, so does the demand for frames.

An alternative approach for controlling stocks with dependent demands is known as material requirements planning (MRP).

Material requirements planning (MRP)
Is a way of planning the flow of materials by calculating requirements from a master production schedule.

MRP was originally designed for assembling complex products, and it breaks the demand for products defined in a master production schedule into requirements for separate parts. For example, if our bicycle manufacturer plans on making 100 bicycles in the first week of March, it will need 100 frames, 200 wheels, 100 handlebars and so on, available at the start of the week. If frames are bought from a supplier with a lead time of a month, then an order must be placed at the beginning of February. Repeating this for all materials gives a schedule for ordering and delivery. In this way, MRP designs a schedule for acquiring all the material needed to meet a production schedule.

There are several requirements before MRP can be used, the first of which is a reliable master production schedule to show the number of products to be made in each period. The next requirement is a bill of materials, or parts list, which lists all the parts needed to make a final product. The third requirement is knowledge of lead times and order conditions of suppliers, so that buyers can arrange the materials to arrive just before assembly of the final product is due to start.

This gives the basic principles of MRP, but the reality can be very complicated. For instance, many of the parts are themselves assembled for other parts, so the operations for each of these also have to be planned and linked to the master schedule.

Distribution resource planning system

The MRP approach has proved so successful that it has been extended in many ways (Waters, 2003). One of these considers distribution resource planning (DRP) which controls the flow of finished goods that have left the production process and are working their way through a distribution system towards the final customer. Instead of starting with a master production schedule, DRP starts with forecast customer orders, and uses MRP methods to plan the need for transport and stocks. This involves:

- Forecasting customer demands for finished goods and translating these into inventory requirements
- Establishing inventory levels at each stocking location
- Determining the timing of replenishments of these inventories
- Allocating items to actual orders – and dealing with any shortages
- Planning transport and vehicle scheduling

Automated inventory tracking systems

Automated inventory tracking systems use scanners and EDI to track the flow of materials throughout an entire supply chain. They monitor suppliers, production plants, distribution centres and customers to show where materials are at any point – in the way that FedEx knows exactly where any package is at any time. Managers can use this information to identify problems such as delays, divert deliveries around problem areas, move materials to cover impending shortages, use links in supply chains that have free capacity, divert items to cover emergencies, inform customers of delivery times and so on.

Such integrated systems rely on item identification systems – predominantly using magnetic strips, bar codes or RFID labels – associated scanners throughout the supply chain, and efficient EDI linking all members. For instance, supermarkets routinely monitor sales through their point of sales check-out systems, and these automatically update requirements with their wholesalers, and then generate orders for replenishment from upstream suppliers. Tracking available stock means that replacement items are found and moved efficiently to replenish the supermarket shelves.

Inventory planner

This is an administrative issue which establishes an inventory planner who is responsible for managing the whole flow of materials, and work towards delivering a perfect customer order. This planner co-ordinates the movement and storage of

LEARNING FROM PRACTICE

SAP AG

SAP was founded in Walldorf, Germany in 1972, and is a 'leader in supplying collaborative business solutions for all types of industries and for every major market'. It employs more than 32 000 people in 50 countries and has '12 million users; 91 500 installations; 1500 partners'.

Forty per cent of SAP's income comes from enterprize resource planning (ERP), with its main product mySAP ERP. In 2004, SAP installed 1335 more ERP systems, bringing its total to more than 20 000 around the world, and making it 'undisputed world leader in ERP software'.

ERP systems have only been available since the 1990s, and the market is clearly growing vigorously, passing $10 billion by 2000. Other companies supply large integrated software, including BAAN, JD Edwards, SSA and PeopleSoft. These have an average installation cost of around $15 million. Of this, 17 per cent is for software, 14 per cent for hardware, 46 per cent for professional services and 23 per cent for internal staff costs. The time to get a system working properly varies from under 18 months to over 30 months. After this, benefits begin to appear in about a year and it takes around 5 years to break even. Peter Burris of META Group makes the comment, 'To say that implementing enterprize resource managment (ERM)/ERP solutions requires an enormous commitment is an understatement. They are expensive, are time-consuming, and require change in virtually every department in the enterprise.'

Source: Brace G. and Rzevski G. (1998) Elephants rarely pirouette, Logistics Focus, 6 (9), pp 14–18; Anon (1999) ERM solutions and their value, Meta Group, Stamford, CT; www.SAP.com; www.metagroup.com

materials, and also liaises between various groups in the supply chain, such as purchasing, materials management, production, inventory control and distribution. Other jobs might include establishing production targets from marketing forecasts, designing efficient production schedules, determining inventory requirements at warehouses and continuously evaluating inventory stock levels.

CHAPTER REVIEW

- Stocks are everything that an organization has acquired and keeps in store until it is needed. All organizations hold stocks, which are a major investment that needs careful management

- Stocks can be classified as raw materials, WIP, finished goods, MRO and pipeline stocks

- There are various costs associated with stocks, including unit, ordering, holding and shortage costs. These are surprisingly high and if inventory management is not done properly the associated costs become excessive

- Stock is often held to hide the effects of problems in the supply chain, such as uncertain demand, variable lead time or unreliable suppliers. This is an expensive option and it is better to solve the underlying problem

- Items should only be held in stock when the benefits are greater than the costs of not holding them. This decision – and subsequent ones about stock levels, ordering policies etc. – need careful analysis to balance conflicting factors

- JIT operations are based on the principle of doing all activities at exactly the time they are needed. This reduces – or preferably eliminates – stocks in the supply chain. This principle of eliminating waste has grown into a broad management philosophy described as leanness

- Lean operations put specific demands on purchasing, as they depend on small frequent deliveries. JIT purchasing extends the lean philosophy into the interactions between buyers and sellers. Related ideas include JIT production and transport

- Managers take several views of inventory including both operational needs and financial impact. Several factors should be considered with the management of stock, including record integrity,

accurate forecasting, standardized and simplified product design, on-site inventory, reducing cycle time, etc.

- A perfect customer order is one that is delivered on time accurately and in perfect condition. Many factors can mean that an order is not delivered perfectly, but managers can take some steps to prevent these, perhaps using materials requirement planning, automated tracking systems, etc.

DISCUSSION QUESTIONS

1 'Higher inventory levels often disguize underlying problems and are a waste of resources.' Explain what this means.

2 How is purchasing involved in the control of a firm's stocks?

3 What operational problems can be suggested by excess stocks of WIP?

4 Why do managers often neglect the true costs of holding stock? What has happened to change our perspective about stockholdings?

5 What are the benefits of finding the total cost carrying stock?

6 Describe the actions that purchasing can take to reduce uncertainty associated with (a) supplier quality (b) supplier delivery (c) order lead times (d) extended material pipelines (e) inaccurate demand forecasts.

7 What problems do errors in forecasting demand create within a supply chain? What can a company do to improve its forecasting accuracy?

8 Discuss the various approaches for the control of inventories.

9 What is meant by JIT operations? How are these related to lean operations?

10 What is a lean supply chain? What changes do lean operations typically make to purchasing and transport?

11 What are the main features of JIT purchasing? How easy is this to implement?

12 What factors must managers consider in the management of stocks?

13 Discuss the concept of a 'perfect order' and how it might be achieved.

REFERENCES

Bowersox D.J. and Closs D.J. (1996) Logistical management, New York: McGraw-Hill.

Bozarth C. and Handfield R. (2008) Operations and supply chain management (2nd edition), Upper Saddle River, NJ: Prentice Hall.

Cox J. F. and Blackstone J. H. (editors.) (2002) APICS Dictionary (10th edition) Falls Church, VA: APICS.

Handfield R. (1993) Distinguishing attributes of JIT systems in the make-to-order/assemble-to-order environment, *Decision Sciences Journal*, 24(3): 581–602.

Handfield R., Bozarth C., McCreery J. and Edwards S. (2006) Design for order fulfillment, Working Paper, Supply Chain Resource Cooperative, North Carolina State University, November.

Hoffman D. (2003) The perfect order: how does your demand fulfilment stack up?, MSI, November, p 37.

Shook J. quoted in Liker J. K. (editor) (1998), Becoming lean, Portland, OR: Productivity Press.

Trent R. J. and Monczka R. M. (1998) Purchasing and supply management: trends and changes throughout the 1990s, *International Journal of Purchasing and Materials Management*, November, pp 2–9.

Waters D. (2002) Operations management, Harlow, Essex: Financial Times Prentice Hall.

Waters D. (2003) Inventory control and management (2nd edition), Chichester: John Wiley and Sons.

Womack J. P. and Jones D. T. (1996) Lean thinking, New York: Simon & Schuster.

Womack J., Jones D. and Roos D. D. (1991) The machine that changed the world: the story of lean production, New York: Harper Collins.

Womack J. and Jones D. (2003) Lean thinking: banish waste and create wealth in your corporation, New York: The Free Press.

FURTHER READING

Briscoe A., Pancerella M. B. and Pleskunas G. (1997) The perfect order initiative, *Pharmaceutical Executive*, 17(7): 82–85.

Dong Y., and Xu K. (2002) A supply chain model of vendor managed inventory, Transport Research, *Part E: Logistics and Transport Review*, 38(2): 75–95.

Fazel F. (1997) A comparative analysis of inventory costs of JIT and EOQ purchasing, *International Journal of Physical Distribution and Logistics Management*, 27(2): 496.

Germain R. and Droge C. (1998) The context, organization, design and performance of JIT buying versus non-JIT buying firms, *International Journal of Purchasing and Materials Management*, 34(2): 12–18.

Gould L. (2003) Automotive supply chain management: as good as it gets? *Automotive Design and Production*, 115(2): 60–62.

Lewis C. (1998) Demand forecasting and inventory control: a computer aided learning approach, Chichester: John Wiley and Sons.

Minner S. (2003) Multiple-supplier inventory models in supply chain management: a review, *International Journal of Production Economics*, 81–82: 265–279.

Orlicky J. (1994) Materials requirements planning, New York: McGraw-Hill.

Silver E. A. (1998) Inventory management and production planning and scheduling, New York: John Wiley and Sons.

Stundza T. (2001) Buyers save money with smart inventory programs, *Purchasing*, 130(23): 8B1–8B6.

Waters D. (2003) Inventory control and management (2nd edition), Chichester: John Wiley and Sons.

Wild T. (1998) Best practice in inventory management, New York: John Wiley and Sons.

Witt C. E. (2003) Economic strategies: inventory management, *Material Handling Management*, 58(5): 31–40.

Zipkin P. H. (2000) Foundations of inventory management, New York: McGraw-Hill.

Chua Cheng Manufacturing

Chua Cheng Manufacturing is a rapidly growing manufacturer of office equipment with facilities in China and the Philippines. A team of management consultants has been advising the company on ways of improving productivity. Their study was drawing to a close when the project manager from the consultancy was called to Chua Cheng's vice president of operations, Sit Yuen Foo, who explained:

'We like your suggestions for rescheduling operations to meet expected demand using less plant and equipment. Now can you do one final study for us? As we will be working with less cushion for safety, it is important that everything continues to work properly. We think that this, in turn, depends on our stocks. We keep a lot of items in the stores and would like some suggestions for improving performance.'

The consultant said that his final report was already suggesting this study. He had talked to the supplies manager for Chua Cheng's plants, who described the present inventory control system as follows:

'We stock 25 000 different items which vary from paper clips to major spare parts for production equipment. There is not really any such thing as a typical item. Demand ranges from zero to 100 000 units a year. Current stocks range from one (we carry the odd spare part for heavy equipment that might break down, but is rarely used) to several hundred thousand (small items such as screws and brackets). Lead times vary from 15 minutes for things bought in a local shop, to over a year for specially designed imported equipment. The unit price ranges from almost nothing to $250 000. The reorder price varies from almost nothing for local suppliers, to very large amounts when we need a specialized piece of equipment designed and delivered from Europe. Shortage costs range from almost nothing to very large sums for things that we absolutely must keep in stock.'

The current inventory management system was installed 10-years ago and has been continually updated – with two complete revisions and many smaller adjustments. The system categorizes items in a number of ways and deals with each category differently. Firstly, the system considers items' importance:

- Five per cent of items are essential and must be kept in stock whatever the cost

- Twenty per cent of items are important and have a notional service level of 97 per cent

- Fifty per cent are ordinary items with a notional service level of 93 per cent

- Twenty-five per cent are low priority items with a notional service level of 80 per cent

A second classification of items looks at how long they had been stocked.

- For new items the expected demand is suggested either by departments requesting the item, or by suppliers

- When an item has been in stock for a few months there is a short history of demand, and forecasts for future demand are made from average values over the past 4 months

- After 9 months, more historical data is available, and forecasting is switched to a more sophisticated method whose performance is constantly monitored

A third classification of items refers to their use.

- Stocks of heavily used items are reviewed at the end of every working day

- Stocks of normally used items are reviewed at the end of every week

- Stocks of lightly used items are reviewed at the end of every month

- Stocks of sporadically used items are reviewed every time there is a withdrawal

- Stocks of items that have no recorded movement in the past year are considered for removal from stock

About 20 per cent of items are in each of these categories.

The system records all transactions and generates a range of reports. For example, at the end of every working day the computer lists the heavily used items and sends suggested purchases to the Procurement Department. The Procurement Department examines these suggestions the following day, makes any modifications they feel are necessary, transmit orders to suppliers and update associated records.

Sit Yuen Foo feels that the system is working reasonably well. It is based on sound principles and the stocks seem to give little trouble, considering the complexity of a system containing $20 million worth of inventory. The consultant's immediate problem is to prepare a proposal for an investigation of the system.

Questions

- Review the features that you think a reasonable inventory management system for Chua Cheng Manufacturing should contain.

- From the limited information given, how well does the current system seem to work? Are there any obvious weaknesses? Where could you look for improvements?

- What could a consultant say in a report to Chua Cheng Manufacturing?

CHAPTER 16
PURCHASING SERVICES

LEARNING OBJECTIVES   After reading this chapter you should be able to:

- Appreciate the importance of indirect spending

- Understand the role of logistics and transport management

- Describe a framework for making transport decisions

- Discuss the concept of third-party logistics

- Describe approaches to improve the purchasing of indirect items

- Discuss the sourcing of professional services

INDIRECT SPENDING

Indirect spending includes all payments made for goods and services that are not actually put into the products delivered to customers. For instance, a manufacturer spends money on transport and legal services, which do not actually form a part of the product and are indirect costs. On the other hand, raw materials and components are part of direct spending. Common examples of indirect spend include professional services, consulting, utilities, logistics, maintenance, repairs, legal costs, advertizing, operating supplies and employee benefits. Obviously, there is variation here, and when a computer manufacturer buys software to add to its machines it is direct spending, but when an accounting firm buys the same software to update its information system it is indirect spending.

Indirect spending is often more than half of an organization's total expenditure, which is the reason why it is being paid increasing attention (Ellram *et al.*, 2004). But there is an underlying difficulty as much indirect spending is not handled by a purchasing function, but is spent directly by other departments. For instance, a company might run a market survey, which involves indirect spending, but is generally organized by the marketing department. Here we describe the role of the purchasing function in managing an organization's indirect spending.

Logistics

Logistics
Is the function responsible for moving materials through their supply chains.

Logistics (Waters, 2008) is one substantial area of indirect spend that has a major impact on customer service.

The Council of Supply Chain Management Professionals defines logistics as 'That part of supply chain management that plans, implements and controls the efficient, effective forward and reverse flow and storage of goods, services and related information between the point of origin and the point of consumption in order to meet customers' requirements (CSCMP, 2008).' Without effective logistics it is impossible to guarantee the standard aims of getting the right product to the right place in the right condition at the right time.

Logistics consists of a series of interrelated activities, including inward transport, warehousing, material handling, packaging, inventory control, delivery and so on. Some people consider 'logistics' to describe the flow of materials through one organization, while 'supply chain management' refers to the overall flow through the whole supply chains. In practice, this is a pointless distinction and most people use the two terms interchangeably.

Transport is often the largest single element in logistics (Bowersox *et al.*, 2007; Coyle *et al.*, 2006), with transport service providers moving materials through four major links (illustrated in Figure 16.1)

FIGURE 16.1

Transport links in an organization

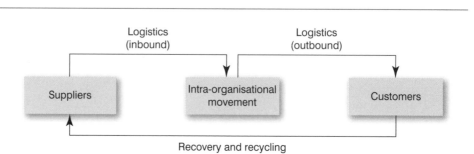

Link 1 Inward logistics – includes all inward shipments moving between supplier and buyers. This element is often included in sourcing negotiations and can be a substantial part of the contractual terms.

Link 2 Movements with the organization – where organizations with multiple facilities have transport moving materials between their separate facilities. This includes movement between production facilities, as well as movement into and out of storage in warehouses, distribution and logistics centres.

Link 3 Outward logistics – forms the link between an organization and its customers. This can be described as physical distribution, moving products through downstream customers.

Link 4 Recovery and recycling – this is described as reverse logistics and brings various types of materials back to the supplier, including waste, recyclable materials, packaging, repairable goods, dangerous goods, reusable parts and so on. This is an area where firms are continually finding innovative methods of recovering and recycling products to minimize their impact on the environment.

This fragmented view of transport often led to different departments controlling different parts of logistics, perhaps with physical distribution responsible for link 3, materials management responsible for link 2 and procurement responsible for link 1. As logistics developed into a single integrated function it absorbed these different responsibilities giving much more efficient operations. The important role of procurement is to acquire the best options for logistics. By moving these indirect purchases from other functions and concentrating them in purchasing, organizations can get much better performance.

LEARNING FROM PRACTICE

Source: Editorial (2001) Money rooms attack Bayer's indirect spend. Purchasing, 129 (12), pp 25–26.

Bayer

To address concerns over its indirect spend, Bayer initiated a programme it called the 'Money Room'. This involved establishing money rooms in plants to act as control centres for procurement.

Requests for indirect spending are typically mapped out into 20 to 25 areas (in columns) and linked to days of the month (in rows). All requests for materials are sent daily to the money rooms where they are consolidated and charted. At given times, money room staff meet to discuss that day's requisitions. If the requisitions meet the day's target spending and no foreseeable savings can be made,

the orders are placed. If the day's requisition exceeds the approved target, staff are responsible for finding ways of reducing, mitigating or eliminating the projected purchases. This can be done by consolidating orders, delaying purchases or by whatever other means seems reasonable. Money room staff are expected to bring costs down to 80 per cent of historical amounts, and they are rotated every 3 to 4 months to bring fresh ideas to the programme. At one location, Bayer reports that the money room programme has saved more than 46 per cent of indirect spend.

TRANSPORT MANAGEMENT

Managers have to make many decisions about their spending on transport. For instance, a basic choice is between company-owned vehicles belonging to their private fleet, or they may sub-contract transport out to third-party suppliers. As organizations focus more on their core competencies, they have increasingly recognized that many transport services can – and should – be outsourced to specialized providers. This moves the responsibility for transport out to expert providers, with purchasing responsible for acquiring services and managing the relationships.

In some countries – though a decreasing number – the options are limited as transport is considered such an important industry that it is either state owned or tightly controlled. Then there is little to distinguish different operators, and service buyers do not take much interest in the evaluation, selection and control of transport. In de-regulated economies, transport is usually a highly competitive business, as it is relatively easy to enter the market (traditionally by buying a single van or lorry) so carriers have to compete aggressively against other established carriers, new entrants, private fleets and other modes of transport. This means that purchasing must consider many more options but buying transport.

Procuring efficient transport services is important for several reasons. Primarily, transport is a major cost to many firms, perhaps amounting to 10 per cent of total operating costs, with logistics expenses that are second only to material costs. Perhaps more important than costs is the impact of transport on operations, where it can affect production schedules, inventory levels, customer service levels, deliveries and so on. Companies that do not effectively manage transport have more waste, higher costs and reduced competitiveness.

As purchasing takes a more active role in transport procurement, it becomes responsible for identifying and selecting service providers, and then negotiating terms, developing relationships, evaluating performance and doing all the other jobs needed to acquire an efficient service. Purchasing does not replace the transport function within an organization, which is still busy developing transport strategies – and day-to-day management of transport operations. The two functions work together, but one acquires transport services and the other manages and controls transport operations; transport decide that it wants to move a load by road next month, and purchasing hire a transport firm to make the move.

Framework for transport decisions

To acquire effective and efficient transport needs a series of decisions, and Figure 16.2 shows a general framework for these, together with the issues faced by procurement managers. This gives a general pattern, as the design and organization of transport networks varies considerably. For instance, moving bulk raw material may need ship, rail or barge movements, while small, time-sensitive components will use faster but more expensive transport, such as airfreight.

Determine when and where to control transport

The initial decision about transport asks how, when and where to control shipments. A related question asks when ownership is transferred. Materials can be shipped FOB to some specified point, which means that the supplier retains ownership of the materials and controls the shipment until it is physically received at the specified point. At this point – which is rarely on board a ship, but the historical

FIGURE 16.2 Framework for transport decisions

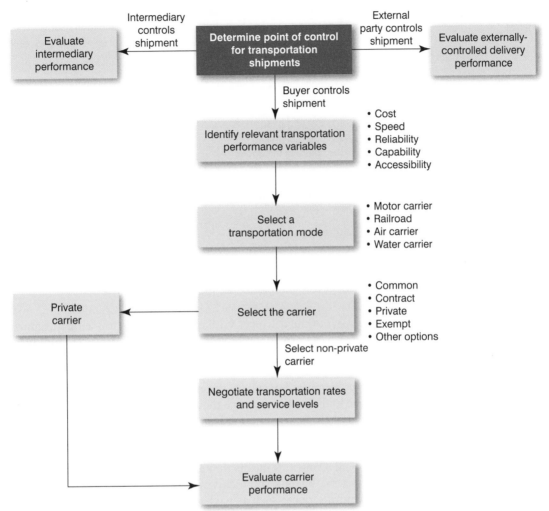

name has stuck – ownership and responsibility are transferred to the buyer. The supplier pays the carrier's freight bill to the point, and these costs are included in the invoiced price for materials. It also means that the seller selects the carrier, arranges the movement, pays the freight bill and files loss and damage claims to this point. Two common points for the transfer of ownership are FOB shipping point and FOB destination (compared in Figure 16.3).

When a supplier includes transport charges in the purchase price (perhaps quoting FOB the buyer's premises) buyers lose the ability to track and control its inward transport expenses. The unit cost is also higher, which inflates the value of the purchase and inventory, and this can have tax and other financial implications. Even when a supplier assumes responsibility for delivery, buyers should ask for a detailed breakdown of the transport costs separately from material costs.

The choice of handover point is basically a choice between insourcing and outsourcing transport: FOB destination outsources transport to the supplier. FOB shipping point allows buyers to manage transport, and then they have a choice of using internal transport, or a specialized transport company – giving third-party logistics, or 3PL. The benefit of internal transport is that an organization maintains

Third-party logistics (3PL)

Has a specialized external provider responsible for logistics within an organization.

FIGURE 16.3

Defining transport
shipping terms

Shipper's facility FOB shipping point	Buyer's facility FOB destination
What does FOB shipping point mean?	**What does FOB destination mean?**
• Buyer controls or directs shipment	• Seller is required at own risk and expense to transport goods to that place and there tender delivery
• Buyer assumes title to goods and risk of loss at seller's shipping point	• Seller assumes title to goods and risk of loss until satisfactory delivery to buyer's facility, unless agreed to otherwise.
• Seller has certain responsibilities:	
○ To put the goods in the possession of the carrier	
○ To make a proper contract for the transport of the goods, taking into consideration the nature of the goods and other circumstances	
○ To obtain and promptly deliver to the buyer any documents necessary for the buyer to take possession of the goods	
○ To promptly notify the buyer of the shipment.	

control over all aspect of the delivery. With external transport – either organized by the supplier or third-party provider – buyers lose control of deliveries and the ability to make any further decisions. In practice, though, they still have some power and might specify a list of acceptable operators. For some shipments, particularly low-volume and low-value ones, buyers are generally pleased to hand over control and not spend the time and effort to manage their own transport.

Another option is to use an intermediary, such as a third-party broker or forwarder to organize the transport. The buyer still gives up control of shipments, but the intermediary is an expert in organizing deliveries and works in the buyer's best interests. In practical terms, this means that an intermediary acts as an agent for the buyer, consolidates the buyer's shipments with those of other customers to get a lower cost, adds extra services such as packaging and expediting, arranges customs clearance, negotiates rates with carriers, provides temporary storage, does any finishing to the product and any other task needed. This option is particularly popular with smaller organizations that do not have the necessary knowledge, skills or resources to manage their own transport.

Identify key transport performance variables

Transport performance must be carefully monitored to compare different operators and types of operations. The criteria more commonly used to measure transport performance are shown in Figure 16.4.

Total cost. This is always important – or else more shipments would arrive by air instead of rail. However, selecting a carrier based solely on the freight rates ignores the total cost and customer service. The lowest-cost carrier may not give reliable deliveries, or may be slower, or lacking in some other features that distinguish superior providers. When other factors are added the carrier quoting the lowest rate may not give the lowest total cost. You can see this effect in airlines, when a budget airline may quote a low price, but by the time you add booking fees, taxes, luggage

FIGURE 16.4

Criteria used to measure
transport performance

Performance measure	Description
Total cost	In addition to the fee charges, total cost includes the cost of extra inventory, warehousing, buffer stock and in the case of international shipments, broker fees, customs, etc. Other cost factors such as extra managerial time may also have to be factored in.
Speed	Measured as time from when the shipment is released at the supplier's facility to the time of receipt at the buyer's receiving dock.
Reliability	Refers to the ability to deliver on time. Can be measured in different ways, but is typically a window of time when the delivery must be made. The measure is then the percentage of deliveries made within the specified window.
Capability	Refers to the ability of the carrier to move the material, including special materials, hazardous materials, etc.
Accessibility	Refers to whether the carrier is capable of picking up the shipment and delivering it door-to-door.

charges, checking-in fees, meals, and all the other charges, the total cost is considerably higher.

Speed. For some items, such as bulk raw materials, the time needed to deliver materials may not be important – but for producers in a time-sensitive environment, speed can be critical. Then ordinary products might move by lorry, while high-value items, such as pharmaceuticals and computer chips, are shipped by air.

Reliability. This refers to the accuracy and consistency of a transport service, with deliveries made at the time agreed. This is an important consideration, with many firms preferring a reliable carrier to a low-cost one. Notice that reliability differs from speed, as it compares actual arrival time against plans – and a reliable carrier with a longer transit time is often preferable to an unreliable one with a faster transit time.

Capability. This refers to a carrier's ability to provide an appropriate service for a given product. This has several aspects. Firstly, does the carrier have the physical capability to transport an item? For example, can the carrier safely transport a hazardous material, or handle large loads? Secondly, does the carrier have the proper equipment in the right location to perform the necessary moves? Thirdly, can the carrier repeat the movement as often as needed, possibly over some extended period?

Accessibility. This refers to a carrier's ability to provide service over a geographical area. A totally accessible carrier is capable of picking up a shipment and delivering it directly to its final destination. But some carriers only work in limited areas. For instance, a rail company can only work over the extent of its lines (though it can work with other carriers to extend its reach). Or a carrier may not have the legal authority to work in certain areas. A carrier that cannot offer total accessibility is not necessarily bad, as it may still give a good service by working with other carriers.

Select a transport mode

The different modes of transport – air, road, rail, shipping and pipeline – have different features that give different levels of performance when judged by the variables listed in the previous section. Then for some items the choice of mode is straightforward. For example, overseas deliveries are usually moved in containers on ocean-going ships; bulk raw materials, such as coal or chemicals, are moved on bulk ore carriers or locally on rail; oil is shipped in pipelines or tankers; small parcels are moved in planes and vans. However, the choice is not always so easy, and often buyers have to look for trade-offs between competing modes and operators. Does the speed of airfreight compensate for its higher cost; is the flexibility of road more efficient than lower-cost rail; do the capital costs of building a pipeline mean that tankers are cheaper? The relative merits and disadvantages of the five principal modes of transport are shown in Figure 16.5.

Road transport. The main competition for transport is often between road and rail. It is not surprizing that road transport is the most common, because its unique ability to provide door-to-door service makes it the most flexible mode. In addition, road transport is best suited to carrying small volumes (often described as less-than-truckload or LTL), and connecting multiple supplies, buyers and their intermediaries.

FIGURE 16.5 Advantages and disadvantages of transport modes

Transport mode	Advantages	Disadvantages
Road	• High flexibility • Good speed • Good reliability • Good for JIT delivery • Can negotiate rates	• High cost • Limited to domestic or regional transport • Cannot be used for large volumes
Rail	• Lower cost • Can handle wide range of items • Piggyback service can increase flexibility • Direct between major cities • Greater inter-modal service • Safe for hazardous materials	• Limited access to rail line or spur • Longer in-transit lead times • Less flexible – do not have rails to all locations
Air	• Quick and reliable • Good for light/small, high-value shipments (e.g. electronics) • Good for expediting/emergency situations	• Very high cost • Location of large airports limits shipping points • Cannot be used for large, bulky or hazardous shipments
Water	• Good for bulk commodities and heavy, large items • Can handle most types of freight • Low cost	• Limited flexibility • Seasonal availability • Very long lead times • Poor reliability (may encounter delays at ports, etc.)
Pipeline	• Good for high-volume liquids and gases • Low cost once installed	• High initial investment and installation costs • Limited to only certain items

Most countries have a well-established road network, and these allow efficient hub-and-spoke movements.

There are disadvantage of road transport, as its flexibility is not universal, and some countries have very poor road networks, while other journeys are either impossible (such as exports from Japan) or infeasible (such as deliveries from China to Europe). It is also has limited vehicle capacity and speed, which make it relatively expensive compared with rail, shipping and pipeline. There are minimal economies of scale – as you cannot simply add more cargo to a vehicle (because of weight, width, and length constraints). This suggests that road transport is characterized by low-fixed costs (because operators can buy small vehicles and do not have to build their own infrastructure) but relatively high-variable costs (typically 70–90 per cent of total cost, due to drivers, fuel, maintenance, tolls, operating fees, etc.).

Rail. An advantage of rail transport is the wide range of items it can carry over long distances, particularly in containers. So while road transport is characterized by relatively small volumes moved over short distances, rail transport is characterized by large volumes moved over long distances In practice, most rail freight consists of bulk commodities, such as coal, ore, steel, oil products and agricultural products.

Another advantage of rail is its relatively low cost, but we have to be more careful here. The costs of owning and operating rolling stock, tracks, freight yards, signalling, and other parts of the infrastructure mean that rail operators have high-fixed costs. However, their low-variable costs give a comparatively low total cost per tonne kilometre. They have flexibility to add extra wagons to a freight train with only a minimal increase in variable cost.

Clearly, firms that use rail must have access to a line, or be willing to use road transport to pick up and deliver from rail terminals. This constraint often limits the use of rail and highlights its major disadvantage of limited access. Rail carriers have attempted to overcome this inherent limitation largely through inter-modal shipments using containers, or sometimes with trucks/trailers driven directly onto flat-bed wagons (known as a piggyback service).

Another disadvantage of rail is that it has to share limited tracks, and working to schedules reduces flexibility ad increases transit times. These delays may be amplified by the need to assemble and later possibly reorganize each train in a marshalling yard.

Airfreight. Because of the high costs – and the limited amount and type of products that a plane can carry – airfreight is not widely used for normal deliveries. It is traditionally used for small volumes of expensive items that are needed quickly, such as pharmaceuticals, lobsters, packages, flowers, gemstones, etc. Included in this list are spare parts that are urgently needed to repair equipment – and when production equipment breaks down, the managers' priority is to get replacement parts delivered as soon as possible, and they are less concerned with the cost. Now that more firms are using JIT operations, they are more likely to consider air transport for a wider range of items. Shipping a high-priced component by air reduces the stocks needed, and it is actually a cost-effective option.

The airfreight industry is highly competitive in most areas, and this ensures low rates and good service levels – but high cost is still its main disadvantage. This occurs because of the high-capital costs (for planes, airports and related facilities) together with a high-variable cost (particularly fuel, staff and maintenance). The other main problems with air transport are its limited capacity (with the dimensions of planes limiting the size and weight of a shipment) and the inflexibility of only having to use airports that are in relatively few locations. One less obvious problem with air transport is its occasional unreliability. Apart from obvious problems like bad weather at airports, freight is often carried in the hold of passenger planes. When a plane reaches its maximum weight, an airline has to decide whether to carry freight or take on another passenger – and the passenger usually wins, while the freight delayed until a later flight.

Water. This includes both inland waterways (river, canal, and lake) and ocean vessels.

Inland waterways typically carry low-value, large-volume items such as raw materials (ores, coal, chemicals, sand, agricultural products, etc.). Inland water carriers rarely transport finished or semi-finished products because of the lengthy transit times. The main advantage of inland waterways is the large volume that a ship or barge can move at one time, at a relatively low cost. The primary disadvantages include the slow speed that gives transit times, inflexibility (being able to call directly at few locations with docks), seasonal shipment in some areas (depending on weather conditions), and the potential for accidents such as oil spills.

The other type of water transport has large ships transporting most of the world's commerce through international shipping lanes. With global sourcing, the choice of transport mode for at least part of the journey is usually straightforward as it needs a containership, bulk carrier, tanker or some other kind of deep water shipping. In recent years, the growth in international trade has steadily increased the amount of freight moving on ocean-going vessels. These are capable of handling virtually any type of goods, and give the lowest unit cost. The disadvantages of this mode include long lead time, inflexibility as large ships only visit a few ports, delays at customs or other points, and risks from accidents and other natural events.

Pipeline. These usually carry oil, petroleum products, natural gas, water, or a small range of other products, such as coal in a slurry. If these liquid products have to be transported over long distance, they can either travel by ocean going tanker, or by pipeline over land. There are really no other options. The total cost of pipelines is broadly similar to rail carriers, as investing in the infrastructure is the major fixed cost, while variable operating costs are relatively low. Although it is not generally a problem, movement through a pipeline is slow, so delivery times for a specific product might be long.

Inter-modal transport. An obvious point about transport is that a single mode is often incapable of meeting the requirements of a delivery. If a company wants to move a shipment from southern China to central Europe it will need a variety of modes and carriers to complete the journey. In China the shipment may be loaded into a container, which is moved by road to a rail terminal, and then by rail to the port of departure. There it is loaded onto a containership which travels to one of the major European ports, where it is loaded onto another rail link to a container terminal where it is transferred to road and delivered to its final destination. In reality, there may be more stages in the journey as the shipment is transferred between carriers, consolidated, sorted, unpacked and so on.

The idea of inter-modal transport is that inter-modal transport uses the best mode for each leg of a journey, with seamless transfers between modes. Each part of a complex journey might be done by a different carrier. If a buyer were to deal with each individually it would be very time-consuming, so many global carriers offer complete delivery services, where they co-ordinate and manage the entire inter-modal journey. The same management service is offered by other intermediaries, with the result that buyers have a single point of contact for the whole journey.

Figure 16.6 shows the relative ranking of different transport modes against our five performance criteria.

	Lowest per-unit cost	Speed	Reliability	Capability	Accessibility
Air	5	1	4	3	3
Rail	3	3	3	1	2
Pipeline	1	4	1	5	5
Road	4	2	2	2	1
Inland water	2	5	5	4	4

1 = Highest rated compared to other modes
5 = Lowest rated compared to other modes

FIGURE 16.6

Ranking of transport modes

Select the carrier

Once a buyer has chosen the best transport mode for a delivery, the next step is to evaluate and select the actual service provider. This itself opens a series of options, as buyers can consider common (or public) carriers, contract carriers, company-owned vehicles (private carrier) – or it can pass all the management to a third-party provider.

Common carriers. These are the standard transport companies who offer a service to anyone who wants to move materials. Operators often publish standard rates, which are controlled by strong competition within the industry. Buyers who decide to use a common carrier often have a wide choice available.

Contract carriers. Shippers that rely heavily on precise and frequent transport might consider a contract carrier. These are companies that do not offer a broad service for any user, but they have longer-term contracts with specific shippers, and they only provide a service to these firms. This offers several benefits to the transport buyer, principally the ability to negotiate favourable, tailored conditions, and the expectation of better service levels than with common carriers.

Private carriers. Some organizations have considerable transport needs, particularly manufacturers and distributors, and it is worth their while to run their own transport fleet. This gives a firm greater control over its own material movements, and it ensures reliable deliveries, and effective cost management. Private carriers often organize their own 'milk runs' which regularly follow the same route to pick up and deliver smaller amounts of materials, perhaps for JIT operations. But the drawbacks to using a private fleet include the capital investment needed, lack of expertize in running transport, low vehicle utilization as they cannot consolidate loads from other users, and inability to consolidate deliveries into larger amounts and get economies of scale.

Negotiate transport rates and service levels

Buyers with small transport needs can choose the best common carrier using their standard purchasing procedures. Buyers with substantial transport needs will probably negotiate with a small number of contract carriers. These contract services may be exclusive, where the carrier is responsible for all of a firm's transport, or the firm may also work with common carriers to compare rates and service. Negotiations between buyers and carriers generally address topics, such as (Dillon, 1988):

- The carrier's performance guarantees, with penalties and rewards
- The firm's commitment to ship a minimum amount of materials during the life of the contract
- How the parties handle freight loss and damage claims
- The type and quantity of equipment used by the carrier
- Frequency and timing of shipments
- Establishment of information-sharing systems
- Freight rates and discounts
- Programmes for joint cost reduction

Performance-based logistics (Vitasek and Geary, 2007) is a collaborative approach that that moves away from the traditional transaction-based model, which pays transport companies for every movement of materials. Buyers may negotiate the lowest cost for each transaction, but operators have little incentive to become more efficient, as any improvement may actually reduce their revenues. This puts the onus for any improvement on the buyer, who must then negotiate new conditions

LEARNING FROM PRACTICE

Saab

As part of a major corporate reorganization in the 1990s, Saab decided to centralize and modernize many of its support functions, including indirect purchasing. This initiative was designed to improve corporate efficiency and increase the firm's profitability. Magnus Strömer, Saab's vice president of corporate sourcing, had the job of centralizing a historically decentralized purchasing organization.

Analyses revealed that Saab had minimal control and visibility of its indirect spending. Based on the results of an internal survey, Strömer and his staff decided that more than 80 per cent of indirect material procurement could be consolidated at the corporate level. Their survey also showed that the company had limited automation in purchasing, high levels of maverick spending and almost no consolidation of its indirect spending.

In the following 18 months, Saab totally revamped its indirect spending by centralizing its staff, introducing a common strategic sourcing process, using a

variety of tools and introducing a new e-procurement system. More than 4,800 purchase orders a month are now placed on the e-procurement system. The next steps include implementing global corporate contracts with many suppliers and evaluating use of the e-procurement system globally. Strömer says, 'If we look at our annual spend of SEK 2.6 billion (€290 million), we have saved SEK 230 million, or roughly 10 per cent, of our total spend per year. This is very important as Saab, like every other company, needs to look at costs to be successful in the market.'

During the implementation, Saab identified 'super users' who set the standard for sourcing performance and can show other users how to use the process to their advantage. When other users see the benefits, it is easy to get them to accept and adopt the new process.

Saab's top management team gave corporate support of the new e-procurement process, and they developed broad policies that persuaded those who were less enthusiastic in accepting the system.

Source: Eames A. (2007) Take-off for new procurement, Efficient Purchasing, 5, pp 38–42.

with the provider. Performance-based logistics argues that the service provider's performance should be judged, not by transaction, but in terms of value-added and total cost. Then the service provider should be compensated by how well it enables the buyer to achieve these outcomes, with rewards appearing as longer-term contracts, performance incentives and increased profitability. This is really a standard approach of procurement, where the rewards of improved performance are not kept by one party, but are shared between the buyer and seller.

OUTSOURCING LOGISTICS TO THIRD-PARTY PROVIDERS

There is a clear business trend for organizations to focus on their core activities and outsource non-core activities to third-party providers. This is particularly noticeable in logistics.

The use of 3PLs is increasingly common, as it provides a convenient, low-cost and reliable logistics services. Its origins are in smaller firms that do not have enough internal resources and skill to run their own logistics, or which do not have sufficient volume to get economies of scale. However, it has become the standard way of working in even the biggest organizations, where it brings considerable advantages (summarized in Figure 16.7).

Select providers

Buyers should be very careful in selecting 3PL providers, as many companies describe themselves as providing a complete, integrated, global service when they do not have the necessary resources. Genuine 3PL companies routinely perform many of the tasks that were previously done in-house, including:

- Routine transport operations to pick up, move and deliver materials

- Running warehouses and logistics centres

- Sorting and consolidating of shipments

- JIT deliveries from local storage points

- International shipping, including customs brokerage, export and travel documentation

- Managing shipments with other carriers and freight forwarding

- Export packaging and containerization

Advantages	Disadvantages
• Economies of scale and increased flexibility • Improve service performance levels • Release capital from sale of assets • Release running costs • Concentrate on core business activities	• Relinquish control, ownership and expertise • Loss of integration between sales and supply • Changeover costs and operational problems • Loss of dedicated in-house managed staff • Sacrifice key business service differentiation

FIGURE 16.7

Advantages and disadvantages of third-party logistics

- Finishing operations for delivery to final customers

- Consolidation of accounts and billing.

They effectively do everything to allows transport buyers to focus on their core activities while the full-service carrier manages the routine details of logistics. This does not mean that the 3PL provider necessarily does all the activities itself, as it can sub-contract and manage the activities of other companies to bring a complete service. Many logistics companies provide such services, and a sensible approach to choosing one has the following steps:

1   *Plan.*

- Define the logistics requirements and how they will be measured and evaluated

- Define the supplier selection process

- Involve key internal people in the decision

2   *Select.*

- Target the best logistics providers

- Choose either 3PL or contract services

- Select the best provider

- Negotiate a mutually beneficial agreement

3   *Implement.*

- Share supply chain information to start the process

- Build relationships

- Work jointly to resolve start-up issues

4   *Improve.*

- Exchange performance and other information to identify opportunities for improvement

- Encourage cross-organization training and projects

5   *Partner.*

- Develop supply chain alliances to share risks and added value

- Involve 3PL partners in joint strategic planning and decision making

Gain access to critical and timely data

It is impossible to manage material shipments properly without critical transport data, so 3PL providers should routinely report information such as:

- Number, identities and locations of carriers providing transport

- Total transport expenditure, broken down by carrier, mode, supplier, location, etc.

- Number, identities and locations of suppliers shipping material inwards to operations

- Volumes and costs associated with shipments from each supplier

- Breakdown of volumes and costs by type of purchased material

- Performance statistics and ratings for each carrier

- Percentage of shipments arranged by suppliers versus buyers (for instance, FOB destination versus FOB origin)

Develop visibility of material shipments

Visibility means that managers have real-time information on the location and status of shipments. This is essential for the proper control of logistics, and it is achieved by shared EDI and communications systems. 3PL operators must have tracking systems to monitor all movements in the supply chain, and record current information about each shipment in transit. Then buyers can access this information from the 3PL supplier's system (or often through a website). An alternative to providing information when requested, is an event-based system, which keeps a log and automatically sends status reports, usually by email. Then a message is sent whenever a shipment passes a particular point in its journey, or an alert is sent when there is a delay or something goes wrong.

Develop closer relationships with fewer providers

We know that buyers and suppliers benefit from closer, more collaborative relationships and this also applies to 3PL relationships. Transport buyers are increasingly reducing the number of 3PL suppliers that they use, with the intention of working more collaboratively with the remaining ones and getting a better service.

Fourth-party logistics

A feature of purchasing is that lower costs and better service comes with higher volumes. A variation on this theme comes with fourth-party logistics (4PL). The principle here is that firms make agreements with outside companies to run parts of their logistics – giving 3PL. But different parts of an organization might sign agreements with different suppliers, for different types of service, with different requirements and so on. Co-ordinating all of these different requirements can become complicated, and it would make more sense if they were consolidated into fewer, larger contracts. This is the aim of 4PL, where another outside company co-ordinates and consolidates a firm's 3PL activities.

The consultancy firm Accenture is usually credited with coining the term 4PL – and registering it as a trademark – and they define it as, 'An integrator that assembles the resources, capabilities and technology of its own organization and other organizations to design, build and run comprehensive supply chain solutions (Accenture, 2009).' This broad definition allows many interpretation of the precise meaning of 4PL, but it generally aims at co-ordinating and improving the management of complex supply chains.

LEARNING FROM PRACTICE

General Motors

General Motors (GM) has a hugely complex logistics network, which includes raw materials providers (such as steel), customs brokers, third-party logistics providers, first-tier and second-tier component suppliers, freight forwarders, assembly operations, original equipment manufacturers, distribution centres, new vehicle dealers, parts and service dealers, third-party logistics distributors of spare parts – and most other activities associated with the motor vehicle industry. Looking at this network, GM's logistics team recognized that neither GM themselves, nor any other company, could handle all – or even a significant part – of the logistics. So they sought a 4PL partner for the following reasons:

- To avoid fixed costs and move towards lower variable costs
- Gain access to specialized logistics resources
- Rapidly develop and deploy state-of-the-art IT solutions
- Provide a single point of accountability responsible for managing all logistics activities

GM signed a contract with Consolidated Freightways to form a 4PL joint venture called Vector SCM, where GM will:

- Retain strategic planning, benchmarking and operational competency
- Have board representation and majority voting rights on critical issues

- Reduce logistics costs through a shared benefits agreement
- Avoid significant IT development costs
- Provide full accountability to GM Global Logistics for all aspects of logistics performance

And Vector will:

- Manage GM's current global network of logistics service providers
- Manage GM's global tactical and operational logistics activities
- Enable logistics capabilities (visibility, speed, flexibility and reliability)
- Provide leading logistics technology
- Provide people, process and technology to support GM global logistics operations
- Work with leaders in the industry to acquire skills and technology

Vector has now assumed responsibility for managing approximately one-third of GM's logistics spending. The gradual transfer of responsibility to Vector has been managed through a procedure of identifying opportunities, building a business case, gaining approval for the transfer of responsibility and then implementing the solution. This required major changes in the way that GM works and allows it to focus on its core capabilities.

Source: Wilkinson G. (2002) Presentation to the Supply Chain Resource Consortium, North Carolina State University, Raleigh, December.

PURCHASING INDIRECT ITEMS

Procurement managers have made great strides in reducing the price of direct materials. Procurement of direct materials is often centralized, with sourcing decisions and contract administration at a corporate or business level. Firms now realize that they have not paid so much attention to indirect spending, which is often devolved throughout an organization. Unless firms put more emphasis on their indirect spending it is unlikely to be managed effectively.

We have defined indirect spending as any expenditure on items that do not form part of the product delivered to a customer. This can be a significant part of total purchases, with surveys suggesting that spending on services was around 11 per cent of total revenue and 30 per cent of total expenditure on purchases (Carter *et al.*, 2003; Wade, 2003), while indirect spending averaged 9 per cent of revenue and

23 per cent of total expenditure on purchases. By comparison, direct spending (where the attention of supply management is most often focussed) accounts for 18 per cent of total revenue and 44 per cent of total expenditure on purchases. Such surveys also suggest that companies expect expenditure on services to increase substantially in the next few years, in part a result of their move towards outsourcing more non-core activities. A breakout of the average percentage of total purchasing spending by category is shown in Figure 16.8.

Continued growth in outsourcing of non–core activities, the expansion of the services sector and increasing cost pressure, mean that the importance of effectively managing an organization's indirect spending is growing. However, the decentralized purchasing and wide variety of items bought, makes it difficult to control indirect spending. Issues often arise when managers try to allocate indirect spending fairly to different functional and budgetary areas. There is an underlying problem when indirect spending is hidden in the price of direct materials. For example, if a supplier pays for shipping, the transport cost (an indirect service) is buried in the cost of the direct material. There are essentially two approaches to reducing the amount spent on indirect materials, which we can characterize as internal and external.

Internal methods of managing indirect spend

Data collection and consolidation. Often, several units within one organization will unknowingly purchase the same items from different suppliers, or even the same

Services spending category	Percentage of total purchase spending (normalized)
Manufacturing	20.24
Inventory	7.93
Professional services	7.61
Construction and engineering	6.04
Information technology	5.24
Marketing	5.13
Logistics	4.94
Real estate	4.25
Advertising	3.00
Project-based services	2.81
Human resources	2.04
Telecommunications	2.00
Travel	1.79
Facilities management	1.86
Printing and copying	1.51
Legal services	1.45
Administrative services	1.15
Temporary staffing	0.97
Research and development	0.78
Call centre	0.76
Accounting services	0.40
Finance	0.29
Warehouse management	0.14
Other	8.49

FIGURE 16.8

Average services spend activity

supplier (often with different terms and prices). For example, John Deere found that it was spending $1.4 million a year on work gloves, with 425 part numbers from 20 different suppliers (Patterson, 2000). Sometimes one supplier was supplying the same glove to different Deere facilities at different prices. Consolidating and standardizing this indirect purchase with the best suppliers would give annual savings of $500,000.

To consolidate items of indirect spending, procurement managers must have a clear understanding of exactly what indirect goods and services are being purchased by each part of their organization. As the example of Deere's work gloves suggests, this kind of information is not available in many organizations. So comprehensive data collection and analysis are the first steps in recognizing materials that might be standardized and consolidated. For example, one company specializing in audits of electricity usage collected information from 2,000 of FedEx's facilities and checked that the correct tariff rates were being used. The facilities varied in size from 2 employees to over 10,000, and using the best tariffs reduced bills by 4-5 per cent. An important result was not just the initial savings, but identification of patterns of electricity use across facilities that allowed FedEx to modify processes and improve energy efficiency (Handfield, 2004).

Restructuring to establish accountability. Establishing a capable procurement structure and setting up accountability for indirect purchases are closely connected with data collection and analysis. By seeing exactly who is spending what, where and when, managers can introduce procedures that deter, or at least control, maverick spending (which is spending by unauthorized people). Then a chain of authority can be established that assigns purchasing authority to match organizational needs. Essentially, appropriate people are given authority to buy materials, with assurances that they follow the correct protocol.

Automating the requisition and sourcing. Electronic requisitioning largely automates the administration of purchases, including the creation and transmission of orders, receipt of materials, updating of stock records and payment of invoices. This automation is common for direct spending, but gives the same advantages for indirect spending. In particular, it allows procurement staff time to consider strategic issues, and problems that need judgement, rather than doing the routine tasks of buying.

Standardization. Automated sourcing, typically associated with e-catalogues on supplier websites, helps to promote standardization of purchases and consolidation of indirect spending. The idea is that the automated systems only allow purchases from approved catalogues which are published after negotiation with approved suppliers. Then purchases are consolidated by suppliers and maverick spending is reduced. Some organizations have taken this further and require every purchase of indirect materials not made from approved catalogues to be submitted to a senior manager for review and approval.

External methods of managing indirect spend

Reverse auctions. The use of reverse auctions – where companies use their websites to solicit invitations to tender for items they want to buy – can greatly affect indirect spending. Reverse auctions are increasing business by an estimated 10 to 15 per cent a year. Among the reasons for this growth is that reverse auctions allow buyers and suppliers to communicate easily in real time from anywhere in the world. Successful buyers have reported price reductions of 10 to 20 per cent. However, this is not such good news for more expensive suppliers, who question whether such cost savings are sustainable after the initial purchase.

Purchasing consortia. Another growing trend is for different buyers to consolidate their requirements for an item through purchasing consortia. These are created by buyers from various businesses who pool their purchases into large orders, thereby increasing their buying power and getting lower prices and better service. The basic aim is to share benefits among purchasers, but some consortia have been so successful that they now charge other businesses a service fee for joining. The main challenge for purchasing consortia is getting members to agree on what to buy. This is inevitably commodities rather than any non-standard items, and each consortium focusses on a certain type of product. But even so it can be difficult to get agreement, and an independent third party is often used to co-ordinate activities. This third party takes all the item specifications from different buyers and develops a product list that best matches their needs.

Purchasing outsourcing. An increasing number of organizations outsource their indirect spending altogether. This passes responsibility for ensuring that indirect items are available when needed to outside specialists. For example, Harley-Davidson wanted to improve the efficiency of its indirect spending, but instead of working on existing procedures, it decided to outsource all indirect purchases to three suppliers. The company's purchasing department conducted a lengthy search to identify suppliers who could best handle the work, and they became responsible for making sure that all indirect sourcing needs were met. This new arrangement saved Harley-Davidson over $4 million in its first year of operation.

Enabling tactics

We have mentioned several ways of improving indirect spending, but these work best – or can only work – when several enablers are in place.

LEARNING FROM PRACTICE

FedEx and Elance

Source: Schoeberger M. (2003) At your service, Forbes, 3 March, p 90.

FedEx Corporation puts a lot of effort into negotiating prices with the 15 firms that provide temporary staff for services call centres, computer programmers and so on. Edith Kelly-Green, their chief sourcing officer, was dismayed to realize that managers were taking short cuts and avoiding the paper jams in the purchasing department by making their own deals with contractors. This maverick spending was often faster, but it missed the discounts that FedEx had negotiated with approved suppliers. Kelly-Green explained that, 'It's one thing to select suppliers and another to make sure employees actually use them.'

To deal with this maverick spending, FedEx introduced software from Elance to automate the hiring, paying and discharging of temporary employees. The efficiency of this new system encouraged managers to use it, and ensured that they used previously negotiated contracts with approved suppliers. FedEx significantly reduced paperwork, and made savings of 10 to 15 per cent of their multi-billion-dollar annual services budget.

Software companies claim that their systems can save somewhere between 2 per cent and 35 per cent off temporary staff costs by tracking hours worked, keeping track of laptops and other company property that temporary employees use and allowing supervisors to evaluate both contract staff and their agencies. Despite this, it was estimated that fewer than 10 per cent of large companies had such systems in place.

Zero-based budgeting. Because responsibility for indirect spending is usually dispersed throughout an organization, it is difficult to identify the savings from improvements. Traditional accounting systems are not designed to systematically track indirect spending. So departments generally start by justifying the same indirect budget they had in the previous planning cycle. Then managers examine the details of spending and look for opportunities to make savings. If they find such opportunities, the department has to reimburse the amount of these savings.

Pre-budget savings. Another way of reducing indirect spending is to force budget reductions, usually reducing a department's budget for indirect materials by some fixed percentage. A firm might reduce the budget for indirect spending by 5 per cent to 10 per cent, and then each department can:

- Negotiate price reductions from suppliers
- Consolidate spending within or across departments to gain price concessions
- Reduce the demand for indirect items
- Use a combination of the above methods.

Organizational structure. We discussed the options of centralized, decentralized, and hybrid procurement organizations in chapter 4. Often a hybrid organization gives central leadership, but allows different business units the flexibility to make their own localized procurement decisions. This model seems a good fit for the indirect sourcing needs of most large organizations.

Integrating accounts payable into procurement. One of the recurring difficulties with indirect spending is contract compliance. Organizations can overcome this by integrating their accounts payable process into the purchasing system. This arrangement gives purchasing the authority not to pay for indirect items that were bought outside the established procedures, meaning that maverick spenders will have their bills left unpaid until they explain their reasons to senior managers.

Power spenders. These are the key individuals or units that control substantial indirect spending and typically have positions of authority. The status and volume of spending of power spenders makes it difficult for purchasing staff to get them to comply with purchasing procedures. Proper training is generally the most effective way of bringing them under control, emphasizing the prevailing sourcing strategies and tools used by purchasing to control the costs of indirect items.

Supplier-managed e-catalogues. Automated requisitioning and purchasing systems encourage broad compliance to existing contracts. However, creating and maintaining internal e-catalogues is costly and time-consuming, so it is better to ask suppliers to provide and manage them. Suppliers have an incentive to agree to this, as they can display their products and increase sales.

Commodity coding for indirect spend. Item coding assigns a unique, identifying code to each product. Assigning commodity codes to indirect items across a corporation can be very difficult, as an indirect item can logically be assigned into different expense categories, allowing inconsistent coding across business units. Often there is a catch-all category, such as 'diverse services' which gives an unclear picture of expenditure. Supplier coding – to identify each supplier – can also be difficult, as suppliers often have multiple locations, allowing multiple codes for the same supplier and the same item. This masks the size of total indirect spending with a particular supplier and prevents buyers realizing the potential for consolidation and negotiating volume discounts.

One commodity team assigned to large suppliers. When a large supplier delivers a broad and diverse range of products, it is often difficult to ensure coherent commodity coding, standardized products – and consistent pricing, terms and conditions. One solution is to assign a commodity team to work with each large supplier. When another buyer is considering using this supplier, a commodity team is already working with the supplier and can ensure that existing contracts with standard products, prices, terms and conditions are used. This co-operative approach helps buyers overcome the common 'divide-and-conquer' approach used by large suppliers.

Outsourcing indirect spending. Outsourcing any part of purchasing can be controversial, but it often brings significant benefits. The main benefit of outsourcing

LEARNING FROM PRACTICE

Bank of America

Source: Handfield R. (2003) Improving the total cost of ownership of document management at Bank of America, Practix, October, pp 1–6.

Bank of America (BoA) is one of the world's leading financial services companies. BoA serves 28 million customers from its 4,200 branches (the most diverse in the USA), and it provides corporate financial services to more than 90 per cent of major US companies.

A major problem for BoA was its document handling, and to improve this, the company created a Document Management department with an aim of reducing the total cost of document handling from their origins through to their end-of-life (archiving, recycling or confidential destruction). Documents are expensive to produce (through print-on-demand, desktop printers, desktop delivery through multi-functional devices, internet delivery, reprographic, etc.) and distribute (through freight transport, post, courier, internal mail, internet, etc.). While looking at the cost of alternatives, some interesting points emerged, For example, the company owned more than 5,000 multi-functional copiers (ones capable of copying, faxing, printing and scanning documents) but only 5 per cent of these were connected to computers; the remaining 95 per cent were used solely for manual copying. As there was no active management of desktop printers, the bank was using them instead of cheaper print shops. The total amount spent on copying and printers was estimated to be around $90 million a year, but nobody knew the exact amount, or even how many desktop printers were used.

Their solution began by centralizing documents, with every document created stored in a digital library. This library included cheques, deposit slips, statements, investment options, standard letters, magnetic character recognition documents – and every other type of document used by the bank. Needless to say, this required a very large database. Once this digital library was established, managers could control how each piece was printed. Some change quickly emerged, such as an increase in documents printed as needed rather than routinely printed and distributed, more use of standard documents and consolidation of different documents.

The Intranet allowed documents to be created in the lowest cost location, distributed to desktop computers and where necessary printing on connected multi-functional copiers. This had some significant implications on operations. By digitizing all documents at their origins, the bank shifted most document delivery from traditional hard-copy to electronic delivery at the desktop. They reduced the number of forms from 45,000 to 6,000, the cost of printing was reduced by more than 20 per cent, the proportion of multifunctional devices connected to the network quickly rose to 35 per cent. As less printing is done, the number of printers almost halved to about one machine for seven employees – which brought complaints from some staff, who now have to walk up to six metres to a printer.

indirect spending is that outside expertise can significantly reduce the costs. But there are other benefits, such as the development of an e-catalogue of items, guaranteed service levels, tighter control of indirect spending, access to real-time data and so on.

SOURCING PROFESSIONAL SERVICES

Many areas of indirect spending have special problems, but we will illustrate some of these by reviewing best practices in an area that is facing increasing scrutiny – the sourcing of professional services, including consultants and software developers. When buying these, some basic steps such as rationalizing and optimizing the supply base, working closely with key suppliers, consolidating requirements across business units, implementing better control systems and implementing new cost savings ideas can save a substantial amount of money (Reilly, 2002).

Professional services are often used quite differently across business units, so procurement has the chance to identify best practices and implement standard procedures. Like most purchasing initiatives, the first step should be to perform an internal audit to see just how much the organization is currently spending on professional services and where those funds are spent. This gives a picture of the current state of sourcing, and shows which areas need improvement. The following steps describe a useful approach to buying professional services.

Have a clearly defined scope

Professional services are often employed to work on a project, such as installing a new e-procurement system. A key point is that the project must have a clearly defined scope, which describes the details of work to be done, aims, deliverables, deadlines and budget.

The scope gives a detailed description of the project and should contain any relevant information. For instance, it might include non-disclosure statements to protect company interests, performance rewards and penalties, details of risk management, how changes to the project are handled and statements about who has operational control over both internal and external staff working on the project. This sort of detail is particularly important with new service providers, but can be relaxed when buyers already have working relations with an established supplier. In the simplest case, work can be arranged by a phone call or email – but it should always be followed by a formal confirmation and scope.

A well-crafted scope can help avoid misunderstandings during the project, and it can also avoid 'scope creep' when repeated adjustments to terms combine to give major changes. When this happens it is probably better to renegotiate the contract.

Move to a centralized procurement structure

Centralizing the procurement of professional services allows buyers to consolidate overall needs, use fewer providers and ensure that they get the best value for money (Avery, 2000). Porter (2001) reinforces the importance of this by saying that, 'Cost reduction is, hands down, the main reason for bringing sizeable purchasing power to bear in the market place.' In practice, there are many examples of cost savings brought by centralizing procurement, such as the $100 million over 5 years saved by Dial (Reilly, 2002).

Centralized procurement of professional service can also increase the accountability of outside consultants by closer monitoring and auditing of their activities, and it can reduce duplication of services and the likelihood of unnecessary charges (Baker and Faulkner, 2003).

Of course, centralized purchasing also has disadvantages. For instance, no single consultant has the expertise to tackle all the variety of consulting projects needed, and while centralization is good at standardizing projects, decentralization is better at tailoring services to specific needs. Some departments may already have good working relationships with specific consultants, and this information is lost when choices are made by a central purchasing group.

Develop a professional services database

For buyers to properly consider professional services, they should have two databases.

A cumulative knowledge database which stores the information already available within the firms, and is needed to prevent duplicate or unnecessary services being sourced. This database typically contains an organized list of past projects, the results obtained, information collected, work quality, accuracy, related work and any other relevant information. If someone is proposing a new project they can search this database to see if a similar project has already been completed somewhere within the organization – and if it has the proposed project will not be needed.

A preferred supplier database which includes supplier performance records and related user comments. This can be very useful for future projects, as it shows which suppliers the organization recommends – and implicitly, those that it does not recommend. The database should generate lists of preferred suppliers based on specific criteria, so that buyers can refine their searches for the best suppliers. Merrill Lynch uses such a system and says that, 'The system's ability to track individual supplier performance, as well as overall supplier performance, allows us to prevent hiring poor performers who leave one supplier company only to resurface under a different corporate umbrella (Porter, 2000).'

Develop a sound procedure for evaluation and selection of suppliers

The central element in procuring professional services is the evaluation and selection of consultants. This is the core task where buyers commit most of their resources. We have discussed supplier evaluation in chapter 7, and the same principles and criteria apply here, with the development of a long list of possible suppliers, pruning this down to give a more manageable shortlist and then final selection of the supplier. This process is summarized in Figure 16.9.

To prune the list of potential suppliers, buyers must decide which factors are important. There are different requirements for each project, firms typically evaluate factors such as consultant's knowledge, costs, experience, likely delivery performance and technological capability. These are very similar to the considerations developed in chapter 7 (summarized in Figure 16.10).

Optimize the supply base

During this process of eliminating suppliers that for some reason are not as good as others, buyers are working to find a small number of supplies they could work with.

FIGURE 16.9

Supplier evaluation and
selection process

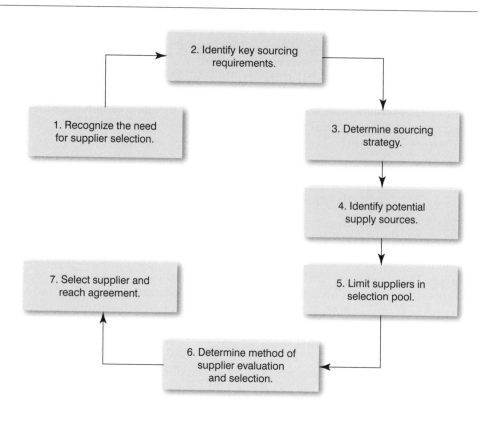

FIGURE 16.10

Criteria for judging
suppliers

Management capability
Employee capability
Financial stability
Costs
Quality management
Process design and technology
Production scheduling and control systems
Environmental regulation compliance
E-commerce capability
Supplier's sourcing policies
Potential for longer-term relationships

In other words, they are rationalizing and optimizing the supply base. The preferred supplier database is an important tool here, as it shows whether a provider's capabilities meet the requirements of the users. The aim is always to work with a small number of the best suppliers.

In practice, firms rarely go to the extreme of using a single source for professional services, because the diverse requirements of their firm need diverse expertise in suppliers. No single supplier would be an expert in all areas, and using more sources allows buyers to tap into specific expertise and increase the flow of new ideas. It can be argued that in a competitive market, considering a new supplier enhances the performance of the others. A rule of thumb is to avoid one-stop shopping, and only use professional service providers for their core expertise – as they are likely to be second rate outside this.

Develop a standardized contract

Specialized buyers understand the requirements of professional services which they meet on a regular basis. This helps them in finalizing details of a contract, which should use a standard format that has been developed in consultation with the organization's legal department. These contracts should be tailored to the specific requirements of professional services, and many firms publish their online templates which contain the clauses most commonly used. These templates allow the scope of the project to be clearly specified in a standard format, forming the basis of the agreed contract.

Monitor results

Firms should have systems in place to measure the performance of professional service providers at various stages of their projects – at the beginning during the selection process, throughout the life of the project, when implementing results, and then monitoring continuing operations. The factors which are used in these evaluations typically include quality of service, cost, schedule, technical support and any other relevant factors – such as how easy the service provider is to work with. The results should be recorded in the buyers' database.

The internal users of a contracted professional service have an important role in the sourcing and evaluation process. Their participation in defining the scope of the project, and providing feedback on progress and services rendered by the provider, and then their assessment of the results, are key facts. These judgements on scope form one view of project success, with the other two related views given by the finance and cost performance, and schedule and timing performance.

Develop policy compliance

The practical success of this seven step approach to procuring professional services depends on how well it is applied. Allstate reduced the number of suppliers for one type of professional service from 300 to 11 and reduced costs by 20 per cent (Avery, 2000). According to a company vice president, 'Effective demand management of professional services depends on establishing clear usage policies, then monitoring and reporting compliance with these policies. Realizing actual savings requires compliance throughout the entire company.'

In practice, many service agreements are not well planned or executed, and they are characterized by imprecise and unclear specifications that make it difficult to see whether a service has actually been performed adequately. The problem is that it is very difficult to write down specific service requirements. For example, how could they describe a contractual agreement for an advertising company to deliver a successful advertising jingle, or what defines satisfactory progress on a software program? Service providers have been known to take advantage of unclear or ill-defined terms, to expand the apparent scope of a contract (and its corresponding fees) or to use a string of change orders (which inevitably favour the service provider rather than the buyer). The answer is to define clear requirements and procedures – and then actually stick to them.

CHAPTER REVIEW

- Indirect spending is the total expenditure on materials that are not a part of the products delivered to customers. These can be expensive and include items like professional services, consulting, utilities, logistics, maintenance, repairs, legal costs, advertising, etc.

- These have often not been controlled by purchasing departments, but have been controlled by other functions. Bringing them under procurement's control gives opportunities for considerable savings

- Logistics is often a major part of indirect costs – and a major part of this is due to transport. The approach to acquiring transport services is important in itself, and it gives some general guidelines for procuring other services

- There is a common framework – or series of related decisions – for planning transport. This makes decisions about the control needed, performance measures, choice of transport mode, choice of supplier and terms

- There is a major trend for organizations to outsource their non-core activities. This is particularly noticeable in logistics and transport, where third parties supply or manage a firm's transport requirements. Selecting the best supplier can be difficult and buyers need to consider many factors

- Several methods are available for improving the effectiveness of spending on indirect items. We characterized these as either internal (such as data collection and consolidation) or external (such as reverse auctions or consortia). To be most useful, these methods need a variety of 'enablers'

- Procuring professional services is an area of increasing concern. We described a general procedure for procuring professional services that starts with defining the scope of their work, through organization and evaluation, and to monitoring the results

DISCUSSION QUESTIONS

1 Why might managers be increasingly aware of – and concerned about – the acquisition of logistics services?

2 What are the benefits of buyers maintaining control over transport for purchased materials?

3 What key items should you negotiate with a logistics service provider?

4 What performance measures are commonly used for transport providers?

5 Compare the relative strengths and weaknesses of each of the major modes of transport.

6 What are the differences between a common and a contract carrier? Can a buyer negotiate with a common carrier?

7 What is third-party logistics? What function does it serve, and what are the benefits?

8 Discuss the conditions under which a buyer might prefer a third-party logistics provider to manage the transport of purchased items.

9 Describe some examples of indirect spending. How do you think it can be improved?

10 One of the biggest problems in managing indirect spend is finding where and how the spending takes place. Why do you think this is? How can managers collect and use this data?

11 Why is it important to have senior management support when implementing a strategy for indirect spending?

12 Can you give some examples of 'power spenders' of indirect items? How do these affect purchasing, and how can they be persuaded to use standard purchasing procedures?

13 Why is it important to clearly define the expectations of a professional services project?

REFERENCES

Accenture (2009) 4PL, website at www.accenture.com

Avery S. (2000) Allstate leverages sourcing to better serve customers, *Purchasing*, 128(2): 12–14.

Baker W. E. and Faulkner R. R. (2003) strategies for managing suppliers of professional services, Tempe, AZ: CAPS Research.

Bowersox D. J., Closs D. J. and Cooper M. B. (2007) Supply chain logistics management (2nd edition), New York: McGraw-Hill.

Carter P., Beall S., Rossetti C. and Leduc E. (2003) Indirect spend, Tempe, AZ: CAPS Research, and website at www.capsresearch.org

Coyle J. J., Bardi E. J. and Novak R. A. (2006) Transport (6th edition), Mason, OH: Thomson South-Western.

CSCMP (2008) About CSCMP, The Council of Supply Chain Management Professionals, Lombard, IL and website at www.cscmp.org

Dillon T. F. (1988) Trends facing transport buyers/carriers, Purchasing World, September, pp 32–34.

Ellram L. M., Tate W. L. and Billington C. (2004) Understanding and managing the services supply chain, *Journal of Supply Chain Management*, 40(3): 20.

Handfield R. (2004) The impact of energy deregulation on sourcing strategy, *Journal of Supply Chain Management*, 40(2): 38–48.

Patterson J. L. (2000) Glove story at John Deere, in Case book: supply management cases, National Association of Purchasing Management, Tempe, AZ.

Porter A. M. (2000) How one firm automated its professional services buy, *Purchasing*, 129(5): S52.

Porter A. M. (2001) Big companies struggle to act their size, *Purchasing*, 130(21): 24–25.

Reilly C. (2002) Central sourcing strategy saves Dial $100M, Purchasing Online, January, p 17.

Vitasek K. and Geary S. (2007) Performance-based logistics: the next big thing? ProLogis Supply Chain Review, Summer, pp 1–12.

Wade D. S. (2003) Managing your 'services spend' in today's services economy, Tempe, AZ: CAPS Research.

Waters D. (2008) Supply chain management (2nd edition), Basingstoke, Hampshire: Palgrave Macmillan.

FURTHER READINGS

Ballou R. H. (2004) Business logistics/supply chain management: planning, organizing and controlling the supply chain (5th edition), Upper Saddle River, NJ: Pearson Prentice Hall.

Bowersox D. J., Closs D. J. and Cooper M. B. (2007) Supply chain logistics management (2nd edition), Irwin, New York: McGraw-Hill.

Carter P., Beall S., Rossetti C. and Leduc E. (2003) Indirect spend, Tempe, AZ: CAPS Research.

Coyle J. J., Bardi E. J. and Langley C. J. (2003) Management of business logistics: a supply chain perspective (7th edition), Mason, OH: Thomson South-Western.

Coyle J. J., Bardi E. J. and Novak R. A. (2006) Transport (6th edition), Mason, OH: Thomson South-Western.

Ellram L. M., Tate W. L. and Billington C. (2004) Understanding and managing the services supply chain, *Journal of Supply Chain Management*, 40(3): 17–32.

Frazell E. H. (2002) World-class warehousing and material handling, New York: McGraw-Hill.

Handfield R. (2004) The impact of energy deregulation on sourcing strategy, *Journal of Supply Chain Management*, 40(2): 38–48.

Lee H. L. and Wolfe M. (2003) Supply chain security without tears, Supply Chain Management Review, 1: 18–34.

Perry C. (1998) Purchasing transport, West Palm Beach, FL: PT Publications.

Reilly C. (2002) Central sourcing strategy saves Dial $100M, Purchasing Online, January, p 17.

Stock J. R. and Lambert D. M. (2001) Strategic logistics management (4th edition), New York: McGraw-Hill.

Vitasek K. and Geary S. (2007) Performance-based logistics: the next big thing? ProLogis Supply Chain Review, Summer, pp 1–12.

Wade D. S. (2003) Managing your 'services spend' in today's services economy, Tempe, AZ: CAPS Research.

Waters D. (editor) (2007), Global logistics and distribution planning (5th edition), London: Kogan Page.

Waters D. (2008) Supply chain management (2nd edition), Basingstoke, Hampshire: Palgrave Macmillan.

CASE STUDY

Best practice in indirect spending

When studying the best practices used in the procurement of logistics and services, several common themes emerge. These include:

- Link service activities directly to the corporate strategy

- Organize indirect spending under a single senior management position, preferably using a hybrid procurement structure when the indirect spending is spread across business units

- Expand the use of IT to capture spending behaviours, costs, maverick spending and other relevant information

- Establish support for new indirect spending processes from senior managers, particularly from the chief financial officer who is often the key person in overseeing compliance

- Tie cost savings directly to actual spending in business units and be sure to capture the savings through a zero-based budget or other appropriate methods

- Form partnerships and alliances with a few service providers to consolidate indirect spending and identify cost-savings opportunities

- Measure service provider performance to sustain superior performance

- Establish benchmarks for service providers' performance and regularly review their improvement against predetermined goals

- Establish the scope of professional services at the start of their work, and follow up routinely to ensure that progress is made in a reasonable and cost-effective manner

- Review indirect procurement strategies periodically to ensure that user requirements and expectations are being met

Buyers are increasingly involved in the procurement of indirect items, where there are opportunities to make major contributions in this important, but often overlooked, area. They must strive to become experts in these areas, to consider user needs, and tailor the sourcing process to prevailing conditions.

Questions

- Buyers' involvement in some services is fairly recent. Give some examples of these and say why buyers have only recently become involved

- Review the list of common themes for purchasing indirect items, and give a summary of what each point involves

- What other factors would you add to this list?

CHAPTER 17
INFORMATION SYSTEMS AND ELECTRONIC SOURCING

LEARNING OBJECTIVES   After reading this chapter you should be able to:

- Discuss the use of information in supply chains

- Review the development of e-procurement and the e-supply chain

- Discuss factors that have encouraged the introduction of new information systems

- Describe the principles of enterprize resource planning

- Discuss the role of purchasing databases and data warehouses

- Appreciate the role of electronic communication between buyers and sellers

- Discuss the functions and contents of e-sourcing systems

- Consider the integration of all aspects of e-purchasing

THE E-SUPPLY CHAIN

e-Supply chain
Refers to any supply
chain that includes
electronic
communications and the
internet – giving a
component of
e-commerce. The
associated management
function becomes
e-SCM.

The revolution in information and communications technology continues to have dramatic effects on purchasing and supply chains in general. In particular, it has allowed the development of e-**SCM**.

The chapter is not a technical presentation of computerized information systems, but instead it focusses on the issues that purchasing managers face in their use of information systems.

Evolution of e-SCM systems

Purchasing managers now expect to have powerful systems at their disposal, but these systems have been developing over some time. Figure 17.1 reviews the evolution of e-SCM systems (Bozarth and Handfield, 2004). Early uses of information systems were in accounting and finance, but in the 1970s more IT resources were allocated to purchasing, operations and logistics. Organizations installed systems such as MRP and distribution requirements planning (DRP) to improve the planning and control of material movements.

These early systems were primarily internal, but in the 1980s EDI allowed the transfer information between remote sites and different organizations. EDI made it possible to share information between customers and suppliers, and when joined by EFT the path was open for automated transactions.

Purchasing managers continually looked for more advances in technology use, and as organizations re-engineered their operations in the 1990s, ERP gave a way of integrating all business functions. By connecting the information systems of different business functions and relating them all to, say, production schedules in a manufacturing company, they would all become more efficient. The principle was that all functions could now work together, with shared, consistent information, joint planning, removal of duplication and waste – and generally working together toward the same ends.

The next developments of e-commerce emerged as the WorldWideWeb – and all the information stored in an organization can now be broadcast on its websites or

FIGURE 17.1   Evolution of e-SCM systems

Solution	Period	Focus	Primary use of system
MRP-DRP	1970s	Internal/managing inventory	Inventory planning, inventory control and distribution efficiencies
EDI	1980s	External	Electronic transmission of purchase orders
ERP	1990s	Internal	Integration of all business functions for processing and reporting
SRM and CRM	2000s	External	Managing and controlling the interface between buyers, suppliers and customers
Collaboration	2000s	External-internal	Systems allow constant communication within supply chains using RFID, EPOS, etc.
Advanced sourcing analytics	2010	External-internal	Sourcing analytics and computerized negotiations

transmitted through the internet. In practice, ERP systems were primarily internal, but the original concept was that they should form links between suppliers and customers. Now the internet provided this bridge and information is visible – at least in principle – throughout a supply chain. Software companies developed new systems to manage the flows of information and materials, not just through each individual organization, but through the broader supply chain. Parts of these systems became popularly known as **supplier relationship management** (SRM) and **customer relationship management** (CRM).

Collaboration among supply chain partners emphasized the need for efficient data capture, and this encouraged the development of EPOS, RFID, biometric identification and other automated data entry methods. For purchasing, new systems came along for computerized negotiation, supplier evaluation, bid optimization and so on. Such increasingly powerful tools are linked in a mobile environment through small computers (palmtops and beyond), personal digital assistants (pioneered by BlackBerry) and sophisticated mobile telephones (extending Apple's iPhone).

We have to give a warning here, and say that although such integrated systems are technically possible, they are far from universal. In 2003, Poirier and Quinn (2003) noted that while most organizations were moving towards external integration only 10 per cent had made any significant progress. Christopher *et al.* (2002) found that, 'upstream and downstream visibility was poor' and, 'end-to-end management of an organization's complex and unstable supply chain network, (particularly upstream into the supplier base), would be an improbable if not impossible task'.

> Supplier relationship management (SRM) and customer relationship management (CRM) Systems to manage interactions with suppliers and customers.

Supply chain information flows

Supply chain information flows (and the information systems that embody them) serve six major functions:

1 Record and retrieve critical data.

2 Initiate and control flows of materials and money.

3 Automate routine decisions.

4 Support planning activities.

5 Support higher-level tactical and strategic decision making.

6 Move and share information across firms and between users.

You can see from this list that information systems cover everything from low-level transactions through to sophisticated strategic support tools. At the most basic level, information systems record and retrieve critical data, and control flows of materials and money (the first two activities in the list). This is referred to as transaction processing. For example, your credit card company has records that include your address, credit limit, payment history and most recent balance, and when you use the card to pay a bill these records are automatically updated.

At a somewhat higher level of functionality, information systems are used for decision making, where routine decisions are automated and the exceptions dealt with manually (activities three and four in the list). For example, a retailer selling 60,000 items will use an information system to automatically forecast demand for each, calculate order quantities, establish reorder points for items and send orders to suppliers when needed. These are routine decisions that can be safely automated.

But sometimes the retailer may have a more complicated purchasing decision – such as a new type of product that does not have any history of customer demand – and he has to make the decisions himself, based on information provided by the system.

Beyond these lower-level decisions, information systems can play a critical role in supply chain planning and strategic decisions in sourcing and supply (the last two activities in the list). For example, a company has to decide on the technologies that it will require for the next generation of products, and identify the supply base, long-term forecasts of demand, capacity requirements and projected cash flows. Then information systems support strategic decision making. They include sophisticated tools to analyse patterns and relationships in the data, and they manipulate and present data in different ways that correspond to the strategic question of interest. They look into the future and plot the long-term consequences of current decisions. Such systems are generally referred to as decision support systems (DSSs), with the name emphasizing that they support, but do not make, management decisions.

To understand the role of information systems in a supply chain, we have to consider not only the level of functionality, but also the direction of the flows. For example, some information flows from an organization to its customers, and these are broadly referred to as customer relationship management flows: and some information flows from an organization to its suppliers, and these are broadly referred to as supplier relationship management flows (illustrated in Figure 17.2). The third type of information flow links higher-level planning and decision making to lower-level activities within a firm, giving the internal SCM flows (Chopra and Meindl, 2004).

A map of SCM systems

The 'map' of SCM systems shown in Figure 17.3 was described by Kahl (1999) and refined by Chopra and Meindl (2004). It distinguishes various applications by the level of functionality (strategic, planning, tactical, routine and transactional) and the direction of links (to suppliers, internal supply chain and to customers). The column of 'logistics' information refers to broad issues in logistics such as determining warehouse locations, optimizing transport systems, and controlling the movement of materials between supply chain partners.

FIGURE 17.2

Flows of information

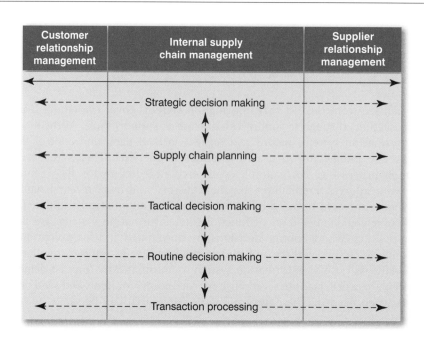

FIGURE 17.3 Areas covered by SCM systems

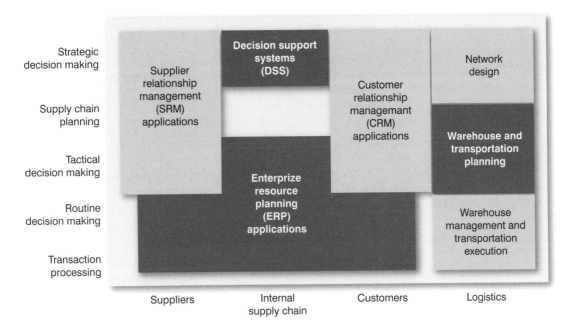

FIGURE 17.4 ERP Systems

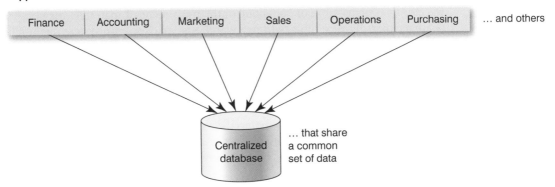

Enterprise Resource Planning (ERP) systems have a central role in this map, and although they come in many forms, they are characterized as large, integrated transaction processing and reporting systems. The primary advantage of ERP is that it pulls together all business functions of accounting, finance, sales, operations, marketing, etc., into a single integrated package that uses a common database (shown in Figure 17.4). To understand why this is so important, you have to consider the alternative. This has every business function with its own software, often running on completely different systems. It is notoriously difficult to share information (perhaps about demand forecasts, customers, suppliers, production plans, etc.) between systems, and it may have to be entered separately into each application.

ERP pulls together different functions, but its strength is in routine decisions and transaction processing, and its scope is largely limited to internal operations. In contrast, SRM and CRM focus directly on managing external links, with Figure 17.5

> Enterprise resource planning (ERP)
> Integrates the flow of information through various business functions.

FIGURE 17.5

SRM/CRM applications

SRM applications	CRM applications
Design collaboration	Market analysis
Sourcing decisions	Sell process
Negotiations	Order management
Buy process	Call/service centre management
Supply collaboration	

giving examples of the types of functions available in these applications (Chopra and Meindl, 2004).

The external focus of CRM and SRM systems use a different approach to ERP, but the major ERP vendors, such as SAP and Oracle, now routinely include all three elements in their systems (which we discuss later in the chapter).

Our map of SCM systems includes three types of 'logistic' applications: network design, warehouse and transport planning and execution.

Network design. addresses such long-term, strategic questions as where to locate warehouses, and how large our transport fleet should be. To find the optimal answers, the system would include some kind of optimizing models and simulation.

Warehouse and transport planning. attempts to allocate logistics capacity in the best possible way. For example, a system could help decide how many units to ship from each warehouse to each demand point. To find the optimal answer, the system would again include some kind of optimizing models that analyse data on warehouse capacities, demand levels, shipping costs, etc.

Execution systems. initiate and control the movement of materials between supply chain partners. For example, within a warehouse an execution system might tell staff where to store items, where to pick them up and how many to pick. Barcodes, magnetic strips, RFID, global positioning and other tracking technology have dramatically changed these operations.

These decisions are important, but in practice there may be surprisingly little integration between them and other areas in the map. The result is unco-ordinated decisions, such as orders for materials made without considering their broader impact. For example, buyers might order materials whenever asked, but without considering the shipping cost – typically giving many small, expensive shipments.

LEARNING FROM PRACTICE

Rolls-Royce

Rolls-Royce is one of the world's leading manufacturers of high-quality jet engines. The company continually updates its range of engines, with a major concern of improving fuel efficiency. New engines are based on advances in design, materials and manufacturing technologies.

Rolls-Royce suppliers have to get the raw materials that they need to make components, including titanium and nickel alloys which are in short supply. Some critical suppliers are smaller specialty manufacturers who do not buy enough volume to have any priority with alloy providers. But if they cannot secure

Source: Securing the future at Rolls-Royce, Case Study, 2007; www.newview.com

the raw materials, then Rolls-Royce customers such as Airbus and Boeing do not receive their engines.

In 2003 Rolls-Royce began an overhaul of its raw material supply chain. The e-sourcing tool, called Material Specification Management, was implemented in 2006 and enables the company to manage the flow of critical raw materials. Benefits of the system include the ability to:

- Understand the total supply chain's material needs
- Generate co-ordinated schedules for tiers of suppliers
- Control material flows
- Identify bottlenecks and work to avoid them
- Help with sourcing decisions
- Measure exposure to material price volatility.

In the past Rolls-Royce only had a rough idea of how much material its suppliers needed to meet their demands for parts. Now a forecasting module estimates the amount of material required at different tiers of suppliers to produce every part for every engine in the production plan – giving visibility of material requirements. This allows managers to check the effects of any price changes on individual engine parts, and hence the final engine. Material price increases can be offset by improved materials management. For example, a key material price increase might be offset by buyers increasing their volume of purchases, or improvements to the transaction processing.

Rolls-Royce have now developed electronic parts and materials catalogues. They can use these to define material specifications and preferred suppliers at every point in the supply chain, and they can capture suppliers' purchasing histories to see how closely they adhere to these recommendations. This allows Rolls-Royce to control sourcing decisions back through the tiers of suppliers, ensuring that its quality requirements are met.

DRIVERS OF NEW SUPPLY CHAIN SYSTEMS

Managers continually look for ways of improving performance, and new information systems offer many opportunities. However, new technology alone does not guarantee benefits, as illustrated by the bursting of the 'dot.com bubble' in the late 1990s. So managers have to be very careful in developing a solid business case for investments in new e-SCM systems, justifying the benefits and carefully analysing the costs. However, there are several key drivers that move organizations inexorably towards new e-SCM systems.

Internal and external strategic integration. As supply chain members increasingly work together, integration must occur between different functions within an organization (purchasing, engineering, operations, marketing, logistics, accounting, etc.), and between external parties (end customers, third-party logistics firms, retailers, distributors, warehouses, transport providers, suppliers, agents, financial institutions, etc.). Both types of integration present challenges. For instance, internal integration requires everyone within an organization to use the same integrated information system. As we have seen, this can be accomplished with an ERP system that links all internal groups. External integration is even more complicated as it needs information shared between diverse organizations. This can be achieved by extensions to the core ERP system, internet links, network communications and e-sourcing. With integrated supply chain systems, one member updating their own system can be a signal for others to follow suit.

Globalization and communication. The idea of a global market is easy to imagine, but actually carrying out business in different cultures and geographies is extremely difficult. Organizations need more sophisticated systems that enable them to manage suppliers and customers in all parts of the world, calculate total global costs, consolidate material flows, standardize materials, improve communications and do all the other things needed to work with global partners.

Data information management. New technology for servers, telecommunication, wireless applications and software are enabling organizations to develop entirely new types of operation. These systems can do many things, including raise the accuracy, frequency and speed of communications. There is now so much information available that systems must be able to effectively sort, filter, analyse and present relevant information.

New business processes. Business processes are constantly being changed to give better performance in a rapidly changing business environment. For purchasing, such processes include supplier evaluation and selection, negotiation, contracting, co-design efforts and inventory management – and they are being analysed, studied and adjusted to remove waste. Flexible organizations respond quickly to changing conditions, and use their agility to gain a competitive advantage.

Replacement of legacy systems. People become familiar with systems, and are often reluctant to invest the considerable effort into learning about new ones. Because of such resistance – and the desire to avoid single large investments – organizations often update systems in a piecemeal way. Then some functions or groups continue to use their old systems, while others use new ones. The old obsolete systems – called legacy systems – should be integrated into the new system. However the two are often incompatible, and then the old systems should simply be replaced.

Strategic cost management. Normal operations in a complex organization involves thousands or even millions of routine information transactions. Related systems automatically capture data throughout supply chains, and they can analyse these to reduce the costs of operations. As more sophisticated systems appear, the capture and analysis of cost – and other – information become more refined, identifying areas for improvement and further cost reductions.

In the remainder of this chapter, we describe the features of four primary types of information system used by procurement:

1   Enterprize resource planning.

2   Purchasing databases and data warehouses.

3   Electronic data interchange.

4   E-sourcing applications.

ENTERPRIZE RESOURCE PLANNING

We have already introduced the idea of ERP, which integrates transaction processing and reporting across functions and locations. There are some different opinions about what exactly is involved with ERP, but we take the view that it gives a single integrated information system throughout an organization. It enables people in very different parts of the business to communicate with each other – in fact it adds a structure to the information flows that effectively forces people to work together. It tracks resources – including people, processes, materials, equipment, money and technology – providing the information and support needed for informed decisions.

Figure 17.6 shows that ERP connects the related areas of customer order management, operations planning and execution, purchasing and financial management and accounting. You can imagine the basic workings of a system, with a sales representative entering customer orders into a company's system via a laptop with access to modules for sales order planning, administration, master production schedule and related modules. Once the orders into the system, the sales representative can tell customers when they will get the delivery. The sale is noted by an operations planning module which may adjust the master production schedule. This, in turn, drives the material requirements system, which automatically generates purchase orders to ensure that suppliers deliver parts, components and services in time to produce the customer's order. When suppliers deliver the materials, this information is passed to the scheduling module, which ensures that the components are linked to the specific production order, and to the inventory management module which controls their internal movements. Once production begins, the salesperson is told that the order will soon be delivered to the customer. Once delivered, customer billing and payment are automatically controlled by the ERP system.

The idea of having a single information system that links all functions seems obvious, but in the past individual systems were designed to meet the specific requirements of each function. They were not linked together because of technical difficulties (it was difficult to design large, integrated systems and get them to work properly) and also because of organizational reasons (different functions had different requirements). There were also problems with legacy systems that had not been updated. The result was fragmented information – followed by fragmented decisions.

ERP systems come in different forms, but a common approach has them designed around four primary business processes (identified in Figure 17.6):

1   Selling a product, with customer order management modules.

2   Making a product, with operations planning and execution modules.

FIGURE 17.6 Enterprize resource planning systems

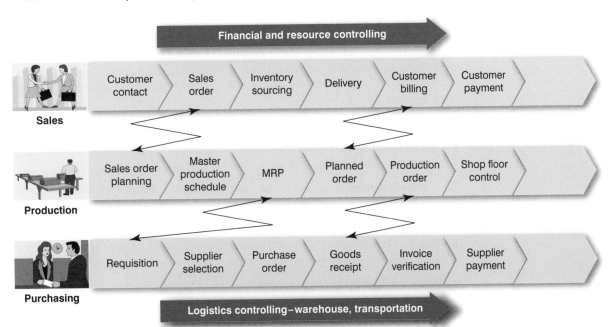

3 Buying a product, with procurement modules.

4 Collecting money and paying bills, with financial management modules.

ERP systems facilitate the integration of these processes through a single customer, product and supplier database. Information is captured only once with standard templates, reducing the chance of inaccurate data entering the database. Then it is processed and transmitted to relevant parts of the business in real-time, eliminating delays in sharing information. Every transaction in each business process is visible and accessible to everyone concerned, so anyone who wants specific information (such as where an order is in the process, or whether a supplier has been paid) can immediately see the latest position. One set of master records is used for the whole enterprize with multiple views.

Implementing ERP systems

The task of implementing an ERP system in an organization where people are accustomed to using their single, familiar legacy systems, has often proved to be monumental. Many implementation efforts have grown into huge projects costing millions of pounds and spread over years.

The basic problem is that the ERP systems are themselves hugely complicated, so getting one installed and working properly is always a major undertaking. The system is, by definition, built around a set of integrated business processes, so before implementation can actually start, managers must have detailed descriptions of every process and the way they work together. The best way of doing this is to use some kind of process charts (Waters, 2002). At this point, managers have a series of maps of how they believe a process works, but they often discover that the real process is quite different from their idea. Sometimes there is actually no formal process, because everyone does a task in their own way. Sometimes the process has just evolved over time. But creating of a set of process charts that actually describe what happens is an essential step in defining the information flows and a system that can provide them.

Describing the current processes is only one step, as managers do not want to install an ERP system around inefficient business processes. Once ERP is installed it defines operations, at least to some extent, so these operations should be efficient. So the next step for managers is to examine the process charts and look for ways of improving the underlying operations, either through adjustments or radical re-engineering. This itself can be a major undertaking that needs organizational and cultural changes.

At this point you can see that implementing an ERP system has four steps:

1 Define the current processes. An ERP implementation team documents the current processes using a variety of process charts and related tools.

2 Design improved processes. The team must have a clear picture of the current processes and their weaknesses, and design improvements that will work better with ERP.

3 Design the ERP system. This is often an iterative process in which the implementation team work with everyone concerned to give a system that meet their requirements.

4 Solve any teething problems and implement the final system. Obvious dangers when switching over from old systems to the new ERP one are that the organization is not properly prepared for the changes, and that the system may not work faultlessly when handling specific activities.

LEARNING FROM PRACTICE

Abide Consulting

Abide Consulting has worked with several organizations to assist in the transition from disparate legacy systems to integrated ERP systems. They have developed an approach to ERP implementation which has seven stages: (1) discovery (2) design (3) system build (4) testing (5) end-user training (6) switchover and (7) post-switchover support.

In the discovery phase, a core team is assembled from both internal and external staff, with knowledge of the areas where ERP is being implemented (for example, operations, inventory management, finance, sourcing). Training sessions reinforce the objectives of the project, schedule, organization, budget, new software functionality and so on. The team then begins a detailed analysis of existing business processes. This includes issues of data integrity (consistency of data within or across systems) and data quality (accuracy and completeness of data). Data delivery can be overlooked, and one company discovered on the first day that its new ERP system went live that the finished product weight data were missing. Then weights for shipping manifests could not be calculated, and outward shipments were brought to a standstill. Trucks and product sat idle in the shipping docks for days until the issue was resolved.

In the design stage, new processes needed to support the ERP are developed and process flow maps are created. Any process requiring IT involvement is documented into functional specifications to show what the ERP system should achieve. These allow a gap analysis to find difference between the existing information supplies and those needed by the new ERP system. Once the core team has identified and resolved these gaps, it can define and document the detail scope of the ERP solution required.

In the third 'build' stage, the IT team takes a larger role. Various modules of the system are established and configured with functional parameters and customized business data. Any re-programming is completed and the IT team completes the initial development of the system.

A typical testing stage involves several iterations of tests to each module, followed by tests with historical information, 'conference room pilots', 'scripts' to isolate specific factors and so on. If these tests are successful then an 'integrated conference room pilot' is performed to rigorously test the whole business process. Key users of the system from all functional areas use the system for training and to test their own parts of the system (referred to as 'user acceptance testing'). This is 'training the trainers' as these key users spread information about the new system and show everyone else how to use it.

The switchover phase enables the organization to take ownership of the ERP system and actually use it. Throughout the development, the organization must have internal champions who support the project and drive the implementation. The new system involves changing people's behaviour, and this needs continuing management support. Users, customers and suppliers are contacted to ensure that any outstanding issues have been addressed, and then the old systems are switched off and the new ones start. Almost inevitably some unplanned issues immediately surface, but contingency plans should have been made well in advance to limit problems (typically including temporary safety stocks, or extra staff on key operations).

In the last stage, the core implementation team resolves any problems (such as software failures, or adjustments to operations). Then they monitor progress to make sure that the system works as expected, and they continue to make adjustments and improvements.

Several factors are likely to enhance the chances of a successful ERP implementation, including:

- Develop a good understanding of the existing business processes
- Make improvements to processes for the future
- Identify inconsistencies and poor quality in existing data
- Ensure that business processes conform to ERP system parameters
- Insist that users replace legacy systems
- Stagger implementations of ERP systems across business locations
- Schedule the switchover to occur in off-peak seasons
- Determine how much additional safety stock and other resources are temporarily needed
- Develop and train a core team of internal staff
- Perform rigorous and structured testing

Source: Personal interviews.

PURCHASING DATABASES AND DATA WAREHOUSES

A prerequisite for introducing ERP is a reliable database – which is an integrated collection of computer files capable of storing the data needed by managers. It is a single, integrated store that collects data from many sources and makes it available to users. The aim of a database is to give efficient storage, updating and retrieval of data, with no duplication or redundancy. You can see the benefit of this by considering a company with data held separately by production and marketing departments; combining data from these into a database may allow insights into the effects of marketing campaigns that would not be evident from either system alone.

Although definitions vary, a data warehouse is generally thought of as a decision support tool for collecting information from multiple sources and making that information available to end users in a consolidated, consistent manner. The need for this arose as organizations began to develop multiple databases, often containing duplicate data. This clearly does not conform to the essential feature of a database – as a single store of organizational data. However, the idea of a data warehouse grew as a means of combining data from all sources in one place and making it available to all of the systems. In most cases, a data warehouse is actually a consolidated database maintained separately from other databases used within the organization.

Purchasing processes need a variety of information from a database or data warehouse, including at least the following:

- **Part number.** The part number that identifies and describes each of the thousands of items that a firm uses

- **Design requirements.** Detailed requirements and specifications for each part number, including quality, tolerances, changes, etc.

- **Supplier name and address.** The names, addresses, contact details and all other relevant details about every supplier that a firm does business with

- **Historical usage.** Information about the past use of items by part number, using location, product used for and so on

- **Production plans.** What the firm tends to make over some period, which determines the needs for parts, storage, purchases, etc.

- **Bill of material.** A structured list of the materials needed to make each product. This is a key requirement for material requirements planning, and links production schedules to purchasing requirements

- **Forecast demand.** Anticipated demand for each item, by location, use, etc. This is based on historical usage data and production plans to forecast future requirements

- **Stock position.** Giving the location, amount, status and related information about all units that a firm has available

- **Pending delivery and overdue due orders.** The status of all material orders that have been placed, and describes them as pending until they are actually received and accepted. Orders not received by their due date become overdue and need expediting

Source: Mitchell P. (2007) Top 10 emerging technologies in procurement, Conference Board Procurement Technologies Conference.

LEARNING FROM PRACTICE

Emerging technologies

Pierre Mitchell of the Hackett Group identified the following 10 emerging technologies for supply management.

1 *Customer relationship management* – to help supply managers better serve their customers. It can include a range of tools that include project management, customer self-service, training, service-level agreements, customer satisfaction measurement and any other methods that help supply managers align their activities to customer requirements.

2 *Guided buying* – a tool that combines ERP and e-purchasing with virtual catalogues, search engines and web agents to guide buyers to preferred sources of supply, and related preferred sourcing procedures.

3 *Advanced supply planning* – links sales and operations plans to supply management. This translates downstream demand into upstream delivery plans across multiple tiers of the supply chain, thereby improving risk analysis, decisions on hedging, avoidance of bottlenecks and other supply trade-offs.

4 *Win-win sourcing optimization* – allows suppliers to better match their capabilities with those of buyers to create more opportunities for both parties to benefit.

5 *Design for supply* – provides a set of tools to manage early design and sourcing. It allows better re-use of existing designs, evaluation of new or alternative designs and the ability to assess the cost of designs on upstream suppliers.

6 *Content-enabled analytics* – are decision support tools that marry internal supply planning processes with external supplier and market data. They allow supply managers to do predictive analyses such as price and cost forecasting, profitability planning and associated risk analysis.

7 *Portfolio management* – periodically assesses the software tools and packages that are used by suppliers. Older software packages and those no longer being used are discontinued, upgrades are installed and future needs are evaluated for acquisition.

8 *Knowledge networking* – is the use of internet-based collaboration tools to capture and disseminate supply knowledge. It shares knowledge of items, procedures, suppliers and best practices with the supply chain community.

9 *Open systems e-tools* – allow internal and external technology providers to provide supply managers with quickly-developed, customized applications that work with software from independent vendors.

10 *Software as a service* – on-demand software that is provided through an internet service. This is being driven by customers' needs for cheaper and more easily upgradable applications, putting pressure on software vendors to provide more cost-effective and modularized solutions.

TECHNOLOGY FOR ELECTRONIC COMMUNICATION

We have emphasized the flows of information within an organization, but purchasing must clearly communicate with external suppliers for:

- Product specifications
- Supplier's bid and terms

- Negotiation and agreement to a contract

- Scheduling of operations and delivery details

- Documentation of product shipment and acceptance

- Accounting audits and billing

- Submission of payment

- Any other information that has to be exchanged

Traditionally, these exchanges of information were slow, inaccurate due to data-handling errors, using excess staff time, expensive and uncertain because of processing and transmission delays. Now, most companies speed-up the process by using the internet, but there are several other technologies that allow purchasing to communicate effectively with external suppliers.

Electronic data interchange

EDI defined a communication's standard which means that users in remote locations, using different systems can transfer information seamlessly between their computers. Since the 1980s, EDI allows sellers – and ultimately buyers – to become more competitive by streamlining communications, eliminating many of the steps involved in traditional information flows. The components of an EDI system include:

- *A standard form (EDI standards)* – include the basic rules of formatting and syntax agreed upon by users in the network

- *A translation capability (EDI software)* – translates company-specific database information into EDI standard format for transmission

- *A mail service (EDI network)* – responsible for the transmission of the document. This forms a connection between the two computers, and in the simplest case can be a telephone line

We can illustrate the typical process that occurs when a buyer and supplier go through an EDI transaction as follows:

1 The inventory management system in a buying company monitors the use of materials using RFID, bar codes, magnetic strips, etc.

2 When stocks of an item fall to a predefined level, the computer recognizes the need to buy more and it creates a purchase order.

3 EDI translation software converts this into EDI form and sends it to the supplier.

4 The supplier's computer receives the order and the EDI software translates the order into the supplier's format.

5 An acknowledgment indicating receipt of the order, is automatically generated and transmitted back to the buyer.

6 When the original EDI purchase order is created, a number of other electronic transactions may occur, transmitting relevant data to the buyer's accounts payable system, to the buyer's receiving file, to the supplier's raw materials inventory file, to the supplier's invoicing file and so on.

7   Once the ordered items have been assembled by the supplier, documents needed to accompany the products are created and a shipping notice is transmitted to the buyer.

8   When the products are received and accepted by the customer, a receipt notice is entered into the receiving file.

9   The receipt notice is also passed to the accounts payable system and to the supplier's invoicing system, at which point an invoice is generated and transmitted to the buyer.

10   Once the invoice is received by the buyer's system, it is translated into the buyer's format and the invoice, receiving notice and purchase order are electronically reconciled.

11   Assuming there are no problems, a payment authorization is electronically created and transmitted to accounts payable, the receivables system is updated, and payment is transferred using EFT from the buyer's bank account to the supplier's.

12   An electronic remittance advice is transmitted to the supplier, and upon receipt, this information is translated into accounts receivable and the buyer is given credit for payment.

EDI and the internet

The problem with this early form of EDI is that it needed a significant investment by companies in dedicated hardware and specialized software. Smaller suppliers found it particularly difficult to justify this investment and they struggled with demands from different companies to adopt differing EDI systems. EDI was never considered an interactive form of communication – each transmission was like normal mail, and signalled the next step in a procedure, but there was no means for buyers and suppliers to exchange ideas in real-time. This problem has now been overcome by the internet.

The WorldWideWeb is a huge network with standard protocols that allow all computers to communicate with each other via telephone lines, optical fibres or radio links. Organizations publish websites that can be viewed by anyone, but for purchasing the key element is B2B (business-to-business) transactions that can be done in private. Figure 17.7 shows how the internet allows organizations to collaborate through a virtual private network (VPN). This VPN is hosted on a third-party's website and server, and does not need any significant investment by either a buyer or supplier.

When you use the internet, you are not aware of any of the electronic activities that are going on in the background. However, they are quite complicated, as you can imagine with a supplier who wants to notify a customer that it is shipping an order. Then a local internet service provider (ISP) has to create a virtual private tunnel through the web using tunnelling protocols (essentially the rules that allow different systems to work together). Using this protocol, data are transferred over the internet from the supplier to the customer's router, which strips off the tunnelling protocols and forwards the message (typically through a local area network) to the right individual.

The internet is clearly an important tool that brings numerous benefits. It is almost universally available, inexpensive and has few compatibility or standards issues. To enhance its internet use, firms can buy e-sourcing tools, which are used by buyers to use technology effectively and streamline processes (Antonette *et al.*, 2002). For instance, SRM and CRM are e-sourcing tools that allow firms to manage

FIGURE 17.7

Internet EDI with virtual
private network

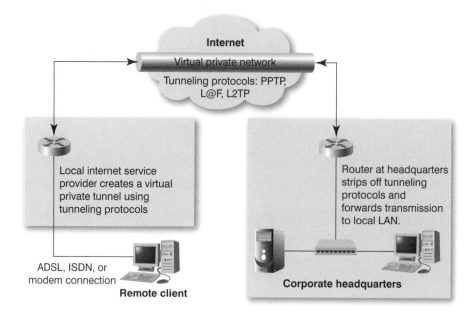

external links with suppliers and customers. However, the internet's true benefits go far beyond basic communications, as it allows buyers and suppliers to achieve greater levels of collaboration and adopt completely new methods of working.

LEARNING FROM PRACTICE

Palniak SGH

On a Wednesday afternoon, Pietro Perlinkso walked into a Palniak SGH store in Prague and bought himself a new white shirt. He paid with a debit card, so the EPOS system initiated the transfer of money from Pietro's bank account to the store's. It also contacted the company's purchasing system, giving details of the shirt requesting a replacement be delivered.

If the shirt had been something unusual, the purchasing system would have used its direct links to their local supplier's production system. This would have scheduled the production of a replacement shirt in its flexible manufacturing facilities, and told the store when it would be delivered. However, the demand for plain white shirts is more stable, and they are made in the Philippines. So the store's EPOS system sent a message directly to the supplier in Manila to add another white shirt to their next scheduled delivery. On Thursday, the supplier had packed a replacement shirt into a shipment for central Europe. This delivery could have been sent by ship to a European port and then onwards by road or rail. However, the delivery to Palniak's store would then have taken several weeks, and there would be a lot of stock tied-up in the pipeline. Instead, the supplier took the shipment to the nearby airport, where it was flown directly to Prague, with a local transport company collecting the shipment from the airport and delivering it directly to Palniak's store.

It seems expensive as airfreight can be 10 times as expensive as shipping. However, this approach removes all the stock from the distribution system (along with its damage, obsolescence and loss), removes the need for warehouses in central Europe, dramatically reduces the amount of handling, allows stores to respond quickly to customers' demands and gives more flexibility in production schedules. Both Palniak and the supplier agree that the benefits far outweigh the additional transport costs.

Source: Based on Wisniek P. (2008) B2B in central Europe, CMNP Resources, Prague.

E-SOURCING

E-sourcing systems include any system that has some element of electronic communication – generally through the internet – to assist procurement. There are three basic types of e-sourcing systems (Antonette *et al.*, 2002):

1 **Sell-side systems** – where websites describe the products of one or more suppliers, and an administrator who guarantees security. Customer register to use the site (which is usually free) and make their purchases. This is the common pattern where most suppliers have websites and allow customers to place orders on them. Sell-side systems have the advantages of needing no investment by the buyer, ease of access and the availability of many suppliers. Drawbacks include the inability to track or control spending by the buyer and questions of security.

2 **Buy-side systems** – where buyers set up websites to describe their requirements and interactions with suppliers in a secure environment. The sites are tied into local networks, so that buyers can manage their purchasing, track spending and control contract management. These are the dominant form of e-sourcing by major companies. Unfortunately, they have the disadvantage of needing an investment by the buying organization – along with training and maintenance of websites.

3 **Third-party marketplaces** – are websites run by independent firms that neither buy nor sell themselves, but provide systems that facilitate electronic purchasing by others. Essentially, these systems are electronic marketplaces that bring buyers and sellers together in cyberspace – the way that eBay has worked for consumers. The e-markets usually specialize in certain industries or types of products. For instance, one might specialize in a commodity such as steel or oil products – giving 'vertical portals'. Another might offer a broader range, such as office supplies or MRO items – giving 'horizontal portals'. In practice, the value of horizontal portals faded as traditional businesses developed their own websites (such as officedepot.com and tesco.com). While some specialized vertical portals have survived by providing expertise and added value, many have simply been taken over by their former customers.

Supplier relationship management

We have already mentioned the purpose of SRM in managing relationships with suppliers. These systems are typically organized around modules that interact with the purchasing database, ERP system, data obtained through external EDI and data from internet-based communications. They analyse the available data and use structured models to support purchasing decisions – perhaps improving supplier selection, contract management, contract compliance and so on.

SRM modules come in many forms, but typically include the following features:

Spend analysis – investigates an organization' expenditure on its purchases. Spend analysis monitor the goods and services bought, which suppliers they are purchased from, where the demand for the items originates in the organization, how much they cost and all related factors. Once a baseline for spending is established, managers can look for opportunities of reducing this, perhaps through consolidation of purchases, reduction in the number of suppliers, elimination of maverick spending, reduction in spending by other departments (such as human resources, marketing and finance), introduction of more efficient contracting methods, reducing risk and increasing supply security. So the approach to a spend analysis:

- Collects at least one year of spending data

- Describes different categories of spending

- Assigns spending to the categories

- Develops plans for reducing the spending

Sourcing – usually including several phases of the sourcing process, including the following.

- **RFQ –** including a request for information, RFP and RFQ. This module helps to identify qualified suppliers to receive RFQ requests. Then it automatically generates, issues and tracks the progress of the RFQs throughout the system

- **E-bid optimization** – extends the traditional bid process to allows suppliers to configure their bids in any number of different ways. Traditionally, suppliers had to submit quotations in the format specified by the buyer; e-bid optimization increases buyers' analytical capabilities enabling them to review bids in different formats. Then suppliers can submit bids in formats that emphasize their strengths

- **Reverse auctions –** are internet processes where multiple sellers of a product are vying for the business of a single buyer, and bidding continues until a pre-established bidding period ends or until no seller is willing to bid any lower. This can significantly reduce the price paid, but suppliers claim that buyers only consider price and forget all the other non-price benefits

  In an open reverse auction, prices are revealed to all sellers, but the identity of the bidders remains anonymous. In a rank auction, sellers are only told their relative rank and not their competitors' bids. A closed auction shows less information, typically saying only that a bid is winning, or it is not. However they are organized, it is critical for reverse auctions to be integrated within the broader sourcing process. Buyers need to prepare properly for the process, which loosely follows these steps (Handfield *et al.*, 2002):

  1 The purchasing company decides which products would benefit from a reverse auction.

  2 Suppliers are initially evaluated and invited to participate in the bidding process. This includes existing suppliers, along with potential suppliers that have been researched and approved.

  3 The company writes a RFQ and sends it by email to the qualified suppliers. Accompanying the RFQ is all relevant information such as when and where the bidding will take place, along with auctioning rules and etiquette.

  4 The bidding process begins at a specified time and usually lasts no more than 30 minutes. The suppliers' identities are always kept confidential.

  5 The company analyses the auction results, chooses the suppliers and awards the business. The winner is not necessarily the lowest bidder.

Reverse auction technology is readily available in different formats. At one extreme sources are self-service systems that are downloaded from a software company and then the buyer organizes and runs the auction itself. At the other extreme are full-service systems, where a company provides websites for the auction, build a list of potential suppliers, gives training, runs the auction, organizes deliveries and generally does all the associated administration.

- **Negotiation and total cost models –** help buyers estimate the total cost of ownership of products, and provide platforms for negotiations that affect this

- **Issuing purchase orders** – generates purchase orders, along with the transfer of purchase order information to the necessary databases

- **Receiving and inspection –** updates system records upon receipt of an item. Most systems hold delivered items in a protected state (unavailable for use) until all related processing is complete, including checking against expected deliveries, inspections, updating databases, material transfer, etc.

Contract management and compliance. This monitors the back-end of the sourcing process. Once a supplier is selected and the contract terms agreed, operations must be monitored to ensure that both the supplier and purchaser are complying with the

Source: Pearcy D., Giunipero L. and Wilson A. (2007) A model of relational governance in reverse auctions, Journal of Supply Chain Management, Winter, pp 4–15.

LEARNING FROM PRACTICE

Reverse auctions

Reverse auctions have been used for sourcing since the mid-1990s led by websites such as the pioneering FreeMarkets. Suddenly, buyers had a new tool to establish prices during the bidding cycle, with bidding organized in a secure, online environment within a specified time and with the goal of obtaining a real market price for an item. It was advertized as an efficient way of selecting a supplier and awarding business.

Despite its benefits, managers have expressed concern about how reverse auctions affect buyer-supplier relationships. The main fear is the message that buyers are only interested in lower prices without any regard to existing or future business relationships, thereby removing any chance of trust and co-operation. However, a survey of 142 purchasing managers suggests that firms which place greater importance on buyer-seller relationships should make the offer and execution stages of reverse auctions independent. In the offer phase, carefully explaining the rules to potential bidders before the auction starts can increase the chances of a successful result. The auction determines the successful bidder and then a separate process starts negotiating an appropriate form of contract and developing a working relationship.

An important point is that purchasers must evaluate the strategic importance of their existing supplier relationship before using a reverse auction. If there is already a successful long-term relationship then a reverse auction may be the wrong way to go. Closer working relationships and the level of co-operation from a supplier depend, at least in part, on its expectation of continuing business.

Strong relationships certainly bring many advantages, but they do not encourage price reductions. If an organization puts a high priority on reducing costs, then a reverse auction is more effective than developing or maintaining relationships. So firms must balance the benefits of lower prices (that may or may not be sustainable) against the potential benefits from non-price-related areas.

The reality is that when they put in the effort, organizations can use reverse auctions and still develop business relationships. If the time savings from reverse auctions are used to build improved relationships – which ultimately lead to lower overall costs, better service and higher quality – then both parties win. On the other hand, if the purchaser uses reverse auctions only to reduce prices, this will be at the expense of supplier co-operation. While much of the time saved will be needed to monitor the supplier's performance to ensure that savings are actually realized. Overall, the long-term benefits from better relationships generally outweigh temporary reductions in purchase price.

terms. Other tasks done by the module might include pricing compliance, changes in terms, volume discount thresholds, payment schedules, due dates and contingencies for non-performance.

Supplier performance measurement and control. This shows the status of items currently being purchased, and analyses supplier performance. It should monitor planned receipts against due dates, thereby showing the status of all deliveries and highlighting those that are either overdue or likely to become so. Then the system should generate reports of supplier performance including reliability, quality, price variances, extra costs, quantity discrepancies and all the other issues.

Total cost reporting. Which generate timely management reports, increasing visibility of the whole procurement process. These reports rely on accurate and current data, so the best results come with real-time records which are automatically updated whenever a transaction occurs. (The alternative uses data buckets, where a process stores information about each transaction in a temporary file and updates the system with a batch of transactions at scheduled times throughout the day.) This module can also do price forecasting, which identifies the factors that affect an item's price (including the length of the item's life cycle, the item's current point in the life cycle, price history, changes in the environment, etc.) and uses these to forecast likely future prices and consequent effects on budgets.

FULLY INTEGRATED SYSTEMS

We have discussed ERP as a way of integrating the various functions and connecting them with consolidated supply of information. Part of this is e-sourcing, which uses the consolidated data to help organize the buying of materials. But it would be a mistake to think that all systems are integrated. The reality is that even when ERP is implemented it may work independently of the e-procurement systems.

In the future, there will undoubtedly be an increased level of integration in these systems, and a convergence of customer-focussed applications that link suppliers seamlessly with internal operations. The requirements of production plants are consolidated and passed backwards to suppliers through a supply module, and forward to customers through a demand module. Then sales representatives can promise exact delivery dates to customers by accessing production schedules and assigning the next unallocated units available. They can check supplier status to check that they are able to deliver the materials needed to meet the schedule.

Another aspect of integration is the use of systems that facilitate transactions between buyers and sellers. For instance, a distribution planning module will identify the transport needs and logistics centre stocks needed to meet customers' deliveries. A demand planning module will check that long-term capacity is sufficient to meet the demand for new products coming from sales systems. A supplier collaboration module will ensure that supplier capacity is in place to meet future demands before they occur. In effect, these linked systems will give access to information about the entire supply chain. Then managers can examine any part, synchronize demand and supply, solve problems and allow smooth, efficient operations.

Such completely integrated systems are technically feasible, but it is fair to say that few firms have made much progress in this direction (Waters, 2007). On the whole, firms have some limited idea of operations in their main first tier suppliers and customers, and virtually no knowledge of the rest of the supply chain. However, integration is a major management theme, and it will undoubtedly increase in the future. An important prerequisite for this integration is information visibility.

Information visibility

Information visibility within a supply chain is achieved by sharing critical data needed to manage the flow of materials. In other words, information available to one member of the chain is made available to all other members. If information is available somewhere in a supply chain but cannot be accessed by people that have to use it, the information has no real value. Information visibility has integrated systems supplying information to everyone who has to use it, and this can help all members of the chain work more efficiently and effectively.

To improve visibility, firms are introducing – or at least exploring the potential of – ways to share information across multiple tiers of their supply chains. Various methods are being considered for moves in this direction, such as business process optimization, and collaborative planning, forecasting and replenishment. Using such methods allows traditional supply chains to evolve into 'dynamic trading networks' (Cole *et al.*, 1999) which consist of groups of independent business units that share planning and execution information to satisfy demand final customer demand.

Of course, introducing visible information needs a lot of effort, and some basic considerations include the size of the supply base and customer base with which to share information, the information shared and the technology used to share it.

Benefits of Information Visibility

Information about forecasts, changes in production schedules, ongoing supply chain performance and a whole range of other information should regularly be passed by customers to suppliers. Information flows from suppliers to customers should include current order lead times, capacity levels, order status and inventory levels. There are many benefits of sharing this kind of information – essentially ensuring that suppliers are aware of what needs to be produced, while buyers know that their orders will be receive as ordered.

Information visibility typically gives the following benefits:

- It does not correct a supply chain problem, but it identifies a problem and makes everyone aware of it in time to take corrective action, and before the problem grows bigger. This reduces the likelihood, impact and costs of potential problems

- Breaks down organizational barriers and enables sharing of critical information about business activities on a real-time basis across the supply chain

- Gives managers a real-time view of supply chain performance

- Uses common performance measures for all processes, with material flows co-ordinated to achieve these measures

- Assigns ownership of operations to identifiable individuals

- Reduces the time for decisions and allows all members to respond quickly to changing conditions

- Encourages collaboration and the inclusion of relevant internal and external stakeholders

- More efficient flows of materials reduce lead times, lower stocks, improve supply chain velocity, reduce wastage – and generally lower costs and increase profits

LEARNING FROM PRACTICE

Dell

Few other companies have been as successful in implementing information visibility as Dell Computers. Although they have since adjusted their operations, Dell pioneered an innovative and flexible approach to production which meant that they could hold only hours of stock yet build and deliver tailored machines for customers within 5 days.

Dell's operations feature lean, build-to-order manufacturing. By widely using the web, Dell collects information from its customers, adjusts its production plans and makes this information available to its suppliers in real-time. The information provided includes details of all requirements, and in return Dell receives information from suppliers that include their ability to

meet the demands. Communication about design changes, component availability, capacity, forecast updates, stock levels and a range of other relevant details flows between Dell and its suppliers.

The original incentive for Dell to develop its model of flexible, customized production was to achieve the benefits of both high customer satisfaction and low costs. But after outsourcing some production to third-party manufacturers, Dell realized that the manufacturers did not have enough information visibility to work efficiently, so this became a major driver of increased visibility. The resulting build-to-order web-based customer model became a benchmark for other organizations and industries.

Source: Based on Lewis N. (2001) Dell portal adds 'value': valuechain.dell.com provides pipeline to info exchange. CMP Media; www.my-esm.com

CHAPTER REVIEW

- An e-supply chain refers to any supply chain that includes electronic communications and the internet – giving a component of e-commerce. The associated management function becomes e-SCM. This chapter focussed on aspects of information systems that purchasing managers should be familiar with

- Procurement managers are continually expanding their use of information technology to improve performance. They now use sophisticated systems to manage the acquisition, processing and distribution of data within an organization and along their supply chains

- ERP is a central element, which integrates data handling for different functions and allows free communications. CRM and SRM focus on external communications

- Many factors encourage organizations to continually update their information systems. These include integration of operations, globalization, use

of new business process, availability of new technology and cost management

- Designing and implementing a new ERP system require systematic analysis of the existing processes, redesign and improvement, development of a new system, testing and implementation. This is a major undertaking that needs rigorous justification, and the resulting system can have profound effects on operations and culture

- The availability of relevant Information is essential for procurement. This is provided through purchasing databases and data warehouses

- Having collected the information, it must be transmitted between partners in the supply chain. EDI systems provided the necessary connections, now largely organized through the web

- The resulting systems for e-sourcing can be complex and include many modules to improve the flows of information and assist with purchasing

● Integrating the flows of information brings considerable benefits. A prerequisite for this is information visibility, where information that is available anywhere in a supply chain is available to all members

DISCUSSION QUESTIONS

1 Why do you think that there is such an emphasis on information systems for purchasing?

2 What information is needed for successful procurement? How is this supplied?

3 Why should supply managers understand the role of information systems?

4 Why do organizations continually update their information systems? What are the dangers of not keeping up-to-date?

5 What is ERP? What are its benefits?

6 Discuss the stages needed to implement ERP. What barriers may hinder the implementation of ERP?

7 'ERP systems take too long to implement and are not worth the cost.' What do you think of this statement?

8 What is a purchasing database?

9 Discuss the benefits that the internet has brought to purchasing. Are these likely to change in the future?

10 What is e-sourcing? How will e-sourcing systems develop in the future?

11 Why are reverse auctions considered controversial? Why would you participate in one as a seller? Why would you organize one as a buyer?

12 What is information visibility? What benefits does it bring? What are the barriers to achieving it?

REFERENCES

Antonette G., Sawchuk C. and Giunipero L. (2002) E-purchasing plus (2nd edition), Goshen, NY: JGC Enterprises.

Bozarth C. and Handfield R. (2004) Operations and supply chain management, Upper Saddle River, NJ: Prentice Hall.

Chopra S. and Meindl P. (2004) Information technology and the supply chain, in Supply Chain Management: Strategy, Planning and Operation, Upper Saddle River, NJ: Prentice Hall.

Christopher M. et al, (2002) Supply chain vulnerability: final report on behalf of DTLR, DTI and Home Office, School of Management, Cranfield University.

Cole S. J., Woodring S. D., Chun H. and Gatoff J. (1999) Dynamic trading networks, The Forrester Report, Cambridge, MA, and at website www.forrestergroup.com

Handfield R. and Nichols E. L. (2003) Supply chain redesign, Upper Saddle River, NJ: Prentice Hall.

Handfield R., Straight S. and Sterling W. (2002) Reverse auctions: how do suppliers really feel about them? Inside Supply Management, November, pp 28–32.

Kahl S. (1999) What's the 'value' of supply chain software? Supply Chain Management Review, 2(4): 59–67.

Poirier C. C. and Quinn F. J. (2003) A survey of supply chain progress, Supply Chain Management Review, September/October.

Waters D. (2002) Operations management (2nd edition), Harlow, Essex: Pearson Education.

Waters D. (2007) Supply chain risk management, London: Kogan Page.

FURTHER READING

Angeles R. (2003) Electronic supply chain partnership: reconsidering relationship attributes in customer-supplier dyads, Information Resources Management Journal, 16(3): 59–84.

Antonette G., Sawchuk C. and Giunipero L. (2002) E-purchasing plus (2nd edition), Goshen, NY: JGC Enterprises.

Beall S., Carter C., Carter P., Germer, T., Hendrick, T., Jap, S., *et al.* (2003) The role of reverse auctions in strategic sourcing, Tempe, AZ: CAPS Research.

Editorial (2002) Auto supplier moves to new quote management system, *Purchasing*, 131(5): S12–S14.

Handfield R. and Straight S. (2003) What sourcing channel is right for you? Supply Chain Management Review, July/August, pp 62–68.

Hope-Ross D., Eschinger C. and Kyte A. (2003) Strategic sourcing applications magic quadrant, 1Q03, Research Note, Gartner Group.

Kaplan S. and Sawhney M. (2000) E-hubs: the new B2B marketplaces, Harvard Business Review, May–June, pp 97–103.

Morton R. (2007) Software on demand, Logistics Today, February, pp 22–23.

Neef D. (2001) E-procurement: from strategy to implementation, Saddle River, NJ: Prentice Hall.

Pearcy D., Giunipero L. and Wilson A. (2007) A model of relational governance in reverse auctions, *Journal of Supply Chain Management*, Winter, pp 4–15.

Teague P. E. (2007) PLM gets buyers under the hood, Purchasing, March 1, and website at www.purchasing.com

Turner N. (2001) Choosing the most appropriate warehouse management system, *Corby*, 3(7): 30–33.

Waters D. (editor) (2007), Global logistics and distribution planning (5th edition), London: Kogan Page.

Waters D. (2008) Supply chain management (2nd edition), Basingstoke, Hampshire: Palgrave Macmillan.

CASE STUDY

Information visibility

The project manager responsible for implementing a new procurement system explained, 'We were looking for a tool that gets our company and its supply chain connected via the internet. We needed to co-ordinate our suppliers with a simple tool to get our feet wet and start working more effectively. Information needs to be shared quickly to establish support.' The information tool the project manager was talking about is expected to do the following (Handfield and Nichols, 2003):

- Provide a view of the same information to suppliers and the company

- Display inventory status, schedules, history of transactions

- Provide a reporting capability

- Display alerts to exceptions

- Communicate replenishment triggers

- Rate suppliers

- Support the next generation of EDI

- Display logistics information.

Some of the benefits that were expected from the new system included:

- Increased customer satisfaction throughout the supply chain

- Supply chain flexibility

- Lower stocks levels

- Less effort needed for expediting

- Fewer production interruptions and changes

- Increased focus on collaboration and proactive activities.

Implementing the new system needed a series of steps. Several software vendors were initially reviewed, and the company chose to run a pilot with one. Several criteria were used to select the vendor, with a major one being the possibility of developing a long-term relationship. As the purchasing manager said, 'We want to improve the product to benefit us as well as other participants across the supply chain. We always run a pilot study to test the product and see how we can work together.'

The project manager described the pilot programme as follows, 'In our pilot, we implemented the system in 2 to 4 weeks, but it really takes a month or so to get the business processes adjusted and the users familiar with the software. The amount of training required varied at each location. We used centralized training sessions, together with site training, and some one-on-one sessions. As a result, everyone in the organization saw the value of information visibility. We realized that a tool is only as good as the underlying business process, and its success depends of acceptance by staff. We also learned that one replenishment method would not work in all situations. Rather, it is better to have different methods that are controlled in the same way across the organization. We also recognized that there were entrenched manual processes in the suppliers' business processes and that would be difficult to change.'

Several barriers and problems were encountered along the way, but purchasing was able to overcome them in the following way:

- Lack of technical expertise in suppliers

  - Solution: The pilot system was designed to be simple, and both the system provider and the company's IT staff gave assistance

- Internal resistance

  - Solution: This was addressed by saying, 'This is a pilot and we want to learn about the software, but we also want to determine where our business processes are working properly.' Participants were encouraged to give their ideas about the system from the start

- Lack of internal resources

  - Solution: This was addressed by trying to prove with the pilot study that fewer resources would be needed for the new system. However, this is a continuing problem as lack of resources will be a major issue for full implementation of the system

- Lack of top management support and understanding

  - Solution: The company organized several knowledge-sharing events with its senior managers, as well as personal interviews. It gave frequent updates on the project status to keep executives in touch with progress

- Lack of standards in the technology

  - Solution: The company does not use a common information processing platform (although this is being developed). The biggest challenge was the different business processes used in different parts of the plant. Training helped to solve this problem

Lessons learned from this pilot study included the following:

- Top level management support is absolutely critical. People will not participate initially unless they are told to do so

- Involvement of all levels of the organization will help people to participate

- Current system transaction processes were not adequate; the company needed to develop new ones

- Efficient business processes must be in place. Without good business processes, the best system in the world will not solve any problems

Questions

- What was the company trying to achieve with its new system? What benefits would it expect?

- What problems did the company meet in increasing its information visibility? Were they technical problems?

- What are some of the important lessons learned by the company?

CHAPTER 18
PERFORMANCE MEASUREMENT AND EVALUATION

LEARNING OBJECTIVES   After reading this chapter you should be able to:

- Appreciate the need to measure purchasing performance

- Discuss alternative measure of purchasing performance

- Describe the steps needed to develop a performance measurement system

- Describe the approach of performance benchmarking

- Appreciate the concept of a balanced scorecard

- Discuss characteristics of purchasing measurement systems

MEASURING PURCHASING PERFORMANCE

Throughout the book we have mentioned the efficiency of operations, and there is an implicit assumption that there is some systematic way of monitoring and evaluating purchasing performance. This may sound easy, but in practice it is difficult to find measures that show exactly how well purchasing is done, whether it is meeting targets and how it can be improved. All firms devize measures, but these are not always helpful, and in some circumstances can even be harmful. For example, the ability to win price concessions from suppliers is viewed as a major objective for some buyers. But when a purchaser continually squeezes short-term price reductions from a supplier, the supplier may not be left with the financial resources to invest in longer-term improvements – or even to survive. So the short-term benefit brings long-term drawbacks.

Managers really need a variety of measures for purchasing performance. Most of these fall into two broad categories – describing **effectiveness** and **efficiency**.

Effectiveness

Is the extent to which managers make decisions that move them towards a previously established goal.

Efficiency

Measures how well the goal is reached, what resources are used to reach the goal or what sacrifices are necessary to reach the goal.

Effectiveness sets the best goals ('doing the right thing') while efficiency shows how well the goals are achieved ('doing the thing right') (van Weele, 1984; Waters, 2002).

Almost all measures include a target against which performance is evaluated. For instance, there is little point in simply saying that a measure will track improvement in supplier quality. What we really need is a pre-established target, and then we can measure actual performance to see if it reaches, or gets closer to the target. So a complete picture requires each performance measure to include a target level, and a timetable within which this target should be reached. Then a reasonable aim might be phrased in terms of, 'reducing purchasing administrative costs by 5 per cent over the next year'.

Why measure performance?

There are a number of reasons for measuring purchasing performance, which we can summarize in the following four points.

1 **Support better decision making.** Measurement can lead to better decisions by making performance visible. Measurement provides a track record of purchasing performance over time, and without knowing exactly how good current performance is it is difficult to know which areas are most seriously in need of improvement, and how to achieve these improvements.

2 **Support better communication.** Performance measurement improves communication across the supply chain, by giving precise information rather than vague statements and implications. For example, a purchaser can let a supplier know exactly what levels of performance are required, what levels other suppliers achieve and how these levels compare with industry standards.

3 **Provide performance feedback.** Measurement is used in feedback, which shows how well a buyer, department, team or supplier is meeting its performance objectives. It also identifies problems and encourages them to be corrected, and prevented from reoccurring.

4 **Motivate and direct behaviour.** Measurement can motivate and direct behaviour toward desired results. For instance, the measures chosen show what priorities the organization has, and informs staff of the activities that managers view as critical. And, managers can directly link rewards and penalties to certain types of behaviour.

Problems with measuring performance

Every manager uses some kinds of performance measures, but this is still an activity that comes with certain problems. The difficulties make Brown (1996) suggest that most managers are like a pilot trying to fly a plane with only half the instruments actually needed, and many additional instruments that measure irrelevant data and serve no useful purpose. Some typical problems include:

The wrong measures. The most common problem with measuring performance is simply using the wrong measures. When a company is trying to reduce its cost, purchasing managers are focussing on delivery lead time; when a company wants to expand it global operations, purchasing is measuring the average order size. The usual reasons for this have managers using the same measures that have always been used in the past, or else they feel that a measure is related to success when it is not, or else they are the easiest or most convenient measures.

The wrong data. Every measurement needs data, and the data available or collected may not allow the measure to be properly calculated. For instance, reducing the operating costs of the purchasing department is a reasonable aim, but the accounts may not actually separate the costs of the purchasing department from the costs of other departments.

Too much data. It is easy to get information from an information system, and there is always a temptation to collect everything that may be relevant. The result is that managers are overwhelmed by data. A rule of thumb says that no-one should monitor more than a dozen measures, half of which are the most critical.

Short-term focussed. Many organizations, particularly smaller ones, rely on measures that have a short-term focus. Typically they emphasize short-term financial and operating data, and this means that purchasing only looks at immediate transactions and workload, while ignoring the strategic concerns.

Lack of detail. Data always has to be analysed and summarized to make sense, but sometimes it is summarized so much that underlying patterns are hidden and the result is to vague to be of any practical use. For instance, any measure that uses a single figure to report monthly supplier quality lacks enough detail, as procurement want to know the specific types of defects, frequencies, causes, costs, variation, trends and so on.

Drive the wrong performance. Unfortunately, some measures encourage behaviour that is not planned or even beneficial. Suppose that buyers are measured on the number of purchase orders they send out; then it is in their interests to divide large orders into smaller ones, split orders between suppliers and generally generate as many purchase orders as possible.

Measures of behaviour versus accomplishments. Some measures look at the way that results are achieved, rather than the results themselves. In other words, they measure behaviour, and there is no guarantee that certain behaviour will lead to desired results. For example, a behavioural measure might track the volume of purchases covered by company-wide contracts, when a better measure would track the savings made by using company-wide contracts. Similarly, a mistaken behavioural measure would record the number of meetings held by a commodity team, while better measures would track the results achieved by the team's actions.

LEARNING FROM PRACTICE

Stoneham

Stoneham had hired a firm of consultants to improve the distribution of their food products. The previous year they had appointed a new purchasing manager who introduced new ideas, but the consultant's were apparently not impressed. They suggested that despite apparent changes in purchasing, there had been no real improvements. One reason was the use of inappropriate measures whose apparent purpose was to show purchasing managers in a good light rather than contribute to company aims.

One aim of the purchasing department was, 'to drive down purchasing costs'. The consultants' comments can be summarized as:

- There is no definition of which costs are to be driven down

- There is no suggestion of how the cost reductions are to be achieved
- No quantifiable targets have been set
- There are no milestones to monitor progress
- There are no comparisons with performance achieved by the department in the past, other parts of the organization, competitors or the industry in general
- No timescale is specified for the savings
- Available cost data is not detailed enough to measure performance

Source: Based on Richmond D. (2009) Performance measurement, RPW, Johannesburg.

TYPES OF PERFORMANCE MEASURE

Organizations should measure those aspects of performance that help them achieve business goals. It follows that the measures should be aligned both vertically (across different levels of management) and horizontally (across different functions). Figure 18.1 illustrates a process where organizational objectives drive the business strategies, such as being a low-cost producer or technology leader. These business strategies then drive appropriate purchasing objectives, strategies and tactics. Performance measures monitor progress towards achieving these.

Strategies actually appear from a combination of top-down strategy design (where senior manages define the strategies) and bottom-up emergence (where internal capabilities grow into business strengths and strategies). Whatever the strategies look like, they rely on measurements to monitor progress. Then there are hundreds of possible measures that can be used for purchasing. A convenient way of categorizing the most commonly used is shown in Figure 18.1, and reviewed below.

Price performance measures

Purchasing uses various indicators to evaluate price performance – or how effectively it spends its money. The most common measure is the difference between actual purchase price and planned purchase price, giving:

Purchase price variance = actual purchase price − planned purchase price

There are several variations on this, including the following.

FIGURE 18.1 Integrated performance measurement process

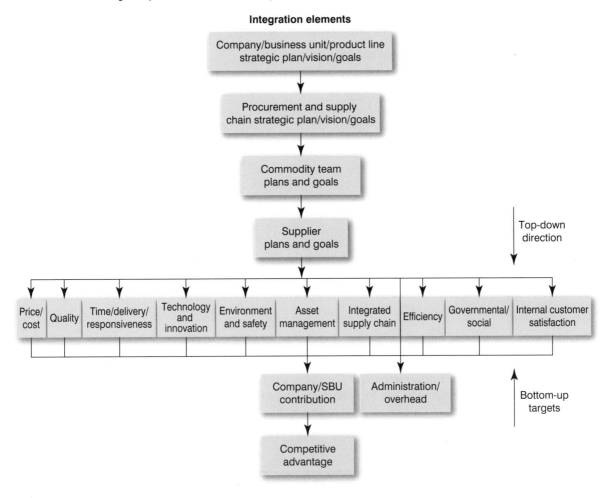

Actual price compared with plan. The amount that is spent on products may, for various reasons, not be the same as plans. In a simple case, inflation may raise prices by more than expected. Then a measure of price performance is the difference between actual and planned purchase prices. This calculation can be done at different organizational levels. Low levels might show detailed comparisons of prices for a single item; high levels might compare expenditure for the entire material budget. Figure 18.2 shows some of the calculations for comparing actual price against plans.

Actual prices compared with market index. This shows how well actual prices paid compare with published market prices. They are most commonly used for products where price is primarily a function of market forces, or to standard and readily available products. The key element is an index which shows how the market price has changed over some designated period (such as a quarter). Then managers can check their actual performance against this.

Price comparisons between operations. This compares the actual prices paid for similar items by the same firm across plants, divisions or business units. These comparisons give visibility, showing who is negotiating the best price. They can also help identify commonly purchased items between units which should be consolidated into bigger orders. When this approach is used to compare the prices paid by different organizations, it can give an interesting view of competitiveness.

FIGURE 18.2 Purchase price variance from plan

Various calculations for measuring purchase price variance:

1   Purchase price variance = Actual price − Planned price.

2   Purchase price variance percentage = Actual price/Planned price.

3   Total purchase price variance = (Actual price − Planned price) × Purchase quantity.

4   Current year impact of purchase price variance = (Actual price − Planned price) × (Estimated annual volume × Percentage of requirements remaining).

Level of reported performance:

Purchase item
Commodity or family group
End product
Project
Buying location or department
Buyer
Management group
Supplier.

Target prices achieved. Target pricing determines the price that external customers are willing to pay for a product, and uses this to assigning specific cost targets to the parts and materials used to make the product. Then for each item:

$$\text{Target price} - \text{Profit target} = \text{Allowable purchase cost}$$

WORKED EXAMPLE

Managers notice that between March and June the price they paid for an item rose from €150 to €152, while the government price index rose from 125 to 128. Has their purchasing department done a good job?

Solution

Considering the government price index:

31 March, market-based price index for Item		125
30 June, market-based price index for Item		128
Market index change	(128 − 125)/125	2.4 per cent increase

Now considering the price actually paid:

31 March, actual price paid for Item		€150
30 June, actual price paid for Item		€152
Price paid change	(152 − 150)/150	1.3 per cent increase
Comparison of actual to market	2.4 − 1.3	Better by 1.1 per cent

The proportion of items that achieve this target gives a positive measure of performance.

Cost-effectiveness measures

The measures in this category focus on efforts to reduce purchase costs, and they fall into two general categories: cost changes and cost avoidance.

Cost changes. Compare the actual cost of an item, or a family of items, over a period of time. These cost changes might be a result of new purchasing practices or policies, or some external cause, notably inflation. Then we can measure the cost reduction achieved:

$$\text{Cost reduction} = (\text{New price} - \text{Old price}) \times \text{estimated volume}$$

For example, if the new price is £9 per unit and the old price was £10 per unit, with an estimated volume of 10 000 units for the next budget period, there is a projected cost reduction of $(10 - 9) \times 10\,000 = £10\,000$. In practice, a change in volume might affect the cost reduction more than a change in price, and inflation may actually increase prices to give a negative cost reduction.

Cost avoidance. Represents the difference between a price paid and a higher price that might have occurred if purchasing had not taken some special action to get the lower price. For example, suppose an item cost €5.00 per unit, but the supplier is quoting a new price of €5.50 per unit. If buyers negotiate a price of €5.25 per unit, then they have achieved a cost avoidance of €0.25 per unit (even though the price is still €0.25 higher than the previous price). Managers are often concerned about such cost-avoidance savings, as they rarely show up in a firm's accounts. The savings are often calculated from some hypothetical future cost, and are sometimes subject to exaggeration, giving descriptions of 'funny money' that is easy to manipulate.

We should give a warning about cost-effectiveness measures, as the method used to achieve any cost reductions is critical. In principle, reducing costs by the co-operation of suppliers is the same as a reduction from heavy-handed pressure on a weak supplier. Both give a cost reduction – but the process used to achieve that result can have longer-term implications. Co-operation may reduce costs through joint improvement and lay the foundation for further benefits in the future; heavy-handed pressure may force a supplier to cut corners, perhaps giving poor quality and growing problems in the future.

Revenue measures

Revenue measures consider the impact of purchasing on positively generating revenue, rather than its usual image as a cost centre, For example, purchasing may uncover new technologies available from suppliers before others firms and gain exclusive rights, or they might help with the design of new products with favourable pricing. Or purchasing might negotiate royalty agreements with suppliers that have rights to use technologies developed for other customers. This direct revenue is a useful measure, but purchasing can have other effects on revenue, such as the increased income generated when efficient purchasing brings a new product to market quickly and allows first-to-market premium pricing.

Some examples of revenue measure include:

● Royalties generated by acquiring new technology and patents initiated by purchasing

- Supplier contribution because of new business generated by business development plans, unique technology found by purchasing, new efficient processes, etc.

- Return on licensing technology driven by purchasing

- Number of patents that have led to royalties

- Value of free samples from suppliers

Although this unusual view of purchasing as a revenue generator makes these measures interesting, it is fair to say that they are not widely used.

Quality measures

As we saw in chapter 11, there are many measures of quality, including:

- **Defects per million** – which states the maximum number of defects allowable in any particular product. As quality management has improved, with the ability to make products to tighter tolerances, this measure has also fallen.

- **Defects per supplier** – which measures the number of defects delivered from each supplier to show the comparative quality of competing suppliers. It is also used as an absolute target for suppliers to reach. It is possible to combine figures to get an aggregate measure across all the different items from a supplier, but this hides the relative importance of each item.

- **Field failure rates by purchase item and by supplier.** This measures the incidence of failures of materials that have been incorporated into products and delivered to final customers. It indicates failures after sale, which organizations are very keen to avoid.

Time and responsiveness measures

- **Time-to-market for new products** – which measures the amount of time from concept to delivery of a product to customers. The objective here is for continuous reduction, to be first to market with a new product and also to lessen the time it takes to break-even and recover fixed costs.

- **On-time delivery** – which show how well suppliers can meet customer schedules. Key aspects of such measures include:

  ○ Due dates, scheduled or promised

  ○ Time slots within which deliveries must be made

  ○ Acceptable range around a due date (for example, no more than 2 days early or no days late)

- **Achieving production schedules** – which show whether procurement is getting materials delivered in time for their use in production schedules. These measures are particularly useful for rapidly changing schedules, such as the manufacture of highly seasonal goods.

- **Cycle time** – monitor the reduction in time taken for various activities, such as order entry, supplier selection and invoice payment. These improvements are achieved through elimination of delays, more efficient procedures or simply doing things faster.

- **Responsiveness** – to schedule changes, product mix changes and design changes. These measures show how quickly procurement responds to changing circumstances – such as their ability to get an emergency delivery, or to change an item's design.

Technology or innovation measures

First view of new technology from suppliers. This measure is typically linked to a contract that ensures a firm gets information about new technologies some time before its competitors. This may be an important point in the choice of suppliers for high technology products. A specific measure might be the number of such agreements, but this gives no idea of the level of success achieved from the early knowledge about the technology.

Standardization and use of industry standards. This measures the amount of standard materials that are bought, or the proportion of current industry standard items, rather than buying special, tailored items. Specific measures include reduction in the number of different items used, percentage of new products made up of currently purchased items and number of industry-unique items used in a new product.

Physical environment and safety measures

Companies are increasingly tracking their achievement of environmental and safety goals. This includes the costs of compliance to both voluntary standards and legislation.

Asset management and integrated supply chain measures

Inventory costs. Organizations use a number of measures of inventory performance such as:

- Value of inventory investment
- Total number of items stored
- Stock turnover
- Time covered by remaining stock
- Inventory carrying cost
- Amount of safety stock held
- Proportion of inactive items
- Accuracy of inventory management system records

Transport cost. These measures track actual transport costs against some pre-established goal, such as demurrage costs, use of premium transport, carrier quality, delivery performance and lead time.

Customer orders. These measures show how well an organization is satisfying its commitment to downstream customers. Of course, virtually every measure might be seen as contributing to customer service, but some more specifically focus on customers, such as the total lead time, returned orders and warranty claims.

E-transactions. This measures the use of EDI or web-based systems to link buyers and suppliers:

- Absolute number of suppliers using e-procurement

- Percentage of suppliers using e-procurement

- Value and percentage of orders

- Percentage of shipping notices

- Funds transferred using EFT

- Meeting customer requirements

- Inventory within the supply chain

Pull systems, supplier managed inventory, etc. These measures establish the number of suppliers that are sharing schedules and other operational data. They also highlight the proportion of suppliers that are not sharing this information.

Administration and efficiency measures

Managers use various administration and efficiency measures to plan purchasing's budget. The two most common methods to establish a budget are 'current budget plus adjustment' and the use of control ratios.

Current budget plus adjustment. Uses the current administrative budget and adjusts this for the next period by an amount that depends on expected business conditions and other departmental requirements.

Control ratios. Where the purchasing administrative budget is a percentage of another measure that reflects purchasing's workload, typically the total spending or number of orders submitted. For instance:

Purchasing administrative budget = Estimated expenditure × Control ratio

The value of the control ratio is usually found from the value used in the past, followed by negotiations to allow for adjustments.

Other approaches. There are other ways of arriving at a purchasing administrative budget, such as the number of purchase orders processed, items bought, headcount and so on. However, firms should always be careful with such measures that they should consider purchasing effectiveness rather than straightforward efficiency.

Governmental and social measures

A growing series of laws is controlling purchasing, such as environmental protection. The aim of this legislation is often to achieve some social goals, and might insist that a certain proportion of business is done with small businesses or minority-owned ones. Managers have to monitor certain activities to make sure that they keep within prevailing legislation, perhaps my measuring:

- Proportion of total spending that is delivered by a certain type of enterprize

- Number of suppliers from certain types of enterprize

- Growth of spending in certain types of enterprize

Internal customer satisfaction measures

Organizations commonly use measures of the satisfaction of internal customers with purchasing. This is typically collected by surveys of internal customers that ask a series of questions presented in a standard questionnaire.

Supplier performance measures

In chapter 7 we saw the importance of evaluating suppliers, and this is an area where considerable progress has been made. Supplier scorecards frequently contain the measures outlined above, with purchasers tracking supplier process, cost, quality, timing and so on. Firms are beginning to quantify the cost associated with supplier non-performance and adding this as part of the total cost of doing business with a supplier.

Strategic performance measures

As well as the direct measures of operations, procurement also requires measures that reflect its support of overall corporate and business strategies. Such measures give less emphasis to efficiency and more to effectiveness. Examples of the strategic measures include early supplier involvement in product design, performance gains emerging from direct supplier development and improvement suggestions from co-operating with suppliers.

Figure 18.3 gives some examples of strategic purchasing measures, which are a combination of actual results and the activities to achieve these results.

FIGURE 18.3 Examples of strategic purchasing measures

- Percentage of purchasing's operating budget committed to supplier visits
- Proportion of suppliers that are quality-certified
- Percentage of receipts free of inspection and material defects
- Total number of suppliers
- Proportion of suppliers participating in early product design or other joint value-adding activities
- Revenue increase from supplier-provided technology that differentiates end products
- Percentage of operating budget allocated to supplier development and training
- Total cost of supplier selection and evaluation measures
- Supplier lead times
- Purchasing's contribution to return on assets, ROI and other financial measures
- Purchasing's success with achieving cost reductions from higher-tier suppliers
- Percentage of purchase spending committed to long-term contracts
- Savings achieved from the use of company-wide agreements
- Purchasing's contribution to reducing new product development time
- Proportion of spending from sole suppliers

FIGURE 18.3 (Continued)

- Proportion of purchases from highest-performing suppliers
- Percentage of purchase transactions using EDI or websites
- Percentage of deliveries on a JIT basis
- Supplier quality levels, cost performance and delivery performance that achieve world-class performance targets
- Supplier development costs and benefits
- Measures for ensuring continuous supplier performance improvement
- Reduction in working capital due to improved purchasing
- Contribution to ROI from strategic outsourcing
- Savings achieved from reducing the number of items bought
- Savings achieved from part standardization.

LEARNING FROM PRACTICE

Purchasing performance

A survey asked purchasing managers to assess, for their most important purchases the performance improvements achieved over the past 12 months. A summary of their responses is given in the following table.

Performance area improvement results	Average
Unit purchase price	4.1 per cent
Transportation and logistics costs	2.6 per cent
Total cost of ownership	3.5 per cent
Overall inventory investment costs	2.0 per cent
Supplier quality	3.3 per cent
Supplier on-time delivery	3.6 per cent
Supplier responsiveness/flexibility	2.3 per cent
Supplier diversity	3.1 per cent
Operating earnings	7.6 per cent
Fixed asset utilization	2.6 per cent

Source: Based on Monczka R.M. and Petersen K.J. (2007), Supply strategy implementation: current state and future opportunities, CAPS Research, Tempe, AZ.

DEVELOPING A PERFORMANCE MEASUREMENT SYSTEM

Performance measurement system Consists of all the procedures to collect, analyse and report current data needed to assess how well a department is performing its prescribed activities.

To measure purchasing performance, a firm needs a **performance measurement system** (Waters, 2009).

The development of a system to measure performance requires the leadership, support and commitment of senior managers. As well as ensuring the commitment of resources, their support also sends a message about the seriousness of tracking and improving performance.

It is also important that all purchasing locations use the same measuring system, as this reduces duplication, as well as the associated development and training costs. But this does not mean that each location must use the same performance targets or even measures, only that they should use the same basis monitoring system.

Developing an effective measurement system needs a sequence of activities. These include determining which type of performance measure to use, the specific measures, standards for each measure, designing a system to calculate the measurers, implementing the system and then continually reviewing the system and each performance measure. Figure 18.4 shows an overview of this process.

Determine which performance categories to measure

We have already listed performance measurements that fall into various categories, and the first step in developing a measurement system is to decide which of these to emphasize. Essentially, managers decide the weight to give to each type of performance, not looking in too much detail at the details of specific measures, but they take a broader view of categories. The categories to be emphasized must relate broadly to organizational and purchasing goals.

Develop specific performance measures

Now managers move on to decide the specific measures to use, and their choice must have the following characteristics:

Objectivity. Each measure should be as objective as possible, which means that it should rely on quantitative facts rather than qualitative judgements. Subjective evaluations invariably create disagreement between people doing the measuring, people setting targets and people actually doing the purchasing.

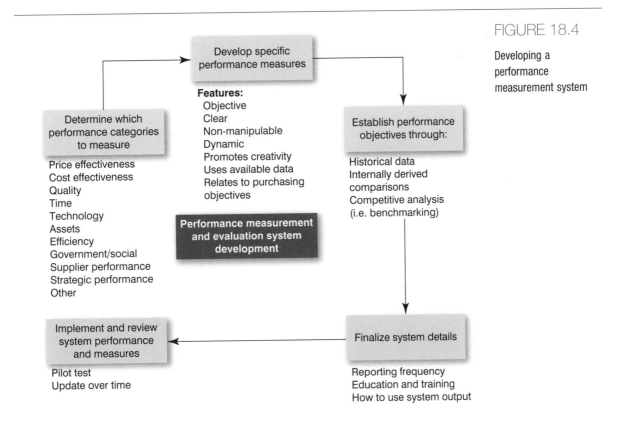

FIGURE 18.4

Developing a performance measurement system

Clarity. People must understand the measure's requirements – which means that each measure should be straightforward and unambiguous, and that everyone concerned must be clear about what is being measured, the reasons for measuring it, what affects the measures, how they can be improved, etc.

Use of accurate and available data. Well-defined measures use data that are available and accurate. Measures that require data that is difficult to find or unreliable, are unlikely to be used successfully or give convincing results. The cost of collecting data should never outweigh the potential benefit of using it in a particular measure.

Creativity. A common misconception is that a performance evaluation system should measure every possible activity. However, this would simply overwhelm managers with information and stifle individual creativity. So many measures would control behaviour so tightly that there would be no room for personal initiative. A successful system measures only what is important, while still promoting individual initiative and creativity. Typically, this means focussing on 5 or 6 important, clearly defined measures.

Directly related to organizational objectives. Figure 18.5 shows how corporate objectives are fed down to influence purchasing goals. The message here is that the business goals have a direct impact on purchasing, and by implication appropriate measures of purchasing performance.

Joint participation. This means that the staff responsible for each measure participate in developing the measure and establishing related targets. Joint participation can go a long way toward getting the necessary support of the people responsible and make the measure work.

Dynamic over time. A dynamic system is one that management reviews periodically to see whether existing measures still serve their purpose and support purchasing's objectives – or whether they should revise the measures and standards.

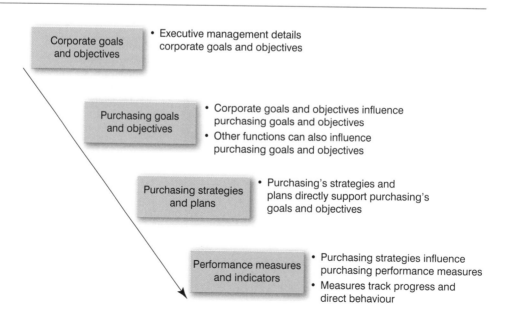

FIGURE 18.5

Linking purchasing measures to corporate objectives

Cannot be manipulated. This means that each measure is based on facts that staff cannot inappropriately influence – to put it simply, the measure is cheat-proof. Ideally, the individuals responsible for the measure should not also supply the data, and automatic data collection is usually easiest and most reliable. Managers want an accurate picture of performance, whether this is good or bad, and they do not want one that is somehow biased.

Establish performance objectives for each measure

It is critical to establish a target for each performance measure, as these define the desired level of performance level. Managers should not specify objectives that are too easy, as they become the accepted, low performance standard. Neither should they specify targets that are too difficult or unachievable, as people become discouraged and accept that they will inevitably fail, so it is not worth spending any effort. Instead performance standards must be realistic and achievable through concentrated effort. In other words, the targets should be 'demanding but achievable'.

The target must also reflect the realities of a firm's competitive environment. A target that is challenging internally but still does not match the level of competitors, needs some attention.

Firms commonly use three methods to establish performance measure targets:

1 **Historical performance –** uses past performance as the basis for establishing a future target. The historical performance is often modified by some improvement factor to arrive at a current objective. Unfortunately, relying on historical data can create problems, particularly when past performance was not very good. Then managers would want a considerable improvement rather than an iterative adjustment. Also, internal historical data gives no idea about the performance of competitors or other leading firms.

2 **Internal comparisons** – where a firm uses performance achieved within its own departments and business units. The best internal performance should then become the target for all other departments. This approach gives a broader view than straightforward historical data, passes lessons for good practice around an organization, uses contemporary data and includes any unusual circumstances. But it also has disadvantages, such as encouraging pointless and unhealthy internal rivalry. However, the main problem is that a firm can lose sight of its external competition as there is no guarantee that even the best-performing internal unit matches the best-performing unit of a direct competitor.

3 **External analysis,** examines the practices and performance objectives of competitors and other leading firms. The advantage of this approach is that it assesses leading competitors and shows how purchasing compares with best practices. This is the basis of benchmarking, which we describe later in the chapter.

Finalize system details

The next step of development adds the remaining details to the system, including the following:

Frequency of performance reporting. Any reasonable measurement system must provide regular reports of its findings. The reporting frequency can differ from measure to measure, and management have to decide the frequency that is most appropriate for each. For example, a measure that tracks the status of inbound transport must be frequent, and preferably report in real-time. A summary measure evaluating overall supplier performance may need only weekly or monthly reports.

Education and training. Employees and suppliers have to be trained to use the performance measurement system. All participants must understand their responsibilities, how to use the system, what its output means, where to look for improvements and so on. The measurement system is a tool, and like all tools proper education and training is needed to use it properly.

Using system outputs. Managers can use the output of a performance measurement system in many ways, and they must give careful thought to finding the most appropriate. Of course, the overall purpose is to evaluate purchasing operations and look for improvements, but some managers rely on the output to evaluate individual purchasing staff or suppliers. Or they may use the results to identify better suppliers that deserve future contracts.

Implement and review system performance

All systems have an implementation phase, which does trail runs to make sure the system works as planned, and then actually installs it. But implementation is not the end of the story, and each performance measure, as well as the whole system, must be regularly monitored to make sure that it continues to work as desired. Having a system that contains obsolete or inappropriate measures can be more damaging than having no formal system at all.

LEARNING FROM PRACTICE

Semionic Communications

Semionic Communications is a medium-sized manufacturer of hand-held communication equipment, normally sold under the brand names of major international companies. They have developed a set of organizational objectives that include being a low-cost producer of high-technology equipment, providing the highest quality to customers and offering the best customer service in terms of delivery and flexibility. The company has also developed a purchasing measurement system that directly supports these organizational objectives.

When implementing its purchasing measurement system, Semionic followed a series of steps that are used in many organizations:

Step 1. Conduct broad discussions and analyses of strategies to identify a sensible set of measures.

Step 2. Use benchmarking and further broad discussions to establish targets for the measures that are demanding but achievable.

Step 3. Put these measures and targets into written policy and procedures.

Step 4. Discuss the measures and objectives with suppliers, showing exactly what is expected of them.

Step 5. Receive feedback from suppliers and modify the measures and targets as necessary.

Step 6. Implement procedures for collecting data and monitoring the defined measures.

Step 7. Analyse performance data, report results and give feedback to suppliers.

Step 8. Continually benchmark, check and update the measures, targets, procedures and analyses.

Source: Based on Scarborough J. (2007) Performance measurement systems, Western Logistics Conference, Leningrad.

Semionic currently use a wide range of purchasing measures that relate directly to the company's objectives. Some of these include:

- **Quality**
  - Supplier defects in parts per million
  - Internal manufacturing defects in parts per million
  - Damage to products
  - Number and cost of warranty claims

- **Price and cost**
  - Trends in actual price to market
  - Overheads
  - Price and cost reductions
  - Industry comparisons

- **Delivery and service**
  - Supplier lead times
  - Supplier on-time delivery
  - New product development time

- **Stocks**
  - Total cost of stocks held
  - Velocity of stock movement through supply chains
  - Reductions in stock achieved

Information to support this system comes from various sources, including internal transactions, data from suppliers and site visits. The frequency of measurement varies between real-time monitoring through to quarterly summaries. New suppliers and those with known problems are monitored more closely than those with a history of good performance.

BENCHMARKING PERFORMANCE

Benchmarking is a method of comparing an organization's performance with the performance of its best competitor, or the best firm in the industry. However, it goes further than a comparison, and not only looks at the superior performance, but how this is achieved. Then managers can see how they can adopt and adapt the practices of leading firms to improve their own performance.

Benchmarking overview

Benchmarking is the continuous measuring of products, processes, activities and practices against a firm's best competitors, or firms recognized as industry leaders (Camp, 1989, part I). Formally, benchmarking measures an organization's performance and compares it with 'best-in-class' competitors, determines how the best-in-class achieve their performance levels and uses that information to establish the organization's performance targets, strategies and action plans (Pryor, 1989).

Benchmarking does not necessarily involve comparisons with direct competitors. Firms often benchmark their operations against non-competitors who have some related process. For example, firms in two completely different industries may both run transport fleets, and they can learn lessons from each other. Understandably, it is usually easier to get benchmarking data from a co-operative non-competitor, than from an aggressive competitor that is trying to gain an advantage.

Benchmarking clearly benefits firms that are not industry leaders, as they can learn where they are weak, and how they can overcome the weaknesses. But it is also useful for industry leaders, as even the best can learn new things and become even better. A firm cannot remain a market leader if it is unaware of the actions and capabilities of its competitors.

Types of benchmarking

There are three basic types of performance benchmarking:

1 The first type is strategic benchmarking, which involves a comparison of one firm's strategies against those of another. By gaining an in-depth understanding of a leading firm's strategies an organization can develop its own strategies to counter and pre-empt the competition.

2 The second type is operational benchmarking, which is the process that purchasing follows when it performs a more detailed benchmarking of activities.

3 The third type is support-activity benchmarking, which sees how the support functions within an organization can reduce their costs compared with external providers of the same services. Firms use support-activity benchmarking as a way of controlling internal overheads, or as a step towards outsourcing when they cannot match external suppliers.

Benefits of benchmarking

There are several clear benefits from benchmarking (Camp, 1989, part III). The most obvious is that it helps identify the best practices that can lead to performance improvement. But benchmarking can also break-down a reluctance to change, as managers can see exactly what it takes to be a leading organization. This, in turn, removes any notion that a firm does not need to change to compete, and reinforces the idea that continuing change is an essential part of survival. Benchmarking also serves as a source of market intelligence. For example, competitive benchmarking may uncover a previously unrecognized technological breakthrough. A less direct benefit is that the benchmarking exercize can develop valuable professional contacts between firms, leading to a useful exchange of ideas.

Critical success factors

Certain factors are critical to benchmarking success. For a start, it must become an accepted, and even routine, process within a firm and not simply another fashionable fad. Employees must view benchmarking as a permanent feature that establishes goals, strategies and new procedures. This, in turn, means that senior management support is critical. This is particularly important as benchmarking needs resources for collecting and analysing information, and senior managers must allocate these resources.

Even when managers look at the operations of other leading firms, it is not in-evitable that they will learn lessons that they can transfer to their own operations (Furey, 1987). Of course, there many be no lessons that are directly transferable. More likely, managers resist benchmarking because of a reluctance to recognize the value of a competitor's way of working – giving the classic 'not invented here' syndrome. One way around this is to benchmark a non-competitor's activities, and when managers get the message that other firms do actually have good ideas, they may start looking more directly at leading competitors.

Another obvious problem with benchmarking is the need for information, and many firms are reluctant to share their ideas. However, this can be surprisingly easy as even the best firms can learn from others, and any exchange of ideas can give mutual benefits. However, this is not always possible, and then firms have to find other sources of information. The obvious one is the World-Wide-Web, which gives a huge amount of information about organizations and the way that they work. The only concern is that not all of this information is reliable, and some can be misleading. An alternative is to use third-party reports, such as trade journals, industry publications, conferences and seminars, which often describe the ways that leading firms have distinguished themselves. These publications can highlight reasons why some firms are most highly regarded, but they are unlikely to include information that is commercially sensitive, and key factors may be missing. Another source of information that is of variable reliability is the word of mouth reports by, say, suppliers, consultants or other industry experts.

The benchmarking process

Camp described five distinct phases before a firm fully receives the benefits of performance benchmarking (illustrated in Figure 18.6) (Camp, 1989, part II).

1 *Planning* – during which a firm considers which functions to benchmark, which companies to select as benchmarking targets (competitors, non-competitors or both), and how to identify data and information sources. Benchmarking plans should focus on methods rather than simply on measured performance, as the methods cause the end results.

2 *Analysis* – which includes the collection and analysis of relevant information. A firm must determine how and why the benchmarked firm is better, asking questions such as:

   ● In what functional areas is the benchmarked company better?

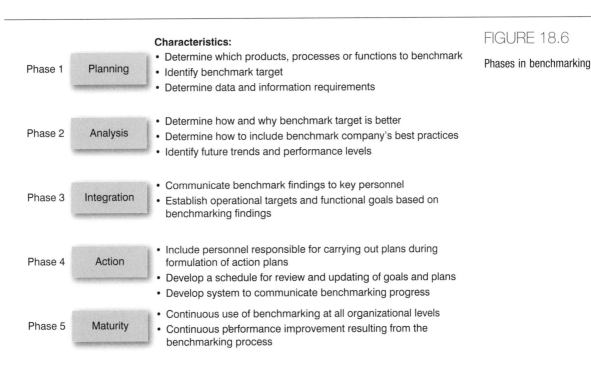

Characteristics:

Phase 1 — Planning
- Determine which products, processes or functions to benchmark
- Identify benchmark target
- Determine data and information requirements

Phase 2 — Analysis
- Determine how and why benchmark target is better
- Determine how to include benchmark company's best practices
- Identify future trends and performance levels

Phase 3 — Integration
- Communicate benchmark findings to key personnel
- Establish operational targets and functional goals based on benchmarking findings

Phase 4 — Action
- Include personnel responsible for carrying out plans during formulation of action plans
- Develop a schedule for review and updating of goals and plans
- Develop system to communicate benchmarking progress

Phase 5 — Maturity
- Continuous use of benchmarking at all organizational levels
- Continuous performance improvement resulting from the benchmarking process

FIGURE 18.6

Phases in benchmarking

- Why is the benchmarked company better?

- How large is the gap between us and the benchmarked company?

- Can we include the benchmarked company's best practices directly in our operations?

- Can we adapt their practices to make them more acceptable?

- Can we project future performance levels and rates of change?

This phase is critical as management has to understand and interpret the benchmarked company's processes, methods and activities.

3   *Integration* – is the process of communicating and gaining acceptance of the benchmark findings throughout an organization. During this phase, management begins to establish targets and functional goals based on the benchmark findings.

4   *Action* – translates the benchmark findings into detailed action plans. Critical points in this phase include nominating staff to formulate the plans, design and finalize details of new operations, prepare for implementation, developing a schedule for updating plans over time and developing a reporting system to communicate progress towards benchmarking goals.

5   *Maturity* – when the results of benchmarking becomes accepted, and a normal part of operations – and when benchmarking itself becomes an accepted way of establishing plans and objectives.

A formal process, such as benchmarking, is essential for establishing performance targets and plans that are externally focussed. Without external comparisons, organizations run the risk of losing sight of what defines best practices or what the competition is doing. Purchasing managers must endorse this practice when establishing plans to continuously improve their performance.

Balanced scorecard for purchasing

The balanced scorecard was first described by Kaplan and Norton in 1992 as a response to their belief that managers were putting too much reliance on financial measures, and this was leading them to make poor decisions. They argued that firms must go beyond financial measures, which are lagging indicators, and use measures that are leading indicators of performance. Specifically, they suggest four key concerns:

1   How do customers see us? (customer satisfaction perspective)

2   What must we excel at? (operational excellence perspective)

3   Can we continue to improve and create value? (innovation perspective)

4   How do we look to shareholders? (financial perspective)

Kaplan and Norton stressed that measurement itself is not the objective, but they clarify thinking and give a strategic focus for performance measurement and improvement. Many organizations have considered a balanced scorecard for their purchasing, with Figure 18.7 giving an example of some results. The results from this analysis would be considered along with purchasing strategies and developed into a set of appropriate performance measures.

FIGURE 18.7 Balanced scorecard for purchasing

Financial

- Revenue

    Revenue from suppliers based on process
        improvements
    Royalty revenue from patents.

- Cost

    Cost for direct material, indirect spend and
        capital spend
    Bill of material cost versus target
    Savings on direct materials used by contract
        manufactures
    Administrative cost per headroom
    Maverick spend.

Operations excellence

- Contract price enforcement

- Audit results and severity of errors

- Payment terms in contracts

- Most favoured customer clauses in contracts

- Not to exceed pricing in contracts

- Keeping pricing current in ERP database

- Strategic sourcing plans in place.

Customer satisfaction

- Internal

    Number of plant shutdowns
    Single-source risk mitigation
    Internal stakeholder survey
    Factory quality incidents
    Suppliers business continuity
    Tool performance
    On-time delivery
    Ramp-up readiness
    Percentage of spend with performed
    Suppliers.

- External

    Customer quality incidents.

Innovation

- New-product development

    Performance versus data milestones in the
        new product innovation (NPI) process
    Current estimated cost against target in
        NPI process
    Cost savings initiated by purchasing/supply
        in the NPI process.

- People development

    Training hours
    Leaderships, development pipeline
    Employee morale.

LEARNING FROM PRACTICE

Procter and Gamble

A perfect order is one that is delivered exactly as requested, with no errors of any kind. Procter and Gamble (P&G), a manufacturer and distributor of consumer products, defines the perfect order measure as, 'on time, to the buyer's requested delivery date, shipped complete, invoiced correctly and not damaged in transit'.

In 1992, P&G began to measure performance in detail, as a way of moving to their aims of achieving perfect orders. Initially, managers were shocked to discover that only 75 per cent of orders were perfect, and the remainder had some kind of problem, even if it was fairly trivial. Since then, substantial improvements have been made. In 1995, 82 per cent of orders were perfect; by 1998, 88 per cent were perfect; and into the 21st century this percentage continued to rise. This has been achieved through continuous replenishment, having customer service representatives work closely with major customers, improved information systems and a range of other actions that improved deliveries.

P&G estimates that every imperfect order costs approximately $200 for redelivery, lost revenue, damage, warehouse and shipping costs, deductions and backorders. The company knows that continuous improvement needs constantly measuring what is really important to the customer – and to the customer, the perfect order is important.

Source: Drayer R. (1998) Presentation to Eli Broad Graduate School of Management, Michigan State University, East Lansing, December.

PURCHASING MEASUREMENT CHARACTERISTICS

A review of purchasing performance measurement systems (typically recording the measures shown in Figure 18.8) reaches a number of conclusions which fall into two categories: system characteristics and human resource characteristics.

FIGURE 18.8 **Strategic performance measures for purchasing**

Financial

- Revenue

- Revenue from suppliers based on process improvements

- Royalty revenue from patents

- Cost

- Cost for direct material, indirect spend and capital spend

- Bill of material cost versus target

- Savings on direct materials used by contract manufacturers

- Administrative costs per headcount

- Maverick spend

Customer satisfaction

- Internal

- Number of plant shutdowns

- Single-source risk mitigation

- Internal stakeholder survey

- Factory quality incidents

- Supplier business continuity

- Tool performance

- On-time delivery

- Ramp-up readiness

- Percentage of spend with preferred suppliers

FIGURE 18.8 (Continued)

- External
- Customer quality incidents

Operational excellence

- Contract price enforcement
- Audit results and severity of errors
- Payment terms in contracts
- Most favoured customer clauses in contracts
- Not to exceed pricing in contracts
- Keeping pricing current in ERP database
- Strategic sourcing plans in place Innovation
- New product development
- Performance versus data milestones in the NPI process
- Current estimated cost against target in NPI process
- Cost savings initiated by purchasing/supply in the NPI process
- People development
- Training hours
- Leadership development pipeline
- Employee morale

System characteristics

1   Measurement is not free. Managers must compare the costs of the measurement system against the benefits – and more measurements do not necessarily mean better performance. The amount and type of measurement should be enough to achieve the intended result but not swamp managers with unnecessary detail.

2   Not all aspects of performance lend themselves to quantitative measurement. For example, negotiating and obtaining supplier co-operation are important for purchasing, but neither are readily quantifiable.

3   Purchasing managers are better served by a few precisely defined and thoroughly understood measures than by many poorly defined and vague ones.

4   An effective measurement system requires a database that provides consistent and reliable data. All staff must have access to the same data when calculating and reporting purchasing performance.

5   Periodic review of the measurement system is needed to eliminate and modify measures that are no longer relevant or have become unnecessary, and to add new ones as required. Performance targets have to be re-evaluated to ensure they encourage positive behaviour.

6 There is no best way to measure performance. Operations – and the most important measures – differ from firm to firm and industry to industry. No universal standards have emerged, but the use of benchmarking means that certain measures are becoming more common.

7 Managers in different levels and positions in an organization need different reports on performance. Careful planning is needed to provide the right information and guarantee effective use of the system.

8 It is not possible to define a single, overall productivity measure that summarizes purchasing performance. Instead managers must collect a cocktail of different measures and balanced the results.

9 Firms should replace measures focussing on activities to strategic measures assessing the achievement of desired end result.

10 The strategies used to produce a performance result are generally more important than the result itself.

11 A balanced scorecard gives an effective method of evaluating purchasing.

Human resource characteristics

1 A measurement system is not a substitute for effective management. The system is a tool that can be used to assist in the efficient and effective management of the purchasing function.

2 An effective system requires communication. Responsible staff must clearly understand the performance measures used, the expectation of them and the role of the measure during performance evaluation.

3 Measures must reinforce positive behaviour and be positively linked to an organization's reward system. However, they should not be used solely as tools to identify non-performing individuals, as this will result in dysfunctional or 'beat-the-system' behaviour.

LEARNING FROM PRACTICE

Hammet Industries

Hammet Industries is a diversified manufacturer of food products with worldwide operations, markets and suppliers. Purchasing is done by several hundred staff at the corporate, business and regional levels, with dispersed purchasing directors reporting to the vice president of purchasing at the headquarters in Switzerland. The corporate function co-ordinates sourcing and contains groups for key purchases, extension of lean operations, organizational development, strategic planning, finance, communications, risk management and other central activities.

The broad purchasing mission is to provide the corporation with a competitive advantage through purchasing excellence. This mission requires vertical and horizontal integration of strategies, and an integrated set of measures to drive and monitor behaviours. Critical measures are cost, quality, availability, global sourcing, effective new product launches and a competitive supply base.

Two measures are most important for cost management – year-on-year price performance and material cost improvement. The company's revenue influences the purchasing cost-reduction target

Source: Based on Scarborough J. (2009) Strategic performance measurement, RPW, London.

because of its need to protect margins. The finance group makes the final judgment on whether cost targets have been achieved. Other important measures include the following:

- Quality and quality improvement
- On-time delivery and availability
- Flawless on-time launch of new products
- Rationalizing the supply base
- Supplier relationships and development
- People development
- Cost management
- E-system applications
- Lean project

The targets for these measures are aggressive, going beyond what has previously been achieved. Hammet regularly reviews measures and targets, and adjusts them to reflect prevailing business conditions.

These adjustments are made at any time, but reviews are done at least monthly.

Measured performance is regularly reported to all appropriate staff throughout the company. Business performance is measurement at the team levels, but appraisals are also done at the individual level, with people expected to stretch themselves to get the greatest rewards.

Purchasing staff have authority to make designated levels of purchases, with specific staff assigned to collect data, check its integrity, report findings and suggest improvements to the system. Various other measures are collected automatically by ERP and other internal systems. Finance staff work to ensure the accuracy and validity of cost savings.

The performance of purchasing is critical to the financial success of the company. Top management regularly review the performance of purchasing throughout the company, while senior purchasing managers work on the issues raised.

CHAPTER REVIEW

- Managers need to measure the performance of purchasing to see how well it is done, how it compares with predefined standards and which areas need improving. The measures should be linked to target levels and timescales to achieve them

- There are some common problems with performance measures, including using the wrong measure, collecting the wrong data, short-term focus, lack of detail, etc. A widely used principle is that measures should focus on results rather than details of activities to achieve them

- There is an enormous number of possible measures for purchasing performance. These can be classified into categories to consider price, costs, revenue, quality, timing, technology, physical environment, safety, asset management, administrative efficiency and so on

- To measure performance, organizations need a performance measuring system. To develop this

needs certain steps. These include determining which performance categories to measure, developing specific measures, establishing performance standards for each measure, finalizing system details, implementing the system and monitoring its performance

- Benchmarking is a method of comparing an organization's performance with the performance of its best competitor, or the best firm in the industry. The key point is that benchmarking not only looks at the performance, but how it is achieved. It looks for ideas that it can adopt and adapt

- A balanced scorecard gives a useful view of purchasing, balancing the four aspects of financial performance, customer perspective, operations perspective and learning and growth

- We can give some general conclusions about performance measurement which fall into two categories: system characteristics and human resource characteristics

DISCUSSION QUESTIONS

1 Why would an organization want to measure purchasing performance?

2 What types of measure are available for purchasing?

3 What is the difference between effectiveness and efficiency? When should a firm focus on purchasing effectiveness? When should it focus on efficiency?

4 In the past, there were certain problems and limitations with measuring purchasing performance. What were these problems, and have they been overcome?

5 'Some companies still rely on measures that harm rather than support purchasing's long-term objectives.' What does this mean? Give examples of this effect.

6 What is the benefit of developing performance measures that focus on cost rather than purchase price?

7 Discuss the difference between cost-reduction and cost-avoidance. Why do some people describe the reported savings in cost-avoidance measures as 'funny money'?

8 Discuss the concept of strategic, rather than operational, performance measurement.

9 Effective performance measurement systems have certain characteristics. What are these and why are they important?

10 How would you set about designing a performance measurement system?

11 What is performance benchmarking and why is it used?

12 If you are made responsible for benchmarking a purchasing process, how would you set about it?

13 Why is it sometimes advantageous to benchmark performance against a non-competitor?

14 How can you establish a balanced scorecard to measure purchasing performance?

REFERENCES

Brown M. G. (1996) Keeping score: using the right measures to drive world-class performance, American Management Association, New York.

Camp R. C. (1989) Benchmarking: the search for best practices that lead to superior performance: Part I, Quality Progress, January, p 66.

Camp R. C. (1989) Benchmarking: the search for best practices that lead to superior performance: Part II, Quality Progress, February, p 71.

Camp R. C. (1989) Benchmarking: the search for best practices that lead to superior performance: Part III, Quality Progress, March, pp 77–80.

Furey T. R. (1987) Benchmarking: the key to developing competitive advantage, Planning Review, September–October, p 32.

Kaplan R.S. and Norton D.P. (1992) The balanced Scorecard, Harvard Business Review, January–February, pp 71–79.

Pryor L. S. (1989) Benchmarking: a self-improvement strategy, Journal of Business Strategy, November–December, p 28.

van Weele A. J. (1984) Purchasing performance measurement and evaluation, International Journal of Purchasing and Materials Management, Fall, pp 18–19.

Waters D. (2002) Operations management (2nd edition), Harlow, Essex: Pearson Education.

Waters C. D. J. (2009) Management performance indicators, RPW, London.

FURTHER READING

Avery S. (2006) GM strives for consistent measures, Purchasing, October 5.

Brown M. G. (1996) Keeping score: using the right measures to drive world-class performance, American Management Association, New York.

Carter P. L., Monczka R. M. and Mosconi T. (2005) Strategic performance measurement for purchasing and supply, CAPS Research.

D'Avanzo R., von Lewinski, H., van Wassenhove, L. N. (2003) The link between supply chain and financial performance, Supply Chain Management Review, November–December, pp 6–7.

Editorial (1995) Inside purchasing: four pillars of supply strategy, *Purchasing*, 118(10): 13.

Kaplan R. S. and Norton D. P. (1992) The balanced scorecard – measures that drive performance, Harvard Business Review, January–February, pp 71–79.

Smeltzer L. R. and Manship J. A. (2003) How good are your cost reduction measures? Supply Chain Management Review, May–June, pp 3–7.

Timme S. and Williams-Timme W. (2000) The financial-SCM connection, Supply Chain Management Review, May–June, pp 33–40.

Trunick P. A. (2007) What you do, start measuring, Logistics Today, August, pp 22–24.

Vitale R. and Mavrinac S. C. (1995) How effective is your performance measurement system? Management Accounting, August, pp 43–47.

CASE STUDY

Avion

Francis Dey and Bill Mifflin, procurement managers at Avion, were reading a troubling performance report concerning a key supplier, Foster Technologies. The report described the deteriorating performance of Foster Technologies in both material quality and on-time delivery. Their conversation went as follows.

Francis: I don't believe what I am seeing. This supplier was clearly a star when we visited before awarding the contract for the new Amrod product line.

Bill: I'm not pleased. I was on the team that performed the audit. Foster's management was so smooth – they definitely said that they could meet all our requirements. I feel like we've been misled by this supplier.

Francis: Didn't you look at their processes and quality systems?

Bill: Of course. Everything seemed good. But now every other shipment has some problem, and the delays are making it difficult to get our product to our customers. What really struck us about this supplier was how innovative they were. Maybe they are too small and lack the qualified engineers. Maybe someone has left the company.

Francis: We have to address these problems quickly.

Bill: I'll tell you what I'm going to recommend. We should begin immediately to look for another supplier. I never was a fan of these single-source contracts. They leave us open to too much risk.

Francis: But won't that take a long time?

Bill: Probably. We'll have to do another supplier search with team visits. New tooling could really cost, too. This could take months.

Francis: Has anyone talked to the supplier about these problems?

Bill: Padraig went over personally today and talked to the production manager. He phoned with his initial reaction, which was that Foster's production manager claimed that we were responsible for a good part of the problems!

Francis: Why us? Are they just trying to shift the blame for their poor performance?

At this point, Padraig O'Donnell, another procurement manager, arrived and their discussion continued.

Bill: Padraig, glad you're here. We were just discussing how Foster's is trying to blame us for their problems. I think we should dump them fast!

Padraig: Possibly – but I think that Foster's production manager is right. I think I would be blaming us, as well.

Francis: How come? We're the injured party here.

Padraig: I spent a good part of the day over at Foster's and learned some interesting things. For example, do either of you remember what we told Foster's the monthly requirements for the product would be?

Bill: I remember exactly. The volumes were projected to be 2,500 units a month.

Padraig: We need to talk with our production group more often. The monthly volumes are now over 4,000 units a month. Our production group now wants material within 10 days rather than the agreed 2 weeks. We have been changing the quantities wanted right up to the last minute before delivery.

Bill: Ah! I remember on our site visit that the most their production system could handle was 3,500 units a month. A 2-week lead time was about as low as they could go.

Francis: But why didn't they tell us that these changes were causing problems? They still have some explaining to do.

Padraig: Apparently they tried. What did your team tell this supplier about contacting us after negotiating the contract?

Bill: We said that any operational problems have to go through our materials management people.

Padraig: Foster's production manager showed me a log detailing seven memos and letters sent to our materials management people outlining the impact of our production and scheduling changes on their operations. He also called us in purchasing several times but got no real response. I get the impression that Foster's is anxious for this contract to wind down so they can dump us!

Francis: What do we do now?

Questions

- What are the problems at Avion? What measures of performance can plot the development of these problems?

- How easy is it to switch suppliers? When should this be considered?

- What is a good customer, and why is this an important concept?

- What should Avion do now? What should Foster's do?

GLOSSARY

Acquisition of materials, procurement, supply management Alternative terms for purchasing.

Agent Is a person or entity who has been authorized to act on behalf of some other person or entity.

Arbitration Is 'the submission of a disagreement to one or more impartial persons with the understanding that the parties will abide by the arbitrator's decision'.

BATNA Is the best outcome one party can get without negotiations.

Bill of lading, Freight bill, delivery terms Types of documents needed for material delivery.

Blanket purchase order Order covering several deliveries over an extended period.

Breach of contract Occurs when one party does not act as agreed in a contract.

Buyer-seller Collaboration Is the process by which two parties adopt a high level of purposeful co-operation to maintain a trading relationship over time.

Centralized purchasing Has all the actual purchasing done centrally, typically in the corporate headquarters.

Clauses and schedules Important elements in a contract.

Commercial law Is that 'body of [the] law that refers to how business firms (parties) enter into contracts with each other, execute contracts and remedy problems that arise in the process'.

Contract Is a legally binding agreement that is the result of an offer and acceptance, with an agreed consideration.

Contract Is a legally enforceable agreement between two or more parties to do specified actions in return for some consideration.

Core capability Key activity that an organisation does particularly well.

Cost analysis Considers each individual element of cost (material, wages, energy, overheads, profit, etc.) that together add up to the final price.

Cross-functional sourcing teams Consist of people from different functions – and increasingly different organizations – brought together to achieve purchasing-related tasks. The tasks can be specific (such as product design or supplier selection) or broad (such as reducing unit costs or improving quality).

Culture Is a very complex idea, but it includes all the understandings that govern human interaction in a particular society. It includes a mixture of language, values, attitudes, customs, social institutions, education, religion and so on.

Decentralized purchasing Devolves all purchasing decisions to local facilities.

Distinctive capability Activities that an organisation does so well that it gains a competitive advantage.

Downstream The tiers of customers after an organisation receiving its products.

Effectiveness Is the extent to which managers make decisions that move them towards a previously established goal.

Efficiency Measures how well the goal is reached, what resources are used to reach the goal or what sacrifices are necessary to reach the goal.

Electronic data interchange (EDI) The automatic exchange of information between remote computers.

Electronic fund transfer (EFT) The automatic transfer of money between accounts.

Entry qualifiers Features that are needed to add a potential supplier to a shortlist.

Enterprise resource planning (ERP) Integrates the flow of information through various business functions.

e-Supply chain Refers to any supply chain that includes electronic communications and the internet – giving a component of e-commerce. The associated management function becomes **e-SCM.**

Ethics Are the set of moral principles or values guiding our behaviour.

Insourcing Means that an organization internally makes a particular material that it needs for its operations.

Integration Is the process of bringing together different groups, functions or organizations, to work together on common business related assignments.

Kanban Is used to control operations by using containers, cards or visual cues to control the production and movement of materials through a supply chain.

Logistics Is the broad function responsible for all aspects of the movement and storage of materials on their journey into, through and out of an organization.

Logistics Is the function responsible for moving materials through their supply chains.

Material release Message to arrange another delivery with a blanket order.

Material requirements planning (MRP) Is a way of planning the flow of materials by calculating requirements from a master production schedule.

Materials Are all the diverse mix of things that an organization needs to perform its operations.

Maverick or backdoor buying Occurs when departments buy materials themselves without consulting the purchasing department.

Mediation, minitrial, rent-a-judge, dispute prevention Methods of conflict resolution

Negotiation Is a process of formal communication, either face-to-face or electronically, where two or more people come together to seek mutual agreement about an issue or issues.

Offer Acceptance and consideration–key elements for a contract.

Operational decisions Are short-term decisions that have relatively minor consequences for specific activities.

Order fulfilment All the activities that combine to satisfy a customer's order.

Organizational design Is the process of evaluating options and selecting the structure, formal communications, division of labour, co-ordination, control, authority and responsibility that best achieves the organization's aims.

Outsourcing Means that it buys the material from an external supplier.

Performance measurement system Consists of all the procedures to collect, analyse and report current data needed to assess how well a department is performing its prescribed activities.

Planning In the context of negotiations planning leads to a method or scheme.

Policies Provide rules or guidance that staff should follow when doing certain activities. They put constraints on staff behaviour. They show how the purchasing function will work to achieve its strategic aims.

Portfolio analysis Classifies different types of purchases.

Position Is the stated demand that is placed on the table by a negotiator.

Price analysis Is the process of comparing a supplier's prices with external price benchmarks.

Principal Is the corresponding person or entity for whom agents carry out their authority.

Procedure manual Is a how-to manual, describing how to do various jobs.

Procedures Are the operating instructions that detail the tasks done in purchasing.

Process capability Is the ability of a process to generate outputs that meet specifications and customer requirements.

Process, logistics channel, value chain, demand chain Give different views of supply chains.

Purchase order Is the legally binding document that triggers the delivery of materials. It is the contract between a buyer and seller.

Purchase requisition Document to request purchasing to buy materials.

Purchasing Is responsible for acquiring all the materials needed by an organization. It consists of the related activities that organize the flow of goods, services and other materials from suppliers into an organization.

Purchasing excellence Suggests that efficient procurement gives a competitive advantage.

Purchasing process Is the set of related activities and procedures that are used to acquire materials for an organization.

Purchasing process The activities used to acquire materials.

Quality In its broadest sense, is the ability of a product to meet – and preferably exceed – customer expectations.

Relationship management Consists of all the activities that organizations use to enhance relations with other parties – including the ability to act ethically, listen effectively, communicate and use creative problem solving.

Request for quotation or proposal Document to collect terms, conditions and other information from potential suppliers.

Reverse logistics Occur whenever materials are returned by customers to their original suppliers.

Reverse or e-auction Auction run through a buyer's website.

Reverse price analysis Considers components of price to check a quoted value.

Six Sigma An approach and set of methods used in quality management.

Social responsibility Is a set of corporate policies, procedures and resulting behaviour designed to benefit the workplace and, by extension, the individual, the organization and the community.

Spend analysis Examines and categorizes the spending done by purchasing.

Statement of work (SOW) Document describing a service that purchasing should acquire.

Stocks Which are also loosely described as inventories – are the stores of materials that an organization has acquired, but it is not ready to use.

Strategic alignment Occurs when all the strategies in an organization support each other and work coherently together to achieve the overall mission.

Strategic decisions Are long-term decisions that have major consequences throughout an organization.

Supplier development Includes any activity undertaken by a buyer to improve a supplier's performance or capabilities to meet the buyer's short and long-term supply needs.

Supplier management and development Includes an array of actions taken to measure, manage and continually improve performance of the supply base.

Supplier quality Represents the ability of a supplier to deliver products that consistently meet or exceed current and future customer expectations or requirements in critical performance areas.

Supplier relationship management (SRM) and customer relationship management (CRM) Systems to manage interactions with suppliers and customers.

Supplier scorecard Review of a supplier's performance in different areas.

Supply base All the suppliers that deliver materials to an organisation.

Supply base optimization Ensures that only the most capable, best performing suppliers are maintained in the supply base.

Supply base rationalization Removes those suppliers that are unwilling or incapable of achieving specified performance objectives.

Supply chain Consists of the series of activities and organizations that materials move through on their journey from initial suppliers through to final customers.

Supply network, supply web Alternative names for supply chains.

Tactical decisions Are medium-term decisions that have less serious consequences for parts of the organization.

Third-party logistics (3PL) Has a specialized external provider responsible for logistics within an organization.

Total cost of ownership (TCO) Is defined as the present value of all costs associated with a product that are incurred over its expected life.

Total Quality Management Has the whole organization working together to guarantee, and systematically improve, quality.

Upstream The tiers of suppliers in front of an organisation moving materials in.

Value analysis and value engineering Check that a product reaches specifications at the lowest overall cost.

Value Ratio of perceived benefits to price paid for an item.

Warranty Assurance that materials are delivered in condition agreed.

Worldwide sourcing and global sourcing Refers to any purchase where the supplier and buyer are in different countries.

INDEX